McKIM, MEAD & WHITE, ARCHITECTS

C. F. McKim

W. R. Mead

Stanford White

McKIM, MEAD & WHITE
ARCHITECTS

LELAND M. ROTH

ICON EDITIONS

HARPER & ROW · PUBLISHERS · NEW YORK

Cambridge Philadelphia San Francisco London Mexico City São Paulo Singapore Sydney

1817

First ICON paperback edition published 1985.

Designer: Margaret M. Wagner

Library of Congress Cataloging in Publication Data

Roth, Leland M.
McKim, Mead & White, architects.

(Icon editions)
Bibliography: p.
Includes index.
1. McKim, Mead & White.   2. Architecture, Modern—19th century—United States.
I. Title.   II. Title: McKim, Mead, and White.
NA737.M4R65   1983   720′.92′2   83–47559
ISBN 0–06–438491–8   83 84 85 86 87 88 89 10 9 8 7 6 5 4 3 2 1
ISBN 0–06–430136–2 (pbk.)   85 86 87 88 89 10 9 8 7 6 5 4 3 2 1

to Carol
who denied herself much
that this might be written;

as Emerson wrote,
the best and truest gift
is a portion of thyself

Contents

Illustrations

(Note: all buildings are by McKim, Mead & White
unless otherwise noted.)

Acknowledgments

Tʜɪs study grew out of courses in modern architectural history I taught at the University of Illinois, Urbana, in 1966–1967. In subsequent seminars with Vincent Scully at Yale I was able to explore the range and contribution of the firm's work, culminating my doctoral dissertation which served as the foundation for this monograph. I owe much to Vincent Scully; his vision of the human environment as a physical and social whole, and his insistence on the architect's obligation to reinforce that unity, continue to challenge me. I owe much to Henry-Russell Hitchcock who, in a seminar conducted at Yale, encouraged me to examine the firm's early work and who has read and reread various versions of this manuscript. I also owe a debt to Heinrich Klotz who, while Visiting Professor at Yale, permitted me to examine the relationship between the firm's work and Italian Renaissance prototypes and the question of "copying." Of many colleagues who have assisted me, provided spiritual support, and asked good questions, I should like to mention Mosette Broderick, John Dryfhout, Christopher Gray, Cynthia Field, Sarah Landau, Walter Langsam, John O'Callaghan, Chiara and Francesco Passanti, Douglas S. Richardson, and Douglass Shand Tucci, among many who, I hope, will forgive me if I forbear reciting a long list. I owe a great debt to the White family of Saint James, Long Island, New York—to Mrs. Lawrence Grant White who had known Stanford, her father-in-law, and her children, Frederick Lawrence Peter White and Robert White, who placed before me all the material they had. Walter O. Cain, the lineal professional descendant of the firm, opened his office records and collections to me. I would especially like to thank Wilson G. Duprey, former Curator of the Map and Print Collection, New-York Historical Society, for his attentive and unending assistance during many years of work. I must also thank the directors and staff of many other libraries and institutions who aided me, including Adolf K. Placzek, then the Avery Librarian, and the staff of the Avery Architectural Library, Columbia University, the curators and staff of the New-York Historical Society, especially Wendy Shadwell, and the staffs of the Amherst College Library, the Manuscript Division of the Library of Congress, the Museum of the City of New York, and the Yale University Library.

The greatest debt is due Carol, for in many ways this is her work as well; she has lived this, accompanied me to innumerable sites, helped take notes, typed and been dispassionate in her editing, and through it all, maintained equable patience. These pages are the fruit of her sacrifice.

Preface

McKim, Mead & White, architects"—printed in small roman characters in terra-cotta brown ink on ivory-colored paper: this was the letterhead of one of the best-known architectural firms in New York, indeed, in the United States, at the end of the nineteenth century. By the early twentieth century their reputation had reached England, prompting Charles Herbert Reilly to write in 1924: "the work of McKim, Mead & White will be found, I think, to be one of the great determining forces in the history of the architecture of our time."[1] His view was shared by many of his generation, both in the United States and in Reilly's native England. Most American critics and architects then, especially the scores the firm trained, would have agreed, for McKim, Mead & White epitomized professional ideals of high-mindedness and civic purpose. They received almost a thousand commissions between 1870 and 1920 and built important public buildings in scores of cities east of the Mississippi. Yet a decade or so after Reilly praised these architects, the general view had changed, and by 1940 McKim, Mead & White were viewed by critics as representing everything wrong with turn-of-the-century architecture. It was relatively easy to accept the judgment proffered, for there was no full account of the firm's work. The handsome folio of 400 plates, the *Monograph of the Work of McKim, Mead & White*, published during the years 1915–20, presented only a fraction of their output, unexplained by any text. The only study to follow, aside from the biographies of McKim and White, was Reilly's slender book, an appreciation rather than a monograph and far from detailed.

Although they had the largest practice in the world for nearly thirty years, McKim, Mead & White have received little of the serious attention they deserve. While the early domestic work has been studied by Vincent Scully and, more recently, by Richard Guy Wilson, the many buildings the firm added to American cities have never been thoroughly examined. Only a small portion, perhaps a dozen of their most famous buildings, are discussed in histories of American architecture. Until recently, in fact, critical opinion prevented us from appreciating the firm's later and more significant urban work, so that the architecture of McKim, Mead & White has not been viewed as a whole or, especially, in relationship to the urban environment it did so much to shape. Nearly all of the major architects of the 1880s and 1890s have had their architectural biographers and scholars—Mariana Van Rensselaer for Richardson and Harriet Monroe for Root—whose work provided a base for later monographs such as Hitchcock's study of Richardson or the work of Donald Hoffmann on Root. A comparable study of Sullivan's contribution had to wait until Hugh Morrison's monograph of 1935. For Richard Morris Hunt there was neither biography nor monograph until Paul Baker's study appeared in 1980. Although biographies of McKim and White were published in 1929 and 1931, respectively, a comprehensive study of their architecture, comparable to Hitchcock on Richardson or Morrison on Sullivan, never followed. This study seeks to redress this.

Critical studies on architecture may take various approaches, being advocatory, doctrinal, interpretive, valuative, or typal. This study—as any work which opens new territory for investigation should be, I believe—is descriptive in character, providing depictive, biographical, and contextual information; it is an examination of the oeuvre of McKim, Mead & White from the early individual designs of the 1870s through the deaths of White and McKim, with a sketch of the continuing work of the successor partners up to the official retirement of Mead in 1919. The primary resource has been the immense archive of drawings, correspondence, photographs, and miscellany deposited at the New-York Historical Society, New York. As large as this archive is, there are important lacunae, for the office was moved twice, in 1891 and again in 1894, and much of the oldest and then apparently superfluous material was discarded.[2] William Rutherford Mead's own correspondence, more concerned with purely business matters than that of the other two partners, is scattered amongst the files, whereas Charles Follen McKim's voluminous letterbooks were given by the firm to Charles Moore in the mid-1920s when he was working on the biography; thus they were preserved and eventually given by Moore to the Manuscript Division of the Library of Congress. Stanford White's equally voluminous letterbooks and correspondence files, so successfully stored away at Saint James, Long Island, as to fade from memory, were rediscovered just recently and deposited in part at the Avery Library, Columbia University, in the summer of 1982. They await a thorough rereading for a new biography of White.

One of the problems in evaluating the work of McKim, Mead & White is how to deal with a nonpolemic architecture. In the case of such architects as Sullivan and Wright, or Philip Johnson and Peter Eisenman, one can read the printed statements (for they all wrote as much architecture as they built) and measure the built work against the written program. McKim, Mead & White, however, like their mentor Richardson, disliked theory by itself and wrote little.[3] Moreover the correspondence that does survive usually tells little of the architect's underlying motif, for it was presented verbally. As H. Siddons Mowbray recalled, "McKim was a firm believer in dinners as a means of carrying out objects he had in view," and many a scheme was arranged in the unrecorded afterglow of canvas-back duck and madeira.[4] Even the firm's drawings were rendered coolly aloof, free of revealing personal idiosyncrasy. But because of the sheer volume of the firm's work, patterns of interest and development become apparent when the whole is viewed, and hence it is critically important to examine the range of the firm's activity.

The Prologue sketches the importance of McKim, Mead, and White in their own time and why they have begun to receive renewed attention. The following two chapters survey the early lives and training of the founders, drawing from the published biographies as well as previously unpublished materials. Chapter 3 deals with the earliest years of practice, years of experimentation and exploration in all aspects of building, and is therefore somewhat more complex in organization than those that follow. By 1890, just as McKim, Mead & White had begun to develop a somewhat clearer hierarchy within their office organization, so too they began to view architectural types (particularly urban types) as series of variations on relatively established themes. Hence Chapters 4 through 6 are themselves more codified in form, with serried discussions of each of the major building types. Chapter 7 treats briefly the succeeding junior partners, and the Epilogue turns to an assessment of the firm's work and impact.

PROLOGUE

America is . . . a young country with an old mentality.

GEORGE SANTAYANA
The Genteel Tradition in American Philosophy
1911

To reflect or reform—which is the proper function of architecture? Should architecture summarize all that has come to make up the culture which produces it, or should it seek to uplift and improve, to redirect that culture? Such questions have polarized critics and architects since Diderot's attacks on immorality in art in the mid-eighteenth century. An even more fundamental question, of course, is why art or architecture must necessarily serve *either* function to the exclusion of the other. American architects have always struggled to develop a true synthesis which alludes to the past, and is therefore indigenous, and yet also stretches technological limits and in some measure reshapes society and technology. This dilemma was all the more pressing just after the turn of the century when European architects were tending to messianic utilitarianism while American architects reemphasized an associational function. In fact, by 1911 it seemed to George Santayana that decades of accustomed reflection in the American arts and literature had enervated the American spirit of innovation. So, when asked to speak at the University of California at Berkeley, he took the occasion to define the "genteel tradition," one component of the dualism he perceived in the American mind and its expression in architecture:

America is not simply . . . a young country with an old mentality; it is a country with two mentalities, one a survival of the beliefs and standards of the fathers, the other an expression of the instincts, practice, and discoveries of the younger generations. In all the higher things of the mind—in religion, in literature, in the moral emotions—it is the hereditary spirit that still prevails. . . . The truth is that one half of the American mind, that not occupied intensely with practical affairs, has remained, I will not say high-and-dry, but slightly becalmed; it has floated gently in the backwater, while, alongside, in invention and industry and social organization the other half of the mind was leaping down a sort of Niagara Rapids. This division may be found symbolized in American architecture: a neat reproduction of the colonial mansion—with some modern comforts introduced surreptitiously—stands beside the skyscraper. The American Will inhabits the skyscraper; the American Intellect inhabits the colonial mansion. The one is the sphere of the American man; the other, at least predominantly, of the American woman. The one is all aggressive enterprise; the other is all genteel tradition.[1]

What distinguishes the work of McKim, Mead & White is the fact not only that it encompasses the complete range of building tasks at the end of the century but also that it combines both mentalities described by Santayana. The firm's work was not progressive in the sense that Louis Sullivan's or Frank Lloyd Wright's is often described as being, for instead of selecting out special types in which rapid change was occurring—the commercial skyscraper and the suburban house—McKim, Mead & White concentrated on public buildings and the urban core. The firm rose to prominence, of course, with the design of spatially open and picturesque country and summer houses, but by the end of the 1880s its concentration shifted to the urban center, and even subsequent summer houses were formal and, with varying degrees of interpretation, classical. Daniel Burnham, too, by the early 1890s, adopted a similar positive view of the city not simply as a place to make one's fortune but as a good place to live. Curiously Burnham himself lived in suburban Evanston, in an old house in the midst of a large heavily wooded lake shore lot, but he moved there in 1886 with his family from the near south side of Chicago. Wright, more significantly, almost from the start of his career, positioned himself in suburban Oak Park. Individually, McKim, Mead, and White took up residence in the heart of Manhattan, each about fifteen minutes walking distance from the offices at 57 Broadway. Indeed, McKim never even owned his home, renting a series of townhouses on West 35th Street. The partners experienced the city as townhouse facades and shop fronts, at close range; Wright saw the city through the commuter train window as a fleeting image, as something perceived at long range, even as something alien.

Wright's wariness and eventual antagonism toward the city was the logical expression of a pervasive Jeffersonian antiurban bias. If the city was basically detrimental, as this view proposed, then social and physical deterioration could only be worsened in places such as New York by the abdication of old Knickerbocker families of their political responsibility and direct social amelioration. George Templeton Strong is a good example, for while his diary reveals his fascination with the growth of New York, it also documents his avoidance of direct action.[2] It was because of their early positive view of city life, filled with gaiety, festivity, light, and color, that McKim, Mead, and White are important. Although they were in no way politically active, they used architecture as an agent in effecting this shift in attitude toward the city, for they played a significant part in reshaping the urban landscape of New York between 1880 and 1910. Well over a third of their nearly one thousand commissions were in the five boroughs of New York City, the prevalent light brick, marble, and glazed terra cotta dramatically changing the color of the city. New York in the 1870s, when the future partners were getting their first practical experience, was not a particularly attractive city. In her autobiography, *A Backward Glance,* Edith Wharton recalled old New York with its "mean monotonous streets, without architecture, without great churches or palaces, or any visible memorials of an historic past," lined with rows of low brownstone houses "of a desperate uniformity of style." She vividly recalled "the intolerable ugliness," the "untended streets and the narrow houses so lacking in external dignity." Because she had spent her youngest and most impressionable years in Europe, when her father rented out their Manhattan townhouse to a succession of postwar business speculators, her mind had been filled, she realized, "with shapes of immortal beauty and immemorial significance." Nevertheless, had not most of her father's acquaintances also traveled in Europe?

> How could I understand that people who had seen Rome and Seville, Paris and London, could come back to live contentedly between Washington Square and the Central Park? What I could not guess was that this little low-studded rectangular New York, cursed with its universal chocolate-coloured coating of the most hideous stone ever quarried, this cramped horizontal gridiron of a town without towers, porticoes, fountains or perspectives, hide-bound in its deadly uniformity of mean ugliness, would fifty years later be as much a vanished city as Atlantis or the lowest layer of Schliemann's Troy.[3]

It was replaced by a city of towers and porticoes, of marble and bright terra cotta, built in large part by McKim, Mead & White.

The partners believed they saw in eighteenth-century architecture a far more sanguine view of urban life, and certainly their early work was instrumental in rediscovering and redefining the native architectural traditions, presenting this classical heritage as a model of civic decorum and balance. If the United States possessed any native tradition, this, they proposed, was as close as it was possible to get. The irony was, of course, that even while they habitually introduced structural and technical innovations in their work, they did not realize that such "invention" was itself very much a native tradition; they thought of tradition as embodied in "style" and certain recognizable forms. Thus, while they attempted to exercise both of Santayana's mentalities, they remained slightly more committed to fidelity to their historical sources rather than giving practical or technical innovations freer rein to determine design and building form.

The myopia that came to affect mid-twentieth-century architects and critics resulted from the extended influence of Santayana's criticism. His "genteel tradition" became an epithet of cultural derision, and because McKim, Mead & White so epitomized the genteel tradition their work became the subject of ridicule and attack. This denigration was all the more pronounced, no doubt, because of the metaphor Santayana had chosen, contrasting a "colonial mansion" with a "skyscraper," the one caught in an artistic "backwater," the other coursing through a "Niagara Rapids." Yet there now appear a number of reasons why this firm deserves renewed study, reasons which caused so many aspiring architects to flock to its office toward the turn of the century, and which still engender respect.

One is directly connected to the use of historic references, for although these architects certainly were eclectics they adhered to a relatively limited historical spectrum; even more important, they developed building plans first around functional requirements. They were what historian Carroll L. V. Meeks has called "creative eclectics," whose plans were carefully molded to utility, but whose internal and external finishes were based on laborious scrutiny of historical sources.[4] While many architects have done this before and since, few have simplified and manipulated form and consciously reduced ornament as effectively as McKim, Mead & White did—Soane, Schinkel, and Lutyens achieved comparable clarity and delicacy, as of course did Richardson. For all his erudition and his greater exposure to the École method, perhaps because of it, Richard Morris Hunt never did. McKim, Mead & White followed prototypes, either ancient or of their own devising, but they navigated the difficult path between uniformity and coherence of plan and form and the conflicting demands for variety and specific adaptation to use. The sense of balance is characterized by the partners' (particularly McKim's) restrained use of ornament. Unlike Sullivan, they did not invent a new ornamental vocabulary, but they shared with him a common ornamental grammar; to McKim, Mead & White, as to Sullivan, ornament was not only to facilitate weathering and promote longevity, but to announce and articulate, to celebrate function. To do that it had to be used with restraint, so that openings, points of transition, approaches, entrances, circulation, were clear. There is one point on which Sullivan and the partners eventually differed greatly, for to Sullivan ornament gradually assumed greater importance while for McKim, Mead & White it lessened in intensity. The firm's work after 1900, for the most part, is its most ornamentally restrained, severe, and sometimes delicate—most notably Pennsylvania Station—while Sullivan's is his most ornamentally complex and personal. Indeed, as his commissions decreased in number and celebrity, his ornament became more and more effusive. Thus, a study of the work of McKim, Mead & White suggests a way of observing precedent without having functional utility or form prescribed by precedent.

This use of precedent is particularly significant, for what sets the historicism of McKim, Mead & White, and of their colleagues such as Peabody & Stearns, apart from that of the early nineteenth century, is the special nature of their references. Instead of following, as A. J. Davis or Richard Upjohn had done, the general associations of Greece, Rome, or fourteenth-century Gothic parish churches, none of which had any particular significance for Americans, they began to examine American public and vernacular architecture of the eighteenth century, which up to the early 1870s was held in very low esteem. The early efforts of McKim, Robert S. Peabody, and Arthur Little, while at the very outset of their careers, to record fast-disappearing colonial buildings helped to create and encourage a popular rediscovery of this architectural heritage and thus to call into being the first architectural preservation efforts in the United States.[5] It is therefore no exaggeration to say that much of what remains of the nation's earliest architecture survives in large measure because of McKim's pioneering efforts to remove the prevailing opprobrium.

Another characteristic which has consistently drawn favorable comment, even from those otherwise critical of the firm's historicism, is its use and manipulation of space. While to some extent this is due to McKim's brief exposure to École design, it also owes much to Richardson's influence. It is not always the sheer volume or perspective of space that impresses, such as one once experienced in Pennsylvania Station or as one may still see in the National City Bank in New York or the Bank of Montreal, but the processional sequence of spaces as seen in those examples and in the Boston Public Library or in the more intimate clubhouses. One even finds such spatial sequences miniaturized in their summer houses, as in the Oelrichs house, Rosecliff. They were especially adept, particularly White, at ingenious adjustments of these formal spatial sequences to irregular sites, as in the E. D. Morgan house, Beacon Rock, on its rocky peninsula in Newport, or the Page house in Washington, D.C.

One attribute of the architecture of this period that continues to elicit admiration and to challenge is its durability. This is particularly true of the work of McKim, Mead & White, for seldom were the lowest-bidding contractors given the job. As a matter of principle and long-term economy, the most reputable and conscientious contractors were awarded work, and the firm repeatedly worked with the Norcross Brothers of Worcester, Massachusetts, who built so much for Richardson.[6] Moreover, the best materials were specified, and detailed construction-site inspections of the quality of materials and workmanship often resulted in rejection of stone or repetition of work because of small, nearly imperceptible flaws. It was an exacting procedure but one which resulted in work of consummate handcraft of extraordinary polish. What makes this all the more appealing nowadays is that the prevailing economic conditions at the turn of the century, the ever-replenished supply of highly skilled immigrant construction labor, and the low prices of rare materials combined to create an architecture, continued by the firm's pupils in their suburban houses, apartments, and Art Deco skyscrapers of the 1920s, which can no longer be duplicated. Such materials and workmanship now inspire wistful longing.

Sullivan and, later, Wright wrote of creating a new architecture, freed of what they viewed as the hypocrisy of drawing from the past instead of celebrating the present. They preached an architecture evolved from lucid guiding principles, but the plutocrats who offered building commissions had little appreciation then for this message. Far more important to the businessmen was their desire to equal the cultural and artistic achievements not only of their contemporaries in Europe but of the merchant princes of Renaissance Italy.[7] So, the traditionalism and historicist allusions of such architects as McKim, Mead & White were most appealing. Business clients, and even more those collective clients such as the boards of directors of libraries, museums, and hospitals which were made up of businessmen, could not help but be reassured by the large, efficient staff of the McKim, Mead & White office (then the largest architectural office in the world); here were architects who organized and operated their business along much the same lines as practiced by the plutocrats. This important lesson was quickly learned by Daniel Burnham, whose office operation by 1910 had surpassed even that of McKim, Mead & White in sheer size and hierarchical clarity.[8]

Because they satisfied prevailing aspirations, because they insisted on durable construction, and because of their efficient productivity, McKim, Mead & White were among the most influential architects of their generation, not only in the United States but in the British Empire as well. The classicism they championed—sober, calm, richly yet discreetly ornamented, and solidly constructed—satisfied a widespread desire for an ordered civil architecture, among a public that increasingly was visually sensitive and culturally alert. The firm was called upon to design a large number of buildings, from Brunswick, Maine, to Portland, Oregon, from Mandan, North Dakota, to Santa Fe, New Mexico, with hundreds concentrated in such major metropolitan centers as Philadelphia, Boston, New York, and Chicago. Altogether the partners received more than 855 commissions before McKim died, and more than 945 by the time Mead retired officially in 1919.[9] Not only did these dispersed works exert significant local influence because of their sheer presence, but through extensive publication in professional journals their impact was felt by hundreds of architects at home and abroad.

Ultimately as important as the buildings themselves was the training given young men in the office. William Boring, who practiced in partnership with E. L. Tilton before being appointed, first, Professor of Architecture and then, Director of the School of Architecture at Columbia University, wrote that during the 1880s and 1890s "it was esteemed by students of architecture, a great privilege to be admitted to the offices of these architects, which seemed to breathe the spirit of the fifteenth century."[10] Since in the 1880s there were as yet only six schools of architecture in the United States, many aspirants felt the best practical training was to be obtained in the offices of McKim, Mead & White.[11] Instead of being displeased with this transience in the staff, the partners considered providing this educational experience to be one of their chief responsibilities. More than five hundred men had worked in their office by 1919, among the best known of whom are Cass Gilbert (architect of the Minnesota State Capitol and the Woolworth Building, New York), A. D. F. Hamlin (Professor of Architecture at Columbia University), Royal Cortissoz (art and architectural critic), John Merven Carrère and Thomas Hastings (architects of the New York Public Library), Henry Bacon (architect of the Lincoln Memorial, Washington, D.C.), John Galen Howard, and John Mead Howells (the nephew of William Mead and architect of the Tribune Tower, Chicago). Scores of young architects who met in the office, such as Carrère and Hastings, established continuing partnerships there.[12] Of the three partners, McKim in particular was deeply committed to the education of architects, spending long hours in the drafting room with his assistants. In addition to this de facto studio in the office, McKim also supervised an atelier, one of two affiliated with the Columbia University School of Architecture from 1905 to 1909. Increasing ill health meant that most of the actual instruction was given by McKim's assistant, John Russell Pope, but McKim's influence reached the other atelier as well, for it was conducted by former office assistant Thomas Hastings, assisted by John V. Van Pelt.[13]

Into the McKim, Mead & White office came a steady stream of requests for advice on the best course of study in architecture. McKim answered each carefully, almost always making the same suggestions: go to a good university for basic education (Columbia was often mentioned); work for several years in an architectural office; and travel in Europe, perhaps attending classes at the École des Beaux-Arts. White, too, received such requests, and to his friend and frequent client, C. T. Barney, he responded in 1901 that Barney's son, James, should go to Columbia but he must concentrate on freehand and mechanical drawing, for "the architects who have made their mark in the world are artists and designers . . . not engineers and business men." As to "historical courses" in medieval ornament, these would be satisfactory, White allowed, "to excite his interest in things, but it don't amount to much in the end."[14]

To McKim, who had been a student at the École, travel and study in Europe were essential for finishing an architect's education, and in order to facilitate such travel he established two fellowships with the estate left him by his second wife, Julia Appleton McKim, the first at Columbia University in 1889, followed by another at Harvard in 1904.[15] To McKim, however, the crowning effort in his crusade to provide "post graduate" education for architects was the establishment of the American Academy in Rome.[16] As an École student he would have been keenly aware of the benefits gained by study at the esteemed French Academy in Rome, but, because he was not a French citizen, admission to the French Academy was impossible. Years later the camaraderie generated among the architects, painters, and sculptors constructing the Columbian Exposition buildings during 1891–1893 renewed in him the desire to provide for artists such a haven for collaborative study comparable to the French Academy. With Daniel Burnham he worked to found such an institution, soliciting support and contributions from fellow architects, friends, and wealthy clients. In 1895 the first architects were dispatched to Rome and housed in temporary quarters—followed two years later by painters and sculptors—but an endowment and a permanent home took twelve years to acquire. In the meantime McKim spent over $25,000 of his own funds to keep the academy alive and functioning.

In addition to these official enterprises, McKim carried on a personal program, aiding young architects. One of his former assistants, Frederick P. Hill, described how McKim unobtrusively observed those who showed promise. If they had plans to go to Europe but had not yet saved enough to go, McKim would produce a check for the necessary amount. To put the recipient at ease, the gift was technically termed a loan. When the money was repaid, if ever, it went directly to help another would-be traveler. Hill said he could not imagine how much money McKim had spent in this way.[17]

There were other more indirect ways in which McKim, Mead & White touched younger generations of architects. In 1881 they assisted in the formation of the Architectural League, devised to give instruction and administer design competitions among students; subsequently both McKim and White served on juries.[18] A few years later, in 1886–87, McKim assisted in raising a fund of $10,000 to establish a *Prix de Reconnaissance* at the École, awarded to French students as a gesture of gratitude from former American students.[19] McKim's concern for his employees and assistants seemingly never ended. Alfred Hoyt Granger wrote that McKim always sensed the struggles of aspiring architects. Without appearing to do so he carefully watched over the professional development of each, and when he felt they had gained the requisite maturity and independence he secured commissions for them.[20] Copies of telegrams of congratulations to former assistants on winning this or that competition appear throughout McKim's letterbooks. It was therefore natural that Cass Gilbert, one of the first office assistants in 1880, should write McKim in 1908, saying "you are the natural leader of your profession."[21] It was an accolade earned over thirty years, nurturing the careers of his former assistants. In a very real sense the office of McKim, Mead & White served as the atelier for two generations of American architects. Even after the founders had gone, the younger partners, who continued to practice under the original firm name, undertook to present the work of McKim, Mead & White to yet a new generation, producing the drawings for the *Monograph of the Work of McKim, Mead & White, 1879–1915*, published in installments from 1915 to 1920.[22]

Not only did those in the office learn the rudiments of running a large professional organization, they also learned that the architect must formulate for himself a philosophy broad enough to apply to each commission. They observed, too, that the architect was not obliged to bow to every whim of the client, but to stand by his professional judgment.[23] The young men learned that what could be done with panache in an isolated country setting most likely would not look well in the crowded confines of the city. The partners had learned this slowly, and with much experimentation, progressing slowly through the use of Richardsonian Romanesque, François Premier French Renaissance, the Italian quattrocento and cinquecento Renaissance, and, ultimately, the sources of the Italian Renaissance in Republican and Imperial Rome. It was a logical exploration in search of the most universal urban prototypes. Yet the young men in the office also learned that the extrapolated abstract universalities of Roman or Renaissance classicism had to be tempered by local traditions. This meant, for instance, that in Boston's Back Bay the firm alluded to the window bays of Beacon Hill; for the Harvard Gates they used burned clinker brick to blend with the nearby eighteenth-century buildings, and for the remodeled Bank of Montreal they restored the dome over the original building. Young architects in the office would have been struck by this desire to enhance rather than alter the unique identities of the places in which the firm built. To be an architect meant to care. Through allusion, too, functional character could be suggested. So, for places of lighthearted activity, the firm used the more plastic, ebullient, and visually complex Renaissance classicism of Spain and northern Italy, but for more formal and serious activities they drew from the High Renaissance of central Italy or from ancient Rome. For educational or domestic buildings they employed variations on Georgian Colonial motifs.

The use of historical allusions, however, did not automatically preclude originality, for as H. H. Statham pointed out in 1898 the Italians themselves had borrowed from antiquity during the Renaissance yet their palaces were hardly Roman.[24] Even when quoting specific European models, McKim, Mead & White consciously and unconsciously modified their sources, introducing a characteristic American quality. When European models had been adapted in the eighteenth and early nineteenth centuries, the variants tended to be more horizontal in line, regularized, visually simplified, tauter, crisper, and more strongly related to the landscape.[25] This is as true of Upjohn's Puginian Gothic as it is of McKim, Mead & White's Renaissance. While specific characteristics such as homogeneity, horizontality, clarity, and tautness have been readily identified in the Georgian architecture of the colonies, as compared to that of England, until lately it has been more difficult to see these same qualities in the Italian or Roman work of late nineteenth-century architects such as McKim, Mead & White. European observers, however, whether traditionalists such as C. H. Reilly, or progressives such as Le Corbusier, long ago recognized and pointed out these distinct and positive qualities.[26]

Perhaps even more important than the training the partners provided or the selective eclecticism they practiced was the principle McKim, Mead & White instilled in their pupils that of all a building's various conflicting responsibilities, its relationship to the street was usually most important. This new positive and broad view of the role of urban buildings in their context was important and timely, for McKim, Mead & White and the two generations of architects trained in their office were instrumental in giving physical form and order to the American city during the very years when it emerged as a dominant force in American society. American cities were growing faster from 1880 to 1910 than they ever had before or were to do again. In 1850 when the three founders were boys, 12.5 percent of the population of the United States lived in what could be termed large towns or cities, that is, 2,897,000 out of a total of 23,192,000. But by the time White and McKim had left the firm in 1910, 37.1 percent lived in cities, or 34,053,400 out of 91,972,300.[27] In other words, during the lifetime of the principals of the firm there was an elevenfold increase in the population of American cities, while the total national population grew slightly less than four times. By 1910 the United States had become an urban nation. Some cities, such as Boston or Philadelphia, had moderate growth rates, while others such as Chicago started from scratch and became major centers of world trade by the close of the century. Americans built cities with a passion; indeed, they had to if they were to provide for their burgeoning urban populations.

The effect of this frantic city-building approached chaos in most established cities, for no city was ever finished but rather was in a constant state of becoming. It was certainly true that in the hands of such trained architects as Hunt and Detlef Lienau, or Frank Furness and Henry Van Brunt, the popular Second Empire and High Victorian Gothic modes were used during the late 1860s and 1870s with particular success. But then as now the great bulk of urban construction was carried out by men who did not have the judgment or educated restraint of these trained few. Thomas Hastings wrote of the great wave of building that swept northward over Manhattan after the Civil War:

> . . . there came such an increase in the number of new buildings as no city had ever seen before. There are many men living today who love to relate to you how they used to take their Sunday

walk into the country as far as 23rd Street! This increase was too sudden for our profession. The work had to be done and it was most of it done by anybody who could draw out any kind of plans. So an immense body of uneducated men tried all sorts of things, exercised their ingenuity in all directions, and we see the resultant confusion.[28]

Outside of the uninspired stretches of monotonous brownstones, buildings were apt to be garrulous individualities; the discrete order and harmony of the Colonial city had broken down.

What McKim, Mead & White contributed to late-nineteenth-century American architecture, helping significantly to change this fragmentation of the visual urban fabric, was not a theory of urban design (which even Burnham's later planning did not do) but rather two exemplars. First, they provided a model of a large architectural office, organized to deal with increasingly complex urban building designs, and second, they established by example a positive view of urban life. Architects such as Frank Lloyd Wright, who espoused Jeffersonian agrarianism and who took to heart the views of A. J. Downing, focused their energies on redefining the suburban single-family house. McKim, Mead & White began their career on this premise, but by 1882 they had cast their lot with the city. So their architecture was developed in accordance with the landscape of the street and not that of the prairie; it recognized the primacy of the corridor of the street and the life of the street. At the same time it recognized that success in the confines of the street would come from subordination to rule, from a return in principle to the decorum of eighteenth-century sources, and from adherence to a transmittable system of design which would foster rather than obviate architectural harmony in the ensemble.

Finding themselves in the midst of a traditional agrarian culture transforming itself into a progressive urban culture, McKim, Mead & White responded by seeking an architecture that was flexible, ordered, and at the same time reflective of a national building tradition. Through the example of their many far-flung buildings, through the influence of the many architects who passed through their office, through the exemplar of their unrelentingly high professional standards, and through their steadfast adherence to excellence in materials and construction, McKim, Mead & White shaped for their generation and the next the character of civic architecture in the United States. Responding quite differently to the social and economic forces that affected Louis Sullivan, McKim, Mead & White created instead an architecture of measured proportion and ceremonial spaces, which was based on the classicism of the native colonial past, but was at the same time distinctly expressive of its own era. Where Sullivan concentrated solely on monuments to commerce comparatively isolated from their social and visual context, McKim, Mead & White attempted to show, particularly in their urban work, that past and present could come together to provide continuity and dignity in the rapidly changing environment.

1

FOUNDATIONS

1840 — 1870

> The youth gets together his material to
> build a bridge to the moon, or perchance
> a palace or temple on the earth.
>
> HENRY DAVID THOREAU
> *Journal*, July 14, 1852

Oɴᴇ grew up in the patchwork farmland of Chester County, Pennsylvania, one amid the rolling marzipan hills of Vermont, and one in the nervous bustle of the nation's largest city. A high-principled Quaker, a jocose and taciturn Yankee, and a blithe ebullient redhead—these disparate three were to form the most active and influential architectural partnership of their generation. They developed a common devotion to art and came to be committed to its cause; eventually they came to be committed to each other.

Of the three, William Rutherford Mead was the eldest, born August 20, 1846, in Brattleboro, Vermont, one of nine children of Larkin Goldsmith and Mary Jane Noyes Mead. His father was a lawyer in Brattleboro, his mother a sister of utopian socialist John Humphrey Noyes.[1] Brattleboro, at that time only slightly larger than 2,800 in population, enjoyed unusual cultural advantages because of a mineral water cure that became popular during the 1840s. The Mead home was visited by some of the luminaries who came to take the cure, providing the children with the acquaintance of intellectuals and artists. Also from Brattleboro were William and Richard Morris Hunt who later achieved prominence in painting and architecture, but when William Mead was born, the Hunts resided in Europe and Richard Hunt was about to enter the architecture section of the École des Beaux-Arts in Paris, the first American to do so. Of the Mead children, several became interested in the arts. William's older sister, Elinor, studied painting, though she never attempted a career. All the Meads communicated visually, for on the sitting room table there were always water color materials and when anyone wished to describe anything they most often drew.[2] In 1862 Elinor married William Dean Howells, who had just been appointed United States Consul to Venice. William's older brother, Larkin, Jr., became a sculptor, studying with Henry Kirke Brown in New York, and then returning home in 1861 to complete the figure of *Vermont* for the state capitol in Montpelier.[3] In a brief statement written about 1918 describing the origins of the firm, William Mead recalled visiting Montpelier with his brother, perhaps about 1862, for the installation of *Vermont,* and he says he was "influenced somewhat toward the study of architecture by my first view, before entering college, of the classic Capitol building." The severity of Ammi B. Young's granite building, as rebuilt by Silloway after burning in 1857, had a marked effect on young Mead.[4]

Mead entered Norwich University in Northfield, Vermont, in 1863, but two years later transferred to Amherst College where he was graduated. "After my graduation from Amherst College in 1867," Mead wrote, "I spent a year in an engineer's office, and in July, 1868, entered the office of Mr. Russell Sturgis. . . . I went into this office as a paid student, for instruction in architecture, and was put directly under the guidance of the late George Fletcher Babb."[5] The identity of the engineer is now lost, but it is clear that from the beginning Mead was interested more in construction than in design. In a further glimpse of Mead's arrival in New York, Peter Bonnett Wight recalled that he and Russell Sturgis had been partners for approximately five years when in 1868 "we were invited one day to go over to Littell's office and be introduced to the new arrival from abroad, Henry Hobson Richardson. It was in that office also that we first met Larkin G. Mead and his brother William R. Mead."[6]

Babb had come into the Sturgis office several years before when it was located across from the Trinity churchyard, at 98 Broadway, but a few months after Mead arrived, in the autumn of 1868, Sturgis moved to 57 Broadway, where Richardson soon set up his office with Gambrill, and where, later, McKim, Mead & White would begin practice. Here Mead worked for three years, leaving in 1871 to study in Europe. He seems not to have been moved by a particular thirst for a sojourn in Europe as much as by a desire to take advantage of fortunate circumstances. Some years earlier Larkin had moved to Florence and established a studio there near other expatriates. Thus William could live with his brother, look at whatever Roman ruins and Renaissance buildings might strike his fancy, and examine the Venetian Gothic buildings which Ruskin and Sturgis so admired. So, Mead recalled, "in 1871 I went to Europe for a residence of a year and a half, living most of the time with my brother Larkin G. Mead at Florence, continuing my studies at the Academie de Belle Arte [*sic,* Accademia delle Belle Arti]."[7] Looking back he surmised, "I suppose I imbibed a love for the Renaissance from my study in Italy." Exactly what the nature of his studies were at the Accademia is not made clear, though they were probably rather informal. Larkin's studio was in the Piazza Indipendenza, while his apartment was in the Casa Grazzini, close to the studios of Hiram Powers, Joel Tanner Hart, and Thomas Ball, whom William undoubtedly met. Occasionally Larkin was called to Venice to assume the role of vice-consul in the absence of Howells, and William may well have accompanied his brother, perhaps with a copy of Ruskin's *Stones of Venice* in hand.

Again for reasons unstated, in 1872 Mead turned homeward; he returned to Sturgis's office

> in the hope that I might continue my services as an architectural draughtsman there. Mr. Sturgis was out of town, and I made a call upon Mr. McKim in his new offices in this same building. I found that he had a quantity of work to be finished before closing with Gambrill & Richardson, and with the two or three country houses that he had on hand, he was very much in need of assistance, so we at once made an arrangement that I should help him out. This was the beginning of our life-long connection.[8]

Why the two had not met before is not clear, for Mead was certain that "up to the time of my departure for Europe in 1871, I had not met him," yet they had worked for architects in the same building for over a year. This sparseness of detail is typical of Mead.

IN contrast to the paucity of information on Mead, there is much more concerning the home environment and education of Charles Follen McKim, for both he and his family saved the many letters which passed between them.[9] McKim was the child of seemingly dissimilar parents. His father, James Miller McKim, was of Scots descent and had been born in Carlisle, Pennsylvania, where he attended Dickinson College. He prepared for the ministry, but before ordination was converted to the abolitionist cause in 1832 on reading William Lloyd Garrison's "Thoughts on Colonization." More temperate in his views than the ardent Garrison, Miller McKim joined with Pennsylvania Quakers such as James and Lucretia Mott, working to bring slavery to an end. He soon resigned his pastorate at Womelsdorf, Pennsylvania, and in 1836 was one of the "Seventy" sent by Theodore Weld to spread the antislavery doctrine. When he became publishing agent of the Pennsylvania Anti-Slavery Society in 1840 he married Sarah Allibone Speakman of Highland Farm, Chester County, Pennsylvania, a Quaker and good friend of Lucretia Mott, and an active abolitionist. The McKims made their home in Philadelphia where Miller was editor of the *Pennsylvania Freeman,* but he was also traveling widely, speaking and collecting contributions for the cause, going to England and Scotland periodically to visit Quaker antislavery organizations in London, Bristol, and Edinburgh.

In 1862 Miller helped set up a relief organization for freed slaves and two years later was instrumental in combining the various regional organizations into the American Freedman's Union Commission, of which he was then elected corresponding secretary. Since the Commission was to have its offices in New York, McKim moved his family to suburban Llewellyn Park, Orange, New Jersey, from which he commuted to Manhattan. Casting about for a way to advance the freedman's cause, Miller McKim learned that E. L. Godkin wished to start a nonpartisan weekly paper devoted to the issues of the day and offered to put up a fourth of the necessary capital. In July 1865 the first number of the *Nation* appeared, edited by Godkin and his assistant Wendell Phillips Garrison, son of the fiery abolitionist.[10]

Though her antislavery sentiments were as fervent as her husband's, Sarah Speakman McKim was less vocal and politically active. In her personal life and manners she was similarly restrained, and was described by Lucretia Mott as being " 'tasty' in her dress, though without much ornament." The McKims had three children: Lucy (1842–1877); Annie, an adopted niece; and Charles, born August 27, 1847, at Isabella Furnace in northwestern Chester County, Pennsylvania, where Sarah was staying with her sister while Miller was once again in England.[11]

Charles McKim's later intensity of artistic conviction is explained, in part, by his home environment. His father was devoted to the cause of the free and educated Negro, undeterred by public condemnation or by any financial or physical risk to himself or his family; he was a man to whom the realization of an ideal was paramount. Indeed, his parents' evangelical abolitionist zeal touched Charles directly, for he had been named in memory of Karl T. C. Follen, who lost his position as the first Professor of German at Harvard because of his outspoken antislavery sentiments; at times, in fact, his father used the German spelling, Karl, when writing about his son to friends. This legacy of commitment had its effect on

Charles, and in later years he was called a "gentle Jesuit of beauty," devoting himself to educating and supporting foreign travel for young architects.[12] Yet Charles's fierce and unrelenting compulsion for perfection and beauty was concealed behind a humble, quiet manner learned from his mother; indeed, even into later life McKim continued to use the Quaker idiom in writing to his mother.

Charles was literally surrounded by abolitionism at Hilltop, the home on Logan Street in Germantown, then outside Philadelphia. Antislavery advocate William Henry Furness, minister of the First Congregational Unitarian Church of Philadelphia (and father of the architect) was a frequent guest, as were Theodore Weld, William Lloyd Garrison, and his sons. Charles became close friends of both Francis (whom he called Frank) and Wendell Garrison, who was married to Lucy in December 1865. Schooling was given first at home, but in 1857 Charles was sent with Annie to Eagleswood, a progressive boarding school run by Theodore Weld at Raritan Bay, Perth Amboy, New Jersey. Weld proved to be a remarkable teacher; his early impetuous zeal for ending slavery had given way to a quiet patience, his own stern self-control inspired his students, so that he inculcated high principles and noble purposes in his students.[13] Sundays brought visitors from New York— William Cullen Bryant, Horace Greeley, various abolitionist Unitarian ministers such as Octavius Frothingham or Henry W. Bellows. Thoreau visited for a few weeks in 1856 just before the McKim children arrived. Moreover, there was a large contingent of Harvard graduates among the visitors, and Weld prepared his students to continue their education there.

Whatever sensitivity toward the landscape that may have resulted from young McKim's walking trip to Gettysburg through southeastern Pennsylvania in 1863 must have been strengthened by the idyllic setting of Llewellyn Park to which the family moved in 1866. There the McKims together with Lucy and Wendell set up a joint household from which both men could commute easily to Manhattan. The families had the added advantage of a wooded suburban setting. Miller McKim's decision to resettle the family in Llewellyn Park is significant, for this was the first American landscaped suburb. It had been started in 1853 by Llewellyn Haskell, a well-to-do chemical and drug merchant and an admirer of A. J. Downing and Calvert Vaux, on a wooded mountainside twelve miles west of New York in what is now West Orange, New Jersey.[14] By 1860 he had assembled over 350 acres and had converted the woods into a picturesque, landscaped park. Much of this, Haskell may have sketched out himself, based on suggestions from Downing, but for later improvements he had the services of professional landscape architects. The roads generally followed the contours of the hillside, and the large irregular house lots were undifferentiated by walls or hedges. The overall effect, as a result, was a densely wooded glen with random open vistas and continuous winding paths. The houses were uniformly picturesque but in a variety of styles, mostly Gothic or Swiss. There were three houses by George Fletcher Babb, but most, including Haskell's and the entrance lodge, were designed by A. J. Davis. Davis himself lived there, and he designed the house at Park Way and Oak Bend that Miller McKim purchased in May 1866 [1]. Originally built for the landscape painter Edward W. Nichols in 1858–59, it was a typical Davis Gothic cottage with a steep center gable whose diamond-paned lancet windows had lighted Nichols's studio. The house was somewhat extreme for Sarah McKim, however, for she wrote to Charles who had remained in Philadelphia:

> The house is rather fanciful for my taste; it was built by an artist; it has a funny pitched roof and clustered chimneys and bull's-eye windows, and niches for statuettes, and all sorts of artistic

arrangements that don't quite suit my plain taste. Still I don't doubt I shall soon be able to accustom myself to them and be quite comfortable. The Park is beautiful and the views from our house are lovely. . . . The roads are so fine that it makes driving pleasant.[15]

Miller McKim seems to have selected Llewellyn Park because of the country setting, but also perhaps because several leading abolitionists also had settled there. McKim also shared the Fourierist views of Haskell, leading the McKims and Garrisons to set up a communal household which, while it helped stretch their limited funds, indicates that they wished in a small way to emulate the examples of Fruitlands, Brook Farm, or even the Raritan Bay Union.

The McKim-Garrison home was visited by many people connected either with the freedman's effort or with the *Nation*, and Miller came to regard the *Nation*'s art critic, Russell Sturgis, as an expert on matters architectural, while Charles became a close friend of Babb. It is uncertain whether Charles actually met Olmsted, whom his father came to know, or Richard Grant White who wrote for the *Nation*. In any case Charles seems to have spent only holidays and the summer in Llewellyn Park, for he was occupied in Philadelphia studying Xenophon and Cicero with a tutor, preparing to enter Harvard in the fall of 1866. Nonetheless Charles puzzled what he would do with a classical education. He wrote for advice to Frank Garrison who had just entered Harvard, considered his prospects, and decided to become an engineer. Thus trained, he reasoned, he could find employment immediately upon graduation, but it would mean intensive study of mathematics during the summer.[16] Once admitted to Harvard's Lawrence Scientific School in September, McKim found he enjoyed mechanical drawing classes, describing many projects in letters to his family. Almost immediately, however, he began planning to complete his engineering training in Europe, at Paris or Freiburg, asking his father's advice. By the end of the fall term it was painfully clear that he had no taste for mathematics, eliminating civil engineering as a career. Drawing, however, he enjoyed and by Christmas Charles had decided to become an architect, but this meant it was even more necessary that he go to Paris to study. Miller McKim preferred Berlin or Munich, for, as he wrote of his son's plans to Wendell, "the temptations of Paris have been found irresistible to stronger men than Charley."[17]

When Charles sent a sample drawing home in February 1867, his father showed it to his acquaintances and began to seek advice from colleagues, including journalist Henry Villard (who had married Wendell's sister, Helen Frances Garrison) and William H. Furness, whose son had become an architect in Philadelphia. Valuing Villard's judgment

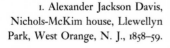

1. Alexander Jackson Davis, Nichols-McKim house, Llewellyn Park, West Orange, N. J., 1858–59.

and his European experience, Miller wrote Charles in March that he would decide nothing "until I shall have heard from Mr. Villard."[18]

During April, then, the matter rested, but the issue was far from settled, as the responses from Wendell Garrison and Villard were rather cautious, as can be surmised by Miller McKim's response later in the summer to Villard:

> I advised Charley to give up all idea of going to France, to give his attention to the subject of architecture here and to enter an architect's office with a view to seeing whether that would not be likely to be the profession best suited to his tastes and talents. He seemed convinced by my reasoning and that of the rest of the family, and, following my counsel, entered himself tentatively at the office of Russell Sturgis. But in a few weeks it became evident that his heart was not in his work. He worked harder out of the office at mathematics, for which he has no aptitude, than he did in the office at drawing, for which he has a positive talent. Soon he told me that his heart was still on *L'Ecole Centrale.*[19]

But, in closing the letter, Miller confessed that Charles would indeed go to Paris, for his close friend William H. Furness had responded most persuasively, saying:

> We meant to strain every nerve and live on potato skins if need were to get Frank off to study in Paris, but the war came and broke up his studies and when his three yrs. service was over he fell in love—was married and had to go to work. He sighs, however, over the loss of Paris advantages. He had 3 years of the best training in Architecture in N.Y. under Richard Hunt who has 15 years in France and 6 in the employ of the French Gov't. A most accomplished architect. I believe he is abroad now, if not consult him. He is known in N.Y. where he resides. My own idea is that if a young man can go to Paris it is the best possible thing he can do, to become a well educated Architect. . . . If Charley could study with Richard Hunt a year or two first making himself perfect in the French tongue, wouldn't it be wise?[20]

Richard Morris Hunt, the first American to study at the École des Beaux-Arts, was indeed in Europe at that moment; the benefit of his counsel thus lost, Miller turned to the only other architect he knew well, Russell Sturgis. Quite unknowingly he consulted an architect who could hardly have been more different from Hunt. Born in 1838, the son of a prosperous New York merchant, Sturgis attended the "Free Academy" (which later became the College of the City of New York), where he met Peter Bonnett Wight. Together they spent long hours examining the plans for All Soul's Unitarian Church by Jacob Wrey Mould, and resolved to become architects themselves, reading Ruskin's *Seven Lamps of Architecture* and his *Stones of Venice.*[21] During 1856–57 Sturgis worked in the office of Leopold Eidlitz in New York, after which he studied in Munich, returned to the United States in 1862, and joined with Wight—who meanwhile had worked in Chicago, returned to New York, and won the competition for the new National Academy of Design in New York with a scheme which was the purest expression of Ruskinian Gothic yet seen in the United States. Wight and Sturgis set up a joint office at 98 Broadway, and were among the seven founders of The Society for the Advancement of Truth in Art, publishing its journal, *The New Path*, which disseminated Ruskin's principles in art and design, Wight serving as editor and Sturgis being the major contributor. The strong Ruskinian character of the journal, reflecting Sturgis's own philosophy, was quite evident in the manifesto printed in *The New Path* in March 1863:

> We hold . . . that, in all times of great art, there has been a close connection between architecture, sculpture and painting; that sculpture and painting having been first called into being for the

decoration of buildings, have found their highest perfection when habitually associated with architecture; that architecture derives its greatest glory from such association; therefore that this union of the arts is necessary for the full development of each.[22]

This was the climate of the office when McKim entered in June 1867. On which of Sturgis's current projects McKim may have been put to work is unknown. Though long since finished, the National Academy of Design by Wight was considered a most important work and would certainly have been studied. He probably examined, too, drawings for Wight's Mercantile Library, Brooklyn, 1867 [2], and perhaps saw early sketches for Sturgis's Farnam Hall, Yale University, built in 1869–70 [3], elements from both of which appeared in McKim's earliest work.

2. Peter Bonnett Wight, Mercantile Library, Brooklyn, N. Y., 1869.

There was one other draftsman-assistant, George Fletcher Babb, whom McKim already knew. Both Babb and McKim were greatly influenced by Sturgis, who was dedicated to developing a functional and rational American architecture based on Ruskinian principles. Mead was to come into the office later, in 1868, and to remain for three years, but ironically it was McKim, who was there less than three months, who appears to have been far more deeply affected. From Sturgis he learned the basic tenets of Ruskinian Gothicism. Architecture should be based on nature, solidly constructed, with no deceptive use of materials or structural shams. Planning should be simple and straightforward, with boldly irregular masses expressive of human use. All of these qualities, Ruskin proclaimed, could be observed in Gothic architecture. "We want no new style of architecture," Ruskin flatly insisted, yet this need not preclude an architecture expressive of its own time, for "originality of expression does not depend on invention or new words." In fact, it was impossible to invent a new style, for style to Ruskin by its very nature meant something that had to be practiced

3. Russell Sturgis, Farnam Hall, Yale University, New Haven, Conn.,
1869–70. *New York Sketch Book*, September 1876.

for ages.[23] By means of its ornament (which Ruskin believed to be the chief part of
architecture) a building could become "the embodiment of Poetry, Life, History and Religious faith of nations."[24] A building should influence its users, or, as Sturgis put it in 1864,
a church "should have just as much to do, in its way, in instructing the minds and softening
the hearts of men, as the minister has in his holy office."[25] Since Ruskin believed that "all
good architecture is the expression of national life and character," so too did he believe that
English Gothic was the national style of England.[26] As McKim assimilated all of this, he
extrapolated that for Americans a national architecture, "as universal and as established as
its language," as Ruskin asserted it should be, would be based on the ancestral Colonial
tradition. This conclusion, only nascent when McKim left Sturgis for Paris, emerged later
when the nation's centennial focused attention on the Colonial period and within six years
had become something of an article of faith. Thus, if one substitutes Colonial Georgian or
a more general Renaissance classicism for Gothic, all the precepts of a national architecture
described by Ruskin appear in the later work of McKim. Like Ruskin, too, McKim was not
primarily concerned with structural expression as the basis of design, though he was introduced to the work of Viollet-le-Duc through Sturgis. This tenuous exposure to structural
rationalism tempered to some extent the purely visual and moralistic approach of Ruskin,
and besides kindling in McKim a desire to translate *Entretiens sur l'architecture*, it prompted
him to seek to meet Viollet-le-Duc as soon as he got to Paris.

His short apprenticeship with Sturgis at an end, McKim prepared in late August 1867
to depart for France. He was already familiar with two of the major influences on nineteenth-century architects—Ruskin and Viollet-le-Duc. Now he set out to experience for
himself the third major influence—training at the École des Beaux-Arts. In mid-September,

having found a room in the Latin Quarter, he began corresponding with his family, hearing in return from his mother that she was pleased he had found William Robert Ware and Robert Peabody, who were already settled in Paris, so that he had at least two friends who spoke English.[27] McKim had already made Ware's acquaintance while in Cambridge, and at the same time he came to know Robert Swain Peabody, who preceded him to the École by several months. "We lived a simple frugal life in the splendid Paris of Louis Napoleon," Peabody later reminisced, "working hard, and he [McKim] especially with a dogged earnestness."[28]

When Charles had first thought of studying architecture in Paris, he planned on entering the École Centrale, soon changing his mind in favor of the École des Beaux-Arts. Since he had learned from Sturgis and from reading Ruskin that architecture was a fine art, it was natural to seek admission to the École des Beaux-Arts rather than the École Centrale where architecture was taught more as an engineering discipline. Indeed, in "The Study of Architecture in Our Schools" of 1865, Ruskin had declared unequivocally that the architect should not be trained with the engineer but with the sculptor.[29]

McKim grasped quickly what was required of aspirants to the École and perfected his French sufficiently to pass the rigorous examinations without great difficulty. He was probably only dimly aware that the school was just emerging from a difficult period of readjustment following an abortive attempt in 1863 by Napoleon III and Viollet-le-Duc to impose more government control over the teaching program.[30] In large part the attempted reform was short-lived, but one major change in the curriculum may have left a permanent mark on McKim and subsequently on his office. During the three years he was at the École, 1867 to 1870, there was no instruction in architectural theory. The chair in theory, which had been occupied by the conservative J.-B.-C. Lesueur, had been abolished and was not reinstituted until 1874. It may be more than coincidence that for McKim and his firm, theory played a very small role; instead, for them, symbolic aesthetics and pragmatic function governed design.

The courses offered within the École proper were appreciated by McKim, though like most École students he seems not to have attended lectures scrupulously. He was content with the atelier he joined, conducted by P.-G.-H. Daumet, and he described it in some detail in a letter home dated August 31, 1868: at the rear of a court off the rue du Four and the boulevard Saint-Germain, on the second floor, was

> a large, square room, lighted by windows reaching from ceiling to floor, and hung about with plaster casts of every description. The inter-spaces, we notice are filled with caricatures of various favorites, many of them executed in good style. On a series of long tables are stretched the designs; and now, if you will figure to yourself above each board a cigarette sticking into the mouth of a long-haired, unkempt, "scrub," dressed in a gray blouse, you may gain some idea of a French Student [4].[31]

What seems to have particularly impressed McKim, as it did many American students, was the friendly hierarchy within the atelier and the esprit de corps this generated, especially at the end of the tedious *rendus,* when the younger students, the *nouveaux,* were conscripted into service working on the large ink drawings of the older students of the First Class, the *anciens.* Indeed, in the normal absence of the *patron* of the atelier the *nouveaux* learned much of the intricacies of design and draftsmanship from the *anciens.* Ernest Flagg said of the atelier members:

4. Alexis Lemaistre, "In the Atelier."
Architectural Record, April–June 1894.

> There is a loyal comradeship among them, also an utter lack of selfishness. The generous way they work for one another is surprising to one of Anglo Saxon blood, who as a rule does not feel called upon to work days and often all night long for a comrade behind in his work, but such devotedness is of continual occurrence at the atelier where it is considered a matter of course.[32]

Before the reform of 1863, during the administration of *secrétaire perpétuel* Quatremère de Quincy, prizewinning designs tended toward a geometrically pure Roman classicism. One of the few lasting results of the reform was to give prize-awarding power to leaders of the self-proclaimed Eclectics, who believed not only that references to the past could and should be present in modern architecture but that these references should reflect a broad historic range. To the Eclectics it was paramount that the character of the design be fittingly appropriate to the literal as well as symbolic function of the building. The plan had to be so modulated in its spaces that movement was directed through it in a logical, effortless way. But once this was achieved the exterior might be expressed in any of a number of ways with historic allusions symbolically appropriate to the function. Hence a church or hostel might be Gothic, or a private house Renaissance of the period of François Ier.[33] One of the Prix de Rome designs much discussed when McKim entered the École was that of Julien Guadet whose Gothic hospice in the Alps was premiated in 1864. Later, having returned to Paris and assuming the chair in architectural theory at the École, Guadet codified the design principles taught there; as with Ruskin's lamps there were seven. First, fidelity to the program, coupled with a diligent investigation of the proper character to be expressed. Second, recognition that site, location, and climate always modify expression. Third, simply constructable compositions. Fourth, truthful architectural expression, with no sham structure or materials. Fifth, effective perceivable visual strength in the structure. Sixth, ample but direct and untortured plans so that light and air could be admitted easily. In his seventh point, Guadet acknowledged that "composition proceeds by necessary sacrifices. Composition must be good first, but it must be beautiful as well. You must therefore compose a building with a view towards its usefulness and its beauty. You will seek character, which contributes to beauty by creating variety."[34]

It was expected that the conceptual parti be sound and logical, the most appropriate synthesis of the practical and artistic; and because the character of the parti was most readily apparent in the plan, most of the student's time was devoted to it. For the same reason, in judging, the jury examined it closely. Graduates of the École would later assert that the chief benefit they derived from their experience was this focus on studying the plan rather than indoctrination in the use of any particular historic style; "it has done much to persuade us that there is such a thing as beauty in [plan] arrangement and not merely convenience—to teach us that there is such a thing as a beautiful plan," wrote Walter Cook.[35] Perceptive students recognized that the chief result of their training was not memorizing formulas, but developing a method of analyzing any problem put before them. "Nowhere do they so thoroughly discourage the mere adaptation of the things that have been done before," Thomas Hastings asserted.[36] Above all, the École stressed a sense of large formal order, and maintained that architecture from its beginnings had been concerned with the most embracing ceremonial elements of life. It was true, of course, that the vast Prix de Rome projects set before the students in the early part of the nineteenth century were impossible, even megalomaniac, but by the end of the century such had become in fact the actual scale of building, particularly in the United States.

Significantly, McKim selected the atelier of Pierre-Gérôme-Honoré Daumet (1826–1911), a graduate of the École and winner of the Prix de Rome in 1855.[37] During his career Daumet had worked under L. J. Duc and had allied himself with the Eclectics who opposed the more orthodox Rational Classicists including Henri Labrouste. It was in 1862, just before the attempted reforms, that Daumet opened his atelier. Like the other Eclectics—Lefuel, Vaudoyer, Charles Garnier, Ballu, and Esperandieu—Daumet favored a more heterodox approach and acknowledged the appropriateness of François Ier, Baroque, or even Gothic for certain uses. McKim may have chosen the Daumet atelier partly because of this, because the sympathies there would have been as close as he could find in Paris to those of Sturgis, but perhaps he was attracted more by the presence of several other Americans, including Peabody, Alfred H. Thorp, Francis W. Chandler, and Sidney V. Stratton. Thorp had already been in Paris for about three years, while Peabody had arrived some time in the spring of 1867. The latitude permitted Daumet's students can be surmised from photographs McKim pasted in a scrapbook.[38] There is a photograph of the casino *projet* [5] assigned in the autumn of 1868, a copy of which McKim had sent home for comment; he had, in fact, not even won a *mention*. McKim's design, as well as those of Stratton, Peabody, and fellow French students Cottreau, Eauline, and Laugier, show a free paraphrase of Louis XIII and Louis XIV elements, and are close in character to the work of Daumet, particularly a house by him at Meaux.[39] In the scrapbook, too, are photographs of church designs by Peabody and Chandler, both of which owe much to Lassus's Gothic Saint-Jean-Baptiste de Belleville of 1854–59 and Heret's Notre-Dame-de-la-Croix of 1862–80. More significant, both are very similar to the prizewinning "Portail d'eglise" prepared by Paul Blondel in the Daumet atelier in 1868.[40] There is Thorp's design for a "Maison d'un peintre" whose boldly scaled masonry distinctly resembles a "hôtel d'un peintre" by Amoudru published in 1868 but perhaps designed earlier.[41] This, and the views of Duban's additions to the Louvre and his additions to the École of 1860–62, would suggest that McKim had some interest in the structural clarity of late Néo-grec work, but such expression was not his central interest and he never experimented with this in his own early work. As did most students of his generation, however, he developed a profound admiration for Labrouste's Bibliothèque Sainte-Geneviève, 1838–50, which appeared a paradigm of library design.

The small number of views in McKim's scrapbook acquire special significance because of their exclusivity. There is a frontal view of the Renaissance headhouse of the Gare de Strasbourg (Gare de l'Est) by Duquesney, 1847–52, and one of the so-called House of François Ier, a pastiche of fragments of an early sixteenth-century house incorporated in a house of 1816 built on the Quai de la Conférence in Paris. There are the views of Duban's

5. Charles Follen McKim, casino project, 1868.

Louvre additions, selected details of some of the new Louvre pavilions by Lefuel, the facade of Notre Dame and the Hôtel de Ville in Paris, the Chateau at Blois, and a detail of the Luxembourg Palace, but of what is called Second Empire Baroque there is nothing. Thus, the most prominent building of the day, the Paris Opéra then under construction, is conspicuous by its absence. Peabody recalled that McKim had some difficulty adjusting to prevailing taste, for his sole exposure to architecture had been through Sturgis:

> That master and Mr. Babb were his arbiters. Ruskin was the prophet of all that was good and true in art. Plunged into a world that did not know these masters even by name and that looked on Victorian Gothic as romantic archaeology, but in no sense as architecture, McKim's inflexible nature had some hard rebuffs and conflicts. It required time and other influences to bring him to a sense of the great worth of the underlying principles of Parisian training, but his sympathies were always more with the later French masters. He never really liked modern French taste and he was in fact more close to Rome than to Paris.[42]

In his letters home McKim had begun to incorporate large block capital letters, causing his mother to ask, "Charlie darling, why does thee make those horrid square capital letters . . . ? I should advise thee to keep to a plain round clear hand as the one to commend thy writing to all sensible persons."[43] Similar printing appeared, too, on the drawings McKim made as he traveled around the countryside, as in the sketch of the house at Lisieux done in the summer of 1869 [6].[44] In these McKim used a slashing line to suggest an atmospheric effect, a technique derived perhaps from his experiments with etching which he had begun studying that spring, with the emphatic approval of his father and Sturgis. While Charles was in France his family continually relayed news to Sturgis and Babb, and when his father wrote back, consoling Charles for not having received a *mention* for his casino *projet*, he added that the drawing had been shown to Sturgis and Babb, both of whom were pleased. "Charley will learn . . . to draw," had been Sturgis's response; "he will make a splendid draftsman."[45] Lucy, however, found "the nude ladies in the niches" gratuitous and offensive. Another reason for contacting Sturgis was for a letter of introduction to Viollet-le-Duc which Miller McKim kept forgetting; he felt it was more important for Charles "to visit the houses and suburban villas of architects who best understand the art of giving the best buildings for the smallest sum. Boston architects have their cheap methods & I presume Paris architects have their cheap methods. *I hope you will study their cheap cottages in detail;* for in doing so you will be able to aid me & others when you come home."[46] There was a stream of advice from home, as in the stern letter from Lucy in the spring of 1869 which expressed little sympathy that Charles had done so poorly in a second peristyle *projet:* "I thought thee had proved satisfactorily to thyself by many trials before thee left home, of the unwisdom of postponing study and then doing it at night with much loss of sleep and consequently of brain power. Yet thee speaks of this truth as if it were a new discovery. . . . Commonplaces have to be rediscovered so often."[47]

6. Charles Follen McKim, sketch of Lisieux, 1869.

The cost of maintaining Charles in Paris was mounting, and Miller became concerned that his son was not gaining any practical experience. Sturgis, he wrote, advocated a trip through France and Italy, but Charles sketched out a trip through England which Miller thought wise, since it offered an opportunity to study with landscape architects, making it possible for Charles to enter Olmsted's office when he returned. Perhaps he could work briefly in an English architect's office, for "Withers, Olmsted and Vaux all agree that a familiar acquaintance with English architecture—suburban and rural—is important to success in the profession here," Miller wrote, adding that he would try to get a letter of introduction to R. I. Withers from his brother Frederick.[48] Meanwhile Miller again asked Villard's advice on a good European itinerary. As a result, during the summer of 1869 Charles toured England, in the company of R. Phené Spiers and Henry Florence, both of whom had been at the École with H. H. Richardson several years before and who showed him the sights of London. Not only did he enjoy the cricket fields, where he played often, he was also made an honorary member of the Architectural Association. With the aid of his father's Quaker friends, McKim was able to visit Bristol and Edinburgh before returning to France. Miller McKim continued to advise studying French landscape architecture.

> City Parks are the rage here now and millions are being [spent] in landscape gardening and ornamentation on them. Phila has a Park of 2800 acres the largest in the world, outside of Russia, and on it she will have to spend vast sums. Keep your eye open for pretty & novel features in the Bois de Boulogne & "when found make a note" of them—in your Portfolio.
>
> If your lot should bring you near M. Schneider's factory village [Le Creusot] take a look at the main features of it with your pencil in your hand. Perhaps his place (iron works) are at too great a distance from Paris; but it is very famous and such places are springing up here. . . . pps. Frank Furness is building a costly Jewish Temple. It is of course of the Saracenic style. Keep your eye out for a beauty of a Jewish synagogue & *note it*.[49]

Charles's time in France was nearing an end, and Miller began examining his son's prospects, again inquiring among his friends. He wrote Charles in September, 1869:

> I found that you were very popular in Germantown and among young Philadelphians . . . so that if you were now to return you would have quite an ovation. You would take a position in society, and if you should choose to "hang out your shingle" in Phila you would do so under the most promising auspices. I saw Frank Furness while in Phila. He is one of the first architects of the city. He has recently had some fine jobs, among them a $150,000 house for Tom McKean (son of Pratt McKean) at the corner of Walnut & 20th, and the conversion of the Market house, which you will remember on 10th above Chestnut, into an edifice for the Mercantile Library. This last he has done most successfully; and the McKean house is a beauty. He wants you to come right to him when you return. He desired me to ask you to make no other engagement. He says he has his eye on you; that he has heard of you through the Boston boys and that he wants you. He says there is a fine opening in Phila; that the Buttons and Huttons & Sloans have had their day, and that real architects are now coming into request. My own judgement is that if you should choose Philada as your location you would find the way to success short & easy. Frank advises that you should go back to school, and not to London, and that an office here is better for practical details than a London office. 3 mos. more of the school he says would be of more use to you than 3 mos. in London.[50]

He was certain that "in the spring you will come home better qualified than most young architects for starting your profession," but as to whether New York or Philadelphia was the best place there was some question. "I think you would sooner make a name and a place for yourself in Phila but New York is a bigger city, and a name and place in it would—when attained—be of more account. As a place to *live* I like Phila best; as a live and progressive city, New York is preferable. The one is a great provincetown, the other a metropolitan city."[51]

Narrowly escaping the outbreak of the Franco-Prussian War, McKim left Paris in April 1870. Apparently he had decided by then to seek a position in New York rather than going to Furness. Whether he actually called at Sturgis's office is not clear, for certainly his architectural ideals on his return were far different from what they had been when he left Sturgis; perhaps his architectural horizons had been elevated to a point where returning to Sturgis would have been difficult. Perhaps, too, Richardson had been recommended to him by Spiers, for Richardson, an *ancien élève*, had been a classmate of Spiers's at the École. Despite the fact that Richardson then had little work, he took McKim on, no doubt because there were few young architects with his training. He was fresh from Paris and England and knew contemporary work that, as yet, Richardson knew only through publication.

McKim came to Richardson to learn; and the office was for him a kind of postgraduate school. Coming from the École he could well appreciate Richardson's insistence that the architect was to defend professed ideals, that his was not a trade but a profession. Thus the architect was entrusted with a near-sacred obligation to supervise all aspects of design and construction. One built, then, looking to posterity, specifying the best in such materials as Quincy granite, and such workmanship as Richardson obtained from his favored contractor, O. W. Norcross. When Richardson started his career it was difficult to incorporate the work of other artists in new work, in contrast to the view advocated at the École that architecture was complete only when embellished by the sister arts, painting and sculpture. It was pure coincidence that the first job given to McKim to draw up in 1870, the Brattle Square Church in Boston's Back Bay, was also the first in which Richardson was able to include sculpture, the tower frieze cut *in situ* by F. A. Bartoldi. Here was the fusion of the arts that McKim (and Richardson) had been taught to expect.

If McKim learned much from Richardson, as he clearly did, perhaps Richardson's own work was affected by the infusion of fresh ideas from Paris. Significantly, the Brattle Square Church is marked externally by a boldness of form and a sharpness of geometric ornament not particularly characteristic of Richardson's work before. McKim also seems to have played a significant part in developing drawings for the Hampden County Court House, Springfield, Massachusetts, which Richardson started to design in mid-1871. Later, in 1874, when McKim edited the *New York Sketch Book of Architecture*, he published a perspective of the court house he seems to have had a hand in preparing [7], his touch suggested in the inscribed "LEX" over the entrance.[52] Richardson may also have been glad of McKim's assistance in handling the volume of drawings for the state hospital complex at Buffalo, on which design started in 1871. McKim seems to have had little effect on the design of the hospital, nor did he on the Trinity Church competition design which Richardson was invited to submit (with the specific exclusion of Gambrill) in March 1872. Richardson met the deadline of May 1, and won the competition, but his worsening Bright's Disease hampered detailed restudy of the scheme when the church bought the lot adjoining the designated site on the east side of Copley Square in the Back Bay. All the while McKim was gradually working more and more outside the Richardson office, establishing his own practice with Richardson's tacit approval. He had, after all, entered the office to gain practical experience, and by mid-1872 apparently felt he had acquired enough to venture out

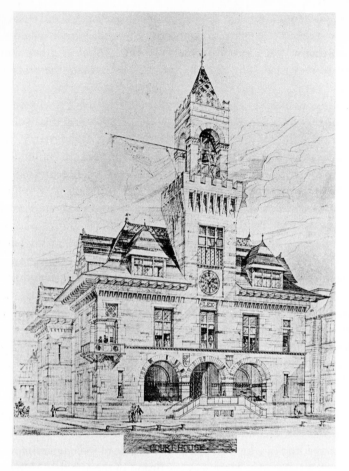

7. Henry Hobson Richardson, Hampden County Courthouse, Springfield, Mass., 1871–73, perspective by C. F. McKim (?). *New York Sketch Book*, January 1874.

on his own. Mead recalled that McKim "had secured a commission for designing several small country houses in the Oranges, N.J., and had decided to start in business for himself. He took two small rooms at 57 Broadway, while closing up his connection with Gambrill and Richardson."[53] Richardson was not exactly being left shorthanded, however, for not long before an amazingly gifted apprentice had entered the office; McKim could leave confident that the Trinity drawings were in able hands.

THE position being vacated by McKim was filled by a redheaded youth of nineteen who had no formal training in architecture, but who had overwhelming enthusiasm and a great natural talent for drawing. Stanford White had been born November 9, 1853, in New York, the son of Richard Grant White, a native of the city who had been educated at the Columbia Grammar School and later at New York University at Washington Square. Unable to pursue a career in law for which he trained, Richard Grant White turned to writing, beginning with art and music criticism in the New York *Morning Courier and Enquirer* (he was a talented amateur cellist). Following the warm reception of his urbane and highly knowledgeable comments, he was named art and music critic for *Putnam's Magazine*, but was replaced shortly thereafter by then acting-editor Frederick Law Olmsted.[54] Subsequently White was a regular contributor to *Galaxy* (and later *Atlantic Monthly* with which it merged), the *Nation,* and *Century* Magazine, writing on music, art, the English language, literature, and the stage. Although his novels were unsuccessful, he became widely known for his essays on English life and manners. For a time he considered writing on architecture, an idea strongly encouraged by his friend Calvert Vaux, who was of the opinion that "tonic medicine in the form of adequate healthy criticism is much needed." One of the few architectural essays White did venture was his strong disapproval of the gates proposed by Richard Morris Hunt for the south end of Central Park, printed in 1866; architecturally, he said, the gates were fine enough, but they were too French and had nothing to do at all with the American spirit of Olmsted's park. Besides Olmsted and Vaux, Richard Grant White was well acquainted with major figures in English and American literature—Emerson, Lowell, Howells, Gilder, Aldrich, Dickens, Browning—and painters, such as John La Farge who lived one block away on Tenth Street. Moreover, Stanford's mother, Alexina Mease White, wrote children's stories and verses. Thus as a child Stanford White was enveloped by the arts and literature.[55]

Even as a small boy "Stanny" showed marked artistic talent. Summers were spent at Fort Hamilton on the Narrows of New York Bay, or at his aunt's home on the Hudson near Newburgh where, sketchbook in hand, he explored the countryside in search of picturesque subjects to draw. Several of the more finished drawings survive, such as the pencil drawing of a house, signed and dated 1864, done when Stanford was eleven [8].[56] In the next several years his touch became more sure, more impressionistic, as is evident in drawings done about 1868–72 [9]. These reveal the wide range of White's interest, from mountain landscapes, to crumbling farm buildings, to urban roofscapes. It is more than likely that White was familiar with English drawings and watercolors, at least at second hand through engravings and etchings, and his style suggests he may even have examined the plates of David Cox's *Treatise on Landscape Painting and Effect of Water Colors* (London, 1813), for such books were in his father's large art library. The boy's early efforts drew

8. ABOVE. Stanford White, sketch of a house, signed and dated "SW 1864."

9. RIGHT. Stanford White, untitled watercolor landscape, c. 1868–69.

favorable comment from those artists who visited the house, and the suggestions Stanford gleaned in this way were the extent of his "formal" training. By the time he was eighteen Stanford wanted to become a painter, but given the limits of his father's income, formal training seemed out of the question. Stanford went to his father's friend La Farge for advice, who answered quite candidly that painting was a risky proposition at best, that recognition came very slowly, and that remuneration was slight—adversities La Farge knew only too well. Meanwhile, Richard Grant White made his own inquiries; through Olmsted he was introduced to H. H. Richardson and arranged an apprenticeship for his son. So it was determined that Stanford White would become an architect.[57]

10. Henry Hobson Richardson, Trinity Church, Boston, Mass., sketch for revised tower design, c. 1873–74 by Stanford White (?). *New York Sketch Book*, March 1874.

In the spring of 1872 White came into Richardson's office at 57 Broadway, working first on the drawings for Trinity Church, which he took over from McKim. Under Richardson's supervision, the scheme was repeatedly restudied during 1873–74 to shorten and lighten the tower, when the engineers warned that the original tower was too heavy for the piles driven into the gravel fill of the Back Bay. Eventually Richardson decided on a stubby tower adapted from the Romanesque lantern of the Cathedral of Salamanca, Spain, and it was White who then drew up the presentation perspective drawing following Richardson's instructions [10].

The Trinity tower rendering is exemplary of White's rapidly maturing drafting style, which was heavily indebted to that of Richard Norman Shaw, much admired by Richardson, whose perspectives began to appear in English architectural journals in 1870. Shaw's technique had much to recommend it to White since it too was concerned with the rendering of texture. This the photograph could do better, of course, but so far, reproducing photographs in professional journals was prohibitively expensive. It is significant, therefore, not only of the rising interest in texture in building materials but also of McKim's interest in Colonial architecture, that the first photograph published in an American architectural journal, in the *New York Sketch Book* in 1874, presented a wealth of picturesque texture. This was a view, not of the austere foursquare front of Georgian Whitehall, built for Bishop Berkeley outside Newport, Rhode Island, in 1728, but of the long sweeping shingled roof to the rear.[58] The following year White made an ink drawing of a nearly identical view, the rear of the Hasbrouck house (Washington's Headquarters), Newburgh, New York [11]. Signed and dated in the lower left corner, "/75 ⚹," it carefully records the texture of the stone walls and most particularly the gentle swells of the sagging shingled roof; a simplified second version redrawn by White was published in the *New York Sketch Book* the next year. In Richardson's office, understandably, White quickly became the delineator of the crisp renderings of the projects which appeared in the *New York Sketch Book* and other journals over the next six years, typified by the views of the Sherman house, Newport, which Richardson started in 1874 [12, 13].[59]

While this work was under way Richardson moved from New York to Brookline, Massachusetts, outside Boston, closer to his clients and friends. Although for some time White had been making periodic trips to Boston to check progress on Trinity Church and other commissions, this commuting now continued since Richardson maintained a nominal joint practice with Gambrill for several years. Following the success of the Sherman house, White was given increasing responsibility for the houses that came into the Richardson office, gradually becoming a virtual collaborator on, if not the actual designer of, the Arthur Blake house, Newton Lower Falls, Massachusetts, 1875, and, more certainly, the Rush Cheney house project, South Manchester, Connecticut, 1876. The latter, particularly, had disparate component elements and an obsession with textured surfaces and ornament that made it unlike the subsequent personal work of Richardson.[60]

In commercial and ecclesiastical work Richardson retained full authority; White, therefore, probably was only minimally involved in the design of the Cheney Building, Hartford, Connecticut, begun in 1875, though he probably executed the published perspective and, as Richardson's agent, visited Hartford to supervise construction.[61] Glenn Brown, then clerk of the works for the contractor, remembered vividly one such visit by White. Tall, lank, and freckle-faced, radiating enthusiasm, White made a rapid survey of the exterior and then went up to the roof. He returned all excitement, demanding paper and watercolors. "There's a beautiful sunset," he said, "so bully that I want to get it down." Brown found the materials and White hurried off again, returning in about an hour, "rejoicing in the beauties he had

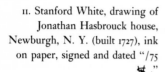

11. Stanford White, drawing of Jonathan Hasbrouck house, Newburgh, N. Y. (built 1727), ink on paper, signed and dated "/75 ₩ ."

12. Henry Hobson Richardson, William Watts Sherman house, Newport, R. I., 1874, perspective by Stanford White (?). *New York Sketch Book*, May 1875.

13. Sherman house, interior perspective, by Stanford White (?). *New York Sketch Book*, May 1875.

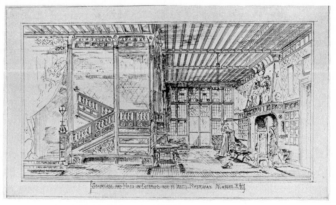

caught in a very effective sketch, with the stone of one of the corner pinnacles in the foreground."[62]

Meanwhile, in New York White began to meet other young adventuresome and idealistic artists. Augustus Saint-Gaudens became one of his closest associates. They met by accident in 1875 when White was on an errand in the German Savings Bank where the sculptor then had a studio. White was drawn to the studio, Saint-Gaudens wrote, upon

> hearing me bawl the "Andante" of Beethoven's Seventh Symphony, and "The Serenade" from Mozart's "Don Giovanni." He was a great lover of music. I gave a false impression, for my knowledge came only from having heard the "Andante" from Le Brethon, ten or fifteen years before, and the "Serenade" from a howling Frenchman in the Beaux Arts who could shout even louder than I, and sang it in a singularly devilish and comic way.[63]

White and Saint-Gaudens became immediate and lifelong friends. They were two of a kind, and one senses in Saint-Gaudens the same mischievous spark that animated White. Saint-Gaudens had begun his studies in New York, continuing at the École des Beaux-Arts during precisely the same years that McKim was there (though they did not meet then), and then in Rome for two years, finally returning to New York in 1872. Commissions, however, were coming in very slowly when White, in his characteristically unselfish way, put Saint-Gaudens in touch with John La Farge, so that in September 1876, when La Farge was engaged at Richardson's urging to decorate the interior of Trinity Church, Saint-Gaudens came to Boston with a number of other assistants. During the winter of 1876–77 he worked on the murals, doing the figure of Saint Paul on one side of the chancel arch.[64] Also working under La Farge in this, the first large-scale mural painting endeavor in the United States, were young artists who later became leaders of the "American Renaissance"—Francis Lathrop, Frank Millet, and George Maynard.

The year before, in 1875, White had begun sketching a large tomb for Edwin Denison Morgan, governor of New York during the Civil War, though how such a prestigious commission came to one so young and unproven is unclear; it may well have been because of his father's influence. White persuaded Morgan that sculpture was needed and that Saint-Gaudens was the man for the job. At almost the same time Saint-Gaudens began making preparatory sketches for a proposed monument to Admiral David Glasgow Farragut to be raised in New York City, and as early as 1876 White joined him in designing a broad base for the bronze figure. These collaborations, and their Robert Richard Randall statue that soon followed, were the first in a long series of works designed jointly. Although sculptors had consulted architects for bases before, it was generally after the figure was completed; never before had an American sculptor and architect worked so closely together, achieving such a harmony between their contributions. In 1876–77 such comprehensive design was unprecedented and not altogether appreciated by those who were asked to pay for it, as the young men soon discovered with the Farragut Memorial committee. Together each enriched and enlarged the other's work, freely offering and accepting criticism, and it is significant that Saint-Gaudens's most vigorous and distinguished creations—such as the Deacon Chapin Memorial in Springfield, Massachusetts, the Adams Memorial in Washington, D.C., the seated Lincoln in Lincoln Park, Chicago, or the Robert Louis Stevenson relief in Edinburgh, Scotland—are those in which he collaborated with White. Work on the Morgan tomb and the Farragut and Randall monuments continued for several years (both monuments were completed in the early 1880s), but Saint-Gaudens, in the meantime, had returned to France, so that during 1877–78 White served as his representative in New York. He met frequently with the committee and Olmsted to select the best site for the Farragut, eventually settling on the placement in Madison Square.

Considering the fact that the young sculptor and architect were breaking new ground in the Farragut—Saint-Gaudens in his straightforward use of contemporary costume and stark realism, and White in his enveloping base with seating—the work progressed fairly rapidly, more so than in some of their subsequent collaborations. Saint-Gaudens not only devised the figure, with timely and pointed criticism from White, but he also sketched the character of the impressionistic reliefs on the bluestone base. And White's base was modified by suggestions by Saint-Gaudens. The details of both parts were settled when White shared the Saint-Gaudenses' apartment in Paris during 1878–79, and upon the sculptor's return the figure was cast and the base cut. Facing west, at the northwest corner of Madison Square, the ensemble was unveiled in 1881 [14].

During 1877–78, White was busy in Richardson's office. He tried to have the decoration of the expansive walls in the New York State Capitol Senate Chamber assigned to Saint-Gaudens for decoration, but this never materialized. In September 1877 the commission for the Oakes Ames Memorial Library came into Richardson's office, and while the large strong masses are clearly Richardson's, the details probably were largely designed by White. The butternut interior woodwork, in particular, has much of the character of Colonial wood-work in which White and McKim were just then becoming interested.[65] Early in 1878 White made his last rendering for Richardson, for a house in South Manchester, Connecticut, for James Cheney [15].[66] The rather awkward plan and the picturesque profusion of gables suggest that this was the pupil's work and not, perhaps, the master's; the turned wooden porch posts, the panels of pebble dash stucco, and the multiple textures of the walls presage what was to come in White's later houses. Of all of White's drawings for Richardson, this is the only one which he signed and dated—"Stanford White del, '78"—and it is the character of this drawing which clarifies, in retrospect, White's contributions all the way back to the Trinity tower and Sherman house drawings of 1874.

As when McKim had been in Richardson's office there had been a mutual influence, so certainly White had learned his profession from the master he affectionately called "The Great Mogul." His frequent field inspections and construction supervision, necessitated by Richardson's ever worsening illness, were invaluable as training. In the office he perfected his drawing, but in the field he learned about materials, how to cajole contractors, and how to persuade clients. Richardson's experience at the École, meanwhile, was exercising a ripening influence, bringing to the master's work increasing unity and cohesion of plan, mass, and detail. Perhaps White's assumption of greater responsibility for detail development freed Richardson to pursue this simplification of form. There was certainly in Richardson's work increasing interest in the use of surface texture as a way of achieving great continuity of surface, and it is indicative of White's influence that as soon as he joined forces with McKim and Mead in 1879, both they and Richardson quickly produced houses critical in the development of the Shingle Style in which surface texture plays so important a part. White learned more in Richardson's office, perhaps, than had McKim, for he was there much longer and occupied in the end a more responsible position. Unlike McKim, however, White had not seen Europe, and though Richardson's extensive library was a great resource, White wanted to travel. While in New York, in February 1878, White wrote Richardson that he wished to leave the office for a time, starting the coming summer, to make a tour of Europe using several hundred dollars he had saved. Richardson was sorry to lose so valuable an assistant, of course, responding: "It is not without regret that I heartily congratulate you on your proposed trip to Europe. And although I can never hope to fill your place to me or in the office, I can certainly think and have for some time past thought it wise and for your best interest to travel and see what the Old World has done for us."[67]

14. LEFT. Augustus Saint-Gaudens and Stanford White, Farragut Memorial, Madison Square, New York, N. Y., 1876–81. *American Architect and Building News,* September 10, 1881.

15. BELOW. Henry Hobson Richardson (with Stanford White?), James Cheney house project, 1878, signed "Stanford White del/ 78." *American Architect and Building News,* May 25, 1878.

Saint-Gaudens had preceded White to Europe, procuring in Paris a studio where he could complete the Farragut. Letters concerning the statue and its base, as well as myriad other matters, criss-crossed the Atlantic, when in June 1878 White wrote that at long last he too was coming over:

> It is like you to offer me a bunk. Do you think I would inflict myself upon you? We shall see. I have been working like Hell and Damnation, and have just been able to finish the drawings [for the Morgan tomb] and put them in such a state that contracts can be taken on them. They are at present estimating and it will take a week before they are in. So you see I have had to put off my passage, and now I sail on the French steamer, Periere, on Wednesday, July 3rd. Who do you think is coming with me? Even McKim. I am tickled to death. He is coming over for but a six week's trip, but it is still perfectly jolly.[68]

At the last minute, a change of plans—White's and Saint-Gaudens's good friend Charles McKim was coming to Paris too.

2

F L E D G L I N G S

1870 — 1879

The important function of architecture
here and now is to lead in the
development and shaping of the most . . .
important of the arts.

American Architect and Building News,
January 1, 1876

BY the time Stanford White had served his "apprenticeship" with Richardson and set out on his tour of Europe in 1878, McKim and Mead had already begun to establish themselves among the younger and more progressive architects in New York City. White, of course, was well acquainted with McKim and Mead, whose small office at 57 Broadway was in the same building where Richardson continued to maintain the New York branch of the office with Gambrill. White came to know, as well, William B. Bigelow, so much like himself, who had started an office in the same building and later entered into formal partnership with McKim and Mead during 1877. While White took care of business in Richardson's New York branch office, he seems to have frequented their chambers, perhaps irrepressibly lending a hand now and then.

As is always the case, the formative years for artists are the most complex and yet the most important for study. So, too, for the young architects whose paths were inexorably converging. During the preceding decade each had been exposed to current architectural trends, exploring and rejecting each in turn. As a result their first independent work during the 1870s matured quickly, so that when the new partnership, McKim, Mead & White, was formed in 1879 it was almost immediately among the leading advocates of a new and yet "traditional" domestic architecture—the Shingle Style. Still young men in 1879, they began to exert an influence on American domestic design that is only slightly less strong a century later. How they came to this early sophistication in design is an intriguing question, and thus the formative years assume special importance and the young architects' first achievements and false starts, in nearly equal measure, invite examination.

From the start McKim had viewed his time with Richardson as simply the last stage of his training. Just how eager he was to strike out on his own is apparent in a drawing of

December 1870, an attic plan presumably from a set of drawings for a suburban house (the only sheet remaining from the set) which McKim signed and dated. In the upper corner of the meticulously colored plan is the round stamp of the Gambrill & Richardson office, bearing the date December 28, 1870, encircled by the hand-lettered inscription, "Charles F. McKim Architect."[1] There are a number of other signed but undated early drawings by McKim in the firm's archive, which have been assigned alphabetical designations according to their apparent chronological order. On stylistic grounds, the next of these appears to have been a stone suburban house capped with a mansard roof, "Project B," perhaps an early experiment. Following this came a series, all of a generic type, of frame construction with clapboard siding below and shingled above. Though the plans of these differ somewhat, they all have a particular crystalline angular hardness which recalls aspects of Sturgis's work, and incorporates some of the character of designs in contemporary builder's manuals such as those by Palliser & Palliser. Various drawings for six such houses survive; the most complete set is that for House D. The perspective [16] exemplifies the hard-edged sharpness of the group, a kind of hardness that appeared simultaneously in Richardson's Brattle Square Church. A plan from this series, apparently an early study for the John Livermore house, Montclair, New Jersey, 1872–73, is equally tight in its clustering of cubical rooms and rigid draftsmanship.[2] It has much more the look of something from a pattern book than the work of someone fresh from Paris. McKim seems to have understood what potential clients wanted, something familiar and not French, and such houses as these started McKim's career. There are at the same time resemblances both in scale and quality of draftsmanship to the elevation of Richardson's Andrews house, Newport, 1872, perhaps drawn in part by McKim [17].

In addition to the Livermore residence, which perhaps was one of the houses in "the Oranges" mentioned by Mead, one of the earliest of McKim's commissions was a house for Joseph Sargent, Worcester, Massachusetts, 1872, whose ample stair hall, "finished in oak, with tiles in the corners of the architraves," was illustrated in the Boston *Architectural Sketch Book* in 1874.[3] In the published perspectives of the Livermore and Sargent stair halls, what was lacking in dashing draftsmanship was made up in attention to detail, with McKim laboriously plotting out the perspectives as he had done in his engineering graphics classes at Harvard.

McKim, rather astutely, had begun to establish himself with the Bostonians who summered at Newport, Rhode Island, and the next year he designed a small schoolhouse seating seventy-five students, presumably an early version of the schoolhouse built for William S. Child in Newport in 1875 [18].[4] It is important not only because it represents a slight reduction in the preceding harsh angularity and incorporates a louvered cupola like those Sturgis placed atop Farnam Hall, but because it appeared in the first volume of a new architectural journal, the *New York Sketch Book of Architecture*, in January 1874. Though officially edited by Richardson, as Montgomery Schuyler noted later, the actual editor was McKim, to whom Richardson delegated the responsibility.[5] Because McKim found himself in a fortunate advocate's position, there soon appeared an inordinate number of plates of Richardson's work, many of the drawings prepared by White, as well as many projects by McKim and Mead. Current work of the most prominent New York architects appeared, such as Richard Morris Hunt's unsuccessful Trinity Church competition entry, his Tribune Building, and his Presbyterian Hospital. The complex pile of Vaux & Wither's Jefferson Market Courthouse and Jail appeared, as did J. C. Cady's Peabody Museum at Yale. Nearly

16. Charles Follen McKim, house design "D," c. 1872.

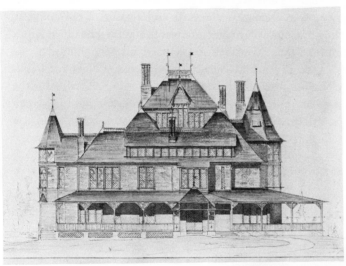

17. Henry Hobson Richardson, F. W. Andrews house, Newport, R. I., 1872, elevation.

18. Charles Follen McKim, School-House project, 1873–74. *New York Sketch Book,* January 1874.

SCHOOL-HOUSE

all of these were highly articulated and colorful High Victorian Gothic, revealing perhaps the lingering influence of Sturgis. Indeed, many of Sturgis's buildings appeared, as did a frontal view of Wight's National Academy of Design. Yet there were plates that suggested a radically new sensibility on McKim's part, photographs of notable old buildings such as Mangin and McComb's French Classic New York City Hall, 1802–11, with a caption identifying it as "the most admirable public building in the city." Even more important were perspectives of proposed new buildings in various classic expressions, such as George B. Post's domed Williamsburg Savings Bank, Brooklyn, and Hunt's Néo-grec Lenox Library, New York. There also appeared sketches of Colonial buildings, such as Bassett Jones's study of the entrance of the Jacob Ford house, Morristown, New Jersey (Washington's headquarters during the winter of 1779–80), apparently submitted in response to McKim's request in the first issue of the *Sketch Book* for "any sketches, however slight, of the beautiful, quaint, and picturesque features, which belong to so many buildings, now almost disregarded, of our Colonial and Revolutionary period." These were needed, he wrote, "to do a little toward the much-needed task of preserving some record of the early architecture of our country, now fast disappearing."[6] The study of Colonial architecture was becoming one of McKim's special interests, and it is significant that he may have planned his schoolhouse to be completely shingled, a clear indication of his study of eighteenth-century Newport buildings. Shortly following the schoolhouse project McKim had built a shingled stable for the Fairchilds in Newport, 1876, its surface relieved by cut patterns in the shingles [19].[7] Such patterning may have derived from Richardson's Andrews house, Newport, but it could also have been adapted directly from Richard Norman Shaw's tile-hung English country houses.

19. Charles Follen McKim, Fairchild stable, Newport, R. I., built 1876.

In the third issue of the *Sketch Book* appeared a design by Mead for a house for John Simpson, Peekskill, New York, even more restrained than McKim's work [20].[8] A comparison of the stair hall detail in that plate with McKim's atmospheric view of the Livermore stair hall [21] and White's interior perspective of the Sherman house hall done for Richardson, all drawn between 1872 and 1874, tells much of the artistic personalities of the three. Mead's is hard, awkward, accurate, but unimaginative; McKim's laboriously attempts to suggest qualities of light and space which White achieved so effortlessly. Mead appears direct but without any particular gift for spatial design; McKim attempts the artistic but not

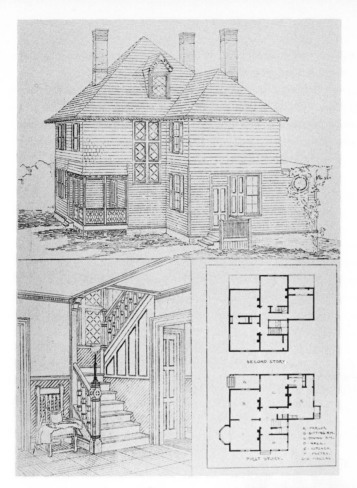

20. William Rutherford Mead,
John Simpson house, Peekskill,
N. Y., 1874. *New York Sketch Book*,
March 1874.

21. Charles Follen McKim, John
Livermore house, Montclair,
N. J., 1874, perspective of stair
hall. *New York Sketch Book*, July
1874.

very successfully while giving a sense of space; and White, while extraordinarily talented, seems to lack a clear sense of the underlying structure.[9]

McKim and Mead had been sharing office space for approximately two years, working independently and assisting each other as Wight and Sturgis had done, when in 1874 they collaborated on an entry in the competition for a new city hall for Providence, Rhode Island [22].[10] There was in this something of Richardson's Hampden County Courthouse, and

perhaps too the recollection of the Trinity Church tower, but overlaid with assorted classical details such as broken pediments. Everything was controlled by a taut correct École manner, though the design was not particularly French. McKim and Mead were not successful in this early venture; the award went to S. J. F. Thayer for a rather conventional Second Empire Baroque design which reveals, by comparison, the "progressive traditionalism" of McKim and Mead's submission.

Late in 1874, perhaps, Mead designed a large resort hotel for the west bank of Cayuga Lake, New York [23].[11] The enterprise of four New York City businessmen, the hotel was to contain parlors, dining rooms, and reading rooms on the ground floor, and fifty bedrooms in the upper floors, with "a lookout in the corner tower, from which an extensive view is had, reaching to Ithaca and Cornell University Buildings, twenty miles distant." The sharp angularity of the tower was typical of Mead, as was the use of shingles only for the upper walls, with clapboards and board and batten siding below. The draftsmanship of the remainder of the perspective, however, suggests another hand, and the barn in the distance with its ancient sagging roof strongly points in the direction of White who was, after all, conveniently available in Gambrill & Richardson's office nearby.

22. OPPOSITE. McKim and Mead, City Hall competition entry, Providence, R. I., 1874. *New York Sketch Book*, November 1874.

23. William Rutherford Mead, Hotel on Cayuga Lake, N. Y., 1875. *New York Sketch Book*, April 1875.

Gradually McKim's houses began to soften in their angularity, and to approach greater overall coherence in plan, but little of this was immediately apparent in the house for inventor-astronomer Francis Blake, Jr., Newton Lower Falls (Weston), Mass., 1874 [24].[12] It recalled strongly McKim's earlier "House D," but the photograph of the parlor, with its paneled fireplace wall, was further evidence of McKim's growing interest in Colonial models. In 1876 there appeared one last residence by McKim in the *Sketch Book,* his cottage for Charles G. Francklyn, Elberon, New Jersey [25].[13] The asymmetrical arrangement of the rooms and verandas around the central hall was pierced by a novel carriage-way running through the center, bringing the visitor directly inside. The entire surface of the building was shingled down to the brick foundation, while on the ocean side the living room was opened to the sea by a wall of glass. Although the published rendering has a softness and fluidity not present in McKim's earlier work, resembling somewhat White's technique adapted from Shaw, the house as constructed was much more angular and sharp-edged. Many hands seem to have been involved in the perspective of the Dwight S. Herrick house, Peekskill, New York, credited to Mead, 1877 [26].[14] Though slightly more fluid in expression than his earlier houses, Mead's Herrick house is still tight and confined, and as in his Cayuga Lake Hotel the lower floor is covered with clapboards while the upper portion is shingled. It is possible that William B. Bigelow, remembered by Montgomery Schuyler as "an amazing sketcher and free-hand draftsman," and who had shortly before opened an office at 57 Broadway, was becoming increasingly involved in the office and may have assisted in preparing the drawing. McKim, however, seems to have contributed the foreground figure for the Herrick house perspective. But the character of the distant landscape, resembling so many in the drawings of Richardson's buildings of the period, suggests White was involved too.

In 1876 McKim commenced a series of seaside buildings in Elberon, New Jersey, that started his and the firm's long association with restaurateur Louis Sherry. It started with the remodeling and extension of an existing house, designed in 1873 by E. T. Potter for Charles G. Francklyn. Francklyn sold this to Lewis B. Brown, engaging McKim then for his new ocean retreat. The design and construction of both the new Francklyn house and the remodeling of the old went on simultaneously. While the new Francklyn house exemplified the gradual movement toward what would later become the Shingle Style, in remodeling the old residence for Brown and Sherry to accommodate the Elberon Hotel, McKim had to deal with Potter's Swiss chalet derivations, so that the end result is not especially characteristic of his work. Nevertheless the extensive porches wrapped around the enlarged building gave the hotel domestic scale [27]; this open horizontality contrasted strongly with the enclosed verticality of contemporary Second Empire Baroque resort hotels such as the Grand Union at Saratoga, New York.[15]

During 1877 the office affairs of McKim and Mead became ever more intertwined and complex. Already active in the New York chapter of the American Institute of Architects, McKim was made a member of the Committee on Architectural Education; more important, he was elected secretary of the national organization at the age of thirty, an indication of his dedication and the respect he had already earned among his older colleagues.[16] As the summer approached it became obvious that Bigelow's practice was so connected with McKim's and Mead's that the three decided to form a partnership, an inevitable juncture, perhaps, in view of McKim's marriage in 1874 to William Bigelow's sister, Annie.[17] Bigelow, who had gone to Paris in 1873 and remained there about a year and a half, had assembled

24. Charles Follen McKim, Francis Blake, Jr., house, Newton Lower Falls, Mass., 1874. *New York Sketch Book,* July 1875.

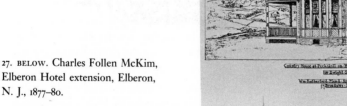

25. ABOVE. Charles Follen McKim, Charles G. Francklyn house, Elberon, N. J., 1876.

26. RIGHT. William Rutherford Mead, Dwight S. Herrick house, Peekskill, N. Y., 1877. *American Architect and Building News,* June 30, 1877.

27. BELOW. Charles Follen McKim, Elberon Hotel extension, Elberon, N. J., 1877–80.

a portfolio of incredibly facile drawings of picturesque medieval French provincial build-ings, and in November 1874, a month after McKim's marriage, a selection of these appeared in the *Sketch Book*. [18] These spirited sketches, so different from the labored perspectives by either McKim or Mead, suggest why Bigelow may have been so readily welcomed into the loose partnership. Meanwhile, McKim maintained a close friendship with Sidney V. Strat-ton, his comrade in Daumet's atelier, a number of whose French travel sketches also ap-peared in the *Sketch Book* in 1876. [19] Nearly as gifted as Bigelow, Stratton too must have lent a welcome hand in making presentation drawings.

The presence of Bigelow changed the chemistry of the partnership, and only weeks after the formation, it seems, dramatic changes occurred in the partners' work. This is demonstrated by the large summer house, Oakswood, for Samuel Gray Ward, Lenox, Massachusetts, begun about mid-1877 [28, 29]. [20] It was the largest house yet to come into the fledgling office; it contained more than twenty rooms on the ground floor alone, and its ground floor stretched nearly two hundred feet. Now destroyed, it was picturesque yet rigorously disciplined in profile, its plan longitudinally extended (and bent at one end to follow the contours of the rolling landscape). The exterior of carefully and asymmetrically balanced gables was entirely shingled, while the interiors and selected details of the exterior employed boldly overscaled Georgian elements. Here, in embryonic form, was the begin-ning of the Shingle Style.

The Colonial Georgian references in the Ward house, more picturesque than archaeo-logical, were a reflection of McKim's developing interest in Colonial architecture. During the preceding three years he had established himself as something of a connoisseur of eighteenth-century relics, as had his good friend Robert S. Peabody. They were the avant-garde of a growing popular interest which had begun to manifest itself in the years just prior to the Centennial celebration. The growing fascination with Colonial architecture was hastened to focus by the presence of Thomas Harris's mock-Jacobean English pavilions at the Centennial Exhibition at Philadelphia. They suggested that a national building tradition could serve as a source of development of a new vernacular, and so in 1877 Robert Peabody wrote in the *American Architect:* "With our centennial year have we not discovered that we too have a past worthy of study? . . . our Colonial work is our only native source of antiquarian study and inspiration."[21] Meanwhile leaving the writing and theorizing to others (as he always did), McKim had already begun to explore traditional sources as a basis of design as early as 1874. Like Harris he first looked to Elizabethan and Jacobean prototypes, first in England and then as transplanted to the Colonies. His library for the Henry A. Page house, Montrose, New Jersey, 1875–76, for example, could be compared to similar living hall interiors by Nesfield or Shaw of the 1860s and 1870s. [22] It is altogether likely that in the company of R. Phéne Spiers McKim had been shown some of these houses while on his English tour in the summer of 1869. McKim's interest in recording the Colonial heritage was declared in the call for drawings in the first issue of the *Sketch Book*. The result of his personal researches became evident when he added a new room in the spring of 1874 to the Thomas Robinson house, Newport (built in 1725), for Benjamin R. Smith who then owned it. He converted the old keeping room into a sitting room, adding a new kitchen wing. As the photograph published in the *Sketch Book* shows [30], the paneled fireplace was among the earliest re-creations of eighteenth-century sources. [23]

McKim was even more successful in evoking the image of the eighteenth century in the extensive additions he made to the John Dennis house (built in 1760), across Washington

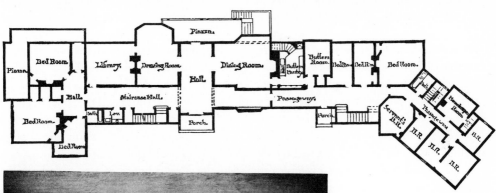

28. TOP. McKim, Mead & Bigelow,
Samuel Gray Ward house,
Oakswood, Lenox, Mass., 1877–78.
From C. A. Morely, *Lenox,* East
Lee, Mass., 1886.

29. ABOVE. Ward house, plan.
Century, June 1886.

30. LEFT. Charles Follen McKim,
Robinson-Smith house,
renovation, Newport, R. I., 1875.
New York Sketch Book, October
1875.

Street from the Robinson house. Again working for Benjamin Smith, McKim added to the rear a new kitchen and large stair hall, with a bedroom upstairs, incorporating in the new work a pediment salvaged from the Hunter house of 1748.[24] McKim's expertise on the subject was sufficiently known so that editor William Rotch Ware of the *American Architect* had only to mention in August 1877 that McKim, whose "researches among antiquities are well known, will shortly forward to us drawings of three stone colonial houses." Although the drawings never materialized, two years later McKim served with Peabody and several others on a committee on the "Practice of American Architects and Builders during the Colonial period and the First Fifty Years of National Independence." Their published conclusions urged the "study of principles that shaped and guided the architecture of the Colonial period," while cautioning against mere copyism.[25]

McKim's and Peabody's expertise came largely from close inspection of old buildings long ignored by public and profession alike; scholarly books examining the earliest national architecture had yet to be written. One of the partners' study tours was described by Mead in his reminiscences:

> In our early days we all had a great interest in the early Colonial architecture of this country, and in 1877 we made what we always called afterward our "celebrated" trip to New England, for the purpose of visiting the towns of Marblehead, Salem, Newburyport and Portsmouth. The party consisted of Messrs. McKim, Bigelow, White and myself. We made sketches and measured drawings of many of the important Colonial houses, which still remain in our scrapbook. I think these drawings represent some of the earliest records of the Colonial period, through native drawings. . . . I think the leaning of this office toward classic form dates from this trip.[26]

They may well have started from Newport, already quite familiar to McKim, with its many examples of both seventeenth-century and eighteenth-century domestic work. In Salem there were many good examples as well, such as the Turner and Crowninshield houses, but perhaps most important was the corpus of work by Samuel McIntire and the quiet decorum of Chestnut Street. The looser ensemble of Marblehead included the King-Hooper house of 1728–45 and the Jeremiah Lee house of 1768. Their headquarters at Newburyport was the rambling house, Indian Hill, owned by Ben Perley Poore and going back to 1650 in some of its parts, but other nearby examples included the Tracy house of 1771 and the Caleb Cushing house of 1808. Portsmouth, New Hampshire, was peppered with excellent houses, some such as the Richard Jackson house going back to the seventeenth century, and others such as the Athenaeum and the Portsmouth Academy dating from the first years of the nineteenth century. There was also the Georgian house of John Langdon, of 1784, to which McKim, Mead & White, much later, would make an addition. Since they were particularly in search of Colonial architecture, they may not have looked at the Italian Renaissance Post Office and Custom House by Ammi Burnham Young, built 1855, but perhaps a vestigial memory of it emerged later in the firm's Villard house complex, so similar in its details.

In December, following this trip, McKim made a rare public address before the New York Society of Architects, in which he lamented the lack of a real antiquarian spirit among American architects; by comparison, he observed, English architects were well versed in their historic buildings. Much could be learned, he advised, by making "accurately measured drawings and notes [which] would offer profitable lessons."[27] The effects of McKim's study in his own designs were twofold, causing first the use of rather Shavian decorative motifs, moving toward Queen Anne or early English Classic, and second, a gradual reduction in massing toward broader, simpler geometric forms. The process was to occupy nearly a dozen years. The most Shavian project, begun in mid-1877, was a summer house for Thomas Dunn, Newport, its rooms arranged in an L and penetrated by an open carriage-way at the bend as in the Francklyn house at Elberon. However, for publication in the *American Architect*, McKim engaged professional renderer L. S. Ipsen to complete a perspective; McKim's own preliminary sketch was much leaner and devoid of the purely decorative half-timbering [31, 32].[28] It is also possible that McKim employed Ipsen to secure a commission that was slipping away, but whatever the circumstances it is significant that by 1877 McKim ceased to make renderings of his own work.

The first steps in the deliberate simplification of massing were made in the suburban house McKim designed in 1877 for Mead's sister and her husband, William Dean Howells, in Belmont outside Boston. Called Redtop because of its covering of redwood shingles, this was the first in a distinguished series of houses, continuing through 1886, in which all of the major compositional elements were gathered under one broad gable so that in elevation the

31. Charles Follen McKim, study for Thomas Dunn house (?), Newport, R. I., 1877.

32. Dunn house, rendered perspective by L. S. Ipsen. *American Architect and Building News*, July 28, 1877.

house became an elemental triangle [33]. Moreover, Redtop was consciously meant to be Colonial, even if it was not quite archaeologically correct; indeed Elinor Howells wrote her brother that "the dining room looks 200 years old."[29] Reductivism of form was the most important, if tangential, result of McKim's investigation of Colonial architecture, and it was to have the most far-reaching effects. One sees a parallel to this in the entrance facade of the Moses Taylor house, Elberon, also designed by McKim in 1877 [34]. In this, too, smaller minor gables were subsumed within the larger gable, but in this the classicism of form was enhanced by classicism in detail, with carved panels looking rather Adamesque. Even the color scheme, yellow clapboards with white trim, derived from eighteenth-century sources, must have looked especially brilliant in the context of the neighboring dark red and brown mid-Victorian summer cottages. If the exteriors of Redtop and the Taylor house suggested abstraction, the interiors were much closer to the irregular "agglutinative" plans of Shaw or Richardson.[30] Redtop, especially, had a commodious central hall with a generous winding stair, while the Taylor house plan was most irregular, bisected by a through central hall, perhaps to allow sea breezes to pass more easily. At this early stage then, only the exteriors were controlled and suggested a new approach; internally these houses were far closer to the progressive mainstream of Richardson.

The house in which the longitudinally extended plan of Oakswood first began to merge with the external abstraction of Redtop was Bytharbor, Saint James, Long Island, New York [35, 36], designed late in 1878 and built early in 1879 for Prescott Hall Butler, a close friend of McKim.[31] As the watercolor drawing made a few years later by White clearly shows, except for a small shed or pantry at the left, all elements were subsumed under a long sweeping gable roof, even more encompassing than that of Redtop. Though the house was later expanded by the firm for Butler, the narrowness of the house suggests that the stair hall at the center originally ran the full width of the house, no doubt with banks of windows to the north providing a panoramic view of Stony Brook Harbor. To the left of the stair hall were the kitchen and dining room, while to the right, perhaps through broad sliding doors, opened the living hall, beyond which was a porch pulled under the continuous plane of the gable roof. McKim's sense of geometric order by now was becoming well developed; pursuing the scheme introduced in the Howells house, McKim produced here a type to which he and his partners repeatedly returned, in the McCormick house at Richfield Springs, New York, and culminating in the William G. Low house, Bristol, Rhode Island [77, 78]. There is no entry in the detailed journals Butler kept of construction of Bytharbor for landscaping, but it is possible that Olmsted may have given some advice since he was already working with the firm. In a letter to a potential client, H. Y. Attrill, in July 1879, Olmsted made it clear he most preferred to work with the few architects who understood his objectives, and among the five architects he listed were McKim, Mead, and Bigelow.[32]

Aside from those for Oakswood, on which work continued well into 1878 when Mead began to keep detailed records of expenses billed to clients, there are no official records of these earliest commissions. One document of the new firm was the publication in the *American Architect* in November 1877 of the perspective of the proposed new Episcopal rectory for Christ Church, Rye, New York, bearing the inscription: "McKim, Mead & Bigelow, Architects, 57 Broadway, New York" [37].[33] The character of this suburban house was far less horizontal than the preceding country houses and even suggested the work of English architects such as Philip Webb or William Butterfield, particularly in its finished state in which brick was substituted for the masonry shown in the perspective. It is possible

33. McKim, Mead & Bigelow, William Dean Howells house, Redtop, Belmont, Mass., 1877–78.

34. Charles Follen McKim, Moses Taylor house, Elberon, N. J., 1877.

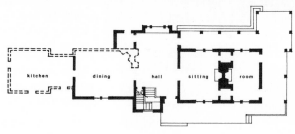

35. ABOVE. McKim, Mead & Bigelow, Prescott Hall Butler house, Bytharbor, St. James, N. Y., 1878–80, watercolor perspective by Stanford White, c. 1884.

36. Butler house, plan (L. M. Roth). Kitchen configuration conjectural due to successive remodelings.

that the proposed masonry reflected Richardson's influence, but it may have been suggested by the High Victorian Gothic masonry church, 1867–69, across the street, by Florentine Pelletier of New York.

Up to this point the work of the young partners had been restricted to country and suburban houses, with the exception of the Providence City Hall project. In 1878 the short-lived firm began to design its first urban buildings, and it was indicative that in this the architects immediately turned to the somewhat more classical Queen Anne, that muted picturesque domestic mode in brick based on English Renaissance Jacobean sources, much favored just then by Shaw and his English contemporaries.[34] They took up this new mode in the Edward N. Dickerson townhouse, 1877–79, and the Frederick F. Thompson townhouse, 1879–81 [38], both in New York. The exterior of the Dickerson house, Montgomery Schuyler felt, looked "less like a work of architectural art than a magnified piece of furniture 'with the Chippendale feeling' [and could] scarcely be called successful."[35] The interiors of the Dickerson house, in part by the firm, were heavy and dark, while those of the slightly later Thompson house were more delicate and taut, alive with a contrast of textures and subtle color combinations, but these interiors were completed by White and differed markedly from the ponderous atmosphere of the Dickerson house.

Perhaps the best of the early urban work was an apartment block, The Benedict, on Washington Square, New York, for Lucius Tuckerman, 1879–82 [39]. Measuring roughly 56 feet across and 100 feet deep, the apartment block had narrow setbacks on the sides for light shafts, resulting in a plan in the shape of a squat I. If the internal plan arrangement with its central, double-loaded corridor was not striking, the facade was remarkable clear in its functional organization. Brick piers rose uninterrupted to the corbeled cornice, with projecting oriel bays between them in the middle floors, recalling somewhat Shaw's New Zealand Chambers, London, 1873. The structural scheme of The Benedict facade was straightforward and rationally clear, in contrast to the comparatively less systematic Borden Block, Chicago, by Adler & Sullivan, built at exactly the same time.[36] This incipient classicism was pursued in the firm's Union League Club, New York, competition entry of spring 1879. Nearly all of the entries were published in the *American Architect* over the next

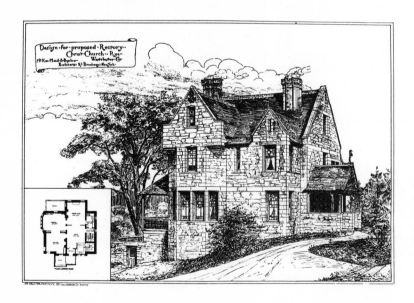

37. McKim, Mead & Bigelow, Christ Church Rectory, Rye, N. Y., 1877–79, perspective by Bigelow (?). *American Architect and Building News*, November 10, 1877.

several months, thus providing a cross section of current architectural ideals as well as permitting close comparison of the young firm's work to that of their peers.[37] Compared to the winning design of Peabody & Stearns of Boston, a Queen Anne confection of chimneys, towers, and gables, the entry by McKim, Mead & Bigelow [40] appears exceptionally subdued. It tells much of the young firm's interests that in so early a work, in the general massing and twin towers, they would allude to the Villa Medici, Rome (home of the French Academy there), a Renaissance rather than an Anglo-Saxon source so preferred by McKim's contemporaries. It is highly significant, too, that of all the published perspectives, only that of McKim, Mead & Bigelow is extended to show a distinctly urban setting of receding residential street corridors. Even in a somewhat rudimentary way, the building was viewed in its context.

38. ABOVE LEFT. McKim, Mead & Bigelow, Frederick F. Thompson house, New York, N. Y., 1879–81.
39. ABOVE RIGHT. McKim, Mead & Bigelow, The Benedict, for Lucius Tuckerman, New York, N. Y., 1879–82.
40. LEFT. McKim, Mead & Bigelow, Union League Club competition project, New York, N. Y., 1879. *American Architect and Building News,* June 7, 1879.

Apparently the last major commission of McKim, Mead & Bigelow was a summer house for Mrs. Anna C. Alden, Fort Hill, near Cold Spring Harbor, Long Island, New York, 1879–80.[38] In plan the house was a linear extension of rooms arranged to lie along the top of battlements remaining from a Revolutionary outpost (other portions of the earthworks framed a garden court in front of the house [41, 42]). The exterior consisted of a masterfully modulated series of turrets, window groups, solids, and open porches, all gathered within embracing gables, the most coherent plan and massing yet devised by the partners—varied and yet ordered. Clapboarding was used on the lower floor with shingles above, and while these and other elements recall the earlier individual work of McKim or Mead, the overall character of the rendering shows the contribution of Bigelow. Indeed, the drawing looks much like those Bigelow later did of his own work.[39] The plan organization was probably McKim's, but the easy collision of forms on the exterior may already show the impact of White, who by now had been in Europe for some months. As the important commissions of mid-1879 suggest, McKim, Mead & Bigelow had begun to define a distinctive style, one that was relaxed and yet was infused with formal clarity and restrained in its Colonial references. Yet behind the solid corporate exterior the mutual trust so necessary for close collaboration was disintegrating.

Sometime during the summer of 1877 McKim's wife took their two-year-old daughter Margaret, returned to her family in Newport, and filed for divorce, which was granted a year later. Why she left, and why thereafter she prohibited McKim from seeing his daughter, still remain mysteries. In his biography of McKim, Charles Moore says with nineteenth-century decorum that it was due to "malign influences."[40] Whatever the causes, real or imagined, McKim was caught completely unprepared and was severely stunned. He must have found maintaining focus on office work impossible and decided to leave for a trip to Europe with White, back to the safe and comforting Parisian environment of his student days. But after six weeks he would return to New York. The travel arrangements were apparently very quickly made, hence the note of surprise in White's letter to Saint-Gaudens.

On July 3, 1878, White and McKim sailed from New York.[41] On reaching Paris they toured the city for two weeks, seeing Sarah Bernhardt on stage and viewing the Salon paintings—which did not particularly impress White, judging from his letters home. On July 15, White and McKim were joined by friends, including Sidney V. Stratton, and they soon developed a daily schedule: mornings making the rounds of the city, afternoons visiting the International Exposition (where White was awestruck by the exhibit of French painting), evenings attending the theater or opera. There were periodic outings to Versailles and other spots outside Paris. The social highlight, in mid-September, was a dinner at Foyot's given by David Maitland Armstrong, then serving as commissioner of the American Art Exhibit at the exposition, who quickly became a close friend of McKim and White.[42] The longest excursion, in which McKim and White were joined by Saint-Gaudens, who had to be pried away from work on the Farragut, was down the Rhone. The group's itinerary is well known from the many letters White sent back to his mother: "We three—viz. Charles F. McKim, secretary of the American Institute of Architects, honorary member etc., etc.; Augustus St. Gaudens, sculptor of great renown; and your dutiful son, secretary of nothing, and of no renown whatever—started Friday afternoon, August 2nd, for a flank movement on the South of France."[43] They traveled overland southeast from Paris, toward Lyon. Everything enchanted White, except heavily industrialized Lyon, where they boarded a boat. Such a passage to Marseilles, White informed his family, is "rarely made by travellers nowadays. The boats go but once a week; and it is sometimes dangerous. In some places the character of the scenery is quite like that of the Hudson, and in parts finer." They steamed downriver to Avignon, where they set out for Arles and Saint-Gilles [43]. Of Nîmes, White wrote:

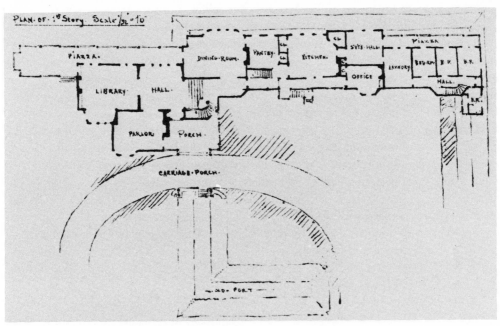

41. TOP. McKim, Mead & Bigelow, Mrs. A. C. Alden house, Fort Hill, Lloyd's Neck, Long Island, N. Y., 1879. *American Architect and Building News,* August 30, 1879.

42. ABOVE. Alden house, plan. *American Architect and Building News,* August 30, 1879.

43. LEFT. St. Gilles, St.-Gilles-du-Gard, France, snapshot from photo scrapbook of Stanford White.

After Verona, the amphitheater in Nimes is the most perfect in the world—they are having bullfights in it to this day. It seats 20,000 persons. We sat in the top row of seats and imagined ourselves ancient Romans, and then I went down (while McKim and St. Gaudens stayed on top) and rushed madly into the arena, struck an attitude and commenced declaiming. They heard me perfectly. I stabbed five or six gladiators—and rushed out with the guardian in hot pursuit.

Soon afterward McKim returned to New York, leaving White in Paris. "Our home," wrote Saint-Gaudens later, "was White's headquarters, whence he darted off in extraordinarily vigorous excursions to the towns surrounding Paris that contain those marvels of Gothic architecture of which he was an adorer."[44] White continued to work on the *Farragut* base when with Saint-Gaudens, but he was frequently absent on extended trips north, to Rouen, Lille, Bruges, and Ghent in Belgium, where he spent long hours studying and making sketches from Flemish paintings. In December White ventured south, stopping at Rheims and Beauvais. After spending Christmas with the Saint-Gaudens family, White was off again, to the south of France, to Bordeaux, to Marseilles, and then to Italy, where he was glad the warmer weather permitted him to continue sketching outdoors.

During the thirteen months White spent in Europe, he dashed off hundreds of sketches and watercolors exhibiting a broad range of interest both in subject matter and in rendering technique.[45] There were many rapid sketches of landscapes and village scenes, and a number of sketches filled with scribbled notes as to building materials and color. In the most rapid sketches there was no attempt at artistic polish, but others, such as the view of the Château de Plecis Macé near Angers [44], were more carefully finished. The soft pencil technique of this, with its rounded outlines and forms, imitated the broken shadows of the various textures of wall and roof surfaces; while other drawings such as the view of the towers of Noyon were done in harder pencil. Still others were embellished with ink washes. In the more finished drawings there was more concern for texture and light effects than for structure. One drawing labeled simply "Courtyard, France" [45], which combined crisp line drawing with watercolor washes, is particularly interesting because of the inward taper of the tower, due perhaps to settling, for in a number of towers built by McKim, Mead & White during 1879 to 1885 this curved taper is reproduced (the towers of the Newport Casino and the R. Percy Alden house are good examples).

Each of the partners—McKim, Mead, and White—collected photographs of buildings, cityscapes, and landscapes when visiting Europe, in addition to making sketches. Their photographs alone eventually filled over 100 scrapbooks.[46] White's photographs of France exhibit a range of interest comparable to that demonstrated by his sketches, from thatched farmhouses to town squares. He saved views of medieval slate-covered houses whose horizontal patterned bands undulate across surfaces warped with age [46]. Almost from the moment of his return to New York and entrance into the new firm, such textures and patterned bands began to appear in White's shingled buildings. There were also views of early French Renaissance houses [47], with areas of low relief in balanced proportion to larger plainer panels; such contrasts also appeared in White's work as soon as he returned home.[47]

Upon his return to New York in 1878, McKim became immersed in office affairs, turning first to resumption of work on the Rye rectory. For the moment Bigelow was still in the office, but after the divorce, relations must have been strained. Bigelow still was formally connected with the firm as late as August 4, 1879, when he signed a receipt for payment toward a summer house for J. M. Cornell at Monmouth Beach, New Jersey, but a few weeks later he formally withdrew from the partnership and moved to separate rooms at 57 Broadway, where he continued to practice through 1880.[48] Even as Bigelow was moving out, Stanford White was preparing to leave France, his money exhausted, his

44. Stanford White, drawing of Château de Plecis Macé, near Angers, France, 1878–79. L. G. White, *Sketches and Designs by Stanford White.*
45. Stanford White, drawing labeled "Courtyard, France," 1878–79. L. G. White, *Sketches and Designs.*

46. Snapshot of unidentified slate-covered house, France, from photo scrapbook of Stanford White.

47. House, Rouen, France, from photo scrapbook of Stanford White.

sketchbooks brimming; he sailed from Liverpool on August 23, 1879. When the end of his sojourn became imminent, White had considered returning to Richardson in Brookline, but then McKim and Mead wrote him of Bigelow's retirement and offered him the position, for they badly needed a delineator and designer. Mead may have hesitated, perhaps, at taking into partnership yet another fiery, energetic artist, but they needed White's skills, so closely parallel to Bigelow's. McKim reportedly persuaded Mead, saying that though White had little training "he can draw like a house afire." On Saturday, September 6, White's ship docked in New York, and on Monday, September 8, 1879, White entered the office; the firm of McKim, Mead & White came into being.[49]

The New York in which the three had apprenticed and in which they had begun their careers was a fertile architectural field, yet what they found and assimilated served more as a base for departure than the model for emulation. Under Sturgis and Richardson, the young men saw the Ruskinian polychromy of Mould's All Saints' Unitarian Church and Eidlitz's Temple Emanu-El; they must have looked closely at Wight's National Academy of Design, measuring its achievement against Ruskin's ideals. When McKim returned from France he could compare contemporary design in Paris to the relatively awkward Second Empire adaptations in New York City, such as the ornate New York *Herald* office, the even more richly embellished Park Bank next to it on Ann Street, the German Savings Bank where Saint-Gaudens had a studio, J. B. Snook's imposing Grand Central Depot, or A. B. Mullett's hulking New York Post Office in front of City Hall. He probably made a point of examining Hunt's few attempts at an Americanized Néo-grec rationalism in the Tenth Street Studio and the Lenox Library (which he published), for besides himself and Richardson, Hunt was the only École student in the city. White frankly expressed his dislike of Bryant and Gilman's mansarded Boston City Hall in a letter to his mother written while on an inspection trip for Richardson.[50] As they evaluated developments in the mid-1870s each of the three came to admire increasingly the civil decorum of early American architecture, of which there were still many important examples in Manhattan besides City Hall, Saint Paul's and Saint John's chapels, and the townhouses of Greenwich Village. If they began to appreciate the sedate and reasoned proportions of such work, what might they have thought of Eidlitz's richly crocketed and highly colored Church of the Holy Trinity, 1870–75, next to Snook's Grand Central Depot pavilions?[51]

Together they knew well the many elements that had contributed to the history of American architecture. Had they been writers like Ralph Adams Cram they might have done for American eighteenth-century architecture what Cram did in analyzing Gothic, for surely they were among the first American architects to have a sense of what the history of their own tradition had been. Individually they had been influenced by both Ruskinian expressiveness of form and Richardsonian mass and commodious order. Accepting none of the preceding stylish modes totally, they were beginning a search for something different, a new and yet traditional American architecture. Exactly what this would be they did not yet know, but it had to combine the good street manners of Federalist New York, the careful functional planning of the École, solid construction as exemplified by Richardson's work, and something of the life of Sturgis's Ruskinian Gothic. By 1879 they knew at least what expressions would not meet their needs; now they began to explore modes rooted in the American past—shingled picturesqueness in the country and, more tentatively, Georgian and Federalist classicism in the city.

3

A NEW FIRM

1879 — 1886

Eager, solicitous, hungry, rabid,
busy-bodied America attempting many
things, vain, ambitious to feel thy own
existence, and convince others of thy
talent, by attempting and hastily
accomplishing much. . . .

RALPH WALDO EMERSON
Journals, 1847

EMERSON'S reflection on the brash American spirit, though written a generation earlier, described the driving energy and ambition of the new firm. The three young architects had good reason to feel confident. Their collective training and experience was thorough, their personal connections with artistic and literary society in Boston, New York, and Philadelphia were the best. They were fortunate, too, to have launched themselves just as the American economy began to recover from the deep depression of 1873. There was now money to be spent—on summer houses, townhouses, corporate headquarters, and, as municipal coffers filled, on civic buildings. Of the younger generation of architects, McKim, Mead, and White not only had the good fortune to appear at that moment when commissions again began to flow, but to offer as well designs whose subtlety and composure made post–Civil War buildings suddenly look old-fashioned. The more prevalent this new perception became, the more work the new firm received. The office at 57 Broadway experienced the first freshets of a flood of commissions. In these beginning seven years alone there were more than 215 commissions; by comparison, Richardson, who worked at a slower pace and whose early career was restricted by the depression of 1873, had about 100 significant commissions during his entire career of twenty years. In 1886 at the end of their first busy period, when H. H. Richardson died, McKim, Mead, and White had only just begun.

One reason for this outpouring of work was that the three quickly developed an efficient office organization. When White was made a partner in September 1879 there were four draftsmen in the office; by 1886 there were more than seventy. Generally Mead was in charge of this staff, and though he did some designing, McKim and White were the primary designers. Stanford White's son, Lawrence, sketched the best description of the founders:

Vogue la Galère [let's chance it] was the motto of the firm; and if McKim was the hull and White the sails of the ship, Mead was both rudder and anchor; for it was his sound judgment, often lacking in the makeup of the other two men, which steered them safely through the shoals, and enabled them to weather the storms. There is a story in which Mead is quoted as saying that it took all his time to keep his partners from "making damn fools of themselves"; and St. Gaudens once drew an amusing caricature of Mead struggling to fly two kites, labeled White and McKim, which were pulling in different directions. But beside his business judgment, Mead's extraordinary grasp of architectural planning was of incalculable value to the firm. He possessed that instinctive sense of scale and proportion which makes the development of the elevations follow naturally and logically from the plan. Although he gave less of his time to actual designing than his partners, he often not only conceived the scheme which was the basis of the whole design, but gave timely criticism which had a vital bearing upon the finished work.[1]

A kindly avuncular man, about five feet seven in height, Mead had deep blue eyes later framed by good-humored creases [48]. He was the balance wheel, the governor of the engine, shrewd, level-headed, with good judgment and an equable temperament; he modified McKim's severity and checked White's enthusiasm. His taciturnity around the office earned him the affectionate nickname Dummy, but it was not for want of knowledge or sensitivity. He was said to possess a critical faculty which mitigated eccentricity in the firm's designs; his counsel was always sought by his partners, his suggestions on plan arrangement and construction carrying great weight. Of the three he was closest to the young men in the office, for he was in charge of personnel and dispensing the payroll on Saturday afternoons.[2]

Idealistic where Mead was pragmatic, McKim sought the best; Mead trenchantly described his partner's artistic objective: "perfection in whatever he undertook." Thus McKim's habitual quest of ideal proportion, fitness, and beauty required unusually long periods of design development and caused changes even as buildings rose.[3] McKim's design process was detailed by Henry Bacon, who had worked closely with him during the 1880s.[4] Delicate sketches would be brought to the assistant's drafting table, accompanied by praise for what was being done; then suggestions would be made, new sketches in gossamer lines would be jotted down by McKim with either right or left hand, with constant smudging of the drawing to create a blurred impression of the form intended—McKim's sketch of 1903 for the central section of Bellevue Hospital is a good example [314]. Innumerable such sketches would follow, each varying slightly from the others, and the draftsman would be instructed to make a finished composite of selected elements. McKim would examine the result, comment, and the whole process would begin again and be repeated over and over until optimum proportions and plan adjustment had been achieved. Although this method, a gradual building up and refinement, was slow, "the results McKim got . . . were of course very fine indeed," observed H. Van Buren Magonigle, "but his way of getting them drove another sort of temperament nearly crazy." Principally one of White's assistants, Magonigle did work for McKim on occasion, and his view of McKim's method differed from Bacon's accordingly. When he entered the office in 1887, Magonigle remembered McKim as standing about five feet seven in height, having a completely bald head with a light sandy fringe and a drooping moustache [48]. He overheard McKim rehearsing a design with an assistant; the snatches of conversation sounded most recondite. Term piled upon term—cyma recta, cyma reversa, dentils, modillions, and so it continued—but when Magonigle later crept over to see the wondrous drawing he found only a top and bottom line framing a few faint pencil marks that bore no resemblance to a cornice. Magonigle describes how once he was asked by McKim to move a line up, erase it, move it back down just a little, erase again, move it up a hair's breadth, and so on, until the drawing was completely smudged; "to repeat that sort of thing for hours on end was hard on the nerves of anyone used to White's lightning decisions and vigorous methods. I always wondered why he [McKim] didn't draw things with his own hands. . . ."[5]

Perspective studies would be made following the same tedious process, change following change, until the project would proceed to plaster models and full-scale plaster detail.

48. William Rutherford Mead and Charles Follen McKim (left and right), c. 1896–97.

As Bacon knew, "it was arduous, but the fatigue of the draughtsman's mind and body was immensely relieved by Mr. McKim's contagious enthusiasm and his unceasing encouragement."[6] After the drawings left the office and went to the contractors' shops, changes might still be made, and even portions of the finished building removed and replaced. "He insisted on having his designs kept in a plastic state far beyond the point at which others would have regarded them as finished," Bacon noted, a procedure McKim and White both learned from Richardson. Royal Cortissoz, also once an office assistant, said that McKim handled building materials with the same feeling and intensity with which artists manipulated pigments and colors, and Granger tells of a time when, having discovered a minor flaw in a portico column, McKim quietly had the column replaced at his own expense even though the imperfection was so slight as to have escaped notice.[7]

McKim would approach a client or a design problem with a quiet, gentle manner which masked his stern determination to achieve the best. If he seemed indirect in speech or action, it was simply his way of gently persuading others of the validity of his point; he invariably won.[8] This desire for perfection led him increasingly to consult Renaissance sources for proportion and ornamental detail. The firm acquired a large library of books and folios, in addition to the photograph and drawing scrapbooks, which the partners and draftsmen freely explored, though Bacon asserted that McKim was "no slave to precedent." Magonigle, however, remembered how McKim and his assistants would "spend hours and hours looking up data, particularly in *Letarouilly,* which was a kind of office bible—if you saw it in *Letarouilly* it was so!" If the right detail did not turn up in the library, McKim started over until he *could* find a precedent, or so it seemed to Magonigle; "he was the most convinced authoritarian I have ever encountered."[9]

Although this approach consumed great amounts of time, the results justified the effort. Frederick Hill recalled a small house in Germantown for which the draftsmen went through change after change until McKim finally gave his approval for preparation of construction drawings; when told that it was the forty-seventh sketch for the house, he replied calmly that even if it still was not perfect "we have avoided at least forty-six mistakes."[10] To Royal Cortissoz, McKim's work represented "the bed rock of pure architecture." Once McKim conceived the central idea he would not alter his course; echoing his father's evangelical zeal, he asserted "you can compromise anything but the essence."[11] Of course such high-mindedness led to the loss of commissions as the firm started, and when McKim was advised to give his clients what they wanted, returning to his high ideals later when the firm's position was secure, he replied that he and his partners would stick to what they believed and either succeed or fail accordingly.[12]

The dogged determination and unfailing patience of this "gentle Jesuit of beauty" caused McKim's clients to build better than they knew or dreamed.[13] In fact, McKim's method was affectionately caricatured by William Dean Howells in *The Rise of Silas Latham,* 1885, whose protagonist planned to build a brownstone front with a "French roof" in the Back Bay of Boston, its principal rooms finished in black walnut.[14] Latham's architect was just able to conceal the involuntary shudder these suggestions sent through him, and then began to propose alternatives, based on "pretty old-fashioned country-houses." Instead of dark walnut the architect gently advised "there is really nothing like white paint" with "a little gold here and there." The house the architect produced in a dazzling deluge of sketches refuted all of Latham's notions, and yet he was soon ready "to swear by the architect" although he wondered afterward whether "that's fellow's fifty years behind, or ten years ahead." Howells not only parodied McKim's celebrated persuasiveness, but the firm's habitual cost overruns as well; for Latham's house, too, far exceeded the estimate, but he was satisfied that "there was no facade as that on the whole street," none with its "satisfying simplicity of the whole design and the delicacy of its detail."

Latham's contagiously enthusiastic architect was also, of course, Howell's thinly disguised portrait of Stanford White. White was the opposite of McKim, yet they were the most intimate of comrades, and together with Mead formed, as Lawrence White said, "a singularly happy combination of men of radically different temperaments."[15] Royal Cortissoz said the three represented a perfect harmonization of talents, each bringing to the union something the others lacked; White, he said, was sheer flame, headlong, a prolific designer who seemed like a force of nature let loose [49, 50, 51].[16] Lawrence remembered his father as

> exuberant, restless, a skyrocket of vitality. He worked at terrific pressure and produced a great many buildings, which are graceful and charming rather than imposing, and often profusely ornamented. He was always striving for new effects, and never hesitated to be architecturally incorrect in order to solve a problem. Once a draughtsman came to him in despair because the axis of a scheme which White had indicated could not be maintained. "Damn it all, *bend* the axis," was the reply.[17]

Unfortunately White did not die peaceably in his bed, and the scandal surrounding his assassination atop Madison Square Garden has often besmirched his architecture and character. The simple truth is that White loved life and beauty with the passionate abandon of a child; to him life was "bully, wonderful, gorgeous." His biographer said White got more

49. Stanford White with full beard, c. 1877–78, while associated with H. H. Richardson.

50. Stanford White, c. 1879–80.

51. Stanford White, 1888, photographed in London by Frederick Hollyer.

out of life in more different ways than did most people; White's own motto, according to Mead, was "a short life and a merry one," a prophecy which tragically came true.[18]

White had a passion for helping people, as is evident from his role in starting Saint-Gaudens's career. White knew nearly every artist in New York, conservative and progressive, ranging from William Merritt Chase, John La Farge, Thomas W. Dewing, Francis Lathrop, to Albert Pinkham Ryder and struggling newcomers like Everett Shinn, whose career he advanced by arranging the artist's first one-man show.[19] Friendship to White was a form of religion; as John Jay Chapman noted: "his attention to the private affairs of people who needed his help—especially of artists—was one of his preoccupations."[20] Once White enlisted the help of painter Edward W. Simmons in the aid of a fellow artist who was about to be evicted from his studio for nonpayment of rent. Taken by Simmons to the studio, White pushed a fistful of money under the door. The unnamed artist was able to keep his studio and later died without ever knowing the source of his mysterious windfall. On another occasion White dove into his pocket to give a notorious begger a handful of change, parrying Simmons's admonition, saying, "You don't understand. Do you suppose I was trying to do him good? I was only trying to justify my own existence."[21]

White was always in a rush; he never stopped. Magonigle remembered him as being

> six feet two or three, with very long legs, broad shoulders, narrow hips, stiff tawny hair standing straight up and cut *en-brosse*, a great red moustache, beetling light eyebrows overhanging little bright grey-green eyes with almost white lashes. His hands were large and strong and hairy with long blunt fingers. . . . He was only 34 years old when I joined the staff. It doesn't seem possible. His reputation was already impressive. Of course a difference of fourteen years at 20 seemed an immense gap and I saw him as a kind of demi-god moving in a world apart. He had a "field" as an electrician would say, and his radiated energy was terrific. . . . White's method of design was as different from McKim's as day from night. He would tear into your alcove, perhaps push you off your stool with his body while he reached for pencil and tracing paper and in five minutes make a dozen sketches of some arrangement of detail or plan, slam his hand down on one of them—perhaps two or three of them if they were close together—say "Do that!" and tear off again. You had to guess what and which he meant. . . . It was grand practice in guessing. A five-minute visit from him left you limp with the reaction from the strain of trying to follow his thought as his fingers flew. Or, he'd suddenly appear at your elbow and say, "That is the goddamdest lookin' thing I ever saw!" stare at it for a while, seize his huge red moustache in both hands and twist it until the hairs came out and fell on the paper, or stick a brand-new pencil into the grip of his big back teeth and twist it and spit out the splinters; then, like as not, he'd say, still staring, "oh, I don't know—that's not so bad," and begin to whistle; finally "All right! All *right!* That's perfectly all right—go ahead! Go ahead!" and disappear. . . . White's way was to load a job on us youngsters way beyond our powers and force a result out of us if it could be squeezed out—sometimes it couldn't. But it was wonderful training if you didn't crack under the strain—it made a man of you—or it didn't.[22]

Exclaiming something "looked like hell" was praise indeed, for often White would grab a drawing and wave it toward Mead if he were anywhere near and say "Look at this, Dummy, swell isn't it." Thus, the draftsman knew that White approved.

To work for White was an exhilarating experience; he inspired loyal devotion, and even though he might curse his assistants when their minds did not follow his nimble flights, they worked themselves all the harder. Many of them spent long hours, nights, and weekends in the drafting room, discovering thereby just how much time White spent there too. He would often appear after the opera in full evening dress, fill yards of tracing paper with sketches, look over the work on the drafting tables and scribble cryptic notes in his bold round hand, usually in the vein of "this looks like hell!" He might pounce on some lone unsuspecting draftsman and start dashing off sketches for some new problem, oblivious to the fact that most people like to sleep. He was just as likely to appear pounding at the door at seven in the morning, his arms filled with drawings.[23] Such nervous energy enabled White to accomplish a great deal. Magonigle tells of a census taken in the office about 1892 which revealed that White had more than ninety jobs in various stages, McKim, seven or eight, and Mead, two.[24] White set this pace for himself quite early, for in a letter of about 1880 to his mother, his father complained that Stanford was hardly ever present for breakfast or dinner: "He is working too hard. . . . I spoke to him about it, and his reply was 'Well father,'—he always calls me father when he thinks I'm a bore, papa at other times—'the work must be done.' "[25] White would have found impossibly constraining the legislation that restricted government architects in France to working on only one building at a time.

Yet there was not always such an endurance race, for at the end of the short winter days, recalled Albert Randolph Ross, after the office lamps had been lit and most of the draftsmen had gone home, the partners would puff cigars while White whistled to himself as he put finishing touches on his work. Then were the partners in their best vein, "then did McKim 'go fishing' as he was pleased to call poring over the old volumes of Roman masterpieces, and then did they admire or aid with criticism each other's work [52, 53]."[26]

White thought with his pencil in hand, sketching and resketching until the result

52. William Rutherford Mead, Charles Follen McKim, and Stanford White, c. 1905.

53. Stanford White, William Rutherford Mead, and Charles Follen
McKim, relaxing on the grounds of White's country home, Box-Hill, c.
1900.

looked right and appropriate for the problem. As with McKim, however, even after drawings were finished, portions might be changed. Handsome drawings were but a means to
an end, and "to work with and under him was to appreciate . . . that the building, not the
drawing, is and should be the architect's chief concern." To White architecture meant color
first, then form, texture, proportion, and plan last of all, and where White thought in
perspectives, McKim thought in elevation and plan; White was considered the Benvenuto
Cellini of the firm and McKim its Bramante.[27]

 These glimpses of the partners pertain, it is true, more to the years between 1886 and
1894, yet they tell something of the young men in 1879. Mead drew up a formal agreement
in 1880, signed by all three on June 21, which stipulated how the monies received were to
be deposited and how the net profits were to be divided—forty-two percent to McKim,
thirty-three percent to Mead, and twenty-five percent to White.[28] The office rooms were
on the top, fifth floor of a narrow cast-iron-fronted building at Exchange Alley and Broadway [54, 55]. Across the front, looking down along Exchange Alley toward the East River,
were a small reception room and three cubbyholes about six feet square for the partners,
each just big enough for a small rolltop desk and a chair. A partition with a single swinging

leather-covered door separated this front section (known by the draftsmen as the "Holy of Holies") from the large drafting room, filled with about a dozen tables and decorated with pieces of wrought iron, plaster casts of ornament, and miscellaneous drawings. Because of the limited space in their private offices, the partners spent almost all of their time in the drafting room, and there arose a compelling esprit de corps in the office. Phillip Sawyer believed that the high caliber of the firm's work during these early years was directly due to the partners' extended presence in the drafting room, and it is significant that this early work from 1879 to 1886 is characterized by a degree of collaboration which makes it difficult to detect an overriding designer's influence.[29]

The caliber of the firm's work was high, too, because of the nature of the clients for whom they built. Many commentators, following the observations of the partners' biographers, have noted that a list of the firm's clients reads like a social directory. When one designed, as they did, for the Amorys, the Astors, the Coolidges, the Fishes, the Goelets, the Stuyvesants, or the Vanderbilts, one was given the means to procure the very best in

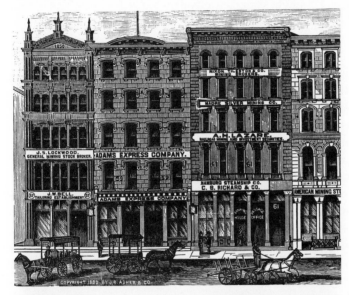

54. 57 Broadway, New York, N.Y., where the offices of McKim, Mead & White occupied the fifth floor. From a print, 1880, by J. R. Ascher & Co.

55. View of the drafting room of the offices of McKim, Mead & White, 1 W. 20th Street, New York, N. Y., c. 1892–93.

materials and craftsmanship. Such clients came from the old established Brahmin and Knickerbocker families of Boston and New York; customarily conservative, they had money to spend on houses or corporate structures, but these were to impress more through restraint and finesse in design rather than through sheer display. Significantly, even the comparatively *nouveaux riches* who employed the firm, clients such as the Mackays, the Oelrichs, the Pulitzers, and especially the Villards, also desired the same classical sobriety in the buildings they commissioned. The firm's clients generally took an active part in shaping their buildings, although few went as far as did Katherine Mackay in dictating to White a specific historical reference; and seldom did White, much less McKim, accede to such mandates.

Between them, McKim and White were able to satisfy the predilections of a broad spectrum of clients. McKim proved skilled at handling building committees and corporate clients, while White was adept at dealing with distaff clients, for although the bills for a house might be sent to the husband, it was the wife with whom White most often dealt directly concerning the design. He might complain privately to his friend Saint-Gaudens of the "small hells" of women who wanted closets first here and then there, but with consummate diplomacy he parried their suggestions. White, too, was a most active clubman, and it was through these connections that many commissions came into the office. His club memberships included the New York Yacht, Racquet and Tennis, Riders, Century, Metropolitan, Union, Players, Grolier, City, University, Brook, and the Ristigouche Salmon club; the latter's piscatorial diversions in the wilds of Quebec seemed to give him keen pleasure. Thus, the partners seemed to meet financiers, moguls, matriarchs, sportsmen, inventors, and industrialists with ease and on common ground.

The partners and several draftsmen regularly ate lunch at an accustomed table in a nearby Italian restaurant, then walked around the Battery and Bowling Green before returning to the office. Mead organized an office baseball team for which there were frequent impromptu warm-up sessions throwing a ball around the drafting room—when the partners were not around. As the office grew, a simple system evolved; the older, experienced assistants were generally associated with either McKim or White, and for each commission the designing partner would select one or more who in turn gathered a work force from the various draftsmen. Magonigle wrote that there were no assigned division heads or squad bosses; " 'efficiency' was unknown; when we had to work overtime, we got a dollar for dinner—nothing for our time—and broke our backs to get the work done; everything was rather happy-go-lucky; but what a place, what an atmosphere for the formation of artists." A few with the natural talent and inclination, such as Francis L. V. Hoppin, or after him Jules Crow, tended to specialize, making presentation perspectives, but another renderer, Egerton Swartwout, recalled "we were all a happy family there, we were proud of the office and its work and appreciated our luck in being there."[30]

In later years, as when the census mentioned by Magonigle was taken, it was White who was largely responsible for bringing the bulk of the commissions into the office, but at the start it was McKim's reputation gained in Newport which attracted clients. From the beginning the firm's summer houses in Newport were covered in shingles, that traditional seventeenth-century envelope which simultaneously was being exploited in the summer houses of William Ralph Emerson. While Emerson and the others interested in shingles looked to Colonial prototypes, photographs brought back from France reveal that McKim and White were also studying slate-covered medieval buildings [46].[31] When architects in the 1870s referred to Colonial sources, their notion of the period was rather fuzzy, merging seventeenth-century picturesque informality and regional variation with the more formal eighteenth-century Georgian. Thus the firm's revival of Georgian elements in the early 1880s, whether relatively pure or in the form of isolated decorative fragments in shingled houses, was an integral part of the Shingle Style. Gradually, however, the geometric logic of Georgian classicism began to infuse all of their work, controlling and organizing even the spatially inventive shingled work.

Among the first buildings designed by the new firm were country clubs, the earliest examples of this new American building type.[32] The Short Hills Music Hall (or Casino), 1879–80, was the first step in the development of an idealistic suburb of New York, Short Hills, New Jersey. The realization of a lifelong ambition of inventor Stewart Hartshorn to build a model community similar to Haskell's Llewellyn Park, Short Hills was started in 1874 on 13 acres near Millburn, New Jersey; eventually it grew to 1,707 acres.[33] The land was thickly wooded, with gently rolling hills through which threaded the Erie-Lackawanna Railroad connecting with Manhattan. With a careful eye for the contours of the land, Hartshorn laid out the streets, installing with them, as they were laid, conduits for water, sewers, and gas. By 1880 there were seventeen families in the village, with twelve new houses under construction; by 1888 there were fifty-two households. Houses were rented for about $750 a year or were sold for about $3,000 on plots consisting of two to five acres. The modest growth resulted from Hartshorn's insistence on approving all plans, ensuring that restrictions on stables and fences were observed, for his primary objective was to augment the natural forms of the land so as to attract "nature-loving people." For Hartshorn, Short Hills was more a hobby than a paying business, and it was not until 1937, the year before his death, that any profit was derived.[34] Two commissions were given to the firm, each integrally connected to this experiment. The first, a small model dwelling started in mid-1879, was meant to attract prospective residents. The second, the Music Hall, begun in November, was to be a community focal point, providing for the social needs of the villagers. Both stood across from the new passenger depot, from which the Music Hall with its tower presented a memorable silhouette to the visitor [56]. The upper part of the tower, clad in shingles in contrast to the masonry below, served as a marker, fixing the center of the community. The building combined an element of playfulness in the gable and tower, with a sense of purposeful abstraction in the conjunction of its parts [57]. Steam radiators were built in behind the seats lining the walls of the second-floor auditorium, and gas fixtures were provided, equipping the room for year-round use. Over the years the Short Hills Music Hall served a variety of purposes: it housed the village school, and the first church held its meetings there until 1884 when the congregation completed their own building; annual town meetings were held there until well into the twentieth century. In addition musical programs and gala presentations of Gilbert and Sullivan operettas kept the hall in nearly constant use.[35] There were few residents of Short Hills who in some way did not come to know the Music Hall well.

The Newport Casino, begun for James Gordon Bennett, Jr., in the autumn of 1879, was the result of pique, for Bennett, ever willful and impetuous, had been disciplined by his more conservative associates of the Newport Reading Room, and finding himself no longer welcome there he decided to build his own club, engaging McKim.[36] Completed in 1881,

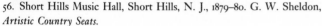

56. Short Hills Music Hall, Short Hills, N. J., 1879–80. G. W. Sheldon, *Artistic Country Seats.*

57. Short Hills Music Hall, detail of entrance.

the Newport Casino was to serve a rather different purpose than the Short Hills Music Hall; this incorporated lounges, restaurants, connecting verandas, and tennis courts to the rear, with offices and shops at the ground floor along the Bellevue Avenue front to provide rental income [58, 59, 60]. The curved veranda not only linked the two wings of the casino, thereby framing the inner promenade court, but also its lathe-turned spindle screens, inspired by Japanese sources, afforded glimpses of the tennis courts stretching off to the right. It was significant that inside the court, where the casino had only its own private functions to serve, the composition is asymmetrical, light, and informal [59], with dissimilar masses and voids played off against each other but focused on the entrance arch and the bell-capped tower whose clock was visible to players on the courts. The Bellevue Avenue front, however, where the building meets the public, is much more ordered and formal [58]. It is a remarkable instance of simultaneity that Richard Norman Shaw designed in the same year the Tabard Inn and Stores, Bath Road, one of his last additions to Bedford Park. This too was a multifunctional building, with shops on the ground floor; but whereas Shaw emphasized the discontinuity of the interiors by a series of slight projections of his facade and by a sawtooth row of sharp gables, McKim, Mead & White emphasized horizontal continuity with a few overlapped broader gables.[37] By slight projections of the upper floors, the long horizontal stretch of the facade is somewhat relieved, but the shingled surfaces are transformed into continuous horizontal bands by means of various patterns cut in their edges, thereby recognizing the fundamental linearity of the street. Here, then, at the very outset of their career, is an indication that to McKim, Mead & White a building has a dual responsibility, not only to its internal functional requirements but to the character of the setting, which here meant the nature of the street.

While Newport had begun to become *the* summer resort of the well-to-do during the 1870s, its rival watering places on the Atlantic Coast were Long Branch and Elberon, New Jersey, where, following the remodeling of the Elberon Hotel, the firm was engaged to design fourteen houses between 1879 and 1886. One of the largest, most innovative, and ambitious was for H. Victor Newcomb, 1880–81 [61, 62].[38] This approached being a longitudi-

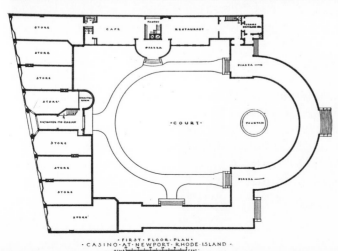

58. TOP. Newport Casino, Newport, R. I., 1879–80, Bellevue Avenue front.

59. ABOVE. Newport Casino, interior court facade. G. W. Sheldon, *Artistic Country Seats.*

60. LEFT. Newport Casino, partial plan (not including playing fields to the right). *Monograph of the Work of McKim, Mead & White, 1879–1915.*

nal plan, but in the living hall there was a sense of continuous, interwoven spaces, for the walls swelled out into inglenooks and window bays. Just to the left of the entrance was a large Shavian window-wall divided into nine squares, a device exploited even further for an entire wall in the larger R. Percy Alden house, Cornwall, Pennsylvania, 1880–81 [63].[39] In this the plan was more decidedly longitudinal, with rooms loosely arranged along the axis which, by means of huge sliding doors, could be opened up from end to end. As in the Newport Casino, the dominant verticals of the Alden house were "optically corrected," for both the bell-capped tower at the rear and the projecting front porte-cochère wing taper as they rise.

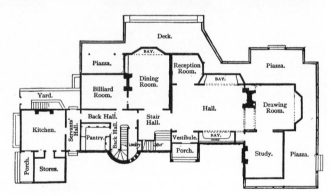

61. H. Victor Newcomb house, Elberon, N. J., 1880. G. W. Sheldon, *Artistic Country Seats.*

62. Newcomb house, plan. G. W. Sheldon, *Artistic Country Seats.*

63. Robert Percy Alden house, Cornwall, Pa., 1880–84.

The overt historicizing references to Shaw's clustering of windows, as at Cornwall, were among the last such references by the firm, but the easy informality of both the Newcomb and Alden house plans was elaborated with variations in a cluster of houses begun late in 1880 at the far eastern tip of Long Island. Because of the excellent ocean fishing there, seven New York businessmen—Alfred M. Hoyt, William L. Andrews, Henry Sanger, Dr. Cornelius E. Agnew, A. W. Benson, Alexander E. Orr, and Henry G. de Forest—formed the Montauk Point Association to purchase a large expanse of land at Cottage Point, just east of the village of Montauk. There, amid the low scrub-covered dunes, they developed a communal summer retreat, engaging Frederick Law Olmsted in the summer of 1881 to advise on the placement of the proposed buildings.[40] Then, in the autumn, the association approached McKim, Mead & White to design a communal central hall to house recreational facilities, stable, and laundry. The following spring the Hoyt, Andrews, Sanger, and Agnew houses were begun, followed in the summer by the Benson, Orr, and de Forest houses [64]. The de Forest house [65] is representative—simple, boldly geometric, completely covered in shingles. Each of the houses was placed on a slight rise, looking out toward the sea; isolated and individual, yet united by common purpose and design, the Montauk houses in their ensemble embody a freedom and spaciousness fitting to their remote and windswept setting.

Had McKim, Mead & White consciously set out to do so, they could hardly have provided a better revelation of what was to come than in the Newport Casino, for in their subsequent Shingle Style work they focused on its several qualities—continuity of space, continuity of surface, and geometric formality. So, in the houses that followed, expression

64. Montauk Association houses viewed from the Henry G. de Forest house.

65. Henry G. de Forest house, Montauk Point, N. Y., 1882–83.

of one of these qualities was stressed. In the Isaac Bell house, Newport, 1881–83, and the Robert Goelet house, Newport, 1882–83, these emphases are clear.[41] While both are completely covered in shingles externally, it is the openness of the plan and the near singular space of the ground floor of the Bell house which are most significant [66, 67]. As in the R. Percy Alden house, the rooms can be thrown open to each other by means of huge sliding doors. In the Goelet house, though the plan is spacious, the treatment of the variously patterned shingles is important. And in the large resort Pocantico Hills Hotel, near Tarrytown, New York, 1882–83, for Lewis Roberts, the firm demonstrated that shingles could be used to sheath even large commercial structures in the country.

66. Isaac Bell, Jr., house, Newport, R. I., 1881–83.

67. Bell house, plan. G. W. Sheldon, *Artistic Country Seats.*

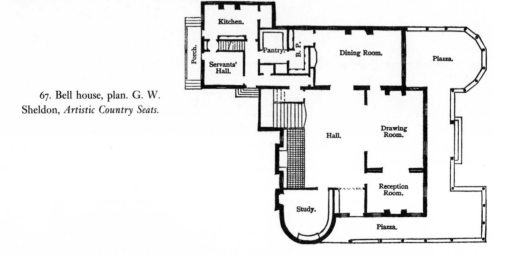

Geometric formality, as essayed in the earlier Howells and Butler houses, was emphatically pursued in Clayton Lodge, 1880–82, the summer house of Cyrus H. McCormick atop a low ridge overlooking the town of Richfield Springs, New York, in grounds planted by

F. L. Olmsted [68].[42] During the 1860s and 1870s this small upstate community enjoyed modest fame for its sulphur springs, and McCormick, then seventy-one, may have held great hopes in the efficacy of the springs; unfortunately he was able to spend only three summers in the house. Clayton Lodge, in its powerful abstract clarity, was among the most progressive houses of the period and could hardly have been in greater contrast to the elaborate Second Empire Baroque house McCormick had built on Rush Street, Chicago, 1875–79, from designs by local architects Cudell and Blumenthal. In addition to the important innovation of its sweeping elemental gable, Clayton Lodge contributed importantly to the emerging Colonial Revival, particularly in White's somewhat exaggerated scroll pediment in the

68. Cyrus Hall McCormick house, Clayton Lodge, Richfield Springs,
N. Y., 1880–82.

upper portion of the gable and the third-floor stucco panels embedded with broken glass.[43] If such picturesque details betray White's hand, the broad triangular composition shows the influence of McKim.

Masonry was not altogether absent in the summer and country houses, as is evident in the fieldstone podium of Clayton Lodge; when it was employed it was rough-faced, recalling that of Richardson. The most extensive use was in the Charles J. Osborn house, Mamaroneck, New York, 1883–85 [69, 70].[44] This was, in fact, not simply a summer house. It was divided into two sections, one intended for year-round living and the other principally for summer residence; hence the interiors were carefully detailed and richly embellished, as with a ceiling panel painted by Thomas W. Dewing. Similar quarry-faced masonry was used in the granite entrance archway of Narragansett Pier Casino, Narragansett Pier, Rhode Island,

1883–86.[45] Organized by local businessmen and New York restaurateur Louis Sherry, this was to compete with Newport for the less wealthy, and this more relaxed informal clientele may have encouraged the development of the rambling, irregular Z-plan extending from the beach road out toward the sea [71, 72]. Its irregular skyline, and seemingly *ad hoc* plan arrangement with its colliding rooms, represents the firm at its most picturesque, but in this instance the partner in charge was McKim, not White. Again inspiration came from the

69. Charles J. Osborn house, Mamaroneck, N. Y., 1883–85. G. W. Sheldon, *Artistic Country Seats.*

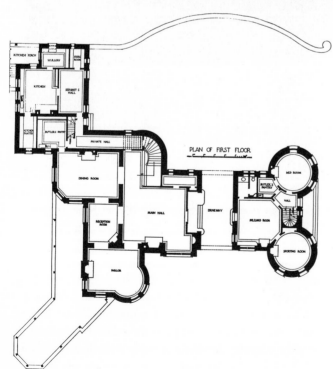

70. Osborn house, plan. *Monograph.*

architects' excursions through France, and there is among White's drawings an unlabeled sketch of a gate in France prefiguring the Osborn house and Narragansett arch [73]. In this, as in many other drawings, White showed the roof slates askew, and in practice the architects took pains to have roof shingles in the casino laid in similar undulating patterns. According to legend, McKim himself joined workmen on the roof, prying up selected shingles with crowbars to achieve the proper picturesque effect.[46]

71. Narragansett Pier Casino, Narragensett Pier, R. I., 1883–86. G. W. Sheldon, *Artistic Country Seats.*

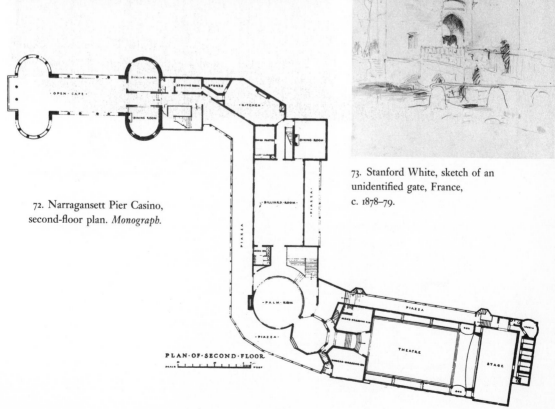

73. Stanford White, sketch of an unidentified gate, France, c. 1878–79.

72. Narragansett Pier Casino, second-floor plan. *Monograph.*

PLAN·OF·SECOND·FLOOR

Because of the virtual omnipresence of the partners in the drafting room and the resulting melding of artistic personalities, those few periods when a partner was clearly absent from the office assume special significance. One of the best documented was White's honeymoon in 1884. In February, after a protracted courtship, Stanford White and Bessie Springs Smith of Smithtown, Long Island, were married, leaving immediately on an extended tour of Europe and the Near East, returning late in August. Among the several houses conceived during this interval, the summer residence for Charles T. Cook, Elberon, New Jersey, is particularly devoid of the fluidity of form and surface by now characteristic of the firm's shingled work, replaced here by a particular angularity.[47] This and the evident antiquarian character of the carved Adamesque ornament suggest the influence of McKim. Yet McKim was able to develop integrated and unified shingled houses on his own, as was apparent in the residence of the Reverend Wynant Vanderpoel, Morristown, New Jersey, 1884–85 [74, 75]. Its plan had an easy pinwheel axiality, the rooms clustered freely around a central hall. On the exterior the windows were fitted into the dominant lines of the house, and the shingled roof and porch surfaces were unbroken.

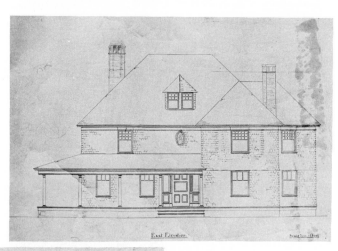

74. The Reverend Wynant Vanderpoel house, Morristown, N. J., 1884–85.

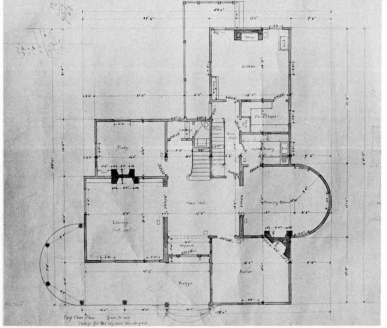

75. Vanderpoel house, first-floor plan.

It was such simple directness and continuity of space, surface, and line which marked the best shingled work of the firm. The sweep of interwoven interiors introduced in the Newcomb house was continued in the stair hall of the Samuel Tilton house, Newport, 1880, and in White's dining room addition to Kingscote, Newport, 1881.[48] It was in organizing the exteriors, however, that McKim's continuing study of Colonial geometries showed greatest effect. It appeared in relatively small houses, square in plan with a large tower pulled into one of the corners, best exemplified by the Mrs. Frances L. Skinner house, Newport, 1882, in which the shingled side wall curves imperceptibly into the corner tower [76]; while in masonry this form was used for the Osborn estate gate lodge. The elemental gable-on-podium form, introduced in the Howells and Butler houses and pursued in Clayton Lodge, was used in less emphatic fashion in the Edwin Metcalf house, Buffalo, New York, 1882, and the George Cresson house, Narragansett Pier, Rhode Island, 1883.[49] The most dramatic restatement and the culmination of this quest for normative form was the William G. Low house, Bristol, Rhode Island, 1886–87 [77, 78, 79].[50] This was a single broad triangular gable, only two rooms deep, or about 40 feet, but nearly 140 feet in breadth, with the rooms

76. Mrs. Frances L. Skinner house, Newport, R. I., 1882.

arranged on staggered floor levels under the outer parts of the roof. A broad hall ran through the house, from the porte-cochère to a bank of windows and a door opening to stairs down to the lawn and an open view of the bay. The classicizing unity was enhanced by the square-cut shingles covering the entire house—walls and roof—for there were no picturesque bands of notched or rounded shingles as in the Bell house. The continuity of that surface, moreover, was strengthened by the way the wall bowed outward to form the bays and the roofs over the bays; even the veranda was pulled under the continuous plane of the roof so that no subsidiary extension or projection would compromise the elemental triangle. To modern eyes it is a particularly powerful design, but it had almost no impact in its own time except perhaps on Babb, Cook & Willard, close friends and colleagues of the architects; it was unpublished and largely unknown except in Bristol and to a small circle in New York. In this summation of all that came before, however, all extraneous elements present in the Butler house and Clayton Lodge are completely controlled by an insistent geometry, so that the Low house represents the fullest expression in shingles of the formal principles inspired by Georgian models with which the firm was simultaneously experimenting in urban buildings.

77. TOP. William G. Low house, Bristol, R. I., 1886–87, ocean side.

78. ABOVE. Low house, entrance front.

79. BELOW AND OPPOSITE, TOP. Low house, first- and second-floor plans (L. M. Roth).

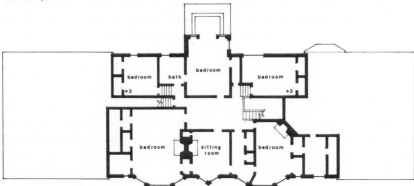

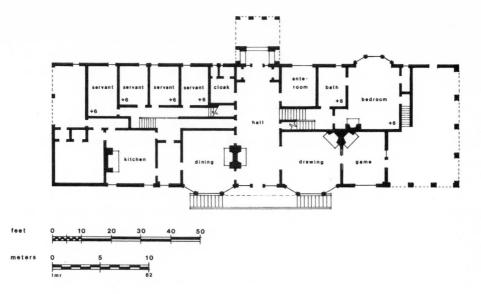

servant +6 | servant +6 | servant +6 | servant +6 | cloak | ante-room | bath +6 | bedroom +6
hall
kitchen | dining | drawing | game

feet 0 10 20 30 40 50
meters 0 5 10
1 mr 82

FROM the start of their practice, McKim, Mead & White recognized the need for different residential types, and while their summer houses and their urban townhouses are relatively well known, their suburban residences are known hardly at all. Prior to 1887 there were relatively few—one for Theodore R. Davis, Brooklyn, 1881–85, another for Robert T. Howe, Mount Vernon, New York, and the more fully developed one for Edwin D. Metcalf, Buffalo, New York, 1882–84 [80]. This rather compact square of brick and stone had portions of the walls, roof, and upper gables covered with red clay tile rather than shingles. Because of the various external details and the elaborate paneling in the main stair hall, this was considered by Buffalonians to be "early colonial."[51]

80. Edwin D. Metcalf house, Buffalo, N. Y., 1882–84.

In these early years, preceding the establishment of clear design hierarchies within the firm, a number of projects continued the free manipulation in plan but now were wrapped in one of various "experimental" external envelopes. One intriguing unexecuted project, a house for Catherine Wolfe at Ochre Point, Newport, circa 1880–81, shows McKim's efforts to translate various Richardsonian and François Ier elements into brick, set off against expanses of blank wall.[52] The most elaborate and carefully finished of this type of "astylar" country house was Naumkeag, for Joseph H. Choate in Stockbridge, Massachusetts, 1885–88.[53] The through central hall, flanked by parlor and library on one side, and dining room on the other, was inspired by Georgian sources, but the plan was complicated by porch indentions and an ell, housing a schoolroom and study on the ground floor. And although the shingling of the gables and roofs suggested the eighteenth century, the round corner towers with "candle snuffer" conical roofs, and particularly the fieldstone construction, came from the architect's sketches of buildings in rural France.

Some of the urban townhouses underway and completed by the new firm—the Dickerson and Thompson houses, for example—had already been termed "Queen Anne" by Montgomery Schuyler, and he used this term as well to describe the firm's William Astor house, New York, 1879–81.[54] An even more experimental expression was introduced in the double house for Charles T. Barney, New York, 1880–82 [81], in which the brick front was organized into structural piers and nonbearing panels laid in a herringbone pattern, making clear the structural action. The overall exuberance which emerged because of the lack of disciplined historical models, perhaps, and the general busyness did not please Schuyler, who felt the Barney duplex was "a mad orgy of bad architecture."[55] Similar but more restrained was the J. Coleman Drayton house, New York, 1882–83 [82]. Again there was a distinction between the bearing wall sections and the nonbearing panels, but the tripartite division of the facade (base, two-story midsection, and attic) was more strongly defined. In this the entrance was emphasized by a broad carved frame, which Russell Sturgis felt resembled the Mycenaean tomb at Orchomenus. There was a certain resemblance also to

81. Charles T. Barney (later Joseph Pulitzer) house, New York, N. Y., 1880–82.
82. J. Coleman Drayton house, New York, N. Y., 1882–83.

Richardson's work, and even to French Renaissance sources, but the Drayton house was a new creation adjusted to urban needs; it was well received, moreover, by most critics, who appreciated its innovation.[56]

In hindsight it would appear that McKim, Mead & White were experimenting with a number of expressions for townhouses, to see which offered a sense of underlying discipline and yet had potential for variation. It was perhaps not so calculated, although the effect was the same; sadly, there is no written account of this process, so the buildings alone must serve to reconstruct the story. One alternative that appeared fruitful was based on French Renaissance sources, and the firm's early experiments with this were only slightly antedated by similar work by their colleague George B. Post, as in his immense house for Cornelius Vanderbilt II, New York, 1879–82. But the firm's adoption of this mode was probably influenced more by Richard Morris Hunt's nearly concurrent house for Cornelius's brother, William Kissam Vanderbilt, New York, 1879–81. McKim, in particular, admired Hunt's design and in later years was accustomed to taking an evening stroll up Fifth Avenue just to see it before retiring.[57]

The firm's first house in this mode was for Charles A. Whittier, Boston, 1880–83, the northern half of a double house the southern half of which was designed by H. H. Richardson for F. L. Higginson [83, 84].[58] Both architects took into account that the houses were to be contiguous, a degree of collaboration rare in American architecture up to this time. Close attention was given to carrying through uniform cornice heights, floor levels, and the continuation of string courses. The Higginson house, however, was not one of Richardson's best, and in the Whittier house the pupils surpassed their former teacher. They employed an adaptation of François Ier with a brownstone base and little or no ornamentation except for the entrance porch, and, in the upper floors, windows arranged so that they formed

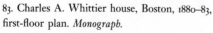

83. Charles A. Whittier house, Boston, 1880–83, first-floor plan. *Monograph.*
84. Whittier house (right half), 1880–83.

vertical bays with spandrel panels treated as nonbearing inserts. The plan was representative of townhouses of the period, with the kitchen in the basement, and living and dining rooms and library on the main floor around a most commodious central stair hall.

This was followed shortly by the Ross R. Winans house, Baltimore, 1882–83 [85, 86].[59]

Except for its greater width and the recessed entrance, this has many features in common with the Whittier house. Though the plan would seem to suggest a compartmentalized separation of spaces, the rooms are connected by large sliding doors, giving the first floor a particular spaciousness. Although an urban house, this was freestanding, permitting at the side and rear a garden with a fountain on the extended axis of the drawing room. For a firm only three years in existence, this was an assured design, clear and simple in mass, with strong horizontals which continued the line of the street. It was gracious to its neighbors, but at the same time was a clear improvement over them. Its crisp and tightly confined ornament, adapted from early French Renaissance sources, as well as the ornament of the Whittier house, may have been developed by the firm's chief draftsman, Joseph Morrill Wells, a great admirer of François Ier architecture, who had just returned from a trip to France and Italy.

85. Ross R. Winans house, Baltimore, Md., 1882–83. *American Architect and Building News*, April 30, 1887.

86. Winans house, first-floor plan. *Monograph.*

It was only natural that during this transitional period the firm should also attempt using the massive masonry of its mentor Richardson. This appeared in the Charles L. Tiffany house group, New York, 1882–85, a cluster of three apartments stacked atop one another [87]. Designing commenced in April 1882 for the client of record, Charles Tiffany, who was to occupy the two floors above the base; the third floor was to be occupied by his daughter. The unique character of the brick mass was a joint creation of White and Louis Comfort Tiffany, the son, whom White greatly admired and with whom he had worked before on the interiors of the Seventh Regiment Armory, during 1880. The firm's earliest drawings for the Tiffany house, in fact, show only the profile of the upper portion, for this section, comprising his own studio-apartment, was designed by Louis C. Tiffany himself. His preliminary sketch shows the conceptual scheme for the roof [88], but the finished building shows that White regularized this scheme by making the upper section one huge

87. Charles L. Tiffany house group, New York, N. Y., 1882–85.

88. Louis Comfort Tiffany, sketch for Tiffany house group, c. 1882? From Charles DeKay, *The Art Work of Louis C. Tiffany*, New York, 1914.

gable supported by a steel frame.[60] Actually there is little in the Tiffany house that refers specifically to Richardson except the broad low-set semicircular entrance arch and the overall amplitude of scale. Whatever sources may have been alluded to—whether Swiss, Netherlandish, German, or even English as suggested by various critics at the time—were so completely merged as to defy separate identification. This authority of expression, added to the great bulk of the house, attracted favorable attention.[61] Now destroyed, the Tiffany house was a careful study in color. The base was of North River bluestone; the upper walls, of speckle-glazed, thin Roman brick then new to New York. White reportedly worked closely with the Perth Amboy Brick Company to achieve a variety of glaze colors, ranging from a soft buff to a deep golden brown, and these bricks were laid in a random fashion to give the walls a rich texture of varied hues. The roof was covered in dark tiles of complementary color.

PERHAPS the most overlooked of the firm's buildings of the period are their apartments and multiunit housing, all now destroyed. The Percival, New York, 1882–83, was a brick residence hotel for bachelors, which offered "the refinement and good service of a private house with the freedom of a hotel."[62] Nearly square in plan, it had suites of rooms grouped around a central hall and vertical circulation core. In 1885 the firm supplied the design for an apartment complex on West 83rd Street, New York, built by prominent real estate developer David H. King. This was followed in the spring of 1886 by a group of houses on Saint Ann's Avenue, the Bronx, New York, for Dr. Theodore G. Thomas. The King houses on 83rd Street were praised by Montgomery Schuyler in "The Small City House in New York" for their unified composition punctuated by alternated roof profiles and the modulation of two brick colors.[63]

THESE urban residences, single and multiunit, seem to have been experiments, for none were repeated. If a harmonious urban ensemble was to emerge, the solution lay in adhering to a more universal discipline, one which architects either already knew in essence or might readily learn—one which had been demonstrated to have worked before. The historical precedents which served this need and which also satisfied the demands of modern functional planning were the Italian Renaissance and its derivative Georgian Colonial; both encouraged flexibility. There had already been tentative allusions to the latter in McKim's "Colonial" interiors and the Union Club competition entry, however loosely the sources were interpreted, but 1882–83 marks the beginning of the firm's definite shift toward Renaissance classicism with the design of three houses, in New York, Newport, and Boston.

Renaissance prototypes had served American architects since the mid-1840s, but this mode had never gained general popularity because it was visually sedate in a period that prized picturesque extremes and variety. It had begun in Germany with the work of Schinkel and von Klenze and in England with Sir Charles Barry's Travellers' and Reform Clubs, London, and his Manchester Athenaeum, all built in the period 1929–39. The *palazzo* was introduced to the United States by John Notman in his Philadelphia Athenaeum, 1845–47, followed by John Cabot's Boston Athenaeum, Thomas Tefft's Tully-Bowen house in Providence, Rhode Island, and Leopold Eidlitz's American Exchange Building, New York, during the next dozen years. A generalized Renaissance expression was used for

Federal buildings across the country after 1853 by Ammi B. Young and James G. Hill, and a theoretical base for its use was proposed by Arthur Gilman.[64] By 1870, however, Renaissance classicism began to appear in somewhat modified form in the work of Henry Fernbach and George B. Post in New York. McKim, Mead & White would have been well acquainted with Fernbach's German Savings Bank, 1870–72, for Saint-Gaudens's studio was there, and McKim published Post's domed Williamsburg Savings Bank, Brooklyn, in the *New York Sketch Book* in 1874.[65] Post had anticipated the firm's move toward Renaissance classicism in his Chickering Hall and the Long Island Historical Society, 1874–79, especially in his New York Produce Exchange, 1881–84, but Post never extrapolated this into a generalized system of urban design as McKim, Mead & White proceeded to do. The building that marked this important change for them was the group of houses on Madison Avenue, New York, for Henry Villard.

There was, in fact, not just one commission from Villard, but a cluster of projects for Villard himself and for the Northern Pacific Railroad, all of which he put in the hands of his young architects—something like a total of $2.5 million in anticipated building costs (1882–85 dollars). The firm had several clients who came to them repeatedly—most notably the Goelet brothers, for their summer house, speculative office blocks, and, finally, their mausoleum—but none like Villard who focused on public structures. The best known of Villard's many building enterprises, however, is the housing complex in which his family's elegant apartments were to be located.

Henry Villard was then at the height of his career, having just consolidated rail lines in Oregon and the Pacific Northwest with the newly completed Northern Pacific. His rise to power and financial prominence, however, had been fortuitous. Born Ferdinand Heinrich Gustav Hilgard in Rhenish Bavaria in 1835, Villard fell into a bitter dispute with his stern father and fled to live with relatives in Illinois, adopting in transit the name by which he was known the rest of his life. In Illinois he learned English and began to write for German- and English-language newspapers; his fervent abolitionist sympathies were apparent in his ardent reporting of the Union cause and drew him to the Garrison family (he married William Lloyd Garrison's daughter, Frances, in 1865), and to other abolitionists such as Miller McKim. Reporting on gold discoveries in Colorado earned him the reputation as an expert on the American West, and his studies of financial operations established him as an expert in business as well. While on a rest visit to Germany, his first trip back to his homeland, in 1873–74, Villard was engaged by Frankfort investors to inspect a railroad in Oregon into which they had sunk large sums with, as yet, no return. When Villard reported favorably, he was instructed to buy a controlling interest and assume management. Villard set about extending new rail lines eastward in the hope of connecting with the approaching North Pacific tracks, and upgrading the steam packets and riverboats that plied the Pacific Ocean, Puget Sound, and the Columbia River (these had been part of the holdings of the railroad over which he obtained control). During 1879–84 he had new ships built on the East Coast, equipped with electric lighting and graced with interiors designed by McKim, Mead & White. These interiors, in fact, were the second commission Villard gave the firm, for, in 1879, when he realized that railroad business would keep him in New York City, Villard purchased wooded property overlooking the Hudson at Dobbs Ferry, New York, bringing in McKim to make additions and alterations to the existing house; this work continued in stages for several years, transforming the original Italianate villa into a rambling, comfortable country house.[66]

If he was to ensure the profitability of his rail and ship network in the Northwest, Villard had to connect it with a transcontinental line to the east, but the directors of the Northern Pacific showed every intention of building their own competing railroad parallel to Villard's, leaving his system with virtually no freight traffic. Quietly, Villard then circulated a letter to his business and professional associates in New York, asking for pledges to a fund of $8 million, the purpose of which he could not yet disclose; the subscriptions quickly exceeded the amount, to a total of $20 million, with which Villard bought up enough stock in the spring of 1881 to control the Northern Pacific. At the autumn meeting he was elected a director and then president of the Northern Pacific.

Early in 1881, as his plan to obtain control of the Northern Pacific appeared assured of success, Villard bought the various lots across the end of the block at Madison Avenue, between 50th and 51st streets, facing Saint Patrick's Cathedral. During the spring he worked with McKim in devising a rather novel plan for six houses forming a group around a central entrance court opening out onto Madison Avenue.[67] Development of the design proceeded during the summer and early fall, when, in October, Villard took McKim with him to Oregon to inspect sites for a series of terminal stations proposed for the railroad. McKim was to stay in Portland, Oregon, through the winter of 1881–82, and the Madison Avenue house project meanwhile was placed in the hands of White, but he too left the office to visit with his brother in New Mexico. The various jobs in White's care were then passed to various members of the staff, the Villard houses being given to the most gifted man in the office, White's principal assistant, Joseph Morrill Wells. Wells is said to have accepted the job on the condition that Mead permit him to throw out everything White had done except the plan arrangement and develop an entirely new exterior. When McKim and White later returned to the office, so this account goes, they discovered he had transformed the group into a Renaissance palazzo, immediately becoming advocates of Renaissance classicism themselves.

This account, relayed years after by friends of Wells, no doubt gives him too much credit, especially for the Villard house complex design development, for it is unlikely he would have had so much latitude in what was the most important single commission yet given the firm. Wells did not decide upon the Italianate character of the house alone. Not only did Villard initiate the arrangement around a court, he wished the group to recall the Hilgard home in Zweibrücken [89], whose restrained Renaissance exterior was typical of much German building of the 1830s—such as the University of Munich, 1834–40, by Friedrich von Gärtner, where the young Villard had studied briefly. Furthermore, in 1881–82 White admired Italian Renaissance architecture far more than Wells. It seems most likely that McKim and White, in conjunction with Villard, had developed the general character of the exterior before their journeys, leaving it to Wells to develop the details. Perhaps it was the crisp and inventively clear details that so affected the partners on their return, for all the members of the firm later readily admitted that Wells was the catalyst in making Renaissance classicism the standard of the office. All agreed too that Wells was entirely responsible for the details of the Villard house group.

It was in connection with the Villard complex that Joseph Morrill Wells (1853–1890) rose to the status of a virtual partner in the firm. A descendant of Samuel Adams, he had been born in Winchester, Massachusetts, near Boston, to a family of limited means, attended the Allen School in West Newton, studied architecture with Clarence Luce, and joined the office of Peabody & Stearns before moving to New York to work for Richard Morris

89. Hilgard house, Zweibrücken, Germany. Photograph in Oswald Garrison Villard Papers.

Hunt.[68] It was while in Boston, apparently, that Wells began to examine Renaissance architecture, preparing two large, detailed renderings of the Palazzo Cancelleria and the Palazzo Farnese, which for many years afterward hung over his drafting table. In September 1879 he joined the office of McKim, Mead & White, but it soon became clear that he was much more gifted than his fellow draftsmen. He became White's chief assistant, but where White thought and designed plastically, Wells designed primarily in two dimensions. He was, however, according to William Mitchell Kendall, a master of detail, bringing to it his characteristic balance, proportion, and perfection of line.[69] In July 1880 Wells left the office for a ten-month tour of Europe, traveling in England during the summer, spending the autumn and early winter in France, and passing the early part of 1881 in Italy. In a series of letters to White he described his preferences; "Gothic I stare at," he confessed in a letter of October 10, "Renaissance I study. Not because I think it best but because it is the most convenient to my taste." What he meant by "Renaissance," however, was François Ier. Later, from Florence on January 24, 1881, he wrote that he wasn't sketching much in Italy because what he saw he did not think would be of use to him when he got back: "Italian architecture is great and grand and dignified. But it seems to me ill adapted for our domestic country where we put three stories to their one." Still, he admitted he had not yet seen Rome, Venice, or other centers of Italian Renaissance culture. Nevertheless, he wrote of his growing admiration of the careful execution, intellectual precision, simplicity, and grandness of Italian Renaissance building.[70] With close friends Wells was good-humored, and he shared with White and Saint-Gaudens a passion for music, helping to organize chamber music concerts at the sculptor's studio. Yet he was often acerbic, as when he replied (only partly in jest perhaps) to an invitation to become a partner in 1889 that he could not afford to sign his name "to so much damned bad work."[71]

When McKim returned from Oregon early in 1882, construction on the Villard houses began, starting with drilling the exposed bedrock for basement excavations, for Villard was afraid that blasting might damage neighboring Columbia College buildings. By the end of the year Villard had the shell nearly completed, and a good start was made on the interiors of his own southern section [90, 91, 92]. The almost immediate impact of the complex was the result of a number of mutually reinforcing factors—the unity and harmony of the block which commanded the street, the studiously correct Italian Renaissance detail, and the unusual arrangement around the central court.[72] The group was no larger than many clusters of townhouses, but because they were so obviously conceived as a single unit, bounded by one cornice and reinforced by other horizontals, they seemed more imposing than their neighbors. Theirs was a monumentality gained through grand and simple form rather than through sheer mass. The court, especially devised by Villard to create a quieter transitional zone between the individual houses and the bustle of the street, was appropriate here, for it mirrored the similar "court" behind Saint Patrick's between the two residential blocks, added by Renwick in the mid-1870s. The result was a suggested cross-axis perpendicular to the street, creating a special sense of focus and arrival. Villard may have had in mind the wide recess of the front of the University of Munich, or even perhaps the court of the replica of Versailles at Herrenchiemsee, near Munich, begun in 1878 by Georg von Dollmann for Ludwig II. The final result, however, indicates the architects studied quattrocento examples such as Peruzzi's Villa Farnesina, Rome, illustrated by Letarouilly. Among modern buildings, McKim admired Duquesney's Gare de l'Est in Paris, surely known to Villard through his extensive travels in Europe after 1873.

Taking advantage of the better exposure and light, Villard had his own apartments in the southern wing; the two center units were sold to Artemas H. Holmes, Villard's business lawyer, and to his close friend, Edward Dean Adams. The front half of the northern wing was purchased by Harris C. Fahnestock, while the rear section of the wing contained two townhouses occupied by other members of the Fahnestock family; these had entrances on 51st Street, while all the others were entered through the court. Part of the terms of sale for each section was a pledge that each owner would engage McKim, Mead & White to complete the interiors, a restriction to which Holmes objected but eventually acquiesced.[73] In sharp contrast to tradition, however, the principal entrance to the main element, Villard's own section, was not on the axis of the court; there were presented three nearly equal entrances, and that on the axis led to a vestibule opening to *two* doors, to the Holmes and Adams sections. This kind of liberty taken with Renaissance and Beaux-Arts planning principles confounded purists and public alike, who thought the entire block was Villard's palatial residence.

Despite the liberties taken, architects and others interested in architecture, such as Samuel A. B. Abbott of Boston, admired the unity and harmony of the ensemble emphasized at every point by the Renaissance moldings, window frames, and entrance architraves. In working out these details Wells apparently spent a great deal of time with Letarouilly's *Rome Moderne*, specifically with the plates showing the Cancelleria, then attributed to Bramante, though he probably examined other volumes on Italian Renaissance architecture as well.[74] This was no copy of the Cancelleria, however, for the pilasters were omitted altogether, and the use of window frames to articulate internal function (that is, the most ornate treatment at the *piano nobile*) was replaced by a simple progression of simplest to most complex, going from the bottom to the top, so that the most embellished frames are those of the windows of the guest and servants' bedrooms.

The external austerity did not extend to the interior, however, and the Villard apartments were richly embellished with marble veneers in the entrance halls, relieved with small-scale, carved ornament also inspired by quattrocento models, murals by Francis Lathrop, and the stair-hall clock by Augustus Saint-Gaudens [93, 94]. Everywhere the work was of the highest caliber. For those with money to spend in ways in which it might show,

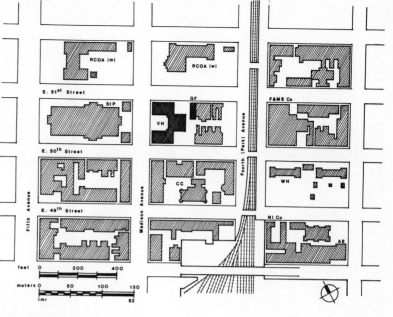

90. Plan of the vicinity of the Villard house group (L. M. Roth, from *Robinson's Atlas of the City of New York*, New York, 1885). Key to symbols: AE = American Express Company; CC = Columbia College; F&MS Co = F. & M. Schaefer Brewing Company; GF = Gibson Fahnestock house; NI Co = National Ice Company; RCOA (m) = Roman Catholic Orphan Asylum (men); RCOA (w) = Roman Catholic Orphan Asylum (women); StP = Saint Patrick's; VH = Villard house group; WH = Women's Hospital, State of New York.

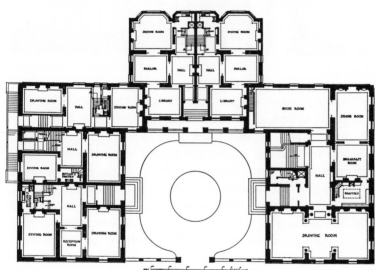

91. Villard house group, first-floor plans. *Monograph.*

92. Villard house group, New York, N. Y., 1882–85.

93. Villard house, dining room, fireplace relief
carving by Augustus Saint-Gaudens.
94. Villard house, upper portion of stair hall.

here was proof that display could be decorous and restrained; more importantly, the unity of the whole was greatly improved when the architect designed the interiors as well. McKim, Mead & White, it was evident, had no need to employ the Herter Brothers or Macotte and Company, the most fashionable decorators of the day. The interiors of the Villard house, begun by White and finished by the firm for the Whitelaw Reids, set a standard of restrained elegance in interior decoration that in turn inspired Edith Wharton to write a handbook on the subject, *The Decoration of Houses,* which appeared in 1897.[75]

Ironically, Villard's business associates who bought the northerly sections lived in the complex far longer than did he. During 1883, to fulfill his goal of completing the Northern Pacific and to make northern transcontinental transit a reality, Villard had severely strained the resources of the railroad, so much so that confidence evaporated and a run began in Northern Pacific stock. In an effort to satisfy creditors of the railroad, Villard sold much of his personal holdings, and by January 1884 was forced to resign the presidency of the railroad. While the Madison Avenue group had been under construction, the Villards had been living at a hotel, and to save on hotel bills the family moved into the incomplete house. Besieged by angry crowds who thought the entire building was a rapacious magnate's palace, Villard and the family left for the quiet of Thorwood, at Dobbs Ferry, after only several weeks of residence, leaving forever the house which so clearly embodied his own ideas of good urban design and which, in many ways, was the best work his architects were ever to do. Villard put the house up for sale and in 1886 sold it to fellow journalist and publisher Whitelaw Reid.[76]

The active part Villard took in planning the Madison Avenue group, the character of the design he encouraged, and the resultant building are illustrative of the harmony and integration Villard tried to achieve in all his endeavors. The Madison Avenue houses alone would have assured for Villard and his architects a place in the history of American architecture, but Villard had in mind a much more ambitious program of building along the length of the Northern Pacific, from Saint Paul, Minnesota, to Tacoma, Washington, and Portland, Oregon. Of all of this the New York houses were only a part, and not even the costliest segment. High on Villard's list of priorities were passenger and freight terminal facilities at Portland (his preferred terminus for the line) and at Tacoma (the terminus previously selected by the Northern Pacific directors in 1873). McKim had remained in Portland during the winter of 1881–82, and after his return in April 1882, a perspective of the proposed passenger terminal was published in Portland [95]. On a site well to the west of the proposed freight yard and terminal, which were next to the Willamette River, the passenger terminal was to be large far beyond the beginning carrying capacity of the railroad. Its arms of offices were to frame a wide entrance court with fountain, a node meant to terminate the broad park boulevard which already extended north from Portland's residential and business center. This expansive passenger terminal was to be a great commodious gate to the city, greeting the long-distance traveler after four or five days on the train with landscaped vistas and splashing fountains; arrival in Portland was to be a festive occasion. The sites for this and the freight yard, however, were marshy and required filling in, and because this work was delayed and attention properly focused momentarily on the river-front freight yards, construction on the passenger terminal still had not started when Villard was forced to resign the Northern Pacific presidency in January 1884. No work was ever to be done on this station. With the change of directors and of president, there was no interest in pursuing Villard's and McKim, Mead & White's ambitious and enormously expensive passenger terminal. Eventually the entire enterprise passed to the Southern Pacific Railroad, which hired Van Brunt & Howe of Kansas City in 1889 to design a smaller, less expensive station along the side of the freight yard, during the design of which Villard was repeatedly consulted; this was built in 1893–96.[77] Villard also had his architects design a small passenger terminal for Tacoma, also arranged around a court, but this station too remained unbuilt.

95. Northern Pacific Railroad Terminal (passenger station), Portland, Ore., 1882. From *West Shore*, April 1882.

Although Villard had wanted to focus his energies on the terminal facilities, he found himself obliged to go into the hotel business after repeated entreaties to Portland business-men failed to spur them to form their own corporation. Good hotels at the ends of the line would be vital for encouraging transcontinental travel when the tracks were completed, and all of this construction had to be finished at nearly the same time. Against his better judgment he committed railroad funds to a hotel in Portland, engaging McKim, Mead & White to prepare the design, which again was published in Portland [96]. Construction of this was delayed, and only the basalt base was finished in 1883 when the railroad's and Villard's finances collapsed. "Villard's ruins," as the hotel substructure was known locally, were a nuisance and eyesore until 1887 when a locally organized company set about finishing the hotel. They used working drawings prepared by the firm in 1885, but McKim, Mead & White turned over supervision of construction to William H. Whidden, who had been in the office, traveled with McKim to Oregon in 1881, and returned later to start an independent practice with Ion Lewis. The completed Portland Hotel, 1880–90, a broad H in plan, with an entrance court, was finished in careful conformity to the original scheme of 1883. The Tacoma Hotel [97], similar in character and detail, was finished earlier, in 1883–84, by the Tacoma Land Company, official developers of the fledgling community, from plans secured by Villard from McKim, Mead & White; this construction was likewise supervised by William Whidden.

Villard had expected to turn the design of many of the secondary railroad buildings over to McKim, Mead & White as well, beginning with a hospital for railroad employees at Brainerd, Minnesota, in 1883 [98]. This frame, shingled building was designed in New York, but the details were developed, specifications written, and construction supervised by Cass Gilbert, who had recently left the office to start his own practice in his native Saint Paul. There were to be a string of such hospitals along the line, part of an extensive prepaid medical-benefits plan for railroad employees; the further prospect of stations and hotels in Montana prompted Mead to write Gilbert in June 1883 in response to Gilbert's suggestion that a branch office be set up in Saint Paul, to be known as McKim, Mead & White, with all work to be credited to Gilbert. Mead was receptive, but before anything could be done the financial troubles of the railroad started and the scheme came to naught; only the Brainerd hospital was finished.[78]

The firm also contributed to the design of line depots, particularly the one formerly in Mandan, North Dakota, as is evident from this bill sent to the Northern Pacific Railroad in April 1884: "for cash disbursements in travel, express, telegrams, etc., for account of Mandan and other stations in superintending building."[79] Surviving railroad records make no mention of the degree to which any of the 150 line depots built during Villard's short presidency might have been influenced by McKim, Mead & White. There were to be no more large railroad-related projects, although Villard did his best in 1883 to have the Dakota capitol given to McKim, Mead & White, for he felt it essential "to promote the erection of a monumental building."[80] The local Dakota capitol-building commission gave the job to Leroy S. Buffington.

Villard was never able again to give the firm any substantial work. His dreams of empire produced no tangible result, or so it would appear today, for the projects failed, the boats sank, the finished buildings burnt or were demolished—not a single one of his Northern Pacific buildings survives. The true impact of his endeavors is found not in his own projects but in the lasting influence of those who came to the Northwest to finish the work he began.

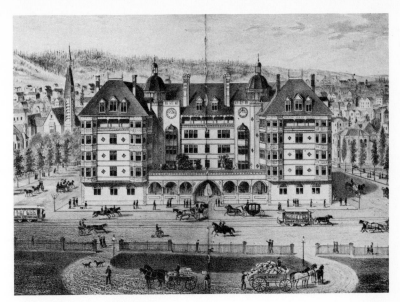

96. Portland Hotel, Portland, Ore., 1883, 1888–90. From *West Shore*, March 1883.

97. Tacoma Hotel, Tacoma, Wash., 1882–84.

98. Northern Pacific Beneficial Association Hospital, Brainerd, Minn., 1882–83.

Whidden and Lewis, after completing the Portland Hotel, designed the Portland City Hall and the Portland Public Library, becoming the city's chief architects; their protégé, Alfred E. Doyle, continued this tradition of excellence well into the twentieth century. Parallel improvements in the caliber of public building occurred in Tacoma, of which a particularly good example is Union Station by Reed & Stem, 1907–11. Such public and municipal architecture as this was Villard's finest legacy.

ONCE the firm had "discovered" Renaissance classicism as a repertoire of infinite variations that virtually assured balance and decorum, they embraced it wholeheartedly, not only in the Villard complex but almost simultaneously in a high-rise commercial block and a hotel designed almost entirely by Wells. This embrace of Renaissance classicism and the resulting greater reliance on established authority came at an opportune time, for the increasing pressure of business, as it forced the partners to relegate more and more work to their assistants, made it convenient, as Richardson had discovered, to send the men to the library to perfect the details.[81] The partners seem to have sensed, too, the parallel of their own age with that of the Medicis. The close collaboration among artists in the Villard house interiors —involving architects, painters, sculptors, mosaicists, and metalworkers—was made possible by an appreciation of the arts and an expansive patronage unprecedented among American businessmen. Industrialists began to think of themselves as "merchant-princes," and as Howard Mumford Jones observed, to find the nearest equivalent to Cosimo de Medici one must look to the end of the nineteenth century.[82]

In time the references to Italian sources would become specific and identifiable, but Wells's RussWin hotel, New Britain, Connecticut, 1883–84, built by two prominent architectural hardware manufacturers, was rather generically classical [99].[83] The exterior owed much to the firm's earlier Benedict apartments in which Wells resided. The brownstone base with its alternated broad and narrow arches housed shops, except in the center where the arch led to a small lobby. Above this base rose brick piers crowned with red terra-cotta impost capitols and arches; the piers varied in width, too, but according to a different rhythm, setting up a degree of syncopation with the base. The red of the terra cotta, the same as that used by Post in his Produce Exchange, was standard for the day, but the crisp quattrocento details were unusual for their authenticity.

Following hard upon the Villard complex came a number of small urban residences that developed some of its features. As the Villard houses were under construction, the firm began work on two houses in Baltimore for Robert and John W. Garrett. The John W. Garrett house is now demolished, but that for Robert Garrett (actually an extensive remodeling and enlargement), incorporates many of the ornamental devices simultaneously used in the Villard complex. Similarly, the Baltimore houses also contained work by allied artists —decorative painting by George Maynard and Francis Lathrop for John, and a frieze mural panel by Thomas W. Dewing for Robert, and finely wrought metal work in the bronze entrance lamps patterned on those of the Palazzo Strozzi by Il Cronaca.[84] A particularly good example of the new type was the townhouse in New York for the brothers Phillips and Lloyd Phoenix, 1882–84 [100].[85] Except for the identical upper bedroom floors for the two bachelors, the plan was typical of townhouses of the period, but the exterior was, by contrast, most unusually severe and restrained. Not only was it classical but it was generically "classic" by virtue of its balance and careful proportions. Moreover, each of its external elements was indicative of some internal function. The main floor, with its dining and reception rooms, was expressed by the simply handled buff sandstone base. A string course set off the upper paired floors for the brothers, in which the brick side walls were clearly the supporting members and the decorated spandrel panel between floors was just as clearly not. The guest rooms above were set apart by the attic "frieze," a fretwork pattern laid up in the brick. Once this basic scheme had been worked out, a number of variations appeared during 1883–86, including houses in New York for Alfred M. Hoyt, Mrs. Edward King, and Gibson Fahnestock [101], the latter even closer to the Phoenix house model. In this variant the base was deeply rusticated and the entrance sheltered by a carved quattrocento hood, but the upper window groups were framed by innovative moldings created by bricks laid to show their corners. This type was then reduced to its simplest in the tenement house for James C. Miller, New York, 1886–87, in which a subtle meander pattern in the upper brick

99. RussWin Hotel, New Britain, Conn., 1883–85.

walls framed the grouped windows and all ornament was derived from patterns laid in the brickwork. All these variants amply demonstrated that within a freely interpreted Renaissance classicism there was a rich potential for coherent urban design.

100. BELOW. Phillips and Lloyd Phoenix house, New York, N. Y., 1882–84.

101. RIGHT. Gibson Fahnestock house, New York, N. Y., 1886–89. *Building,* April 1889.

As the firm began to explore the Italian Renaissance in 1882, McKim became increasingly interested in the native derivative, Georgian Colonial. Freely interpreted Colonial allusions had been present in his own work since 1874, of course, and Adamesque ornament had been used in the Moses Taylor house and the Newport Casino front. In 1882–83 McKim began work on a second house, for the son, Henry A. C. Taylor, this time at Newport, adhering to Colonial models in plan and detail far more closely than ever before, perhaps because of the proximity of eighteenth-century prototypes. Construction was delayed, however, for in 1884 Taylor instructed his architects to translate what had been started as a masonry house to one of wood; as a result the house was not finished until 1886, though it appears to represent a scheme four years old.[86] The house was obviously based on the local Colonial heritage, and the library, in fact, incorporated elements from a room in an eighteenth-century house in the old section of Newport [102, 103]. Even the color scheme, of yellow with white trim, was based on nearby sources, but the scale was greatly enlarged, approaching true English Baroque, especially in the clustered chimney tops. The romantic element was present too, for the roof shingles were laid in undulating patterns to simulate the settled sags of venerable local buildings.

102. Henry Augustus Coit Taylor
house, Newport, R. I., 1882,
1885–86. *American Architect and
Building News*, July 23, 1887.

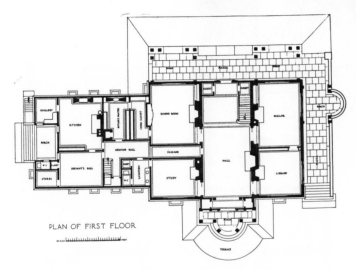

PLAN OF FIRST FLOOR

103. Taylor house, first-floor plan.
Monograph.

At first, most such eighteenth-century allusions were restricted to Massachusetts, and the house which perhaps most clearly illustrates the rationale behind these allusions is that for John F. Andrew in the Back Bay of Boston, 1883–86 [104, 105].[87] In its basic parti and general severity, McKim's design referred to the well-established domestic traditions of Beacon Hill, but the specific details were drawn more closely from Italian sources, so that although individually the cornice, window frames, paired porch columns, or the thin Roman brick have little to do with Beacon Hill, the generic resemblance is strong, especially because of the broad swelling bays. Not so long ago this was viewed as a Colonial "Revival," which is to say something imposed and thereby replacing an architectural expression more indigenous, but in fact, because of the pronounced conservatism in Boston's domestic architecture and the expressed wish of the early 1880s no longer to import the French (that is, mansarded) house, the firm's Andrew house is not so much a *revival* as a *survival* of a valued native architecture; the Andrew house or the even more chaste Alexander Cochrane house on Commonwealth Avenue, 1886–88, could easily fit into the old quarter of Boston.[88]

In September 1883, not long after starting the Andrew house, McKim was introduced to Julia Appleton, of the venerable Beacon Hill family. With her sister, Marian Alice, Julia commissioned McKim to design a country house in Lenox, Massachusetts [106, 107].[89] Since a number of eighteenth-century fragments and antiques were to be incorporated in the house, McKim carefully followed Colonial precedent, particularly in the details, but the random window arrangement and particularly the "broken plan," its axis bent to fit around

104. John F. Andrew house, Boston, Mass., 1883–86.

105. Andrew house, ground-floor and first-floor plans. *Monograph.*

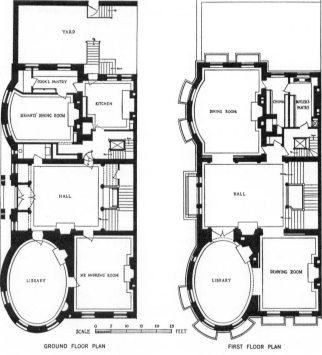

GROUND FLOOR PLAN   FIRST FLOOR PLAN

an ancient elm on the grounds, showed that tradition did not necessarily dictate form. The insouciant plan is in fact close in spirit to those of the shingled houses, and the sensitive response to the uniqueness of a site is a corollary to the bowed front of the Andrew house and its reflection of the special character of Beacon Hill.

106. Julia and Marian Alice Appleton house, The Homestead, Lenox, Mass., 1883–85. G. W. Sheldon, *Artistic Country Seats.*

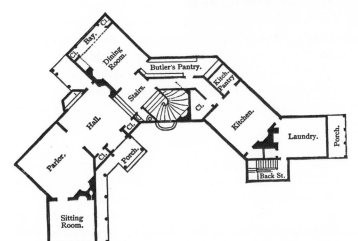

107. Appleton house, plan. G. W. Sheldon, *Artistic Country Seats.*

DURING the second half of the nineteenth century the upper middle class gentleman had the advantages of two homes—his physical domicile and his club. Indeed, as publisher Henry Holt claimed, aside from the home, the club was one of society's most important institutions.[90] As active clubmen, McKim, Mead, and White would have heartily agreed. The firm's clubs, both their earliest and the more widely known clubs of later years, such as the Century, Harvard, or University clubs, were built in the developing residential sections where new townhouses were being built. Typically they were within easy walking distance, so that members might retire there after dinner to enjoy a cigar and some conversation. Accordingly, in their club houses, McKim, Mead, and White introduced a domesticity of scale that soon established a standard. This was not the case, however, with their early YMCA of Newburgh, New York, 1882–84, which was not purely a social club. This was in downtown Newburgh, contiguous with the Turner Building by Babb, Cook & Willard, which was designed in collaboration with it.[91] The firm's Freundschaft Club, New York, 1885–89 [108], to house a German fraternal association established in 1879, was built well to the north of developed Manhattan, in the new residential area rising along Park Avenue north of 42nd Street. The upper windows of this Italianate block were grouped in tall arcades, expressive of the auditorium within. Whereas the Villard houses and their immediate derivatives had been dark in color, and therefore close to the palette of High Victorian Gothic architecture, this club was built of buff Scotch sandstone, with buff speckled Roman brick and matching terra-cotta trim. The firm also built a new classical house in limestone for the Deutscher Verein on 59th Street, facing Central Park, in 1889–91, but although this was one of the oldest and wealthiest organizations in the city, having been founded in 1842, the design was not nearly as ambitious as that of the earlier Freundschaft. Soon after the Freundschaft Club was started, the firm designed the only club of the period to survive, the Algonquin Club, on Commonwealth Avenue, Boston, 1886–89 [109].[92] The firm won this commission over local architects, participating in a closed competition, because of the success with which they adroitly fitted the many requisite activities into an intricate H-shaped plan on a greatly restricted site. Considering the date and what the partners had already done, the exterior was a bit awkward, hard, and angular, and the superimposed porches at the entrance appeared to be even more top-heavy when the original projecting basement had to be pulled back to comply with zoning regulations. The rather harsh and ill-proportioned exterior was a curious contrast with the assured classical work of the preceding years, and even more with the Boston Public Library begun the following year, but the light gray stone anticipated the granite of the library. All the clubs of the period (except the Newburgh YMCA) were built in residential sections, as alternative "homes," and the Algonquin Club retains this domestic character, forming part of the north wall of the Commonwealth Avenue corridor and flanked by ranges of townhouses facing a similar range across the broad boulevard.

BETWEEN 1879 and 1887, McKim, Mead & White completed several churches which constitute the sole and brief medieval interlude in their otherwise classical oeuvre. Some of the historical references were specific, but the First Methodist Church of Baltimore (Lovely Lane United Methodist Church), 1883–87, is intriguing because it was quite intentionally archaic in character, rather more Romanesque than Gothic. In some of its exterior details it was even more nonhistorical than Richardson's Romanesque was becoming, but the interior details, rather curiously, were based on Early Christian sources. This was White's commission, begun in August 1883, but well developed in construction drawings before his departure on his honeymoon. The cornerstone was laid on October 29, 1884, and the building dedicated on November 6, 1887. Specific details are sparse, but the church seems to owe much of its form and detail to its dynamic minister, John F. Goucher, and because of the strong emphasis on choral music and preaching on the part of the congregation, the church focuses in plan on a large oval auditorium, around which are arranged subsidiary classrooms and offices [110, 111].[93] Behind the auditorium is a chapel, while to the right is the parish house. In the sanctuary the decorative motifs, especially the stained glass window designs, are based on mosaic patterns in Saint Piaceta, Rome. Why White should have drawn on Romanesque and Early Christian sources, and why he should have employed such purposively crude rough-faced granite masonry, is unclear, except perhaps because of a

108. Freundschaft Club, New York, N. Y. 1885–89.

109. Algonquin Club, Boston, Mass., 1886–89.

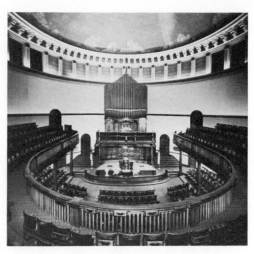

110. LEFT. First Methodist Episcopal Church
(Lovely Lane United Methodist Church), Baltimore,
Md., 1883–87. *American Architect and Building News,*
March 26, 1887.

111. ABOVE. First Methodist Episcopal Church, view
of the sanctuary interior.

112. BELOW. View looking south along St. Paul
Street, Baltimore. *Brickbuilder,* March 1906.

rather curious desire to indicate that this was the "mother church" of Methodism in the New
World.

   If the exterior was intentionally crude, the sanctuary was far more comfortable and
genteel, with a carpeted floor, upholstered seats in place of the more traditional pews, carved
black birch woodwork, and a ring of 340 gas jets at the spring line of the ovoid vault. Forced
ventilation was also incorporated, with foot-operated registers below each seat, with the
incoming air artificially cooled during the summer months, making the church a kind of
testing ground for the mechanical equipment used in the Madison Square Garden, begun
just months before the church was dedicated.

The corner tower, 186 feet high and based closely on that of the eleventh-century abbey church at Pomposa, Italy, was disproportionately tall in relationship to the body of the church, but it was apparently intended to be so [112]. It was conceived as part of a large ensemble of buildings that Goucher and White projected to house a new women's college. Although perhaps as many as a half dozen buildings were designed by White, only two were built using the firm's drawings (the gymnasium and the Latin School); figure 112 shows the entire complex in 1895, including White's gymnasium and Goucher Hall by Charles L. Carson. Apparently there was no thought given to shaping a planned campus quadrangle, but the buildings were united in character by a common rough-faced masonry.[94] Since this institution was specifically developed for women, the question arises why White did not use a more effeminate architectural expression. Perhaps the boldness of the masonry was meant to counter the prevailing popular notions regarding women's education. Goucher College was the first of several such facilities which the partners were to design, and as McKim's later comments regarding his plan for Radcliffe College suggest, women's education, then a very novel idea, was to them a serious matter.

Also during mid-1883 the firm began work on designs for Saint Paul's, Stockbridge, Massachusetts, for which the cornerstone was laid in August and which was dedicated in 1884 [113].[95] McKim's commission, this had come to the firm from Prescott Hall Butler as a memorial to his mother. While the general character of the limestone building is Norman, the entrance porch is patterned specifically on one at Canterbury Cathedral. The plan is untraditional in that it was given only one transept arm, two bays wide, while opposite it is a shallow baptistry, but the scale is intimate and the overall character much like that of English parish churches carried to completion and modified over centuries. It was natural for McKim to observe such sources since he was housing an Episcopalian congregation, but he may have directed special attention to this small chapel not only because it was for his good friend but because it was here, on September 3, 1883, that this once-ardent Quaker was confirmed and became an Episcopalian communicant.[96]

Whereas work on the Stockbridge church was rapid, construction of Saint Peter's,

113. St. Paul's Church, Stockbridge, Mass., 1883–85. *American Architect and Building News*, February 15, 1902.

Morristown, New Jersey, 1886–92, was protracted; it is the only other example of the firm's use of medieval forms during these early years [114].[97] Among the members of the building committee was the Reverend Wynant Vanderpoel, who had no regular parish at the time and was asked to serve on the committee because of his experience in church design and construction. Of the several architects Vanderpoel asked to submit preliminary sketches, only McKim, Mead & White and John H. Sturgis of Boston responded; the commission eventually went to the firm which, together with Vanderpoel, drew up a scheme based on typical English parish churches, particularly Saint Cuthbert's, Wells, a perpendicular Gothic parish church of the fifteenth century, for again the congregation was Episcopalian. Vanderpoel and the firm devised a systematic construction sequence, beginning with the chancel, vestries, and side chapel; when this section was completed, the old church, still standing and in service, on the site of the new nave, would be pulled down and the new nave started, leaving the tower as the final element to be built. However, by the time the chancel and new nave were actually finished in 1892, the congregation had grown to the point where another bay had to be added to the nave, throwing out of proportion the design of the original tower. Consequently, construction of the tower was postponed until 1905–08, during which time McKim prepared designs for a larger tower.

Of greater portent for the future was the collaboration in the remodeling of the chancel of the Church of the Ascension, New York, 1885–88 [115]. The project was initiated by the rector, the Reverend E. Winchester Donald, who had come in 1882 (he later was called to Trinity Church, Boston). He felt strongly that the flat chancel wall of Upjohn's church, ornamented solely by three plain lancet windows, needed further embellishment, and in 1885 the Rhinelander sisters provided a gift of $20,000 for the work.[98] Near the church happened to live John La Farge, who showed Donald a sketch for an *Ascension* in stained glass he had been asked to design some years earlier for another church. Here, Donald was certain, was the desired finishing touch for the chancel, but La Farge deferred, saying that it would be better if Saint-Gaudens were to model the design in low relief. As the scheme became more complicated, it was turned over to White for organization, with the end result that the *Ascension* was to be by La Farge, but now a mural on canvas set in a low relief gilt frame,

114. St. Peter's Church, Morristown, N. J., 1886–90, 1890–92, 1905–08.

filling the upper chancel wall; below it were to be a marble reredos and altar, with low relief angles to the sides by Augustus's brother Louis Saint-Gaudens, and incorporating in the reredos, angels in mosaic and a zone of tightly curled rinceaux also in mosaic, of lavender-colored tesserae inlaid in the amber Siena marble, all executed by D. Maitland Armstrong. La Farge began work in mid-1886, but then developed qualms concerning the hovering

115. Church of the Ascension, New York, N. Y., chancel renovation, 1885–88. Mural, *The Ascension of Our Lord,* by John La Farge; relief angels by Louis Saint-Gaudens; mosaic work by D. Maitland Armstrong; pulpit designed by McKim; the entire work supervised by White.

figures in his large canvas and the character of the background landscape. When his friend Henry Adams proposed a trip to Japan, La Farge readily agreed, certain the renewed contact with the Orient would provide the necessary spiritual and artistic inspiration to finish the mural. So work on the mural stopped from June through early November 1886, but even after painting ended there was a further delay when the chancel wall failed to hold the canvas and new and better anchored plaster had to be prepared. The ensemble, finished during 1887–88, was a success, improved perhaps by La Farge's delay, for his canvas had an ethereal quality given substance in deep saturated color. La Farge had worked before with Richardson in decorating Trinity Church, and with Saint-Gaudens in Saint Thomas's, New York, but the contributions of the artists in finishing the chancel of the Church of the Ascension were more fully integrated. This collaboration then provided the impetus for McKim's even more extensive embellishment of the Boston Public Library.

Since joining forces to design base and figure of the Farragut Memorial in 1877, White and Saint-Gaudens had continued to collaborate.[99] At almost the same time that the *Farragut* was dedicated in 1881, the two began work on the *Standing Lincoln* for Lincoln Park, Chicago, 1881–87 [116].[100] In addition to Saint-Gaudens's fee of $30,000 for an eleven-foot bronze, there was a separate appropriation of $10,000 for a seat by White. As the project grew in scope, as White's schemes invariably did, the seat became a broad setting in the form of a large semicircular bench, in the center of which would stand the bronze figure. In conception, the setting was similar to that of the *Farragut,* except for the greater scale and the fact that the seating nearly encircled the figure, bringing the observer completely behind and around the figure, rather than simply to the side.

More complex was the setting for the Deacon Samuel Chapin Monument which Saint-Gaudens began modeling in 1880.[101] Chester William Chapin, president of the Boston & Albany Railroad and a descendant of the pioneer settler of Springfield, Massachusetts, wished to commemorate his Puritan forebear. After several preliminary experiments, Saint-Gaudens developed a twelve-foot figure, clutching a massive Bible to his chest, grasping a walking stick, and vigorously striding forward, his cape billowing around him. Upon returning from his honeymoon trip late in 1884, White was engaged to design a base, but after visiting the site in Springfield's Stearns Park he expanded the original scheme to include a landscape enclosure, a fountain, and a stone bench [117]. The elder Chapin, meanwhile, had died in 1883, but his son, who carried the project forward, liked White's proposal; the enlarged setting was completed and dedicated on Thanksgiving Day, 1887. To Saint-Gaudens the ensemble was admirable in every respect:

> At the opposite end of the little park from the statue, and balancing it, stood a fountain, and between the two, in the center, a stone bench. Along each side of the open space we planted white birches, and the whole we enclosed by a pine hedge. If this could have remained, and the buildings around the square have been carried out as Mr. Chapin expected, the result would have been unusually effective. At the time we placed it there, however, the quarter of the city was poor, and in a few weeks the boys had destroyed everything in the way of vegetation.[102]

The buildings referred to were part of an urban renewal project of Chapin's and a number of Springfield businessmen, but since nothing further was done the park embellishments eventually were removed to other parts of the city. In its fusing of differing elements, including water and plantings, and its combination of materials as in the malachite-brown of the bronze and the pink granite of the broad base, the Chapin Monument was classic,

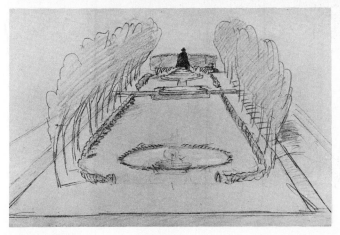

116. ABOVE. Augustus Saint-Gaudens and Stanford White, *Standing Lincoln*, Lincoln Park, Chicago, Ill., 1884–87.

117. LEFT. Augustus Saint-Gaudens and Stanford White, Chester William Chapin Memorial, *The Puritan*, Springfield, Mass., 1884–87, sketch by White showing complete setting. L. G. White, *Sketches and Designs.*

and the bronze elements of the fountain, the frogs and fish, even recalled Renaissance work. But the proportions of the base, nearly thirty percent wider than the ensemble was tall, were original, and even more inventive were the Celtic interlace patterns of the broad cyma recta base. As in the Church of the Ascension chancel, what was most important was the merging of artistic temperaments, so that, although the work of two individuals, the result is the expression of one artistic mind.

ALLUDING to Italian Renaissance sources in the sculptural collaborations with Saint-Gaudens was not difficult, but the partners' decision to incorporate classical principles of design in their commercial buildings of the early 1880s proved to be a far greater challenge. To a large degree this was because commercial blocks in New York, as in Chicago, kept increasing in height and general scale, whereas the palazzi which served as the models had never been more than two or three stories in height. There were a number of projects that never materialized, including unsuccessful competition entries for the Mount Morris Bank and Safe Deposit Company late in 1881, and the Manhattan Company and Merchants Bank in 1883. The firm did build a mill for the Poidebard Silk Company in North Bergen, New Jersey, in 1882. One large project lost must have been a particular disappointment, a hotel in Baltimore, estimated at $200,000, done for H. Guinand in 1886.

118. American Safe Deposit Company and Columbia Bank building, New York. N. Y., 1882–84. *American Architect and Building News,* January 30, 1886.

One of the firm's early important ventures was the American Safe Deposit Company and Columbia Bank, New York, 1882–84 [118].[103] Safe deposit institutions were relatively new, a response of the banking industry projecting an image of greater security; in this instance two small companies joined forces to house themselves and to build rental office space. In the lower half of the rusticated sandstone base was the American Safe Deposit Company, entered by means of stairs down from the long 42nd Street facade; the Columbia Bank was on the upper level of the base, reached by stairs from the short Fifth Avenue side. As in the Phoenix house, designed that same year, the windows of the upper brick section were gathered in framed vertical bays, with terra-cotta spandrel panels between floors—one way of expressing the increasing height of commercial blocks—while the differentiated base and attic-level loggias created a classical tripartite organization in the whole. If this was not an especially well-proportioned whole, it was at least a coherent and creditable early effort in giving order to a tall commercial building, more than comparable to the contemporaneous efforts of Adler & Sullivan or Burnham & Root during 1882 to 1885.

In 1885 the firm began the first of a series of speculative commercial buildings for prominent Manhattan real estate developers Ogden and Robert Goelet, for whom White had already designed the expansive shingled country house, Southside, at Newport, 1882–84. The base of their real estate operations was the diminutive office structure on West 17th Street, done by the firm in 1885–86, a confection of Dutch Renaissance motifs with stepped gables, in brick with light stone trim [119].[104] Shortly after beginning the small office headquarters, the firm commenced work on the larger Goelet Building at 20th Street and Broadway, 1886–87, the first of the speculative buildings [120].[105] Like the American Safe Deposit Company and Columbia Bank, the tripartite Goelet Building consists of a base, midsection, and crown. Along the sides the tall arches of the base rest on rather substantial piers, but at the rounded corner curved arches bear on single polished granite columns, a curiously weak-appearing resolution of the accumulated forces at the corner. As in the bank, here too the upper windows are grouped into vertical bays framed in specially patterned brick and dull-gray glazed terra cotta, with spandrel panels of patterned brick. The uppermost floor (later removed during upward expansion) was treated as an attic with panels between the windows filled with brick fretwork, and the whole capped by a prominent cornice.

Although this newly developed articulation, employing Italianate arcades and details combined with François Ier paneled walls, was at this point unique to McKim, Mead & White, it was their response to the problem of rational expression of the structural bearing wall, engaging so many Eastern architects of the period. George B. Post had initiated this interest with his arcaded Long Island Historical Society, Brooklyn, 1879–79, and his important Produce Exchange, New York, 1881–85, its huge mass organized in great arcades and incorporating an internal metal frame.[106] Contemporary with the paneled American Safe Deposit Company and Columbia Bank was Peabody & Stearns's R. H. White warehouse, Boston, 1882–83, whose midsection gathered in tall three-story arcades had an immediate impact on Burnham & Root's McCormick Building, Chicago, 1884–86, and on Richardson in his celebrated Marshall Field Wholesale Store, Chicago, 1885–87, and his Ames Building on Harrison Avenue, Boston, 1886–87. If the arcaded version of this structural rationalism is better known today, during the late 1880s and 1890s the paneled variant enjoyed even more popularity in Boston, New York, and Philadelphia. In subsequent buildings for the Goelets the firm used the more massive expression, celebrating the heaviness of the outer walls demonstrated by Babb, Cook & Willard in the De Vinne Press building, New York, 1885.[107]

119. Goelet Brothers Offices, New York, N. Y., 1885–86. R. Sturgis, "The Works of McKim, Mead & White," *Architectural Record*, Great American Architects Series, 1895.

120. Goelet Building, New York, N. Y., 1886–87. *Building*, May 26, 1888.

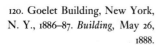

But most significantly, neither McKim nor White felt any compulsion to devote his energies to fully rationalizing the tall commercial building as Sullivan was drawn to do. On the dense mica schist underlying Manhattan it was still highly economical to build heavy bearing-wall blocks of eight to sixteen stories, and there was therefore no internal metal frame to announce in the Goelet Building. Still, the Goelet Building was a departure from the disjointed commercial buildings common in the 1870s and early 1880s, with its clear articulation of functional parts and its special treatment of the wall.

Just as there had been domestic work impossible to classify as Shingle Style nor yet truly classical, so too there were several small public and quasi-public buildings that can only be called "transitional." One was the Lambda Chapter house of Delta Psi at Williams College, Williamstown, Massachusetts, 1884–86, a curious aggregation of elements built in random ashlar masonry.[108] Work on the design began just after White left on his honeymoon trip, and it is possible that its angular junctures might have been softened had he been able to contribute. Too much should not be made of his absence, however, for the Phelps Association building (Wolf's Head Society) at Yale University, New Haven, Connecticut, 1884–85 [121], apparently designed by McKim, is a carefully balanced mass of varied parts, its brownstone masonry closely detailed. In a small public library at Manchester-by-the-Sea, Massachusetts, 1886–87, commissioned by Thomas Jefferson Coolidge (and later given his name), McKim gave a final expression to playful picturesqueness [122]. A loving evocation of Richardson's small-town libraries, this had, to the left, a wing for the reading room; a cavernous central, arched entrance flanked by an assertive cupola-capped tower containing vertical circulation; and, to the right, a memorial room for the Grand Army of the Republic, later converted to library use. Even the flinty brown masonry has a slight Richardsonian batter in the foundation.[109] It would be easy to overlook these "deviations" while trying to concentrate on easily recognizable trends of this period, were it not for the evident care in design, detailing, and construction in these smaller works, in such things as the decorations and window of the Phelps Association by Louis C. Tiffany, the memorial window of the Manchester Library, done jointly by D. Maitland Armstrong and Tiffany, and the oak screen of the library, said to be built of fragments from Morlaix, Brittany, brought back by McKim. Though small, these buildings were not treated as minor commissions.

Even more intriguing, during this period McKim, Mead & White had several commissions for vehicles, including the interiors of Villard's Columbia River steamers mentioned previously. There were also White's interiors of 1885 for *Namouna*, the yacht of James Gordon Bennett, Jr., sumptuously delicate and colorful, fittingly appropriate for flamboyant Bennett. The railroad passenger car project done by White in 1886 begs to be compared to Richardson's cars for the Boston & Albany two years earlier, but unfortunately no drawings survive. This is not as frustrating, perhaps, as the absence of drawings for a commission of 1882 for James P. Leverich, described as "plan for Portable House. $30.00." Whether this was a collapsible house or an early form of mobile home remains a mystery.[110]

These first years of practice for the partners were years of domestication as well; within a year and a half all were married. White, the youngest, was married first in 1884, to Bessie Springs Smith, to whom he had been introduced in 1880 by McKim. Bessie was the youngest

121. Phelps Association (Wolf's Head), Yale University, New Haven, Conn., 1884–85. *Inland Architect*, October 1890.

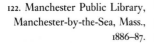
122. Manchester Public Library, Manchester-by-the-Sea, Mass., 1886–87.

of a large family and part of an extended group of Smiths who had settled the central part of Long Island and lived there, in and around Smithtown, since the seventeenth century. The Whites leased a farmhouse on Carmen's Hill in adjacent Saint James, next to Prescott Hall Butler's Bytharbor. Soon White began making the never-ending alterations to the house and gardens of Boxx-Hill, which they eventually purchased in 1892, turning it into a charming and relaxed country house. Here, increasingly, Bessie preferred to stay, near her family, rather than in the townhouse at 121 East 21st Street, Gramercy Square, New York. While White had been courting Bessie Smith, Mead had met a young Hungarian, Olga Kilenyi, in New York; they were married on November 13, 1884, in Budapest. They had no children and lived at 118 East 25th Street, New York. McKim's introduction to Julia Appleton in 1883 resulted initially in the commission for the Lenox country house, but more than discussions of the plans drew them together, and on June 25, 1885, in Lenox, both of the Appleton sisters were married—Marian to George von Lengerke Meyer of Boston and Julia to Charles McKim. Since McKim had been married before, the ceremony was not celebrated in the church but in the summer house designed for the sisters but which now became McKim's home as well. The McKims left immediately for a honeymoon trip through Europe, but what should have been a time of unalloyed joy was saddened by news from Wendell Garrison that the Whites' first child, named Richard Grant White II, had died (a second son, Lawrence, was born in 1887). McKim was soon bereaved himself, for unexpectedly, on January 3, 1887, his beloved Julia died; several years later he had a stained-glass window by La Farge installed in her memory in the south wall of Trinity Church, Boston. McKim's enforced separation from his daughter was now compounded by the loss of what his biographer called "the great romance" of his life. He never removed the gold band, a family heirloom, given him by Julia, and ever after when in deep thought he would slowly, unconsciously turn the ring around his left little finger.[111]

THE earliest work of McKim, Mead & White from 1879 to 1887 was concerned in nearly equal measure with picturesque effect and abstract geometry. These often conflicting interests are not only apparent in their shingled houses but also in their many urban buildings. In the firm's summer houses this quest for clarity of form and order focused on the elemental gable form, culminating in 1886 in the Low house of Bristol, Rhode Island. Parallel to this, and bound up with it, was the quest for an equally appropriate urban idiom, documented by successive experiments with Richardsonian Romanesque, François Ier French Renaissance, and various nonhistoric or identifiable inventions such as the Barney and Drayton houses.

By 1882, as a result of these investigations, the firm came to a rediscovery of the ordered calm and clarity of the Italian Renaissance of the fifteenth century, first and dramatically announced in the Villard house group, as an analogue to America's Colonial classical tradition and as an expression of the new Medicean cosmopolitan culture. For certain uses, and in particularly appropriate places such as Newport or Boston, this Italianate manner was transmuted to its Georgian variant or even to the closely related attenuated Federalist architecture of the early Republic. Further, in adapting this Italianate classicism for vertical commercial blocks, the partners evolved a rational if derivative expression of the bearing wall, each element, whether structurally bearing or not, clearly articulated. Such a traditional but nonhistoricist idiom served the small residence such as the Phoenix house as well as the larger business block such as the Goelet Building. This shift toward classical organization and form, whether specifically historical or more innovative, occurred in all areas of the firm's work, prompted by a growing concern for buildings as part of the larger urban context. Such a concern, however, can only be surmised since the partners wrote so little; there are no day books, diaries, or journals, and McKim's surviving letterbooks date after 1890. Nonetheless, the nascent response to the street, suggested in the Newport Casino front, merged with classical allusions, and continued in the Villard houses and their gesture toward the street—all this was raised to a new level of urban sophistication in the buildings that followed in 1887, most especially the Boston Public Library. The firm's buildings were made to fit well into the urban fabric. They respected and augmented the necessary corridor of the street by means of their horizontal divisions and emphasized bases. They were defined by clearly delineated envelopes that were either closed or open, and inviting to the degree appropriate for their internal functions. While it is true that Chicago architects did much the same while also perfecting a new framing system to lighten their speculative buildings, McKim, Mead & White attempted to develop a canon of design, rooted in ancestral architectural traditions, applicable to all types of urban building. What set the firm apart in 1887 was the way it extrapolated this emerging urban sensitivity to include the city's spaces as well as the building's spaces. The fact that their work was Italianate or Georgian, ultimately, was rather less important than the way it enhanced urban form.

4

RENAISSANCE

1887 — 1892

Nationality is a good thing to a certain
extent, but universality is better.

HENRY WADSWORTH LONGFELLOW
Kavanagh, 1849

The work of McKim, Mead & White during the years 1879 through 1886 gradually moved toward a generic classical formality, particularly in the city, and by degrees in their country houses as well. Classicism, the firm came to believe, was allied with a national building tradition evolved in the eighteenth and early nineteenth centuries, but, even more, it was part of the rich European architectural tradition to which the United States considered itself heir. While continuing in some measure the free expression of interwoven spaces developed in their earlier shingled houses, the partners gradually emphasized more this trans-Atlantic connection, seeking ultimately to reinvigorate the native classicism of the eighteenth century now embellished with the collaborative work of painters and sculptors as the Georgian and Federalist models had never been. They sought a new "Renaissance" or at least a resurgence of the variant of the Renaissance carried across the Atlantic.

In the six years beginning with 1887, McKim, Mead & White received more than 185 commissions, and, though less in number than in the beginning years, the buildings of this second period were larger and more important; contracts for 1879–86 had totaled about $4,550,000, while contracts for 1887–92 totaled $13,407,393.[1] The mounting pressure of work necessitated moving the office, first to a temporary location at 1 West 20th Street [55] in 1891, and then to larger quarters filling almost the entire fifth floor of the Mohawk Building at 120 Fifth Avenue, in the spring of 1894. Not only did this permit expansion of the staff, which grew to nearly 120 by 1892 when the firm was at its busiest, but the enlarged staff in turn created a need for clearer hierarchical organization. The loose camaraderie of the early years necessarily became somewhat more systematic. The partners now spent more time out of the office, and when they were in the office they were more likely to be in their own chambers. Thus, because of the tighter organization, the stylistic maturation of the firm, and the physical absence of the partners from the drafting room, the fusion of personal styles which had marked the first period changed toward more individualized expressions characteristic of the partners. Whereas White had protested vigorously in 1886 that "no member of our firm is ever individually responsible for any design which goes out from it," by 1893 this was no longer literally true. Later, in 1920, before Mead had entirely withdrawn from office affairs, William Mitchell Kendall (who joined the office in 1882) drew up a list of the founders' principal work, noting the names of the partners in charge; attached to this attribution list, concerned largely with buildings done after the first move in 1891, is a note that all members of the firm had checked it. Moreover, when the partners were traveling or were in Europe, the work remaining on their jobs in hand had to be carefully anticipated. For two such absences by White in 1892 and 1894, checklists prepared for his many assistants survive in the firm's archive, specifying exactly what was to be done and which of the younger men was temporarily in charge.[2]

THESE changes, both in personal style and in the firm's decisive adoption of Renaissance classicism, were dramatically announced in four large buildings all begun in 1887, each supervised by one of the partners—McKim's Boston Public Library, White's Madison Square Garden, and Mead's twin office blocks for the New York Life Insurance Company in Kansas City and Omaha.

Of the three, the most important as a symbol of the resurgence of American classicism was the Boston Public Library. It was also, coincidentally, the first designed. The construction of the Boston Public Library was the keystone of an integrated system of educational and cultural institutions which genteel Bostonians viewed as making their city a center of European culture. The building of the library reflected at the same time a municipal "populist" movement which had been gathering force for a period of ten years, whose aim was to provide the best reading material for the greatest number.[3] This spirit of public and private munificence is part of the background of the library, started in 1852 when Joshua Bates, a native of Weymouth, Massachusetts, who had built a fortune in London, offered to buy books for a public library for Boston provided the city would erect a building and maintain it. Three years later a building was put up on Boylston Street, and similarly public-spirited citizens donated specialized collections, so that by 1878 the library was filled to capacity, mandating larger quarters. The trustees of the library were urged to petition the state legislature for a lot in the newly reclaimed lands in the Back Bay, a request granted in April 1880. The trustees received the end of the block west of Copley Square, facing Richardson's Trinity Church, on the condition that construction begin within three years.

During 1880 and the early part of 1881 the trustees developed a program for the proposed building, and in their report of June 1881 they took a pragmatic position: "No elegant edifice is to be designed in which books are to be deposited in conformity to the architectural or ornamental structure of the building, but it should be erected over the books, the arrangement and classification of which for the convenience of use must determine the form and details of its great hall."[4] At first the trustees hoped to convert the existing English High and Latin School for use as a library, but they were advised by both George A. Clough, then the city architect, and by architect Henry Van Brunt that such a conversion was not practicable. Subsequently, Clough and Van Brunt individually submitted sketch plans for a library on the Copley Square site.[5] Both proposals were simple and severe, so much so that Clough estimated that his scheme could be built for as little as $450,000.

To enlarge the building site, the trustees purchased the adjoining lot to the south in 1883, making the building area nearly square, fronting on Dartmouth Street and running from Saint James (now Blagden) to Boylston Street. In view of this larger site, and because Clough's and Van Brunt's designs had proved unsatisfactory, the state legislature extended the construction deadline by three years. Taking advantage of the reprieve, in January 1884 the trustees announced an open competition for a three-story brick building with brown-stone trim. By August twenty entries had been received, and although prizes were awarded none of the designs was judged suitable for construction.[6] McKim, Mead & White apparently decided against competing, establishing an office rule against competitions they seldom waived. The outcome might well have been anticipated, for in the 1880s construction contracts seldom resulted from competitions, and when they did the completed building often bore slight resemblance to the architect's winning design. Since the second deadline was now fast approaching, the new city architect, Arthur H. Vinal, was instructed to prepare plans which could be carried out for the predetermined sum of $450,000. Vinal's incomplete drawings satisfied no one, and his design was later described by Ralph Adams Cram as "an example of what Richardson's own style could become at the hands of a sincere but incompetent disciple—it was a chaos of gables, oriels, arcades and towers, all worked out in brownstone."[7] Nonetheless, construction had to begin not later than April 21, and at 4:18 P.M. that very day the first piles were driven into the gravel fill of the Back Bay for the foundations of Vinal's building.

In December, after numerous piles had been placed at a cost of $73,600, Professor T. M. Clarke of the Massachusetts Institute of Technology discovered that errors in Vinal's engineering computations made further construction indefensible. This, coupled with the growing dissatisfaction with Vinal's design, led to a cessation of work, and the foundations were covered over for the winter while the situation was reassessed. Since the trustees had been incorporated by the state, the legislature intervened, and on March 10, 1887, they amended the act of incorporation, giving the trustees of the Boston Public Library full control over the design, construction, erection, and maintenance of the central library building. The trustees also were empowered to select and employ architects of their own choice on the condition that no work be initiated until complete plans and specifications had been approved, to prevent any more false starts.

Meanwhile there had also been shifting within the board of trustees, the central figure and president now being Samuel A. B. Abbott, who was acquainted with the work of the firm, admiring particularly the Villard houses. He was, moreover, a cousin of McKim's second wife, Julia, who had died shortly before, in January. Hurriedly Abbott set off for New York to confer with McKim; their first discussions, on Saturday, March 19, 1887, were so successful that McKim spoke with several other members of the board on Monday, while in the meantime he discussed the impending commission with White and Saint-Gaudens on Sunday. On March 26 the trustees voted to engage McKim, Mead & White with a proviso that they operate a branch office in Boston until construction was completed, for they correctly anticipated a storm of protest over hiring "foreigners" from New York in preference to established Boston architects. On March 30 McKim signed the contract and, soon after, turned the better part of the Appleton townhouse on Beacon Street into a temporary office.[8]

This history explains the sense of purpose McKim and the trustees felt, for nearly a decade had passed and over $83,000 wasted. Nonetheless, both McKim and the trustees clearly understood that nothing would be gained by acting in haste. The problem set before

McKim was to design a large public circulating library on a major urban square, to contain a large reading room and stack storage for at least 700,000 volumes, attendant service facilities, and a number of special collections. Although the library was to be a public collection for home borrowing, it was to be at the same time one of the major reference collections in the United States. None of the large metropolitan libraries in the United States, nor the famous national collections in Europe, were lending institutions, and though some of these provided formal inspiration, nowhere was there a library whose collection and function were similar to those of the Boston Public Library. Neither McKim nor the trustees knew precisely where to begin, a problem which was compounded because the trustees did not as yet have a firm idea of what they wanted nor did they always heed the advice of their librarian.[9] This lack of a clearly formulated program was to cause numerous problems later, when new rooms and functions were forced into a shell which by then was well along.

In addition to the functional problems, the proposed site offered a great challenge. The broad expanse of Copley Square was enclosed by the widest variety of buildings, among which the library had to be judiciously fitted [123]. The major building on the square was Richardson's Trinity Church to the east, whose pyramidal, craggy bulk and massive central tower dominated the square. To the north was a block of unobtrusive brick and brownstone houses, punctuated by the low facade of the Gothic Second Church. On the northwest corner, at Boylston Street, was the vigorously High Victorian Gothic, new Old South

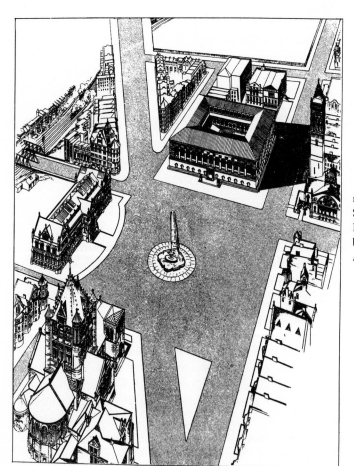

123. Aerial perspective of Copley Square showing relationship of Boston Public Library to existing buildings. *American Architect and Building News*, June 9, 1888.

Church by Cummings & Sears, its bristling tower a strong vertical element that had to be recognized. To the south stood the Museum of Fine Arts by Sturgis & Brigham, a Ruskinian Gothic block of red brick and buff-yellow terra cotta. And at the southwest corner was the S. S. Pierce store, a parody of Richardson's Romanesque. As Walter Muir Whitehill noted, it was no easy matter to create a building that would have architectural integrity and not swear at its neighbors, that would be the first American "ideal library," built within the confines of another architect's foundations.[10]

As the site was challenging, so the aspirations of McKim and the trustees were equally high. The general desired character was sketched out for McKim in the spring of 1887 and summarized by the trustees in their report for 1888. As before, they "insisted that convenience and usefulness should not be sacrificed for show, and that internal arrangements of the building should be considered first," but they also insisted that the building was to be a *"palace for the people"* and as such should be a monumental building, worthy of the City of Boston.[11] Reportedly McKim first considered the Louvre pavilions, the Farnese Palace, and Duban's École des Beaux-Arts facade as formal models, devoting several months to this, but eventually settling upon Labrouste's Bibliothèque Sainte-Geneviève, Paris, which he considered "the best type and the best scheme in its outward expression and also its arrangement."[12]

Using the Bibliothèque Sainte-Geneviève as a starting point was quite natural, for not only was it generally regarded by architects as an exemplary modern library, it had been the paradigm of libraries for several generations of École students. Many of the formal requirements of the Boston Library were similar to those faced by Labrouste. McKim's building, too, was to form a defining wall for a major urban space; he, too, had a large reading room which was to be at the upper level and needed to be expressed externally. By using a continuous arcade a horizontal emphasis could thus be given to the facade, complementing the verticality of the Old South Church tower and Trinity Church. Indeed the neighboring buildings continually appeared in the firm's early studies and perspectives [125]. Despite the differences in historic references, McKim's austere arcaded facade was a logical extrapolation of what Richardson had been doing in his last buildings, in its monochromatic material, its suppression of detail, and continuous arcade.[13] McKim's dual concern that the library complement the buildings around the square and still be unobtrusively dominant is evident in an interview given to the Boston *Herald* early in 1888, in which McKim observed that "the restful character of its lines will act as a counter and a balance to the already abundant variety of form in the square."[14] He wanted the library to appear solid and durable without being somber or heavy, and to achieve this he contrasted the solid base against "free, open lines at the top of the building."

By the end of the summer the basic design had taken form, and on September 28, 1887, McKim wrote that he was having a perspective prepared to present to the trustees. The initial design, approved on November 3, determined the essential outlines of the building, but a number of details subsequently were restudied [124]. The emphatic separation into two major stories—a severe rusticated base and the continuous upper arcade—appeared in the first rendering, but the eleven openings of the arcade were framed by engaged Tuscan columns carrying relatively light architraves; the entrance was a single square-headed door, similar to that of the Cancelleria in Rome. Compared to the florid expressions typical of public buildings during the preceding fifteen years, the library design was plainly simple; too much so for some. The Boston *Globe* was greatly disturbed "by the resemblance it bears

124. Boston Public Library,
Boston, Mass., initial design, 1888.

125. Boston Public Library,
perspective across Copley Square.
*American Architect and Building
News*, May 26, 1888.

126. Drawing room of the
Appleton-McKim house, Boston,
c. 1888, converted to a temporary
branch office. On the wall to the
left is the rendering of the initial
design [124]; below it is the
perspective of Copley Square [125].
Photo: L. M. Roth; MM&W
Archive, NYHS.

to . . . the city morgue, where all the unknown and unclaimed dead of Boston are placed, prior to final interment. Let the trustees look at it well and then decide if they want a morgue in the Back Bay."[15]

The trustees were little affected by such clamor, though James F. Clark was bothered by the single door. He felt the entrance was rather uninviting, that it appeared more a door for keeping people out than inviting them in, and when the drawings were presented to the trustees he suggested that the entrance be embellished with sculpture—figures symbolic of literature, the arts, and sciences. To McKim, Clark's comments seemed "forcible and just," and his proposal for sculpture "an inspiration."[16] The entrance was carefully restudied and given the form of a triumphal arch, fronted by sculpture on pedestals.

Other refinements were required, but McKim increasingly felt unable to pull the design together; if he went to Paris, he wrote Mead, the atmosphere might result in an improved design. His partners, however, were strongly opposed, and Mead was certain, as he wrote back to McKim, that postponing work would prove disastrous:

> . . . if you leave it, and get under the influence of Doumet [*sic,* Daumet] or anybody, you will simply come back and knock into fits the accepted design and all the work done in your absence.
>
> I know you pretty well and I say this because I do. If the Library is to be built or started under this committee you may be sure it had better be started in early spring. Once started it cannot be stopped. It will require all your efforts to get everything ready for a start.
>
> It is now nearly the first of January. The three months you would be away would bring you to the first of April, the time you ought to have your contracts signed. I say most firmly —complete your drawings, get your contracts signed and then if it is necessary to go abroad to refine the design in its details, go.
>
> I tell you, with your temperament, you are in great danger of getting in doubt about the design and suggesting all manner of changes, even thinking you have an altogether better scheme, if you leave it for a moment. You stand in a good position now, and we are all ready to back you, but nobody but yourself can take care of the Library for the next three months.
>
> I do not say anything about the financial condition of the office, and the necessity of pushing all work we have on that account. I say all I have said because I want the library to be a success, and I know that it cannot be left in other hands without great danger.[17]

Such was Mead's function in the office. Partly as a result of this firmness and, no doubt, because he knew all his partner said to be true, McKim remained in Boston at the Beacon Street office [126]. There he struggled with perfecting the design during the winter of 1887–88. His assistant, William T. Partridge, remembered how one evening they returned from dinner to confront the library drawings once more, passing in the lower hall a large transparency of the Colosseum in Rome. Absently McKim turned on the light behind it and sat gazing at it, when suddenly "he jumped up and said, 'Partridge, look how much better the right hand part looks with its severe piers, than the left-hand with the Greek orders plastered on; how much more dignified. That's the trouble with our library, we've got too much on it.'" Far into the night they erased the engaged Tuscan columns.[18] The end result not only approached the severity of the Colosseum piers shorn of their orders but even more the massive sculptural quality of Alberti's Roman exterior for San Francesco in Rimini. The final design, then, was not only "thrice blessed" but had the benefit of four venerable authorities—Richardson, Labrouste, Alberti, and the Roman Colosseum.[19] The inertia thus overcome, the remaining adjustments in the design followed quickly. Final presentation

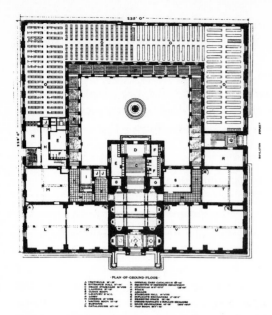

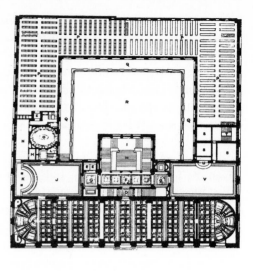

·PLAN·OF·GROUND·FLOOR·

127. Boston Public Library, plans of ground floor and first floor, 1888. *American Architect and Building News*, May 26, 1888.

128. Boston Public Library, plaster model of final design as presented to the public, 1888.

drawings were prepared and approved by the trustees on March 30, 1888, exactly one year after the signing of the contract [125, 127]. During the next month the drawings and a ten-foot-square plaster model [128] were displayed in the Old State House, eliciting favorable public comment; many Bostonians were simply relieved that experimentation and indecision had finally come to an end.[20]

Although the city long before had appropriated $450,000 for city architect Clough's proposed building, after awarding competition prizes, paying for Vinal's foundations, and meeting other obligations, $358,000 remained. Clearly, McKim's new design could not be carried out for that sum, so, following the trustees' approval of the scheme, McKim and his staff worked rapidly to prepare a realistic estimate. On April 23 they submitted an estimate of $1,165,955 for everything except the ornamental sculpture in front of the building, an average of $0.4085 per cubic foot. McKim also appended a table showing the relative costs of other public buildings of the period, which ranged from a low of $0.433 per cubic foot for the Albany Post Office to a high of $1.00 per cubic foot for the Connecticut State Capitol at Hartford. Though the Boston Public Library would cost less per cubic foot than any of the buildings listed, there was an overrun of $800,000 beyond the funds already appropriated. Not surprisingly, there were vigorous objections to this increase in cost, but the trustees gave McKim solid support. The trustees, city officials, and most of Boston's influential citizens wished to memorialize the city's civic consciousness, its pride in her past, and confidence in her future; all of this McKim's magisterial building promised to do. On May 7, 1888, the city council authorized the additional expenditure, proposals for bids were advertised in July, and on the 23rd that of Woodbury & Leighton of Boston was accepted. Construction of the foundations and lower walls started almost immediately, allowing the cornerstone to be laid on November 28.

However, as construction of the lower level progressed upward from street level, the tone of public approval changed, for many Bostonians were rather unprepared for the unrelieved starkness of the walls and the blunt square windows at full scale. Although it had looked satisfactory in the plaster model, now it appeared as plain and as bald as the morgue, as the correspondent of the *Globe* had warned. This aggravated the long-standing irritation with the trustees for having selected out-of-town architects. Then, as construction of the arcade progressed, showing the embellishment of the upper level, and after full-scale mock-ups of the cornice were raised to allow detailed study of the final appearance, public approval once more began to return. As the more delicate upper stages appeared, it was apparent that the library had precisely the "stately aspect" that Bostonians were beginning to prefer in their urban architecture.[21]

As for the high estimated cost, this continued to cause problems. At first, when the bids came in, it appeared that the firm's estimates had been rather liberal and that the building could be finished for less. But building costs began to rise, and simultaneously the trustees made substantial changes in the architectural program; both required adjustments to the working drawings. Whereas the original specifications had called for Milford granite for the walls of the internal court, identical to that of the exterior, this was changed in 1889 to buff Roman brick with granite trim, and the overall height of the building was lowered nine feet. Alterations were made in the arrangement of the special library floor, reading room, vestibule, roof, and interior finishing. Even so, in spite of these measures, the total cost of the building rose steadily; by 1892 contracts had increased to $1,908,519.

It was not simply the quality of materials and exacting workmanship which were driving up the cost. The aspirations of McKim and the trustees were rising also, and the trustees felt that the library should be embellished with the finest works of art, commissioned especially for the building. In the initial flush of excitement Saint-Gaudens had been approached about several figures at the entrance, but then the mayor rescinded the appropriation. Undaunted, Saint-Gaudens continued work on three relief panels proposed over the entrance arches, but it was not until 1892 that funds for them were restored to the budget and a contract signed. While these were finished and installed, Saint-Gaudens also worked on two freestanding groups for pedestals on the front terrace. Progress on these was excruciatingly slow, and work was continuing in 1899–1900 when the sculptor learned he had an intestinal tumor. Saint-Gaudens then closed his Paris studio, packed all the models, and returned to New York and his studio in Cornish, New Hampshire, but when the crates were opened it was discovered that the maquettes for the library terrace groups had been so poorly packed that the plaster was in hundreds of pieces. The ailing sculptor was never able to summon the energy to rebuild them, so the library groups, perhaps the most important he ever attempted, remained unfinished. There was, in any case, some concern in Boston as to the paucity of their clothing for so public a setting. The pedestals, intended for Saint-Gaudens's bronzes, remained empty for several years; later, reclining figures of Art and Science by Bela Pratt were installed, in 1912.[22]

Many of the other projected embellishments were completed as planned, though not all. In the grand stair hall were placed recumbent lions carved by Louis Saint-Gaudens, commemorating Civil War regiments from Massachusetts. Few of the artists earned much from their commissions, nor intended to, because of the time and care they expended on their work for the library. For instance, early in 1890 both Edwin Austin Abbey and John Singer Sargent promised McKim and the trustees murals for the library, but official contracts were not prepared until 1893. Abbey's *Quest of the Holy Grail,* for the delivery room, was not finished until 1902, and the last panels of Sargent's mural cycle were not installed until 1916. For the upper walls of the grand staircase McKim wanted panels by Pierre Puvis de Chavannes, and as early as the summer of 1891 approached the French painter. Because of advanced age, Puvis de Chavannes demurred, but McKim urged repeatedly, sending to Paris a model of the stair hall, in April 1892, via John Galen Howard, who was then at the École. Finally a contract was signed in July 1893, and Puvis de Chavannes's murals, *Les muses inspiratrices acclament le génie, messager de lumière,* were installed in 1896, well before Abbey's or Sargent's. James A. McNeill Whistler and John La Farge also were asked to do murals, in 1894, though these never materialized. For the entrance vestibule Daniel Chester French was engaged in 1894 to model low-relief bronze doors, which were installed in 1904; these strikingly simple and unornamented panels suggest parallels to European Symbolist art.[23] Such enrichments, plus the increasing expense of materials, caused the final cost of the library to reach approximately $2,203,178 in 1898 when the last bill was submitted to the trustees.[24] Significantly, the trustees' and the city's vision of the library continued to expand as the fabric of the building rose.

Within five years from the start of the Boston Public Library the notion of painters, sculptors, and architects working so closely and unselfishly together was commonplace for public buildings. But prior to this, aside from La Farge's hurried decorations in Richardson's Trinity Church in 1877–78, such collaboration had been almost unknown in American architecture. To McKim, with his École training, such close association not only was natural but brought out the best of each artist. That so many artists were called upon to embellish the library was due first to McKim's initial image of what the building should be, and second, to the trustees' unending support in search of funds to see that the embellishments were realized. Scions of merchants and Boston Brahmins, the trustees saw themselves as latter-day Medicis, and in providing the opportunity for architecture and its allied arts to flourish together once again they truly believed that a new Renaissance had been started.

When the foundations and basement walls had been completed in 1889, the firm turned to a new structural system for the floors of the library, using vaults of flat tiles in an extremely tenacious mortar developed in Catalonia by Raphael Guastavino.[25] This technique, well known in Catalonia but only just brought to the United States, was promising but untried for a large building. Essentially, the structural basis of these vaults is the same as that of modern thin concrete shells—it is the curvature of the thin membrane, not mass, that provides strength. Thin tile arches running from pier to pier carry even thinner tile vaults [129]. The gently rounded surfaces are covered with lightweight concrete and finished to provide flat floor surfaces. When cured, this construction is in every way as solid and as monolithic as modern poured concrete, and like it, too, is nearly untouched by fire. Exploiting the versatility of this new technique, Guastavino contrived different vault forms for each of the major rooms. Although the Guastavino system was "new" it produced a "traditional" solid floor that required bookcases in the "stack" storage area, whereas the newest innovation in libraries in the 1880s were self-supporting cast-iron metal stacks (as

129. Boston Public Library, construction of Guastavino vaults for ground floor, c. 1889.

were then being introduced at Harvard) that provided much greater density in book storage. Unfortunately the metal stack system allowed for only one use for an area, whereas McKim knew that any area of his building was likely to be converted to a different use; even as construction progressed, the functional operations in different parts of the building were radically changed. For maximum building flexibility he chose the strongest multifunctional and fireproof floor system available; and, as it has turned out, his choice was the wisest in the long run, for operations in the library have continued to change over the past three quarters of a century, and the vaulted floors have proved more than strong enough for each successive adaptation. The most strictly "utilitarian" solution of the day would have long since proved least practical.

During the winter of 1894 the first books were transferred from the old building, and on March 11, 1895, the Boston Public Library opened to accolades from Boston's citizens and the architectural fraternity. The exterior of pink Milford granite had been modified in a number of subtle ways from the published design of 1888 (compare figures 125, 130).[26] The generic resemblance to Labrouste's Bibliothèque Sainte-Geneviève was apparent to critics, but there were significant differences.[27] McKim chose to emphasize the lower story by changing the proportions, eliminating the garlands, using a stronger molding below the windows, rusticating the wall, and using rectangular windows, creating a less fluid rhythm.[28] Where Labrouste had a single door McKim had opened a recessed vestibule behind three arches. Since in both libraries the books in the reading room were arranged along the walls, both arcades were closed at the bottom by panels, but those of the Boston Library are shorter since the books are only on one level. In both, the panels are inscribed with the names of luminaries in the arts, literature, and science. Generally McKim sought to create a texture more richly scenographic than directly functionally expressive; even the windows, screened by Roman lattices, continue the plane of the wall up to the tiled roof, whereas Labrouste's windows read externally as dark voids.

Labrouste's library, pressed tight against older buildings to the rear, similarly serves to define a major urban space, the Place du Panthéon, but his building is not deep. McKim's, in contrast, is nearly square, 225 feet across and 229 feet deep, its center hollowed out to form a large court [131]. The presence of the court made difficult any purely functional plan arrangement and precluded the kind of orderly procession of hierarchical spaces as taught

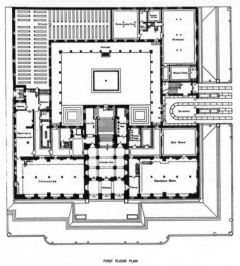

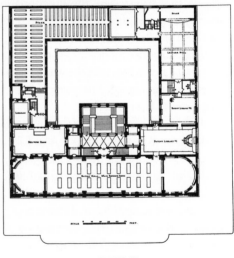

FIRST FLOOR PLAN　　　　　　　　　　　　　SECOND FLOOR PLAN

130. Boston Public Library, 1887–95.
131. Boston Public Library, ground (first) floor and first (second) floor
plans, as built. *Monograph.*

at the École. The approach is clear enough, across a raised terrace to the three deep arches
hooded by immense wrought-iron lamp clusters, through a vestibule graced by French's
bronze doors, into a low dark vaulted inner vestibule. Here, however, one faced a conflict
of paths, for one could take the perpendicular axis and move sideways to specialized reading
rooms and, eventually, by sideways movements, into the court, which comes as something
of a surprise. One is drawn more strongly by the flood of light, however, to the central arch
and up the grand staircase through whose windows one has a glimpse of the upper walls
of the court. At the top of the staircase one faces a wall, so that again lateral movement is

132. Boston Public Library, view of court. *Monograph.*

required to reach the delivery room and, eventually, the reading room. As was standard for the nineteenth century, the library used a closed-stack system, so that users would consult the card catalog, place an order for a title, and take a seat in the delivery room waiting for the book to be sent from the stacks. The richly appointed room, encircled overhead with the deeply colored Abbey mural, with its paneled ceiling, marble fireplace, and paneled walls, served as a club room for all of Boston. Once the book arrived one could take it for home reading or retire to the barrel-vaulted reading room. Readers might also snuggle up on the built-in seats at the landing of the great stair, next to the windows overlooking the court, if they did not go into the court to find a quiet seat.

Though it presented considerable functional problems, the court proved to be one of the most appreciated public spaces in the city [132]. On three sides it is framed by an arcade which, according to the original drawings, was to be carried on square piers—later changed to Tuscan columns much like those of the Cancelleria court. In fact the court serves a very functional purpose by screening out the noise of the city and creating a quiet, sunlit well; here readers may relax and find a peaceful cloistered retreat and listen to the gentle splash of the fountain. Here, Henry James felt, a wealth of science and taste had created the feeling of "one of the myriad gold-colored courts of the Vatican."[29]

Another of the elements of the library most enjoyed is the grand staircase, seen best in the afternoon when the light slants through its arcaded windows and strikes the amber-hued marble walls [133]. The extreme care taken in the selection of materials for the stair hall exemplifies the pains taken in the construction of the entire building. The floor and stairs are of French *echallion,* an ivory-gray "marble" filled with fossil shells, inlaid at the landing with geometric patterns of red Numidian marble. The walls, pilasters, and arcades are of a golden Siena marble veined with black. Frederick P. Hill, McKim's assistant, was assigned the responsibility of supervising its painstaking assembly:

> . . . richer and darker tones [were used] for the lower part of the staircase and gradually shading off to lighter ones as it was carried up to and around where the Puvis de Chavannes paintings were to be. The marble for the lower part was to be the Monte Riete, or Convent Siena, a very beautiful and rather rare marble that came only from a quarry owned by some Monks who would not allow any contractor to work the quarry nor any modern machinery to be intro-

133. Boston Public Library, view of the stair hall, c. 1894, before installation of the Puvis de Chavannes murals.

134. OPPOSITE. Boston Public Library, Bates Hall (reading room).

duced. As a result of this policy the supply was limited, for the Monks only got out a block now and then, when in need of funds. They used primitive methods in prying it out, then rolling it down the hill and selling it to some dealer.

This meant finding and getting hold of all such marble as had been brought into the United States, was being brought in, or was likely to be brought in during the progress of the work. It was not only a question of getting that particular marble, but of matching the coloring and markings and also grading it so that it would lead up gradually to the lighter toned Sienas of the upper parts of the gallery. [The marbles were exactly matched, in paired panels, on the left and the right side of the stair hall.]

Visits had to be made to the different marble yards where there happened to be blocks of it and also to Corlears Hook [in New York City] where blocks of marble were landed in those days. The blocks were brought over from Italy by ships which used them for ballast and landed them at the Hook, then the marble was sawed into slabs, inspected, accepted or rejected.

This procedure was followed until the work was finally completed. It was found, on checking records, that in order to produce the desired results, four hundred tons of slabs had been handled in the manner described above, accepted or rejected, mostly the latter, and that sixteen months had elapsed since the work was started.[30]

Royal Cortissoz was referring to this care in the selection and precise placement of the marble when he wrote that McKim was dealing in marble "as an artist deals in paint and he would no more submit to a change in the appearance of the surfaces he had planned than a painter would allow his color-man to dictate the final condition of a picture."[31]

Having ascended the stairs, ordered and received a book, one turned to the large reading room, Bates Hall, a long barrel-vaulted room divided into five bays by major transverse ribs [134]. In the vaulted ceiling is the greatest contrast to the Bibliothèque Sainte-Geneviève, for where Labrouste desired to exploit expressively his cast-iron structure McKim used plaster. Labrouste designed the roof support system of the reading room first, so to speak, and let that determine the building, whereas McKim seems to have decided first

on the spatial volumes.[32] The room ends in apses covered by half domes. In the north apse the large rectangular panel was to have been painted by Whistler, and along the west wall were round-headed panels where it was hoped murals would be painted by George DeForrest Bruch, Frank D. Millet, and Abbott Thayer, projects that were never realized.

Behind the delivery room and its adjacent offices extended the stack area, reduced to half its original size by the inclusion of new functions before the building was finished (compare Figs. 127 and 131). The original plans provided for a capacity of two million volumes, equal to the Congressional Library and twice that of the Bibliothèque Nationale and the British Museum; however, with the insertion of a porte-cochère on Boylston Street, a bindery, newspaper files, an enlarged patent library, and an auditorium, the stack area was cut in half. Since the books extended awkwardly around the rear of the building, a pneumatic tube system was devised to deliver requests to stack attendents and a miniature cable railway created to bring the books to the delivery room.

On the third floor, originally devoted to special collections and study rooms, the large central corridor has murals by Sargent showing the history of religion. Sargent became absorbed in this, the largest single commission he had been given, and he worked on the canvases from 1890 up to 1919 but was unable to complete the last portion. It was his best mural work, deeply colored and shrouded in an aura of mystery, intensified by the dim lighting Sargent specified.[33]

With the Boston Public Library, the firm adopted Italian Renaissance classicism as its preferred mode of design. Though various historic sources had provided inspiration, the library was a well-integrated ensemble. The building was also sensitive to its site, its even rhythms and horizontal stretch embracing and making comprehensible the vast space of Copley Square. In doing so it affirmed a new professional and municipal desire to shape and improve the urban environment. Admittedly there were functional utilitarian problems resulting from the desire for a grand building, exacerbated by the trustees' indecision and their indisposition to consult their librarian. Nonetheless the Boston Public Library immediately established a standard of excellence and restrained elegance in public buildings, contributing to a climate that soon gave rise to the New York and Chicago public libraries and scores of others. Its plan became the model for many which followed, whether municipal or collegiate, though almost always minus the central court. The Boston Public Library offered civic excess and public splendor to all; the marble staircase was an invitation to grand ascent, as though the quest of knowledge would elevate the mind. One critic wrote in 1892 that the building should have been made severe and devoid of ornament since it was to be used by plain people, "mechanics, laborers and their families"; on the contrary, perhaps it is properly resplendent for this very reason.[34] The library suggests that beyond utilitarian functionalism there are civic and aesthetic requirements which the architect may appropriately satisfy in the broadest, most generous way.

ITS severe classicism and remarkable restraint during a period otherwise noted for exuberance quickly set the Boston Public Library apart, but it was remarkable too for the unprecedented contributions of so many artists. Almost overnight artistic collaboration became the hallmark of good public architecture. But if this was announced on a grand scale in the Boston Public Library, it was also evident at the same time in the intensely personal expression of the secluded Adams Memorial in Rock Creek Cemetery, Washington, D.C., 1886–91.[35] This was truly a collaborative work, conceived in its broad outlines by a historian and painter, translated into three-dimensional form by a sculptor, and given its setting by an architect. Ostensibly created in memory of Henry Adams's wife, Marian Hooper Adams, it soon transcended that limited meaning to become one of the most potent images in American art. Its meaning lies in an understanding of the character of Marian, for so unlike her reflective and analytical husband, she was intuitive and sought in art "the victory of spirit over matter, and the peace of infinite love."[36] Marian became a skilled amateur photographer and was much involved in directing the design of their new house in Washington, D.C., by Richardson, but she never lived in it, for on December 6, 1885, in despair over the death of her beloved father, she drank potassium cyanide from among her darkroom chemicals. It was a blow which Adams said cleaved his life in two parts, opening a wound which never healed. For years afterward he never spoke of his wife, suffering deep depression as the anniversaries of her death came and passed, but gradually during 1886 the idea of a memorial took shape in his mind. It was definitely not to be the usual Western or European funereal monument, neither a portrait nor sentimentalized grief. Simultaneously his friend La Farge was reaching an impasse in laying out the miraculously hovering figures in his Ascension mural, and in June 1886, Adams suggested they leave for Japan, for "a bath for the brain in some water absolutely alien." They told an inquiring journalist while crossing the continent for San Francisco that they were "in search for Nirvana," to which came the naïve but perhaps accurate rejoinder that it was out of season. Before leaving New York Adams may have breathed some word of the proposed memorial to Saint-Gaudens whom he saw, but while in Japan at Nikko he discussed with La Farge the nature of monuments, the problem of art and nature so apparently resolved in the landscapes around him, the meaning of the great bronze Buddha at Kamakura, and of the Kwannon image of compassion. La Farge wondered if any American artist could create a true monument, "pure, by itself," for American artists were held hostage by a society devoted to "usefulness, and getting on." What was needed, La Farge said, was an antidote for what "Stanford White once called our 'native Hottentot style.' "[37] Adams came to realize the memorial he wanted would embody what he saw in Japanese Buddhist art, the beauty of Nirvana, "self absorption into the universal and the infinite, in anonymity, in the extinction of the restlessness of the will."[38]

By mid-November 1886, Adams and La Farge had returned and the first sessions began, with Saint-Gaudens, in search of a suitable figural but nonrepresentative image. Meetings continued through April 1888, when the concept of a seated figure was agreed upon, and toward autumn separate contracts with Saint-Gaudens and White for figure and base were signed. But as the figure and its setting became more precisely defined, Adams began to experience trouble with the artists, and after a brief session in the sculptor's studio in New York in December 1888, while en route from Boston, Adams noted in his diary: "we discussed the scale, and I came away telling him I did not think it wise for me to see it again, in which he acquiesced."[39] Even Saint-Gaudens's specific requests to check the final modeling Adams turned down; he advised that any help that was needed could be offered by La Farge. With the artists working together some progress was made and various studies prepared and rejected, based on Michelangelo's Sistine ceiling sibyls, Socrates, and Buddha. On a sketch Saint-Gaudens scribbled, "Adams/ Buddha/ Mental repose/ Calm reflection in contrast with the violence or force in nature."[40] However, once Adams and La Farge had departed for Japan and the South Seas a second time in mid-August 1890, Saint-Gaudens was able to bring the figure to completion. Meanwhile White had been experimenting with enclosures of varying shapes, finally settling on a hexagon within a rectangle, the hexagon formed by a slab behind the seated figure and facing bench seats. Between the rectangular curb and the slab and seats were to be plantings of cedar and holly.

Once away from it Adams became enthusiastic about his "Buddha monument," as he called it. There were details, however, only he could settle, such as the finishing of the slab which Adams had preferred be perfectly plain, but which Saint-Gaudens and White felt should have a subtle cornice. Saint-Gaudens wrote Adams:

> You asked that, in whatever was placed back of the figure, the architecture should have nothing to say, and above all that it should not be classic. White and I have mulled this over a great deal,

with the enclosed results. . . . This matter must be settled immediately, and I cannot do that without asking you. I do not think the small classical cornice and base can affect the figure and, to my thinking, the monument would be better as a whole.[41]

Adams relented, and once the bronze was cast and the ensemble installed in Rock Creek Cemetery in 1891, glowing reports were forwarded by friends to Adams, still in the South Seas, including photographs which gave Adams a slightly false impression. In June he replied to John Hay, who had written that the memorial was "indescribably noble and imposing . . . full of poetry and suggestion . . . a peace to which nothing matters"; Adams confessed that although he found it "not exactly my ideal, it is at least not hostile." He realized that "St. Gaudens is not in the least oriental, and is not even familiar with oriental conceptions. Stanford White is still less so. Between them the risk of going painfully wrong was great. Of course White was pretty sure to go most astray, and he has done so."[42] But, as Adams admitted to his brother, "As my friends are determined that I shall be satisfied with the work, I am at least relieved of a heavy anxiety on their account, though I can't help still looking forward with a little dread to my own first sight of it, not because I doubt that his artistic rendering of an idea must be better than my conception of the idea, but because the two could hardly be the same, and what is his in it might seem to mix badly with the image that had been in my mind."[43]

As soon as Adams reached Washington in mid-February 1892, he went to Rock Creek Cemetery and found his opinion of the figure and setting greatly changed; the photographs had not done them any justice [135, 136]. To the sheltered enclosure, ever more so as the plantings matured, he returned again and again, so much so that it became a kind of second home. He might slip into the shrubbery to listen to the comments and explanations of those who sought the memorial out and wondered what it meant:

> Most took it for a portrait-statue, and the remnant were vacant-minded in the absence of a personal guide. None felt what would have been a nursery-instinct to a Hindu baby or a Japanese jinricksha-runner. The only exceptions were the clergy, who taught a lesson even deeper. One after another brought companions there, and, apparently fascinated by their own reflection, broke out passionately against the expression they felt in the figure of despair, of atheism, of denial. Like the others, the priest saw only what he brought. Like all great artists, St. Gaudens held up the mirror and no more.[44]

Saint-Gaudens himself, when once visiting the memorial with John Hay and Mrs. Barrett Wendell, was asked what the figure meant. Pausing momentarily, he replied, "I call it the Mystery of the Hereafter," and when questioned if that meant happiness, he expanded, "No, it is beyond pain and joy."[45] Only once, it seems, did Adams himself reveal his own interpretation, in a letter to Richard Watson Gilder in 1895:

> The whole meaning and feeling of the figure is in its universality and anonymity. My own name for it is "The Peace of God." La Farge would call it "Kwannon." Petrarch would say: "Siccome eterna vita è veder Dio," and a real artist would be very careful to give it no name that the public could turn into a limitation of its nature."[46]

When the project got underway, Adams had thought of his "Buddha monument" as a personal expression, but it became equally personal for all who worked on it. When Adams

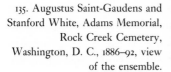

135. Augustus Saint-Gaudens and Stanford White, Adams Memorial, Rock Creek Cemetery, Washington, D. C., 1886–92, view of the ensemble.

136. Adams Memorial, figure and stele.

first saw the photographs he realized the degree to which he was now alienated from it; it was no longer only his. But later, when in the bower itself facing the figure, removed to a space somehow out of time, he saw it was no longer a personal memorial but a statement collectively created and offered to all who would seek it out; it belonged to them all. It is still an intensely personal experience. Seated across from the silent figure, one is completely enclosed by the green vault. No longer elevated on a differentiating pedestal, the figure confronts the viewer, and in its still, dark, arboreal room makes imponderable mysteries visible. There are no inscriptions, no references to individuals or a specific time, nothing to introduce limits. Instead, as Adams wished, La Farge, Saint-Gaudens, and White created a simulacrum in stone, bronze, and foliage of the peace Marian Adams finally attained. And as Adams recognized, the memorial exists not in time past, but in the present; it changes and nears fuller realization with each passing season.

Despite Adams's concern over Saint-Gaudens's slow start on his memorial, the ensemble was completed in a relatively short time for the sculptor. Aside from the never-completed Boston Library terrace figures, the work which occupied Saint-Gaudens longest was the Shaw Memorial, 1881–97, on which he was laboring before and after the Adams Memorial was conceived and finished. In 1863 Colonel Robert Gould Shaw, a Bostonian, was killed while leading his volunteer black troops in an attack on Fort Wagner, Charleston, S.C., and soon after the war several Bostonians formed a committee to raise funds for his memorial. In 1880 initial studies for a statue were made by Anne Whitney, but when these were found unsuitable, H. H. Richardson helped direct the commission to Saint-Gaudens early in 1881. Eventually a contract was signed with the committee in 1884, with delivery of the statue promised in two years. It took thirteen years to complete, however, and was not dedicated until 1897. Saint-Gaudens's original concept had been an equestrian figure in front of a masonry screen carrying a long inscription and a tree in low relief.[47] When the Shaw family objected to such a heroic figure, the sculptor translated the whole into a bronze relief, including a group of soldiers. Aside from the change, another reason for the protracted development was that Saint-Gaudens modeled the horse himself, so insistent was his desire for total unity of expression (later he would collaborate with animal sculptors as was often the practice); each of the Negro soldiers also was painstakingly studied from living models. McKim's white granite and marble setting, designed in 1890–91 and embellished with insignia and emblems, came much later as the final details of the sculpture were being clarified and once the site for the relief had been settled [137]. Largely through McKim's efforts, the edge of the Common, directly facing the entrance stair of Bulfinch's State House, was selected for the Shaw Memorial; the decision to incorporate trees into the setting was his also, and fountains once played to the rear as well, so that here too were combined sculpture, architecture, planting, and water.[48]

137. Augustus Saint-Gaudens and Charles Follen McKim, Colonel Robert Gould Shaw Memorial, Boston Common, Boston, Mass., 1890–97 (figure begun 1881). *American Architect and Building News*, September 11, 1897.

The embellishments on the white marble frame and base of the Shaw Memorial were cut in relief, but during 1889 White and McKim both began incorporating bronze intarsia inserts in the reddish granite they began to prefer. White, for instance, used this combination for the rather simple cylindrical base for Frederick MacMonnies's *Nathan Hale,* 1889, and the more elaborate Battell Memorial Fountain, Norfolk, Connecticut, 1889, which combined a fountain, seating, and lighting in a way reminiscent of the Chapin Monument.[49] Much more expansive in feeling was the West Point Battle Monument, 1891–96 [138], whose red granite Tuscan column, surmounted by MacMonnies's *Fame,* placed on a broad podium at the edge of the bluff, commemorated officers and soldiers of the Regular Army lost in the Civil War.[50] Particularly effective in this are the studied color contrasts of the buff and dusky-red granites and the verdigris bronze inserts.

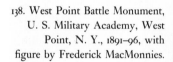

138. West Point Battle Monument, U. S. Military Academy, West Point, N. Y., 1891–96, with figure by Frederick MacMonnies.

Park embellishments and furniture, such as the Battell Fountain, the partners evidently felt were important to the spatial definition of edges and the creating of focal points. The single largest project of this kind was the Washington Memorial Arch, Washington Square, New York, 1889–95 [139]. There were, in fact, two arches, the first dashed off by White as one of many ephemeral fete ornaments to commemorate the centennial of George Washington's inauguration in New York in 1789; this first version was of wood, tall and spindly since its piers were not to obstruct the sidewalks at the foot of Fifth Avenue, where it stood against the backdrop of Washington Square. But the image of the arch at the terminus of the street so imprinted itself on the residents that even before the festivities were concluded subscriptions were being taken to underwrite the construction of a permanent masonry arch, for which White provided the plans gratis. This second version was built inside the park at the point where Fifth Avenue begins, and because of its ample surroundings the proportions of the second version are more substantial.[51] Perhaps White was drawn to antique models because the arch was to symbolize the triumph of republican democracy; whatever the reason his sources were revealed in a rare written commentary:

> In style this monument is distinctly classic, and by this term is meant Roman in contradistinction to the less robust, more fanciful and more "personal" style of the Renaissance. Although

having a discreet flavor of its own, this quality has been kept in abeyance to the conservatism which seems proper in the designs of a structure intended to stand for all time and to outlast any local or passing fashions. When brought in close comparison, however, with the triumphal arches of Rome and the Roman Empire, many differences are to be noted—that of the size of the opening being the most striking, though not the most important. No arch of antiquity containing but one opening has a span as great as that at New York [30 feet 2 inches], the nearest approach to it being the arch at Aosta, which has a span of about 29 feet 8 inches. The arch at Salonika has its central opening 36 feet wide, which is the largest span of all Roman triumphal arches—this, however, is a construction with three openings. In architectural treatment the Washington Arch differs from its classical predecessors in being generally lighter, in the prominence of the frieze, in the reduced height of the attic, and lastly and most important, in the absence of the Orders. Of the few remaining Roman examples of arches without orders, perhaps the best known is that at Alcantra.[52]

Clearly it was not unfamiliarity with antique models that differentiated White's work from McKim's, but rather choice. For this commission White evidently felt a severe neoclassical Roman symbol was appropriate, to honor the man who founded the nation.

The most extensive park embellishment program undertaken by the firm was in Prospect Park, Brooklyn, the first parts of which were designed in 1888 and on which work continued well into the twentieth century. As a landscape design, Olmsted's Prospect Park was superior to the earlier Central Park, partly because of better natural features in the topography but also because the site was not crossed by major thoroughfares. To define the edges of the park and to complement the random, irregular vistas created by Olmsted,

139. OPPOSITE. Washington Memorial Arch, Washington Square, New York, N. Y., 1889–92. Judson Memorial Church, 1888–93, visible across the square.

140. ABOVE. Prospect Park, Brooklyn, N. Y., entrance from Grand Army Plaza, 1888–89.

141. Prospect Park, entrance from Parkside and Ocean Avenues, 1890.

McKim, Mead & White were engaged in September 1888; they started with the major northern entrance at the Grand Army Plaza, where four Doric columns were erected, topped by bronze eagles by MacMonnies, flanked by subsidiary lamps, pavilions, and balustrades [140]. In 1890 the other principal entrance at the south, at what is now Parkside and Coney Island Avenue, was framed by large pedestals designed to support MacMonnies's *Horse Tamers* [141]. In the next several years came the statue of James Stanahan and miscellaneous "fences, columns, shelters, houses, pedestals, balustrades, etc." inside the park, including an outlook tower, rose garden, and the Maryland Society Battle Monument.[53] The basis of Olmsted's original design had been to contrast the increasingly mechanized urban fabric with the re-created natural landscape; although in failing health, he vigorously opposed any attempts to soften this contrast, to "construct" within the boundaries.[54] In hindsight, however, it might be argued that his picturesqueness and the firm's classical allusions combined rather successfully in Prospect Park, giving it a rather pastoral Virgilian aspect.

ONCE the decisive move toward Renaissance classicism had been taken during 1887 in the design of the Boston Public Library, the entire production of the firm moved in that direction. Indeed in White's new front for the Edwin Booth house in Gramercy Square, New York, remodeled to house the Players Club, the large wrought-iron lamps were very much like those developed for the library entrance.[55] Urban residences were ready subjects for the decorum this historical allusion promoted. Still, as White had noted in his description of the Washington Arch, a good deal of freedom was possible within this mode, and he certainly exploited it in a series of richly embellished houses beginning with that for J. Hampden Robb, New York, 1889–91 [142].[56] In this the color scheme was still dark, the terra cotta matching the dark reddish brown brick; and though there is a wealth of small-scale ornament—escutcheons, garlands, moldings, and architraves—all of it is held in check. Other houses recalled the sobriety of the earlier Villard and Phoenix houses, such as that for the Reverend John F. Goucher, Baltimore, 1890–92. Although this was directly across Saint Paul Street from the women's college complex and the Methodist Church just designed by White, it had nothing of the dark rough masonry of those buildings, but rather, had walls of ochre-colored Roman brick with limestone trim. During the early 1890s, McKim's involvement with the World's Columbian Exposition resulted in two residences by the firm in Chicago. Of these the Bryan Lathrop house is Georgian, while the Robert W. Patterson house, 1892–95 [143], by White, had many of the features of the Robb house but was lighter in color—ochre Roman brick walls with slightly darker terra-cotta window architraves and string courses. While the center is dramatically emphasized by superimposed porches of which White was fond, the interior spaces are not as grand as the exterior might suggest.[57]

The urban "home" existed in various forms, and the firm was involved in redefining or modifying all types, including the large residence hotel. The firm made extensive alterations to two in New York: Carl Pfeiffer's Savoy Plaza, 1884 (on the site of Hardenbergh's Plaza later), on which the firm worked during 1888–91, and the Park Avenue Hotel, which they remodeled in 1890–91. Demolished along with both of these was the Yosemite, New York, 1888–90, commissioned by the New York Life Insurance Company [144], the first of several commissions which came from that company; this was also the first prestigious apartment block on upper Park Avenue following the closing over of the New York Central railroad tracks.[58] More sumptuously embellished was White's Hotel Imperial for Robert and Ogden Goelet, New York, 1889–91 [145].[59] In the white Tuckahoe marble base were shops, with a mezzanine level above. The whimsical manipulation of window openings in the base contrasted with the more orderly sequence in the upper floors, which were clad in white glazed brick and matching terra cotta. Because of the public nature of its ground-floor spaces, the interiors were embellished with murals by T. W. Dewing and Edwin Austin Abbey.

Together with the Robb and Patterson houses, the exterior treatment of the Hotel Imperial illustrates White's desire for greater texture in tight zones of crisp ornamentation.

142. J. Hampden Robb house,
New York, N. Y., 1889–91.
*American Architect and Building
News,* November 7, 1891.

143. Robert W. Patterson house,
Chicago, Ill., 1892–95.

Generally, however, this expression was reserved for New York, while similar buildings elsewhere were more restrained. A good example is the bachelor's residence hotel designed for T. O. Browne and J. M. Meredith, Boston, 1890–91 [146].[60] Facing the Boston Common, the entire block is comparatively more restrained and reserved, commensurate with its setting at the foot of Beacon Hill. Because fire safety was of paramount concern, the entire block was built of solid brick masonry, with brick arches and vaults supporting all floors; no metal framing was used. The plan had suites of rooms arranged around the central elevator and stair core; the only break in the rectangular plan profile is a small ten-by-eleven-foot light shaft at the rear. The materials used externally recall those of nearby houses, red brick with limestone quoins and trim, while the eighty-foot bulk of the block effectively terminates the row of houses descending Beacon Street and forming the defining wall of the Common.

During 1890 to 1892 a number of commissions came into the office for multiunit housing blocks or complexes, and of them certainly the most important was the group called the King Model Houses in Harlem, 1891–92, designed by David H. King, Jr. During the 1830s and 1840s Harlem had been a sleepy suburb of a New York well to its south, for it was too far from lower Manhattan for effective commuting by coach; but by 1879, when the elevated railroad had been extended into the area, increasing numbers of tenement blocks and apartments were built for the middle class. Schools, clubs, theaters, and commercial buildings soon followed, giving rise to a fully developed community. King, a well-known

144. Yosemite Apartment Building, New York, N. Y., 1887–90. *American Architect and Building News,* February 21, 1891.

145. Hotel Imperial, New York, N. Y., 1889–91. *American Architect and Building News,* October 25, 1890.

building contractor and wealthy developer of Manhattan real estate, saw the potential in acquiring a large tract of Harlem property and building a harmonious townhouse complex emulating the high design standards of the upper-middle-class townhouses of lower Manhattan. A brochure he produced asked: "Why should not the homes of New Yorkers be sunny, tasteful, convenient, and commodious, even if their occupants are not millionaires?"[61] On a portion of the former Watt estate, on a tract lying midway between 137th and 140th streets and running from Seventh to Eighth avenues, King laid out a complex of 160 housing units "on such a large scale and with such ample resources as to 'Create a Neighborhood'

146. Browne and Meredith Apartment Building, Boston, Mass., 1890–91.

independent of surrounding influences. It is the largest enterprise of its kind ever undertaken by one builder on Manhattan Island," a boast which seems to have been accurate.

Along Eighth Avenue, apartment houses were built, with townhouses everywhere else, all set back at least thirty feet from the curbs of the north-south thoroughfares and twelve feet from the east-west streets [147]. King also provided asphalt-paved alleyways through the center of each block, each crossed by two paved walkways closed by ornamental wrought-iron gates; where the walkways intersected the alleys there were fountains. Because the alleys were wide, allowing for the passage of two carriages, it was here, rather than on the street, that much of the daily business of the households took place—ash collection and milk and ice deliveries, for example. The housing of the complex was portioned out to three prominent architects; the units along 138th Street and on the south side of 139th Street were by James Brown Lord and Bruce Price, while McKim, Mead & White designed the townhouses on the north side of 139th Street. Compared to the units by Lord and Price, those by the firm are slightly wider, and where the former used yellow brick with white terra-cotta trim, McKim, Mead & White used brownstone for the bases with glazed speckled Roman brick with matching terra-cotta trim above. Because of the length of the blocks, the rows were divided into groups, and McKim, Mead & White further subtly accentuated the ends by projecting the terminating units forward about one foot [148]. Their townhouse units are

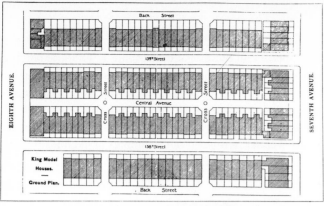

PLAN OF BLOCKS SHOWING CROSS STREETS.

147. King Model Houses, New York, N. Y., 1891–92, general plan. From *King Model Houses.*

148. King Model Houses, oblique view of houses on north side of 139th Street.

149. King Model Houses, 259 W. 139th Street, facade. 150. King Model Houses, floor plans of typical house on 139th Street. From *King Model Houses.*

FLOOR PLANS OF A HOUSE ON 139TH STREET.

particularly good representatives of the middle-class urban residence of the period [149, 150]. The plan is commodious while being highly efficient, and although the main floor is elevated there is no high stoop. On the interior and exterior, ornament is held to a minimum; except for the delicate terra-cotta rosette and a single string course, the exterior wall surface is blank, the variegated brick providing the only necessary visual enrichment.

"From whatever point of observation the buildings are viewed, their aspect is harmonious, well proportioned, and tasteful," extolled the prospectus brochure, and the contrast between the King houses and the far more typical dumbbell tenement of 1879 or even the New Law tenement of 1901 is striking. Compared to these officially legislated standards the King houses were generous indeed, with ease of access to the various rooms and good ventilation. King was well aware of what might become of the complex through speculation, and by building on the entire tract at once there was no room left for subsequent inharmonious additions. Moreover, through covenants in the purchase contracts, additions or alterations to the units which blocked light or air were prevented. And to ensure longevity and reduced maintenance, King purchased the best materials in bulk and insisted upon the best workmanship.[62] Such townhouses were not unusual in New York as the city expanded rapidly to the east, west, and especially northward, nor were the plans used radically different from those developed before. What set apart the King Model Houses was the scope of the project and the artistic ambitions of the developer; McKim, Mead & White's units in particular demonstrated that a concern for the budget need not preclude good design.[63]

HAVING already begun to stress the domestic character of the clubhouse prior to 1887, the challenge before the firm now was to reconcile this with their preferred Renaissance classicism. In the small Players Club across Gramercy Park from his own home, White had only to make minimal modifications to the former home of Edwin Booth, reserving the strongest classical touches for the entrance porch replacing the stoop. In their other, larger clubs of the period the firm introduced something of the character of London clubs, but handled spaces with more freedom and creatively unorthodox ways. Like Decimus Burton and Sir Charles Barry they tended toward the Italian Renaissance references, not the Georgian. The most significant club of the period, establishing the type for those which followed, was the new home of the Century Association, New York, 1889–91, to replace outgrown facilities at the edge of Greenwich Village [151, 152].[64]

Inasmuch as the partners were Centurions, the Association simply appointed them architects for the new building in May 1889, stipulating a modest budget of $150,000. Since the Century Association had evolved from an informal "Sketch Club" a generation earlier, there were to be in the new building, besides the customary lounges, library, and dining facilities, special day-lit galleries where members could hang their latest paintings. The scheme was developed in a collaborative way reminiscent of the early years, the plan developed by McKim, the facade organized by White, and the details carefully studied by Wells. Because the club was home to so many artists and literary figures, White devised an especially rich facade based on variations of several northern Italian palazzi, but recalling most specifically the Palazzo Canossa, Verona. Where Sanmichele, however, had divided the base of his palazzo with a single emphatic molding, White substituted a change in material from smooth masonry to richly textured terra cotta, and introduced in the upper level a Palladian loggia. Most characteristically, on the facade he alternated stretches of

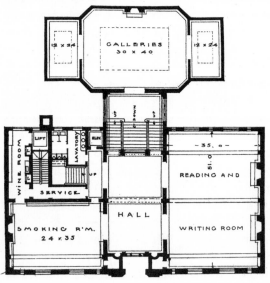

151. Century Club, New York,
N. Y., 1889–91.
152. Century Club, second-floor
plan. *American Architect and
Building News*, February 23, 1895.

smooth buff Roman brick with zones of incredibly saturated ornament much like that of palazzi in Cremona or Brescia. The richly framed window clusters had the character of the Palazzo Dati, Cremona, or the Palazzo Malvezzi-Campeggi, Bologna, but instead of literally copying these, White devised a variant splashed with his own dense ornament so easily rendered in terra cotta. The Century Club was highly regarded in the 1890s for its combination of invention and restraint, apparent in several notices in the professional journals and in comments from *Architecture Review* (Boston) in 1892, which warmly approved the "admirable proportions and delicate profiles," and the "picturesque distribution of the masses of light and shade throughout the whole design." To the reviewer "it is such work as this, rather than the Babel-tower office buildings or the striking novelties, which are promising for the future of American art."[65] Even with the festive character of the building, the construction estimates of Norcross Brothers, the contractor, were only slightly over the figure originally set by the club officers.

Where the Century Club was demonstrably lighthearted and festive, the second major club of the period was sumptuous but grave; this was the Metropolitan Club, New York, 1891–94, founded by a disgruntled J. P. Morgan when business associates of his were denied membership at the prestigious but conservative Union Club. Because of the nature of the initiators, the entire conception of the Metropolitan Club was more elaborate than that of the Century. The exterior, for instance, was built of two varieties of white marble, and the cost of the building as a whole was almost ten times that of the Century Club [153]. Although the palazzo block of the Metropolitan Club is on Fifth Avenue, the entrance is to the side, in a recessed court screened from 60th Street by pairs of columns, a Mannerist inversion very similar to the entry to Raphael's Palazzo Pandolfini, Florence [154, 155]. But here, too,

153. Metropolitan Club, New York, N. Y., view from Central Park, 1891–94.
154. Metropolitan Club, first- and second-floor plans. *Monograph.*

FIRST FLOOR PLAN

SECOND FLOOR PLAN

METROPOLITAN·CLUB NEW YORK CITY.

the historical reference is generic rather than specific, for while the Metropolitan Club is decidedly Italianate it is far from a copy of a specific building. What is ostensibly a masonry building in fact has an internal metal frame, but because the framing was rushed in advance of detail drawings of the internal finishing, the Pavonasso marble columns around the upper part of the central hall had to be sawed in half and hollowed out to fit around the metal

155. Metropolitan Club, entrance on 60th Street.
156. Metropolitan Club, Main Hall (Marble Hall). *American Architect and Building News*, February 13, 1897.

columns then already in place [156]. If the exterior has specific historic allusions, the major internal spaces are more original, especially the immense central hall, fifty-two by fifty-five feet, rising through two stories and paneled in polished Pavonazzo, Skyros, and Vermont marbles. As the hall clearly shows, if the Century Club is intimate, the Metropolitan is unquestionably regal in scale and grandeur.[66]

WHILE Italian Renaissance classicism was being explored as a source of images of coherent urban architecture, McKim, Mead & White continued to expand on their use of Georgian models. Now, however, these eighteenth-century references were combined increasingly with allusions to native Federalist architecture, that severe and attenuated conservative variant of Georgian Baroque which flourished in New England after the Revolution, up to about 1815. As before, plan arrangements were determined far more by functional requirements than by emulation of the past, and the historical allusions were determined by regional associations or the influence of the immediate environment.

This is best illustrated, perhaps, by one of the first efforts in this mode of the period, McKim's gates for Harvard University, which eventually resulted in a return to Georgian brick and mortar that continued to shape Harvard's architecture for nearly two generations. The Johnston Gate was built through a bequest of Samuel Johnston, Class of 1855, who provided $10,000 specifically for a gate between the oldest campus buildings—Massachusetts Hall, 1718–20, and Harvard Hall, 1764–66. Given the restrictions of the gift, McKim reasoned that a gate presupposes a fence, and in 1888 he began sketching out some general ideas for a new enclosure for the Harvard Yard, proposing brick piers supporting wrought-iron fence panels. He then turned his attention to the gate specifically, studying such Georgian prototypes as those at Saint-John's College, Winchester, and the Banqueting House at Kensington Gardens.[67] The final result, because of the broad open site, was a large recessed central gate flanked by smaller gates and brick and wrought-iron panels [157]. The materials McKim wanted posed problems since there was little available commercially that corresponded to those used in the eighteenth-century buildings. He made the rounds of Boston brickyards, selecting blackened overburned clinkers and underfired brick in various buff, salmon, and reddish hues, which, laid in Flemish bond in a thick buff-colored mortar bed, simulated the variegated color and texture of the weathered walls of neighboring Massachusetts and Harvard halls. Reportedly the iron work was similarly handled: standard machine-rolled bars, larger than necessary, were reheated and hammered down and made as true as possible by hand, giving the bars irregularities more in sympathy with eighteenth-century work.[68]

This meticulousness pushed the cost beyond the amount bequested. As a result McKim was instructed by the Harvard trustees to prepare a second and more circumspect design, but his reply explained how he approached the problem of devising a gate for the one-hundred-foot opening between the two venerable buildings: "Our effort was to accomplish, always with a view to simplicity and economy, the most appropriate design we knew how to make and not the most appropriate $10,000 design, and we saw, and see now no other or better way to accomplish a successful result."[69] His view of the architect's role, then, was to design with a view to optimum response to function and site and not strictly on the size of the budget, confident that for the best design for the circumstances the necessary money somehow would be found. It usually was, as in this case when the necessary subvention was given by his brother-in-law, George von Lengerke Meyer; the Johnston Gate was finished 1889–90.

157. Johnston Gate, Harvard University, Cambridge, Mass., 1889–90.

Looking at Harvard University now it is hard to visualize how it changed during the presidency of Charles Eliot, but when Eliot was inaugurated in 1869 Harvard was a relatively small college, and when he retired in 1909 it had become a major center of graduate studies in the humanities and natural sciences. So McKim's advocacy of an ancestral expression can be understood as a way of maintaining focus, identity, and a clearer sense of Harvard's history at a time when it was being radically transformed.[70]

Soon after the Johnston Gate was underway, McKim received commissions for two more gates leading into the Harvard Yard. The second, commissioned by Meyer himself, was built in 1890–91 on the north side, and the third, commissioned by the Porcellian Club in 1890–91 for the south side, was not built until 1900–01 after revision of the design. Once these three were started, a desire began to grow among the alumni for the construction of a new enclosure around the yard, opened at strategic locations by memorial gates. The accumulation of building funds through donations, however, was greatly protracted by the business depression of the 1890s, so that building did not begin until the turn of the century.

The reflection of local tradition was also the basis of McKim's Germantown Cricket Club, 1889–91 [158], a commission directed to the firm by McKim's boyhood friends in the community. In this McKim may have been referring generally to the brickwork of Philadelphia, but he was specifically influenced by the eighteenth-century Price house on the club grounds, which had been converted into the Ladies Club House.[71] There were thus both specific and generic associations in the Georgian mode. Similar in general massing was the Edwin D. Morgan house, Wheatley Hills, near Wheatley, Long Island, New York, 1889–90 and enlarged later [159], with its extended central block and "hyphenated" wings, but this was clad in shingles not brick. At almost the same time Morgan, the grandson of the New York banker who had commissioned Saint-Gaudens's and White's ill-fated mausoleum in Hartford at the outset of their careers, also commissioned a large house, Beacon Rock, Newport, 1889–91, on a rocky peninsula on the southeast shore of the island, whose crest had to be leveled by dynamite to form a flat building platform. Its plan was U-shaped with a formal entrance court, in marked contrast to the rustic northern face of the house which rises up from the rock, culminating in a circular veranda formed of massive archaic-looking Doric columns laid up in rough field stone [160, 161]. Internally the plan was marked by the

158. Germantown Cricket Club, Germantown (now Philadelphia), Pa., 1889–91.

159. Edwin D. Morgan house, Wheatley Hills, Wheatley, Long Island, N. Y., 1890–91.

160. ABOVE. Edwin D. Morgan house, Beacon Rock, Newport, R. I., 1888–91. *Monograph.*
161. LEFT. E. D. Morgan house, "Beacon Rock," plan. *Monograph.*

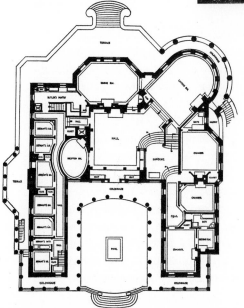

PLAN OF FIRST FLOOR

suggestion of formal symmetry playfully turned awry by studied irregularities, with a diagonal axis leading to the living room and its Doric veranda.[72]

Both of the Morgan houses, particularly Beacon Rock, had a generosity and freedom in plan that reflects relaxed summer life, but in the urban house the Georgian-Federalist exteriors are more reflective of an inner formality, as in the J. Arthur Beebe house on Commonwealth Avenue in the Back Bay, Boston, 1888–89. While the Beebe house does have two swelling bays framing an Ionic portico whose fanlight greatly resembles that of Bulfinch's house at 39–40 Beacon Street, the double-hung windows with the large sheets of plate glass are typically nineteenth-century and compromise the Federalist character of the design.[73] This was greatly improved upon in the double house on Commonwealth Avenue for Francis I. Amory and Richard Olney, 1890–92 [162].[74] The two units are treated as one facade, the entrance porticoes joined together, and throughout, the details are much more delicate, as in the windows with their small panes and shutters, true to eighteenth-century models. This double house established a type which the firm returned to for a number of variations, beginning with the wider Bryan Lathrop house, Chicago, 1891–93 [163].[75] Designed by McKim, and resulting from the many trips to Chicago in connection with the World's Fair, this was one of the firm's few Georgian-Federalist buildings outside the Northeast. Lathrop's childhood in Alexandria, Virginia, or his wife Helen's recollection of Washington, D.C., may have had some part in determining the character, but it may have been that by 1890–91 this mode was viewed by the partners as being a universal American rather than a regionally limited New England urban type.

There were few opportunities to employ this newly rediscovered "national" expression in ecclesiastical work, with the exception of the remodeling of the chancel of the Church of Christ at Dartmouth, Hanover, New Hampshire, 1889, based on drawings donated by White.[76] The church, built 1794–95 by Colonel David Curtis, was a good example of the disseminated conservative meetinghouse design rooted in James Gibbs's Saint-Martin's-in-the-Fields. In order to create a recessed choir, White took as a planning module the Palladian motif in Curtis's tower, placing a new wall in front of the existing flat sanctuary wall, piercing it with Palladian arcades. As a result, the exterior and new interior were clearly related and White's attenuated alterations disrupted the original interior as little as any changes might have done.

The largest of these Georgian-Federalist evocations, the Rhode Island State Capitol, 1891–1904, was to assume great importance almost from the day the design was first put down on paper, for it became the model for a generation of new state capitol buildings across the country.[77] Remarkably, Rhode Island had not built a new state house following the Colonial period, although there had been growing interest since mid-century in replacing Richard Munday's Colony House, Newport, 1739. Thus, the Rhode Island legislature was one of the few which continued to meet in an eighteenth-century building through the following century. McKim was well acquainted with the original state house, and his years in Newport may have familiarized him with the functional arrangement of the upper principal floor, with council and assembly rooms on either side of a central "middle room," which opened out onto a carved balcony overlooking the major public space of the town, Washington Square. It was from this balcony, for instance, that the Declaration of Independence was read to the citizens of Rhode Island, so that this rostrum had a particularly rich imagery.

Early in 1891 the state legislature decided to erect a new building in Providence. This decision coincided with and was spurred by the Providence Public Park Association, which advocated putting the new capitol atop Smith's Hill, approached by a new mall three hundred feet wide extending to a new passenger railroad station below. The mall approach was to be a "magnificent boulevard . . . designed in the perfection of landscape architecture."

162. Francis I. Amory house (right half) and Richard Olney house (left half), Boston, Mass., 1890–92.

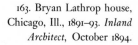
163. Bryan Lathrop house, Chicago, Ill., 1891–93. *Inland Architect,* October 1894.

The new capitol, embellished by "lawns, promenades, beds of flowers, fountains, and other works of art," was to be an "ornament" to the city and state, representing "its wealth, its culture, and its thrift."[78] A preliminary competition was held for Rhode Island architects in 1890, and the winner of this was then included in a second competition in 1891 among nine specially invited architects. Despite the partners' avowed policy against participating in competitions, the State House Commission had so constituted the competition program that McKim, Mead & White agreed to enter. Among other provisions, the program stipulated that all drawings submitted were to remain the property of the individual competitors, there were to be reputable judges, accurate estimates were to be part of each submission, any competitor attempting to influence the decision was to be expelled, and the winning competitor was to be appointed architect and superintendent of building construction, all in accordance with rules formulated by the American Institute of Architects.[79] Moreover, the firm had a special invitation from Governor Herbert W. Ladd, chairman of the commission. By December 17 the firm's drawings were ready for final inking for shipment to Providence, and on January 14, 1892, while Mead waited in Providence, the firm was declared the winner. Indeed, Mead had played a large part in developing the plan, although McKim worked on the elevation and details, leaving construction supervision to his principal assistant, Henry Bacon.[80] The firm won in part because of the exceptional clarity of their plan, which provided for Senate and House chambers surrounded by auxiliary offices and council rooms; at the center were a library and, at the crossing of the axes, a domed rotunda that served double duty as the principal stair hall [164]. It was a tightly focused composition, as sharp and abstract in plan as it was on the exterior. The general conceptual model was, quite naturally, the National Capitol with its clearly expressed wings and domed rotunda, but now translated as a simplified whole rather than a collection of aggregated parts. McKim also had in mind another prototype, for in writing to Cass Gilbert about his own unsuccessful proposal for the Minnesota Capitol, Lyman Farwell said he remembered being told by Bacon that "McKim took his ideas & his exterior treatment from the little city hall in N.Y.C."[81]

The capitol was far from construction when Farwell wrote in 1894, but he knew the design through publication in the *American Architect* in 1892. The building, above a broad podium enriched with substantial bronze lamps and sculpture groups, was subdivided into three large blocks, linked by recessed "hyphens" corresponding to the circulation around the dome piers. There was an emphatic base, but in place of a dividing string course there was a series of balconies, each carrying a pair of electric lamps. The dome was loosely patterned after those by Wren and Soufflot on Saint Paul's, London, and the Panthéon, Paris. Additions which the Capitol Commission greatly admired were the four tourelles at the corners of the dome base. In general the austerity of the plan and exterior recalled more the Boston Public Library than the delicacy of the New York City Hall, but perhaps what Farwell had been told was that the central stair had been inspired by that in New York, for the double helix in the original scheme did indeed resemble the remarkable staircase in New York.

Construction was delayed as the drawings were modified several times, and by July 1894 a model was prepared for display in Providence [165]. Among the changes, perhaps to reduce costs, were the elimination of all ornamental sculpture, the heavy *chéneau,* and all but the centermost balconies; the four tourelles were also deleted, to the displeasure of the commission. Added, however, was a projected arched center bay in each side wing, perhaps a reference to Thornton's National Capitol, and this then provided a basis for an enlarged triumphal arch motif in the central block, its deep barrel vault leading to the rotunda.

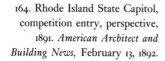
164. Rhode Island State Capitol, competition entry, perspective, 1891. *American Architect and Building News,* February 13, 1892.

165. Rhode Island State Capitol, plaster model, c. 1895.

    Additional restudy of the plans was then required in 1894–95, with the addition of restrooms and cloakrooms at the entrances to each of the legislative chambers, adding sixty feet to the building's length. Revised estimates were obtained from Norcross Brothers, the contractor, and on September 16, 1895, ground was broken on Smith's Hill. The final design called for an emphasized central section in each wing, framed by pilasters and engaged columns, a device modified for the projecting elements of the ends of the wings and for the balcony loggia at the center opening off the governor's reception room, a clear reference to the Newport Colony House [166, 167]. At the suggestion of Richard Morris Hunt it was decided to build the superstructure of white Georgia marble, with a matt sand-rubbed finish; moreover, the dome was to be of solid masonry and self-supporting, with no internal metal skeleton, the structural details of which were worked out by the builder, Norcross Brothers.
    As construction of the Rhode Island Capitol commenced, other capitols based on it also

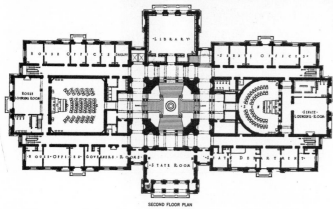

SECOND FLOOR PLAN

166. Rhode Island State Capitol,
Providence, R. I., 1891–1903.
167. Rhode Island State Capitol,
second-floor plan. *Monograph*.

were started, beginning with Cass Gilbert's far more richly embellished Minnesota Capitol.
The firm's interiors in the Rhode Island building, however, were as severe as the exterior.
The offices and council rooms were especially plain, and the two principal legislative
chambers were severely classic in a way that recalled Benjamin Henry Latrobe. The most
embellished interiors were the central rotunda and the governor's reception room, the major
public spaces. In these McKim took care to simplify the results, as is evident in his written
response to Mead concerning an inspection visit in August 1901:

> I write this simply to let you know how really well things are coming out, and I am sure that
> you will agree with me, when you see it, that we were wise in not going outside for assistance
> [for decorating the interiors]. The Senate is about half completed, and looks so much more
> simple, as well as appropriate and dignified, in that part in which gold has not yet commenced,

that I suppressed the gold altogether, depending on the white marble and green to do the trick, and if any gold is to be used at all, confine it to the drapery, or an eagle behind the Lieutenant-Governor's seat. Fortunately the gilding had not proceeded too far. From the Senate, we went to the library, which is really a fine room, now practically completed, and which we left with hardly any change. It is both sumptuous and sober, and is sure to be popular. The State [reception] Room is too much pink, white and gold, too liney, and too ballroomish, but this I think will be overcome by the introduction of grey in the panels and stiles and rails, giving the walls more body, the coved ceiling dark and strong in color, cut to the central panel, which will be left for clouds or figure composition. . . . The State Room seemed an appropriate place —if any place in the building—to have figure decoration. It will also be a relief from the succession of architectural decoration everywhere else in the building.[82]

Work on the landscaping had only just begun when McKim wrote to Mead, but he "was most astonished at the change which came over the grounds, since I saw them last. Already, the grading gives the building a different setting, and *is the greatest possible improvement.*" A broad esplanade was being extended down the hill to the Woonasquatucket River and the train station, but although work continued on the grounds three and a half years after the building was occupied in 1901, the landscaped connection to the station below was never made. It was expected that the setting would acquire special importance since the enterprise had been set in motion by the Providence Park Association, and although the proposed landscaping was not entirely finished, in the concern for the setting and the original inclusion of sculpture one sees in the Rhode Island Capitol the first stirrings of the City Beautiful Movement, sketched out even as the Columbian Exposition and its Court of Honor were being designed.

The impact of the Rhode Island Capitol was immediate, preceding actual construction. Although Minnesota had been considering building a new capitol since 1881, the legislature acted soon after the Rhode Island plans were published. The first Minnesota competition of 1894, which Lyman Farwell entered, was inconclusive, while the second was won by Cass Gilbert, now established in Saint Paul. Though Gilbert's design was inspired by the Providence model, it was far more ornate inside and out, incorporating a great deal of sculpture, including a gilded quadriga by Daniel Chester French. The dome, moreover, was virtually a duplicate of that of Saint Peter's, Rome; but because of the severe Minnesota winters Gilbert was obliged to use a three-shell structure comprised of an inner hemisphere, a steel-framed brick-infill inner cone carrying the lantern, and a self-supporting white Georgia marble outer shell.[83] The Minnesota Capitol, 1895–1905, was but the first of many derivatives. A number of existing buildings were enlarged in the spirit of the Rhode Island model, as in Virginia, Florida, and Alabama, for which McKim was engaged as a consultant in 1906.[84] The new capitols closest in sobriety and clarity of form to that in Rhode Island were those for Arkansas, 1899–1916, by George R. Mann, who had been an office assistant, assisted by Cass Gilbert; for Mississippi, 1901–03, by Theodore R. Link; for Kentucky, 1904–10, by Frank Andrews; most especially for Wisconsin, 1906–17, by George B. Post & Sons; and the cluster of buildings in Olympia, Washington, 1911–28, by Wilder & White, who had been office assistants. The new capitols for Montana, South Dakota, Pennsylvania, Idaho, and Utah also bore the stamp of the Providence model. So, in Rhode Island the firm gave form to a vision of public architecture that was shared by a great number of their countrymen, noble in expression, capable of supporting allegorical embellishment to enhance its meaning, and rooted in what was seen as American classicism.

CONCURRENT with the vigorous economy after 1886, philanthropic donations and church building increased. Of the firm's ecclesiastical work the most ambitious project was their entry in the competition for the Cathedral of Saint John the Divine, New York, 1889. Their submission, however, was very hastily drawn up, and later in the year, when William Rotch Ware assembled drawings for publication in the *American Architect* and wrote McKim requesting the firm's perspective, White refused, saying the work had been too rushed.[85] Nor has a reproduction of their entry survived, so how they may have adapted Renaissance classicism, which they clearly now favored, for such a large church remains unknown. Besides White's Hanover church renovation, there was Mead's Tudor Gothic Revival parish house, 1893, for the First Presbyterian Church, New York, its externals determined by the adjacent church, 1845, by Joseph C. Wells. It was only because of the proximity that the firm turned to this expression; McKim's aversion to the Tudor revival is evident from his terse comment on first seeing the drawings: "My God. Gothic!"[86] Parallel to McKim's incorporation of various arts in the Boston Public Library, White did much the same in his chancel renovation of the Church of the Paulist Fathers, New York. The original building, 1876–85, was a rather stark Gothic revival structure by Jeremiah O'Rourke; the renovations of 1887–90 consisted of stained glass windows by La Farge and a new main altar and subsidiary altars by White.[87] The main altar, the focal point, White patterned on the monumental baldacchinos of early Christian basilicas of Rome and Ravenna [168]. In addition to exotic materials —porphyry, Numidian jasper, Mexican onyx, alabaster, gold-backed mosaic on the inner

168. Church of the Paulist Fathers, New York, N. Y., altar and ciborium, 1887–90. L. G. White, *Sketches and Designs.*

169. Judson Memorial Church, Washington Square, New York, N. Y., 1888–93.

surface of the baldacchino dome, and marble mosaic in the baldacchino gables—White incorporated the work of several sculptors, including Philip Martiny and Frederick Mac-Monnies, who did the kneeling angels.

The largest church of the period, the Judson Memorial Baptist Church, New York, 1888–93, had a prominent site at the corner of Thompson Street and Washington Square South, facing Washington Square [169, 139]. Taking advantage of the corner site, White divided the complex into a foursquare sanctuary block linked to a tall campanile by an entrance "hyphen," with auxiliary facilities behind the tower. As in the Boston Public Library, artists were engaged to enrich the building, with stained glass windows by La Farge and relief sculpture in the sanctuary by Saint-Gaudens but carved by Herbert Adams. Classically inspired throughout, the design mixed elements from early churches in Rome and quattrocento churches in Florence. Overall, the Judson church suggests Santa Maria in Cosmedin, Rome, but the campanile strongly resembles those of San Giorgio in Velabro, Rome, of the thirteenth century, and of San Lorenzo in Lucina, Rome, of the fifth century.[88] The hood over the entrance, however, is drawn from such Renaissance sources as San Alessandro, Lucca, built about 1480. In general the tight crisp ornament suggests that White was studying the work of sculptors such as Bernardo Rossellino or Desiderio da Settignana, but there appears no iconographical reason why these Romanesque and Renaissance allusions should have been used for a church in memory of Adonirum Judson, the first American missionary sent to Asia. Perhaps the generic Renaissance expression was viewed somehow as being more modern than the deprecated Gothic Revival (this note of contemporaneity was furthered by an electrically illuminated cross atop the campanile). Despite the classical elements and the warm tawny terra cotta and brick, the Judson church had little immediate influence, for Gothic still conveyed an image preferred by Roman Catholics and most

Protestant denominations; indeed, within less than a decade the successful efforts of Henry Vaughan and Ralph Adams Cram to reinvest Gothic with formal, iconographical, and structural meaning were to limit the influence of McKim, Mead & White in developing a Renaissance ecclesiastical style.

AT the close of the nineteenth century New York was symbolized in the public mind by three structures—the Statue of Liberty, Brooklyn Bridge, and Madison Square Garden. The Garden was by far the most famous of the firm's buildings for amusement, public or private; it was perhaps even more widely known than Pennsylvania Station during the first quarter of this century. It was White's counterpart to the Boston Public Library, for its complex combination of theatrical amusements and elegant divertissements characterized its architect just as the sobriety and studied erudition of the Boston Public Library characterized McKim.[89]

Madison Square had begun as a playing field and parade ground in the upper part of Knickerbocker New York, but in time its restrained townhouses were replaced by fashionable hotels as society moved ever northward. The New York & Harlem Railroad, meanwhile, had penetrated deep into the heart of the city, building a terminal at Prince and Center Streets in 1832, but coaches to this had to be drawn by horse below Madison Square because of state ordinances. Accordingly, the railroad acquired the entire block northeast of the square, building there a combination car barn, freight shed, horse stable, and passenger depot. When Cornelius Vanderbilt later combined the Harlem, the New Haven, and the New York Central and Hudson River Railroads, building for them the immense Grand Central Depot, 1869–71, the car barn and stable on 26th Street became obsolete. While retaining ownership, the railroad leased the property first to P. T. Barnum, who operated there his "Monster Classical and Geological Hippodrome," and then to Patrick S. Gilmore, who booked everything from religious revivals and temperance meetings, to flower shows, balls, beauty contests, the Westminster Kennel Show, and, most popular of all, boxing "demonstrations" conducted by "professors," since there was a strict state law forbidding pugilistic contests. Gilmore modified the drafty structure, festooning it in the summer with so many plants that it became a veritable garden amid which Theodore Thomas's orchestra played. At the end of 1878 the lease on what was now known as "Gilmore's Garden" ran out, but the enterprise was reopened the following season by William Kissam Vanderbilt and rechristened the "Madison Square Garden." It limped along, barely surviving except for the ever-popular boxing "demonstrations" given by "professor" John L. Sullivan, and, beginning in 1883, the annual meetings of the National Horse Show Association of America, which appealed to wealthy and more genteel society. Otherwise the Garden stood empty frequently, its high operating expenses not offset by rentals.

In 1884 Vanderbilt reluctantly announced that the Garden would be demolished and the site converted to other uses, whereupon various groups, especially the horse show interests, raised a howl of protest and formed a syndicate to buy the property and build a new facility. By the summer of 1887 over $1.5 million in stock had been sold by the Madison Square Garden Company, which was organized by Hiram Hitchcock and included, among others, J. Pierpont Morgan, Frank K. Sturgis, Andrew Carnegie, James Stillman, Herman Oelrichs, James T. Hyde, Adrian Iselin, W. W. Astor, Edward S. Stokes, and Stanford White.[90] Designs for the new Garden were solicited, to be submitted to William R. Ware for evaluation; not surprisingly, perhaps, that proposed by McKim, Mead & White was declared the winner in July 1887.

To retain their audiences, events normally scheduled for the Garden had to resume with only one postponement, so speed of construction was absolutely essential. Demolition started August 7, and by having crews working round the clock, under lights at night, the debris was cleared away in three weeks and construction started. The entire operation was personally supervised by contractor David H. King, Jr., and at any given time about a thousand men were at work. In addition to excavating for foundations, rock had to be blasted along the Fourth Avenue side for the extensive basement power plant. Once the brick walls were up, construction proceeded quickly and was complete enough for opening in eleven months. With such haste, of course, changes were made in the design even as building commenced, so that the tower, for a time eliminated, was restored at White's insistence but moved from the Madison Avenue front to the 26th Street side. Since comfort of the public was vital for success, and because the necessary functional spaces completely filled the building site, it was decided to put arcades over the sidewalks to provide sheltered corridors for assembling and strolling; this, however, required special enabling state legislation permitting New York City to cover its sidewalks.[91]

The new Garden was a marvelous collection of heterogeneous functions brought together under one roof [170, 171].[92] The principal space was the great amphitheater on the Fourth Avenue side, reached from Madison Avenue by a broad central hall-lobby flanked on the left by a large theater seating 1,200 and on the right by a restaurant. The theater, with its two balconies, went through the full three-story height of the building, but above the restaurant was a ballroom/concert hall with adjoining supper room/foyer, with separate men's and women's withdrawing rooms ideally arranged for social functions. The Garden Theater, as it was called, was officially a separate business, specializing in comic opera; its interior, hung with silks in cream and pale yellow, was warmly praised by Mrs. Van Rensselaer, who greatly appreciated the air-space acoustical barrier between the theater and the rest of the building. "I remember only two theater interiors in this country," she wrote, "which I should care to visit in cold blood by daylight for the mere sake of their architectural interest. One is Mr. Atwood's Music Hall . . . at the World's Fair (alas! already destroyed), and the other is the Garden Theater—with the graceful swing of its curved lines, its stately columns, its delicately modeled decorations, and its unusual air of joyousness combined with refinement."[93] Above the ballroom and theater, screened by open colonnades and corner tourelles, was a large café and roof garden, protected by a glass roof, in sections which could be removed for the warm summer months. Here, amid a festive display of incandescent lamps, "cabaret" musicals were performed starting late in June.

The Garden Theater prospered moderately, but the other operations on the Madison Avenue side contributed little to the astronomically high overhead; in fact, none of the fashionable restaurateurs such as Sherry or Delmonico would move into the Garden restaurant, where champagne would be requested by the horse show crowd one week and beer and sausages would be demanded by boxing devotees the next. The fortunes of Madison Square Garden hinged on the great amphitheater. Measuring nearly 188 by 304 feet, covered by an exposed steel truss roof with clear spans of 167 by 277 feet, it could seat five thousand around the arena, and twelve thousand with seats on the arena floor, for political conventions [171, 172]. The six main trusses of the roof, with sixteen radial-end trusses, were carried by built-up Phoenix columns; at the center of the roof was a skylight, 55 by 135 feet, with ten

170. Madison Square Garden,
New York, N. Y., 1887–91.
Monograph.

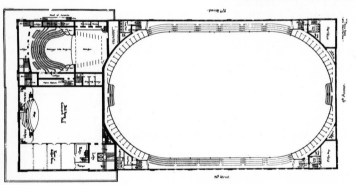

171. Madison Square Garden,
first-floor plan (bottom) and
second-floor plan (left). *Building*,
November 16, 1889.

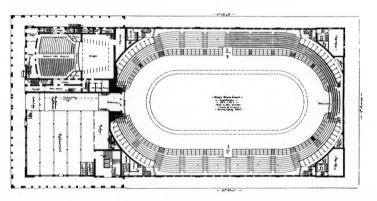

movable sections which could be rolled back for ventilation. The iron and steel of the trusses was frankly exposed, with no fire insulation, and were painted a light buff; iron also was used for the seats. To increase fire safety the entire building was illuminated by incandescent lamps powered by a self-contained generating station, an extensive use of electricity that attracted considerable curiosity.[94]

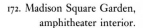
172. Madison Square Garden, amphitheater interior.

Although wrought iron and steel were used in the amphitheater and for major floor girders and joists throughout the building, these rested on brick walls, for Madison Square Garden employed traditional bearing walls. Externally the walls were embellished with a rich encrustation of deeply modeled terra cotta. Even the great tower was a shaft of solid brick, resting on a mat of concrete, with foundation walls 12 feet thick tapering to 3 feet 6 inches above; the width of the tower at the sidewalk was 38 feet, while at the level of the terra-cotta loggias it was 34 feet 6 inches, giving a degree of entasis [173]. The tower's upper loggias were framed in steel, the terra cotta there being a protective sheathing, with the base of the frame tied into the brick shaft.[95]

Madison Square Garden was meant to be a place of joviality and lightheartedness, and accordingly White chose a light exterior color scheme of buff and yellow brick with buff and brown terra-cotta trim. For the details of the terra cotta, White studied northern Italian examples of the trecento and quattrocento; the saturated ornament is much like that of the Certosa, Pavia, while the street arcade resembles closely the grand cortile of the Ospedale Maggiore, Milan. The tower was unmistakably based on the Moorish Giralda, Seville, Spain, but White elongated and simplified the shaft, and in place of the richly modeled surfaces of the original he substituted a smooth surface broken only by a subtle diaper pattern in the brick.[96] The upper stages of the tower were much closer to the Renaissance additions of 1568 to the Giralda, but again everything was elongated. Atop the original is a weathervane, a rotating figure of Faith *(giraldillo),* which White changed to a figure of Diana, perhaps in an oblique reference to her sometime association with athletics. The hollow copper figure by Saint-Gaudens, the only ideal nude he ever did, is poised on one foot. Initially he and White decided on a height of 18 1/2 feet, but when it was completed, raised, and unveiled in September 1891, they were both dismayed to see that she was much too large. At their own expense, architect and sculptor had the original *Diana* lowered and a smaller figure of 13 feet hoisted in her place in late 1893. After this costly experience, both agreed never to complete another figure before a full-scale model first had been carefully scrutinized in place, a resolve to which they held.[97]

The upper portions of the tower were open to the public and reached by a pair of elevators that extended to the lowest loggia; stairs ascended from there. Above the circular Corinthian colonnade was an observation platform 289 feet above the street, and a higher circular platform, just below the feet of Diana and big enough to hold two people, was 304 feet above the street. Only the New York *World* building at Park Row and Frankfort Street to the south was taller, so that the views from the loggias of the Garden tower were unexcelled.

173. Madison Square Garden, detail of tower.

This much of the tower the public could see, but the middle section was reserved for seven floors of private studios for White and his friends. Here White played host to a select company who attended openings of the shows below. Each of the studios was U-shaped, wrapped around the elevator and stair core. In her memoirs, Evelyn Nesbit described White's "Snuggery," and how she often watched him set to work after the guests had left, piling mounds of crumpled sketches until the morning light broke. The walls were heavily curtained with tapestries, with Oriental divans and Renaissance chairs from Spain or Italy for furniture. Strewn about were bear, tiger, and leopard skins, and everywhere, in the least expected places and often hidden from view, were light bulbs casting a rosy glow. It was, she thought, a scene straight out of the Arabian Nights; "it would take Scheherazade to describe it adequately."[98] At night White would take guests up the winding stairs to the observation platform below *Diana*, where they could reach up and feel the figure turn in the wind. The public function of the tower was a beacon, for during the performances its pinnacles would be atwinkle with light bulbs, and searchlights would sweep across it, so that all New York knew there was something playing at the Garden.

Even before the Garden was finished there was an upwelling of popular acclaim. *Harper's Weekly* ran a series of articles, one of which praised the Garden as "unrivaled as a place for summer entertainments," and observing that those responsible for it "have done much to merit the endorsement of an appreciative public." New York, Clarence Pullen concluded, "can take pride and find pleasure in the New Madison Square Garden." Charles De Kay declared the building "a great gain to the city in every way"; he particularly liked "its walls glimmering pale yellow through the trees of the square, its tower rising in rich yet refined beauty above the tree tops." The incorporation of street arcades [174] and the tower, both embellishments with no compelling utilitarian function, drew special commendation from William A. Coffin, who hoped "the money thus spent to beautify our city will speedily come back to the directors, so that their example may be followed, and the claims of beauty be considered along with those of utility when other enterprises of the sort are projected."[99] Unqualified praise came from Marianna Griswold Van Rensselaer in the *Century* in 1894. The Garden, she wrote, "asserts itself without a rival. Nothing else in all New York has done so much to dignify, adorn, and enliven its neighborhood; nothing else would be so severely missed by all New-Yorkers were ruin to overtake their dearest architectural possession." The genius of the building, she believed, was that it was unforced and spontaneous, that it appeared in answer to a genuine need, "and now we hardly understand how we lived so long without it." She felt confident it was "so big and so beautiful that it will never be removed." Or so she hoped, forewarning that when *Diana* ceased to turn "it will mean that her feet have rusted to her pedestal, that the tower and the Garden have fallen into decay, that the life and laughter of New York have departed."[100]

Despite such praise the Garden had limited influence, for it was truly inimitable; its function was too specialized. The terra cotta, which the *Architectural Review* thought "worthy to be compared with much of the best architecture of the world," did contribute to the shift away from "the dull red and lugubrious chocolate of former years," not only in New York but in such a removed example as the Jewelers Building, Chicago, 1924–26, by Thielbar & Fugard, which is covered in glazed buff terra cotta. The Garden tower may also have influenced somewhat Richard Schmidt's tower of the Montgomery Ward office building, Chicago, 1897–99.[101]

Mrs. Van Rensselaer was convinced the future of the Garden was bright, but it was not; *Diana* did cease to turn. Madison Square Garden was doomed from the moment it was

174. Madison Square Garden,
detail of sidewalk arcade.
Monograph.

conceived, for none of the popular entertainments brought in sufficient revenue to support a building so lavishly equipped. Originally a few shops had been included to bring in some income, but the pressing need for additional stables caused their displacement. The failure of the company's stock on the eve of opening bode ill, and J. P. Morgan and Stanford White were obliged to purchase large blocks of stock to bolster the price. Madison Square Garden lost $18,000 the first year and $16,000 the second, although it did better after that, but except for four or five good years the Garden showed a deficit every season. Few shows brought in enough to cover operating expenses, which ran to $20,000 a month, so the company consistently failed to pay dividends on its stock. Inevitably, in 1908 the Garden was put up for sale and bought by an operating company with the mortgage secured by the New York Life Insurance Company; in 1913 when the operating company failed as well, ownership of the Garden passed to the insurance company, which for several decades attempted to keep the enterprise alive.

Much history was made in Madison Square Garden—the twenty-one-round fight between John L. Sullivan and Jim Corbett, the later fights of Jack Dempsey, the first professional football game in 1902, the first American Automobile Show in 1900, theatrical and musical performances by Sarah Bernhardt, Adelina Patti, and Paderewski, the presidential nominations of Grover Cleveland, William Jennings Bryan, Theodore Roosevelt, William Howard Taft, Woodrow Wilson, and Warren G. Harding. The Democratic Convention of June 1924, however, was the last political gathering in the Garden, which closed in

May 1925. Shortly thereafter demolition started, and when the season opened that fall it was in a new building at Eighth Avenue and 49th Street; but so strong was the identification by now that even several blocks away the new structure, and even subsequently the third amphitheater above Pennsylvania Station, have had transferred to them the name "Madison Square Garden."[102]

SEVERAL important educational buildings were produced during this period, and one of the earliest is of special interest since it did much to initiate the revival of Spanish Colonial architecture as a regional expression in the Southwest. This was the Ramona School for Indian Girls, Santa Fe, New Mexico, established in memory of Mrs. Helen Hunt Jackson, named after one of her memorable fictional characters, and supported largely through the gifts of Katherine Drexel of Philadelphia. When White began work on the U-shaped complex with kitchen and refectory enclosing a court to the rear is not recorded, for once again he donated his services; the surviving drawings are dated November 1887.[103] In general the building combined Richardsonian solidity and references to a generic Spanish Colonial tradition [175]. These allusions were not wholly romantic musings, for White had explored the region in the spring of 1882 while visiting his brother, Richard Mansfield White, a mining engineer working in New Mexico. Stanford wrote back of the unique beauty of the landscape, and in the school he designed five years later he devised what he considered a style of architecture "suited to the history, climate and surroundings of New Mexico," a rather Mediterranean hacienda with low tile roof, porticoes, and projecting vigas.[104]

175. Ramona Industrial School for Indian Girls, Santa Fe, N. M., project, 1887.

This exercise celebrating regional traditions paralleled the firm's efforts to renew the Georgian-Federalist traditions of New England, but on the whole during this period the partners adhered to a broadly interpreted Renaissance classicism for collegiate building, no matter what their location, because of the didactic function. The art gallery at Bowdoin College, Brunswick, Maine, 1891–94, was decidedly Renaissance [176, 177]. Commissioned by Mary and Sophia Walker as a memorial to their uncle, Theophilus W. Walker, it was to house the important Bowdoin College art collection, which had been shunted from place to place around the college for over half a century. Largely the work of McKim, the gallery plan was quite simple: galleries to either side and beyond a central domed rotunda. In the lunette panel of the rotunda opposite the entrance was first projected a mural painted in Rome of *The Art-Idea* by Elihu Vedder, but once this was started additional murals were devised for the remaining three lunette areas, and together the four were to represent allegorically the centers of European art and thought. Thus Vedder's group became *Rome*, flanked by *Venice* by Kenyon Cox, a red-hued group of three, and *Florence* by Abbott Thayer, a brown-toned group of five, in contrast to Vedder's more complex, stylishly linear, pastel-colored composition. The best of the four and the last completed was John La Farge's *Athens,* over the entrance, with contemplative figures in deep glowing colors so much like those of his windows.[105] Because of its artists, the Walker Gallery panels are a more representative cross section of American mural art than the decoration of the Boston Public Library.

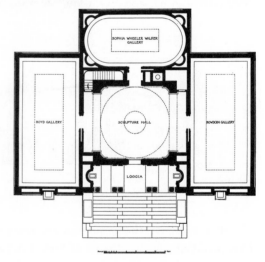

176. Walker Art Gallery, Bowdoin College, Brunswick, Me., 1891–94.
177. Walker Art Gallery, plan. *Monograph.*

　　　Although built of standard red brick with limestone trim, the Walker Gallery is closer to the Italian Renaissance than the English Georgian, especially because of the carefully detailed Palladian entrance loggia. By the turn of the century the firm began to prefer Georgian for collegiate building, having established by then a strong link between that expression and their work at Harvard, but in the early 1890s the rediscovery of Renaissance classicism influenced all their collegiate building, whatever the location. Another example, even more Italianate in the details of its terra cotta, was the Fayerweather Science Hall for Amherst College, Amherst, Massachusetts, 1892–94.[106]

Concurrent with the Walker Gallery the firm worked on a small public library, the Whittemore Memorial Library, Naugatuck, Connecticut, 1891–94 [178], based on the same plan. In these two small buildings, in fact, they established a type to which they returned a number of times for buildings of related function. In the Whittemore Library the domed central rotunda was flanked by a reading room to the left, book stacks to the right, and librarians' offices to the rear. Although it had no murals, its pink granite walls, Ionic portico, Siena marble paneling, fireplace in the rotunda, and coffered gilded inner dome suggest a Boston Public Library in miniature.[107]

178. Howard Whittemore Memorial Library, Naugatuck, Conn., 1891–94.

A much more ambitious project for the Chicago Public Library, if it had materialized, might have redirected the work of the firm by involving them more in architectural developments in Chicago. On October 6, 1891, over a week after the library competition had been announced, the directors of the library wrote McKim, Mead & White, formally urging the firm to enter.[108] Although thirteen sets of drawings were received by the library in January 1892, when the awards were announced later that month and all submissions acknowledged, the firm's name was not listed. A memorial museum for the Grand Army of the Republic required in the building may have led the firm to decline to prepare an entry, in view of the impossibly restricted and complex program. The prize went to their colleagues, Shepley, Rutan & Coolidge of Boston.

DURING the mid-1880s commercial building was down somewhat because of a comparatively mild business recession, but it resumed with vigor about 1886. Just as McKim and White had made important declarations of artistic character in major buildings started in 1887— McKim in the sobriety of his Boston Library and White in the festive gaiety of his Madison Square Garden—so did Mead manifest his interests in the twin New York Life Insurance Company buildings. During the 1880s the company had built a number of regional buildings, both to decentralize operations somewhat and to realize profits from speculative real estate development. To economize, the projected buildings for Kansas City and Omaha were to be duplicates, and for the commission four firms were invited to compete—George B. Post; Babb, Cook & Willard; Van Brunt & Howe; and McKim, Mead & White, which was awarded the job.[109] Built concurrently in 1887–90, both buildings had basements extending down to bedrock, two-story bases of brownstone, with upper walls of brick and terra cotta, 133 feet high at the main cornice and reaching 170 feet in the center tower [179]. The lower floors were occupied by New York Life Insurance Company offices, with rental space above. Except for the crisp quattrocento Italianate details in the terra cotta, the general organization of the upper walls parallels Richardson's Marshall Field Wholesale Store being completed the year these were started. The tripartite division into base, midsection, and

179. New York Life Insurance Building, Omaha, Neb., 1887–90. R.
Sturgis, "The Works of McKim, Mead & White," *Architectural Record*,
Great American Architects Series, 1895.

cornice-crown, as well as the quickened rhythm in the attic level, had already been employed in the office building for the Goelet brothers and in Wells's Russell and Erwin Hotel, but the more innovative wall articulation developed for the American Safe Deposit Building and the Goelet Building was abandoned here in favor of the authority of the Italian Renaissance.

What set this apart from the firm's previous commercial blocks, too, was the immense scale, but despite their great height, the New York Life Insurance buildings were structurally traditional, with load-bearing exterior masonry walls and internal cast-iron columns, for bearing walls had been stipulated by the company in the competition program. In 1887 a metal frame carrying all the loads of a building, including its outer skin, was still quite novel among New York architects and clients. It was not until the following year that Bradford Lee Gilbert began his Tower Building, New York, partially framed in iron and steel; this was at 50 Broadway across from the firm's offices.[110] Although only eleven stories, the Tower Building appeared to be much taller because of its narrow width of 21 1/2 feet. By the time it was completed in 1890, G. B. Post had started his Union Trust Building, 1889–90, and this was quickly followed by his Havemeyer Building, and Price's completely steel-framed American Surety Building, both built between 1891 and 1895, rising fifteen and twenty-two stories respectively. Despite their familiarity with the new technique, the firm had no pressing desire in 1887 to employ what was for New York still an experimental and very costly structural alternative; clients even less so. Moreover the New York City building department was slow to formulate code requirements for the new technology, so that in April 1892, when the firm submitted their entry in the competition for the Home Life Insurance Company Building, New York, they noted they had based their design on conventional bearing-wall construction in the absence of clear code requirements from the city, even though it meant sacrificing a percentage of the ground-floor area.[111] Boston clients were even slower to adopt the metal frame. The massive Second Ames Building, Boston, built by Richardson's successors, Shepley, Rutan & Coolidge, in 1889, has solid walls of granite and sandstone, and only in 1893–94 did C. H. Blackall's steel-framed Carter Building go up—incidentally, it employed paneled walls and terra-cotta trim much like the work of McKim, Mead & White in New York of a decade earlier.

The external expression developed for the New York Life buildings was also employed by the firm in their entry in the competition for the State Street Exchange, Boston, 1887 [180], a solution also similar to the design entered by Babb, Cook & Willard in the Kansas City–Omaha New York Life competition and published just three weeks after the firm's State Street Exchange design appeared.[112] Such strong resemblances in this and in other commercial buildings by the two firms in the late 1880s suggest that Babb's close friendship with the partners was such that many of these business blocks were designed in virtual collaboration. McKim, Mead & White's Judge Building, 1888–90 [181], designed by White for the Goelets, was remarkably like Babb, Cook & Willard's De Vinne Press, 1885, but regularized somewhat by a repeated bay module.[113] Its corner was similarly rounded and richly quoined in modeled terracotta to emphasize the turning of the wall, and at the top was a slight gable formed by an open brick arcade, both features which had appeared in the De Vinne Press.

White's passion for rich surface textures nearly overpowered him in the heavily encrusted office building he designed for George H. Warren, New York, 1890–91, but his Cable Building, New York, 1892–94, was much simpler [182].[114] Built for the Broadway Cable Traction and Seventh Avenue Railway Company, it made use of a straightforward tripartite

180. State Street Exchange,
Boston, Mass., competition entry,
perspective, 1887. *American
Architect and Building News,*
October 22, 1887.

181. Judge Building, New York,
N. Y., 1888–89. *Building,*
March 1, 1890.

division into arcaded base, tall arcaded midsection, and attic story with cornice, but here
the slender arcade piers reflect an inner steel skeleton, perhaps the first use of a complete
metal frame by the firm in a commercial building. Its plan was a variation of the hollow
"square doughnut" then becoming standard for Chicago office blocks, for here superim-

posed glazed corridors divided the huge internal court into two rectangular light wells. Equally restrained but of a different type was the tall, narrow speculative office block on Beekman Street, New York, for Cornelius and William Kissam Vanderbilt, 1891. Also tripartite, its base was especially chaste, but the midsection was sheathed in a more massive-looking brick wall; its L-shaped plan opened onto a light shaft at the rear. For small commercial blocks, such as the Park & Tilford branch store on the Upper West Side of New York, 1892, the firm might employ a pilastrated block, but for larger buildings the tripartite formula was preferred, as in the firm's unsuccessful entry in the Home Life Insurance Company competition, 1892, which had a tall base and an equally tall attic crown. Not nearly as splintered by numerous embellishments, the exterior of this approached the clarity of Bruce Price's Sun Building project of 1890. But by 1892, the towers of Price, and even the more conservative Post, were far better than those designed by McKim, Mead & White.

182. Cable Building, New York, N. Y., 1892–94.

In addition to his Madison Square Garden complex, one other building of the period established White's ability as an organizer of competing functional demands and a master of ornamental embellishment—the New York *Herald* Building, 1890–95. This was designed for James Gordon Bennett, Jr., whose father had made the *Herald* one of the first dailies to achieve mass circulation by treating society gossip as news. To the younger Bennett, who exploited yellow journalism even more, the Second Empire Baroque office his father had built on Park Row was far too staid and the location far too prosaic for a paper of the *Herald's* reputation. He was convinced the only proper location was at the edge of the "tenderloin" district, and he knew exactly what he wanted—a low building rather than a great soaring tower that seemed to swallow up people, as he felt G. B. Post's Renaissance tower for Pulitzer's *World,* then abuilding, would do. On the narrow trapezoid where Broadway crosses Sixth Avenue he wanted an exact duplicate of the Palace of the Doges in Venice! As Bennett and White discussed the project during the period 1890–91, the architect resisted Bennett's design suggestions, for there was already P. B. Wight's adaptation of the Palace of the Doges in his National Academy of Design. Gradually White persuaded Bennett that the smaller and less well-known Palazzo del Consiglio, Verona, could serve just as well as the model. There remained, however, considerable problems in trying to fit all the necessary functions into the trapezoidal site, particularly since Bennett stipulated two stories and no more.

Constructed in 1892–95, the *Herald* Building combined in a crazy-quilt pattern all the necessary facilities, with the major entrance at the narrow 34th Street end leading to a vestibule and stairs up to Mr. Bennett's personal office [183, 184]. The press room, one level below the street, ran through two floors and was visible from the plate glass windows sheltered by the long loggia along Broadway. Although White had derived much from the Palazzo Consiglio, this was not a copy. Said to have been designed by Fra Giocondo in 1476, the Consiglio has one facade, facing the Piazza dei Signori in Verona, and what at first appears to be purely modular is actually a play of subtle irregularities, of adjustments between seemingly identical units unequal in dimension. In contrast, the *Herald* Building is freestanding and much larger, and the bay module, repeated all around the structure, is regularized. Furthermore, White changed the flat polychromatic fresco painting in the upper story of the original to low relief panels of lemon yellow and buff terra cotta. On the roof stood bronze figures by Antonin Carles of bell ringers poised under the watchful eye of Minerva, so although Bennett did not get his Palace of the Doges, a hint at least of Venice was suggested by this group inspired by the bell ringers on Caducci's clock tower on the Piazza di San Marco. There were other decorative touches on which Bennett absolutely insisted, so that bronze owls—Bennett's personal totem—were required along the eaves, their eyes wired with electric lamps.[115]

The *Herald* Building was set down in the midst of the teeming theater district in what was then New York's tenderloin [185]. Here flourished all manner of dance halls and cafés, and any building which hoped to secure its own place in this environment had to be as brazen as its surroundings. The *Herald* Building was a success, for it combined a modicum of order and balance with panache and audacity; it met the tenderloin on its own terms. It was a theatrical spectacle itself, even at night when its owls' eyes blinked down on the square; indeed, its presence was so strong that the square was given the name of the building. Though the building was demolished long ago, after the paper moved from a building which soon grew cramped, the bronze bell ringers were lowered to the vest-pocket square, and to this day, surrounded now by towering skyscrapers, "Stuff" and "Guff" still ring out the hours watched by Minerva, on Herald Square.

As the proposal for the Home Life Insurance Company indicates, the firm had limited success in competitions, and among other important commissions they failed to win were those for the Central Railroad of New Jersey in 1889 and the Erie County Savings Bank in 1890. Despite some setbacks, pivotal commissions were gained and the firm embraced fully

183. *Herald* Building, New York,
N. Y., 1890–95.

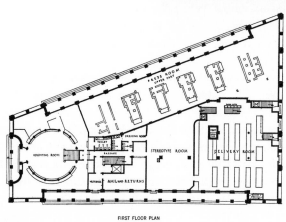

FIRST FLOOR PLAN

184. *Herald* Building, first-floor
plan. *Monograph.*
185. *Herald* Building and the
Herald Square area, c. 1900.

classical principles of design. Always original, even when they referred to specific prototypes, the partners modified and adapted. The dominant horizontality they now championed contrasted with the standards of architectural distinction promoted a decade earlier by
High Victorian Gothic bumptious display and verticality. Following the Boston Public
Library, architecture of status now was distinctive by its sobriety and breadth, and the
character of the American cityscape began to change accordingly. This espousal of classicism also resulted in a change in the palette of building materials, away from the brownstone
and red brick of the "brown decades" toward pink and white granites and marble, glazed
Roman brick and terra cotta. The firm's architecture became filled with color, as one has
but to walk through the Boston Public Library to discover. McKim's own work tended
increasingly toward abstract order, to parallel that of Alberti or Bramante with an assertiveness studied from Roman monuments, while White for the moment was caught up in
exploring the flexibility and freedom possible in the Renaissance idiom; his work was
marked by richly textured surfaces and ornament which increased in extravagance through
the mid-1890s and then began to wane.

The firm had also developed a massive, arcaded commercial block type. Had they
continued in this, working in concert with Babb, Cook & Willard who pursued a similar
course, and had they then incorporated the structural articulation of the paneled bearing wall
they used in the early 1880s as in the American Safe Deposit Building, it is possible that a
New York type of commercial architecture might have come to maturity. But for the
bearing wall, no matter how directly or forthrightly expressed, there was no immediate
future; the metal frame was certain to overtake it through sheer economic determinism;
labor-intensive masonry was becoming ever more expensive while metal frames were
becoming less so.

A GENERATION ago the fact that McKim, Mead & White did not seize upon the development
and rationalization of the metal frame was sufficient to condemn them. Now it seems more
important that their buildings responded so sensitively to their urban settings, that there was
an anticipated interaction between building and environment, as is evident in the Boston
Public Library and the *Herald* Building. Both were shaped by their settings and, in turn,
exerted a strong influence on their surroundings. Both attempted to benefit their place, to
bring a sense of order and purpose. As yet, neither the partners nor any other architects,
for that matter, had any practical experience in what would now be called city planning;
their participation in designing the World's Columbian Exposition was to change this, just
as it affected all those who worked on it, giving rise to the City Beautiful movement and,
ultimately, to modern American city planning. Although the firm was not involved in the
earliest stages of planning the grounds, McKim's subsequent activity, his close association
with Daniel Burnham, and his insistence on the highest standards left their mark on the
architects and artists with whom he worked. Indeed, Burnham was always quick to ac-
knowledge his indebtedness to McKim, his "right hand man," for the artistic success of the
fair.[116]

Plans to celebrate the discovery of the New World by Columbus were first formulated
in 1882, initiating a contest between New York, Chicago, and several other cities for the
honor of being the host. Finally, in the spring of 1890 Chicago was selected by Congress,
and local and national committees were appointed.[117] Once Chicago had been officially

designated, the local committee engaged Frederick Law Olmsted to advise on the best site for the fair and appointed Burnham & Root as consulting architects.[118] Before the end of the year Burnham had been reappointed chief of construction, in charge of all building and landscaping in preparation for the celebration. Because of the delays caused by the initial indecision as to the host city, as well as the great size of the proposed fair, it was impossible to have one architect design all the buildings, so in December 1890 Burnham requested permission to select designers for the most important buildings. Then, to squelch rumors that the fair was to be little more than a bumpkin's cattle show, Burnham adroitly called upon architects from New York, Boston, and Kansas City as well as the principal firms in Chicago.[119] The Eastern architects, including McKim, Mead & White, were at first hesitant to accept Burnham's invitation since construction would take place far from their offices, and according to the organization of the fair they would have no voice over construction supervision, a professional prerogative for which they and the American Institute of Architects had battled for several years. Burnham stressed, however, that they were to have full artistic control over their designs, and by the end of the month all had agreed to participate and to gather in Chicago in January for an initial planning session. At this meeting, which started January 10, the firm was represented by Mead, and although the Eastern architects were especially disheartened at the swampy condition of the proposed site in Jackson Park on the city's south side, they were buoyed up by Burnham's contagious enthusiasm, resolving in their first session that all the buildings be "in harmony with one another."[120]

Root was not present at these opening deliberations, however, for while entertaining the assembled architects on Sunday he caught a cold which rapidly developed into pneumonia; he died the following Thursday while the architects continued to meet. There was nothing to do but continue, and by the end of the week the architects had confirmed the general plan established by Olmsted and Burnham, agreed on a common cornice height and arcade module, and portioned out the buildings among themselves. As Louis Sullivan recalled, "by an amicable agreement each architect was given such building as he preferred, after consultation."[121] By mutual consent it was agreed that the major exhibition buildings around the Court of Honor basin would be classical in expression, for this was the only mode in which all the participants had been trained. Richard Morris Hunt was given the focal Administration Building; Peabody & Stearns chose Machinery Hall; McKim, Mead & White selected the Agriculture Building; George B. Post drew Manufactures and Liberal Arts; Van Brunt & Howe had Electricity. The remaining building on the Court of Honor, Mines and Mining, was selected by S. S. Beman of Chicago. Adler & Sullivan chose the Transportation Building at the edge of the Court of Honor next to the rail lines; Henry Ives Cobb took Fisheries; and William Le Baron Jenney drew the Horticulture Building at the northern end of the lagoon [186, 187].

In February the architects met again in Chicago to present preliminary sketches, and from this meeting onward the firm was represented by McKim. Peabody and McKim jointly requested extending a canal between their buildings, and Saint-Gaudens, who had been brought out to advise on sculptural embellishment, suggested closing off the eastern end of the court with a columnar screen. When the designs were then presented to the group they displayed a remarkable unity except for Post's Manufactures Building with its 400-foot dome that competed with Hunt's domed focal building, but Post interjected that he had only been considering the dome and would modify the design. McKim then presented his

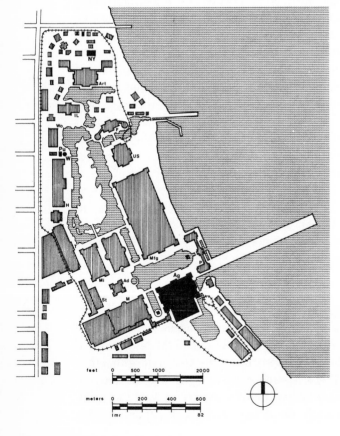

186. World's Columbian
Exposition, Chicago, Ill., Court of
Honor looking west, 1893.
Agriculture Building in left
foreground.

187. Columbian Exposition, plan of the grounds
(L. M. Roth).
Key to symbols:
Ad = Administration Building (Richard Morris
Hunt); Ag = Agriculture Building (McKim, Mead
& White); Art = Art Pavilion (Charles B.
Atwood); E = Electricity Building (Van Brunt &
Howe); F = Fisheries Building (Henry Ives
Cobb); H = Horticulture Building (Jenney &
Mundie); IL = Illinois Pavilion (W. W.
Boyington); M = Machinery Building (Peabody &
Stearns); Mfg = Manufactures and Liberal Arts
Building (George B. Post); Mi = Mines Building
(Solon S. Beaman); NY = New York State
Pavilion (McKim, Mead & White); P = Peristyle
(Charles B. Atwood); Pu = Puck Pavilion
(McKim, Mead & White); St = Passenger Station
(Charles B. Atwood); T = Transportation
Building (Adler & Sullivan); US = United States
Pavilion; W = White Star Line Pavilion (McKim,
Mead & White); Wo = Women's Building
(Sophia G. Hayden).

Agriculture Building, beginning with the comment that the proposed projecting portico would be removed. "Thus was the feeling for unity manifested," noted Charles Moore, "and the willingness of those two men to subordinate their individual ideas in order to produce a single harmonious effect illustrates the spirit which made possible the artistic success of the Fair. Where those two led all others were willing to follow."[122]

As construction started, Burnham had a log cabin built on the island in the lagoon, where he stayed until the fair opened. Gathered around him were many of the artists and architects working on the building, including frequently McKim. It was the warmth and cordiality of their evening discussions concerning the interrelationship between the arts that convinced McKim a similar academy must continue after the fair and resulted in the American Academy in Rome.[123] At dawn each morning Burnham had all the artists driven around the grounds so they could see the day-to-day progress of the whole. Gradually McKim relinquished all other office business to devote himself to the exhibition, acting as Burnham's liaison with most of the other architects. Between February 1891 and the opening of the fair in 1893, McKim made twenty-three trips to Chicago, and after June 1892 he stationed his assistant, Henry Bacon, in Chicago to oversee construction of the firm's four buildings on the grounds.

The largest of the firm's contributions was the Agriculture Building, measuring 300 by 550 feet, on the southern side of the Court of Honor [188].[124] The facade, like those of all the buildings, was a wood and plaster shell around the internal utilitarian steel shed covering the exhibits. In the festive spirit of the fair, McKim's exterior was more Baroque in its plasticity than most of his other work of the period. Atop the center dome, 130 feet high, was the first eighteen-foot version of *Diana*, which had just been removed from the Madison Square Garden; the ornamental sculpture was by Philip Martiny and the pediment group by Mead's brother, Larkin. Because of the extensive sculpture and heavy modeling of the Agriculture Building and virtually all the other pavilions, there was no great problem when at the last minute, as time ran out, the buildings had to be spray painted a uniform white instead of being done in polychrome by hand, as originally planned. All the buildings, that is, except one, for Sullivan had decided to rely on painted ornament rather than modeled

188. Agriculture Building, World's Columbian Exposition, Chicago, Ill., 1891–93. William Henry Jackson, *The White City*.

surfaces (except in his central entrance), and he insisted that the Transportation Building be painted polychrome to break up the large flat surfaces. McKim also made last-minute changes, insisting that an attic story be added to the Agriculture Building to improve its harmony of design, and though there was no money left for construction, the "gentle Jesuit of beauty" got his attic.[125]

The other significant fair building by the firm was the New York State Pavilion, not commissioned until April 1892 due to political delays in New York. Because the pavilion was to be under construction in time for dedication of the grounds on Columbus Day, there was no time for a general design competition and the officials appointed McKim, Mead & White, who were known for sound design and speedy construction. By April 29 their preliminary design was ready and construction started in June. "Primarily intended for the comfort, accommodation and convenience of the people," the building was to house receptions and other public gatherings as well to be "a convenient and comfortable club house for New Yorkers."[126] Since the site was directly opposite Charles Atwood's Fine Art Pavilion, the northernmost principal classical building, McKim was able to use a preferred classical expression in contrast to the highly varied idioms that appeared in neighboring state pavilions. He reasoned that "the broader treatment, the more festal and palatial characteristics and grander proportions of the Italian Renaissance, in which the use of Allegory and Symbol is possible, adapt it most admirably to all requirements." To McKim's mind, the priorities of design for the fair, and perhaps all urban architecture, were order and harmony first and then, within these limits, festivity.[127] With the Villa Medici in Rome as his model (the home of the French Academy there), he achieved the desired balance and grand proportions with provision for extensive sculptural ornament [189]. As in adapting the Veronese Consiglio for the *Herald* Building, many of the features of the Villa Medici were regularized.[128] The ground floor had a large hall, but the principal room was on the second floor, a ballroom covered by a barrel vault and lavishly ornamented in white and gold; this proved to be one of the most popular halls on the grounds and was in almost constant use.[129]

189. New York State Pavilion, World's Columbian Exposition, Chicago, Ill., 1892–93.

A quarter century after the fair, Sullivan viewed the classical resurgence after the fair as a pathological aberration that had swept him and his architecture before it; "the damage wrought by the World's Fair," he prophesied, "will last for a half a century from its date, if not longer."[130] And for half a century after Sullivan's imprecation the opprobrium lingered. Considered as pragmatic or rational structural expressions, the major buildings around the Court of Honor in particular *were* deceptive, their lath and plaster shells attempting in no way to express the internal, light-metal skeletons, even in the case of Sullivan who did nothing to express the wooden frame of his building. And it was true that the historicist allusions of the fair buildings rekindled a romantic eclecticism that lasted until the middle of the twentieth century, but there were distinctly positive aspects to the fair. For the first time in American history, government, business, and the arts collaborated in the creation of what was literally a small city. Circulation was well planned, incorporating a centrally located rail terminal, served by an elevated electric railway that extended around the perimeter of the grounds. Also powered by electricity were the double-belt moving sidewalk on the lake pier and battery-powered launches which plied the canals and lagoons.[131] The fair had its own fire department, police force, telegraph and telephone systems; it was illuminated entirely with incandescent lamps incorporated in the fabric of the buildings, with all wires and cables in underground conduits. When the gates closed at night an army of groundsmen swept through the fair, picking up debris, cleaning, straightening, so that by morning the exhibition was once more bright and fresh. It was a "city" so clean, beautiful, and efficient that visitors from the corners of the nation carried away with them an image of what their own towns and cities might become.[132] Critic Montgomery Schuyler concluded the fair had been a success because of its unity of expression, generosity of scale, and thoroughness of illusion. Without doubt, the whole was superior to any of its parts, but the careful organization of the buildings around broad spaces allowed their order to be perceived and permitted easy circulation, giving the ensemble a cohesiveness, which was reinforced by uniform building height and style. Henry Adams, for all his misgivings about what the fair portended, observed that the Columbian Exposition "was the first expression of American thought as a unity."[133]

Through his important contribution to the exposition McKim gave expression to his belief that the architect's paramount responsibility was to furnish the amenities; they would not happen of their own accord, but once they had been provided the rest would follow.[134] That the fair was beautiful, every visitor granted, and many unfortunately concluded that its beauty came from its classic allusions rather than its planned order. If one result, as Sullivan foresaw, was a classical resurgence, a more progressive influence was the momentum given the fledgling discipline of city planning, inaugurating the City Beautiful movement and leading to the creation of hundreds of public buildings and civic centers. Within a decade many cities had either set up permanent planning departments or had commissioned special plans, so that the ultimate and most positive effect of the fair was to reform the urban consciousness of America, changing the popular notion of urban development from laissez faire to informed and reasoned amelioration.[135]

AT the time Mead and McKim began work on the fair, it must have seemed that the economy, now recovered from the disastrous depression of the 1870s, would move ever upward, but as was equally clear when the fair closed in the autumn of 1893, another depression was well advanced. The years of affluence, for a time, had ended. What had the partners accomplished since they propelled themselves to the front of their profession with the Boston Public Library? They had regularized their work, adhering to a limited but flexible range of classically derived types which, they were now convinced, could serve the range of American building functions while alluding to national building traditions more than a century old. They had taken a clear position in the Boston Public Library that urban life was good and that urban spaces were to be graced by monumental buildings recalling Rome and Renaissance Florence. In that library, in the Bowdoin Gallery, and in the pavilions of the Columbian Exposition they proposed that such monumental urban architecture served its function to the fullest and best when embellished with the work of fellow artists. The new city would be built not in brownstone but marble, in the lighter and more ascendant tones of glazed terra cotta. It would be a good and beautiful place, better than the graft-ridden city of dark Gothic revival spires and Second Empire mansards. It would recall the decorum of the vanished, and perhaps apocryphal, ancestral Colonial city; it would be, as Katherine Lee Bates imagined in 1893 after visiting the "White City," the realization of the "patriots dream/ That sees beyond the years," whose "alabaster cities gleam,/ Undimmed by human tears."

5

ENSEMBLES

1893 — 1899

". . . nowhere in the civilized world are the
practical concerns of life more engrossing . . .
and the love of beauty less diffused."

CHARLES ELIOT NORTON
Educational Review, 1895

". . . the thing of first importance in architecture
is beauty."

CHARLES FOLLEN MCKIM
to his Columbia atelier students, circa 1905

IF the year 1887, with its cluster of important commissions, marked the beginning of an especially happy and prosperous period for the firm, the subsequent period was one filled more with frustration. Exactly when this shift toward the negative began is more difficult to pinpoint, and the partners themselves were probably not aware of it because of the flurry of work connected with the Columbian Exposition. But during 1893–94 the economic climate of the United States changed, and the remainder of the 1890s were lean years; only for a few were these "the gay nineties." McKim, Mead & White, like so many architects, had to weather a long and severe business depression which was well established by the end of 1893; they, however, were fortunate in being well established in the profession by then and were able to survive.[1] Except for this seven-year interval, McKim, Mead & White enjoyed uncommon prosperity, partly because of the chemistry of their combined personalities, and partly because their architecture had an increasingly popular appeal, but also because they appeared at a most propitious time, their long practice spanning the last two periods of economic expansion before enactment of the graduated federal income tax in 1913. Just as the young firm began their experiments in shingles, the national economy emerged from the deep depression of the 1870s, and the economic upsurge of the first years of the twentieth century was more vigorous, in some ways, than that of the 1880s. The intervening seven years, on the contrary, were rather grim. Statistically, the picture is not so bleak, for the firm received 168 commissions, the dollar amount value of which was $23,385,820, during a time when building costs actually dropped slightly from what they had been during the

1880s. In their correspondence, however, the partners present a different picture. McKim, for instance, complained to Mead in mid-1894 that the firm needed "about a dozen large jobs to keep out of the poor-house."

Repeatedly the partners turned away promising young men who wished to enter the office for the experience; in fact, they were forced to lay off many experienced assistants who had been in the office for several years, as McKim informed Montgomery Pickett, who wrote asking for work in late 1893. The strain of the times sufficiently disquieted those kept on, to prompt them to draw up a petition, sometime during 1896, complaining of the lack of ventilation in the drafting room.[2] At the height of their office activity in 1892, when drawings were being done for the private work as well as the Columbian Exposition buildings, the firm employed perhaps as many as 120 people, but by 1895 this number had dropped to less than 80, and it dwindled still further with the outbreak of the Spanish-American War. Because of these reductions a young English architect was prevented from seeing how the office functioned at close hand. Banister Fletcher, recipient of the Godwin Bursary Prize, had stopped at the office in 1893, hoping to see McKim who then happened to be conferring with a client. McKim later wrote Fletcher saying that although he thought the idea of studying American architectural practice a good one, he regretted being unable to add to the office staff at that time. To compensate, he offered to write letters of introduction to his colleagues Peabody and Post.[3] As this indicates, opinion among the English regarding the firm's work was high.

Operations within the office were further complicated by the second relocation in the spring of 1894, to the Mohawk Building on Fifth Avenue. Shortly thereafter, the partners offered to pay their principal assistants, Kendall, Richardson, and Bacon, a percentage of the profits rather than a fixed salary, an offer Bacon turned down to his later regret.[4]

Part of the firm's frustration during the late 1890s was their poor record in competitions. They had often refused outright to participate because winning architects did not supervise construction or because the fee stipulated was below the five percent level advocated by the American Institute of Architects. McKim wrote admonishingly to former assistant Thomas Kellogg, who was submitting a design in the New York City Hall Annex competition for which the fee was three and one-half percent, reminding him that H. H. Richardson had instructed *his* pupils, "never under-estimate your own services; your client is going to estimate you at exactly your estimate of yourself."[5] To rectify this the partners supported passage of the Tarsney Act in February 1893, which provided for (but did not require) competitions for federal buildings. Since the law was not put into effect until 1897, when President McKinley took office, there was no immediate benefit. The firm did enter one of the first competitions under the aegis of the Tarsney Act in September 1897, for a new immigration station on Ellis Island in New York harbor, but they lost to a new firm formed by former assistants in the office, Boring & Tilton.[6] Indeed, the partners encouraged their staff to enter properly organized competitions and to use office facilities after hours; one example is the entry by Teunis Van der Bent and Albert Ross in the Baltimore Courthouse competition of 1894, in which they placed fifth in a field of 73 entrants with their sober but well-modulated classical design.[7]

Except for contests under the provisions of the Tarsney Act, conditions specified in almost all prestigious competitions had become so objectionable that in early 1897 McKim, Mead & White joined with a number of prominent architects, including G. B. Post, Bruce Price, Carrère & Hastings, and Babb, Cook & Willard, in drawing up a list of the conditions under which they would agree to compete: if a group of architects was invited, then any architect later added to the list had to be approved by those already agreed to compete; professional consultant architects were to be engaged to draw up the competition program; competitors were to be paid a fee to cover their expenses in preparing their entries; and the winner was to be paid the standard five percent fee and to supervise construction.[8]

Presumably it was because of the threat to professional prerogatives that White refused to contribute to a publishing experiment undertaken by Edward Bok in 1895. As editor of the *Ladies' Home Journal,* the popular magazine with the largest circulation at that time, Bok wished to improve the general quality of middle-class housing by publishing a series of house plans by prominent professional architects, and White was one of scores of designers canvassed. Although there was to be an honorarium, there would be no fee based on construction, since plans were to be sold to readers. Exactly when Bok contacted White is not clear, but later, when the architect saw the published results by such architects as Ralph Adams Cram, Wilson Eyre, and Bruce Price, he wrote Bok he "would not only make plans" but "would waive any fee for them in retribution for my early mistake."[9]

White was also busy selecting and designing frames for his painter friends such as Thomas W. Dewing, earning the grateful thanks of painter and patron alike. As the economy recovered toward the end of the decade, White stepped up his forays to Europe in search of art work and furniture to be used in his interior decorating. A decade earlier, as this aspect of White's work began to flourish, he encountered difficulty trying to get some of the items past customs, and he contacted Charles C. Beaman, a client and prominent lawyer, for assistance:

> I brought over some copies of antique statuettes. You know the character of work that I do with St. Gaudens, sculpture and architecture together, and I use these as models in my work. I entered these as "tools of trade" and the Treasury Department refuses to allow them . . . and proposes to charge me 55% duty.
>
> Now this is a trivial matter but at the same time it contains the kernel of the business. . . . Will you kindly give me your advice.[10]

McKim also was making a contribution to the fledgling profession of interior decorating, for he had received from Edith Wharton in 1897 a manuscript of her *Decoration of Houses,* with a request for comments. "I would not have troubled you about the matter at all," she apologized, "if I had not fancied from some talk we have had together that you felt that there were things which needed saying on this very subject & had I not hoped that, if Mr. Codman & I couldn't say them in the right way, we might, in a slight degree, co-operate with the work you are doing in your Roman academy."[11] McKim was warmly supportive in his response, although he differed on a few minor points. He advised that sixteenth-century Italian architecture needed to be discussed in preference to palaces and hunting lodges, but concerning her insistence that the interior of a house should have classic proportions, harmonious treatment from room to room, and overall restraint, he was in total agreement. Such were the very principles he had been taught at the École, he wrote. The aim there was to capture "the spirit of a style rather than its literal delineation," aiming at "a modern style based on classic composition." Hence there was no need to adhere slavishly to the letter of tradition, he advised her, but rather,

> by conscientious study of the best examples of classic periods, including those of antiquity, it is possible to conceive of a perfect result suggestive of a particular period, if you please, but inspired by the study of them all.[12]

Because of the general economic depression, those commissions which relied most directly on philanthropy fell off most sharply. Most notably, there were no churches started by the firm during these seven years, and construction of the firm's Brooklyn Museum was postponed for several years. Furthermore, the number of collaborative sculptural works was dramatically reduced, and it was not until 1895 with the first stirrings of economic recovery that White and Saint-Gaudens began new projects, beginning with White's first studies for the architectural frame of the Phillips Brooks Memorial in 1895. The sculptor had been at work on the figural group for about two years, and though contracts were signed by both sculptor and architect for completion of the memorial during 1897, this was yet another of the sculptor's greatly protracted endeavors, and the finished work was not unveiled until 1910 when both creators were dead.[13] Also in 1895 White was asked to persuade Saint-Gaudens to accept the proffered commission for an equestrian monument to General Henry W. Slocum in Brooklyn, but he demurred and eventually the commission went to his former assistant, Frederick MacMonnies, with a base designed by White; this ensemble was executed in 1903–05. Two years later, in 1897, White was asked to advise on the placement of MacMonnies's Woodward statue in front of the Brooklyn Museum, but these activities were far from the expansive collaboration White had enjoyed during the 1880s. Two bases were designed for equestrian statues during the nineties, however, White's low, spreading base for Saint-Gaudens's *General Logan,* Chicago, 1894–97, and McKim's tall base for the *George Washington* by Daniel Chester French, with horse by Edward C. Potter. McKim worked hurriedly on the base in 1899, and the completed statue was unveiled on the Place d'Iena, Paris, France, in 1900.[14]

WHAT greatly aided the firm in surviving these years of retrenchment was a series of commissions for planned building groups, especially college campuses, and in these projects the firm applied the lessons they had abstracted from working on the Columbian Exposition —careful balance between building masses and open spaces, hierarchical composition, focus, and coherence and harmony in expression.

One of the striking features of the exposition had been its carefully designed and tended grounds, a demonstration that openings between buildings were not simply leftover spaces but environmental areas equally deserving of artistic attention. Even as the exposition was being prepared for opening early in 1893, a group of concerned architects and civic leaders in Boston began organizing a competition for the architectural finishing of Copley Square, then an inchoate expanse ringed by an increasingly distinguished group of buildings, most recently McKim's library then under construction. McKim worked closely with William R. Richards and C. Howard Walker and the Boston Society of Architects which sponsored the competition. Their program was printed in late February and published in the *American Architect* the next month, but then the matter languished. When McKim, Walker, and Frederick O. Prince launched the campaign again in 1896, once more with the support of the Boston Society of Architects, it again foundered because of the depressed economy. Thus, sadly, the city lost an opportunity to complete the square in a manner consonant with its principal framing buildings, perhaps even to have had it done by McKim, Mead & White, who prepared drawings in 1893 and 1896, and so the architectural treatment of Copley Square was delayed for more than seventy years.[15] Perhaps a bit more sanguine after this, McKim declined an invitation from the mayor in 1898 to sit on a beautification committee for New York City.[16]

Far more fruitful were the partners' efforts on behalf of two universities in New York City, plans for which were prepared by the firm and carried out almost simultaneously, but starting by a matter of months with White's plan for the new campus of New York University on Fordham Heights in the Bronx. As the area around the original Washington Square building of New York University (then the University of the City of New York) became less residential and more commercial toward the close of the century, and as the school grew in complexity and enrollment, it became clear, by the end of the 1880s, that some portion of the school should be moved northward. Henry M. MacCracken, then vice-chancellor, made this his special project and in November 1890 reported to the governing council of the university that the undergraduate portion of the school should be moved closer to the residential area, to the vicinity of 42nd Street, leaving the law, education, and graduate schools at Washington Square. In February 1891, when this idea was formally presented to supporters of the school, the site indicated for the new University College, as it came to be called, was now well to the north in the vicinity of 150th Street. But it was not until MacCracken happened to discover that the 40-acre H. W. T. Mali estate on Fordham Heights overlooking the Harlem River was for sale, that a definite site presented itself. From the moment the university acquired the first section of the Mali property in May 1891, MacCracken began to imagine a group of buildings on the edge of that bluff, so that this campus plan, more than any of the others by the firm, perhaps, is stamped by the high-mindedness and moral purpose of the university president.[17]

Henry Mitchell MacCracken (1840–1918) had been in charge of several small schools in his native Ohio after receiving his baccalaureate, but at the age of twenty-one he began the study of theology, finishing with a year at the Princeton Theological Seminary. Following ordination he served several churches, interrupted by a period of study of philosophy at the universities of Tübingen and Berlin, Germany. He then saw that his calling lay in education, and in 1881 was appointed chancellor of the Western University of Pennsylvania, and three years later was appointed professor of philosophy at New York University. Within a year he was made vice-chancellor, and he then began a program of transforming the institution, building up the graduate school and the other professional programs. Since it had been MacCracken who so effectively initiated the northern move, as soon as the first portion of the Mali property had been acquired, Chancellor John Hall resigned and MacCracken was immediately named to fill the position.[18]

Perhaps MacCracken had been in contact with White already as to plans for the proposed uptown University College even before the site had been acquired (White's father was a distinguished alumnus and White himself had been given an honorary degree by the school in 1881). On January 2, 1892, MacCracken wrote White to reschedule a trip to inspect "the heights beyond the Harlem," and three days later another letter asked White to prepare sketches "of the group of buildings" on the new site.[19] Virtual appointment as the university's architect came from MacCracken on January 22, 1892:

> I solicit such aid in connection with our present movement as you can give, and especially in the way of professional suggestions. At this juncture, I should be very glad to have your judgement in respect to the architecture of our proposed University College buildings on "University Heights," as well as of the proposed university building on Washington Square.[20]

Three days later White responded with a proposal, as requested, for removing the original Town & Davis Gothic Revival building of 1832–37 on Washington Square, stone by stone, to the new site. The interior would then be completely rebuilt to accommodate a chapel, museum, and library; the existing Mali mansion would be converted for classroom use.[21]

There the matter rested as the university endeavored to find funds. A larger question had arisen, in any case, that required investigation. During 1890 Columbia University, faced with similar restrictions on expansion at their location at Madison Avenue and 49th Street, also had begun looking northward and in April 1892 had purchased a large parcel on the Upper West Side of Manhattan. Even before the sale had been made final, potential donors, perceiving they would soon be approached for substantial gifts to both schools, called for a merger or federation of the two institutions. Consequently both schools quietly pursued their own goals during 1892–93 while examining proposals and counterproposals for some sort of "union."[22] There seems to have been a tacit understanding, however, that both institutions should proceed with their respective relocations, since any "merger" was most likely to take place at the administrative level, if at all. So, New York University obtained estimates on the cost of moving the Town & Davis building and Columbia appointed a trio of architects to study its new site. Within weeks of the inevitable collapse of the merger negotiations, in November 1893, both schools had taken decisive steps: Columbia appointed McKim, Mead & White as their campus architects, and New York University, upon discovering that the cost of moving the old building was equivalent to building four or five new buildings, had White prepare sketches for a new campus.

White had prepared alternative schemes, for in notifying White that reconstructing the old building would cost too much, MacCracken wrote they could use the "square plan," but with the change of shifting the science laboratories to the south side and dormitories on the north, for electric trolleys, likely to be built along Sedgwick Avenue, would otherwise disturb scientific experiments.[23] A week later MacCracken informed White, "our thought about the central building is that it would be as you suggest, Library, Chapel, Museum, and nothing beside except perhaps the administrative offices. On the north of it, balancing the language building we would expect to have another recitation hall in the future, the Philosophy Building."[24] By February 1894 the general character of the main cluster of buildings had been established: a domed central block flanked by two classroom buildings, all to be built of limestone and buff-yellow brick [190]. Concerning the design, MacCracken requested colored presentation drawings on February 28, 1894, allowing White to restore the connecting colonnades between the buildings he desired, and reassuring the architect:

> We understand of course, that the scheme will depend largely for effect upon the Central Building and that the other buildings will depend on dignity of line and of proportion for their effects. . . .
>   My impression is that after we have chosen our Plan, that if we have a fairly large elevation made of the Central Chapel and Library building, that there are two or three people who are thinking of making large subscriptions, one of whom will very probably give us the building. This will give them the right to name it, and with its lofty dome, will make a Memorial that will be seen for miles.[25]

In April, following approval of the firm's drawings for the Hall of Languages, Norcross Brothers started construction, aiming at completion in time for the start of the fall term when operations could be transferred to the new campus. In the autumn, as this was finished, final drawings were prepared by the firm for the library, for MacCracken had indeed found

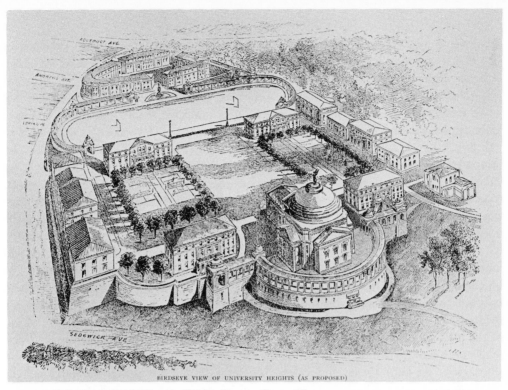

BIRDSEYE VIEW OF UNIVERSITY HEIGHTS (AS PROPOSED)

190. New York University, University Heights Campus, Bronx, New
York, N. Y., planned 1892–94. From J. L. Chamberlain, ed., *A History of
New York University*, Boston, 1901.

191. Gould Dormitory, New York University, built 1896–97. *American
Architect and Building News*, September 14, 1901.

his donor. Since mid-1892 he had received promises of large donations from railroad financier Jay Gould, promises which faded with Gould's death in December, but in May 1895 Mac-Cracken was pleased to announce that the daughter, Helen Miller Gould Shepard, had expressed the wish to continue what her father had begun. Then, when all seemed settled as to the library, the university library committee informed MacCracken they desired a competition, inviting R. M. Hunt, G. B. Post, and Henry J. Hardenbergh, in addition to the firm.[26] Knowing the background of this invitation, however, the other architects demurred, and by mid-June MacCracken was asking White to push the library back as far as possible so as not to project beyond the front of the Hall of Languages; the result was an immense substructure beyond the base of the library and into this it was decided to place the museum. Ground for the Gould Library was broken on October 19, 1895, when the campus grounds were formally dedicated.[27]

Mrs. Shepard had also given funds for a dormitory, started early in 1896, which was intended to be the first in a cluster of five around a circular dining hall at the east edge of the campus [191]. During the period 1895–97 a dozen or more plan arrangements were studied in detail for future buildings and for the final placement of the athletic field, uniting the western academic complex with the College Close of dormitories at the east end.[28] Meanwhile MacCracken continued to suggest building alignments and changes in grade levels while the executive committee considered the master plan proposals, admitting to White in April 1897, "the more I study the schemes, the more I incline to change my mind in favor of the central scheme" [192].[29] There was still no decision concerning the master plan, however, even when the colonnade around the Gould Library was finished in 1901.

When Columbia University and New York University first began looking in a northerly direction, the areas into which they moved were still largely suburban neighborhoods; the steep banks above the Harlem River and Fordham Heights were sparsely settled, and stands of wood were still prevalent. It had been the residential atmosphere that attracted MacCracken, for he believed faculty could now live close to the new campus. The Mali estate occupied one of the highest points of the bluff above the Harlem River, and from there one could see through the Harlem valley to the Hudson and across to the New Jersey Palisades. At the point where the ground began to drop, White placed the academic building cluster. The focus of the entire ensemble was the centrally planned library with a saucer dome of Guastavino tile [193, 194].[30] On the upper level was the reading room, enclosed by a circular colonnade of sixteen highly polished green Connemara marble columns; beyond the colonnade on the main floor and on the mezzanines above, were the book stacks and eighteen seminar rooms, one for each of the departments of instruction. Below the reading room, in the base, was an auditorium seating six hundred. Around the auditorium ran the semicircular museum, lit by ranks of skylights, and a passageway linking the Hall of Languages, the Library, and the projected Hall of Philosophy to the north.

If, as it now appears, White had developed his centralized scheme with its domed library early in 1894 before McKim had yet settled his design for Columbia, what might he have considered as possible references or models? Clearly he was not interested in medieval cloisters as was Henry Ives Cobb, then beginning work on the new University of Chicago, but rather he and McKim both had Jefferson's classical University of Virginia much on their minds. Perhaps, too, White recalled the general organization of Joseph Jacques Ramée's Union College, Schenectady, New York, 1812. As shown in several mid-nineteenth-century lithographs based on Ramée's original drawings, a central rotunda was to be flanked by

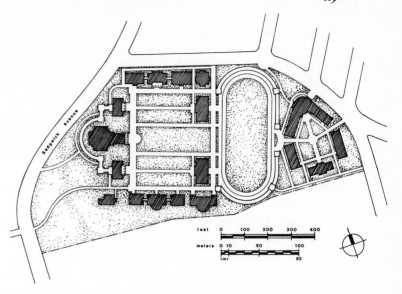

192. New York University,
comprehensive scheme for
University Heights campus, 1894.

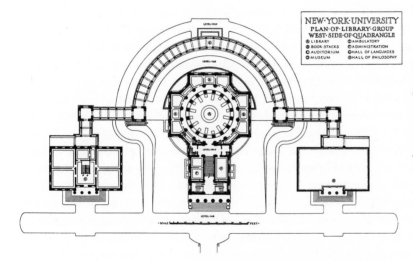

193. New York
University, plan of
Gould Library, Hall of
Languages, Hall of
Fame, and proposed
Hall of Philosophy.
Monograph.

194. Gould Library, built
1896–1903, and Hall of Fame, built
1900–1901.

rectangular blocks, all facing a front court.[31] Nor could White have avoided being influenced in some way by the various sources being studied by McKim's assistants in their development of the Low Library for Columbia during 1894.

White had wanted to connect the library and its flanking buildings with a colonnade on the podium as early as 1894, but the idea had been rejected by the executive committee; by 1896 he had been able to reintroduce it in the drawings. It was clearly needed on artistic grounds, as a means of softening the edge of the massive substructure, but what functional purpose might it serve sufficient to interest a donor? In 1900 it occurred to MacCracken that it might house a Hall of Fame commemorating Americans who had made significant contributions in statesmanship, the law, science, literature, and the arts, and again he was able to persuade Mrs. Shepard to finance the finishing touch to the library. In 1901, with the completion of the colonnade, the basis of the New York University plan had been established, and though there was much left unconstructed, White was never again to build there. From this windswept aerie glimpses of the river below and, on clear days, a bit of the Palisades to the west still can be seen; although the pastoral landscape has changed drastically since the turn of the century, the library of New York University and its encircling diadem is still a splendidly heroic response to what was once an equally splendid landscape.[32]

There was in White's focused academic cluster for New York University something of the centripetal character of Hunt's domed Administration Building in the Court of Honor at the Columbian Exposition. There was a similar influence on the focus of McKim's plan for Columbia University. As had New York University, Columbia College (as it then was) faced the problem of construction around its midtown campus at Madison Avenue and 49th Street, much of which had only recently been built from designs by Charles C. Haight. During the late 1880s the Columbia trustees considered several options, looking closely at the area then occupied by the Bloomingdale Asylum far to the north at Broadway and 116th Street. At almost the precise moment that New York University bought the first section of the Mali estate, the Columbia trustees formed a committee to examine the ramifications of "a change in the site of the College," and in November 1891 they decided in favor of rebuilding on the Bloomingdale Asylum site. One of the questions with which they wrestled was whether to move only the undergraduate division to "the country," but the decision in the end was to relocate everything, for of paramount importance was their concept of an urban university with all its parts physically united.[33] In April 1892, the asylum property was purchased, and the next month, even while negotiations with New York University were in progress, President Seth Low of Columbia invited three architects to study the site and devise a general scheme for a new campus. The members of this trio were Richard Morris Hunt, Charles C. Haight (architect of many of the buildings then occupied by the college), and Charles F. McKim; they had the assistance of William R. Ware, who had left M.I.T. to set up a school of architecture at Columbia in 1881.

The new Columbia site, on what became known as Morningside Heights, was a broad rectangle between Broadway and Amsterdam Avenue, from 120th Street down to the ungraded right-of-way for 116th Street, rising to a prominence at the center. A survey had been prepared in January, and from this topographical models were prepared for the committee to study during the winter of 1892–93; it was at this time that, at the original trio's request, Frederick Law Olmsted was added to the committee. As early as February 1893 a formal classical scheme suggested itself to McKim, for he wrote to Olmsted of the rise at the center of the site as "the crowning feature of the island," and because of the "commanding view . . . of the Palisades to the Narrows and over both rivers, no problem could be more admirably suited to monumental treatment."[34] McKim also asked Olmsted to stop by the McKim, Mead & White office to see their model, in the hope of finding a solution to a rift that was gradually opening among the members of the committee. To get the fullest use of the site, McKim was proposing a bilevel podium on which all the Columbia buildings would stand, an arrangement similar to but more extensive than White's podium for New York University. Hunt and Haight strongly disagreed. Hunt had devised a rather French plan comprised of a number of connected pavilions enclosing numerous small courts; his plan had its principal entrance on Broadway facing the Hudson. Haight had developed a Gothic plan with its entrance on Amsterdam Avenue looking east. McKim felt strongly that the campus should face south, toward the heart of the city, to have better sunlight and less winter exposure. Of the three consultants, he particularly stressed what he called the "municipal" or urban character of the problem and the consequent need for a formal plan: he specifically urged using "pure Classic forms . . . embodying the principles of the early Renaissance masters" in order to achieve "unity at all points . . . in the simplest and most monumental way."[35] Ware was concerned as to the expense of McKim's terraces and made estimates of the cost of all three proposals, causing McKim to write Olmsted that although he understood the need for economy,

> it strikes me that [Ware's] method of getting at the merits of each composition by *arithmetic* is just a little ludicrous, as when you built the great terrace of the Capitol, in order to accomplish a distinct purpose, you would have immediately rejected any plan which might have been presented at less cost as unwisely economical if it failed to accomplish this.[36]

Through the spring and summer the committee continued to meet, while Ware and Olmsted tried to fabricate a composite plan, which prompted McKim to ask Hunt what he thought "of 'Uncle William' Ware's block plan based, as stated in his report, upon the plums offered in yours, Haight's and ours. It seems to me a pudding—and a very indigestible one indeed."[37]

By November 1893, when it was apparent that the negotiations with New York University would produce no good result, the Trustees' Committee on Buildings and Grounds drew up its report, which coincided with McKim's views, recommending formation of two terraces with the primary campus entrance on the south at 116th Street. The focal element was to be the library, surrounded by various classroom and dormitory buildings which, though separate, were to be unified in character and built over a period of time as need arose. After comparing the relative merits of both the Gothic and Renaissance styles, the committee recommended Renaissance and the appointment of McKim, Mead & White as university architects.[38] Accordingly, on December 4 President Low wrote the firm offering the appointment, and the formal contract was signed two weeks later on December 28, 1893.[39]

During the winter and early spring of 1894 the firm worked on the Columbia plans, and by the middle of April a scheme had been approved by the trustees. This proposed a rectangular library block at the center, flanked by symmetrical groups of buildings, with a large student union to the rear [195]. The library, however, was the subject of continued and intensive study, for it was not sufficiently distinct from the other buildings to hold the center. Several models were constructed in search of a solution, when finally, in July, McKim had good news for Mead, then in Europe:

Dear Dummy:

... Columbia had passed their scheme before you went, since when we have been working on the Library and the two Faculty buildings. The scheme for the Library has undergone many changes and at one time I felt as sick of it as you did of [the Twombly estate near Morristown, New Jersey], but last week we struck it and are now awaiting official notice to commence working drawings which Mr. Low expects to send next week.[40]

Much of the work had been done by William Mitchell Kendall and Austin W. Lord; and Egerton Swartwout, then a draftsman working under Kendall and Lord, recalled they first studied Gibbs's Radcliffe Camera, Oxford, which they modified from a circular plan to an octagonal plan and finally to a cruciform plan [197]. It was during this last phase that Swartwout himself suggested moving the stairs to the reentrant corners, forming the angled intersections suggestive of the work of C.-N. Ledoux, as in his Porte d'Ivry, although it is most unlikely they would have known this building.[41] McKim and White were due to sail for Europe as well, but the pressure of the Columbia work forced McKim to postpone his departure, prompting a note of regret to White, July 24, 1894, on the back of which was lightly sketched in soft pencil the outline plan and front elevation of Low Library almost exactly as built.[42]

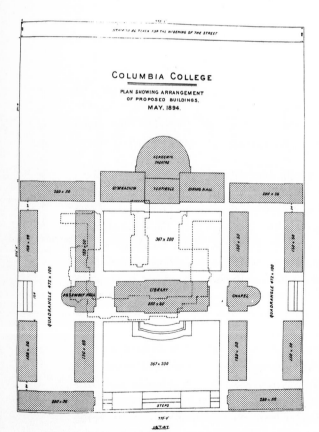

195. Columbia University, Morningside Campus, New York, N. Y., proposed plan, dated May 1894. (Shading added.)

196. Columbia University, final plan, 1894. *Monograph,* detail.

In using a domed library, based indirectly on the Roman Pantheon, McKim may well have had in mind the library Rotunda by Jefferson for the University of Virginia, but for the overall arrangement and character of the ensemble he was also looking at contemporary French work, especially Nénot's new campus for the Sorbonne begun in 1885.[43] Instead of Jefferson's parallel ranks of pavilions, McKim devised two clusters of seven buildings flanking the library, with the large student union behind it [196]. On the east-west axis through the library were small centrally planned buildings (an assembly hall and the chapel) which divided the flanking groups and helped define small internal courts.

Once the library design was settled in November 1894, preparation of working drawings for it and the adjoining buildings progressed rapidly, so that bids were taken and ground broken June 18, 1895. Initial building activity centered on the library and its south court terracing, and in 1896 construction started on the Engineering Building and Havemeyer Hall in the northeast corner and on University Hall (the union) but this never progressed beyond the ground floor. Except for University Hall, all the buildings in this first phase of construction were completed by 1898 [198].[44] It should be noted, parenthetically, that the university did not yet own the lower ground south of 116th Street, so that the original plan was only for the nearly square area to the north; the southern parcel was not acquired until 1902, and the firm planned the south campus in 1903.

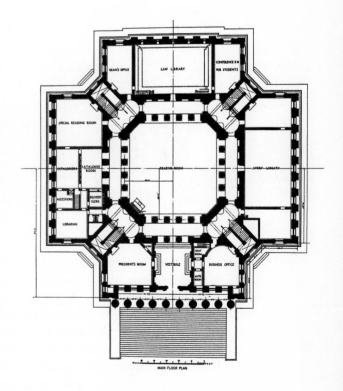

197. Low Library, Columbia University, plan.
Monograph.

Why it took McKim so long to achieve the final form of the Columbia Library, when White had already arrived at his centralized Gould Library for New York University, is not clear, but once the final plan was arrived at, like a keystone, the library held the rest of the ensemble together. Its focal importance was emphasized by its being constructed

198. ABOVE. Columbia University, aerial photograph of completed construction, 1898. *American Architect and Building News*, November 5, 1898.

199. Low Library and South Court approach.

entirely in limestone, in contrast to the surrounding brick blocks with limestone trim; it was clearly, as McKim wrote, the "common laboratory and work shop of the college."[45] Although not purely circular, the reading room was similar to White's, even having concentric circular work tables with individual reading lamps. These worked well with the soft even light admitted through the four great lunettes in the octagonal drum, but supplementary illumination was required at night. McKim wanted this as diffused as the reflected daylight, and after much experimentation a sphere was suspended from the dome, off which eight spotlight beams were reflected. Pleased with the result, McKim then used indirect lighting in the gymnasium and swimming pool, where glare was a problem.[46] If McKim had envisioned forming the library dome in Guastavino tile, the early drawings specified a steel frame covered with limestone plaques. Norcross then suggested a solid concrete shell, but the onset of cold weather in November 1895, as construction proceeded, forced the substitution of a brick outer dome with an inner metal lath and plaster shell.[47]

Unlike the University of Virginia, Ramée's Union College, or even White's New York University, the Columbia campus from the start was viewed by McKim as urban in character [199]. He insisted that the entrance court and its terraces be paved and formally landscaped, with retaining walls, balustrades, and other architectural elements. When the trustees had first objected to the size and starkness of the court in the early designs, McKim explained it was a vestibule, "a kind of ATRIUM upon whose correct expression the Library and adjoining buildings absolutely depend. It should be formal and it should be paved, in our opinion, and not carpeted any more with grass than with rugs. . . . The problem is not suburban in any sense, but distinctly municipal."[48] This formal approach, so in contrast to Jefferson's Lawn at Charlottesville, was even refined by an optical correction inspired by the west approach to the Parthenon. There, the slight curvature of the temple and its stereobate was extended to the western stairs cut into the rock of the Acropolis, and at Columbia the broad steps leading to the library from 116th Street similarly had a slight rise at the center to counter any visual sensation they might be sagging.[49]

The high regard in which McKim and White both held Jefferson as an architect, because of his intelligence and erudite classical allusions, and the importance of his University of Virginia as one of the first American colleges whose buildings and spaces were consciously *planned,* would have made the library Rotunda there a particularly important model for the libraries they were planning in 1893–95. It was one of those remarkable coincidences of history that at the very moment both their libraries were underway the firm should be engaged to rebuild Jefferson's Rotunda. For in October 1895, the prototype for the central buildings of both New York University and Columbia University was almost completely destroyed by fire. Designed by Jefferson in 1817, the Rotunda had been expanded to the rear by his protégé, Robert Mills, in 1851 when the pressing need for more classrooms required construction of "the annex."[50] In time even this proved too small, and during 1893–95 the Rector and Board of Visitors (comparable to president and trustees) discussed what was needed and where new buildings might be situated. Then, early in the morning of October 27, 1895, a fire started in the far corner of the annex. Students and townspeople tried to arrest the fire and in vain dynamited the connection to the Rotunda, but the fire leaped the gap and before the afternoon was over had consumed the wooden dome and gutted the interior.

A building committee was quickly formed, and it engaged Harry P. McDonald, an architect from Louisville, Kentucky, who happened to be supervising a job in Charlottesville at the time of the fire, to rebuild the roofs of the front terraces and to prepare the gutted Rotunda for the winter. Meanwhile, on October 31 the faculty prepared a comprehensive assessment of the university's needs and suggested some priorities. They recommended to the Visitors that the ruins of the annex be removed, the ground leveled, and an esplanade laid out. The Rotunda should be rebuilt externally following the lines created by Jefferson as closely as possible, but with the addition of a portico on the north face echoing that on the south facing the Lawn. As to the treatment of the interior, the faculty was unclear whether it should be restored exactly as it had been built under Jefferson's direction with two floors, or opened up with only one floor. They were certain, however, that the architect should give "especial attention to the problems of *heating, lighting,* and *ventilation,* which in the old building were inadequately solved." To replace the destroyed facilities, a new classroom building was to be constructed, with a large central lecture room, with additional buildings to house physics laboratories and engineering, but the boilers supplying power to these were to be in a separate building for fire safety. Indeed, fireproof construction was a requirement, particularly in the rebuilt Rotunda. A new law building was to be designed by the architect, and a general plan devised indicating where future buildings might be situated. The recommendations concluded with concern expressed for the style and quality of the new buildings:

> The faculty is deeply impressed with the propriety of following in these buildings classical types of design and of locating them so as to create a harmonious combination with the Jeffersonian group. As we examine the additions made to this system by Jefferson's successors, we are forced to confess with a certain shame, that not one of them has added in the least degree to the harmony and beauty and magnificence of the original composition. We recommend, therefore, that the Visitors select as their professional advisor, a man not of local repute only but of broad and national consideration, that he be instructed to consider in his designs not merely the convenience and elegance of the single structure, but its effect as a member of our general architectural system, and that he submit to your Board a comprehensive scheme which shall embody his advice on the location not only of the buildings recommended in this report but also of such additional dormitories, hospital buildings, official quarters and so on as the Visitors may contemplate. The study of our grounds as a problem of landscape gardening should at the same time receive some attention.[51]

Meanwhile McDonald had begun roofing over the front terraces of the library and even developed a set of drawings for the rebuilding of the Rotunda, but during January it was discovered that steel beams in the terrace roofs were so small for their loads that they were already buckling. There were those within the university who favored a competition for restoring the Rotunda, and a group went to New York to contact Carrère & Hastings, McKim, Mead & White, and eventually Shepley, Rutan & Coolidge in Boston, but the conditions proposed for the competition were not satisfactory. Mead and Carrère discussed the matter and suggested that university officials simply make a direct selection from among the three firms. In addition to wanting any competition operated along the lines suggested by the A.I.A., should the university insist on a contest, Mead and Carrère agreed that the winning architect should design all the needed buildings, not just restore the Rotunda, "so that the scheme may have some unity."[52] The Board of Visitors then appointed McKim, Mead & White architects for the entire enterprise on January 18, 1896, and on the same day McDonald withdrew, turning over his measured drawings of the Rotunda. Ten days later White, whose special responsibility this job became, visited Charlottesville and inspected the grounds. Progress on the designs was extremely rapid: preliminary drawings were finished February 21 and sent to Charlottesville five days later with a letter describing the alternative proposals. For the Rotunda itself, White had drawings showing an exact duplication of the several floors built by Jefferson, but there was also a proposal for opening up the Rotunda with one large room. This approach the firm preferred, for it was deemed "a nearer approach to a classic and ideal treatment of the interior of such a rotunda. It is one which is much the most sensible where a library and reading room to meet the enlarged needs of the University is required; and it is one which we believe Jefferson himself would have adopted had the Rotunda been intended solely for use as a Library."[53] As for the new additional buildings, White offered two arrangements, one option showing a cluster to the side of Jefferson's quadrangle, and the alternative showing a group at the end of the Lawn, but this the firm did not prefer, for "we should regret blocking the beautiful vista at the end of the present campus."

White then made a formal presentation of the proposals to the building committee, on March 2, followed almost two weeks later by a similar presentation to the Board of Visitors. Despite some opposition from a faction within the faculty who wished the Rotunda interior archaeologically restored, the Visitors decided instead in favor of the single large space and determined as well that the new building group should be at the end of the Lawn. Unfortunately, for opening the Rotunda interior and for closing off Jefferson's open composition, the architects alone have been excoriated for almost thirty years, some even speaking of "the mutilations of 1896–1898."[54] Once the Visitors had made their decisions, working drawings were quickly prepared, bids obtained, and a contract awarded to Charles H. Langley and Company of Richmond on May 23. Compared to the extended deliberations and design studies for the other two universities, this was lightning speed. Construction was rapid as well, and all work was completed in the spring of 1898.

Of highest priority was the restoration of the Rotunda, using fireproof construction throughout. As the faculty had wished, the ruins of the annex gave way to a landscaped esplanade. The exterior of the building was returned to its appearance before the fire [200], and the original southern terrace wings were rebuilt. New matching wings were built on the north side of the Rotunda, connected to the southern wings by arcaded walkways enclosing diminutive courtyards. On the north face of the Rotunda a new shallow porch was built echoing Jefferson's on the south. The destroyed laminated wooden dome was replaced by a double-shell Guastavino tile vault whose low profile oculus approximated that in Jefferson's original drawings. As the faculty and Board of Visitors decided, the interior was rebuilt as one large room with colossal Corinthian columns supporting encircling mezzanine galleries.[55] At the south end of the Lawn, on sites determined by the building committee and the Board of Visitors, were the three new buildings [201, 202]. On the axis of the Rotunda is the largest, Cabell Hall, and flanking this are Cocke Hall (engineering) and Rouss Hall (physics). These in turn were to be part of a comprehensive scheme comprising eight other buildings, including the refectory (built by the firm 1906–07) and a proposed law building (designed in 1908). Because the ground fell away so sharply at the end of the Lawn (about thirty-five feet), White was able to push the three new buildings against the slope and build what are, from below, two- and three-story blocks, but which present only one low story to the new terrace. White was highly sensitive of the relationship of his additions to the Jefferson campus. Upon White's return from Virginia in January, his friend, the mural painter Edward Simmons, noticed he seemed particularly quiet. "I've just seen *his* plans," White uttered with marked deference. "They're wonderful and I am scared to death. I only hope I can do it right." The new buildings, with conspicuously low profiles and modest pedimented porticoes, were built of brick which, White specifically instructed the on-site superintendent, had to match Jefferson's brick in color and texture; moreover, the unfluted columns also had to "conform entirely with the character of the old work."[56] Because the budget for the three new buildings was so restricted, they were not fully fire-resistant in construction, and to reduce the risk the boilers and generators were housed in a separate powerhouse below Cabell Hall, about one hundred feet down the hillside. Nonetheless, there was extensive masonry, and the semiconical floor of the mandated horseshoe-shaped lecture room in Cabell Hall was built of ramped Guastavino vaults [203].

Despite the criticism McKim, Mead & White have received repeatedly for closing the Lawn and opening the Rotunda, as is now clear, the architect had little to say about the sites

200. Library Rotunda (as restored, 1896–99), University of Virginia, Charlottesville, Va.

201. University of Virginia, general plan showing reconstructed Rotunda and positions of proposed new buildings, 1896. *Monograph.*

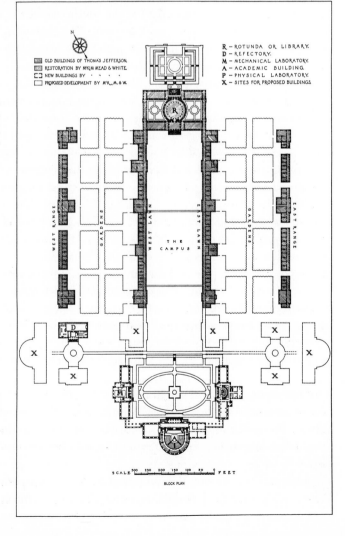

selected by the building committee and Board of Visitors. Rather White used every architectural device at his command to minimize the effect of the new buildings on the originals, beginning by depressing the new southernmost terrace more than eighteen feet below the level of the Lawn at the foot of the Rotunda stairs. The new buildings were restrained in character and not so powerfully elemental as Jefferson's. From the open pergolas connecting the new buildings one can still see the vista of the Blue Ridge Mountains, so that the prospect has not so much been obliterated as modified. Given the restrictions placed on them by the faculty and Board of Visitors, the firm attempted to build in a way that expressed their own interest and respect for the heritage of American classicism, but was also sensitive to the character so strongly established by Jefferson's original campus. So successful were they in returning Jeffersonian classicism to favor that subsequent university buildings by Fiske Kimball, Paul J. Pelz, and Eggers & Higgins continued in this mode from 1899 through the 1950s.

Although the sites of Columbia and New York universities were fixed and hence conditioned their plan organizations, the style and character of the buildings was not

202. University of Virginia, aerial view from the south showing the Academic Building (Cabell Hall) and power plant in the foreground, flanked by the Mechanical Laboratory (Cocke Hall, left), and the Physical Laboratory (Rouss Hall, right).

203. Cabell Hall (Academic Building), University of Virginia, ramped handkerchief Guastavino vaults supporting floor of lecture auditorium, construction photograph, c. 1897.

preconditioned. However, when the firm then worked at the University of Virginia, Jefferson's buildings determined both expression and scale. In the firm's planning for Radcliffe College the tone was set by the institutional connection with, and the physical proximity to, Harvard and its eighteenth-century architectural heritage. For years, wives of Harvard faculty had urged that comparable instruction be made available to women. Finally in 1879 an arrangement was made whereby some Harvard faculty members might teach classes for women, leading to degrees certified by Harvard.[57] As the experiment proved successful, the link between Harvard and the "Harvard Annex" strengthened, and in 1893 the name Radcliffe was formally adopted by the young college in honor of Ann Radcliffe, Lady Mowlson, who had given Harvard its first scholarship endowment in 1643. There were still no buildings or campus until 1885 when the Fay house, a well-proportioned Federalist brick house of 1807 at Garden and Mason Streets, was acquired. It was an excellent location, just one block from the Harvard Yard, overlooking the Cambridge Common; bit by bit the adjoining parcels were obtained until by 1897 almost the entire irregular block was Radcliffe property. At this juncture, Mrs. Henry Whitman, a staunch benefactress of the school, decided that a master plan was needed, and her interest coincided with the gift from Mrs. Augustus Hemenway of a gymnasium. Sarah Whitman had courageously taken up a career as an artist, studying painting in Boston with William Morris Hunt and then in Paris with Couture; eventually, like La Farge, she turned her creativity to stained glass.[58] Perhaps through her artistic interests she had made McKim's acquaintance before, for in February 1897 she contacted McKim to draw up a plan for the development of the Radcliffe campus, incorporating the gymnasium which was being given to the firm to design.

The small area posed considerable problems for arranging the necessary buildings, and in March McKim wrote Mrs. Whitman "we have found it no mean task to bring about a symmetrical relation in a territory of such irregular form; and, in fact, until a common center of reference for the whole system of buildings was reached, by the adoption of the library as the central feature, from which and to which all lines should radiate, we failed, notwithstanding numerous studies, to accomplish much of value" [204]. Now that the focus had been established, the plan was falling into place, centered on the library, what McKim called "the common laboratory and workshop, so to speak, of the college, circular or polygonal in form, facing all the buildings, and practically equi-distant from all. This building should be broad and low, with a central reading room lighted by an entire clerestory, and surrounded by a series of stacks and special libraries for students, through two stories in height." At the apex of the site he felt a theater should be placed, "with which building we have associated the gymnasium and refectory, as dependent functions, especially at Commencement time."[59]

As for the general character of the proposed buildings, they would be like those at Charlottesville, McKim wrote. Soon drawings were shipped to Cambridge [204, 205], but some questioned the wisdom of a central library, to which McKim suggested to Mrs. Whitman that she let the matter rest, for once the gymnasium was built he was sure the logic of the plan would become apparent. As for the appearance of the library, he suggested "some day, *after dinner*, and when you are not harassed by the outside world, please turn to Raphael's 'Marriage of the Virgin' and let me know if the little temple in the background . . . does not appeal to your imagination as an appropriate theme for a library for a Radcliffe girl. . . ."[60]

The Hemenway Gymnasium, 1897–99, was the only building constructed at this time, with offices and locker rooms on the first floor, and the gymnasium floor above [206].[61]

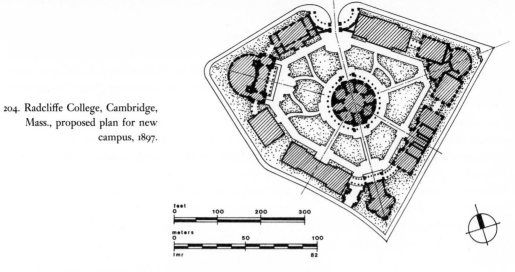

204. Radcliffe College, Cambridge, Mass., proposed plan for new campus, 1897.

feet
0   100   200   300

meters
0   50   100
1mr   82

205. Proposed Radcliffe College campus, aerial view, c. 1897.
206. BELOW. Hemenway Gymnasium, Radcliffe College, Cambridge, Mass., 1897–99.

Georgian-Federalist in style, it is of deep red brick with limestone trim, and in its overall expression refers to the long and venerable Harvard architectural tradition to which Radcliffe was now heir. Although the firm never had any further Radcliffe work, McKim's plan was a decisive influence in later building, for an auditorium (1904) and a library (1907) were built to the left of the gymnasium, forming a group much like that proposed by McKim.

For Harvard itself, the firm's work was limited at first to the gates. But the completion of the Johnston and Meyer gates brought into focus two related problems: the lack of coordination among the various buildings in the Harvard Yard, and the absence of any clear formal approach to the university. In 1891, as an exercise for himself, McKim had sketched out an entrance corridor leading to the Yard from the Charles River, and though the drawings remained in the office, various members of the Harvard Corporation knew of them, prompting university treasurer Edward Hooper to write for copies. McKim's reply of July 8, 1896, explains and describes the plan, now lost:

> I sent you today by Adams express the plan you asked for, designed some years ago to present the possibility of a front door or connecting link between Harvard University and the Charles River, the area thus proposed to be planted with elm trees four abreast, forming a broad alleyway, whose length would afford numerous plots for the development of the University upon a definite system. . . .
>
> What difficulties may stand in the way of this plan I do not know, but this I do know— that *some* plan is woefully needed at Harvard, to restore at least in a measure, the sense of order and repose which belong chiefly to her early buildings [although he added hastily in a postscript] Fogg Museum and others excepted!![62]

If nothing came of McKim's project, it seems to have drawn the interest of Charles Eliot Norton to the problem, and prompted preliminary discussions between President Eliot and Frederick Law Olmsted. When failing health prevented Olmsted from pursuing the project, his son, Frederick, Jr., designed an entrance corridor, in 1896, incorporating some of the elements described by McKim.[63]

The popular reception of the McKim gates, meanwhile, spurred interest in additional gates, so when the corporation resolved in February 1899 that an enclosure was needed around the Yard the firm was approached by a number of alumni groups wishing to erect memorials. In restudying his earlier gate and fence design, McKim was concerned that the height of the fence be coordinated with the Phillips Brooks House, just then being completed at the northwest corner of the Yard from plans by A. W. Longfellow. A fence around the Yard, to be successful, had to "seem to be the natural boundary of the old buildings," McKim wrote Longfellow, but this should prove "easy of attainment, provided we adhere to a system of alternate pier and open iron panel construction of the simplest sort." In this way, McKim continued,

> familiar vistas would be retained, while uninteresting ones could easily be screened by turning from pier construction into stretches of actual wall. To save expense and in view of the plain character proposed, the iron work need only be partially wrought, the larger part being cast, the piers being made without panels and capped with a flat moulded stone. . . . Perhaps you will send a rough sketch at scale of what you think would . . . be most in harmony with the old buildings, and we can study up any modifications which may seem desirable and likely to bring about the most unity. As regards the scale of the general fence, it should be diminished, I think, considerably, from that of the lower side panels of the front [Johnston] gate.[64]

After the design of the fence had been circulated in the spring of 1900, objections were voiced by Charles Eliot Norton, who complained that there were not enough locations for memorials. He preferred that the lower half be brickwork, the upper half, iron, so that at irregular intervals the brickwork could be heightened to contain a memorial plaque or some other device. McKim retorted that this inconsistency would destroy the entire concept:

> the success of the fence depends upon the very abstract and impersonal character to which objection has been raised, and which would, we fear, be lost by the introduction of a variety of elements of an individual character such as you propose. In other words, we regard the fence *simply as an enclosure* and have sought to keep it as simple in its parts as possible, relying upon the gates for emphasis and concentrating memorials at these points.[65]

With President Eliot supporting the McKim fence the controversy dissipated and work began. Altogether McKim and his assistants designed thirteen individual memorial gates in 1899–1900, with the first and second groups built in 1901 and a third in 1902 [207, 208]. Others followed in the early years of the new century, including, finally, the revised Porcellian Club (McKean) gate.[66] The fence and gates were well received, especially by the older alumni

207. Map of the Harvard and
Radcliffe Yards showing locations
of buildings and gates by McKim,
Mead & White (L. M. Roth).
Key to symbols:
Radcliffe Yard:
G = Radcliffe Gymnasium
F = Fay House
Harvard Yard (Class Gates are
identified by Class Year):
B = Bradley Memorial Fountain
J = Johnston Gate
M = Meyer Gate (Class of 1879)
P = Porcellian Club Gate
R = Robinson Hall
S = Sever Hall
U = Harvard Union

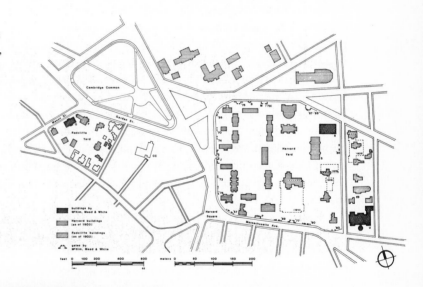

208. Porcellian Club Gate,
Harvard University, Cambridge,
Mass., 1890–91, 1900–01.

who saw the intimate scale of the old Harvard being replaced by Eliot's new, more diversified university. True, the gates were a change, but they had the character of the old Harvard, and Henry L. Higginson, class of '55, thanked McKim for making the Yard "a new place and yet old."[67]

In the Harvard enclosure, but most especially in the plans for Columbia, New York University, the University of Virginia, and Radcliffe, the firm attempted to expand on the rational planning of the Columbian Exposition. Each of these ensembles exhibited comprehensive organization, unity of conception, propriety of scale, and sensitivity to site. Meanwhile the firm applied similar principles in more circumspect undertakings which manifested a broader social concern, for during the 1890s the firm also designed workers' housing near Niagara Falls and in North Carolina.

The first industrial community, begun in 1892, as part of the electrical generating plant at Niagara Falls, New York, was called Echota. As early as 1757 attempts were made to use the water-power potential at Niagara Falls to operate a sawmill, and during the nineteenth century industrialization at the falls increased.[68] Since there were no nearby centers of population, industrial development was limited, and though Buffalo was only twenty miles away there was no practical method of transmitting even a fraction of the falls' power such a distance. In 1886 engineer Thomas Evershed proposed cutting a discharge tunnel beneath the city of Niagara Falls, and the quantity of power to be realized by this scheme, for the period, was immense. New York City investors were solicited to underwrite the construction and to find a means of transmitting the power; in 1890, however, there were considerable differences of opinion, even among the world's most renowned scientists, how this might be done. In the autumn of 1890 construction began on the tunnel, even though the method of power conversion had yet to be settled. Generation of direct current electricity was quickly ruled out, despite strong protests from Lord Kelvin and Thomas Edison, for it cannot be transmitted. Then in demonstrations at Pittsburgh and in the lighting of the Columbian Exposition, George Westinghouse showed that alternating current electricity was practical, transmittable, and economical. Alternating current generation, then, was the answer.

Even before this had been settled, in mid-1892, the firm was given the task of designing the shells of the generating station buildings at a point almost a mile and a half above the brink of the falls.[69] There a deep inlet was cut into the bank of the river; a powerhouse was to run along its west side and (once alternating current generation had been decided on) a separate transformer building was to be erected at the end of the inlet. Edward Dean Adams, then president of the Niagara Falls Power Company, admitted the problem given the architects was difficult. Nothing like this had ever been built before, yet the structures had to be attractive, "artistic in grandeur, dignified, impressive, enduring and monumental," protecting the delicate machinery inside from fierce winters; moreover, the machinery would provide nothing visible to suggest the enormous power being captured.[70] The architecture had to convey symbolically the harnessing of the Niagara; and it may have been for this reason that the firm used rough-faced masonry, returning to a Richardsonian idiom which had not appeared in their work for five years [209, 210].[71] The buildings were completed in 1895 just as the first Westinghouse generators were installed, and electricity was transmitted to Buffalo on the night of November 15, 1895.

While the tunnel was being cut and the powerhouses built, the Niagara Falls Power Company also began development of another section of the lands it had assembled. Confident that the volume of cheap electricity soon available would draw scores of electrically dependent industries, and faced with the need to house their own employees, the company set up a subsidiary to develop a workers' housing village. The name adopted by Adams for the community was Echota, from the name of the ancient Cherokee capitol city, which Adams liked to interpret as meaning "place of refuge."[72] The location was roughly in the middle of the L-shaped holdings of the company, and because the eighty-four acres were absolutely flat, the company first had engineer John Bogart design and install a subsoil drainage system before completing the street system.

209. Niagara Falls Power Company, Generating Station (right) and Transformer Building (left, behind rail cars), Niagara Falls, N. Y., 1892–94.

210. Niagara Falls Power Company, Generating Station, interior.

The utilities installed, McKim, Mead & White were engaged to design an initial group of sixty-seven frame houses. Some of these were single-family, more were duplexes, and some were three- and four-unit townhouses; in all this first phase of construction accommodated 112 families [211, 212, 213, 214, 215, 216]. On Sugar Street, the principal thoroughfare, was a large communal building containing a general store, assembly hall, and bachelor apartments. As in Short Hills, Echota Hall housed the first church meetings and served as a primary day school. The houses of Echota combined abstract aspects of the firm's shingled houses, with elements of contractors' vernacular housing, but through the use of several plan types, some inverted, considerable variety was obtained within the overall unity of character; not surprisingly, electric lights were installed in each home (a most uncommon luxury in workers' housing then).

The activities of the Niagara Development Company in building the housing were not particularly unusual for the time, for many companies built housing, much of it quite good, as a way of attracting and retaining skilled labor.[73] What set Echota apart was that such a prominent architect as White was employed; the only comparable examples prior to 1900

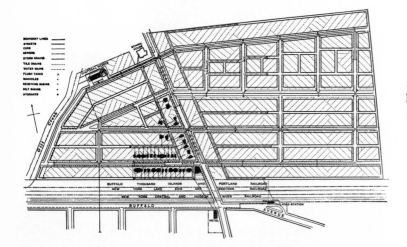

211. Echota, Niagara Falls, N. Y., plan. *Cassier's Magazine,* 1895.

212. Echota, view on "A" Street, c. 1895. *Cassier's Magazine,* 1895.

213. House on Sugar Street,
1891–95.

FRONT ELEVATION.

FIRST FLOOR.

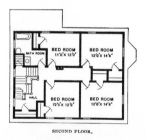

SECOND FLOOR.

214. ABOVE LEFT. House on Sugar
Street, elevation and plans.
Cassier's Magazine, 1895.
215. ABOVE RIGHT. Three-unit row
house, "A" Street, elevation and
plans, 1891–95. From G.W.W.
Hanger, "Housing of the
Working People," Bulletin No.
54, U.S. Bureau of Labor, 1904.

216. Three-unit row house,
"A" Street.

are the duplexes at Hopedale, Massachusetts, partly designed by Peabody & Stearns in 1896. Equally significant was White's refusal to take the standard fee for his work, charging only for draftsmen's time and expenses.

More limited in scope was White's work for the Roanoke Rapids Power Company in Roanoke Rapids, North Carolina. In the autumn of 1894 he designed for the company a knitting mill and scores of frame houses, of which only two now survive; again he declined the standard fee [217].[74] The houses have a broad gambrel roof spreading the length of the house so that the short porch is tucked under the eave [218]. The houses, shingled over the upper walls, in the gables, and on the roof, with clapboards below, must have seemed well-protected, so that locally they were called "turtle-top houses."

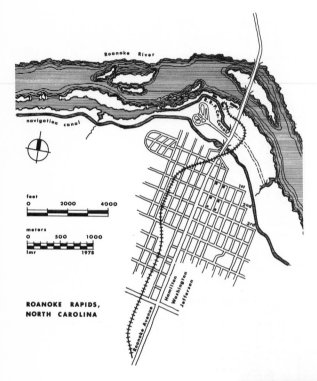

217. Roanoke Rapids, N. C., plan (L. M. Roth). The symbol ■ represents position of original "turtle-top" houses.

218. "Turtle-top" house, 1st and Hamilton Streets, Roanoke Rapids, N. C., 1894–95.

White's work at Echota and Roanoke Rapids, as well as that of Peabody & Stearns at Hopedale, inaugurated a pattern that continued for over fifteen years, in which prominent architects increasingly turned their attention to the design of industrial housing. Only once more was the firm itself involved in such work, and only in a small way, in 1905, when they were asked by Robert Cheney to design a house costing $6,000 for a superintendent in the Cheney silk mill at South Manchester, Connecticut. By then, McKim, Mead & White had already made their principal contribution, but in the decades that followed other architects applied the lessons of the Columbian Exposition, of focus, coherence, and clarity in planning, to the design of industrial communities across the nation.[75]

ALTHOUGH the firm's first two college campus plans were begun in 1892–93 as the depression set in, extensive building operations did not commence until 1895, when some stirrings of economic recovery were apparent. Much the same is true for the urban townhouses of the period, and even as wealthy a client as H. A. C. Taylor thought it prudent to wait a few years between design studies for his New York residence and actual construction. In style, two principal types of townhouses were produced: the Italianate, referring to Florentine sources, and Georgian-Federalist, which are discussed presently. Of the Italianate, the H. A. C. Taylor house was not only the first but the best during these years.

Taylor and McKim had begun planning a residence on 71st Street, New York, in the spring of 1892. Having made several studies, McKim suggested that since the house was to be Italian in character, the main floor containing drawing room, library, and dining room ought to be raised to the second floor, the traditional *piano nobile* in Renaissance palazzi. To do this required introducing an *entresol* as a base, to house reception room, kitchen, and service rooms, so that one might enter at ground level rather than going up a long external stoop. He cited for Taylor an example: "the most perfect house I was ever in is the little Barbaro Palace [in Venice] purchased some years ago by Mr. Daniel Curtis of Boston, who lives in it with immense satisfaction to himself and his family and to the envy of all comers."[76] Once the design was settled, however, construction was delayed until 1894–96. The house, of four stories with an attic, was based closely on the Palazzo Bartolini-Salembeni, Florence, by Baccio d'Agnolo, 1517–20 [219].[77] The basic scheme was worked out by McKim, but detailing was done by his chief assistant, William Mitchell Kendall, and although they introduced a number of changes, the adherence to the model was significantly stronger than in previous adaptations. To what extent this is due to Taylor's influence is impossible to say, but it may be significant that Kendall had such a large part in developing this design. The Taylor house was not a townhouse in the literal sense, contiguous with adjoining residences; it was exposed on all sides, sharing small enclosed yards with neighboring houses. Thus the side walls were as carefully detailed as was the facade.

Aside from what might be termed the "classic" Georgian-Federalist townhouses, the other urban residences were hybrids of Florentine and Colonial allusions, and of these the most austere was for the former minister to France and Governor of New York, Levi P. Morton, New York, 1896–98.[78] This too had a ground-floor entrance in place of the traditional New York stoop, and the chaste, light-colored facade was not only contrasted with the adjoining houses but was far from the exuberance one would have expected from its designer, Stanford White, in the nineties. It was, however, as were other buildings of the end of the decade, a harbinger of a new severity in his work.

219. Henry Augustus Coit Taylor house, New York, N. Y., 1892–96.

Other urban residences of the period were more even in their blend of sources, such as the red-brick Georgian Philip A. Rollins house, New York, 1899–1902, or the yellow-buff brick Stuyvesant Fish house facing it across 78th Street, 1897–1900.[79] These references were blended in the contiguous and unified Butler-Guthrie houses, New York, by White[220].[80] To the front, facing Park Avenue, was the Prescott Hall Butler residence, 1895–97, for a longtime friend and client of the firm. A variant of their Andrew house, Boston, this too had oval corner bays, but it was built of mottled yellow-ochre Roman brick, with crisp subdued Italian Renaissance details. On 35th Street, behind the Butler portion, was the narrower William D. Guthrie townhouse.

220. Prescott Hall Butler–William
D. Guthrie houses, New York,
N. Y., 1895–97. *American Architect
and Building News,* June 10, 1899.

Contemporaneous with the combined Butler-Guthrie houses was the cluster of houses by the firm that arose at the intersection of Delaware and North avenues, Buffalo, then the most fashionable residential district in that city. This too was viewed by White, who designed all three, as a kind of ensemble, if limited in scale. First built was the Georgian Robert K. Root house, 1894–96, in red brick with gambrel roof. Next, two doors north of the intersection, was built the red brick Georgian Charles H. Williams house, 1895–96. Between them, and sharing a common yard with the Charles Williams residence, rose the largest of the three, for George R. Williams, 1895–99, a formal Italianate block of yellow-buff Roman brick with limestone trim. Its plan opened with remarkable breadth and clarity, the rooms on the periphery focused on a spacious three-story central stair hall; in structure it typified the larger houses of the firm from the early nineties onward, for its thick structural masonry walls supported an internal steel frame that carried both masonry and wooden partitions.[81]

By the end of the nineties, with economic recovery well advanced, the firm received a rush of commissions for large country estates and summer houses, perhaps the finest of their type ever done by the firm. Among these were: the Frederick W. Vanderbilt house, Hyde Park, New York, 1895–99; the Herman Oelrichs house, Rosecliff, Newport, 1897–1902; the court and outbuildings added to the Edwin D. Morgan house already begun at Wheatley Hills, New York, 1898–1900; the James L. Breese house, The Orchard, Southampton, New York, 1898–1907; the Alfred A. Pope house, Hill-Stead, Farmington, Connecticut, 1898–1901; and the most ambitious of them all, Harbor Hill for Clarence and Katherine Mackay, Roslyn, New York, 1899–1902.[82] Only the Morgan house court additions incorporated aspects of the now-dated Shingle Style; the others were classic, either reflecting Colonial Georgian models as the Breese and Pope houses did (which were inspired by Washington's Mount Vernon), or Italian Renaissance and French Baroque sources as in the Vanderbilt and Oelrichs houses. The most distinctive of the group, perhaps, is the Oelrichs house, for in contrast to other Newport "cottages," it is low, seemingly of one story, and patterned by White on Mansart's Grand Trianon at Versailles [221, 222]. White's use of a French source was itself unusual, but even more so was the use of white glazed terra cotta for the entire exterior. It was sufficiently unusual to cause Elinor Patterson to ask White if Tessie Oelrichs had left the house because, as had been rumored, of a problem with moisture getting into the terra cotta, to which White was happy to reply that the terra cotta was quite dry; Mrs. Oelrichs had remarried.[83] If appearing compact externally, the interior opened onto one of the largest living/ball rooms in Newport, thirty-nine by seventy-two feet, and a curving, heart-shaped imperial staircase that was perhaps White's most graceful and plastic creation [223]. The Mackay house also deviated from the preferred sources, but White was obliged by the client to model the house on Mansart's Château de Mainsons outside Paris [224]. The firm was also involved in the design of the grounds immediately around the house and in the landscaping of the Morgan house at Wheatley Hills.[84]

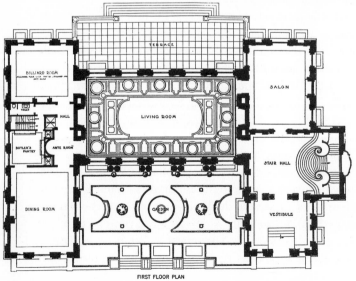

221. Herman Oelrichs house, Rosecliff, Newport, R. I., 1897–1902.
222. Oelrichs house, first-floor plan. *Monograph.*

223. Oelrichs house, staircase.
Monograph.

224. Clarence H. Mackay house,
Harbor Hill, Roslyn, Long Island,
N. Y., 1899–1902.

THE Georgian-Federalist urban residences of the period were part of a larger body of work which included extrapolation of these sources for the design of public and quasi-public buildings. These houses, too, tended to be designed after 1895. The first and again the most austere of the group was McKim's residence for George A. Nickerson on Commonwealth Avenue, Boston, 1895–97 [225].[85] Constructed entirely of white granite, it was a direct allusion to the Federalist traditions of Beacon Hill, specifically Alexander Parris's Sears house, 1818, 42 Beacon Street, which was only a few doors removed from the Appleton house that McKim had been using as the Boston branch office while the library was under construction. While adapting the basic forms of the Sears house, McKim made numerous variations, so that despite its relatively small size the Nickerson house appears to have breadth of scale and monumentality, enhanced by the uniform material and restrained ornament. The optical refinements, such as the studied reduction in window size toward the top of the house and the slight entasis in the swell of the bay, increase its visual impact and suggest that within the classic parameters of the firm's work less could be more.

225. George A. Nickerson house,
Boston, Mass., 1895–97.

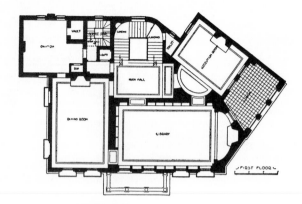

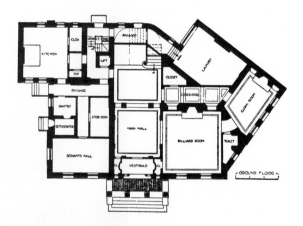

226. ABOVE. Thomas Nelson Page
house, Washington, D. C.,
1896–97, ground (first) and first
(second) floor plans. *Monograph.*

227. LEFT. Page house.

The use of Georgian-Federalist references in Washington, D.C., was especially natural because of the strong architectural traditions of neighboring Georgetown and Alexandria. Two houses begun by the firm there in 1896–97 indicate how this idiom could be adjusted to the awkward polygonal sites encountered in Washington. Both were located in the northwest sector, then being built up with large residences; both were on irregular corner lots that had resulted from L'Enfant's overlay of grid and diagonal street patterns. The larger of the two, by White, was for Thomas Nelson Page, 1896–97 [227]. The main facade recalls the Amory-Olney duplex, but the plan is more complex [226]. and the jigsaw intricacies of the interlocking rooms are characteristic of White's spatial inventiveness. The other house, for Thomas O. Selfridge, Jr., 1897–99, was smaller and resembled The Octagon, the John Tayloe house, 1799–1800, by William Thornton, much admired by McKim.[86]

At the same time that the Florentine H. A. C. Taylor house was started on 71st Street, McKim drew up plans for Taylor for a double house to go up behind it, fronting on 72nd Street, for other members of the family [228]. This facade, however, was based closely on the Boston sources, especially the Amory-Olney duplex; it was among the firm's best Georgian townhouses of the period, slightly more chaste and restrained in its embellishment than the double house for James J. Goodwin on 54th Street, New York, 1896–98, by both McKim and Mead [229]. This duplex, too, recalled the Amory-Olney model, but rather than having two equal halves this had wider and narrower sections for father and son. Consequently, the balanced Georgian facade has one major centered entrance with a subdued entry to the right.[87]

228. Henry Augustus Coit Taylor houses (double house), New York, N. Y., 1892–96. Museum of the City of New York.

229. James J. Goodwin houses (double house), New York, N. Y., 1896–98. *Monograph.*

The most quietly elegant and well-proportioned Georgian townhouse of the period, attributed by his biographer to White, came at the end, built for Henry B. Hollins, New York, 1899–1901 [230]. A smaller variant of the now-familiar Amory-Olney paradigm, it had a limestone base and carved stone tympani panels in the arched second-story windows. Here especially the reduction in size and number of elements served to sharpen proportions and clarity of form. It was also White's and Hollins's goal to work with Whitney Warren, architect of the adjoining Edey house, for "these houses should be more or less in accord, and it certainly would add very much to the street if this were done," wrote Hollins.[88]

230. Henry B. Hollins house, New York, N. Y., 1899–1901.

Of the large public buildings drawing on eighteenth-century sources, the largest was the most derivative; and whereas in other instances there were historical if not obvious reasons for making such stylistic allusions, there was no obvious compelling reason for basing the Garden City Hotel so closely on Independence Hall, Philadelphia. Garden City had been started by merchant A. T. Stewart in 1869–70 as an ideal residential suburb. Critical for success in such ventures were accommodations for visitors and potential buyers, and the first hotel there, 1871–73, was a modest Second Empire block by Benjamin Fowler and Robert Stewart. The community then foundered during the depression of 1873–77, partly because all of the property became encumbered in the probate of Stewart's estate, and it was only in early 1893 that a greatly protracted legal battle among the heirs was settled and the Garden City Company formed to develop and manage the town.[89] Among White's first undertakings there were the enlarging of the Casino and then construction of a large new hotel. Located in the middle of a twenty-two-acre park, directly opposite the Long Island Railroad station, White's U-shaped Georgian brick building, 1894–96, had a gambrel roof ornamented by a wooden cupola [231]. In 1899 the hotel suffered extensive damage by fire, and the firm enlarged and refurbished it, 1899–1901. The center of the building was restored and wings added to it, but since the greater breadth made the original cupola too small, the center of the restored building was rebuilt with a tower adapted from that of Independence Hall, large enough to give proper vertical accent to the greater length [232].[90]

231. Garden City Hotel, Garden City, Long Island, N. Y., original building, 1894–96.

232. Garden City Hotel, reconstructed with tower, 1899–1901.

One of McKim's purposes in returning to the Georgian idiom had been to integrate the Johnston Gate with its eighteenth-century neighbors at Harvard, and he understandably continued to use this for the firm's first major building on the campus. The Harvard Union resulted from Henry Lee Higginson's dual desires to commemorate the Harvard volunteers

233. Harvard Union, Harvard University, Cambridge, Mass., 1899–1901.

234. Harvard Club, New York, N. Y., 1893–94, with additions, 1900–05 (to the rear), and 1913–16 (tall section to the left). *Monograph.*

who had fallen in the Spanish-American War as well as to provide a meeting place for all Harvard students. As the curricular structure of the university was being changed by Eliot in favor of elective courses, such a common ground was keenly needed. In September 1899 Higginson asked McKim to study the recently completed student union at the University of Pennsylvania and make some preliminary designs for a similar building for Harvard. After Frederick P. Hill had been to Philadelphia, sketches were prepared which McKim presented to Higginson and Professors Hollis and Coolidge. The general scheme was approved and construction started, so that the Union was completed in 1901 [233].[91] Because of its rather difficult position at the southeast corner of the campus, crowded in among existing houses, the large building was studied and restudied to bring it into such harmony with its neighbors as it could reach. This too was built of the deep red brick which McKim had now made synonymous with Harvard, with somewhat more embellishment in the form of limestone quoins, escutcheons, and other details than was typical of his work. The final result, particularly the interiors, was well liked by students and faculty, as is evident in George Santayana's comment to a friend regarding "the chorus of praise we are raising about the big new room at the Union. It is the only noble room in the college and will give many people here their first notion of what good architecture means."[92]

A Georgian-Federalist building was also natural for the Harvard Club in New York, begun by McKim in June 1893. In this way he could claim an associational link between the university and the club. Completed in 1894, this first section occupied a small lot in 44th Street, and was originally quite compact (it was later expanded twice by the firm). It looked more like an elegant if slightly overscaled house than a club, and its tall basement and engaged Ionic columns at the second floor seemed to recall Sir William Chambers's Somerset House, 1776, rendered in brick [234]. The interiors were especially intimate in scale, and the club proved to be very popular. When the building was dedicated in June 1894, it was described as conveying the spirit of Harvard's architecture, and for one member its interiors had the general effect of "age, refinement, and tranquility"; and even when it was later greatly enlarged by the firm, McKim was able to retain this intimacy of scale.[93]

IT was only the connection with the university that caused the Harvard Club to be Georgian; in other public and quasi-public buildings the historical references were to Italy. The times were not conducive to club building and aside from the small Harvard Club, there was only one other. In McKim's University Club, New York, 1896–1900, as a result, there is an intense and perhaps compensatory concentration of artistic effort. The officers of this organization of university graduates had attempted to purchase the Stokes residence next to their existing clubhouse on Madison Avenue at 26th Street in May 1894, and McKim, one of the members, made studies showing how the adjoining house could be converted to the club's use.[94] After negotiations for the Stokes house collapsed, in May 1896 five lots were purchased at Fifth Avenue and 54th Street, well uptown, and on June 25, McKim, Mead & White were formally appointed architects. McKim's preliminary sketch, one of the few to survive [235], shows a tall rectangular block of seven-by-five bays, but as built the club was somewhat taller, because of the insertion of mezzanine floors in each of the major stages; moreover, the 54th Street facade was also made planar instead of having the recessed center [236]. The corners, however, were slightly emphasized by pilasterlike piers, and the whole block decisively terminated by a bold cornice, combining features from many Florentine palazzi such as the Palazzo Strozzi and ancient sources such as the Temple of Mars Ultor.[95] The entire exterior, except for the cast-bronze balustrades, was built of pink Milford granite, the same as used for the Boston Public Library, but its rough surface soon acquired a blackening film of pollutants. Recalling Renaissance palazzi, it was not a copy so much as an erudite *pasticcio,* incorporating many features which, though they may have come from disparate sources, were organized in a coherent whole of thoroughly assimilated elements.

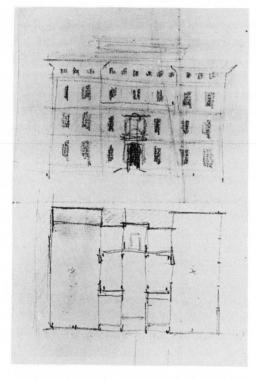

235. University Club, New York, N. Y., McKim's original sketch, 1896.

236. OPPOSITE. University Club, New York, N. Y., 1896–1900, photograph of c. 1899 showing original color and areaway with balustrade. *American Architect and Building News,* August 26, 1899.

The appeal to authority became evident when difficulties arose concerning the panels of Knoxville marble, which were being carved with the seals and mottos of the eighteen colleges whose alumni made up the membership. There had been some reticence among the building committee over the propriety of the carved panels, and after the first inscriptions were cut it was decided that the writing had to be removed as it seemed to the committee too novel. At a meeting of the club in February 1899, McKim argued in favor of the inscriptions, documenting his appeal with photographs of many Renaissance and Roman buildings bearing inscriptions, including the Palazzo Spada, the Porta del Popolo, the Fontana dell'Acqua Paola, and the Porta Maggiore in Rome, supported with a written statement (prepared by Kendall) listing other examples of carved shields with inscriptions. In the face of such venerable authorities, the building committee relented and the remaining shields were carved by Daniel Chester French, complete with inscriptions.[96] In this instance, the sources were marshalled after the fact to support what had been designed intuitively. In addition to the shields, another embellishment McKim felt essential to the success of the building was the heavy sculptural balustrade along the sidewalk, which helped in the transition from the street to the massive block. Much to McKim's dismay this had to be removed in 1910 as part of widening the street because of increasing traffic; he wrote

disgustedly to Lawrence Grant White, then in Paris: "Volumes have been written on 'how to beautify New York' and this is how they are doing it."[97]

The University Club was intentionally large to facilitate growth of the membership, and while several of its rooms, such as the lounge and dining room, were expansive, there were many smaller chambers. The main hall at the first floor [237], with its colonnade of green Connemara marble, is a good example of an amplitude which is, at the same time, carefully scaled.[98] Of the many facilities of the club, the library was one of the most important to its members, and on its design McKim devoted great care, devising a long

237. University Club, "rotunda" lounge. *American Architect and Building News*, July 29, 1899.

238. University Club, library, with completed vaults.

groin-vaulted room with five transverse barrel vaults forming alcoves, its walls lined up to the spring line of the vaults with walnut bookcases [238]. The library was opened in 1899, its unpainted plaster vaults stark white.[99] McKim intended they should be painted to complement the rest of the room, and in the spring of 1902, at his recommendation, the building committee engaged H. Siddons Mowbray to do the work. Using Pinturicchio's Borgia apartments in the Vatican as his model for composition and color, Mowbray worked on the canvas panels in Rome, and during the summer of 1904 they were installed in the library.[100] Consequently, in form and decoration, the library, as an analogue to the club in its entirety, summed up not only McKim's studied erudition but the accumulated body of knowledge to which modern scholars are heir.

THE one large hotel designed by the firm during the nineties was also the focus of intense artistic energy. This hotel, for Louis Sherry, New York, 1896–98, was one of the tallest structures by the firm to date, only slightly shorter than the New York Life Insurance Buildings in Kansas City and Omaha [240]. The tripartite exterior was devised by White to terminate in a massive cornice seemingly scaled to the total height of the building. The upper two thirds of the building contained bachelors' apartments, providing rental income, reached by a modest entrance on Fifth Avenue. Below were the public spaces frequented by fashionable society—a café, one of the best restaurants in the city, various reception rooms, and a grand ballroom [239], all sumptuously decorated by White.[101]

Because the public buildings of the period were so dependent on private funding, they too were greatly affected by the economic slump of the period. The firm's first, in fact, was delayed in its construction by seven years, but that delay, as it turned out, made all the difference in its success. This was the Boston Symphony Hall, another of the many benefactions of Henry Lee Higginson.[102] Dissatisfaction with the Music Hall, home of the Boston Symphony since 1881 when it had been established by Higginson, was growing, for despite very good acoustics the building was a fire hazard and had inadequate ventilation. When it was rumored that the city might cut a new street through the site of the hall, Higginson and "two or three of us" bought the only suitable lot for a new hall. "I know of no one, but you," Higginson dashed off to McKim in late October 1892, "to whom I shall entrust the work. Possibly others are as good, but not for me. Nor do I know if Mr. White is as good—nor if you will take the job." Higginson assumed, too, that the bulk of the cost of this would fall on his shoulders, so he made it clear from the outset that "if anything is done, it must be done at low cost."[103] The letter was handed to McKim as he boarded a train for Chicago on exposition business, but he replied with delight two days later that working on the new hall would be a great pleasure. A month later Higginson then sent McKim a detailed description of the requirements of the new hall.[104] It was to seat 2,200 to 2,500 (an increase of fifty percent over what the old hall accommodated), with a stage for 90 musicians and the possibility of 300 singers, plus all necessary auxiliary rooms for offices, rehearsals, instruments, and storage. Most of the seating was to be at street level, with safe easy exits, and two small galleries. Whatever windows there might be should be as high as possible to keep out street noise. The room was to have good response for quiet as well as loud passages: "our present hall gives a piano better than a forte, gives an elegant rather than a forcible return of the instruments, noble but weak—I want both." He also related that "*the* authority on sound here—Prof. Cross—tells me that an angular sounding-board [over the stage] is

239. Sherry's Ballroom.
240. Sherry's, New York, N. Y., 1896–98.

better than any other shape." Higginson again emphasized the need for absolute economy, "as I will bear the burden of the new hall, perhaps quite alone," and he therefore liked McKim's early suggestion of including rental spaces, provided they could be fitted into the restricted site. Among European halls that might serve as exemplars, Higginson mentioned those he knew well, including the Musikvereinsgebäude in Vienna, the Dresden Opera, the new Gewandhaus in Leipzig, and Wagner's opera house in Bayreuth, whose deep side pilastrades were said to greatly improve acoustical response. He even suggested the material for the new building: "I rather incline to brick and brick ornament. I always like the severe in architecture, music, men and women, books, &c. &c."

Consumed with exposition business, McKim had to put off development of the music hall design until the end of 1893, and then construction was indefinitely delayed when the city suspended action on the proposed street; then no buyer could be found for the old hall. McKim prepared several alternate designs, one of which was based on classical Greek and Roman theaters. The memory of Nîmes, when he and Saint-Gaudens sat in the uppermost row of the amphitheater while White playacted and dashed about below, and how easily they heard him, convinced McKim that the new hall should resemble classical auditoriums. In July 1894 McKim furnished Higginson with three sets of plans which had already been sent to John Galen Howard, then a student at the École, so they might be checked by

241. Boston Symphony Hall, original "Greek Theater" scheme, perspective, 1893–94.

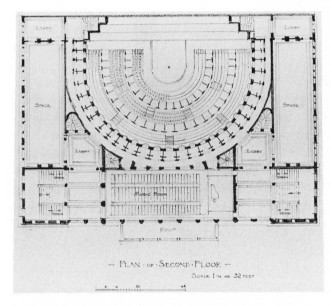

242. Boston Symphony Hall, original "Greek Theater" scheme, second-floor plan, 1893–94.

Professor Laloux. One set showed a traditional rectangular-box auditorium much like the old hall and the Leipzig Gewandhaus, another showed an elliptical plan which Laloux believed would have the best acoustics, and the third was McKim's preferred classical semicircular hall, a building wider than it was deep, with a long vestibule across the front and large staircases in the corners [241, 242]. At either side of the semicircular hall were rehearsal rooms, and under these, at ground level, were shops which would bring in rental income. The steeply sloped floor accommodated most of the seats, although there were boxes on four levels, and a gallery. The facade somewhat resembled that of the Paris Opera but was without its Baroque plasticity. A model of this was sent to Boston and displayed in the public library, generally meeting with favorable comment, but since this was such a radical departure from traditional music halls it raised doubts in the minds of the symphony's directors.[105]

There matters rested for a time, until the old hall was finally sold in October 1898 with the provision that it be vacated by April 1, 1900. Suddenly there was the need for great haste in putting up the new building. A decision had been made, however; as Higginson informed McKim, "while we hanker for the Greek theater plan, we think the risk too great as regards results, so we have definitely abandoned that idea. We shall therefore turn to the general plan of our [old] Music Hall and of the halls in Vienna and Leipsic [sic], the latter being the best of all. . . . We have eighteen months in which to complete our work, and we have, at the outside $200,000 (probably somewhat less) to spend."[106] Subscriptions later raised the figure to $400,000, still a limited budget. If McKim had to give up his favorite scheme, he was reassured by the comment of the first violinist, who told Higginson they always got the best sound in rectangular halls.[107]

Just as working drawings were being finished in 1898, Higginson chanced to comment to President Eliot that the objective in the new hall was to make it as acoustically perfect as possible, with their model the Leipzig Gewandhaus. Eliot observed that he had asked a young physicist at Harvard to investigate acoustical problems they experienced in several auditoriums there, and he suggested that Higginson might ask the architects to confer with Wallace C. Sabine. Even as McKim had been perfecting his Greek theater scheme, Sabine had been carefully measuring the acoustical response of three Harvard lecture halls, with the result that by 1898 he had "invented" the science of acoustical engineering. It had been only weeks before Eliot's conversation with Higginson, that Sabine had informed Eliot he had at last determined the mathematical basis for predicting sound absorption and reverberation time. Rather quickly it was arranged for Sabine to examine the architect's drawings and suggest changes that would guarantee the desired acoustics.[108] This was an extraordinary challenge, for the new hall was to be seventy percent larger than the Gewandhaus. Customarily, achieving good acoustical response was a matter of luck and rule-of-thumb designing. To propose that architect and physicist work together to *design* for a predicted acoustical performance was brash indeed, and it was remarkable that such well-known architects should have put the success of their building in the hands of a thirty-year-old physicist whose theories had yet to be proven.

As it became generally known that the acoustics of the new hall were being designed for predicted results, anticipation and skepticism mounted. Sabine made calculations based on dimensions in the plans, determined loudness, interference patterns, resonance, and reverberation time, and then proposed a number of changes, including placing pilasters in the side walls and reforming the orchestra box to make it smaller and megaphone-shaped to reinforce the attack of the music [243, 244]. So important was this configuration that Sabine insisted the organ chamber be modified and the organ, by a long-established builder, be redesigned. Meanwhile, he toured with the symphony, measuring the reverberation times of Carnegie Hall, New York, and the Academy of Music, Philadelphia. The result was that Sabine suggested further modifications in the firm's drawings, introducing sufficient sound-absorbing material—so that Sabine was confident the reverberation time on the finished hall would be 2.31 seconds, just 0.01 second longer than that of the Gewandhaus.[109] While Sabine was suggesting the final adjustments, the building was constructed, 1899–1900, and formally opened with a dedicatory concert on October 15, 1900. The acoustics that opening night were exactly as Sabine had predicted, and by the end of the concert he found himself the acclaimed authority; the hall, likewise, immediately became a paradigm of acoustical design.[110]

The Boston Symphony Hall is a rather plain building externally, a large rectangular brick box flanked on either side by long wings containing the auxiliary rooms.[111] The slope of the floor is slight, in contrast to that in the rejected Greek theater scheme. To provide proper base resonance, the floor is of wood laid over masonry and a steel frame, but otherwise the building is of noncombustible materials, a significant improvement over the old hall. McKim also included a large heating and ventilation system, with provisions for

243. Boston Symphony Hall,
Boston, Mass., built 1899–1901.

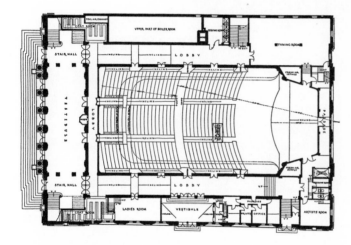

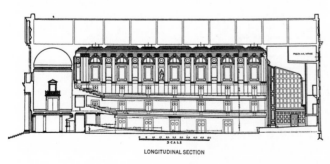

LONGITUDINAL SECTION

244. Boston Symphony Hall,
first-floor plan and section.
Monograph.

cooling the air during the summer months. The exterior was not given the sculptural embellishment McKim intended, nor were the large blank stone panels ever cut with the inscriptions planned, so the building has a rather Spartan appearance (which Higginson may have preferred). The skyline, too, seems especially severe since the decorative *chéneau* was never installed. Perhaps to modern eyes this very simplicity enhances the way the hall serves its primary function so well, for the Boston Symphony Hall is still the acoustical yardstick by which newer halls are judged.

Finances and restricted donations also affected the largest of the public building projects
of the period, the Brooklyn Institute of Arts and Sciences, now called the Brooklyn Museum. The idea for the building had developed in 1888, when Brooklyn was still a separate
city, and hence the museum was a response to the growing Metropolitan Museum in Central
Park. The site selected in Brooklyn was better, in than it was not *in* Prospect Park, but
adjoining it in the separate enclave set aside by Olmsted and Vaux for just that purpose. By
1891 the necessary enabling legislation had been passed, and in May 1893 a competition was
held for a building to cost $300,000. The design with which the firm won was ambitious

245. Brooklyn Institute of Arts
and Sciences (Brooklyn Museum),
Brooklyn, N. Y., 1893–1915.
Monograph.

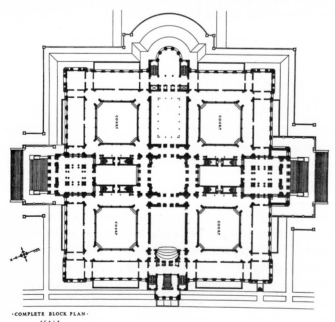

246. Brooklyn Museum,
comprehensive plan. *Monograph.*

far beyond the program, but so composed in segments that it could be built in sections as need and contributions permitted. Then, just as the firm was to start on construction, the deepening depression brought work to a halt. The comprehensive plan consisted of a large quadrangular building arranged around internal courts [245, 246], with subordinate pavilions at the corners and major entrance pavilions at the center of each side. It was a typical, large Beaux-Arts plan from the early part of the nineteenth century, with arms extending inward from each entrance pavilion, merging under the domed rotunda at the very center.[112] In 1895, as the economy revived somewhat, construction began on the first section of the museum, the northwest wing, and when this was finished the museum was formally opened. The center pavilion of this front, with its Guastavino-tile dome, and the hall behind it were added in 1900–1905, and the eastern half of the front was completed in 1904–06.[113] Also in 1906 the grand staircase in front of the building was finished. Then, in 1909, the master plan was restudied by the younger partners added to the firm, resulting in the elevation of the dome on a taller drum and the addition of a tall lantern; although the great dome was not built, the revised plans were used for further additions made in 1913–15. Since McKim was in charge of the first phase of construction of the museum, it is not surprising that it so strongly resembled his Agriculture Building at the Columbian Exposition, opened just as the competition drawings were done. Aside from the required permanent construction, the only significant difference between the two schemes was the projection of the cornice of the museum over each pilaster, achieving slightly more plasticity and providing a clearer pedestal for the attic sculpture by Daniel Chester French, Herbert Adams, Edward C. Potter, and Attilio Piccirilli.

Just as the lack of donors prevented the Brooklyn Museum building from being carried out at the scale hoped and planned for, so too the decline in giving halted church building. There was some correspondence early in 1893 between Mead and the Reverend Winchester Donald, now rector of Trinity Church, Boston, regarding completion of the porch of the church and the addition of electric lighting. Of all the architects who had worked with Richardson on Trinity, Donald felt White understood the building best. The building committee, however, favored Richardson's successors, Shepley, Rutan & Coolidge, who were engaged. Nonetheless, Donald wanted White to have some hand in renovation, and McKim relayed a proposal to White who was then traveling, saying that Donald wanted "a bully sketch for a pulpit which he can use to raise funds for construction. He wants something big, broad, ample, and simple, but rich in the right places—just what it ought to be—SEE!"[114] But even this came to naught.

The firm's education buildings of the nineties also came at the end of the decade; all, that is, but Cullum Hall, West Point, 1893–98, which resulted from a special bequest. The severe and rational classicism of this is all the more remarkable because this was White's [247].[115] Made possible by a provision in the will of Major General George W. Cullum, a graduate of the academy in 1833 and a former superintendent of the post, the building was to house formal receptions and cadet dances. Won by the firm in a limited competition, the design had to be restudied during 1894 to lower the cost and, according to McKim, the final design owed much in its details to Albert Randolph Ross, one of White's principal assistants.[116] Of pink Milford granite throughout (which in the cleaner air of the Hudson valley has remained rather bright), Cullum Hall is an austere box, with slightly recessed screen walls behind engaged Ionic columns on the front and pilasters on the sides and rear. The engaged columns are actual structural bearing elements, for the cornice load is carried to them by means of flat arches in the architrave. Accordingly, the wall behind the vertical supports is merely a screen. This rational use of the classical orders strongly appealed to Montgomery Schuyler, who compared this to Néo-grec architecture in France and to the Greek temple of Zeus Olympios at Akragas (Agrigentum), Italy.[117] As at New York University, White pushed the building to the very edge of the plateau on which the academy is built, raising it on a massive substructure.

Another of White's educational buildings was his Cornell Medical School, New York, 1898–1901, a teaching and clinical institution paid for entirely by Colonel Oliver Hazard Payne. The building was a large massive block, bold in its components but sparsely ornamented except for two projecting entrance bays. These served to emphasize the dual functions of the school, and in his description of the building, White wrote that the "bays, with engaged columns running through two stories, serve to mark two entrances, one to the main building [the teaching section], and the other to the Dispensary." To aid in asepsis, he specified minimal detail inside, with materials "specially fitted to the purposes of a Medical College, glazed brick and tile predominating."[118]

At nearly the same time McKim was given the commission for his last major building for his alma mater, Robinson Hall, 1899–1902.[119] The gift of Mr. and Mrs. Nelson Robinson whose son had entered Harvard in the class of 1900 but who died before graduation, the building was to house the department of architecture. President Eliot and the Harvard Corporation had discussed the site for the new building and intended to have it designed by Herbert L. Warren, head of the architecture department, when Henry Lee Higginson persuaded them to give the commission to McKim. Higginson, a member of the corporation since 1893, wrote Eliot that the university should have an "outside" architect since outside funds were involved; when Harvard was to build with its own money, then, he wrote, they should turn the work over to Warren. "I do think it just the case for McKim," urged Higginson:

> The needs of the department, Professor Warren can set forth better than anybody. Mr. McKim has a great eye for proportions, and if he is looked after, he will restrain his desire for ornament. Such is my opinion. He can also do work economically if he wishes. Mr. Norcross's criticism of Mr. McKim's Music Hall plan was this: that it was a very economical building and that he, after several days, could only cut off $300 in the expenses, and that only in the foundations. I think this speaks pretty well for Mr. McKim.[120]

Having received the commission, in August 1899 McKim inspected the proposed site at the north edge of the Harvard Yard, near Hunt's old Fogg Museum, then writing to Eliot that the site presented several difficulties which required study. Two months later a preliminary design and perspective of the proposed building were sent to Eliot with McKim's statement explaining why the position of the building deviated from that specified by the corporation. If the relocation was approved, McKim argued, a number of trees would be saved that served to screen the juxtaposition of the differing architectural styles, the proposed arrangement would make Richardson's Sever Hall the focus of a new quadrangle, and this group would in turn conform to the main axial lines of the university, thereby extending the general system of the campus.[121] With this Eliot and the corporation were persuaded, and Robinson

Hall was constructed accordingly. As a whole the building was not as striking as the Boston Library nor even Symphony Hall, but this was the result of the subordination to the existing conditions and particularly Sever Hall [207, 248].[122] Charles Eliot Norton, ever a critic of McKim's work at Harvard, wrote disparagingly of Robinson Hall, saying it was not beautiful, that it violated rules of good architecture, and that it was out of harmony with Sever Hall.[123] Certainly in style it was different, although in material and color it was complementary. What Norton seems not to have considered, however, was the important role McKim gave Robinson Hall in forming the spaces around Sever Hall. Like White's building at the University of Virginia, this was to be a background building, defining spaces but not dominating them. Once this definition was begun by Robinson Hall, the quadrangle east of Sever Hall was completed by Guy Lowell's Emerson Hall to the south, and the new Fogg Museum of Art by Coolidge, Shepley, Bulfinch, & Abbott across the street to the east.

247. Cullum Memorial Hall, U. S. Military Academy, West Point, N. Y., 1893–98.

248. Robinson Hall, Harvard University, Cambridge, Mass., 1899–1902. *Monograph.*

THE public buildings of the period and of the years preceding had been disparate creations; although in urban settings, none had any special relationship to any larger grouping other than its relationship to the street. Through the nineties, however, the firm was engaged in an enterprise which, even if the individual buildings were simple and unprepossessing, is significant because of the ensemble. In Naugatuck, Connecticut, beginning in 1891 and continuing through 1905, McKim, Mead & White built a group of six public buildings that represent most of the types architects were asked to do at that time. All were commissioned or directed to the firm by Naugatuck industrialist John Howard Whittemore, who commissioned of the firm an additional three houses, two projects, and two buildings in nearby Waterbury. All together then, Whittemore was responsible for bringing the firm thirteen commissions.[124]

Whittemore had grown up in Naugatuck, a small New England village that had been established in the seventeenth century and slowly began to industrialize in the mid-nineteenth, beginning with small textile and notions factories and then rubber shoe manufacture in 1843. As a young man, Whittemore, with his partner, Bronson Tuttle, established a malleable iron works which specialized in producing small parts used in huge quantities in Union Army wagonwheel hubs, farm wagonwheel hubs, and washers used in fastening railroad rails; the sheer volume of these essential parts soon made Whittemore a wealthy man. By 1885 he was able to withdraw in large measure from day-to-day management of the company and devote himself to building a large house at the edge of Naugatuck near the factory. Not built until 1888–90, the house he had the firm design was quite spacious, its wide paneled halls and staircase used to display the impressive collection of Monets, Morisots, Cassatts, and Whistlers he had begun to assemble. Whittemore later had the firm design two more houses, one in the mid-nineties, outside Naugatuck, and one for his son, Harris, in 1901, next to his own in Naugatuck, but these private commissions fade in importance next to his activities in enriching and defining the town center. Here he gave the firm six separate commissions, and later, two projects. Taken together, the completed and projected buildings include two schools, a public library, two banks, a church, a new town hall, and the landscaping and furnishing of the town green [249]. While the individual buildings are not of the caliber of the firm's most notable buildings, their ensemble merits special attention, for in few other industrial communities was any architect given the opportunity to create such a varied selection of buildings over an extended period. What McKim, Mead & White attempted to do in Naugatuck was to interrelate their buildings with the growing town as a whole, as each work was designed. Their goal was a coordinated yet varied "urban" center, and the attempt was so successful that one observer called Naugatuck "an architectural oasis."[125] The partners attempted a rich mixture of balanced order and irregularity, the old patterns made stronger and more comprehensible through the new additions.

Although the Naugatuck green was ringed with churches and houses of various vintages, it lacked coherence. In November 1891 Whittemore engaged the firm to amend this with the first building he placed next to the green, the Howard Whittemore Memorial Library, finished in 1894, and similar in its parts to the Bowdoin Gallery but built entirely of pink Milford granite [178]. The marble-paneled rotunda with its gilt-coffered dome made this far superior to what most industrial towns of this size were afforded. Then, in his capacity as a board member of the Naugatuck National Bank, Whittemore directed the commission for a small bank building to the firm, 1892–93. The site also faced the green, next to the library, then abuilding. The large details were oversized, but the color scheme was light so that the two buildings formed a visual termination to the street on the north side of the green.

In September 1892, while both library and bank were under construction, the firm received the commission for the third building on the green, the Salem School, 1892–94, a gift to the town by Whittemore, west of the green but centered on its axis [250]. The school was laid out with clusters of rooms around an extremely broad spacious hall and generous staircase, but externally the classicizing formality of the preceding buildings was modified by a shift away from the pink granite and buff brick to red brick and brownstone, perhaps in an effort to stay within a restricted budget.

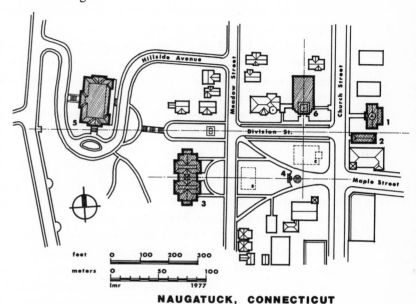

249. Naugatuck, Conn., map showing locations of buildings by McKim, Mead & White around town green, 1891–1905. Key to symbols: 1. Howard Whittemore Memorial Library, 1891–94; 2. Naugatuck National Bank, 1892–93; 3. Salem School, 1892–94; 4. fountain on the green, 184–95; 5. Hillside High School, 1901–05; 6. Congregational Church, 1901–03; s = location of original Salem School; c = location of preceeding Congregational Church.

NAUGATUCK, CONNECTICUT

250. Salem School, Naugatuck, Conn., 1892–94.

In 1893 Whittemore momentarily turned his attention away from the center of the town to focus on a large project. Concerned about landscape preservation in the corridor between Naugatuck and Waterbury, during the early 1890s he began to purchase large tracts between Naugatuck and Middlebury, a hamlet seven miles to the northwest. The area was still largely wooded, for Naugatuck lay at the very edge of the industrialization that stretched northward from Bridgeport on Long Island Sound. To supervise the landscaping, Whittemore engaged landscape architect Charles Eliot (the son of Harvard's president), but when Eliot succumbed to pneumonia at the age of thirty-seven in 1897, the work was continued by Warren H. Manning. The goal was to create a large managed preserve in Middlebury, connected to the Naugatuck green by a landscaped parkway.[126]

On a ridge overlooking Lake Quassapaug just west of Middlebury, Whittemore had Eliot lay out a large country estate with adjoining farms, and in October 1894 McKim, Mead & White began designs for the principal buildings. The site was unexcelled—an open windswept ridge looking down on the lake and rolling wooded hills that stretched away toward the Berkshires. The main house was placed on a low terrace at the edge of the hill, with the maximum possible view [251]. It resembled the Morgan house at Wheatley Hills, but here the whole composition is contained within one single geometric envelope; even the porches are subsumed under the continuous sweep of the roofs. Only seven miles from Naugatuck, the Middlebury house was elevated to catch summer breezes and provide a comfortable refuge. Unlike most of his contemporaries, Whittemore chose not to escape to Newport or take to the high seas during the summer; his ties to his home and to the town were strong. It was the good fortune of Naugatuck that virtually all its industrial leaders felt likewise, so that it was not until well into the twentieth century that the town began to suffer the indifference of absentee-ownership of its companies and of their transient managers.

While providing for his own comforts in Middlebury, Whittemore was also keenly aware of the public needs in Naugatuck. Although the library, bank, and Salem School had helped transform the green into a true village center, the green itself was still ill-defined. While the approach from Middlebury and the green itself were landscaped by Eliot, Whittemore engaged the firm in the winter of 1894–95 to design walks in and around the park, the defining bollards, and a public drinking fountain at the center [252]. This and other projects undertaken by the town put to work many of those laid off in the rubber and malleable-iron plants. Completed the following autumn, the landscaping and architectural treatment crisply defined the town center.

In 1900, when it was obvious that the educational needs of the expanded town population could no longer be served by the single Salem School, Whittemore offered to build a high school for Naugatuck. The problem of location then arose, for in the earlier undertakings all the available space around the green had been used, yet this new building was to be related to that newly defined center. Behind the Salem School the ground rose steeply, and Mead and White, who worked on this together, placed the high school on a leveled terrace halfway up. Built in 1901–05, it had a high pink Milford granite base with upper walls of light buff brick and limestone trim [253]. Because of the helical rise of the street around the school, each of the three floors could be given direct access to ground level.[127]

Even as Whittemore began to see the need for the high school, in the mid-nineties the Congregational Church began to show signs of aging. The white frame structure, built in 1855, had been allowed to deteriorate to the point where, by 1894, a new building was needed. Pledges were obtained for the necessary funds, and in 1899 Whittemore, a member of the building committee, donated the lot next to the parish house on Division Street, facing the green. Early in 1901 McKim, Mead & White completed plans and construction started; the church was dedicated in May 1903. Since for over forty years the steeple of the frame church had been a landmark in the community, the firm modeled the new church closely on the old building, changing the materials to deep red brick with limestone trim [254].[128] At the same time they looked to other archetypal New England meetinghouses, such as the Park

251. John Howard
Whittemore house,
Middlebury, Conn.,
1894–96.

252. Fountain, Naugatuck town
green, 1894–95.

253. Hillside High School,
Naugatuck, Conn., 1901–05.

Street Church of Boston, 1809, although for the steeple itself (and for some interior details), the firm drew on the source of all such meetinghouses, James Gibbs's Saint-Martin's-in-the-Fields, London, 1721–26. The Naugatuck steeple is not a copy of Saint-Martin's; the brick and stone tower is shorter and squatter, giving a strange sense of scale, emphasized by the overly large details of the whole building. It is altogether possible that these adjustments were conscious attempts to make the church appear more massive than its true physical dimensions would indicate, reinforcing a sense of permanence and stability. Because of the scale and placement of the church, all of the buildings around the green, new and old, are subtly knitted into a coherent whole. More important for the residents of the town, its tall spire, recalling centuries of denominational and regional associations, told the people of Naugatuck who and where they were.

254. Aerial view of the Naugatuck town green, c. 1906.

In 1906 a large classical project, meant to replace the High Victorian Gothic town hall, and a small bank were designed by the firm, but a brief recession in 1907 seems to have stopped construction. Had they been built, the effect of the firm's work in Naugatuck would have been more direct, perhaps, yet even without them the physical and cultural change was marked. What Whittemore and his architects had achieved after fourteen years of building was a town center both ordered in plan and picturesque in appearance. Following Whittemore's death in 1910 the town continued the development he had begun, further defining the enclosure of the green. Along Church Street north of the library were built two banks and a post office, all classical and small in scale; since that time the example of

Whittemore and the architecture he commissioned of McKim, Mead & White has continued to foster a unique and sensitive civic consciousness in Naugatuck.[129]

DESPITE the depression the firm did complete a number of important business and office buildings, including three major banks, all under the direction of White. The first was the Bowery Savings Bank, New York, begun in February 1893 just before the crash and built during 1893–95 [255, 256, 257].[130] The site was particularly challenging, occupying the northwest corner of the Bowery and Grand Street; unfortunately, the critical corner parcel, owned by the rival Butcher's and Drover's Bank, was not for sale, so the space available for the new bank formed an L around the competitor. Accordingly, White developed two entrances from each principal street, with vestibules leading to the large square banking room. The long corridor entrance White was able to put to good use, for since this bank served wage earners and not wealthy depositors, and since it encouraged a volume of small deposits, he used the L for customer seating. Whereas the outer walls hugged the polygonal sidewalk line, the square banking room was set inside this irregular rectangle, a room within a room. This opulent room, gilded and richly colored in its materials, was nonetheless restrained and attracted customers through the sheer luxury it afforded them of being able to explore its colorful and expansive spaces. As in the Boston Public Library and the Columbian Exposition, the architecture and its attendant sculpture (such as the pediment figures by Frederick MacMonnies) were designed to stimulate and elevate; as a result the bank soon became and remained "an architectural and economic anchor through the Bowery's years of hard times."[131]

Even richer embellishment was to follow. In 1894 White began sketches for the renovation of the headquarters of the New York Life Insurance Company, for which the firm had already done so much work. The company's operations were becoming ever more crowded in the long narrow four-story building designed by Griffith Thomas, 1868–70.[132] When that building was erected, the company had been unable to acquire the rear of the long trapezoidal block, but in succeeding years as portions became available they were purchased. Early in 1893 the company considered adding to the rear and enlarging the old building, setting up a closed competition, inviting besides the firm, Babb, Cook & Willard, G. B. Post, D. H. Burnham & Company, and C. D. Hatch. When the contestants protested the low fee, the company agreed to the American Institute of Architects' (A. I. A.) standard five percent. High on the company's priorities was piling as many floors as possible on the old structure to assure "the largest possible income . . . consistent with proper light and air."[133] White's winning design added eight stories to the old front section, attaching a new twelve-story addition to the rear, gutting the interior of the original building to provide for a new banking room and executive offices, and, on the twelfth floor, new rooms for the Merchants' Club. Construction was carried out in 1896–99 in a series of overlapping campaigns, front and back. The original Broadway facade was greatly changed, with the incorporation of colossal columns screening the entrance [258]. Above this the midsection of the building was resurfaced, producing an alternating rhythm of paired floors and mezzanines; this terminated in an arcade, a massive cornice, and a clock tower incorporating sculpture by Philip Martiny. The enrichment was even more heavily concentrated, however, in the new banking room and especially the corporate offices.[134]

In view of this heavy embellishment, the stark severity of the State Savings Bank of

255. Bowery Savings
Bank, New York, N.
Y., 1893–95.

256. BELOW. Bowery Savings Bank, plan. *Monograph.*

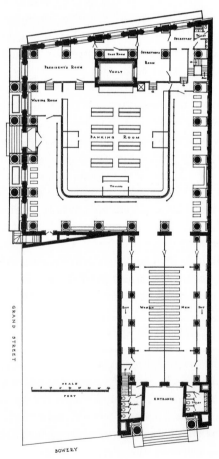

257. Bowery Savings Bank, main banking room,
interior.

258. New York Life Insurance Company Building,
headquarters, New York, N. Y., 1893–99.

Detroit, 1898–1900, comes as something of a surprise [259, 260].[135] Along Shelby Street the marble wall was divided into five broad arched bays between pilasters; on Fort Street the arcade device was repeated, but hollowed out at the center to form an entrance portico which opened into the bank vestibule and, on either side, to rental offices. The airy, spacious, brightly day-lit banking room was toward the rear, surrounded by offices, so that it was reached only by passing through the external and internal vestibules. On the second floor, to either side of the entrance, were additional rental offices, reached by stairs and a bridge over the vestibule. This unusual arrangement allowed for a single, more secure entrance and made the building visually uncomplicated. The structural system was directly expressed, for since this was to be a low building a complete metal frame was not required; the marble walls, with their pilasters, are structural, and within the arches are steel box girders as lintels.

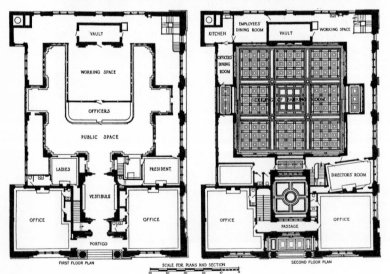

259. State Savings Bank, Detroit, Mich., 1898–1900, perspective rendering.

260. State Savings Bank, first- and second-floor plans. *Monograph.*

The arcades were then opened up with glass, bronze mullions, and thin panels between floors. If the encrusted New York Life headquarters was typically White of the 1880s, this elegant austerity and that of the Cullum Memorial, so much more like McKim's work, opened a new and more settled phase for White.

For all the commissions won and successfully carried to completion during the nineties, there were many disappointments, commissions dropped, and competitions lost. The firm entered and failed to win the competition for the Massachusetts Mutual Life Insurance Company Building in Springfield, Massachusetts, in 1894. They also lost in the competition for the American Surety Building at Broadway and Pine, New York, 1893–94, but a faded photograph of their lost drawing survives [261].[136] It is surprising that the firm entered this competition at all, considering the design was bound to result in a slender tower and McKim's growing discomfort with skyscrapers as they reached beyond fifteen stories. The proposed twenty-one-story building was to fill the cramped site formerly occupied by the old New York *Herald* Building, now that the paper had moved to White's new building on Herald Square. The firm quite appropriately lost to Bruce Price, who handled the problem of the slender tower far better, for instead of a clear tripartite organization, they awkwardly piled up repeated stages with trebled stages and mezzanines much as White did in the New York Life headquarters. Curiously, there was none of the simplicity of their Home Life Insurance project of two years earlier. The firm also lost the competition for the New York Clearing House, 1894, for which White prepared a tall, high-waisted four-story design. More disappointing, no doubt, were the losses in the competitions for the College of the City of New York above the new Columbia campus on Morningside Heights and for the new immigrant station on Ellis Island, both of 1897. Indeed, McKim confided to Burnham "the ambition of this office is to keep out of competitions and so long as we can make our bread and butter otherwise, I think it most unlikely that we shall go into competitions for combined libraries or anything else."[137]

McKim was referring to the important competition for the New York Public Library, the loss of which was a keen disappointment. The library had just been formed in 1895 by the merger of the Lenox and Astor libraries and the Tilden Trust. Large and valuable collections in themselves, the combination promised to be one of the most significant in the country. The competition for a grand new building, announced in May 1897, was open to all aspirants with only sketches to be submitted; from this group twelve finalists would be selected to complete and expand on their schemes, the final drawings to be due in November.[138] The requirements for the library had been stipulated with precision by the trustees in an effort to obviate difficulties as had arisen during construction of the Boston Public Library, but to McKim these restrictions threatened to stifle exterior and interior beauty. As the site in Bryant Park was one of the most important in the city, McKim felt he must have absolute freedom in organizing the firm's entry. As a result they forfeited the prize. It must be admitted, too, that their proposal was not as boldly modeled in its parts, not as richly sculptural as the winning entry by their former assistants, Carrère & Hastings. Still, McKim was glad to see the award go to young men who had been in the office; and even if the French character of their design was not his métier, he appreciated its merit, sending this congratulatory letter:

261. American Surety
Building, New York,
N. Y., competition
entry, perspective, 1893.

I have seen your Fifth Avenue facade for the great library, and while a building can only be fairly judged in execution, and one may well demur at this or that, I want to write and tell you how much I think, taken as a whole, your design is fine and worthy to be built.[139]

During the last decade of the century, McKim, Mead & White came squarely to the forefront of their profession, an arrival announced by the publication of the first extended analysis of their work in 1895. Russell Sturgis's essay, "The Works of McKim, Mead & White," was the first in the Great American Architects Series published by the *Architectural Record*—a series that shortly included studies by Sturgis and Montgomery Schuyler on Adler & Sullivan; Henry Ives Cobb; Shepley, Rutan & Coolidge; Peabody & Stearns; George B. Post; Bruce Price; and Charles Coolidge Haight. Sturgis's assessment was not positive; he much preferred contemporary French architecture, and he warned the reader that in looking at the work of McKim, Mead & White "there will be but few evidences of that modern spirit." While he most admirably examined the broad range of the firm's production (indeed, some of his illustrations are now the only surviving visual record), his compliments were consistently backhanded. He concluded, after III pages of discussion, that it was fair to say "that in general the buildings which we have been considering, taken together, are as good as can be expected of a firm which is doing all the work it can get."[140] How the partners reacted to this sneer from their former mentor, they did not bother to record, but it must have stung.

For McKim the decade brought physical trauma offset by great personal happiness. Like many others during the mid-nineties he was swept up by the bicycle craze, but unfortunately had an accident that resulted in a hernia. In October 1895 he underwent surgery to repair the damage, and although the operation was successful, McKim's health afterward was never what it had been; it slowly began to deteriorate. Increasingly he suffered from acute attacks of what was called "gastric neurosis" or dyspepsia that often made it impossible for him to take any nourishment.[141] Compensation came, however, in the permanent reunion with his only child, Margaret, in 1899, from whom he had been cut off for twenty years; they now became frequent companions and correspondents.

If, as the partners often wrote, the nineties were a trying period, they nonetheless produced important work. Many of their individual buildings were distinguished either for the combination of sobriety of form and decorative intensity, as in the University Club, or for technical contributions, as in the Boston Symphony Hall. Despite some errant creations, heavily embellished, the work of both of the designers tended toward greater austerity, as in McKim's Nickerson house or White's Cullum Memorial. In some cases this may have come about because of restricted budgets, as was certainly a factor for Symphony Hall, but it also reflected closer observation of ancient and High Renaissance models, as in the Taylor house in New York, where one clearly sees the effect of poring over the plates in Letarouilly and d'Espouy.[142] More intriguing, because unexpected, is this shift in White's work, as clearly evident in the Hollins house and the Detroit bank but especially in the Cullum Memorial. Gradually, White stripped away the more florid ornament of the Spanish and North Italian Renaissance, turning toward Republican Rome, as presaged in his Washington Arch, but now keyed to a more rational expression of structure.

The firm's most important contribution, however, was in the design of ensembles. Certainly, McKim, Mead & White were never planners in the sense that Burnham became after 1893, for they remained more interested in architecture at a smaller, more immediately perceivable, scale. Yet from the beginning of their partnership they were concerned with larger spatial and visual relationships. It is important that such a large percentage of their energies from 1892 to 1900 was concentrated on designing buildings in groups. Even more significant was the symbolism they added to this concern for urban design, so that each ensemble could be read as a family of buildings devoted to a common purpose. The Columbian Exposition, for all its stylistic conservatism, was an experiment in urban design at full scale, the first that American architects ever were accorded, and the firm quickly put its practical lessons to use in their own work. The fair and the subsequent ensembles of McKim, Mead & White helped define a new role for the American architect. He was no longer simply the designer of individual buildings, but rather the shaper of places and spaces, the choreographer of spatial experience. His proper province was the whole of the built environment.

6

PINNACLE

1900 — 1909

The will to grow was everywhere written
large and to grow at no matter what or
whose expense.

HENRY JAMES
The American Scene, 1907

FOR Americans the new century began full of energy and promise. The United States had become a world power, and its economy was again strong. There were high expectations and money for building. As a result, the decade after 1900 was most productive for McKim, Mead & White. They received more than 210 commissions amounting to construction contracts worth $36,379,768. The office staff was increased gradually, to 92 people in 1902 and reaching 110 by 1909. Because of this expanded and well-trained staff, some of whom had been with the firm since before the Columbian Exposition, these later buildings are marked by extremely high quality of design and execution. Indeed, these late works have become so representative of the firm's efforts that, of any dozen or so buildings selected to illustrate their work, the great majority by far would come from this decade.[1]

His time taken up with supervising the expanding and busy office, Mead had little left for designing [262], but he did work with Whitelaw Reid in 1908, laying out a tent camp, Camp Wild Air, in the Adirondacks, then building a two-story lodge there of cedar logs.[2] McKim led an especially hectic life despite increasing problems with his health [263]. He was persuaded to serve two terms as President of the American Institute of Architects, 1902–03, devoting his energies to convincing public and government officials of the benefits of well-designed buildings and of the value of preserving historic structures and natural scenery. Through McKim's initiative the institute was persuaded to purchase Thornton's Octagon house in Washington for its national headquarters. Little of this activity was publicized at the time, for as institute secretary Glenn Brown observed, "McKim was retiring and seldom took an apparent active part in large meetings, and for this reason a large part of the membership failed, I believe, to appreciate the great work he did for the Institute."[3] His remarks to the institute at the annual conventions were customarily spare and

262. William Rutherford Mead,   263. Charles Follen McKim,   264. Stanford White,
c. 1918. C. Moore, *Life and*   c. 1903.   c. 1905.
Times of Charles Follen McKim.

brief, summarizing developments in architectural education, professional relations with the government, and the far-reaching effects of the Senate Park Commission's work. In closing his address in 1902 he asserted that "great opportunities demand thorough training. Confidence comes not from inspiration but from knowledge. The architect who would build for the ages to come must have the training of the ages that are past."[4] This sentiment helps explain the decided shift to sober High Renaissance and Augustan Roman sources in his and his partners' work at the opening of the new century.

More of McKim's time was occupied in bringing to a final resolution the logistic and economic difficulties of the American Academy in Rome, which he steadfastly supported during the nineties and early 1900s. Particularly needed were an endowment to support a continuing program of study, the acquisition of a suitable building as a permanent home, and official recognition by the American government, which would promote the fullest cooperation of Italian officials. Through McKim's persistent and considerable efforts, all of these objectives were reached by 1909, and the Academy began to function smoothly.[5]

So high was English regard of the firm's work, in 1903 McKim was awarded the Gold Medal of the Royal Institute of British Architects. In his acceptance speech, he called attention to the familial relationship between Colonial architecture and that of Wren and his followers; unfortunately, he noted, many of the American buildings were being swept aside before advancing commercial prosperity, resulting in the loss of historic monuments and "the lesson they invariably teach of sound proportion, simplicity, and good manners."[6] Nonetheless, he was heartened to see some growing interest on the part of his countrymen in the preservation of significant buildings, which the A.I.A.'s purchase of the Octagon exemplified, and he was glad to report increasing cooperation between government and architects. During the ceremonies, McKim repeatedly said he was happy to accept the medal not for himself but on behalf of all American architects, to whom it had really been awarded.

After his presidency McKim remained active in A.I.A. affairs, and he served on the Municipal Art Commission of New York.[7] Little by little, however, as he threw himself into these endeavors and into his many building projects, his nervous equability and physical stamina began to break down. Spring trips to South Carolina and excursions to the moors of Scotland became necessary annual therapy, but the relaxation came too little too late. Mead, who like White enjoyed the best of health, observed to a colleague late in 1905 that although many of McKim's projects had begun to bear fruit, he "at last sees that he has been overdoing it."[8]

During the first years of the new century White produced the most carefully composed and detailed work of his career [264]. Meanwhile he continued his annual forays to Europe in search of the many paintings, carvings, pieces of furniture, and other objects that then found their way into his clients' new homes. He was especially busy collecting art work for the interiors of the Payne Whitney house, begun in 1902. His Gramercy Square townhouse, the subject of endless alterations, began to resemble a storehouse as objects piled up and covered the walls, and in fact at the turn of the century White was obliged to rent a warehouse to hold the paintings and sculpture that were pouring in. Then, in March 1905, the warehouse and its contents were consumed by fire—Holbein portraits for Henry VIII and Edward VI were just two of the hundreds of priceless objects that were destroyed. At the time White was with McKim, shooting near Garret, South Carolina. "Stanford has behaved and bore up like a soldier in the loss of his things," McKim reassured Bessie White, but "after two days of stony misery poor old Stan broke down completely, and sobbed at the breakfast table like a child. Then he made up his mind to it and threw it off, so that one would think he had forgotten all about it."[9]

For White, too, there were picture frames and book covers to design, such as the elaborate cover he sketched for a book planned by Robert Russell, which was to have a figure of the Naples Venus deeply embossed at its center.[10] And there were always the party settings to design, the most elaborate of which was the transformation of Sherry's ballroom into a version of the Hall of Mirrors at Versailles for the James Hazen Hyde Ball in 1905.

There were more collaborations with Saint-Gaudens as well, but nothing like the flurry of activity that marked the 1880s. Since 1893 the sculptor had been working slowly on a memorial to Phillips Brooks next to Trinity Church, Boston, and in 1895 White had obtained drawings of the church to make a start on the ciboriumlike setting. Since the figure was progressing so slowly, White put this work aside. Not until 1902 did Saint-Gaudens finish the pair of figures, but then the model was destroyed in a studio fire at Aspen in 1904, forcing the sculptor to reconstruct it. As a result White was able to complete his design for the setting only shortly before his death; construction drawings were finished by his assistants in 1907, but the entire ensemble, resembling the Scagliere Monument in Verona, was not finished until 1910.[11]

The last setting White designed for Saint-Gaudens, for the *Seated Lincoln* in Grant Park, Chicago, was begun in 1904 when the figure was first sketched; White wrote Burnham about the location of the natural history museum Burnham was proposing for the Chicago waterfront so the *Lincoln* ensemble might be most advantageously located.[12] The earlier *Standing Lincoln* in Lincoln Park had represented the man, but the seated figure was to represent the head of state. Saint-Gaudens had anticipated flanking the figure with allegories of Justice and Charity, but after discussions with White this was changed to a broad semicircular podium and bench, backed by a tall clipped hedge, the whole framed by Doric columns taking the place of the auxiliary figures [265]. This project too was delayed by the

265. Augustus Saint-Gaudens and Stanford White, *Seated Lincoln*, Grant Park, Chicago, Ill., 1904–c.1920.

266. Detroit Bicentennial Memorial Column, Detroit, Mich., project, 1899. *American Architect and Building News*, June 16, 1900.

studio fire of 1904, but the figure was reconstructed and completed by Saint-Gaudens shortly before his death in 1907, just as construction drawings for the setting were prepared by the firm. Eventually the ensemble was finished, although landscaping in Grant Park remained incomplete through the mid-1920s. If the Brooks Memorial, finished in 1907–10, in its crowded figures and claustrophobic ciborium, is awkward and uncharacteristic of the collaboration of these two artists, the *Seated Lincoln* is far more successful; it has an amplitude and severity that contrasts appropriately with the more intimate *Standing Lincoln*.

The stark Greek Doric columns employed as the framing ends of the *Seated Lincoln* were relatively new in White's work, for before he had favored the lighter Ionic and Corinthian orders. But for memorials and monuments White had begun using the heavy austere Doric order in 1900, beginning on a monumental scale with his proposed Detroit Memorial Column. The project had been initiated in 1899 as a memorial of the founding of the city in 1701 by Antoine de la Mothe Cadillac. A Detroit World's Fair was considered, but as one was already being prepared in Buffalo, Charles Lang Freer suggested a memorial, to be designed by a group of artists. The participants chosen were architect Stanford White, sculptors Saint-Gaudens and Frederick MacMonnies, and painters Dwight W. Tryon and Thomas W. Dewing. Donating their services, the committee visited Detroit and inspected the proposed memorial locations; a design, prepared by White, was presented at the Detroit

Museum of Art on February 22, 1900 [266]. Of all the possible locations, the committee felt the area at the base of Belle Isle in the middle of the Detroit River was most commanding and historically appropriate, for a monument there, easily visible from the city, would signify the importance of the early trade routes on the Great Lakes. White proposed a huge Doric column, framed at its base by a colonnade and sculptural groups, carrying on its enormous capital a tripod incorporating a flame of natural gas and electric beacons. The committee believed that "if such a design is artistically and properly carried out the Detroit column would forever stand as a sign and insignia of the city the world over, and rank with the famous monuments of all time.[13] The white marble column, 24 feet in diameter at the base, was to be 220 feet high. To provide a proper forecourt, nearly 38 acres were to be reclaimed from the marshy land at the southern tip of the island; a portion of this was to be laid out formally along the axial approach. It was hoped the cost of one million dollars would be contributed by Detroit citizens, but public interest waned, and even before the city celebrated its bicentennial, plans for the memorial had been shelved.

Even so, the basic concept was not lost altogether, for White adapted it for the Prison Ship Martyrs' Monument, Fort Greene Park, Brooklyn. Nearby, in Wallabout Bay, more than 11,500 American prisoners had died in chains in the holds of English ships during the Revolutionary War. As early as 1898, E. R. Kennedy had wanted to have White and Frederick MacMonnies design a monument to their memory, avoiding a competition, but funds were raised only with great difficulty, and not until 1904 was a limited competition finally held. Upon getting the award in 1905, White had working drawings prepared, but actual construction was further delayed until 1907, after White's death. The grand colonnades of Detroit were eliminated and the slightly reduced Doric column of 143 feet was set on a terraced hill ascended by broad flights of stairs; the tripod atop the column, once bearing a perpetual flame, was modeled by Adolph A. Weinman [267].[14]

While Daniel Chester French had been expeditiously finishing his equestrian *Washington* during 1899 and McKim its base, Saint-Gaudens had yet to finish his equestrian *General Sherman*, although he had begun work in 1892 and restudied the figures in 1897. It was only in 1902 that he asked McKim to design a base for it. Saint-Gaudens's progress had been so slow because he had done much of the modeling of the horse himself, although this time he worked with R. Phimister Proctor, who had also assisted Saint-Gaudens on the *Logan* monument for Chicago. Work was delayed too because neither the Sherman Memorial committee nor the sculptor could agree on a site; even when the figure was finished in 1900 the location had not been fixed. The location Saint-Gaudens, White, and McKim all preferred was adjacent to Grant's Tomb on Riverside Drive, far to the north in Manhattan, but their second choice was in the center of the Mall in Central Park. Neither was acceptable to the Grant family or other sculptors of pieces in the park, who rightly feared the *Sherman* would dominate everything. While McKim was hunting in the South in January 1901, White wrote the memorial committee that "any site which does not face the statue south, I know Saint Gaudens could not assent to, as it has been modeled for a southern light."[15] Within months, however, all parties agreed to the site at the *rond-point* at the southeast corner of Central Park, where Fifth Avenue and 59th Street intersect. While the bronze was being cast and prepared for its multiple layers of gold leaf, the details of the pedestal were studied; a rounded rectangular base of red Stony Creek granite was given an encircling bench seat; and the whole was placed on a broad podium. At long last the statue was unveiled in May 1903 [268].[16]

267. Prison Ship Martyrs' Memorial, Fort Greene Park, Brooklyn, N. Y., 1904–09, with sculpture by Adolph A. Weinman. Perspective signed and dated "Jules Crow 06."

268. Augustus Saint-Gaudens and Charles Follen McKim, General William Tecumseh Sherman Memorial, Central Park, New York, N. Y., 1902–03 (figure begun 1892).

269. Washington, D. C., photograph of the Mall, looking east, c. 1895.

WHEREAS White's Detroit column project at the start of the century had come to naught, McKim's contemporaneous planning activity in restoring L'Enfant's scheme for Washington, D.C., was to have an impact on the remainder of the century. Although the firm had been able, in a small way, to extrapolate from the Columbian Exposition in the collegiate planning, the reorganization of the national capital acquired greater significance as the first expression of the City Beautiful movement inspired by the fair, and as John Reps has noted, the official report of the Senate Park Commission for Washington was "the country's first modern city planning report."[17]

The city's original plan, drawn by L'Enfant during the critical period when the national government was created, was intentionally designed to express in a symbolic way the balance of power in the Federal Constitution, yet no sooner had the nineteenth century begun when this symbolic system was dismantled, piece by piece. First, President Jackson had Robert Mills's Treasury Building, 1836–39, placed east of the executive mansion, blocking the line of sight to the Capitol; and twelve years later, when Mills's Washington Monument was begun, its position had to be shifted to a point 120 feet south and 380 feet east of the crossing of the President's house and Capitol axes, where the subsoil could bear the weight of the colossal obelisk. The Mall was vitiated even more when Renwick's Gothic Smithsonian Institution was built perilously close to the center line in 1847. Then in 1859, President Fillmore had Andrew Jackson Downing prepare a romantically picturesque landscape plan for the Capitol Mall and the President's grounds, a scheme totally at variance with L'Enfant's vision. The most grievous intrusion was made in 1872 when Congress granted the Baltimore & Ohio Railroad permission to lay tracks across the Mall and construct a train shed and terminal station fronting on B Street (Constitution Avenue). L'Enfant's symbolic order had become cacophony [269]. The problem of restoration was intensified when, in 1881, an expanse of land was reclaimed from the tidal flats of the Potomac, so that whereas the Mall had previously ended just west of the Washington Monument, by 1900 over six hundred acres had been created through dredging, moving the shore of the river more than a mile west of the obelisk.

During 1890 some proposals for reorganizing the Mall were suggested as the approaching centennial of the city stirred interest in some sort of memorial. There was, furthermore, the pressing need for additions to the President's house, especially for executive offices. In an attempt to satisfy all needs, President McKinley appointed a committee to study the creation of a permanent memorial of the city's centenary, and this centennial committee, chaired by Senator James McMillan of Michigan, recommended building a new executive mansion and reorganizing the Mall leading to a memorial bridge over the Potomac to the Arlington National Cemetery. But then the appropriation bill for this ambitious project was so trimmed in the House of Representatives that it allowed for only $6,000 for a study of additions to the President's house and minor modifications to the Mall, under the direction of Colonel Theodore A. Bingham, Chief of Army Engineers, and an unspecified landscape architect. Bingham prepared several schemes showing streets cut through the Mall and designed immense domed wings for the President's house.[18] Bingham's proposal, presented in December 1900, were greeted by a storm of protest from architects across the country, orchestrated largely by Glenn Brown, secretary of the American Institute of Architects, who had just completed a comprehensive study of the Capitol building and L'Enfant's plan and thus was thoroughly familiar with the original planner's intent. Since the annual convention of the Institute was scheduled for Washington in December 1900, Brown selected as the theme of the sessions the artistic and unified development of Washington. In the wake of Bingham's hapless proposals, a number of prominent architects offered designs showing how the grandeur of the Mall could be restored. Among the speakers was Frederick Law Olmsted, Jr., who made it clear that landscape architecture was not restricted solely to the creation of planned informality in apparent imitation of nature, but was concerned with the relationship of buildings to the spaces around them and the conscious ordering of those spaces. Whether a particular design was formal or informal, he said, depended on the circumstances of the place; great public edifices ought to be strongly formal, and this formality should be recognized in the plan of their surroundings. L'Enfant's Mall, he observed, had been specifically designed

> to relate directly and visibly to the Capitol; while it has been planned and planted for the most part in utter disregard to this primary purpose. Its details . . . have arrogated to themselves the control of the design.[19]

To circumvent the penny-pinching of the House of Representatives, at an executive session of the Senate, March 8, 1901, Senator McMillan secured the passage of a resolution directing the Senate committee on the District of Columbia to report on the development and improvement of the District's park system, securing such professional advice as it might require. Since the expenses of this committee were to be paid out of the Senate contingency fund, McMillan's true intent to replan the entire city was cloaked in a study of only the "park system," requiring no approval from the House. Within two weeks the Senate District Committee met with the American Institute of Architects to select the professional advisors for the "park" study. The first name put forward was Burnham's, followed by that of Olmsted, Jr., as the landscape architect. These two then asked that McKim be appointed as the second architect. By March 25 all three had accepted their appointments to an ad hoc Senate Park Commission. Meanwhile, McMillan, eager to foster cordial relationships which would help ensure that plans would result in building projects, introduced the commission members to Secretary of War Elihu Root and President Roosevelt, who expressed their interest in preserving the works of Washington's time.

Burnham arranged with Senator McMillan for the commission members, accompanied by McMillan's secretary, Charles Moore, to travel to Europe to survey the examples of urban design and the parks and cities L'Enfant had considered when planning Washington. McKim cautioned that they should concentrate on a selected number of cities rather than wasting too much of their month's traveling time going from place to place. Because of his greater experience in Europe, McKim was put in charge of the travel arrangements. Prior to sailing from New York in June, however, they toured plantation houses and cities in Virginia that also had served as models for Washington, particularly Williamsburg. Meanwhile, the commission had already begun sketching out some proposals, and the matter of placing sculptural memorials arose; McKim suggested that Saint-Gaudens be added to the commission, but because of the late date and ill health he was not able to join the group in the trip to Europe.

As the ship left New York harbor, maps of Washington were spread out, and the four set to work. Moore began to feel that the architects' ideas were becoming too grandiose to receive serious consideration in Congress, to which Burnham asserted "it was the business and duty of the Commission to make the very finest plans their minds could conceive. The future . . . will prove even those plans all too small; and that the time (if ever) to compromise was after the large plans had been made."[20] The group toured Paris, turned to Rome where they studied the great Piazza of Saint Peter's, then, to Hadrian's Villa at Tivoli, and from there, to Venice, a plan of which had been among the papers Jefferson lent L'Enfant. In Vienna they toured the Schoenbrunn and the Ringstrasse. Some time was spent in Budapest before the group returned to Paris, where they measured the grounds at Fontainebleau and Vaux-le-Vicomte. The gardens and *grandes allées* and the great basin at Versailles, one of L'Enfant's primary sources, were also carefully studied.[21]

In July the group separated, Burnham going to Frankfort to inspect the new railway station there, and McKim and the others going to England. Burnham detoured at the request of Alexander Cassatt, president of the Pennsylvania Railroad, who had commissioned Burnham to design a new station in Washington, D.C., for the Pennsylvania and Baltimore & Ohio railroads. The projected Washington station weighed greatly on the minds of the commission, for the location on the Mall posed the most serious obstacle to the full restoration of L'Enfant's plan. Burnham had been instructed by Cassatt not to concern himself with the site for the new station, but the commission decided that if Cassatt would not relocate the station they would take him to the Avenue des Champs Élysées in Paris and ask him to visualize a train shed across it. One can only imagine the amazement Moore, Olmsted, and McKim must have experienced when Burnham rejoined them in London with the news that the Pennsylvania and Baltimore & Ohio railroads were willing to vacate the Mall, building their new station north of the Capitol, provided Congress would help finance a tunnel under the Capitol building. The commission's sweeping reorganization of the Mall was now feasible, and they set to work with renewed vigor. Before leaving England they examined the parks and gardens of several estates, including Bushy Park and Windsor Great Park.

After returning to New York in August, the four separated, each to his own office. The general features of the plan had been laid out on board ship on the way home; all that remained was to prepare final drawings and models for presentation to Congress. Moore had the task of forwarding to Olmsted and McKim accurate measured drawings of the city and Mall. While supervising the whole enterprise, Burnham was largely occupied with the many engineering and design problems of the new station. Olmsted, in Brookline, was in charge of the proposals for expanding and connecting the District's parks. McKim had charge of redesigning the Mall and the new buildings in the central section of the city; of the four he was most concerned with building design. Realizing that extensive visual materials would help win support for the new plan, McKim rented office space on the floor above the firm's offices and there gathered a team of draftsmen who, under the direction of William T. Partridge, began preparing the large drawings of the Mall and its enclosing buildings. They also constructed a model measuring nine by seventeen feet, showing the center of Washington as redesigned by the commission, with a more detailed companion model showing the grounds around the Washington Monument [270, 271]. A second nine-by-seventeen-foot model was constructed under George C. Curtis in Boston, showing the existing conditions in Washington. McKim also assembled a corps of artists to prepare large colored perspectives; among them were Jules Guerin, Otto H. Bacher, Henry McCarter, George de Gersdorff, A. R. Ross, Robert Blum, Carleton T. Chapman, and F. L. V. Hoppin.

On January 15, 1902, the commission's report was formally presented. While McKim supervised installation of the perspectives and models in the Corcoran Gallery, McMillan and Moore presented the final draft of the report to the Senate District Committee. As he toured the exhibit of drawings and models that evening, President Roosevelt became appreciative and then enthusiastic as the scope of the plan became apparent.[22] Parklands were proposed by Olmsted throughout the city, especially along the valleys of existing waterways such as Rock Creek. Together with existing parks, these would form an interconnected network across the city. Around the Capitol building were to be judicial offices and new office buildings for members of the House and Senate [271, 272]. Besides providing badly needed space, with the existing Library of Congress (not actually shown in the drawings!) these would create a proper architectural frame for the Capitol. The system of streets around the Mall was retained as it existed, but the axis of the Mall was shifted slightly to the south so that it would run through the center of the Washington Monument. Along this realigned Mall, from the Capitol westward, were new carriage drives and closely spaced rows of trees defining the new axis; on either side of the axis were various departmental buildings and museums. In the triangle between Pennsylvania Avenue and the new Mall were to be new municipal office buildings for the District government.[23]

As it was impossible to swing the axis south of the President's house so as to run through the Washington Monument, McKim devised a large formal garden terrace framed by a square of trees west of the obelisk; at its center was a round pool of water marking the crossing of L'Enfant's axes [273].[24] The President's house was untouched, but rather a ring of executive office buildings enclosed Lafayette Square to the north. At the other end of the axis to the south was to be a formal cluster of museums dedicated to national heroes, focused on a centrally planned domed structure much like White's library for New York University.

West of the Washington Monument the new Mall was extended through the reclaimed land, with carriage drives and rows of trees framing a long reflecting basin inspired by that at Versailles.[25] At the end was to be a monument to Abraham Lincoln, an open portico sheltering a seated statue [274]. For this, for the first time in his work, McKim proposed using the Greek Doric order (which White had just used for his Detroit Memorial). Radiating out from the drive around the Lincoln Memorial were several avenues leading to Olmsted's

270. Senate Park Commission, model of Washington, D. C., showing existing conditions, 1900.

271. Senate Park Commission, model of proposed development of the Mall and reclaimed lands, Washington, D. C., 1901–02.

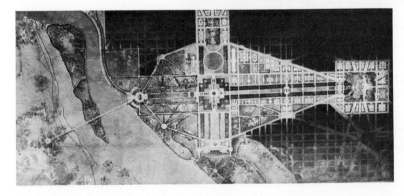

272. Senate Park Commission, plan of treatment of the Mall and reclaimed lands, Washington, D. C., 1901–02.

Rock Creek Parkway and to the bridge across the Potomac to Arlington Cemetery, so aligned that it pointed directly toward the Custis Mansion, the home of Robert E. Lee. The river crossing, then, was a symbolic link between the leaders of North and South.

The commission's plan was simple and bold. Like the original, which it endeavored to restore, this plan was to provide, in L'Enfant's words, a guide for "embellishment which the increase of the wealth of the nation will permit it to pursue at any time however remote."[26] The scope of the work was staggering to congressmen accustomed to thinking of individual buildings, or at best, city blocks. The cost seemed astronomical, but as Montgomery Schuyler observed:

273. Senate Park Commission, perspective of proposed gardens and terraces around the Washington Monument, signed "Graham/1902."

The point is to have a plan that you believe in. . . . Whatever it may cost Uncle Sam to do all this, it will cost him nothing to say now that he believes in it, that he means to do it in good time, and that in the meantime whatever he does in the way of public architecture or public embellishment he will do it in accordance with it.[27]

Indeed, some of the proposed changes were already underway. Burnham's Union Station, begun in 1902, on Massachusetts Avenue, faced the Capitol, and the grounds between the two buildings were cleared and landscaped so that the station truly became the vestibule to the city. On March 22, 1902, the first steps were taken to fix the location of the planned Lincoln Memorial, for prior to a meeting with Senator Shelby M. Cullum of Illinois, McKim explored the marshes of the western edge of the landfill with Saint-Gaudens and Moore until they found the point on the Capitol–Washington Monument axis, and there they drove the first stake in the reorganization of the Mall.[28]

In an effort to begin the Lincoln Memorial, Senator Cullum asked McKim to prepare estimates of the cost of the building. Drawings were given to Norcross Brothers, and on March 29, 1902, McKim forwarded their estimate to Senator George P. Wetmore, noting that in the absence of detailed drawings no completely accurate figures could be established, so the figure he was quoting was tentative. To this undisclosed sum, he cautioned, should be added Saint-Gaudens's fee of $250,000 for the figure. Later, in writing to O. W. Norcross, McKim noted that, using the Doric order, the memorial would cost $1,957,480, but that changing the design to Corinthian would add $350,000.[29] Although Cullum's bill was passed in 1902, McKim did not live to see the end of the matter, for the Lincoln Memorial Commission did not hold its first meeting until 1904 nor make its report until 1909, when it came to the conclusion that the most fitting memorial would be a highway! This digression from the Park Commission's recommendations opened the floodgates for all manner of other memorial proposals, and the controversy was not settled until 1912 when a newly constituted Lincoln Memorial Commission returned to the location and basic form of the memorial first proposed by the Senate Park Commission. Since by this time both originating architect and sculptor were dead, Henry Bacon, once McKim's close associate, was asked to submit designs for the building, and Daniel Chester French modeled the figure, drawing on Saint-Gaudens's *Seated Lincoln* in Chicago; although varying slightly from the original proposal of 1902, the Lincoln Memorial was finally completed in 1914–22.[30]

274. Charles Follen
McKim and the Senate
Park Commission,
perspective
of proposed Lincoln
Memorial, 1902.

Concurrently McKim had been asked to supply drawings for the Potomac bridge, and on forwarding drawings to Secretary of War Elihu Root in October 1902, he pointed out that his scheme called for a low bridge of multiple segmental arches, for the landscape, he emphasized, was not sufficiently bold to warrant a great single suspension or trussed span. To allow for river traffic, one of the center spans could be "a skeleton bascule bridge, balanced as indicated, and worked by electric machinery under the road bed."[31] The relationship McKim perceived between the bridge and the landscape was significant, with the undulations of the arches suggested by the gently rolling banks of the river. As with the Lincoln Memorial, the bridge proposal was tabled until pressing automobile traffic in the mid-1920s forced action. In this instance, the bridge commission was given to the younger partners continuing the office, and the Arlington Bridge was constructed in 1926–32 with only minor departures from McKim's original scheme.

The delays encountered in building the Lincoln Memorial were typical of the impediments thrown in the way of implementing the Senate Park Commission plan, beginning with the construction of the new Agriculture Building in 1901–04. Before the commission members left for Europe in June 1901, McKim wrote to James Knox Taylor, federal supervising architect, requesting not only that the proposed Agriculture Building be built behind the existing building on the Mall so as to conform to the new street alignment being considered, but also that a classical expression be employed due to the proximity to the Capitol.[32] Government officials, however, felt it their special prerogative to determine the position of the new building, and the architects, Rankin, Kellogg & Crane of Philadelphia (former assistants in the McKim, Mead & White office), were instructed to disregard the 800-foot Mall being proposed by the commission and to place their building 100 feet closer to the center line. When, during the spring of 1904, Burnham and McKim wrote President Roosevelt to resolve the matter, they were informed it now rested with the Senate. Accordingly, a hearing was conducted in March by the Senate District Committee, at which officials of the Agriculture Department, Burnham, McKim, Saint-Gaudens, and others testified; the result of this was that the committee ruled in favor of the 800-foot Mall. By this time, however, the foundations had already been started, and again the President and Secretary of War William Howard Taft were asked to rule on altering construction. Fortunately an engineer reported that making the changes would reduce the cost and so the repositioning of the Agriculture Building was ordered. In the end, the recommendations of the Senate Park Commission had been upheld and the broad lines of their scheme established, but it had been particularly wearing on McKim. After the final hearing concerning repositioning, Secretary Taft congratulated McKim on his victory, to which McKim replied, "Was it a victory? Another such and I am dead."[33]

The Senate Park Commission had accomplished a great deal. They had drawn up a plan for Washington that incorporated the basic features of L'Enfant's original scheme, reconciling to it the various additions and changes that had been made during the nineteenth century. The breadth, simplicity, and logic of their plan gradually inspired increasing numbers of government officials. Just as the Columbian Exposition had revealed the theoretical potential of planning, so the Park Commission's plan demonstrated the successful reshaping of a real city. In particular, the impact of the written report, the exhibition of the drawings and models, and the subsequent dispute over the placement of the Agriculture Building made President Roosevelt keenly appreciative of the wisdom of comprehensive preliminary planning. To ensure that the projected new office buildings for members of the Senate and the House of Representatives would be in accord with the Park Commission's plan, and to preclude any confrontation such as had arisen over the Agriculture Building, in the spring of 1904, at McKim's suggestion, President Roosevelt appointed an ad hoc Consultative Board to review and advise on future designs. The members were those formerly on the Park Commission, with the addition of Bernard R. Green, Superintendent of the Library of Congress. President Roosevelt made clear his views concerning adherence to comprehensive plans in speaking to the American Institute of Architects in 1905. If the nation was to have good architecture, he advised,

> whenever hereafter a public building is provided for and erected, it should be erected in accordance with a carefully thought-out plan adopted long before, and that it should be not only beautiful in itself, but fitting in its relations to the whole scheme of the public buildings, the parks and drives of the District.[34]

Then, on the eve of leaving office, on January 19, 1909, President Roosevelt issued an executive order formally creating a permanent Council of Fine Arts to advise on design and placement of future public buildings. Among the twenty-one appointees to the Council were Burnham and McKim, but McKim was by then too ill to serve. Despite resistance from some parties, the Commission of Fine Arts was reaffirmed by Roosevelt's successor President Taft in 1910.[35] In surveying the gradual development of Washington over half a century following the establishment of the Fine Arts Commission, one discovers that, except for the clearing and planting of the Mall, few of the Park Commission's *specific* proposals have been carried out literally, yet their basic scheme (and L'Enfant's original design) have been consistently reinforced. The essential qualities of space, order, formal clarity, and harmony among the many parts have been maintained and "reciprocity of sight" restored. Even the exigencies of two major world wars have not materially altered the pursuit of this plan. Fortunately, before the chance to reclaim this legacy had passed altogether, Burnham, Olmsted, and McKim rekindled L'Enfant's vision.

After 1902 Burnham turned to urban design and planning almost exclusively, and McKim too received offers to participate in planning commissions. In 1903 he was again asked to serve on a New York City planning committee, but even the entreaties of Mayor Seth Low were to no avail. McKim explained to Charles Moore that the way the New York committee was set up virtually precluded any positive result, nor was there any fee or salary.

Perhaps most important to McKim, the committee's inquiry was limited to Manhattan and did not take in all five boroughs of the newly consolidated city. Nor were they to consider the interrelated problem of transportation. "The difficulties to be overcome here, are, so far as the Borough of Manhattan is concerned, insuperable," he wrote Moore, "and with but a few years of breath left to hope for, there are several ways in which I could put in my time more effectively."[36] McKim also declined an invitation in 1907 to participate in planning the area around the green in New Haven, not only for reasons of health but because this was a competition.[37]

McKim's participation in the Senate Park Commission was an auspicious beginning of the new century, and in the firm's individual buildings this same spirit of confident expansiveness and artistic generosity was amplified. Particularly in their private houses, the careful allusions to historical sources became more pronounced, markedly so in White's work, beginning with the vexing commission from Joseph Pulitzer. The firm had already remodeled the C. T. Barney house in New York for the Pulitzer family, 1891, and four years later had added a tower to the Pulitzer summer house at Bar Harbor, Maine.[38] In January 1900 fire completely destroyed the Barney-Pulitzer house on 55th Street, and although all of the family were safely evacuated, two servants were killed and an invaluable library and numerous arts works were consumed. Pulitzer had engaged the firm by September to design a new house, although he had not yet purchased the lots he wanted off upper Fifth Avenue. By mid-April 1901, however, he had acquired three adjoining lots on East 73rd Street, and construction commenced the following month. Pulitzer taxed his architects, requiring numerous visits to Chatwold in Bar Harbor and the preparation of ink drawings of "the blackest black on the whitest white," as well as plaster models of the facade which he could study with his fingers; for, since he was going blind, delicately shaded perspectives were useless to him.[39] Of the various preliminary designs a few photographs of drawings survive, indicating that White experimented with a high-crowned French Renaissance scheme similar to G. B. Post's Cornelius Vanderbilt II house of 1882–94, which Pulitzer rejected as being far too gaudy. White also prepared a Florentine palazzo similar to McKim's H. A. C. Taylor house but covered with relief sculpture; this too was turned down. White then turned to the palazzi of Baldassare Longhena in Venice from the end of the seventeenth century, in particular the Palazzo Pesaro and the Palazzo Rezzonico, although he seems also to have studied the Palazzo Labia by Andrea Cominelli of the mid-eighteenth century [275].[40] The firm wrestled with the obstreperous Pulitzer every inch of the way. First, the client did not want to pay for all the rejected preliminary studies, and then when White was designing the interiors, he kept changing his mind. White reminded him: "I know one thing, and this is we have certainly made twice as many studies, and done twice as much work on this as we have ever done on any interior work before, and it is pretty hard where so many contrary orders are given, and so many changes made to know where you stand or what to do."[41]

Because of Pulitzer's special requirements, the plan was not typical of the firm's other urban residences [276]. The site was much broader, and hence the house is more expansive (it has since been divided into three luxury apartments), and there were a number of unusual spaces such as the glass-roofed circular breakfast room. The interlocking complexities of the plan, however, were typical of White, as for example the servant's passage over the breakfast room with its glass wall and glass block floor to admit light into the room below. The interiors were elegant but restrained in accordance with Pulitzer's instructions that there be "no ballroom, music room, or picture gallery under any disguise." He had flatly in-

275. Joseph Pulitzer house, New York, N. Y., 1900–03.

276. BELOW. Pulitzer house, first- and second-floor plans. *Monograph.*

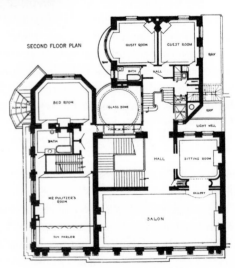

structed White there was to be no French furniture, for he wanted "an American house for comfort & use not for show or entertainment."[42] In his own rooms, isolated from the rest of the house by a thick masonry wall, Pulitzer insisted on absolute quiet. As luck would have it, the lots he had purchased included a spring, and since nothing could stop the water it was conducted into a sump emptied periodically by an electric pump. The firm turned to Wallace Sabine for assistance in damping the noise, and one can detect a trace, perhaps, of testiness in a letter to Sabine from the otherwise unflappable Mead: "We have been building a house for Joseph Pulitzer, who is a nervous wreck and most susceptible to noises, and he has discovered many real and imaginary noises in his house. Some of them are real and can be obviated, and we have great confidence that you can discover the cause and a remedy for them."[43] All seemed well, for, as Mead later reported to Sabine after his recommendations had been followed, Pulitzer had been living in the house since mid-October 1903 when a small fire broke out in the basement: "the fire department was out and rushing about the house and he did not wake up. I am satisfied of one thing—that nerves are his trouble and that it is not part of an architect's business to supply the client with a proper set of nerves."[44] Unfortunately, Pulitzer was convinced the noise of the pump was still present, being concentrated somehow in his bedroom. Finding no peace in the house he had a separate wing added to the rear by Foster, Gade & Graham, so effective that Pulitzer's secretaries dubbed it "the vault." Its double walls had mineral wool packed in the air space, and the floor rested on ball bearings; here at last Pulitzer found silence.

The embellished Florentine scheme Pulitzer rejected was almost immediately adapted by White for the Robert Wilson Patterson house in Washington, D.C., 1900–03 [277].[45] In 1899, when Joseph Medill died and Patterson became editor-in-chief of the many Medill publishing enterprises, he and Elinor set about building a festive second house on Dupont Circle suitable for the life they now planned to lead. In keeping with the desired character, the house was built of white glazed terra cotta, once White had allayed Elinor's concern as to the resistance of the terra cotta to moisture. Especially intriguing is the plan, devised to fit the irregular lot, using two wings forming a **V** and joined at the center by a typical Whitian two-story porch with doubled columns [278]. The ground floor had a central stair hall flanked by reception and billiard rooms, but most unusual was provision for an automobile, making this one of the first houses equipped with an internal garage.

A house which received even more of White's attention, both in planning and internal furnishing, was for Payne and his bride, Helen Hay Whitney, on Fifth Avenue, New York, 1902–09 [279], a wedding present from Whitney's uncle, Oliver H. Payne.[46] The gently bowed facade was actually the southern half of a double house, the northern half of which was built by the J. C. Lyons Building and Operating Company. The white marble exterior was in the spirit of the Pulitzer house, then under construction, and like it, similar to Longhena's Palazzo Pesaro. The masonry bearing walls, as in other large urban houses by the firm, braced an internal steel frame. The greater part of the enormous cost of the house was incurred by the rare materials, architectural fragments, antique furnishings, and art works with which the house was sumptuously finished [280].[47] Small wonder that the house cost nearly a million dollars, well over the estimate, causing Oliver Payne to protest. White apologized to Payne, acknowledging that

> all kinds of small extras have crept in and . . . the changes I have made in the treatment of the smaller rooms have added over a hundred thousand dollars to the price of the house, and I have

277. Robert W. Patterson house, Washington, D. C., 1900–03.

278. BELOW. Patterson house, first- and second-floor plans.

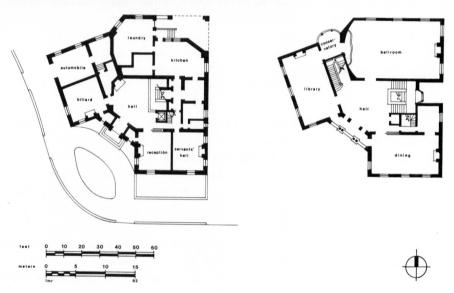

dreaded to speak to you about it until the house was far enough finished for you to see the result, as although I feared that you would be angry at first, I thought if you saw the money had been wisely spent and that I had given Payne and Helen a house to live in which is really of the first water and could stand in beauty with any house in the world, that you would forgive me and I believed in my heart that you would in the end approve of what I had done. . . .[48]

Helen and Payne were delighted with the house, and Helen comforted White, promising to write Oliver Payne "such a letter about the house that he will forgive you anything."[49] In the face of such gratitude, Oliver Payne relented and forgave White. Such was White's effervescent enthusiasm that clients and critics could forgive him anything—all but one who began to plot against White's life even as the Whitneys rapturously took possession of their new house.

In striking contrast to the opulence of the Whitney house was the chillingly austere

279. Payne Whitney house, New York, N. Y. (bowed front portion), 1902–09; townhouse for J. C. Lyons Company (left half), 1902–05. *Monograph.*

280. Whitney house, stair hall, interior.

Italianate John Innes Kane house, New York, 1904–08, by McKim and William S. Richardson [281], as Spartan on the inside as it was outside.[50] Curiously, it was the ground floor, here, not the *piano nobile* where the principal rooms were located, which received the greatest emphasis, with shallow rustication and paired pilasters recalling Peruzzi's Palazzo Massimi in Rome. For one other residence, a unique setting dictated a radically different

281. RIGHT. John I. Kane house, New York, N. Y., 1904–08.

282. BELOW. Vanderbilt houses complex, New York, N. Y. William Kissam Vanderbilt house (forground), 1878–82, by Richard Morris Hunt; Mrs. William Kissam Vanderbilt, Jr., house (to the right), 1904–07. W. J. Roege photograph, 1924.

treatment using a style the partners had not employed for twenty years. White's house for Virginia and William Kissam Vanderbilt, Jr., New York, 1904–07, the most archaeologically correct François Ier house he ever did, was on Fifth Avenue immediately next to the famous "château" Richard Morris Hunt had designed for William's parents in 1879 [282], and White wisely chose to emulate Hunt's example.[51] In the grill work of the door, the carved frames of the windows, and especially in the rich roofscape, White showed his love for concentrated detail, but in contrast large stretches of wall were left blank. Yet, so closely did White follow

Hunt, it is easy to read the two houses as one building. The Vanderbilt house was a clear gesture of respect toward an architect White and his partners held in high esteem; having taken an evening stroll up Fifth Avenue to see it once more, McKim would say, he was ready for another cigar before going to bed.

For the most part the other residences of the period alluded to Georgian-Federalist traditions, but one country house by White warrants special notice not only because of its external severity but also for its interesting function and structural solutions. The firm built very little for the Astor family (even relatively little for the Vanderbilts), and perhaps the only Astor who could fathom the Bohemian side of White's nature was John Jacob IV who far preferred the country life at Ferncliff up the Hudson at Rhinebeck, built by his father, William Backhouse Astor, Jr., who also had disliked the stuffy conventions of fashionable society. Here Jack and his spirited wife, Ava, had White build a guest house and recreational pavilion incorporating squash courts, swimming pool, and enclosed tennis court, 1902–04 [283, 284].[52] From the entrance drive the one-story building distinctly recalled Mansart's Grand Trianon at Versailles, but in the two-story wing to the rear White used light metal parabolic arches to carry Guastavino tile vaults and skylights the length of the tennis court. It was an interesting spatial experiment, but as White wrote Wallace Sabine, the curvature caused acoustical problems.[53]

283. ABOVE. Tennis Court Pavilion, addition to Ferncliff for John Jacob Astor IV, front, 1902–04. *Monograph.*

284. Astor Tennis Courts, Ferncliff, interior. *Monograph.*

THE remaining urban residences at the start of the century belonged to the Georgian-Federalist type the partners had been developing for a decade and a half and which, by now, had been widely adopted by other architects. Two houses, not urban, clearly demonstrate the associational links that frequently suggested this style. One was the elongated summer house of Thomas Jefferson Coolidge, on a bluff overlooking the Atlantic at Manchester-by-the-Sea, Massachusetts, 1902–04. A "hyphenated" house, this referred to Georgian plantation houses of Virginia, but its classicism and brick construction were meant to recall the ancestor whose name Coolidge bore.[54] The second house was for Joseph Willard and also drew from eighteenth-century sources. Built in a residential section of Richmond, Virginia, 1906–10, its high hip roof and brick walls greatly resembled such plantation houses along the tidewater as Westover and Carter's Grove. Among the freestanding city houses were White's Benjamin W. Arnold house, Albany, New York, 1902–05, with twin bays framing a delicately detailed entry portico.[55] Even more delicate was the townhouse White designed for his close friend, the art and antique collector and dealer Thomas B. Clarke, in New York City, 1902 [285]. Clarke's need for abundant light for his collections presented White with a problem, for the lot was extremely narrow and the house would have only one usable open side.[56] Instead of using multiples of individual windows which might have broken up the wall, White employed a fully glazed oriel like those used so often by Richard Norman Shaw during the 1870s, as in his New Zealand Chambers, Old Swan House, and his own home in Ellerdale Road, London. The detailing, however, as in the iron railing and the Ionic columns of the porch, recalled White's other Georgian-Federalist work.

In two houses White and McKim seemed to have exchanged temperaments momentarily, White being more geometrically severe in the C. D. Gibson house and McKim more delicate in the Percy Pyne house. White seems to have prepared the plans for the house for

285. Thomas B. Clarke house, New York, N. Y., 1902.

his good friend, the artist Charles Dana Gibson, very quickly. Built on East 73rd Street, New York, in 1902–03, the house delighted Gibson; it was simple and yet well proportioned and only modestly embellished internally as well as in the austere facade [286].[57] Whereas the Gibson house was designed and built within twenty months, McKim's last Georgian-Federalist residence was protracted in design and construction. McKim started sketches for the Percy Pyne house, New York, in January 1906 at the request of Pyne's uncle, H. A. C. Taylor.[58] Once test borings had been made, little was done as the drawings were studied and modified during the next four years. Delicate and refined in proportion and detail, the proposed house recalled once more the Amory-Olney model and the duplex for Taylor on 72nd Street, but as constructed in 1910–12, under Kendall's direction, several alterations were made [287]. The slight bowed front on Park Avenue was flattened, and a modest corner entrance on the avenue replaced the more elaborate porch planned for 68th Street. Although these changes mitigated somewhat the force McKim had intended in the design, the Pyne house was nonetheless a fitting conclusion to McKim's long campaign to reinvigorate the Georgian-Federalist idiom as a national architectural expression.[59]

The true capstone of McKim's adherence to Georgian-Federalist classicism, however, was his timely restoration of the White House in 1902. Burned by the British during their occupation of Washington in 1814, the Executive Mansion (as it was known until 1901) had been slowly deteriorating after a hasty refurbishing which had included the first of many coats of white paint to cover the evidence of fire. When James Hoban had designed the President's house in 1792 the functions of the executive branch were so limited that the office in the house promised to be fully adequate, but by 1890 the executive's activities had become so numerous that crowds of congressmen and office seekers constantly thronged the halls waiting to see the President. These conditions had prompted Mrs. Benjamin Harrison to have Frederick Owen draw up plans for a vastly enlarged Executive Mansion; these preliminary plans were then modified by Owen and Colonel Bingham, providing the basis for the plaster model which so shocked the architects assembled in Washington in 1900. Some observers even suggested abandoning the dilapidated if historic building and starting anew elsewhere—a proposal which met with much criticism and was definitely put to rest when Theodore Roosevelt assumed office in 1901 and announced that "the President should live nowhere else than in the historic White House," using the popular name for the building.[60] In April 1902 when Mrs. Roosevelt was drawing up a list of proposed repairs to the house for the annual Sundry Civil Appropriations Bill, she asked McKim, now a familiar figure in Washington due to his participation in the Park Commission, to look over the house and suggest what was needed. Shocked to see the decrepit condition of the building, McKim bluntly pointed out that the annual appropriation of $16,000 would not even cover the cost of a thorough cleaning, much less provide for structural repairs. Unwilling to see so important a project undertaken in a niggardly way, he suggested that nothing be done at that time.[61]

Before leaving Washington McKim stopped at the Senate District Committee office to inform Senators McMillan and Moore of his discussion with Mrs. Roosevelt. McMillan asked if $100,000 would do the job properly, to which McKim replied it would make a good start. As McKim forgot the matter and boarded the train, McMillan went straight to the appropriations committee, and by the time McKim arrived at his office in New York there lay a telegram from Moore saying that the Senate had approved the construction of temporary executive offices and the expenditure of $165,000 for the restoration of the White House.

286. Charles Dana Gibson house,
New York, N. Y., 1902–03.

287. Percy R. Pyne house, New
York, N. Y., 1906–12.

Thunderstruck, McKim arranged with O. W. Norcross to go to Washington, inspect the fabric of the White House, and prepare more accurate estimates of the cost of restoration.[62] After meeting with President Roosevelt, in New York on April 19, 1902, McKim was formally given the commission for rehabilitation of the old building and construction of temporary offices outside the house.

Concerned that the Sundry Bill would be stopped in the House, Moore cautiously approached penurious Illinois Congressman Joseph G. Cannon, who informed him that neither Cannon nor the American people cared how much it might cost to repair the White House so long as requests for money did not dribble in year after year; he wanted the full cost laid before Congress in time for the pending bill. Working hurriedly with Norcross, McKim submitted a revised estimate for the entire job—$369,050. Somewhat surprised at how the cost was growing, Roosevelt approved the estimate, and then added $100,000 for furnishings! By June 20 the bill had cleared both houses and was signed; it allotted $65,196 for construction of temporary executive offices and $475,445 for rehabilitation of the White House, the funds "to be expended by contract or otherwise at the discretion of the President."[63]

Meanwhile work had already started, for McKim had been given strict instructions by Roosevelt that all construction had to be finished within six months in time for the next social season; furthermore, the private quarters of the family on the second floor had to be ready by October 1. Repeatedly Roosevelt referred to the work as "McKim's restoration," finally compelling McKim to write the President explaining it was the work of all the partners and requesting that all correspondence from the Corps of Engineers be addressed to "McKim, Mead & White," and not to him personally.[64] Drawings were being dashed off and rushed to the workmen; the general confusion McKim described to his friend Thomas Newbold in July:

> The house is torn to pieces, and all the trades are working in there at once, for dear life, with night shifts. The President stood it for a week, and then retired to a safe distance, at 22 Jackson Square. Dirt and Bedlam let loose, does not compare with it! The work of destruction is now pretty well completed, and there are indications of reconstruction beginning to be seen, but the time is terribly short, and the demand for drawings, to keep ahead of the men, will make it an anxious time for a month to come. Whether or not we shall be able to keep our pledges to the President to be ready Oct. 1st remains to be seen. It will be nip and tuck if we do. . . . With only 90 days ahead of us, to get through at least six months work, it is hard to keep from getting rattled.[65]

With so little time, McKim was unable to do all that was required, but the worst structural and visual faults on the ground and first floors were corrected. His primary object was to restore the White House externally and internally to the character of Hoban's period. Inside the house this required the complete reconstruction of the underpinning of the first floor, for the original wooden floor beams had been so cut through for plumbing, heating, gas, and electrical piping they were sagging; new steel beams were inserted and failing utilities were replaced.[66] The major spatial change was the removal of the original formal staircase at the western end of the central hall, for the upper rooms had, by custom, become the family's private quarters, and thus the grand staircase served no real function. With its removal, McKim was able to nearly double the State Dining Room in size [288]. The first floor was also redecorated, and the Victorian embellishments removed, revealing in many

288. White House, Washington, D. C., new State Dining Room, 1902–03.

instances traces of Hoban's original delicate moldings, which then served as the basis for new work. With no time to spare, the interiors were finished on schedule, the debris cleared away, and the Roosevelts installed in a house that reflected its beginnings more clearly than it had in almost three quarters of a century.[67]

The changes on the exterior were even more dramatic. As first planned by Hoban, the President's house was a simple rectangular box with no dependencies, but, at the request of President Jefferson in 1807, Latrobe had constructed low terraces on either side. Of the same height as the basement, barely visible from the higher ground to the north (and thus similar to the subterranean dependencies at Monticello), these terraces defined a garden and lawn to the south of the house. In 1857 the first of successive greenhouses was added to the west terrace, and subsequent presidents added to the greenhouses as they fancied flowers or grapes or cucumbers, until the aggregation was said to resemble a commercial florist's [289]. The greenhouses were removed, bringing to light the remains of Latrobe's wings; using these as a basis, McKim designed extended wings on both sides of the house.[68] The East Wing, ending in a large reception hall and porte-cochère, provided a formal entrance for guests, coat room, and public washrooms [290].

The corresponding West Wing contained the temporary office and auxiliary spaces. Both Burnham and McKim felt most strongly that the White House could not be put in proper order until the President's office had been moved off the grounds; accordingly they both had grave reservations about building temporary accommodations in the new wings.[69] Their hope was that permanent facilities could be built on Lafayette Square in accordance with the Senate Park Commission's proposals, and Burnham wrote Moore in April 1902 that he was "very much opposed to any structure in the present White House grounds, because although called 'temporary,' it would be left there for a lifetime."[70] To *require* eventual construction of a permanent office McKim assured Moore that he was not going "to provide anything better, either in design or construction."[71] Even so, construction of a permanent office seemed far in the future, so McKim was asked in 1904 to provide drawings for an interim office to be added to the West Wing.[72] Nothing came of this proposal, much less construction of a complex of new buildings around Lafayette Square; the "temporary" office was eventually enlarged, repaired, and repaired again, so that Burnham's prophecy has proven all too accurate.

289. White House,
West Wing,
photograph of August
1901 showing
accretion of greenhouses.

290. White House, new East
Wing entrance, 1902–03.

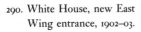

During 1903 all work on the White House exterior was finished. Much had been accomplished in so short a time, and few now realize that the White House today is largely the product of President and Mrs. Roosevelt's spirit of enlightened conservation and the opportune historicism of McKim. The restoration of the White House and the newly extended wings were so unified that Montgomery Schuyler believed

> the original architect, could he visit the scene of his labors, would be as delighted as surprised to see what has come of the development of his ideas. . . . The President's house is at last, as it ought to be, the dwelling in the United States best adapted to dispense, with convenience and with dignity, the national hospitality.[73]

McKim's long study of the early American architectural tradition had especially prepared him for such restorative work, and perhaps in the White House the most telling indication of McKim's view of the architect's role in such undertakings is that he left no discernible trace of his own hand.

WITH the full recovery of the national economy by 1900, commissions for hotels and clubs once more came into the office, including one intriguing project in 1901–02 for a hotel for Louis Sherry. With his eye on an international business, Sherry was proposing to put up a large luxury hotel in London, and had the firm prepare a perspective painted by Hughson Hawley. Although the project fell through, the breadth, general character, and some aspects of the classical ornament of the project bear a strong resemblance to Shaw's Piccadilly Hotel, London, 1905–08, suggesting that reproductions of Hawley's rendering may have been circulated in England.

Aside from McKim's addition to his Harvard Club in 1900–05, all the other clubhouses were by White, such as the Brook Club, housed in a remodeled townhouse on 40th Street, New York, 1904–05, and the new building for The Lambs, New York, 1903–05, a society of actors and theater aficionados named in memory of Charles and Mary Lamb, and the large Harmonie Club, New York, 1904–07, directly across 60th Street from the Metropolitan Club.[74] Especially intriguing is White's Colony Club, New York, 1904–08 [291]. Perhaps because it was to contain reading, meeting, and recreational facilities for socially prominent women, White favored a Georgian expression with what might be termed "diminutive" brickwork, using header courses. In a contemporary account, Anne O'Hagan related that White used the houses of Annapolis as models, even taking the club's building committee there to see selected houses. She does not indicate which ones, but the John Brice house, circa 1772 by William Buckland, and the Reynolds Tavern are likely examples, for both have similar header brickwork with only the small ends of the brick showing. Ironically, when the club was completed, one wag claimed this brickwork was "immoral."[75] If the brickwork was not actually immoral, it was certainly unconventional, and in this, White may have been making a conscious reference to the club's flouting of social conventions—it even had a bar and rooms for transient women guests, which shocked some polite members of society. The bricks themselves were rough (much like eighteenth-century brick), giving the wall an uneven, tweedy texture that catches the light. Added to this were diaper patterns laid in darker brick, and the most unusual device of brick headers laid diagonally in the tympana panels of the windows of the second floor. This feeling of lightness was enhanced by the original porch supported by extremely attenuated cast-iron columns; when Madison Avenue was later widened, the porch had to be removed, but slim pilasters and a reedlike entablature attached to the wall still survive. In the private houses then abuilding, White took special care with the interior finishing, but in the Colony Club, perhaps because it was a women's club, he urged that a number of the rooms be designed by Elsie de Wolfe, who was just then beginning to perform this service for some of her friends. When there was reluctance on the part of the club organizers to give this interior work to a virtual unknown, White insisted "give the order to Elsie, and let her alone. She knows more than any of us."[76]

WITH the recovery of the economy there came to White two major church commissions, both in New York: the portals of Saint Bartholomew's, 1900–03, and the Madison Square Presbyterian Church, 1903–06.[77] The Saint Bartholomew doors were a memorial to Cornelius Vanderbilt, II, a communicant and active supporter of the church who died in 1899, given by his widow, Alice Gwynne Vanderbilt, and her children. White's task was to fit the doors and a new portal onto the church by James Renwick, built in 1872 at Madison Avenue and 44th Street, a rather curious Lombard Romanesque amalgamation of somewhat

291. Colony Club, New York, N.Y., 1904–08.

strident reddish brown, and gray-green sandstone. Using the Romanesque church as a point of departure, White began studies in 1900. Desiring an expression both consonant with the rest of the church and yet essentially classical, he developed a Provençal Romanesque scheme, based on the portals of Saint-Gilles-du-Gard, France. He had long admired this facade, describing it in a letter to his family in 1878 as the best piece of architecture in France. While following the overall form of Saint-Gilles, he made numerous adjustments and changes, all aimed at reinforcing the horizontal line [43, 292, 293].[78] So that all arches might spring from the same line, for example, the center arch was tilted. Because the center doors were to be nearly equal in width to the outer doors, he added broad pilasters to make up the difference. In general, the complexities and inconsistencies of the model were made more uniform. Once the basic outline had been determined, the three portals were assigned to individual sculptors, who were to work out the details of the tympana, lintel, architrave, and bronze door-valve relief carving. The central portal was given to Daniel Chester French, who was assisted by Andrew O'Connor, the south portal to Herbert Adams, and the north portal to Philip Martiny. Although White laid out the basic design, the configuration of figures was left to each sculptor, subject to White's approval. (This union of architecture and sculpture gives some hint of how White might have completed the portals of Richardson's Trinity Church, Boston; Shepley, Rutan & Coolidge, who were given the job, subordinated all carving to the architecture frame.) Who determined the iconographic program for the Saint Bartholomew facade is not clear, but there is a casual similarity to the disposition of scenes at Saint-Gilles.[79] Adams's panels portrayed the childhood and ministry of

Christ; Martiny's, the birth of Christ, John the Baptist, and Christ's Passion. French's and O'Connor's central section was most successful, the tympanum showing Christ in Glory and the lintel dealing with the Crucifixion. Perhaps the most significant technical consideration was that each of the bronze door-valves was cast as a solid leaf, not a collection of separate narrative panels attached to a structural frame.

Despite all the various sculptors, White brought all the parts into harmony, earning the approbation of both Sturgis and Schuyler, who wrote that the architect had responded with sensitivity and sympathy to Renwick's facade. Schuyler, who had no tolerance for copying, called the new portal

292. St. Bartholomew's Church, New York, N. Y. (original building on Madison Avenue by Renwick, Aspinwall & Russell, 1872), new portal, 1901–03.

293. St. Bartholomew's Church, new building on Park Avenue by Bertram G. Goodhue, 1917–30, portals moved from previous building.

a beautiful success, and as congruous with the old work, perhaps, as is compatible with success-fulness. The only unfavorable criticism it suggests is that it is perhaps too visible an application and an afterthought, a sheathing and screening of the old front, upon which however, it does not pour any unnecessary contempt.[80]

It seemed to Schuyler that White had shown how Romanesque might express elegance and refinement as well as the massiveness evident in the work of Richardson.

The other ecclesiastical commission was for a new Madison Square Presbyterian Church, the pulpit of Charles H. Parkhurst, who had attracted considerable attention for his earlier attacks on Tammany Hall. During the late 1880s and '90s, Parkhurst waged an unending battle against crime in New York, especially the graft of city officials who secretly protected saloon and brothel owners. He was chosen president of the New York Society for the Prevention of Crime and helped form the National Law Enforcement League. Since 1854 the congregation had met in a tall-spired brownstone Gothic church at the southeast corner of Madison Avenue and 24th Street, facing Madison Square, only two blocks south of Madison Square Garden. In 1890, on the large lot south of the church the Metropolitan Life Insurance Company built new offices, and the fate of the church was thrown into question. The church wrestled with the possibility of moving elsewhere but decided not to flee to the more polite neighborhoods uptown, as so many other congregations were doing, but to remain in the heart of the city. Beginning in 1896 attempts were made to find three contiguous lots on Madison Square, with no success. Then, in October 1902, members of the church met with representatives of the Metropolitan Life Insurance Company and reached an agreement in which the company offered to build a new church on the northeast corner of Madison Avenue and 24th Street in exchange for the existing building. The offer was accepted on the condition that the church be allowed to act on its own behalf. The following February the transaction was made official, the congregation conveying the old church in return for the new site and the sum of $325,000. Meanwhile a building committee was formed, and in April 1903, at the recommendation of Robert de Forest, chairman of the committee, McKim, Mead & White were appointed architects. The following month White met with the committee and presented a general scheme for the new building, including the bold portico, dome, and brick and terra-cotta exterior that became its distinguishing features. Development of the design proceeded quickly, the drawings and specifications were prepared, and in May 1904 the contract was signed with Charles T. Wills; on October 14, 1906, the church was dedicated [294, 295].[81]

White prepared a description of the new building, noting its major features and explaining the reasons behind the design.[82] Instead of the customary Gothic, White selected Early Christian sources, specifically the Church of the Hagia Sophia, since Gothic represented medieval Catholicism whereas the Greek cross plan was better suited to the spoken word of the Protestant service. Moreover, he noted, eighteenth-century American churches had been classical. As in Byzantine churches, the dome was covered with gold mosaic, with light from hidden lamps bounced off the curved surface, supplemented by hanging fixtures. Because the area around the church was certain to become filled with skyscrapers, he chose to make the entrance portico especially bold in scale so it might hold its own against the larger buildings to come.

In plan the church was a compact Greek cross, seventy-four by eighty-four feet [296, 297], with low blocks at the corners containing stairs to the galleries.[83] The sanctuary walls were simply treated with contrasting plain panels and areas of dense ornament. To correct anticipated problems with echoes, Wallace Sabine recommended felt panels in the upper walls, but, balking at the cost of this, the church opted instead for a silk net, fabricated by the Tiffany studios, suspended over the sanctuary. Although the net turned out to be ineffective acoustically, the other furnishings by the Tiffany studios—stained glass windows, organ case, pews, and altar furniture—were well designed for their functions. Behind the sanctuary was the Parish House and offices. The body of the church was bound by a richly modeled terra-cotta cornice, its edges trimmed in a *chéneau* incorporating the Greek cross. While the ground color of the terra-cotta and brick walls was light buff, the backgrounds and recesses of the moldings and entablatures were glazed in various hues—moss green, yellow ochre, light raw umber, and a muted blue-gray—forming delicate horizontal bands of color. Purportedly, this was the first use of such multiple colors in architectural terra cotta in the United States. Under White's direction, and at his request, the Perth Amboy Brick Company, one of the major manufacturers of face brick and terra cotta on the eastern seaboard, had already developed various white and buff clay bases and numerous glazes, but attempts to recreate the polychrome glazing of the Della Robbias had met with little success. Only about 1903 did the continuing experiments begin to show promise, and it was after inspecting the results of these trials that White specified the color in the ornamental moldings of the church. In firing some of the first pieces, however, yellow and green glazes ran together in the kiln, creating brown. When White saw what the ceramicists considered a disaster he became rhapsodic, ordering the "accident" repeated for several portions of the church.[84] Polychrome glazing was used in the relief panels of the pediment as well, but though White sketched out the design for the panels he was unable to develop the design further before his death. The modeling was done by Adolph A. Weinman with the assistance of painter H. Siddons Mowbray, the figures representing a knight (the church militant) and a shepherd (the church pastoral) at the shrine of Truth. The panels, with their cream-colored figures against a light blue background, in the manner of the Della Robbias, were installed in 1910.

For its simple plan, forthright expression, carefully balanced proportions, and daring use of color the Madison Square Presbyterian Church was well received by the public and architectural critics. As with other boldly colored churches in New York, White's was

294. Aerial view of Madison Square, New York, N. Y., c. 1910, showing Madison Square Presbyterian Church (far right), 1903–06, with Madison Square Garden in the background.

295. Madison Square Presbyterian Church, New York, N. Y., 1903–06. *Monograph.*

affectionately given a sobriquet—"The Church of the Holy Stein." In 1907, the year after its completion, the building was given the medal of honor by the New York Chapter of the American Institute of Architects. Yet despite its popular appeal and professional acclaim, like the Madison Square Garden nearby, the church was doomed from the moment of its inception, for while the refusal of the congregation to flee its urban ministry and seek haven in the genteel neighborhoods to the north may have been ecclesiastically and socially commendable, it placed the building in a financially untenable position. The Madison

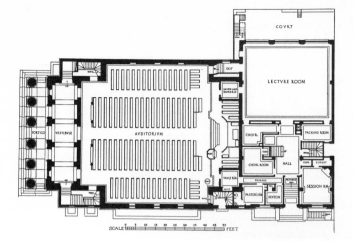

296. Madison Square
Presbyterian Church, plan.
Monograph.

297. Madison Square Presbyterian
Church, interior of sanctuary.

Square Presbyterian Church stood for only thirteen years. By 1919 it was completely surrounded by skyscrapers, and the property was actively sought by the Metropolitan Life
Insurance Company. The construction of yet another church became mandatory. When
plans for the demolition of White's building became known, a storm of protest arose in the
press. Gilbert Fraser, a visiting British architect, pleaded: "I cannot imagine such a thing
happening. How do you expect to have a beautiful city if you have no regard for your old
buildings?" The church was one of White's masterworks, he asserted. "It was exquisite, as

fine as anything I have ever seen. And you tear it down, and build one of your hideous, if useful skyscrapers. It is as if we in England were to tear down one of Sir Christopher Wren's churches."[85] Similarly stirred, White's close friend John Jay Chapman denounced its destruction:

> The demolition of the Presbyterian Church on Madison Square makes one feel as if our very monuments and triumphal arches were merely the decorations of a parade, or a scaffolding dressed for a holiday. Lath and plaster they were, and to lath and plaster they return. There is no room in America for a past—no not for a yesterday. This particular church was one of the most careful pieces of work in the city. It was like a Byzantine jewel, so concentrated, well-built and polished, so correct, ornate and lavish that a clever Empress might have had it built. It represented wealth and genius and was one of the few buildings left by Stanford White in which every stone had been weighed, every effect unified. It was brilliant yet solid. It was a little princess of a building, and it did not, as Stanford White's work was apt to do, greet you charmingly and bid you pass on. It brought you to a full stop of admiration. . . . The Americans change buildings every few years as one changes cars in traveling. Hawthorne said that the American would no more think of using his father's house than of wearing his father's coat. The pressure of space in our cities has left no corner for anything except for the trick-buildings and extravaganzas of commerce. The very merits of these office-buildings and apartments are a ghastly comment on the age. They emphasize our detachment from the past by the very links into which they bind us to the past. This kind of building is *architecture*, because it is learned, talented, logical and beautiful; and yet it is *opium*, because learning, talent, logic and beauty have been subordinated to the fantastic needs of a queer period, to a moon-race of whirl-people, who develop and change faster than men have ever changed before, so fast, in fact, that any abstract of their mind shows distortions and gyrations as of a thing in motion. . . . Good architecture is the mightiest artistic power in the world. It passes on the shadow of humanity from one age to the next as no other art can do. It speaks to the mind of the infant without the need of an interpreter. It does not merely hark back to the past. Any great building *is* the past—an enduring unescapable, present reality. It creates literature, feeding the world with ever more imagination, and growing more potent in its decay than it was in its prime.[86]

If the Madison Square church represented what White could provide a wealthy urban congregation, his Trinity Church and Parish House, Roslyn, New York, 1905–07, commissioned by Mrs. Clarence Mackay, showed what was possible for a smaller suburban church.[87] Its broad Latin cross plan was covered by a large trussed roof braced by massive buttresses. Although the general feeling was Gothic, there were no pointed arches. The low ground-hugging mass and the rough materials gave Trinity Church a sense of solidity and permanence.

THE return of prosperity invigorated gifts to colleges and universities, and the firm began to receive numerous commissions of this type. Not only were there individual buildings, but several new campuses were designed as well, beginning with a general scheme for the University of Cincinnati in 1902. For many years the university had occupied a portion of the McMicken estate close to the center of Cincinnati, but this area became industrialized, and in 1889 the university was granted a section of Burnet Woods Park for a new campus. Although the first of several buildings went up in 1895, no survey was made of the grounds nor any comprehensive plan prepared. At the request of President Ayres, during early 1902

William S. Richardson, White's principal assistant, made several trips to Cincinnati. The sketch plans then prepared showed existing and proposed buildings organized around two major axes terminated by clusters of new buildings resembling the group for New York University. Little came of the proposed plan, however, although the formal approach to McMicken Hall from Clifton Avenue was constructed.[88]

Soon after, in 1903, Mead and McKim were asked by alumnus Charles Day Norton, a Chicago businessman acquainted with Burnham, to serve on a commission to prepare a comprehensive plan for Amherst College. Inspired by the Washington plan, Norton was persuaded something similar should be done for his alma mater. Mead thought Norton and his associates were "very ambitious," but to realize their goal Norton and five classmates had pledged $5,000 to underwrite the expenses of the Amherst planning commission.[89] During 1904–05 the Amherst commission worked with the firm to prepare the comprehensive plan, which Norton then presented to the college trustees in 1906. Not only did this serve to guide subsequent campus development, but the commission itself, on which McKim and Saint-Gaudens served, continued to advise the college for many years thereafter under Mead's chairmanship.

Implementation of the firm's scheme for the University of Cincinnati was limited, and at Amherst they served only in an advisory capacity. In the second phase of planning for Columbia University in New York, however, their work was considerable. The Columbia trustees had let expire an option on the block of property south of 116th Street, below the entrance to the Low Library, but in the autumn of 1902 they were able to acquire the parcel stretching down to 114th Street. In July 1903 McKim and his assistant, Kendall, began to develop an extension to the original campus; by Christmas the new model and perspective were completed [298, 299].[90] Since the land sloped down from 116th Street, McKim and Kendall formed a southern terrace, recalling the one north of 116th Street. This new South Field, flanked by two classroom and ten dormitory buildings (providing 3,200 rooms), mirrored the original campus and the buildings echoed the heavy Renaissance classicism. In May 1904 work commenced on Hartley Hall, on Amsterdam Avenue, followed by work on Livingston Hall. Soon there went up Hamilton Hall, 1905–09, and Kent Hall for the School of Law, 1907–11, in the southeast corner of the original campus.[91] It was a mark of the skill of the designers that the sequence of courts and terraces appeared to be one composition, forming an enlarged ensemble as complete and contained as the original group had been, standing by itself. Up to this point, however, none of the small interior courts outlined in the original plan had been enclosed, but with the construction of Earl Hall (an assembly hall used by the campus YMCA) west of Low Library, 1901–02, and Saint Paul's Chapel by Howells & Stokes, east of the library, 1903–06, and later the Avery Library and School of Architecture, 1911–12, the first of these courts was defined.

Just over a year before expanding the Columbia University plan, the firm began work on a series of new campuses for military institutions, none of which were as successful in their ensemble as Columbia, however. The first of these was the United States Army War College, Washington, D.C., 1902–07. The college was barely two years old, born of a growing concern over the lack of cooperation and coordination between the branches of the army, graphically illustrated by operations during the Spanish-American War. In 1901 Secretary of War Elihu Root established the War College to which selected officers from various service schools would be sent for special instruction in coordinated large-scale deployment of men and materiel. Initial training was given in temporary quarters on

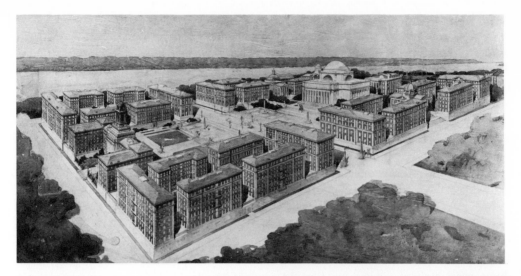

298. Columbia University, aerial perspective of expanded campus plan, signed "Jules Crow," 1903.

299. Columbia University, rendered plan of expanded campus plan, 1903.

Jackson Place in Washington, while Congress appropriated funds for permanent headquarters on the grounds of the Washington Barracks (now Fort McNair) on the peninsula between the Anacostia and Potomac Rivers.[92] The southern half of the peninsula was already dotted with a disparate collection of barracks while the northern portion of the base was still open. Colonel William M. Black, in charge of laying out the War College, at first planned to build in the open area, close to the city, and he referred to the scheme he had in mind during lunch with Secretary Root, McKim, and Senator McMillan, as they discussed the work of the Senate Park Commission. Whereupon McKim ventured the opinion that Black had "the heel of the stocking where the toe ought to be." He pointed out that the college buildings would be in an inelegant location, while the barracks, which needed to be close to the city, would be at the "commanding point of land looking off towards Mount Vernon, down the broad Potomac pathway—more spacious than the Thames at London, the Seine at Paris, the Tiber at Rome, or the Danube at Vienna." The two locations, he believed, should be reversed. And, he advised Colonel Black, in building the officers' houses, "have regard to the climate and build them with broad piazzas looking off on the water." Such observations were enough to convince Secretary Root that McKim should design the War College.[93]

The peninsula, somewhat irregular in outline, is approximately 1,000 by 3,800 feet. In order to exploit fully the scenic potential, as well as to put the barracks nearest the city where need suggested they should be, McKim proposed clearing the entire site and starting anew. At the north end, flanking a monumental gate, were to go the barracks and various administrative and supply buildings, all to be built of red brick [300]. Beyond the barracks the grounds were to open onto a broad lawn defined by rows of closely spaced trees. Behind these, to the west, were to be the officers' houses, with duplexes on the east side for noncommissioned officers. These, too, were of dark red brick with white colonnaded porches and latticed "piazzas." While the residences and the officers' mess were eventually completed, other portions remained unbuilt. At the far end of the peninsula, with a view across the Potomac, was the focus of the entire composition, the War College Building. Centered on the axis, it was intended to be visible from the main gate. Simple and straightforward, the external massing corresponded directly to internal functional arrangements [301].[94] For permanence and fire safety, the internal flooring, vaults of the map room and library which constituted the central volume, and both inner and outer shells of the rotunda dome were built of Guastavino tile. As a result, the building is masonry throughout, including the slightly arched floors of the galleries around the central rotunda [302]. Moreover, between the shells of the dome are diagonal flying buttresses of Guastavino tile much like those used by Antonio Gaudí in the crypt of the Colonial Guell Chapel in Barcelona, begun in 1908 [303].

In June 1902, when plans had been completed and construction was about to begin, McKim was ready to call a halt to the entire operation because the Corps of Engineers (the contractor for this work) attempted to dictate conditions. The Corps expected to supervise construction, meaning that once the working drawings were turned over, the firm would have no way to ensure compliance. In addition, since there seemed to be so much repetitive work, the army wanted to trim the architect's fee well below that stipulated by the American Institute of Architects. McKim protested vigorously to Captain John S. Sewell, stating that under such terms the firm could not continue. Secretary Root mediated, asking McKim to clarify his firm's position, and in July McKim responded that, as designing architects, they expected to be the authority in all questions of design and disposition of the buildings and grounds, to prepare all preliminary and construction drawings, and to supervise construction, although they were willing to agree to an inclusive fee of three and one-half percent. When this proved acceptable to all parties, work proceeded.[95]

While McKim was occupied with the Fort McNair project, White was busy with the other military school, laying out a new comprehensive plan for West Point. Even as he worked on that plan, White was busy supervising construction of the Officers' Mess, a granite block next to his Cullum Memorial Hall, and one of a pair meant to flank the memorial. In 1901, a year before the academy's centenary, the Board of Visitors had reported on the disgraceful condition of the academy's physical plant, calling for a "complete tearing down and a new building up." In April 1902, over dinner at the University Club, McKim suggested the advantages of a comprehensive plan for West Point to Colonel Albert L. Mills, then Superintendent of the Academy.[96] Two months later Congress authorized a competition for such a master plan among a selected group of architects including McKim, Mead & White, D. H. Burnham, Peabody & Stearns, Carrère & Hastings, Cope & Stewardson, Hines & La Farge, Charles C. Haight, and Cram, Goodhue & Ferguson. Several of the architects, especially Carrère & Hastings, Burnham, and White, who represented the firm,

300. Army War College, Fort McNair, Washington, D. C., 1902–08.

301. Army War College Building, 1902–08.

302. ABOVE. Army War College Building, diagonal "flying buttresses" between inner and outer shells of rotunda domes.

303. LEFT. Army War College Building, interior of rotunda.

were concerned that the winning architect would have little control over construction and would be paid a fee less than the professional standard. Furthermore, White was concerned that Montgomery Schuyler, a consultant to the War Department, might attempt to impose a "Carpenter's Gothic" on all contestants. Such conditions, White wrote Burnham in November 1902, would "make any architect of independence of thought withdraw from the competition."[97] Not that White felt all designs had to be classical to conform to his Cullum Memorial and Officers' Mess. If Burnham felt these had to be removed, White reassured him that it was paramount "there should be one great whole concentric scheme." This might be medieval in accord with some of the existing buildings, or classic, but "if the style is not to be classic, I think, for the sake of the whole scheme, the Cullum Memorial and its adjacent buildings should be taken away."[98]

The competition program, however, was quite specific on this point; all of the existing barracks and other buildings were to be retained and incorporated in the new plan. Judging the entries were Lieutenant-General John Schofield, Colonel Mills, and three architects selected by the contestants—George B. Post, Walter Cook, and Cass Gilbert, all classically oriented. White's plan provided for a number of detached officers' houses arranged along the hillside above the drill plain, with new barracks and academic buildings clustered to the south of the parade ground [304].[99] At the far western edge of the plain, White placed the chapel, a centrally planned building, similar to the New York University library, which soon after provided the point of departure for the design of the Madison Square Presbyterian Church. Below the existing Officers' Mess, at the east edge of the plain, was the largest building in the proposed plan, the riding hall, an immense covered space for full-scale cavalry drill [305, 306]. Realizing that erecting such a mammoth building anywhere close to the plain would utterly destroy coherence in the ensemble, White proposed placing the riding hall against the face of the bluff, using the roof as a large terrace extending from the plain, "giving the appearance to the Post at this point somewhat the character of the magnificent Citadel at Quebec," as he wrote in the statement meant to accompany the drawings.[100] Such placement would also permit the masonry walls to blend with the rock of the cliff. The internal structure was to consist of six intersecting paraboloidal Guastavino vaults, 150 feet in diameter at the base and approximately 52 feet in height at the apex, opened by 35-foot skylights at the crown, enclosing a hall 150 by 625 feet. The five arches formed by the intersections of the paraboloidal shells would have had a span of 125 feet, rising 39 feet. The clear floor space for maneuvers would have been roughly 102 by 595 feet, with a continuous viewing gallery around the hall. In the space between the curved vaults and the outer walls, offices were to be fitted. In his statement White pointed out that $65,000 could be saved using Guastavino vaults instead of more conventional steel trusses, and without doubt, if constructed, the riding hall would have been the single largest project undertaken by Guastavino, a remarkable engineering feat, and one of the most striking covered spaces of the twentieth century. White's overall scheme for the academy, however, was neither coherent nor unified and much less suited to conditions than was the winning scheme by Cram, Goodhue & Ferguson, which took much better account of the existing Gothic buildings.

The remaining campus plan of the period would probably have been White's but for his untimely death; as a result the Mackay School of Mines building and the reorganization of the University of Nevada was taken on by William S. Richardson. The dual commission came about as a result of the gift of the Mackay School of Mines building by Clarence H.

Mackay and his mother in memory of his father, an Irish immigrant who had discovered and developed the famous Comstock lode in Virginia City, Nevada. Richardson visited Reno in June 1906, and immediately upon his return, plans for the mines building and the surrounding campus were developed. The University of Nevada then consisted of eight buildings loosely defining a quadrangle; using these, Richardson proposed enlarging an existing building at one end, making a domed library, adding several new structures to better define the quadrangle, and placing the new School of Mines at the other end. The Mackay mining building was a relatively austere two-story red brick block, built 1906–08, and although the firm was never retained to design any of the subsequent additions to the quadrangle, the example of the classical Mackay building and Richardson's plan shaped the growth of the university for a quarter of a century thereafter.[101]

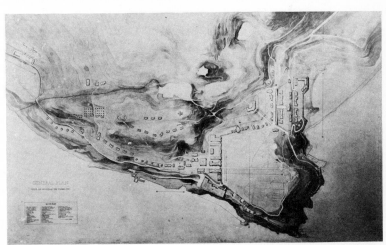

304. RIGHT. U. S. Military Academy, West Point, N. Y., competition entry for comprehensive replanning, plan, 1902.

305. BELOW. U. S. Military Academy, West Point, competition entry for comprehensive replanning, east elevation, 1902.

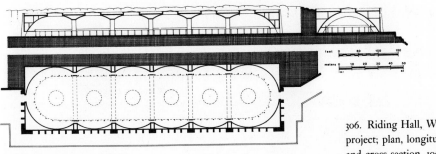

306. Riding Hall, West Point, project; plan, longitudinal section, and cross section, 1902.

The remaining collegiate work consisted of individual buildings, all of which were variations of the Georgian-Federalist type introduced at Harvard; this included, in a more Roman vein, McKim's architectural casing for the Harvard Stadium, finally built in 1902–03.[102] A basic type was developed in Rockefeller Hall, Brown University, 1902–04. The building, donated by John D. Rockefeller, was to house the campus YMCA and the student union. Although the firm was selected because they were considered to be sympathetic to the architecture of adjacent Hope College, the trustees did not grant them complete freedom but supplied floor plans.[103] Rockefeller Hall (now Faunce House) is a reduced and modified version of the oldest building at Brown, University Hall, 1770–71, but with individual details made more elaborate and emphasized with brick quoins and heavy stone frames at the openings. While Rockefeller Hall was being constructed, McKim began studies for the Women's Building at the University of Illinois, Champaign, built 1904–05, on basically the same plan. Up to the turn of the century Illinois's major land-grant university had been predominantly male, with the emphasis on agriculture and engineering, but during the 1890s growing numbers of women were attracted to the university as it broadened its liberal arts offerings. As at Radcliffe, this necessitated proper facilities, especially for physical education and recreation. In June 1903 a site for a special women's building was set aside by President Draper. Again the basic plan requirements were drawn up by the school, this time by the head of the university's architecture department, Nathan Clifford Ricker. Through the influence of Ricker, who was anxious to demonstrate to McKim the stature of the architecture program, the entry of McKim, Mead & White in a limited competition among six architects was selected. The site was south of the nucleus of the university, far from the heterogeneous buildings of the old campus, on broad lawns and fields where McKim could use the favored Georgian-Federalist mode unencumbered [307].[104] U-shaped, its projecting end pavilions came forward toward the lawn of the new quadrangle. Even more than in

Rockefeller Hall, each of the salient elements, reflecting internal functions, was carefully articulated and emphasized. No doubt McKim and the firm intended this as an "architectural lecture," as Jefferson had intended for his pavilions at the University of Virginia, and indeed the Women's Building had a profound effect. Its Georgian civility influenced nearly every subsequent campus building at Illinois over the next half century, for the scores of new buildings by campus architect James M. White, and by Charles Adams Platt (who also prepared the campus master plan), owe their form and expression to McKim's example.

The fencing of the Harvard Yard inspired comparable work at Princeton, and in 1903 McKim and Kendall began designs for a new gate framing the entrance to Princeton at Nassau Hall. This gate, of limestone piers and wrought-iron panels, was the gift of Augustus Van Wickle, whose forebear, Nathaniel FitzRandolph, had contributed the property for the original campus in 1753; it replaced a lower iron fence that had enclosed the campus since 1838. In spite of the eighteenth-century heritage of the college and town, McKim's design is closer to French late Baroque types than to American sources and does not make as direct an associational reference as the work at Harvard. As the gate was being constructed, 1904–05, McKim designed the Cottage Club on Prospect Street, Princeton, 1904–08, based partly on local eighteenth-century sources and perhaps most directly on Sir John Turner's School, Kirkleatham, England, 1709.[105]

ONE of the distinguishing characteristics of the nineteenth century was its pervading interest in public education, not just in building privately and publicly funded universities, but in raising countless libraries in great cities and small towns. McKim, Mead & White had already played a pivotal role at both ends of the spectrum of this enterprise in Boston and Naugatuck, and this work continued into the new century with McKim's design for the Orange Free Library, Orange, New Jersey, 1899–1901. Residents of the town had been raising funds for a new library since 1890, and some preliminary sketches had been prepared then by the firm. Progress in gathering the money was hampered by the depression, but in 1899 Joseph W. Stickler offered to build the library as a memorial to his son.[106] Because the library trustees had since acquired additional footage next to the designated site, in 1900 McKim, Mead & White began enlarging the earlier design, referring back to the type they had established in the Whittemore Library and the Walker Art Gallery—a central octagonal hall opened to symmetrical reading rooms with a stack room to the rear [308]. In this instance, however, the entrance was strongly emphasized by being projected forward.

307. OPPOSITE. Women's Building, University of Illinois, Champaign-Urbana, Ill., 1903–05.

308. Orange Free Library, Orange, N. J., 1900–1901.

As it happened, this was a "trial run" for the finest private library and gallery McKim was ever to design, the Morgan Library. With the patronage of J. Pierpont Morgan, McKim was able to realize a level of carefully studied form and consummate workmanship that had always been his ideal. Well known as perhaps the most important international banker and financier at the turn of the century, Morgan was also one of the most inspired and successful of modern collectors; his perspicacity in the selection of art objects was matched by a shrewd business sense, which brought him the means to build his enormous collections. These were not the grabbings of a *nouveau riche* but the exercise of a carefully educated artistic sensibility.[107] When Morgan's father had transferred his banking office to England, the boy was sent to schools in Europe, where he acquired an early appreciation for the art of the Old World. Within seven years of entering the business at the age of twenty, Morgan had organized his own banking house and within another seven years was associated with the respected banking house of the Drexels in Philadelphia; thus was founded one of the strongest and most influential banking organizations in the United States. Before the death of his father in 1890, Morgan acquired art objects only irregularly and on a modest scale, but with his father's fortune added to his own, he began a concerted effort to develop his collections. The rare treasures which he accumulated rapidly—incunabula, gold and jeweled bindings, paintings, sculpture, drawings, manuscripts, and the finest examples of the minor arts of the ancient world and middle ages—were crowded in a basement vault in the modest family brownstone at Madison Avenue and 36th Street, New York. Although he relied on his own judgment in making purchases, he also had the advice of his nephew, Junius S. Morgan, and such astute experts as Thomas B. Clarke.

Morgan's purpose in buying in such quantity was twofold. Not only was he satisfying an intense personal love of art to the fullest degree his wealth permitted, he was also assembling a major collection for his countrymen. As a founder of New York's Metropolitan Museum of Art, he was keenly sensitive to the teaching role an art collection plays in a large city. Yet, ironically, for many years he was unable to bring the bulk of his collection to the United States because of the prohibitively high tariff on art works (as Stanford White had also learned), so many items remained in his London house or were loaned to selected British museums for the interim. Meanwhile the basement vault in New York, the house, and even a warehouse on 42nd Street became so stuffed with paintings and books that by 1900 the collection was inaccessible even to the collector. Confident that eventually the tariff would be changed, Morgan began to make preparations in 1900 for "suitable disposition which would render [the collections] permanently available for the instruction and pleasure of the American people."[108] Gradually Morgan acquired parcels on 36th Street adjoining his home to make a place for a suitable library, and as early as 1900 had Whitney Warren prepare some preliminary designs.

At the same time, McKim had begun to solicit Morgan's aid in endowing the American Academy in Rome. When Morgan phoned him on the evening of March 26, 1902, asking McKim to pay a visit the next morning, McKim assumed it was concerning the academy, but the next day Morgan told him he wanted the firm to design the library. McKim then faced a professional dilemma, for he could not take a commission away from a colleague. Later he explained what had transpired in a letter to Warren:

> Knowing that you had already prepared plans, I at once stated to Mr. Morgan that we could not, under the circumstances, undertake the work; that you were a friend of ours, and expressing my surprise and regret. In reply, Mr. Morgan informed me that he had determined not to make

use of your plans and that he had already reached this decision before he called us in, and it was only upon this definite assurance that we consented to undertake the work.[109]

Jubilant, McKim dashed off a letter to Mead, then traveling, saying the office was prospering, for Morgan had asked him to call at his house whereupon he

> informed me that he had purchased all the property between his house and Park Avenue on the north side of 36th Street, to be laid out architecturally and turned into a garden (135 × 100) adjoining his house to the east. He proposes to cut off 28 feet at the eastern end of this purchase for a house for his daughter Louisa (who married Satterlee) and in the interval between the two, build a little museum building to house his books and collections [309]. . . . today he sailed for Europe, having authorized us to go ahead on both jobs.[110]

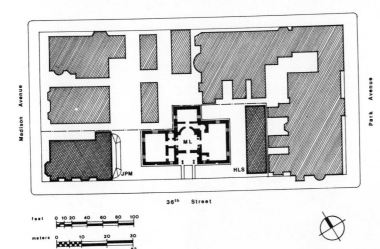

309. Morgan Library, New York, N. Y., site plan (L. M. Roth, based on *Bromley's Atlas of the City of New York*, Philadelphia, 1909). JPM = J. Pierpont Morgan house; ML = Morgan Library; HLS = Herbert L. Satterlee house.

As for the library, the requirements were straightforward. It was to be fireproof and solid, with an office where Morgan could meet with business associates, art dealers, and personal friends. It was to be uncomplicated, classical, and built of marble. Morgan instructed McKim, "I want a gem," and in few other commissions was the architect spurred to the point he was in this work, in every detail.[111] For two years the plans were meticulously studied, most often over breakfast at Morgan's house, for Morgan was involved in every decision; he informed McKim that no design was to be fixed, "nor do I wish anything done until I have definitely decided upon same."[112] As Richardson had so often done, McKim based his first studies on his last library, so the initial scheme for the Morgan Library greatly resembled the Orange library [310]. The projecting central block contained the main collection, and smaller offices were at the sides and rear—a rather ungainly arrangement for Morgan's purposes. In the second proposal the center block was reduced and the entrance recessed. The final version was slightly elongated with the facade made flush; the plan was rearranged as well, with the books to one side, Morgan's private office on the other, and a circulation rotunda and librarian's office in the center [311, 312, 313]. While the final design is decidedly Italianate, it is unclear if McKim considered specific sources, although the general composition of the facade greatly resembles the upper stage of the Nymphaeum of the Villa Pappa Giulia, Rome, circa 1550–55, with the stucco features rendered far more crisply in marble.

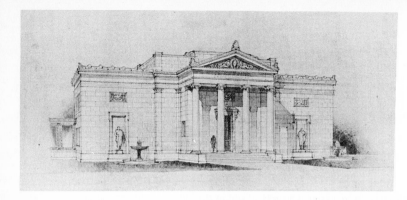

310. Morgan Library, initial scheme, 1902.

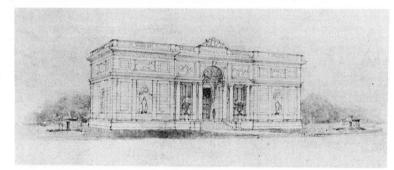

311. Morgan Library, final design, 1903.

312. Morgan Library, exterior. *Monograph.*

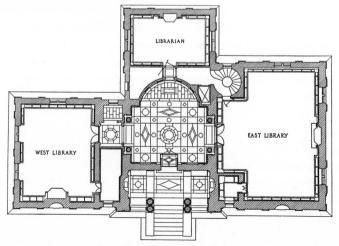

313. Morgan Library, plan. *Monograph.*

Once marble had been selected as the principal material, McKim began to envision using Greek *anathyrosis* masonry with precision-ground mortarless assembly. On a recent trip to Athens, he related to Morgan, he had tried to insert a knife blade between the stones of the Erechtheum with no success. Building in this way would ensure the soundness and longevity of the structure, McKim told his client, but it would be very expensive, and no one would be able to see where the money went. When told the increase in cost would be $50,000, Morgan instructed McKim to proceed.[113] The process entailed filing and grinding the surfaces of each individual block to make them absolutely square, doweling the blocks together with a cement mortice in the center, providing a cup chamber for condensation, and adding a thin lead film in the horizontal joints. To get a sample of Greek work for comparison, McKim wrote one of Mead's former assistants, Gorham Phillips Stevens, then in Athens as the first Architectural Fellow of the American School of Classical Studies. The masonry of the library was going up slowly, he wrote, but "more perfect jointing has not been executed, so far as I know, since the Greeks."

> Were it possible for you to procure and send us a squeeze, at our expense, showing one or two joints of the Erechtheion, indicating its minuteness on the surface of the ashlar, it would greatly interest our patron, Mr. Morgan, and this office. Possibly a wax or paper pulp squeeze could be made so as to be sent by mail. Any accompying [sic] observations as to the nature of the bed and face of the joint that would throw light would add to this interest.[114]

The squeezes duly arrived, and the following summer Stevens was repaid by similar squeezes from the firm that showed the joints of the Morgan Library. "The extremes of climate," McKim explained to Stevens, "have made it wise to introduce a film of lead one-sixty-fourth of an inch in thickness in the horizontal bed and they are, therefore, somewhat more apparent than the Greek joints of the Erechtheion, our vertical joints are nearly, if not quite as good as the best of the Greek, it being impossible to insert a knife blade into them."[115]

Construction of the Morgan Library began in April 1903 and was substantially complete by November 1906, when Morgan used his office for a reception of the purchasing committee of the Metropolitan Museum, of which he was now president. Some portions of the interior, however, were not completely finished until January 1907, and in the autumn of that year the books and collections were transferred. The East Room, the largest, was the main repository for the books, with shelves on three levels and a large Flemish tapestry over the fireplace depicting the Triumph of Avarice, proudly displayed without any apparent concern over the obvious irony. The West Room, smaller and with a lower ceiling, was Morgan's study; in it were gathered the pieces which gave him the greatest pleasure. The walls were covered with red silk damask from the Chigi Palace in Rome, the marble mantelpiece was from the studio of Desiderio de Settignana, the coffered ceiling was purchased by McKim in Italy and may have come from the palace in Lucca of Cardinal Gigli (after installation it was lowered to improve the proportions of the room). Carefully arranged therein were portraits by Memling, canvases by Perugino and students of Botticelli, Bellini, and Tintoretto, entrancing pieces of Florentine sculpture including one by Rossellino, majolica ware, a red porcelain Chinese vase of the seventh century, delicate pieces of faience, a Chou Dynasty bronze as well as Renaissance bronze pieces, exquisite gold and enamel reliquaries, and the Stavelot Triptych. In the windows were incorporated those fragments of stained glass that had been among the first things collected by Morgan as a child.[116]

For the exterior stone carving and the interior vaults, McKim gathered prominent sculptors and painters as he had so often done before. The lionesses on either side of the entrance stair were carved by Edward C. Potter, while Andrew O'Connor did the attic panels depicting Tragic and Lyric Poetry as well as the lunette panel over the entry based on the Aldus hallmark. The interior vault painting was done by H. Siddons Mowbray, then also at work on the University Club library vaults, using allegories of art and literature, figures of writers and philosophers, gods and goddesses, painted in a low key so as not to draw attention away from the art works and books. As in the Boston Public Library, stones and marbles from around the world were employed. The exterior of white marble is accented by the geometric mosaic of the loggia floor laid in Knoxville levanto marble and verde antico. In the central hall the colors in the veined skyros and cippolino marble columns are more pronounced, and in the floor are incorporated pieces from the Roman Forum and the Forum of Trajan.[117]

The Morgan Library was the most complete demonstration of McKim's controlled aesthetic sensibilities. It was an intensely personal building for both architect and patron. To it Morgan increasingly retired after 1906. His biographer and son-in-law, Herbert Satterlee, said no one could really know Pierpont Morgan if they had not seen him seated in silence before the fire in his study, smoking a large black cigar, perusing the latest acquisition or playing solitaire. Morgan the financier may have been at once the terror and savior of Wall Street, but Morgan the man lived in the West Room.[118] The library and its surroundings were clearly one of McKim's significant successes, and the superlative craftsmanship and studied design were praised in numerous publications.[119]

Concurrent with building an opulent sanctum for the world's richest collector, the firm was also busy designing a series of public library branches for the citizens of New York. Long before Carrère & Hastings's majesterial central library was completed, it was clear that continued growth of the city would soon put large segments of the population well beyond reach of the main repository. To facilitate the goal of building branch libraries scattered throughout the city, Andrew Carnegie made the city a generous gift in 1901 to build sixty-one branches, at an approximate cost of $80,000 each, provided the city would supply building sites and maintain operation. Library trustees then appointed an advisory board, consisting of John M. Carrère, Walter Cook, and Charles F. McKim, to draw up guidelines for the proposed buildings. Their report of September 1901 recommended that all the branches be of a distinctive type, basically the same throughout the city, using a standardized plan, with as much uniformity as local conditions would allow. They specifically deprecated what they called the general trend toward "too much variety; really variety for variety's sake." They suggested the trustees appoint two to five architects to design all the branches and that the architects selected be instructed to develop all designs in collaboration to ensure uniformity of type. Three firms were appointed, and not surprisingly these were Carrère & Hastings, Babb, Cook & Willard, and McKim, Mead & White. Of the forty-two branches built in this first phase of construction, eleven were by McKim, Mead & White, ten of these designed under McKim's general supervision from 1902 to 1908, and the last, by Kendall.[120]

The branches by McKim, Mead & White reflected the standard plan adopted by all, with circulation and general reference works on the ground floor, children's books on the second floor, and general reading on the third floor farthest removed from street noise. The exterior presented a problem in facade design, for all the libraries were built contiguous with adjoining townhouses in residential areas. The basic palazzo type, opened up by large arched windows, is typified by the Tompkins Square branch on East 10th Street [314]. For one variant on 115th Street the masonry was deeply rusticated in the manner of the Palazzo Strozzi, Florence. In several others the upper floors were set apart by colossal pilasters, and in the Rivington Street branch these became structural piers allowing the wall to become a screen of glass and metal spandrel panels [315]. These more skeletonized examples showed a desire to admit as much light as possible. Russell Sturgis, by this time a vituperative opponent of the firm's classicism who was certain that the Renaissance idiom of the branches precluded satisfactory lighting, noted in a review of the library branches that the 125th Street branch by the firm had skylights and that the Tompkins Square branch, one of the more closed and conservative variants, was well illuminated.[121] The branches were designed to serve two purposes: to be both specific to their neighborhoods and yet universal in character, to be individually identifiable and yet expressive of a municipal type. They largely succeeded because they were derivations of urban residences, and thus fit well among the brownstones of their respective neighborhoods; at the same time their greater breadth of scale and restraint make them distinct from their surroundings.

314. Tompkins Square Branch, New York Public Library, New York, N. Y., 1903–05.

315. Rivington Street Branch, New York Public Library, New York, N. Y., 1904–05.

THE New York library branches were public buildings as well as educational buildings. The firm's two major public buildings at the start of the century were, in contrast, so vast in scale, compared to the branches, that neither was ever fully executed. Both had to be built in sections over a period of many years; one was Bellevue Hospital and the other the enlarged Metropolitan Museum of Art, New York.

The new Bellevue, begun late in 1902, has come to mean psychiatric care, but it is actually a full-service hospital, having originated in the seventeenth century as a city alms-house located not far from present-day City Hall.[122] In 1816 it was moved to what was then a remote location, Belle Vue Farm, north of the city on the East River. There it remained even as the city gradually spread past it, a cluster of assorted buildings in the area enclosed by First Avenue, 26th Street, 29th Street, and the river. By 1860 Bellevue had evolved into a large general hospital that included a medical college offering some of the best clinical training in America. During the last half of the century the hospital was enlarged and the college expanded, but in 1897 fire destroyed nearly all of the teaching facilities, precipitating the merging of the Bellevue Medical College with the New York University Medical School a year later. Reconstruction was mandatory, and late in 1902 (or perhaps very early in 1903) the firm was asked to prepare a master plan for Bellevue and Allied Hospitals. Though the entire hospital plant was to cost $5 million when completed, it was understood from the outset that it would be built in increments as funds were available and as space for the new buildings was cleared.

Given the number of necessary facilities and the land available, some of which was already built on, there was no alternative but to stack the facilities, departing from the tradition of isolated pavilions, well established in hospital design. Even though Pasteur, Lister, and Koch had proved the germ-basis of disease by the mid-1880s, in 1905 when Dr. Albert Ochsner spoke before the Association of Hospital Superintendents, advocating stack-ing of facilities in new hospitals, his idea was considered startling, since it precluded natural ventilation believed to dispel disease-carrying vapors. The plan which McKim and the Bellevue hospital directors developed in 1903 played an important part in the transition from G. B. Post's modest three-story stacked New York Hospital of 1876–77, to the immense multilevel Mount Sinai Hospital planned by Dr. S. S. Goldwater in 1910.[123]

From the start McKim felt it necessary to have a central focal point in so large a composition, although not for compelling medical reasons. Since the compound was nearly square, he arranged the various departments and pavilions in the form of a large **H** whose arms reached out to the corners of the site. At the center was to be a great rotunda surmounted by a dome, as shown in the faint preliminary sketch, one of the very few to survive [316]. During 1903 the mechanical and functional details were worked out by Van der Bent while the formal aspects of the design were studied by McKim and Kendall. Late in the year a large rendering of the complex, viewed from across the East River, was prepared by Jules Crow (Fig. 317).[124] At intervals in the outstretched wings were recesses for verandas, so that patients had generous light and ventilation on three sides of many of the larger wards.

Although the dome was a powerful visual device, it was a luxury and soon disappeared from studies; the central section was transformed into a broad pavilion whose corners were crowned by low belvederes. During 1905 the scheme was restudied and the belvederes lowered still more; by the end of 1906, with further redistribution of some of the elements, the master plan was finally settled [318].[125] The pavilions were so arranged that construction could begin with the outlying portions, at the corners, and proceed inward, postponing demolition of the existing buildings on the site. In May 1907 work started on the Pathological Wing, Pavilion N, at the far northwest corner, and in the subsequent years additional sections were completed in a process that was carried on by the younger partners.

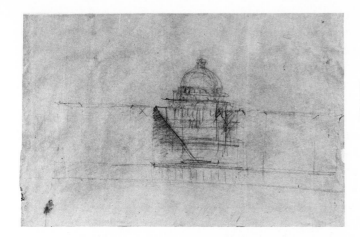

316. Bellevue Hospital, New York, N. Y., original conceptual sketch by McKim, 1903.

317. Bellevue Hospital, perspective of initial comprehensive design from the East River, signed "Jules Crow/03."

318. Bellevue Hospital, aerial perspective of final comprehensive design, 1905.

The other large public building project was a comprehensive scheme for enlarging the Metropolitan Museum of Art in Central Park. The first section of the building, a colorful Ruskinian Gothic block of 1874–80 by Calvert Vaux, had been erected at the edge of the park at 82nd Street. As the collections grew, additional sections were added to this: Section B to the south in 1888 by Theodore Weston, and Section C to the north in 1894 by Arthur L. T. Tucherman. Each addition deviated further in style from Vaux's example, so that the whole became an assemblage of ill-adjusted parts. During 1890–95, Richard Morris Hunt was engaged to develop a master plan to rectify this dissonance, and he devised an immense neo–Baroque scheme which proposed wings enclosing courtyards stretching from 79th to 85th Street, screening the original parts of the museum complex from view along Fifth Avenue. Hunt died, however, before construction was advanced, and only his central entrance pavilion, Section D, was completed—in 1895–1902 by his son, Richard Howland Hunt, assisted by G. B. Post.[126]

By 1904 the need for still more gallery space became pressing because of two factors; first, the bequest of $6 million from Jacob S. Rogers, the income from which was to be used to purchase works of art, and second, the election of J. Pierpont Morgan to the presidency of the museum. This made it virtually certain that Morgan's vast collections would someday come to the Metropolitan. Morgan's annual purchasing expeditions to Europe now intensified as he made Rogers Fund purchases. The result was that in a very few years the Metropolitan became one of the major museums in the world, making New York an art center. More than ever a broad comprehensive plan for expansion of the museum was needed, and in the early spring of 1904 the firm was given the task of developing this master plan. Progress was rapid, and by June the trustees had given authorization for construction drawings for a new wing north of Hunt's entrance pavilion; at the same time a plaster model of the entire museum complex was built. Although McKim was nominally in charge of the entire operation, the master plan was a true product of the office: design details were developed by Kendall and William S. Richardson, while Burt Fenner handled organizational and administrative matters. Even Saint-Gaudens contributed, warning McKim " 'For God's Sake' remember that proper lighting is an important consideration. I speak of this again with emphasis as my attention has been drawn to the dismal failure of Hunt's hall for sculpture there. It may be good architecture and a glorious bath of Caracalla thing, but it's a damn bad gallery for the proper disposition of works of art."[127] By the end of 1906 all particulars of the master plan had been agreed upon, and construction started in Section E.

Even though expansive in scale, the general plan by McKim, Mead & White was more economical of material and space than Hunt's master plan had been [319, 320]. The classicism of Hunt's entrance pavilion was continued in the new wings proposed along Fifth Avenue but toned down; the general sequence of masses and spaces was mirrored by an extension to the west into the park. As section after section was added by the firm along Fifth Avenue, the critical view was that these were among the most successful additions yet made to the museum. Only two sections were added under McKim's personal direction—Section E to the north, finished in 1910, and Section F, 1907–10, the Hall of Decorative Arts built to house the Morgan armor collection—but the remaining additions along Fifth Avenue were done by the younger partners. The western extension, mirroring the Fifth Avenue pavilions, was never built although it was the more interesting of the two halves, for it included ornamental sculpture, fountains, and terraces, connecting it with the park [321].[128]

One disappointment of the period was the failure of McKim's entry in the New York Customs House competition in 1900. Since 1862 the federal customs offices had been in Isaiah Rogers's neoclassical Merchant's Exchange at 55 Wall Street, 1836, but in 1899 the building was purchased by the National City Bank, setting in motion a competition for a new customs house under the provisions of the Tarsney Act. As he had done in the New York Public Library competition, McKim refused to adhere to the restrictions of the program and again disqualified the firm's entry. The competition was won by Cass Gilbert, but McKim was comforted, perhaps, by the commission to enlarge and renovate the Merchant's Ex-

319. ABOVE. Metropolitan Museum of Art, New York, N. Y., additions, 1904–16. Photograph of Fifth Avenue front, c. 1920.

320. RIGHT. Metropolitan Museum of Art, comprehensive plan for expansion, 1904–06. *Monograph.*

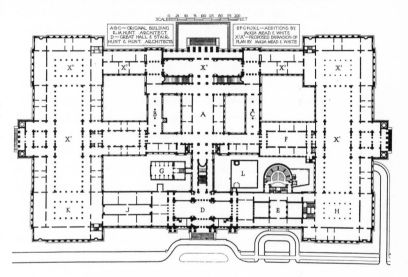

321. BELOW. Metropolitan Museum, perspective of proposed expansion on west side facing Central Park, signed and dated "Jules Crow 07."

change to house the National City Bank once the Federal offices had been moved to Gilbert's new building facing the Battery Park.[129]

THE improved business conditions, understandably, resulted in many commercial commissions, which largely fell into two categories: banks and mercantile or office buildings. Of the banks the first was the expansion of the Bank of Montreal in Montreal, Quebec. A landmark for over half a century and the focus of Canada's economy, the original bank, 1845–47, by John Wells, was a close adaptation of the contemporary Commercial Bank of Scotland, Edinburgh, 1845–46, by David Rhind. The main features of the facade on Saint James Street were a colossal hexastyle Corinthian portico and a low saucer dome of wood which, after a few bitter Montreal winters, had to be removed [322]. The central banking room, open to the dome above, was flanked by subsidiary offices, but as the economy of Canada expanded during the second half of the nineteenth century, the interior of the bank had to be modified in 1887, and although this was sufficient temporarily, by 1899 the bank needed to double its space.[130] Expansion was restricted by several factors. There was no question of vacating the Saint James Street location, but the land to the south of the bank was then occupied by the General Post Office, while the parcel to the north was similarly unavailable. There were several lots to the north behind the bank, but they were on the other side of narrow Fortification Lane which the city refused to close, even for so important a petitioner as the Bank of Montreal. Furthermore, the land fell away quickly in that direction, dropping approximately twenty-five feet from Saint James Street to Craig Street.

When McKim inspected the proposed expansion site north of the bank in 1900, he found he was dealing with one of the most important buildings in the city [323]. The land the enlarged bank was to cross had once been the northerly line of fortifications, and in front of the bank was the Place d'Armes, a square dominated by the Gothic Church of Notre Dame, 1824–29, by James O'Donnel. Aside from the Champ de Mars and the adjacent City

322. Bank of Montreal, Montreal, Quebec, Canada, St. James Street building, with dome restored, renovated 1903–05. *Monograph.*

Hall and Court House, the Place d'Armes was one of the most identifiable spaces in the city. In view of this, McKim felt that the old bank had to provide the basis for the new work. His solution was to abstract a bay module from Wells's Corinthian portico as the principal planning element in the new wing. The original building would be retained and refurbished, its dome rebuilt, connecting to a link to the new banking room along Craig Street [324, 325]. Because of the drop in ground level, the banking room would be on the upper floor of the Craig Street addition, its immense volume broken down into three cubical bays using the module derived from the portico. This room would lie across the axis of the original building and the hall-bridge link over Fortification Lane, but since the irregular Craig Street lot was not precisely perpendicular to the axis, McKim used a device employed by White in the Bowery Bank, placing a room within a room, using the various interstices around the banking room for auxiliary offices, stairs, and other service facilities.

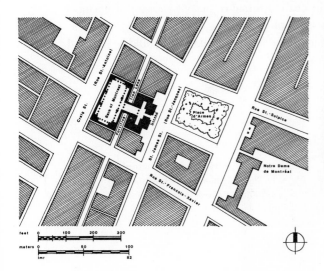

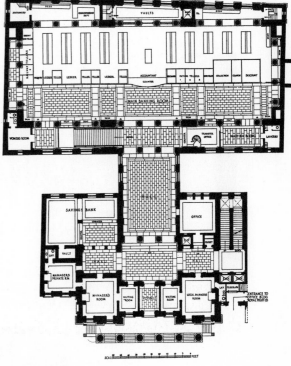

323. ABOVE. Bank of Montreal, site plan.

324. RIGHT. Bank of Montreal, plan. *Monograph.*

325. BELOW. Bank of Montreal, longitudinal section (L. M. Roth).

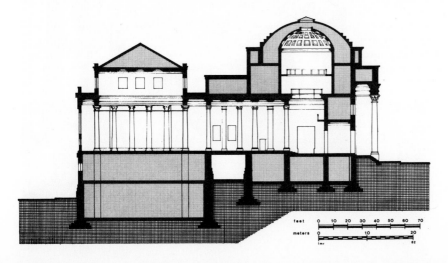

Construction, begun in May 1901, was supervised by associate architect Andrew T. Taylor of Montreal, and while excavation proceeded for the new Craig Street addition, the walls of the original building were shored up and its basement rooms renovated. Work then shifted to the massive walls of Chelmsford granite for the Craig Street building, its broad, external Tuscan pilasters corresponding exactly to the Corinthian columns within [326]. Finished in 1904, the banking room is one of the largest spaces by the firm, measuring 156 by 57 feet; the Corinthian columns are 31 feet high, while the ceiling rises 26 feet higher still [327].[131] The materials were the finest available: walls and floor of dull pink Knoxville granite with some limestone accents; columns of highly polished green syenite with bases of black Belgian marble and cast-bronze gilt capitals. Although no specific antique model was followed, the color and scale of the room suggest early Roman basilicas such as Santa Maria Maggiore or San Paolo Fuori de Mura, Rome.

Once the Craig Street addition was sufficiently finished to permit transfer of business operations in June 1903, work began on the second phase, 1903–05. The hall-bridge link was extended into the old building, which was then gutted so new steel beams could be inserted

326. Bank of Montreal, Craig Street extension, 1900–04. *Monograph.*

327. Bank of Montreal, new banking room, Craig Street extension. *Monograph.*

into the existing structural walls. The functional arrangement of the original building was completely revised, but on the new steel underpinning a dome of Guastavino tile was built [322]. Viewed from the newly restored rotunda, the columns of the hall and the great Corinthian columns of the banking room serve as a series of screens obscuring the view of that main room and heightening the sense of anticipation and surprise as one proceeds toward the huge space. Indeed, the entire sequence of spaces along the entry path is most carefully controlled, and the visual experience expanded through the coordinated materials and colors [325]. The interiors of the Bank of Montreal are among the most magnificent in Canada, but just as important is McKim's restoration of the dome, thus giving back to this landmark the silhouette which had become synonymous with banking in Montreal.

At almost the same time as drawings were started for the Bank of Montreal, Stanford White began the first sketches for his Knickerbocker Trust Company, New York, 1901–04. The commission came to the firm from White's good friend Charles T. Barney, president of the bank. Preliminary drawings called for a thirteen-story building on the corner of Fifth Avenue and 34th Street, with a hotel or offices on the upper floors [328].[132] The drawings

328. Knickerbocker Trust, New York, N. Y., perspective of initial scheme, thirteen-story skyscraper, 1901.

had been completed and estimates prepared when, late in 1901, Barney's associates, who were putting up the money for the upper floors, withdrew from the project. Despite the setback, the bank decided to go ahead with the project, building only the lower four floors, but, as White noted,

> the masonry walls, the iron work, and all constructional work, the elevator wells, the feeds, and all necessary chases, and everything which would enable the balance of the stories to be built are included in this specification; but the building is to be considered as a four story building —that is, no temporary roof, but a permanent roof, as the probability is that the remaining stories may never be built.[133]

The small but imposing white marble templar block had a force and presence which helped to make this one of the most famous financial institutions in the city [329].[134] McKim, among many others, transferred his personal funds here. In this White not only expressed his increasing clarity of form but also revealed the extent of his archaeological studies, for although the Knickerbocker Trust was obviously adapted from a Roman temple, it combined references to many antique sources: the colossal Corinthian order was close to that of the Temple of Mars Ultor and the Pantheon in Rome; the rinceaux patterns in the frieze recalled a fragment from the Forum of Trajan and also the Maison Carrée in Nîmes; the putti growing out of the rinceaux at the corners may have been inspired by similar motifs at Pompeii.

The Knickerbocker Trust Company building was praised by Montgomery Schuyler at the same time that he was also applauding the work of Wright and Sullivan. Unaware, no doubt, that the bank had intended to erect a tall building with the temple as its base, Schuyler was greatly pleased that the architect did *not* pile offices floor upon floor above the banking room, and he particularly liked the colossal Corinthian columns which visually and literally supported the roof. These and the nonsupportive screen wall behind the columns Schuyler compared to the Néo-grec rationalism of the Faculté de Médecine in Paris by P.-R.-L. Ginain, White's Cullum Memorial, and the ultimate source for such work, the Temple of Zeus Olympios at Akragas. The Corinthian order was correctly handled, he noted, with the intercolumniations being neither too wide nor too narrow. This, plus the sheer size of the columns and the strong ornamentation, enabled the bank to hold its own against the towering and floridly embellished Astoria Hotel across the street. What Schuyler was suggesting was that the Knickerbocker Trust was successful not solely because of the logically expressed function but because it was also visually rewarding. As he observed, it was "one of the most impressive visual objects on Fifth Avenue, or indeed in the street architecture of New York, and we ought to feel very much obliged to the architect for giving us something so good to look at."[135] Whether it was because the building was intended as a base for an office superstructure, or because of White's desire for texture, the Knickerbocker Trust was given a richness and assertiveness which made its larger neighbors appear rather mean by comparison.[136] Even in its truncated form, it was a better building than most others on the avenue. The upper nine floors were never built, despite some interest in doing so in 1920; so, like the Madison Square church, the Knickerbocker Trust stood only a short time before it was replaced by a taller, more productive building. There was virtually no place for small gems in the vertical city.

Meanwhile McKim received a number of similar commissions, such as the New England Trust Company, Boston, 1904–07. The site, in the heart of the Boston business district, was relatively small, and McKim decided to make the bank one large rectangular room covered by a single Guastavino vault, lit by a tall window arcade in the exterior walls [330].[137] In deference to his Boston clients, perhaps, McKim used little embellishment, but by means of the large windows he was able to suggest the volume within, topped by suites of offices in the attic story. In its own way, it was comparable to the functional expression of Sullivan's small Midwest banks designed during these same years.

329. Knickerbocker Trust, New York, N. Y., 1901–04.

330. New England Trust Company, Boston, Mass., 1904–07.

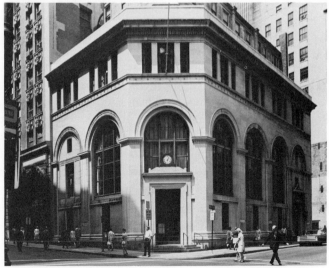

At the same time McKim started work on the New England Trust, he became involved
in the design of the Girard Trust Company, Philadelphia. The project had been initiated
in June 1904 when E. B. Morris, president of the bank, asked Allen Evans to submit a
proposal for a new building, specifically asking that this be Evans's work and not that of
his partner, Frank Furness. The new building was to stand next to the West End Trust on
Broad Street, which Furness & Evans had done in 1898. Nine months later McKim and his
firm were brought into collaboration on the bank.[138] Unlike the Bank of Montreal, much
of the work for the Girard Trust was done in Philadelphia. Built in 1906–08, the entire
exterior is of dense white Georgia marble [331]. As the site was nearly square, Evans and
McKim developed a centralized plan with a single large, domed, central volume flanked on
three sides by tiers of offices; a fourth side was devoted to the entry vestibule. Thus the
external dome announced the central volume, and the base block reflected the surrounding
auxiliary spaces, so that given the syntax of the classical language, here too function was
expressed by form.[139]

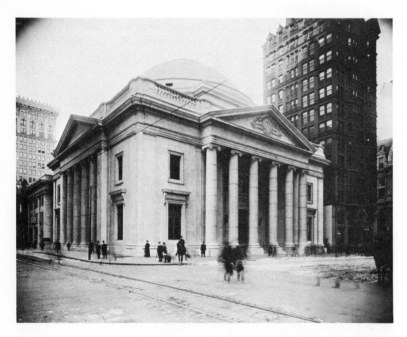

331. Girard Trust Company,
Philadelphia, Pa., 1904–08.

In building for the National City Bank, McKim had to modify an existing landmark
in New York's financial district to fit the needs and aspirations of the city's most powerful
bank. Bank president James Stillman had long wished to occupy the old Customs House,
Rogers's Merchant's Exchange, and during a meeting in Washington with Secretary of the
Treasury Lyman Gage, arranged to buy the building for $3,265,000. In mid-1899 there was
held a sham public auction at which the "sale" was made official. At first there was much
public concern that this admired building would be torn down, but Stillman announced it
would be saved. He had been attracted to the building not only because of its long Ionic
portico on Wall Street but also because it filled an entire city block and few New York banks
could claim the distinction of being freestanding buildings. At first Stillman and McKim
planned to incorporate Rogers's eighty-foot-diameter rotunda and brick dome into the
renovated interiors, but then for a time serious consideration was given to using the old

building as the base for a twenty-three-story skyscraper; but despite the income potential this scheme was set aside. By 1904 the design had been settled and working drawings prepared, as Gilbert's new Customs House was being completed. Then remodeling of the building was postponed because of the financial panic of 1907, but shortly thereafter work commenced on gutting the vacated Merchant's Exchange; the interiors were sufficiently advanced to permit formal opening for business in December 1908, although work continued in parts of the building for two years.[140]

The remodeling consisted of two distinct parts; gutting and completely rebuilding the interior of Rogers's original building, and then adding four stories above, using a Corinthian order proportioned to Rogers's Ionic columns below [332, 333, 334].[141] Accommodated in the new upper stage were rental offices and dining and library facilities for bank employees. Because the granite removed in the lower part was reused in the upper stage along with new Rockport granite that matched the old, the juncture between old and new construction is nearly impossible to detect; the building gives the appearance of having been constructed in one operation. The vast cleared space of Rogers's building was reshaped as a great cruciform hall, 123 by 187 feet and 59 feet from floor to coffered ceiling, lit by a glass-covered oculus 52 feet in diameter. Although there was no spatial procession and hence no sense of anticipation as in the Bank of Montreal, the sheer magnitude of the room makes it one of the great spaces in the city.

Although McKim prepared the design for the National City Bank, its construction was supervised by William S. Richardson, as was true also for the Downtown Building for the Knickerbocker Trust Company, designed by White just before his death in 1906 [335]. The construction history of this was also troubled, for building was halted during the panic of 1907, and after reorganization of the bank, work resumed but only to the ninth floor of what had been designed as a twenty-two-story building; two years later the remaining floors were finished.[142] The base was much like the Knickerbocker Trust on 34th Street, with a colossal order, and light glass and metal screen walls. For a skyscraper, this was a conservative tripartite design, but it is significant as one of the few true skyscrapers completed by the firm and one which set the pattern for those designed by the younger partners during the next decade and a half.

Other commercial work consisted of office and mercantile buildings, ranging from small shops to large office blocks. Soon after remodeling the showrooms of the Duveen galleries in 1902, White designed a small elegant showroom for the American Tobacco Company (later the Havana Tobacco Company), New York, 1902–05. Occupying the ground floor of the James Building at Broadway and 27th Street, the room was completely redone in selected white marbles [336]. The outer walls were almost entirely of plate glass, so that the marble surfaces glistened in a flood of light. There was little more to the room, for the total effect depended more on the carpets, potted plants, and a few selected antique chairs and tables than on the architecture per se. Perhaps it was the bright airy quality that caused one observer to call this "the finest store in the world."[143]

While White was completing this small shop he was also expanding on this theme in two large mercantile buildings. These two, the Gorham and Tiffany buildings, along with the colorful Madison Square church, made these years hum with an intensity of work. Could White have pushed any harder had he known these years were also to be his last? The eight tall stories of the Gorham Building in Fifth Avenue, New York, 1903–06, stood well above the surrounding buildings [337].[144] This too was tripartite in organization, the arcaded base taking in the display floor and a mezzanine level. Above this decorated zone was a much plainer middle zone of office floors, and above that the terminating two-story section, richly embellished in correspondence to the base arcade, with Corinthian columns, entablature, and a great cornice cantilevered eight feet from the face of the building. The cornice was

332. National City Bank, New York, N. Y., 1904–10 (enlarged from Isaiah Roger's Merchants' Exchange, 1836–42).

334. National City Bank, banking room, interior.

333. National City Bank, plan.
Monograph.

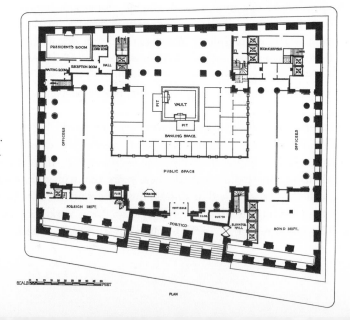

335. Knickerbocker
Trust Company, Downtown
Building, New York, N. Y.,
1906–09, perspective, signed and
dated "Jules Crow/07".

336. American Tobacco Company
(Havana Tobacco Company)
salesroom, New York,
N. Y., 1902–03. L. G. White,
Sketches and Designs.

built up of copper sections, and originally the components of the Florentine double modillion profile were enameled in various colors, with parts gilded, but weathering has stripped this away and left an even, green patina. As in earlier commercial buildings, the turning of the corner was given special attention, here recalling the solution used in the Judge Building and referring to seventeenth-century palazzi in Rome such as the Palazzo Almagia'-gia Fiano.

If White drew from a broad range of Italian sources for the Gorham Building, in Tiffany's, New York, 1903–06, he was clearly inspired by one Renaissance model [338].[145]

Seldom did White replicate his sources, but the Tiffany store was quite obviously patterned after Sanmicheli's Palazzo Grimani, Venice, 1556. Why he used this particular model is not indicated, but perhaps he wished to make a parallel between the splendor of Venetian art and the treasures of the nation's best-known jeweler. Even in following a model so closely, however, White demonstrated his audacity in making changes. He eliminated the superimposed syncopated rhythms of Sanmicheli's facade, changing the a-b-b-b-a sequence of varied bays to a uniform module, on Fifth Avenue, enclosed by double columns, although in the longer 37th Street side he introduced single columns in the center bays. Furthermore he

337. OPPOSITE. Gorham Company Building, New York, N. Y., 1903–06.

338. Tiffany's, New York, N. Y., 1903–06.

subdued the ornamental keystones and stripped away the fluting of the doubled columns, simplifying the sculptural enrichment of the facade.

White may have been attracted to Venetian sources because of their relatively larger proportion of window to solid wall, but he increased this ratio still more by introducing large show windows on the ground floor, and in the middle level he removed the spandrels of the arches, putting a skin of glass behind the free-standing curved architraves.[146] All of these changes tended to emphasize the lightness of the structure and the presence of an internal steel frame, all part of White's increasing interest in structural expression. He was especially interested in the visual properties of pure structure, as is evident in the Guastavino vaults of the storage room on the topmost floor.

Tiffany's, like the Knickerbocker Trust, was a powerful presence on Fifth Avenue, not simply because of its great height, but because of its classical sobriety. Henry James said the building presented itself with a "great nobleness of white marble," and he praised the "sociable symmetry" of its three easily perceived stages (containing seven floors).[147] In contrast to the exterior, the ground-floor showroom was richly embellished in colored marbles, with pockets of dense ornamentation. But sobriety was the essence of the Tiffany stables which the firm did in 1904 [339].[148] Tucked in the middle of the block on 41st Street, the building housed the fleet of wagons and the horses used for deliveries (later it was converted to accommodate gasoline-powered trucks). The wide central opening of the Palladian motif conveniently provided for the larger vehicles, while the smaller flanking openings provided for those on foot. Now destroyed, it epitomized the best of the firm's restrained but well-proportioned street architecture.

Whereas the firm's heavier commercial blocks of the 1880s pointed in the direction of a coherent expression of a structural bearing wall, White's commercial work at the start of the century approached a skeletonized modular type, as is demonstrated in the Tiffany

339. Tiffany's stables (garage), New York, N. Y., 1904–05. *Brickbuilder*, February 1906.

340. Munsey (*Times*) Building, Washington, D. C., 1905–07. *American Architect and Building News*, May 12, 1906.

building. Once this had been developed it was adapted for smaller office blocks, such as that for Frank L. Munsey in Washington, D.C., 1905–07. The building site was narrow but deep, so that the upper floors were pulled in along the sides, creating an I-shaped plan with light wells on either side. The facade was reduced to a frame of thin pilasters and entablatures holding a skin of glass and bronze spandrel panels and mullions [340].[149] The sheathing at the base was white marble, but the upper frame members were covered with white-glazed terra cotta. As in the Gorham Building, the surmounting cornice was proportioned to the total height of the building. Munsey had created a publishing empire, beginning with the *Golden Argosy* in 1882, to which was added a number of other magazines and newspapers across the country, including the Washington *Times*. The *Times* Building, as this also was known, was to house the consolidated headquarters of Munsey's many enterprises, and he planned to build a series of similar office buildings in Baltimore, Boston, and New York, where he had publishing interests. These never materialized, but the studies for those buildings were used in developing the plans for the Eastman Kodak building, New York, 1906–07, with its reinforced concrete frame.[150]

One of the smaller of the commercial buildings was for John Howard Whittemore and was another of his many philanthropic gestures. Because McKim and White were so occupied with other work, this design was developed by Kendall and Van der Bent. The Buckingham, named for Mrs. Whittemore's family, was built in aid of the Waterbury, Connecticut, hospital; Whittemore constructed the building at his expense provided the hospital raised for itself an endowment equal to the building's cost. When finished, all rents from the offices were to go to the hospital. Built fronting a small park in Waterbury, 1903–06, The Buckingham had shops on the ground floor and three stories of offices around the perimeter above; inside all of this was a public auditorium [341]. The external walls were of white terra cotta with a matt white glaze. Around the smaller windows inset in the arcades above was sgraffito work in the plaster.[151] Because of its foursquare solidity and simplicity, The Buckingham controlled the small plaza in front of it; it had a graceful urbanity that was decidedly horizontal in line.

341. Buckingham Building, Waterbury, Conn., 1903–06.

As always, there were a few commissions, invariably by White, which are difficult to categorize, such as his interiors for C. T. Barney's yacht *Invincible,* 1900. It was a wistful gesture, for Barney was far from invincible; his Knickerbocker Trust failed in 1907 and he took his own life shortly thereafter. Of all White's many design experiments, without question the most extraordinary was the tower and transmission station he designed in 1900–02 for his friend Nikola Tesla. He had met Tesla through Edward Dean Adams when all were working on the Niagara Falls generating station (Tesla's work on polyphase alternating current equipment was vital to its success). While Tesla had been working in conjunction with George Westinghouse on that project, he had also been experimenting with the resonant response of tuned electrical coils (his famous "Tesla Coil") and a related system of transmitting not only Morse code messages without wires but electrical energy as well. Initially these experiments were conducted in his laboratory on Houston Street, New York, where he gave demonstrations to White and prominent society investors, who he hoped would underwrite the high cost of his investigations. White admitted to Tesla the demonstrations "made a deep impression on me, as they did on everyone."[152] Through the efforts of such supporters, in 1899 Tesla was able to pursue his experiments on a large scale at a specially built laboratory outside Colorado Springs, publishing a rather philosophical account of his work.[153] As he saw it, single channel wireless telegraphy was merely one of the cruder applications of a method of transmitting energy, even if it was the one that seemed most practical at the moment. Late in 1900 Tesla was able to persuade J. P. Morgan to advance him $150,000 for an experimental wireless station, but what Tesla really had in mind was the construction of a full-scale power transmission plant for what he called his "World System." This was to combine interconnected radiotelephone networks, synchronized time signals, stock market reports from around the world, and a full range of private communications, as well as the wireless transmission of electrical energy to all parts of the globe. He boasted of inaugurating the system by powering and controlling an electrical boat at the Paris World's Fair in 1903 from his base in New York.[154]

As the site for the transmission station, James S. Warden, manager and director of the Suffolk County Land Company, offered Tesla two hundred acres of flat scrub-covered sand at Shoreham, on the north shore of Long Island about sixty-five miles east of Brooklyn. A portion of this was cleared, and White's first two buildings went up in 1901; these consisted of a low brick laboratory and the adjacent wooden transmission tower, but he may also have designed the Long Island Railroad depot built there as well. The enterprise was christened Wardenclyffe by Tesla in honor of his benefactor, and it was projected that when the "World System" was in full operation, approximately two thousand people would work and live there; presumably White would have designed the entire community. The tower was as strangely mysterious as the laboratory was plain and unassuming [342]. A tapered double-octagonal shaft of wooden trusswork, one frame inside the other and fastened entirely with wooden dowels to eliminate any metal, it rose 187 feet into the air, carrying an ovoidal metal frame 68 feet in diameter, which was later to be covered with copper plates; its exaggerated mushroom shape served to increase speculation among local farmers. Below the octagonal concrete foundation ring was a tubular pit 120 feet deep containing a telescoping steel column that could be extended up through the full height of the wooden tower. Before construction in 1902, wind pressure on the structure was calculated by White and engineer W. D. Crow.[155]

In the meantime, of course, Tesla had lost the race for demonstrating simple wireless

342. Tesla "World System" Transmission Tower, Wardenclyffe, Shoreham, Long Island, N. Y., 1902.

telegraphy; appropriating several of Tesla's patents, Guglielmo Marconi had transmitted the letter *S* across the Atlantic on December 12, 1901. Having spent Morgan's advance to build the basic equipment, Tesla could find no more financial support; his assistants at Wardenclyffe were laid off and work there came to a halt. For a few nights Tesla conducted some tests, astounding the local residents who saw great bolts of blue lightning, hundreds of feet in length, flung from the top of the mushroom tower, and felt the air bristle with static electricity and ozone. Then there was silence. In 1905 Wardenclyffe, the tower and the laboratory filled with strange apparatus, was abandoned. The tower stood moldering until dynamited for scrap in 1917, but Tesla never ceased to believe in his "World System."[156]

While White was at work on the fantastical Wardenclyffe project, he also assisted in the design of a more prosaic powerhouse for New York's first subway, the Interborough Rapid Transit (IRT). Although a subway had been proposed in 1868, pressure from established transit companies blocked progress until 1897, when the IRT company was formed; even so, legal and financial problems delayed the start of construction until 1900.[157] A single large central generating station was to provide electricity for the entire network, with scattered transformer substations. The central powerhouse was to fill the entire block at the west end of 59th Street on the Hudson River, where coal could be delivered by barge. The internal arrangements and machinery were designed by contractor John B. MacDonald and engineers for the IRT, while White designed the external envelope. Built in 1900–04, the powerhouse measured 964 by 200 feet and housed six independent generating stations consisting of coal hopper, boiler, engine, alternator, and auxiliary equipment. To conserve room, coal was stored in hoppers above the boilers and fed down partly by gravity; the weight of the coal necessitated immense steel girders and trusses over the boilers. The chimneys, one for each station, went through the center of each hopper, and were likewise supported by the massive steel substructure. These details were all decided by company engineers, who also worked with White to develop an appropriate exterior, "architecturally attractive and in harmony with the recent tendencies of municipal and city improvements."[158] The base was of pink Milford granite with upper walls of buff Roman brick and matching terra cotta [343]. To subdivide visually the long side walls, White devised a bay system whose paired rusticated pilasters carry a heavy entablature below the roof line, exactly at the point corresponding to the massive internal girders carrying the hoppers and chimneys. The six chimneys, supported 76 feet above the floor, rise 162 feet above that platform and have an entasis varying from a 21-foot diameter at the roof line to a 15-foot diameter at the top. Through such visual devices and the ornamental embellishment, White attempted to mitigate the impact of this behemoth on its surroundings, for since the powerhouse could not practically be made small, at least it could be made pleasing to look at.

BESIDES this, White worked on one other rail facility, his Grand Central Terminal project of 1903. This and McKim's Pennsylvania Station both grew out of the continuing contest between the New York Central and the Pennsylvania Railroads for the traffic of New York, and although White's project followed McKim's by nearly nine months, it is instructive to view the development of Pennsylvania Station in the context of the rebuilding of Grand Central Terminal.

In 1832 the New York and Harlem Railroad began operation on tracks laid on the Bowery from Prince to 14th Street, and over the years extensions were made northward and

343. Interborough Rapid Transit Company (IRT) Powerhouse, New York, N. Y., 1901–04.

southward. The first depot was built at Chambers Street, but as residential areas pushed farther north, the depot was successively relocated, first, in 1860, at 26th Street (where the train sheds were later rebuilt to house Gilmore's Garden and then the first Madison Square Garden), and finally at 42nd Street, where Snook's Second Empire station was finished in 1871. In that station Cornelius ("Commodore") Vanderbilt consolidated the New York and Harlem, the New York and New Haven, and the New York Central and Hudson River Railroads, making it the most important point of entry into the city, bringing traffic from New England, upstate New York, and points west. In 1899–1901 the building was enlarged and modernized by C. P. R. Gilbert.[159] Earlier, during the construction of the depot on 42nd Street, the tracks running down Fourth Avenue (later renamed Park Avenue) were repositioned in a cut which was roofed over for a distance of nearly three miles north from 42nd Street (with vent holes at intervals). Through this tunnel coal-fired, steam-powered locomotives pulled the trains into Grand Central.

Meanwhile, as the New York Central was acquiring controlling interests in roads reaching through Ohio and Indiana to Chicago, the Pennsylvania Railroad also was extending its line of operation, absorbing smaller lines in a countereffort to reach Chicago; it also obtained right-of-way to Jersey City, where its trains came to a halt. Manhattan was less than a mile away, but the intervening Hudson River could neither be bridged nor tunneled under with available technology, so for thirty years, while the Pennsy's directors wrestled with the problem, passengers on the Pennsylvania Railroad had to be ferried from Jersey City to Manhattan, not an arrangement to induce traffic away from the rival New York Central.[160]

In 1874 and again in 1879 attempts were made to tunnel under the Hudson, but when a caisson blowout killed twenty workmen this stopped. Then in 1884 Gustav Lindenthal proposed a gigantic suspension bridge over the Hudson, several times longer than the Brooklyn Bridge opened the year before, but as the cost was to be shared by several railroads, some of whom balked, the project was dropped. In 1892, gaining entry into Manhattan became the special interest of Samuel Rea, assistant to the president of the Pennsylvania Railroad, who scrutinized all available options, concluding that at that time the best solution was a shorter tunnel under the Narrows between Staten Island and Brooklyn with a connection back across the East River onto Manhattan somewhere in the vicinity of Madison Square. Rea's report spurred interest once more, only to have it dampened once again by the depression of the nineties. In any case, Rea's proposal was predicated on the use of smokeless electric traction, and so far there were no electric locomotives capable of pulling standard long-haul trains. By the close of the century, however, a number of technical advances had been made, in the use of heavier caissons and shields for tunneling, and the perfection of heavy and more powerful electric locomotives; moreover, by 1900 the economy was once again vigorous. The first large-scale application of electric traction was the extension of the Orléans railway into Paris to the new Gare d'Orsay, built 1897–1900 in anticipation of the world's fair. The last two and one-half miles of track, much of it below street level, was electrified. At the suggestion of Rea, Alexander J. Cassatt, then president of the Pennsylvania Railroad, traveled to Paris specifically to see this installation, becoming convinced that the problems so far preventing entry of the Pennsy into Manhattan were now solved.[161]

During 1901 the railroad began acquiring the necessary properties in New Jersey and rights-of-way in Manhattan, while detailed plans for the tunnels and track layout were

developed by company engineers. The immense project was then divided into three opera-
tional divisions, two purely engineering and one engineering and architectural: the North
River Division to go under the Hudson, under chief engineer Charles M. Jacobs; the electric
traction and station under chief engineer George Gibbs; and the East River Division to go
under the East River, under chief engineer Alfred Noble. This East River tunnel had been
added because in the spring of 1900 the Pennsylvania Railroad acquired an interest in the
Long Island Railroad, a merger which worked to the advantage of both, for the Pennsylvania Railroad wanted a potential connection to New England which this linkage provided,
and the Long Island wanted to reach Manhattan. The combination, however, was to greatly
exacerbate the traffic flow patterns to be accommodated by the architect in the station. Not
only would he need to provide for periodic crowds of long-haul passengers and baggage,
but he would now need to allow for the circulation of surging hordes of Long Island
commuters twice daily.

Essentially the proposal for the Manhattan connection was this: two tracks would leave
Jersey City and cross the Hackensack Meadows on a causeway, descend into two tubes
under the Hudson and then proceed under the streets of Manhattan to a station at Eighth
Avenue and 33rd Street. From the east side of this station four tubes would continue below
street level across Manhattan, under the East River, return to the surface, and connect with
the Long Island system at Long Island City. Of the 5.1 miles of tunnel, 1.5 miles were to
be under water. The railroad received the necessary authority from the City of New York
in December 1901 to build and operate a terminal, with the stipulation that no combustion
of any kind be used for locomotion in the tunnels.[162]

Just when the directors of the New York Central understood what the Pennsy was
undertaking is not clear, but by 1901 they must have been aware that the New York Central
was soon to face such competition as it had never faced before. It would take very little for
the new Pennsylvania Station to outclass the weak refurbishing of the old Grand Central
Station in 1899. Then came tragedy and legislative mandate. On the morning of January 8,
1902, while moving through the tunnel under Fourth Avenue, inordinately filled that cold
morning with steam and smoke, a New York Central commuter train plowed into the rear
of a standing New Haven train; the engineer had been unable to see the signals. Seventeen
people were killed and scores injured. Under public pressure, the state legislature passed a
law forbidding any steam-powered locomotives to enter Manhattan on any line used
predominantly for passenger service after July 1, 1910. The New York Central now entered
the race to see which of the two major railroads soon to be in Manhattan could electrify
first. Realizing that this would entail extensive rebuilding of the tracks, chief engineer
William J. Wilgus of the New York Central pushed the bold proposal of rebuilding the
entire station, with two levels of tracks and a completely new station above them. In
December 1902 Wilgus's plan was approved, and replanning the track fan began; in addition,
proposals for the design of the new station were sent out to four selected architects, the
finished drawings due March 1, 1903. The four invited architects were: D. H. Burnham &
Company; McKim, Mead & White; Samuel Huckel, Jr., of Philadelphia; and Charles Reed
and Allen Stem of Saint Paul, Minnesota. Eventually the prize went to Reed & Stem,
although Whitney Warren and Charles D. Wetmore were then added, to design the shell
of the station, an arrangement which was not without legal difficulties later; their well-
known Grand Central Terminal, begun in 1903, was completed in 1913.[163]

The firm's Grand Central Terminal proposal was prepared by White. Above the track
fan devised by Wilgus was to rise a large square block fourteen stories high and towering

above this a sixty-story tower [344, 345]. The tallest building in the world, the Grand Central tower would have been visible from all parts of the city, the last sight of outbound seafarers and the first of those inbound. At the base the existing streets penetrated the building through five-story vaulted arcades, maintaining the flow of vehicular traffic. The belvedere tourelles and the general massing of the tower recalled White's Madison Square Garden tower. This project, a few years later the basis for the younger partners' Municipal Building design, further demonstrated White's growing interest in the skyscraper and the expanding urban scale of building. But White's scheme was "far too extensive," in the view of New York Central president William H. Newman, and "impracticable." Parts of the design he liked, just as he thought the peristyle around Burnham's proposal handsome, but he preferred the Reed & Stem design taken as a whole.[164]

There appears to have been no great disappointment in the office when Grand Central was awarded to Reed & Stem, for their attention was already focused on the single building which for years symbolized the best of McKim, Mead & White—Pennsylvania Station. The

344. Grand Central Terminal, New York, N. Y., competition entry, 1903, perspective from the south, signed and dated "J. A. Johnson 03".

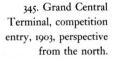

345. Grand Central Terminal, competition entry, 1903, perspective from the north.

commission had come as a complete surprise the year before. While inspecting the site for Burnham's projected Union Station in Washington, D.C., with members of the Senate Park Commission, McKim received a telegram from Cassatt asking for a meeting on April 24, 1902. McKim quipped to Moore that Cassatt probably wanted a new stoop for his Philadelphia townhouse; he had no idea that instead of a stoop Cassatt wanted a grand portal to New York and that McKim, Mead & White was to be its architect.[165] When handed the commission, McKim immediately thought of a grand monument gateway, and when Cassatt proposed it include a high-rise hotel McKim gently but unwaveringly disabused him of the idea; this may have been the fatal flaw in McKim's scheme, for had there been this additional income McKim's masterwork might have lasted longer than fifty years. From the moment the hotel was eliminated, this station, like so many of the firm's best works, was foredoomed.

Elated at the new commission, McKim wrote Burnham, thanking him for his congratulatory note, interjecting that his friend Daniel S. Newhall said they had been employed because they were New York architects.[166] Despite this disclaimer, it was true that, besides Burnham, then at work on his Washington Station, there were few other architects in the United States with the breadth of experience and vision to undertake as large a complex as Pennsylvania Station. Aside from its great size, necessary to handle the volume of long-haul passengers, commuters, baggage, freight, and mail, McKim faced the challenge of making the station a fitting gateway to the city, symbolically representing the power and position of the railroad, in a building where the trains themselves would never be visible from the street. Engineering necessities placed the level of the tracks forty-five feet below street level, or about nine feet below the mean level of the Hudson, and this meant that all the usual visual attributes of great train stations of the nineteenth century—the soaring arched train sheds and the trains themselves—would not be present. Through architectural means alone Pennsylvania Station had to impress passenger and passerby.

Once the various legal issues regarding franchises and rights-of-way had been resolved, McKim worked out the basic plan, with the advice of Samuel Rea and William H. Brown, the chief executive officer and engineer of the railroad. His objective was to achieve "operating efficiency" with an "outward expression of the station's use" but conveying the image of a "monumental gateway" to the city.[167] By 1904 the specifics for the layout of the tracks were settled, and work began on the tunnels and the huge excavation for the station. The eight-acre hole for the building excited almost as much curiosity and awe as the Brooklyn Bridge—according to one estimate three million cubic yards of earth and mica schist were removed—and like the bridge, it inspired several paintings by members of the Ash Can School. In the spring of 1905 the granite work was started on the lower levels, while the adjacent cubical granite powerhouse on the south side of 31st Street was rapidly completed. On October 16, 1906, the tubes from Hackensack reached the station excavation, but completion of the East River tubes was delayed by construction problems until March 1908, by which time the station superstructure was well advanced.[168]

At the critical point when the details of the design had to be developed, deteriorating health forced McKim to delegate much of this work to Richardson, while organizational and engineering supervision was taken over by Van der Bent.[169] Though the station was eventually completed by them and other members of the firm, the design was McKim's. The final step was to have a large plaster model made, complete with every molding and belt course; but for the absence of people, it is easy to confuse some photographs of this with views of the finished building. Besides being a powerful presentation device, the model permitted study of the lighting of various rooms, and one photograph shows that for a time the firm experimented with large globes suspended in each of the three bays of the central waiting room.

Pennsylvania Station was a large rectangular building, 430 feet by 780 feet, filling two entire city blocks from 31st to 33rd streets between Seventh and Eighth avenues [346]. Covering nearly eight acres, the station stood over a broad fan of tracks that extended back to Tenth Avenue and reached halfway through the blocks east of Seventh Avenue; at the widest point there were twenty-one parallel tracks [347]. Already 45 feet below the street, the tracks were undercut in several places by subtunnels for baggage handling, drainage, and electrical conduits. The three northernmost tracks were reserved for Long Island commuter trains, reached by a sequence of special concourses extending to the rapid transit lines at each end of the station under Seventh and Eighth avenues (these subways, unbuilt when the station was constructed, were put through shortly afterward). This commuter concourse, with its special access staircases to the street, was 18 feet above the tracks; branching off from it was a broad exit concourse 60 feet wide that ran the width of the station and had special exit stairs separate from those used by other passengers. This critical element of the pedestrian traffic flow does not appear on most plans of the track level, nor do the 650 steel columns which supported the superstructure, for despite its massive-looking external masonry cladding, the building was steel-framed to accommodate the maze of tracks below [348].[170]

346. Pennsylvania Station, New York, N. Y., 1902–11. L. H. Dreyer construction photograph, March 4, 1910.

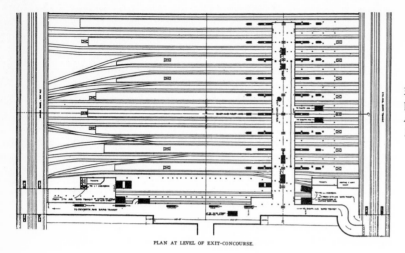

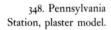

PLAN AT LEVEL OF EXIT-CONCOURSE.

347. Pennsylvania Station,
plan, commuter concourse level.
*American Architect and Building
News*, May 26, 1906.

348. Pennsylvania
Station, plaster model.

The next level [349] was the main working floor, still fourteen feet below the street. Among the novel features were the wide ramps descending from entrances on Seventh Avenue to long cul-de-sacs in the middle of the station where passengers alighted; vehicles then continued to a wide baggage drop at the east end of the building and from there could rejoin the ramp and return to the street. Electric trucks carried freight and baggage via a separate southerly passage to the far western end of the station, where elevators descended to the baggage cars. Thus, passengers were given the shortest, most direct traffic route, while baggage was conveyed mechanically on the longer route.[171] At this main concourse level were the general waiting room, with separate smaller men's and women's waiting rooms, and the large glass-covered concourse with stairs leading down to the trains.

McKim felt, to be justly proportioned, such huge spaces had to stretch vertically. To divide the space into easily understood units and to provide proper visual scale, he modeled the general waiting room on the tepidarium (warm room) of the Baths of Caracalla, Rome. As Moore recalled, when the Senate Park Commission was in Rome in 1901, they spent an

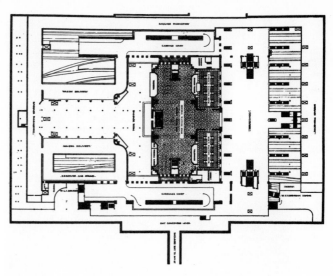

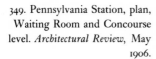

349. Pennsylvania Station, plan,
Waiting Room and Concourse
level. *Architectural Review*, May
1906.

afternoon studying the ruins of the baths, and McKim even hired groups of people to stroll around so he could observe the scale and see how the building had been adapted to the movement of crowds.[172] The central room of the baths was approximately 80 feet wide by 175 feet long, divided into three rectangular bays and covered by a massive concrete groin vault which, at its apex, was about 110 feet above the floor (this gives ratios of width to length to height of 1 to 2.2 to 1.4). McKim enlarged all the absolute dimensions about twenty percent, making the general waiting room 102 by 278 feet, with vaults 147 feet from the floor (1 to 2.75 to 1.45) [350]. In Pennsylvania Station, however, the vaults were a space-defining shell of plaster suspended from the structural steel frame rather than structural masses. The great room was intended as a visually coherent civic space and depended on certain structural simulations to achieve this end. Besides its Roman spatial source, the room was sheathed in material also Roman, for the travertine was quarried in Campagna near Tivoli, which had once supplied stone for the emperors. Its warm mellow buff color was matched by the beige of the plaster vaults.[173]

The giant Corinthian columns, 59 1/2 feet high to the top of the capital, visually supporting the vaults, rested on pedestals whose tops marked street level. This truly colossal order was complemented by a smaller Ionic order of pilasters and columns around the room —here an open colonnade, here an articulation of the otherwise plain wall—which corresponded to the muscular Tuscan Doric colonnade around the exterior of the building. Lunette windows 68 feet in diameter, recalling the arched train sheds of Paris, Frankfort, and Dresden, lit the waiting room, and immediately below them, in large rectangular panels, were mural maps by Jules Guerin showing in light hues the routes of the Pennsylvania and Long Island railroads.

Beyond the general waiting room and its segregated lounges opened the concourse, a vast room 208 by 315 feet, covered entirely by a steel and glass umbrella 90 feet from the floor. Like the general waiting room, it was divided into three groin vaults with extensions to the outer walls [351, 352]. The Concourse was one of the marvels of early twentieth-century engineering, its airiness in contrast to the more massive Roman waiting room. Despite a seemingly awkward juxtaposition of two apparently incongruous expressions, McKim was probably closer to the baths than he knew, for later excavation of the large frigidarium next

350. Pennsylvania Station,
Waiting Room, interior. L. H.
Dreyer construction photograph,
c. 1910.

to the central tepidarium revealed portions of large iron trusses with bronze fittings bolted
to them, the remains of what was once a system of bronze reflectors used to direct sunlight
onto the bathers below.[174] Clearly the concourse frame was heavier than necessary to carry
the glass vaults, and the form of the vaults depended more on Roman concrete models than
on engineering statics, but these were conscious design decisions. McKim's intent, wrote
Richardson, was to provide "an appropriate transition between the purely architectural"
character of the waiting room and "the purely utilitarian and structural treatment" of the
tracks below, to give "an easy and unconscious gradation of effect from the monumental
side of the station to the utilitarian." As a result the general shape of the vaults was
determined first and then translated by engineers Purdy & Henderson into glass and steel;
even the lattice work of the built-up columns and the cross section of the ribs were varied
and made lighter toward the top to avoid monotony.[175]

      At street level the massive building was tied together by a uniform Tuscan Doric order,
used as an open colonnade on the east, north, and south sides, and as a pilaster order
elsewhere [353]. As in studying the Boston Public Library cornice, full-scale models of the
main cornice and the attic story were lifted onto scaffolds for examination in perspective.
Across the front the colonnade provided shelter over the entrances of shops and a bank on
Seventh Avenue. Leading from the major central entrance pavilion was a barrel-vaulted
arcade 216 feet long and 45 feet wide, a covered street lined by small shops; at the end was
a vestibule opening to a restaurant and cafeteria, and, down a flight of stairs, the general
waiting room. This sequence of spaces, varying from narrow to wide, small to large, moving

351. Pennsylvania Station, Concourse, interior. L. H. Dreyer construction photograph, October 7, 1909.

352. Pennsylvania Station, glass roof of Concourse. L. H. Dreyer construction photograph, February 18, 1910.

through portico, arcade, and vestibule to the vast waiting room and concourse, was the most carefully calculated in all the firm's work.

Circulation was well organized, for besides the vehicular ramps descending from Seventh Avenue, at the sides were pedestrian bridges over the ramps [354], leading to stairs to the waiting room. Similar stairs descended into the Concourse, giving ready access to the train for commuters who had no need for the ticket and information windows in the general waiting room.

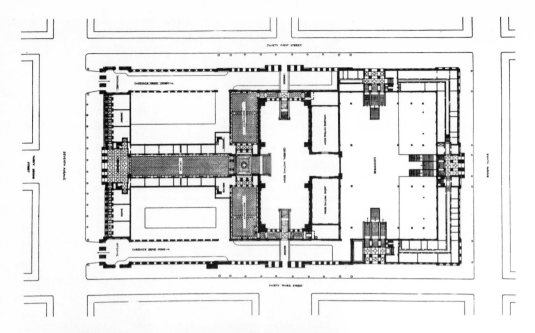

353. ABOVE. Pennsylvania Station, plan, street level. *Architectural Review*, May 1906.

354. LEFT. Pennsylvania Station, pedestrian bridge over vehicular roadway. L. H. Dreyer construction photograph, c. 1910.

The insistent horizontal procession of the continuous external colonnade, inspired by Bernini's Piazza di San Pietro and Soane's Bank of England (pictures of which McKim kept pinned above his drawing board), was broken only by the lofty attic of the waiting room with its peaked roof and lunette windows. Nearly one million cubic feet of pink Milford granite were brought to the site in 1,140 railroad cars, to sheath the exterior of the station.[176] Although this intractable material tended, of itself, to keep ornament simple, the exterior was made purposely severe, Richardson indicated, to mitigate the variegated character of its surroundings. The intent, inside and out, was "to maintain a unity and simplicity . . . so that the structure will count as a whole of many inter-related parts."[177] What little sculpture there was in the clock faces and the ornamental eagles atop the attic story was done by Adolph A. Weinman.

355. Pennsylvania Station, erection of steel framing
for Waiting Room. L. H. Dreyer construction
photograph, April 8, 1908.

Construction, begun in May 1904, proceeded without serious incident [355]; Pennsylvania Station was dedicated on August 1, 1910, not quite a year after McKim's death. Long Island trains pulled away from the station in September, and the first Pennsylvania trains arrived from New Jersey two months later. Only a few small items remained to be done, so that by October 1911 the station was completed in all its details [356].[178] Ironically, both the man who had conceived it and the architect who designed it never lived to see the building finished, yet McKim had succeeded in planning a station which, in its original state, was bright, clean, spacious, orderly, and efficient in operation. It provided for separation of various kinds of incoming and outgoing traffic; pickups and deliveries were made well away from the street. Admittedly, there could be confusion in trying to meet incoming visitors unfamiliar with the station, for there were so many entrances and exits, but the plan was very well suited to the needs of daily traffic in and out of New York.

Published both during and after construction, Pennsylvania Station was widely admired in the United States and England.[179] It did much, along with Grand Central Terminal finished soon after, to establish the sober classical image of early twentieth-century train stations, large and small, providing the model for Chicago's Union Station designed in 1914 by Graham, Burnham & Company and built in 1916–25. There was nothing, it was agreed, to compare to Pennsylvania Station. European observers, especially, took special note of the liberties taken with classical rules of design, such as the round bases for the Tuscan columns at the entrance to the vehicular ramps, which were much better suited to traffic. Some wrote the firm directly upon seeing the plans reproduced in the professional journals, as did Welles Bosworth: "I know that though so independent of the opinion of younger men in the profession, it still must be pleasant to hear how profoundly some of us respect you."[180] The station was, as McKim and Richardson had designed it to be, "a welcoming portal where at last one has come to rest, in pleasant surroundings, after a tedious journey."[181]

As the times and the fortunes of the railroads changed, however, the neoclassical

356. Pennsylvania Station, east front. L. H. Dreyer construction
photograph, February 18, 1910.

symbolism of the station was supplanted in the public mind by the utilitarian functionalism
of International Modernism, and approbation gave way to indifference and then contemptu-
ous neglect. No serious attempt was made to keep the station clean of the soot that turned
its beige and amber walls an ever-darkening dun-colored gray. Then, in 1956, as if to
intensify the increasing dinginess, the railroad constructed a large ticket counter, tricked up
with numerous television consoles, in the middle of the waiting room, blocking the entrance
to the concourse. Covering the new counter was a huge elliptical translucent plastic shell
filled with fluorescent tubes, suspended by cables attached to the dark Corinthian columns.[182] The optical contrast between the luminescent shroud and the now-blackened walls
was too much for the eye to take in; one focused on the bright shell, and the befouled classical
vaults withdrew into deeper obscurity. The interiors were gradually stuffed with display
cases, finned automobiles on revolving platforms, flying signs, illuminated advertisements,
and other assorted bibelots. Lewis Mumford could still see in 1958 the basic richness and
clarity of McKim's plan. For Mumford the classical forms were symbolically dead and
functionally meretricious, but the essential design of the station was to him superb:
"McKim's plan had a crystal clarity that gave the circulation the effortless inevitability of
a gravity-flow system, with pools of open space to slow down or rest in when one left the
main currents. Movement is the essence of transportation, and movement is what McKim's
plan magnificently provided for." It was, Mumford declared, a beautiful ordering of
space.[183]

A few years later Pennsylvania Railroad officials announced a plan to replace the station
with an office skyscraper and a new Madison Square Garden.[184] A shock ran through the
architectural world, for it seemed impossible to be so callous. Friends of the station offered
a counterproposal, which would have provided new income property and kept the station

intact, to no avail. Pennsylvania Station would come down.[185] Compromise, persuasion, and reason were ineffective—not in the cold light of profit and loss tables. Vigorous protest against the scheduled demolition now arose. Aline Saarinen's suggestion that "a good architect could make this building work," was restrained, but seething outrage compelled Mumford to call the proposed "reconstruction" of the station "an act of irresponsible public vandalism." The traveler in the flattened remains of the station beneath the new sports palace, he wrote, would "be mashed into subterranean passageways like ancient Christians, while the wrestler and fight promoter will be elevated to the vast arena."[186] Week after week Ada Louise Huxtable launched scathing editorials in the New York *Times.* If an impoverished society wished to kill a city, this, she said, was how to do it. In the architecture of expediency which replaced the station, the human environment reached zero.[187] Once, Mumford noted, McKim had dissuaded Cassatt from building a hotel over the station, and "professional and civic pride won out over cupidity"; now it was just the reverse.

Some who looked only at the supposed logic of the balance sheet said that Pennsylvania Station had failed, and to a point they were correct, for during the fifty-two years of its existence, while the function of the railroad changed, imaginative and sympathetic use of the station had not. It had been made to fail. The power to perceive or even comprehend its public grandeur, the magnificent spatial release from the crowded streets, its civic excess, was lost. When destruction loomed, it proved impossible to save it, for the station and the kind of architecture it epitomized had been ridiculed too long. Of the demolition in 1963–65, there are now only four mute stone eagles as witness, gallingly displayed in front of the gutless pattern-book skyscraper facing Seventh Avenue. Even the silent indictment of the smashed fragments dumped in the Secaucus marshes was apparently too much [357]; the pieces were pulverized for landfill. Where once stood Pennsylvania Station, public indifference and expedient meaninglessness took the place of civic symbolism and public splendor. Our greatest loss is that we will never be able to build its equal.

As the construction of Pennsylvania Station pressed inexorably onward, quietly and without fanfare the torch was passed; what had begun as McKim's great commission was completed by William S. Richardson and the firm—this esprit de corps and consensus of mind that allowed someone to take up a job if a partner or his assistant was suddenly called away had always been the strength of the firm. Just as McKim had passed the responsibility of Pennsylvania Station, so the decade up to 1906 was one of leave-taking, as one after another of the staunch patrons came to the firm for their mausoleums. As each was finished—many of them in Woodlawn Cemetery, New York, or Graceland in Chicago—for the Goelets, 1899; H. A. C. Taylor, 1900; Louis Sherry, 1906–07; and C. J. Osborn, 1909—one part after another of the firm's activity was rounded out. An end must have been sensibly near.

McKim had to parcel out his ebbing energies carefully. One last major planning enterprise, despite its cost in time and effort, commanded his attention, for he understood that the replanning of the area around Niagara Falls would have extended ramifications. So, despite his failing health, in 1907 he consented to serve on a board to advise on reclamation of the scenery around the falls. Since 1875, when Frederic E. Church had painted his sweeping curve of the Canadian rim of the falls, increasingly fewer painters were drawn to capture the awesome panorama as tourist hucksterism and growing industrialization tainted the once wild and romantic scenery. Alerted by Church to the despoliation of the falls, Frederic Law Olmsted campaigned for preservation of the scenery, proposing a state reservation in a report written with James Gardner in 1879–80. The resultant park, estab-

357. Fragments of Pennsylvania
Station dumped in the Secaucus
Meadows, N. J., 1966.

lished in 1883–85 as part of a joint New York–Canadian effort, comprised only the shore line
and islands in the rapids above the falls.[188] On the crest of the gorge on the American side,
however, industrial development continued unabated, and by 1893 eight large mills along
the cliff spewed tail water and industrial wastes down the walls of the gorge. At the bottom
of the cliff was a ninth mill supplied with water from the surface canal by a large exposed
penstock tube. Beginning in 1895 even more water was diverted for the first of four American
electrical generating plants, and by 1904 the volume of water being withdrawn by the two
rival American companies—and the nearly equal volume being used by Canadian electrical
companies—prompted fears that industrial expansion would eventually cause the falls to run
dry. Within a year, rising sentiments for protection and preservation of the falls led to the
framing of the Burton Act, passed in 1906, "for the control and regulation of the waters of
the Niagara River, [and] for the preservation of Niagara Falls."[189] Through the provisions
of the act, the President was directed to seek cooperative treaties with Great Britain and the
Canadian government, and in this way the preservation of the falls came within the jurisdic-
tion of the War Department and the Corps of Engineers.

   To survey conditions and advise on remedies, in January 1907 Secretary of War William Howard Taft appointed McKim, Frederick Law Olmsted, Jr., Frank D. Millet, and
Captain John S. Sewell of the Corps of Engineers "to consider the preservation of natural
scenic effects at Niagara Falls; [and] to recommend remedial measures of reasonable cost
which would result in improving conditions on the American side of the Gorge."[190] At
McKim's suggestion, the commission commenced an inspection tour as soon as the snow
melted, traveling to Niagara Falls in April, but then McKim was forced to return home
when he suffered food poisoning which confined him to bed for five weeks. On June 24 the
commission met to discuss its findings, and during the ensuing summer and autumn their
report was drafted.[191]

   Presented in January 1908, the Niagara Commission's report made a number of recommendations. Some of these dealt with existing bridges and their eventual replacements, but of central importance was the restoration of the natural appearance of the falls. All waste material dumped from the cliff was to be cleared away and indigenous vegetation restored. As soon as possible the buildings clustered along the cliff were to be removed, but until this could be done they were to be electrified and the smokestacks rendered smokeless. When the power station at the foot of the gorge became obsolete it was to be removed, but in the meantime, it and any additions to it were to be faced with rubble stone masonry and the penstock tubes enclosed in a concrete screen wall also faced with rubble stone from the talus at the floor of the gorge; thus the building would have the color and something of the texture of the cliff face. Their intent, wrote the commissioners, was that the natural beauty of the rapids, the falls, and the gorge below "should not be despoiled to promote the material welfare of even many individuals," and they expressed the hope that the entire gorge area, up to three hundred feet back from the face of the cliff, could be purchased and set aside as a national park. Although this sweeping proposal was not economically feasible, many of the other recommendations were followed. The power companies that were affected voluntarily took action to implement the suggestions regarding the lower powerhouse and penstock tubes; dumping and tail-water discharge was discontinued; and the operating smokestacks were made smokeless. Subsequent charters granted companies locating along the gorge had clauses requiring restoration and preservation of the scenic elements of their properties. Unfortunately, the factories along the cliff were not removed until 1945, nor was the old power station in the gorge removed until the collapse of the crumbling cliff face in 1956 destroyed two thirds of the installation. Yet significant steps toward restoration of one of the world's natural wonders had been taken, both through government action and private initiative.

PENNSYLVANIA STATION was the culmination of the art of civic architecture begun by the partners nearly a generation earlier and was rightly regarded as the firm's finest work, by their contemporaries. However, the decade from 1900 to 1909 was one of incredible activity and to focus too closely on the complexities of Pennsylvania Station and the tragedy of its destruction is to lose sight of the remarkable achievements of McKim, Mead, & White during the early years of the twentieth century. In each of the principal areas of design, the partners arrived at a synthesis of classical allusions which seemed the result of a certain irreducible logic, what Royal Cortissoz described in speaking of the Morgan Library as the bedrock of architecture.[192] Certainly many of the designs, such as the Percy Pyne house, Madison Square Presbyterian Church, the Morgan Library, the Bank of Montreal, the Knickerbocker Trust, and Tiffany's, were among the best ever produced by the firm and were greatly admired. Each possessed a distinctive clarity of plan combined with strong sculptural massing. Ornamentation and detailing was resplendent but carefully held in check. Construction was impeccable, detailed to weather long and well. McKim's work, as might be expected, had become more severe; but more surprising, White's work also revealed an intensive study of ancient and Renaissance sources, as shown in his Pulitzer house and Tiffany's. It may be that this increasingly archaeological approach was a response to the poor record of architectural preservation of eighteenth-century buildings. It may also have been that this new classicism, Roman in scale, was a reflection of the rising international stature of the nation. In large building complexes such as Bellevue Hospital, the Metropolitan Museum of Art, and especially Pennsylvania Station, the firm developed the capacity to handle large systems and interrelated services, but with the exception of White's towering

Grand Central Terminal project, these were horizontal compositions. If the newly elevated junior partners wished to seek out skyscraper commissions, the founding partners tended to avoid skyscrapers, preferring to turn the ingenuity of the twentieth century to solving other problems.

The firm's campus plans, particularly McKim's War College, continued to reveal the influence of Jefferson's University of Virginia, but it is tempting to see Jefferson's influence, too, in the expanded campus of Columbia University, although this is the result more of circumstance than intent. Of more portent were McKim's participation in the Senate Park Commission and the way both he and Burnham applied the lessons of the World's Columbian Exposition to solving the needs of a real city. The effect of the commission's report was to make urban planning practical and desirable, thus ushering in a new era in the development of the American city. Through his participation, too, in the Niagara Falls Commission, McKim demonstrated a concern for the quality of the environment as a whole, both manmade and natural, an interest in conservation that might be paralleled with President Roosevelt's contemporaneous national forest program. His insistence that the physical environment not be spoiled, even for the advantage of many individuals, acquires increasing urgency in an age when it is ever-tempting to postpone careful planning in deference to cheaper expedients.

The scale of the twentieth-century city was radically changing; urban America was becoming decidedly vertical. White alone seems to have welcomed this challenge. The destruction caused by the San Francisco earthquake on April 18, 1906, deeply troubled him. He grieved at the hundreds of deaths, and as an architect he was appalled at how easily whole blocks of buildings had toppled onto their inhabitants. Immediately his attention turned to devising ways of mitigating injury in future disasters, dashing off telegrams to Burnham with proposed building code revisions, hoping they might find their way into Burnham's plan for San Francisco.[193] Would not riveted steel frames, thoroughly braced and tied to their piles, with cladding interlocked and tied to the frame, he wrote, be able to ride out such quakes? And would not similarly integrated reinforced concrete, thoroughly tied together with T-irons and wire mesh, also be quakeproof? There was no question in his mind but that standard brickwork should be absolutely prohibited in a new code. White's normal whirlwind pace seemed to quicken as summer neared. He had numerous commissions in hand, such that McKim wrote Mead that "Stanford is alternately in seventh heaven and the other way around," and that he was "full of schemes and projects," referring perhaps to a project in Washington, D.C., where White was to have headed Tuesday morning, June 26, after dining with his son and some friends and attending the season opening of a new musical at the roof theater of Madison Square Garden on Monday night.[194] White never got to Washington, he never even saw the end of the show, for as the chorus sang the closing number, at 11:05 P.M., June 25, 1906, Harry Kendall Thaw walked up to White, seated by the stage, and shot him three times. Slumped under the table on the roof of his most playful creation, White lay dead.

AT a meeting in memory of Charles F. McKim, Walter Cook said that the words engraved on Wren's tomb in Saint Paul's, London—"If you seek his monument, look about you"— could equally be said of McKim. Surely one feels this, standing in front of French's seated *Alma Mater* on the terrace in front of Low Library at Columbia University; McKim's biography *is* written in his architecture, for his whole being was invested in what he built. But as became graphically clear during 1907 and 1908, to write White's biography, one had to look not only at his professional life and his architecture, one had to explore the byways of old Chelsea and backstage Broadway, one had to see not only his family and country house at Saint James and his richly appointed townhouse on Gramercy Square, but also his out-of-the-way private studio in the Madison Square Garden tower and another, secret, studio on 24th Street, its bedchamber paneled in mirrors around the walls and across the ceiling. Was the White who, as Edward Simmons described, shoved a fistful of currency under the door of a destitute painter, and who urged Burnham to rewrite the San Francisco building code so hundreds more need not die again, the same White who, after his death, was portrayed in the yellow press as a satyr with an insatiable appetite for young women, as someone who forced a pubescent girl to rise virtually nude from a giant pie at a stag party? There were, it seemed, two Whites, one readily acknowledged by those prominent in business, artistic, literary, theatrical, and architectural circles, and another whose more-than-avuncular interest in young showgirls was known to only a handful of his closest friends. White had a passion for all that life offered, especially the theater and the pretty butterflies who charmed its chorus lines; those whom he especially liked he showered with gifts, dresses, music and drama lessons, even corrective dental work. It was, he would say, simply his way of perfecting in some small way what was already beautiful.

White's special protégé during 1901 and 1902 was Evelyn Nesbit, a stunningly beautiful girl of sixteen who had come to New York from Pittsburgh via Philadelphia, where she had begun posing for various artists. Since her widowed mother was able to earn little as a dressmaker, the child continued to pose in New York for artists recommended by those she knew in Philadelphia, among them J. Wells Champney, George Gray Barnard, Carroll Beckwith, and Charles Dana Gibson whose ink sketch *The Eternal Question* is her portrait [358]. She began to get small parts in the chorus on Broadway, and, through a stage friend, Edna Goodrich, was introduced to Stanford White in August 1901 at a private lunch in the 24th Street studio, where they were joined by Thomas B. Clarke. White showered more than the usual attention on her, taking her to the office to meet his partners, and introducing her to prominent photographers Sarony, Gertrude Käsebier, and Rudolf Eickemeyer, Jr. [359]. When his wife, Bessie, was at Saint James, Evelyn would spend long hours after the theater in the tower studio, often until dawn. White particularly liked pushing her ever higher in a red velvet swing in one room of the 24th Street studio until her feet broke through a Japanese paper parasol fastened to the ceiling. They sipped champagne, and, as Evelyn would write later, one night one glass too many was shared, and as she put it, she awoke in the mirrored bedchamber no longer a girl but a woman.[195]

What the true relationship was between Evelyn and Stanford can be surmised only from what she testified at Harry's trial and later expanded in two autobiographies; White never had a chance to speak in his own defense. Even when Thaw's defense counsel tried to make White look as bad as possible, Evelyn felt compelled to put into the record that Stanford was most gentle, that he "had a very fatherly way," and that he was "kind and considerate and exceedingly thoughtful." No one, certainly not Thaw, seemed to understand she had loved him. In any case, it made no difference what had truly happened, for as Thaw's lawyers made certain at his murder trial, it mattered only what Evelyn had *told* Harry had happened, or more accurately, what he had *heard* her say.

Harry Kendall Thaw, aged thirty-four when he shot White, was the heir to a fortune of $40 million accumulated by his father in Pennsylvania Railroad securities. He was so unstable his father stipulated in his will that Harry's inheritance could come to him only in small allowances through his mother. That made not a whit of difference, for his mother

358. LEFT. Charles Dana Gibson,
"The Eternal Question," c. 1902.

359. Rudolf Eickemeyer, Jr., "In My Studio" (Evelyn Nesbit),
carbon print photograph, 1901.

had never denied him anything; he was vain, a wastrel, and upheld by his mother in every whim. *No* had never entered his vocabulary. Even before he ever met Evelyn, Harry grew to hate White, when some chorus girls he had invited to a party at Sherry's decided they preferred a gayer party being given in White's tower studio. Harry then became infatuated with Evelyn, who saw in Thaw, if not a particularly handsome or balanced suitor, at least one who could give her great wealth and social position she could never hope to find with Stanford. Evelyn consented to travel through Europe with Thaw, first in the company of her mother but, after a quarrel between them, unchaperoned and as Harry's "wife." At first all went well, but abruptly she was brutally exposed to the dark side of Harry's labyrinthine character. He had taken her to a *Schloss* high in the alps, and one night burst into her room, high on cocaine, and whipped her into bloody unconsciousness.

Once back in New York, Evelyn could not escape Harry's entreaties for forgiveness and pledges of love. By now he had learned from Evelyn of her affair with White, but to him it could only have happened if White had drugged and raped her. Now, not only was White responsible for denying him entry into the city's fashionable clubs, he had ruined his future wife, or so Harry came to believe. Then Thaw became convinced that White had hired thugs to pick a fight in the street and beat him to death; he took to carrying a pistol. Evelyn, alternately mollified by Harry's fawning and expensive gifts, and then terrified by his extreme manic-depressive states and threats, enlisted White's help in freeing herself of Thaw. But these few gestures of friendly aid Thaw took as direct insults. Then, for a time, he improved, to the point where, worn down by Harry's incessant proposals, Evelyn agreed to marry him. Increasingly he forced Evelyn to recite how "The Beast" had drugged and deflowered her when she was but a girl; each time he would be satisfied only if she embroidered the tale with ever more lurid details. It was all fabrication, but to Thaw's crazed mind White had dared assault the sanctity of his home and wife (he did not recognize that he had himself had Evelyn as his mistress for several years before their marriage and had so displayed her across Europe). White had no idea how far Thaw was slipping from reality, his brain burned out by drugs. He did not see the Thaws the evening of June 25 when he and Larry and several of his son's friends down from Harvard had dinner at Martin's, one of the fashionable restaurants, but the Thaws saw him come in; nor did he see the Thaws a few hours later on the roof of Madison Square Garden. The musical opening that night, *Mam'zelle Champagne,* was generally regarded as rather dull, and the Thaws rose to leave early, but Harry must have been listening to the lyrics, at least subconsciously. The male lead had boasted, "I could love a thousand girls," the soprano had asked, "Can I fascinate you," and the chorus was singing the last number, "I challenge you/ I challenge you to a duel," when Harry slipped to the other side of reality. Was this White's challenge, issued over the bottle of champagne, that had led to Evelyn's ruin? He left the others on their way to the elevator and walked toward White, reaching for the revolver in his overcoat pocket. A few seconds later, a most illustrious architectural career had come to an abrupt end.

Before Harry's trial in 1907, the denizens of Broadway quickly discovered that the newspapers were far more interested in yarns of White's depredation than in accounts of his kindness and generosity; even before the first juror was empaneled, White was judged and found guilty by the press. White was certainly not the devil he was made out to be by the yellow press, but neither was he an angel; he was, as Edward Simmons described him, a child and an artist who never grew up. Nor was Evelyn the innocent Harry's defense presented in court. Saint-Gaudens rightly recognized her ambitiousness in describing the events to Alfred Garnier, speaking of "an idiot that shoots a man of genius for a woman with the face of an angel and the heart of a snake."[196] Scores of letters came to McKim and Mead, from Cass Gilbert, Daniel Chester French, and from Richard Harding Davis, who offered to write something in White's defense, "because he is being damnably represented." Davis did write, but all of White's other friends suddenly disappeared or were unavailable; there ensued a conspiracy of silence, lest they become besmirched as well.[197] Thaw's trial for murder became a legal circus, hinging on what Evelyn had said, and not on what White had done (or had *not* done), and on a definition of legal insanity. White was portrayed as a roué, and Evelyn's character was ruined by the questioning of both defense and prosecution. Her demure costume and pained emotions were superbly presented; on the stand, she was, so Thomas Beer wrote, "a trumpery woman tricked out as a schoolgirl." Samuel Hopkins Adams wrote in the New York *World* that Evelyn's testimony was "a memorable, a magnificent, and a profoundly wicked triumph of dramatic art."[198] When at last the jury had to decide, seven thought Thaw guilty of first degree murder, and five thought him innocent by reason of insanity. A second trial in 1908 resulted in his being declared insane and committed to a state hospital, where his wealth enabled him to live in grand style, interrupted by an escape to Canada, followed by a brief return to the hospital, before being declared sane in 1915 and released.

So, White died because of his reckless abandon and an unquenchable desire to savor all of life's pleasures, while Thaw lived because he killed a man and could pay enough to be officially certified as crazy in doing so. How could such inverted values be understood by McKim, whose entire life, public and private, had been rooted in decorum and balance? He and Mead attended the funeral, and he designed White's headstone for the grave in Saint James. In the months after June 1906, he and Mead and the stunned office staff endured with

Spartan determination, but the animating force was gone. The vicious "whispering campaign" mounted by the Hearst and even the Bennett papers to discredit White deeply hurt McKim, even more than the deadening silence among White's friends. In life White had been the cynosure of fond attention; now, dead, he was anathema. Those few brave souls who did raise their voices, such as Davis, were themselves likely to be attacked.

Perhaps White's death, as sudden as it was, was opportune. Many of White's friends and clients perished on the *Titanic* six years later; had he dined elsewhere that fateful evening in 1906, or had he decided not to attend the opening of the roof theater, given his fondness for European travel in high style, he might well have gone down in the Atlantic with them. In 1913 the federal income tax was enacted, drawing off some of the wealth that had once built White's architecture, and the next year a world war erupted that swept away the confident positivism, the *joie de vivre,* that had made White's kind of architecture possible. By 1918 White's world was gone. It may have been merciful that he already had departed.

McKim's health, impaired since the bicycle accident in 1895, steadily deteriorated. The six years since the turn of the century had been the most busy of his life, but White's murder and the yellow-press vilification seemed to make further such exertion impossible. There was, besides, McKim's growing feeling of being at odds with prevailing trends. He had once written Saint-Gaudens about the "new elevated railroad" when it was just started in 1878, saying "I am sure that as time passes, it and similar inventions jar more and more upon me."[199] Unlike White, who embraced innovation and was beginning to explore skyscraper design, McKim had been unable to adapt, mentioning to one inquirer in 1907 that he felt the office "fortunate in keeping out of the business of skyscrapers thus far." Similar were his comments to his friend, English architect Sir Aston Webb, lamenting the eruption of skyscrapers at the tip of Manhattan. "It only goes to prove that the contracted area of the island and the almighty dollar outweigh all other considerations. With your preference for skyscrapers, I only wish that you were in charge of the two that have, unfortunately, come into the office, in order that you might have an opportunity to carry out your prophecy, that it is possible to make these abnormal developments beautiful."[200]

McKim gradually curtailed his office work, trying to spend more time out-of-doors. He even hired an automobile so he could drive out to Smithtown and Saint James to take the air.[201] But he grew steadily weaker, and even a change of scenery in Europe had limited effect when Saint-Gaudens then died, another loss keenly felt. Ill health forced him to cut short his inspection trip to Niagara Falls in April 1907. A few months later when the financial panic forced the Knickerbocker Trust to close its doors, his funds were frozen until the bank reopened. On January 1, 1908, McKim formally withdrew from the office, and anyone asking for him was told he had gone on an extended vacation. As for the office, McKim was assured that the work would continue. Not only was Mead still in vigorous health, but three new partners had been added in January 1906, and White's son, Lawrence, was pursuing studies at the École des Beaux-Arts in Paris before joining the firm. In April McKim closed his home on 35th Street, stored his few pieces of furniture, and traveled first to Washington and then to Narragansett Pier with his daughter. During the summer of 1909 he moved to a small cottage in the woods below the house he had designed for Prescott Hall Butler so many years before. There, as Indian summer cast a veil over Stony Brook Harbor, on September 14, 1909, McKim quietly died.[202] The partnership of McKim, Mead & White had come to an end.

7

THE NEXT GENERATION

1910 — 1919

When you get through with your work on the other side and come home ready to build, you will find opportunities awaiting you that no other country has offered in modern times. The scale is Roman and it will have to be sustained.

McKIM
to LAWRENCE GRANT WHITE, 1909

Oᴺᴇ of the developments that set late-nineteenth-century American architects apart from their predecessors was the rise of the "perpetual organization," the office large and complex enough to continue operation without the founding partner. Governmental building departments from the time of Louis XIV up to the nineteenth century, such as the U.S. Office of the Federal Supervising Architect (which had 148 employees in 1891), had already achieved this continuity, but by 1880 private architects had begun to do the same. Richardson had been forced to do so since his Bright's Disease made it increasingly difficult for him to move about; he had to rely on his assistants. McKim, Mead & White pursued organization still further, setting up a practice which rivaled in size that of the Supervising Architect. So, even if the original partnership ended with the deaths of White and McKim by 1909, the firm did not. The work of the office continued without pause under the new partners added in January 1906—Kendall, Richardson, and Fenner—who were augmented by Van der Bent in 1909 and Lawrence Grant White in 1920 [360]. Except White, all had been in the office many years, serving as virtual project architects for such buildings as the Morgan Library and Pennsylvania Station. Consequently there was no abrupt change in the character of the work of the office, a continuity emphasized by the retention of the name "McKim, Mead & White" well past the middle of the century. Indeed, the succeeding partners emphasized this continuity, for in publishing the *Monograph of the Work of McKim, Mead & White* during 1915–20, nearly a quarter of which deals with their own work, they made no distinction between the founders' buildings and their own. As a result, a number of these later buildings are still mentioned periodically as designs by McKim or White.[1] Another factor accounting for the lack of clear demarcation between the founders' work and that of the succeeding partners is that extensive responsibility had already been given them by 1904, when White and McKim were still active. Including the commissions clearly identified as having been put in their hands before McKim's death, between 1904 and 1920 the younger partners carried out 111 commissions.[2]

Mead, who enjoyed continued good health, was less and less involved in office affairs, being consulted as a kind of senior advisor when in New York, but increasingly he traveled to Europe; by the time of his death he had crossed the Atlantic as many as sixty times. He was directly responsible for only three designs before his complete withdrawal from the office in 1919: the Hobart J. Park house, Portchester, New Jersey, 1906–08; the Student's Building, Vassar College, Poughkeepsie, New York, 1912–14; and the Converse Memorial Library, Amherst College, Amherst, Massachusetts, 1915–17. He did work closely with Burt Fenner in organizing a group of architects as clients to build The Architects' Building at 101 Park Avenue, where the office moved, once again, in 1912. He had his own private office there, and his name continued to appear on the letterhead, but he was most often in Europe, and it was while there, in Paris in 1928, that he died. He was buried in the Protestant Cemetery in Rome.[3]

Each of the successor partners had been particularly close to one of the founders. William Mitchell Kendall (1856–1941), a native of Jamaica Plain, Massachusetts, Harvard class of '76, had studied architecture for two years at M.I.T. and had then spent a year and a half in Europe before he entered the office in October 1882. He quickly became associated with McKim and was largely responsible for the detailing of the Low Library and Earl and Hamilton halls at Columbia University, many of the Harvard gates, the Morgan Library, the Naugatuck High School, War College, Bellevue Hospital, and The Buckingham, to cite only a few.[4] Burt Leslie Fenner (1869–1926), a student of the University of Rochester and M.I.T., was admitted to the office in 1891, reportedly at the request of his father, once a classmate of Mead's at Amherst. Fenner then assisted Mead, eventually assuming his position as manager of the office. Because of his administrative skill, Fenner was asked to serve as secretary and general manager of the United States Housing Corporation during 1917–1918, overseeing the construction of war housing for more than 141,000 people.[5] William Symmes Richardson (1873–1931) was a native of Massachusetts but moved as a child to California, where he began his architectural studies at the University of California (Berkeley) in 1890–92. He then transferred to M.I.T. and after graduation in 1894 spent a year and a half at the École des Beaux-Arts. Upon returning to the United States in June 1895 he joined the firm; although he was chiefly White's assistant, he also worked with McKim on many projects, most notably Pennsylvania Station, the National City Bank, and the Girard Trust Company.[6] Teunis J. Van der Bent (1863–1936), a native of the Netherlands and a graduate of the University of Delft, 1885, had been in the office since 1887. His special concern was planning, construction, and engineering. He was not made a full partner until 1909, but in 1928 assumed the responsibilities formerly Fenner's and thus became business manager of the firm as well.[7]

Lawrence Grant White (1888–1956), the son of Stanford White, was the last partner admitted before 1921. Educated in private schools, he was in his junior year at Harvard when his father was shot. After graduation he went to Paris and enrolled at the École des Beaux-Arts, joining the atelier of Henri Deglane in 1909; in 1914 he entered the office, becoming a full partner in 1920.[8] After White's death, McKim became for Lawrence a kind of second father, sending him long letters full of advice. When he returns from Paris, McKim tells Lawrence, he must see Washington and the new Senate office building by Carrère & Hastings, as well as Burnham's railroad station and the new buildings on the Mall.

360. McKim, Mead & White, partners and office staff, 1924. The four seated figures, front and center, are (left to right): Teunis J. Van der Bent, Bert Leslie Fenner, William Rutherford Mead, and Lawrence Grant White.

"Enough pegs driven to make it impossible for anybody to pull them up" and debase the Senate Park Commission plan. But there was still much to be done: "the scale is Roman and it will have to be sustained." The changes in New York's architecture, he lamented, were not for the better. The new soaring Metropolitan Life tower on the site of the old Gothic Madison Square church "has the merit of bigness and that's all. I think the skyline of New York grows daily more hideous."[9]

It is ironic that, in the general confusion over the division of work between the founding and the younger partners, the Municipal Building in New York should be considered the work of the former, for it so clearly represented what McKim felt was making the skyline "daily more hideous." The Municipal Building, 1907–16, the firm's first *true* skyscraper, was the result of the younger men's overriding enthusiasm. When the mayor telephoned the office in October 1907, asking the firm to participate in a limited competition for the building, McKim made no committal, passing on to Mead the mayor's desire that the building "be a worthy achievement." Although he knew of the firm's reluctance to participate in competitions, the mayor asked them to consider it. The newly elevated partners were eager to try, but McKim confessed to Mead "we have more to lose than gain in going in. I have consulted with both Kendall and Richardson. They would like to go in...."[10] The younger men carried the argument, and during the winter of 1907–08 Kendall made his first studies; the firm won the competition in 1908.[11] The problem was most complex, calling for a building of up to twenty-five stories in an irregular hexagonal site, its ground floor penetrated by Chambers Street, and with its basement levels opened up to accommodate a major subway station. The layered stages of Kendall's tower recalled both Madison Square Garden and White's Grand Central Terminal project [361]. According to Lawrence White, Kendall also hoped to recall the adjacent City Hall of 1802–11.[12] This was the largest vertical building ever undertaken by the firm—twenty-four stories to the main cornice with nine levels in the tower; 320 feet to the cornice and 552 feet to the top of the

361. Municipal Building, New York, N. Y., 1907–16.

362. Hotel Pennsylvania, New York, N. Y., 1915–20. Photograph by I. Underhill, 1919.

figure of *Civic Fame* by Adolf A. Weinman.[13] The building exemplified the kind of organization which had gone into making Pennsylvania Station a success, but now turned vertically. As with the founders' major buildings, this too had a strong impact, the lower section greatly influencing Albert Kahn's massive headquarters building for General Motors, Detroit, 1922, while the elaborate tower reappeared in 1915 as Carrère & Hastings's Tower of Jewels at the Panama-Pacific Exposition.

With the downtown Knickerbocker Trust under construction and the Municipal Building started, the firm had definitely entered the field of skyscraper design. Others followed soon, including the eighteen-story Munsey Building in Baltimore, 1908–13, and the fifteen-story Fayette National Bank, Lexington, Kentucky, 1912–15. Perhaps even more complex than the Municipal Building was the Hotel Pennsylvania, New York, 1915–20 [362].[14] Facing Pennsylvania Station on the east, it, too, was built over the subterranean tracks. This, the realization of Cassatt's dream now based on the model developed by George B. Post & Sons in the Statler Hotel, Buffalo, 1907–11, had serried wings of rooms, each with its own bath. To provide light and air to each of the 2,200 rooms, the twenty-two-story building was divided into four parallel brick slabs set on a tall stone-clad base. The Hotel Pennsylvania, however, was more elaborately equipped than Post's had been, making it not

363. 998 Fifth Avenue, New York, N. Y., 1910–14, perspective dated 1910.

only the largest but the most modern in the city. At $12,116,099, it was certainly the single most expensive building ever done by the firm. The other major tall building by the younger partners is still known simply by its address, 998 Fifth Avenue, New York, 1910–14. This is a series of superimposed luxury apartments, and for this reason, perhaps, Richardson based his design on superimposed Italian palazzi, with the emphasis not on the vertical but the horizontal [363].[15] The huge block was divided into three major stages, each articulated by intermediate mezzanines and strong belt courses, the whole terminated by a massive cornice. Because of the severity of surface and line, the astylar building attracted much favorable comment, even causing it to be occasionally credited to the founding partners, for it does show their legacy at its best.

In these tall buildings the younger partners deviated most from the practice of their mentors, but in their urban townhouses they followed the general type sketched out in the Kane house of 1904–08. Kendall had assisted McKim in that, and he continued to use its austere Italianate Renaissance classicism in his Edward T. Blair house, Chicago, 1912–14, and the Thomas Newbold house, New York, 1916–18.[16]

Much of the successors' activity involved continuing the large-scale commissions started by the founders. It was the younger men who put the last addition on the Harvard Club, New York, 1913–16, and they carried out a series of buildings at Columbia University, 1907–19, both on the original campus and in the South Field planned by McKim and Kendall in 1903. They also did additional gates at Princeton, and added a number of sections to both the Metropolitan and Brooklyn museums, 1909–16. There was also some minor work in

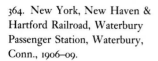

364. New York, New Haven &
Hartford Railroad, Waterbury
Passenger Station, Waterbury,
Conn., 1906–09.

Prospect Park, and two branches of the Bank of Montreal in western Canada, 1909–14.[17]

Among the successors' churches was Richardson's Andover Free Christian Church, Andover, Massachusetts, 1907–08, suggestive of eighteenth-century meetinghouses, and Kendall's more elaborate First Presbyterian Church, Chattanooga, Tennessee, 1909–11, derived from White's Madison Square church.[18] Their commercial work, in addition to the Bank of Montreal branches, included Richardson's abundantly fenestrated Italianate Second National Bank, New York, 1907–08, and a second Munsey Building office block in Washington, D.C., 1912–18, next to the earlier one of 1905–07 and merged with it by means of new refacing.[19]

For John Howard Whittemore, Richardson designed a passenger station in Waterbury, Connecticut, 1906–09, to serve the New York, New Haven & Hartford Railroad, one of the largest projects undertaken while Whittemore was a director of that line [364].[20] Its central waiting room was covered by a broad elliptical Guastavino vault. Originally designed without the tower, this was incorporated about 1907, based on the tower of the Palazzo Pubblico, Siena, 1288–1309, but with the clock shifted to the top of the tower.

The office policy against participation in any of the major world's fairs after 1893 was changed by the younger partners, and during 1912–14 Richardson contributed to the planning development of the Panama-Pacific Exposition in San Francisco; his particular responsibility was the Court of the Universe, a large oval space at the center of the contiguous exhibition building complex.[21] The encircling Corinthian colonnade was richly embellished with architectural carving and sculpture, the last attempt to employ such neo-Baroque in an American world's fair [365]. Richardson and his fellow fair architects may have thought

365. Court of the Universe, Panama-Pacific Exposition, San Francisco, Calif., 1912–15. *Monograph.*

366. U. S. Post Office, New York, N. Y., 1908–13.

they were expanding on the tradition of the Columbian Exposition, but to later eyes it was evident that what freshness and novelty there had been in the Chicago fair was not to be recapitulated.

In competitions for public buildings the younger partners had mixed success. Several they lost, but they had been more fortunate in what were probably the two most important they entered in 1908, for the Municipal Building and for the new central New York Post Office, built in 1909–13 over the Pennsylvania railroad tracks west of Pennsylvania Station.[22] Kendall's winning design called for a broad colonnaded block, 377 feet across and 330 feet deep, raised on a 14-foot podium ascended by a broad staircase nearly 275 feet wide [366]. The twenty columns of the Post Office portico corresponded exactly to the Doric pilasters on the west wall of Pennsylvania Station. Behind this entrance colonnade was a long public lobby and behind that a vast sorting room. At the back were not truck-loading docks but chutes by which the bagged mail could be dropped to the mail cars in the trains below. Kendall was apparently alone responsible for selecting the passage from Herodotus, describing the messenger service of the Persian empire, which was then emblazoned along the full width of the facade frieze, thus giving an unofficial motto to the postal service: "Neither snow, nor rain, nor heat, nor gloom of night stays these couriers from the swift completion

367. Minneapolis Museum of Fine Arts (Minneapolis Institute of Arts), Minneapolis, Minn., 1911–14. *Monograph.*

of their appointed rounds."[23] Richardson's winning entry of 1911–12 in the competition for the Minneapolis Museum of Fine Arts (Minneapolis Institute of Fine Arts) marked a new austerity, even a Spartan classicism, that McKim and White, no doubt, would have softened. Where the earlier Brooklyn Museum had combined various Roman and Baroque attributes, this was severely Grecian, with a central hexastyle Ionic porch intersected by a traverse block much like von Klenze's Glyptothek, built in Munich a century earlier and perhaps the immediate model for Cass Gilbert's U.S. Supreme Court, Washington, D.C., 1935. The comprehensive scheme for the entire museum group included a concert hall and an art school, providing for an inclusive arts center, but only the frontal element was built [367].[24] This shift toward a more orthodox neoclassicism was also evident in the winning competition design for the McKinley Birthplace Memorial, Niles, Ohio, 1915–18.[25]

The last and best work of this transitional decade for the firm was also the most historically derivative, as exemplified in the Racquet and Tennis Club, New York, 1916–20.[26] In a general way, Richardson drew upon quattrocento palazzi, such as the Palazzi Spannocchi and Antinori in Florence, for the heavy rustication of the base and the heavy pointed arches, but he also used brown brick for the walls and a bold series of blind arches at the fourth floor to indicate the internal presence of the tennis courts [368]. Thus were historicism and functionalism fused, with much of the balance of color and textural contrasts that had characterized McKim's work. It was also instinctively and properly scaled to the breadth of Park Avenue, and helped to make this one of the most urbane streets in the country prior to 1948 and the arrival of the glass-wall office tower. The last major public building started before Mead's official retirement was the Butler Art Gallery, Youngstown, Ohio, 1917–20.[27] For his exterior, Kendall used the casino in the garden of the Villa Farnese at Caprarola, by Vignola, circa 1555, but changed the material from rough stucco on brick to cut stone, with a corresponding sharpening of the details [369]. The casino parti was widened, and the windows closed for better overhead lighting and security. Kendall also substituted broad stairs, creating a more inviting approach. The final result was a building crisp in line and carefully balanced in form, but without the rhythmic complexities that had given McKim's Morgan Library its character. Nonetheless, the cool clarity of the Butler Gallery had a certain appeal, and it served in turn as the model for Albert Kahn's William L. Clements Library at the University of Michigan, Ann Arbor, 1923.[28]

368. ABOVE. New York Racquet and Tennis Club, New York, N. Y., 1916–19.

369. LEFT. Butler Art Gallery (Butler Institute of American Art), Youngstown, Ohio, 1917–20.

THE successors in the firm were clearly aware of the responsibility they carried, of the cachet which the name still possessed. Like the founders they, too, were high-minded, taking on the protracted and costly job of preparing the hundreds of ink line drawings for the plates of the *Monograph,* presenting the best examples of the work of their mentors (and some of their own) before a new generation of architects. Surveying the accomplishment of both the founders and the younger partners in 1922, Lionel Moses, himself long a member of the staff, suggested that a comparison of the work of the former and the latter "reveals little to allow of differentiation. The same scholarly knowledge is evident. The same dignity of design is appreciable. The same conception of scale and proportion is discernible. . . . No break in continuity is evident between what was and what is."[29] He may have believed this was so, but something had gradually slipped away. The concentration, energy, contrast, exquisite refinement, the eccentricity, the sheer élan of the founders' work was gone. No longer was there the tension between firebrand and aesthete; all the younger men were moderates, consumed neither by a passion for attempting the unheard-of, nor a religious zeal for endlessly refining form and detail. The new men took to the middle of the road, and although they still proudly displayed the motto of the firm, *Vogue la Galère* ("Let's chance it"), in their publications, the adventurousness implicit in that impish phrase did not manifest itself in their work.[30] So, the subtleties of proportion, the vigorously modeled ornament, the rich polychromy were muted as the decade passed, in favor of more conventional and safer formulas. Yet, there were flashes of the old character in 998 Fifth Avenue and the Racquet and Tennis Club. After 1920 the firm came to specialize in educational and medical complexes, perhaps even earning in part the label "plan factory" suggested of them.[31] Still, the quality of design and construction remained high, so that the successors were able to accomplish much through the momentum created by the founders.

EPILOGUE

The work of McKim, Mead & White
sums up the finest aspirations of a great
people at a great epoch.

C. H. REILLY
McKim, Mead & White, 1924

THE sheer output of McKim, Mead & White, as well as the significance of their best-known work, made this firm one of the most important in the development of American architecture. Yet the critical and general lay perception of their position in the architectural world has been far from unvarying, shifting from acclaim to denigration and back to a rather balanced appreciation. Perhaps to assess the work of this firm properly it is necessary to understand their objectives in design and building. There remains for us, then, the question of what the work of such architects as McKim, Mead & White might teach the next generation of builders.

The passage by C. H. Reilly clearly indicates the high regard he had for McKim, Mead & White in the twenties. It was logical for the British to be receptive to the work of the firm, for the way had been prepared by the attention given to the work of Richardson in the 1880s with the publication of some of his buildings in English architectural journals and his design of Lululand, Hertfordshire, for the painter Sir Hubert von Herkomer.[1] English writer Edmund Gosse also generated much interest, following his lecture tour of the United States in the 1880s. He was interviewed by *The Critic* of New York and expressed great surprise and delight with American architecture, particularly the Tiffany house, saying it was a "most beautiful modern domestic building." He was also impressed by the happy collaborations of White and Saint-Gaudens, since his countrymen had had little success in that direction.[2] Perhaps more influential among British architects was the opinion of Robert Kerr, Fellow of the Royal Institute of British Architects, critic, and historian, who asserted flatly in 1893 that Europe had lost the lead in architecture, certain to be taken up by the United States. American architects, he noted, were quite willing to tackle mundane problems and the intricacies of construction which Kerr said his London counterparts were increasingly reluctant to do. American architects, he said, were adventurous, unafraid of novelty, eager to do "big things."[3]

With such approbation, English clients began to approach the firm, beginning with James Crowdy, who wrote in 1893 asking for the design of a hotel to rise next to the Royal Opera House.[4] Alexander Koch had written asking for illustrative material for his *Academy Architecture*, saying, "your firm's name has been *specially given to me* as doing the best work in the States," and in 1903 he wrote again asking for photographs of houses for a forthcoming issue.[5] Young English architects and students, such as Banister Fletcher, began appearing at the office, eager for experience in the largest and most celebrated firm in the world, so different from the one-man offices at home. Some carried letters of recommendation, such as young Frederick Ramsey, who had a letter from Richard Harding Davis, which also contained a request of White for photographs of Madison Square Garden for the use of a visiting Englishman.[6] In 1898, in his *America the Land of Contrasts*, James F. Muirhead agreed with Kerr that architecture in the United States had surpassed that of Europe, and among the important firms he named McKim, Mead & White.[7] The next year, McKim was happy to relay to Seth Low a letter from John M. Brydon, formerly of Nesfield & Shaw, asking for information concerning the Low Library at Columbia. McKim was especially pleased to inform Low that the Royal Institute of British Architects had formally requested illustrations of American work, which they admitted was in advance of their own, for an exhibition intended as "an object lesson."[8]

In 1899, de Gersdorff, McKim's assistant, was sent to England to pursue negotiations with a prospective client, and although this produced no result there followed, shortly after, the Sherry hotel project of 1902.[9] Subsequently, McKim corresponded frequently with such leading British architects as Aston Webb and Reginald Bromfield in his official capacity as president of the American Institute of Architects. When word came early in 1903 that they had nominated him for the Royal Gold Medal, it must have been a great satisfaction, but not perhaps a total surprise. Esteem for the firm's work in Britain continued to rise, as Cass Gilbert discovered in 1908 when he attended the annual dinner of the Royal Institute of British Architects, writing to McKim: "You probably do not realize the great appreciation of your work which exists in England as well as in America. It gave me very great pride as an American to hear your name and work so enthusiastically praised in England, and I basked in a certain amount of reflected light when I announced myself as one of your early pupils."[10]

The most ardent English advocate was Charles Herbert Reilly (1874–1948), director of the School of Architecture at the University of Liverpool. Early in 1909 he wrote to the firm, requesting photographs of their public work for the use of his students, but even before Mead could respond Reilly crossed the Atlantic and toured the eastern seaboard, visiting various architects' offices, including that of McKim, Mead & White.[11] The result was a paper he read before the Architectural Association of Ireland in February 1910, entitled "The Modern Renaissance in American Architecture."[12] He noted that, while still on ship, a fellow architect had attempted to persuade him that the firm's University Club was worthy to be ranked with the Farnese or Massimi palaces, a comparison Reilly was convinced was surely exaggerated. Having seen the club, however, he now agreed. He was impressed by the public interest in architecture and the degree to which the public was conversant with the work of major architects. He praised the development of rigorous architectural education, but what interested him most was the efficient operation of large American offices such as that of McKim, Mead & White, whose operation he described at length. Following his return, he placed six of his Liverpool students annually in American offices for experience, and in this way (as well as through his publication of the firm's work) he helped to extend the restrained classicism of McKim, Mead & White to the far reaches of the British Empire.[13]

Particularly welcome, therefore, were the first installments of the *Monograph of the Work of McKim, Mead & White* which began to arrive in England in 1916, occasioning an article by Stanley C. Ramsey.[14] But the culmination of this British acclaim was Reilly's small book, *McKim, Mead & White* (1924), in the series "Masters of Architecture," edited by Ramsey. Of the nine titles in the series, this was the only one devoted to an American firm, the others dealing with English, French, and German architects.[15] A small but sensitive study, it came as a complete surprise to the younger partners; Lawrence White, who chanced to see a copy in London, greatly appreciated Reilly's praise.[16] In the brief eighteen pages of text, Reilly accurately gauged the import of the firm's work, both in England and the United States, noting the many young architects who had passed through the office. He commented on the attention English architects were paying to the work of the firm, saying, "one has only to compare some recent buildings in this country by certain of our younger architects . . . to realize how much this country has been enriched by such study." As to the general influence of American architects in England, "we recently had given to us in the Bush Building in the Strand a work by a student of the McKim atelier . . . and it has taken its place at once with us. It does not seem exotic, it only seems better than our own work."[17] He stressed the collaborative nature of the office, saying it was impossible to speak of a given building as being McKim's or White's or Kendall's. In this he was overly cautious, perhaps, but his observation was accurate that through their work the firm helped American architects adhere to a bold, simple, and severe classicism in large public buildings, thus avoiding picturesque digressions. In confronting and surpassing European standards, Reilly believed "for American architecture McKim, Mead and White may be said to have done a similar work to that which Henry James did for American literature."

It was in suggesting ways of judging the work of McKim, Mead & White that Reilly was most perceptive. "We must measure them by the general character of their total output and by their influence rather than by any individual building," he rightly asserted. It is impossible to take any single building and extract from it the whole philosophy of the firm as one might of Alberti or Mies van der Rohe by scrutinizing San' Andrea, Mantua, or the Seagram Building. Reilly understood correctly, too, that although the work of the firm was by and large classical, it can be readily distinguished by "its greater breadth of treatment, its finer scale, and more reticent manner." He also saw that for any given building, the firm sought the solution "which has its roots in the general history of civilization. The greater the problem they had to attack, not only the simpler and more monumental was the final result, but the further back into history they went for its inspiration."

The major agent in making the work of the firm available outside the United States was *A Monograph of the Work of McKim, Mead & White, 1879–1915*, initiated late in 1913. The 400 plates, published in lots of twenty, started to appear in 1915, and the first three volumes of 100 plates each were issued by 1917. The firm provided the services of its best draftsmen —August Reuling, John Vegessi, and Philip Merz—in the preparation of the inked drawings, and new photographs were prepared by Robert Tebbs. Unfortunately, by 1918 the office draftsmen were so fully occupied with war work, and photographic materials and paper were so hard to obtain, that the last installments did not appear until 1920. After the war, however, there was such interest in the folio that a smaller Students' Edition of 136 plates was issued in 1925 containing all of the line drawings of the original. Copies of both were widely distributed, and a letter from a reader in Osaka, Japan, who was missing one plate, indicates that the *Monograph* found its way around the globe.[18]

The view of the firm's work in France and Germany was more critical and reserved than in England. Still, Werner Hegemann had ample praise for the building groups, campuses, and city plans by the firm and other American architects in *The American Vitruvius: An Architect's Handbook of Civic Art* (1922), written with Elbert Peets and richly illustrated with examples of the firm's work.[19] These showed what Hegemann believed was the major contribution of American architects and planners—a new awareness of urban design. The title was carefully phrased to place this volume in the tradition of *Vitruvius Britannicus* and *Vitruvius Scotius,* the reference works of the eighteenth century, for this was to be the source book for the urban architecture of the twentieth. Three years later, Hegemann produced a modified edition in German, followed by a laudatory article examining the firm's use of Renaissance sources.[20] Jacques Gréber also wrote on *L'Architecture aux Etats Unis* (1920), and although he drew upon many examples by the firm, it was not so much an examination of their inherent virtues, but, as the subtitle made clear, *preuve de la force d'expansion du génie français* (proof of the expansive power of the French spirit).[21] If printed illustrations left doubts in the minds of Europeans, like Reilly they were struck when confronting the buildings *in situ,* as was Le Corbusier during his visits to New York in 1935 and 1936: "In New York, then, I learn to appreciate the Italian Renaissance. It is so well done that you could believe it *to be genuine.* It even has a strange new firmness which is not Italian but American."[22]

If some Europeans praised the work of McKim, Mead & White, this had little impact on European design, but in the United States the firm's dispersed architecture had a pronounced effect. Although the work of the graduates of the office—such as Cass Gilbert, Carrère & Hastings, York & Sawyer, Henry Bacon, John Mead Howells, Austin W. Lord, or John Galen Howard—was similar to but not wholly imitative of the work of their mentors, there were many who replicated this or that design for a new use. So the Duquesne Club, Pittsburgh, 1891, by Longfellow, Alden & Harlow, is based on the firm's Algonquin Club, and the Reid Memorial Library, Passaic, New Jersey, 1902–03, by Jackson, Rosencrans & Canfield, is based on the Cullum Memorial. Some well-known architects were also rather literal in their borrowings. John Russell Pope's Union Station, Richmond, Virginia, 1917–19, is modeled on the Low Library, and James Gamble Rogers's Brooks Memorial Art Gallery, Memphis, Tennessee, 1925–26, is an enlarged version of the Morgan Library.[23] The Knickerbocker Trust proved to be a particularly potent exemplar. Although Latrobe's Bank of Pennsylvania, 1799–1801, had established the image of banks as solid, foursquare temples, there had been a Gothic interlude in mid-century, and the Knickerbocker Trust reasserted the classical image. Its simple yet richly ornamented block was adaptable to many uses other than banking, and variations began to appear all over the country. A random sampling might include the Dayton Daily News, Dayton, Ohio, 1908, or Mundie & Jensen's First National Bank of Champaign, Illinois, 1915. Even closer adaptations included Albert Kahn's Detroit Trust Company, 1915; Bliss & Faville's Bank of California, San Francisco, 1909–11; and Doyle & Patterson's U.S. National Bank, Portland, Oregon, 1916–17.[24]

In 1879 when the partnership was formed, a building was considered eminently symbolic and fitting a public institution if its elements strongly contrasted in color and texture and its silhouette bustled with complexity. By 1900 the far-flung work of the firm had done much to transform this image, so that public architecture was considered successful in proportion to the understatement, restraint, and sobriety of its design. If the rows of sedate Georgian-Federalist townhouses that now filled newly developed residential sections in the major cities were red brick in construction, in other buildings the entire palette of materials shifted away from the deep reds and browns of the 1870s toward brighter colors, to marble and glazed terra cotta.[25] Ochre- and amber-colored Roman brick became standard building materials, so that one can find in small farming communities of the mid-continent, such as Mason City, Illinois (population 2,000), a bank of 1904 with a carved stone hood over the entrance much like that of the Gibson Fahnestock house and another down the street with salt-glazed Roman brick walls. Frequently there arises the notion that a building is not only *like* the work of Stanford White, it *is* the work of Stanford White. In rare cases there may be some truth to the legend, for White indeed may have left behind a sketch scribbled on a luncheon napkin which a local builder may have tried to decipher. There is no way of knowing how many designs White may have dispersed in this or similar ways to friends and acquaintances. Some of his best work does not appear in the official bill-book record; there is no entry, for example, for his base for the Adams Memorial. When the building in question is dark, heavy, and angular in character, not classical, it almost invariably came from a different hand. The best investigated instance of such misattribution concerns the National Bank of Salem, Oregon, long said to be White's; careful study of local sources revealed it to be the work of a Salem architect patterned after a bank by Frank Furness![26]

The reach of the firm's influence suggests the high professional and popular regard for their work. It was never unanimous, however, and even during the partners' lifetimes there were antagonists. Russell Sturgis began to level sharp criticism in his essay of 1895 and later roundly discredited their work.[27] And Montgomery Schuyler, who vigorously opposed copywork and wrote biting satires on the growing practice of designing by the pattern book, nonetheless praised the firm's Knickerbocker Trust, calling it a "modern classic" in 1904.[28] Upon White's death most of the professional journals ran adulatory editorials (even if the yellow press newspapers took exactly the opposite stance), and *Brickbuilder* even devoted its entire issue for December 1906 to a series of biographical articles by his former assistants. *The Critic* had an especially laudatory column, praising White as "our first architect of real genius."[29] Others took a more balanced view, such as the editor of *The Nation* who believed White had been undone not only by his own frailties but by the follies of the time: "His own aesthetic standards were the highest; but insensibly, as he sold his taste to a wealthy but untrained society, he condescended to their ignorance and vanity."[30] This lapse was evident in White's own Gramercy Square townhouse, claimed the editor of *American Architect*, for the interiors showed no synthesis, but rather the rooms appeared to be a collection of odds and ends.[31]

After the First World War, the first historians of American architecture attempted to determine just what the American spirit in its architecture was, and if the classicism of the 1890s had contributed to or hindered its expression. In his *Story of Architecture in America* (1927), Thomas Tallmadge made the dilemma clear, for while he respected McKim greatly, Tallmadge had practiced in Chicago and knew Sullivan and Wright personally, and therefore could write as a participant in the development of Chicago's "commercial style" and Wright's "Prairie Style." He entitled his ninth chapter "Louis Sullivan and the Lost Cause," not because he thought Sullivan or Wright had been fundamentally wrong, but because what they had propounded was at variance with what the American and especially the midwestern public wanted. Neither architect had developed (up to the time Tallmadge wrote) a base broad or deep enough to carry the Chicago work forward into the 1920s. In his later *Architecture in Old Chicago* (1941) he observed: "An artist's reputation with posterity depends on the vividness of his personality, on the power and popularity of his work, and most of all on the influence he wielded on his contemporaries and on his successors. If his power was so great that he changed . . . the course of architecture, creating a new expression which the people accepted, then he becomes one of the immortals. The men who have done this in America are Thomas Jefferson, Benjamin Latrobe, H. H. Richardson, Charles F. McKim, and Louis Sullivan."[32]

It was Fiske Kimball, however, who went to the heart of the problem then beginning to cloud understanding of "Academic" architecture. In his *American Architecture* (1928), he defined two poles of modernism: the love of science and respect for abstract form. Kimball drew a parallel between Sullivan's architecture and "realism" in nineteenth-century painting and literature, all of which "emphasized the novel element in modern life rather than its continuity with the past." The counterpart to this was a movement to restore the supremacy of abstract form, centered in New York and led by McKim, Mead & White. By viewing this as a conflict in "an interpretation of architecture . . . in terms of mass and space" and an alternate interpretation of architecture as a "realistic" expression of structure, Kimball avoided questions of style and the idea of "classicism," already in 1928 becoming a pejorative term. He was correct, for to McKim and White it was far more than a matter of which style, but a question of a building's responsibilities to revealing internal functions or augmenting the larger context. For them, context and abstract form always were the determining factors. By 1900 the drive toward abstraction was in ascendancy, and, as Kimball notes, "McKim and his followers went on from triumph to triumph, finding in the early buildings of the Republic a supporting tradition and a national sanction." McKim's followers, those practicing as Kimball and his colleagues wrote, faced a quandary, for it appeared that "the great problems of our time have been attacked and solved with such perfect conformity to [classical] ideals that little room is left for further creative effort." So, Kimball realized, "the disciples of McKim are condemned to ring the changes on the models already established. These tend to harden into formulae, sometimes relieved in their application by subtle restudy of proportion and detail."[33]

Within a few years of the appearance of Kimball's book, of course, opinions changed, so that functional "realism" in architecture came to be preferred to "abstract form." European progressives and radicals during the 1920s had been fascinated with the "realism" of Sullivan's buildings, seeing in them the realization of the realism advocated by Semper, Choisy, and Viollet-le-Duc. This led to the apotheosis of structural action, mechanical function, and industrial process, in the service of social reform, that shaped the early work of Gropius and Mies van der Rohe. Once this utilitarian-social theory was developed, it made "Academic" or "Beaux-Arts" architecture appear fallacious, since structural action was hidden and the building process was not pointedly celebrated. To this then was added a Marxist stigma, for it was the fruit of capitalism. "Our Imperial architecture," wrote Lewis Mumford in 1924, "is an architecture of compensation: it provides grandiloquent stones for people who have been deprived of bread and sunlight and all that keeps men from becoming vile."[34] Architecture, according to the new definition, was simply to be an envelope, sheltering in the most forthright and structurally rational way essential environmental and physical needs. Richly ornamented public buildings were adjudged "imperious" and, *ipso facto*, oppressive. The groundwork for the popular notion of the "anti-monument" was laid.

It might be supposed that turn-of-the-century classicism would have been readily subjected to Veblenian analysis, but surprisingly few charges of "conspicuous consumption" were leveled at such public architecture even late into the 1920s. Later, when it was examined from a Marxist point of view, it was noted by Michael Klare that while such architects as McKim, Mead & White built for the wealthiest of capitalists, what they built for the most part were public buildings generated by the strongest expression of *richesse oblige* the nation had yet seen.[35] To a degree, this outpouring of hospitals, sanatoriums, museums, libraries, schools, and even entire colleges and universities, compensated for the slow progress of municipalities in providing such services. As Klare observed, one might say such buildings as Carnegie's hundreds of small libraries were undertaken to assuage guilt, reduce proletarian discontent, or effect something of a redistribution of wealth. The reason most cited by the participants, however, was to raise the standard of general intelligence, so that such architecture was judged by its donors not according to its utility merely but for its capacity to inculcate morals and social values. Consequently, buildings for institutions were regarded as vehicles for social symbolism, and this virtually required the return to an allegorical language in architecture and its attendant figural sculpture.[36] This was precisely the reason given by McKim for using the Renaissance idiom for the New York State Building at the Columbian Exposition, for in such architecture "the use of Allegory and Symbol is possible."

In his autobiography Louis Sullivan asserted that such classicizing allegory was alien to the American spirit and had been forced on a duped public. When the *Autobiography of an Idea* appeared in 1924, Mumford shared this view, and soon he was joined by Henry-Russell Hitchcock and Philip Johnson in proselytizing for the bare European modernism that was supposedly entirely *sachlich* and culture free. In 1936, Hitchcock presented the work of H. H. Richardson as leading the way to modernism, tending to dismiss any positive impact McKim or White may have had on their teacher; he believed that on leaving Richardson in 1878 White "left the position of a one-eyed minister to become king among the blind."[37] The general acceptance of the "International Style," as Hitchcock and Johnson christened it, was reinforced by recurrent attacks on pictorial formal design during the 1940s, as in Siegfried Giedion's *Space, Time and Architecture* (1941), which claimed that the academics had contributed absolutely nothing to the Columbian Exposition.[38] In 1947 James Marston Fitch wrote how Sullivan's ideals had been betrayed by the substitution of the classical architecture of the "Wall Street autocracy," and that after the Columbian Exposition "American architecture was undermined by the most dangerous reaction since its birth."[39] The complete shift in public opinion was signaled by John Kouwenhoven's pronouncement in 1948 that "the work of men like McKim . . . had less relation to the vital contemporary forces of American life . . . than even the crudest, least ingratiating examples of small-town dwellings or the most materialistically functional office buildings."[40]

Then, unexpectedly, following the Second World War, when the utilitarian doctrine was fully embraced by the public, the theorists and critics who had propounded the theory in the twenties and thirties began to change their position, calling for a return to monumental formalism in the new architecture required in devastated Europe, for an architecture of dignity and fundamental emotional impact, an architecture representing ceremonial life, going beyond mere functional fulfillment and expressing "aspirations for joy, for luxury,

and for excitement." What was needed now were buildings which could *not* be justified at
all by sheer necessity.[41] Conversely, postwar public opinion had now been conditioned to
support the wholesale demolition of Beaux-Arts buildings across the country, even though
the qualities they incorporated were precisely those being advocated by the critics. In his
encyclopedic *Architecture: Nineteenth and Twentieth Centuries* (1958), Hitchcock presented
a view of traditionalist academic architecture just the reverse of that in his study of Richardson. McKim, Mead & White, in their Boston Public Library, were described as not refuting
what Richardson had done but in fact pursuing a course he had already sketched out.
Traditional or academic architecture was not meretricious or nonfunctional, as we had
earlier been told to believe, nor was it to be dismissed with derision; it was simply necessary
to evaluate it by the humanist standards of the nineteenth century rather than utilitarian
standards of the twentieth.[42]

Vincent Scully's *Shingle Style* (1955) marked the beginning of a genuinely positive view
of at least the firm's summer and country houses. And Philip Johnson even went so far as
to suggest the following year that "McKim of New York, in his Boston Public Library,
contemporaneously with Sullivan, erected a design far purer, and much more inspiring to
look at (at least for me), than nine-tenths of Sullivan's buildings." Is Sullivan the father of
functionalism? he asked.[43] When the new editions of Hitchcock's *Richardson* and Fitch's
American Architecture were published in the 1960s, the original pejorative passages were
qualified, toned down, or stricken out altogether. Indeed, in *Architecture and the Esthetics of
Plenty* (1961), Fitch cast a withering eye on the work of the modernists, noting:

> We are quick to criticize the formalism of Alberti and Palladio, of Charles Follen McKim and
> Stanford White; but we are oddly blind to the same tendencies in Mies van der Rohe's campus
> for the Illinois Institute of Technology or Le Corbusier's Unité d'Habitation in Marseilles. They
> make just as many concessions to preconceived ideas of the facade as Palladio ever did.[44]

Eventually, quasi-official approbation came in 1964 with the publication of the *Encyclopedia
of Modern Architecture* in which Arthur Sprague's entry on McKim, Mead & White observed: "Now largely and unjustly unappreciated, the buildings produced by the firm were
among the finest and most graceful of the period." In the subsequent architectural biographical dictionaries, *Who's Who in Architecture* (1977) and the massive *Macmillan Encyclopedia of
Architects* (1983), the entries on McKim, Mead, and White were among the longest and most
detailed.[45]

In his history of American architecture (1969), Vincent Scully declared that the Beaux-
Arts movement produced "highly competent architects, better trained in many ways than
those of any generation and, in some ways, than those of this"; they generally built "better
monument and urban spaces than the later period, at least in America, has yet been able to
do."[46] And in an extended analysis of the Boston Public Library (1972), William Jordy wrote:
". . . in the cause of Art, and in the conviction that the highest calling of wealth was its
civilizing effect on society, of which magnificent patronage of the arts was a cardinal aspect,
McKim cajoled millions from his clients. . . . he, more than any other American architect,
deserves to be honored as the great professional, in the institutional sense of the label. The
Boston Public Library commemorates his high-mindedness."[47]

The much-publicized exhibition of drawings from the École des Beaux-Arts, Paris, at
the Museum of Modern Art, New York, in the autumn of 1975, organized by Arthur Drexler,
was the most striking indication of this change in critical and public attitude. This bastion

of modernism reversed its position of forty-five years, affixed the twenty-foot-long colored renderings to its walls, and published a compact catalog and then a sumptuously illustrated book, all aimed at presenting the inherently important and positive characteristics of Beaux-Arts methods of design.[48] Suddenly Beaux-Arts and academic architecture became eminently respectable. What criticism there was of Beaux-Arts and academic architecture focused on the overemphasis of sheer draftsmanship, but one essay sparked by the exhibition declared that American architects represented the best of the École, since they alone had the opportunities to build at precisely the scale at which they had been taught to think, and more than the French they showed a willingness to abandon precedent and to invent.[49] Following by a few months the actual day of the firm's centenary, Ada Louise Huxtable called attention to the one-hundredth anniversary of the founding of McKim, Mead & White, saying it was time for a thorough investigation of the buildings which had once symbolized for architecture what the name of Morgan signified for banking or Dom Perignon for champagne.[50] So, by 1980, the course of critical and popular perception of the work of the firm had come nearly full circle, approximating something of what it had been three quarters of a century before: first, the firm could do no wrong; then they could do no right; now they are seen as having built a remarkable number of astoundingly good buildings which warrant closer study.

WHAT removing the blinders of orthodoxy has finally enabled us to perceive are those qualities which McKim, Mead & White infused in their architecture, arising from their study of history. The three architects had come from families of education and conviction, not from families of wealth, and although they built for the wealthy, they designed primarily for the community as a whole. As White believed, the city's streets belong to the people and their domain extends as far as the eye can see.[51] They built with a deep respect for the American building tradition, a fervent Ruskinian and Vitruvian idealism to build well, and a conscious desire to achieve order and harmony in the urban fabric at a time when it seemed the entire American culture was in flux. It is true that in a few instances, as in restoring the White House, they disturbed or even destroyed some fraction of the Federalist architectural heritage, that they were extremely selective in what they incorporated from the lessons of Ruskin and the École, and that they declined to shape a new architecture in response to changes in building construction. Yet to concentrate on these allegations is to miss the overriding positive contributions they made.

They viewed architecture and the building of cities as an art which depended for its greatest success on the participation of all the arts, an attitude derived from both Ruskin and the École. From Richardson and their direct contact with the École, they came to value the clarity of the plan based on movement through spatial sequences. Even so, there could be no ideal or prototypal solution, for contingencies always impinged on the ideal. Moreover, an individual plan never existed by itself but was the outline of the larger relationship of the building to its context, to the larger urban ensemble. McKim, Mead & White were dedicated traditionalists, drawing from the past those elements which seemed to them to enhance and amplify function and experience. Unlike the architects of the previous generation, they maintained a relative purity of historical allusion, thus laying the groundwork for the "period" eclectic revivals of the early twentieth century. They avoided replication, so that an intriguing character of their work is the result of their reference to recognizable models—their audacity, in fact, in boldly alluding to models—but they also reshaped these allusions to make of them something quite different.

Consciously as well as intuitively they emphasized those historical references which augmented a sense of place or which had become associated with a particular building type. They adapted from Greek architecture the clear articulation of parts, and they seemed to sense, too, the critical importance of *topos,* of place. So they avoided prototypal solutions in favor of specialized designs adjusted to client and site. The Bank of Montreal, with its restored dome, and the bowed fronts of the Boston Back Bay houses are clear examples. As did the Greeks, they sought conceptual order—*rhythmos* and *symmetria* (pattern and commensurability)—as a safeguard against chaos.

They looked to the large public buildings of Augustan and Hadrianic Rome rather than the heavily ornamented and more plastic work which came after. They adhered to the Vitruvian triad of commodious planning, sound construction, and visual delight, and like Roman architects they favored organization around perpendicularly arranged axes leading to clearly defined focal points and nodes. Like the buildings of Rome, those by McKim, Mead & White conveyed a symbolic message to an audience educated to comprehend their meaning, at least more so than to mid-twentieth-century users. Their architecture was similarly meant to inspire civic virtue. Just as the architects of Imperial Rome took full advantage of the increasing division of labor in the building trades and of the panoply of materials made available by the far-flung imperial trade network, so too McKim, Mead & White exploited the benefits of a complex building industry, teeming with skilled European artisans pouring into the United States, and the wealth of materials carried by rail and ship from all parts of the world.[52] So, as William S. Richardson noted, Pennsylvania Station was consciously patterned after Roman sources because these too had been buildings conceived to accommodate moving crowds and because the complexity and cosmopolitan character of the modern city so nearly approximated that of ancient Rome.

The Italian Renaissance was particularly studied by McKim, Mead & White since it was based in a flexible yet highly ordered system of design in which differing elements could be combined to form a coherent whole. For McKim as for Vignola and Palladio, beauty rested in order, harmony, proportion, and propriety or decorum. The firm's tendency, therefore, was to give clarity of form and response to the physical and historical context priority over purely utilitarian organization. Neither McKim nor White felt a need to rationalize their preference for Renaissance forms; they simply drew from Italian, French, or English examples, since such architecture seemed to them to embody qualities of intellect, imagination, clear order, balance, and civic amenity. And such sources lent themselves to visual enrichment where appropriate.

It is not difficult to see the work of McKim, Mead & White as the conclusion of the neoclassicism inaugurated by Jefferson, Soane, Durand, and Schinkel. Like the Roman architecture which inspired that of the Enlightenment, the firm's "neoclassicism" was meant to impress upon the observer a moral lesson, to expand his capacities for civic responsibility, a didactic function advocated by Denis Diderot, who wished to make art and architecture means to inculcate virtue and purify manners. McKim and White viewed architecture as had Archibald Alison, not only as "an innocent and elegant amusement to private life" but a force that might "increase the splendor of national character."[53] Their attitude is paralleled by the advice given Howard Van Doren Shaw in 1918 by Eastern colleagues who urged him to use the Choragic Monument of Lysicrates as a model for a funerary monument, for, they said, "a beautiful thing like that couldn't fail to be educational."[54] There is a difference, however, between the neoclassicism of the turn of the eighteenth century and that of a century later. The first, *romantic* classicism, was nostalgic and meant to refer the observer's mind back to an equivalent period, just as Jefferson's Virginia State Capitol is meant to draw a parallel between the modern Republic and its model in Republican Rome. In contrast the later resurgent classicism was a response to current conditions, an attempt to introduce order and clarity in an urban environment which was growing exponentially and chaotically. This is why it appeared at exactly that moment in the United States when transit lines were laid down and skyscrapers began to rise. It was not so much a conservative retrenchment as a positive assertion of alternatives for public and domestic architecture.[55] So the Georgian-Federalist "revival" championed by McKim, Mead, and White had a dual purpose; it was not only a resurgence of the national architectural character but also the suggestion of a method of giving to the dense urban settlement a modicum of order.

In a sense, too, as antithetical as it might at first appear, McKim and White may have been urged to Georgian-Federalist allusions by Ruskin. In his *Seven Lamps of Architecture* (1849), Ruskin observed that where once nature's silent skies and slumbering fields had brought a measure of quietude to man, the increasing crowding into cities was screening nature out; "we are thrown back in continually closer crowds upon the city gates. The only influence which can in any wise *there* take the place of that of the woods and fields, is the power of ancient Architecture." Ruskin, of course, was referring to medieval buildings, whose destruction he expressly forbade; "it is again no question of expediency or feeling whether we shall preserve the buildings of the past or not. *We have no right whatever to touch them.* They are not ours. They belong partly to those who built them, and partly to all the generations of mankind who are to follow us."[56] When the Centennial focused attention on Colonial architecture, Robert S. Peabody proposed that in scrutinizing the "Georgian Houses of New England" an architect might observe ways of harmonizing a building in its own elements and with its surroundings.[57] In 1883, in commenting on the rising interest in the domestic architecture of the Colonies and early Republic, Montgomery Schuyler had to admit that it was not surprising that architects turned their backs on the "wild work of Broadway and Fifth Avenue," casting instead "long and lingering looks at the decorum of the Bowling Green and Washington Square, and to sigh for a return of the times when the common street architecture of New York was sober and respectable, even if it was conventional. . . ."[58]

In using Italianate and Georgian-Federalist allusions, McKim and White were following the spirit if not the letter of Ruskin, in considering architecture a civilizing force, symbolically as well as functionally expressive. They took more literally, however, Ruskin's injunction for preservation. In 1894 McKim roundly denounced a scheme for remodeling Bulfinch's Massachusetts State House, in letters to Henry Lee Higginson and George von Lengerke Meyer, McKim's brother-in-law, then speaker of the Massachusetts House. "It makes me wrathy," he wrote Higginson, "that as a people we have so little reverence, care so little for tradition, and are so blind to the value of the work of a master—the only one the country has thus far produced in our profession, and to whom we owe the best examples of good proportion we possess."[59] In 1906, when he was asked to advise on additions to the Alabama State Capitol in Montgomery, McKim wrote his physician, Dr. Charles Hitchcock, that "possessing, as we do, so few landmarks and so little that will really stand in the present day architecture, every effort, as far as possible, should be made to preserve our past."[60]

If McKim's early interest in the "ancient" architecture of his own country can be attributed, however obliquely, to Ruskin, so too can his relative disinterest in structure, for to Ruskin "if a thing stands, that is all that is wanted."[61] Ruskin passed over or ignored much. Most significantly, he never seemed to view even small buildings in their entirety, much less large buildings or groups of buildings. The detailed study of plan relationships and forms in large masses, which was cardinal to McKim, came from his study in Paris. Although McKim attached great importance to the conceptual scheme, the parti, and gave commensurate importance to the development of the plan, he was not as rigorous in this pursuit as his French teachers or counterparts. This is why it is difficult to describe the work of McKim, Mead & White as typically "Beaux-Arts," if this is taken to mean precisely representative of the thinking of the École and completely realizing its design principles. Many liberties were taken, especially in the relaxation of absolute bilateral symmetry in formal plans, but the functional clarity, spatial progression, conceptual order, and symbolic expression characteristic of Beaux-Arts design are nonetheless present. These same qualities are evident, too, in Sullivan's skyscrapers in which, in the best École tradition, "form follows function," just as it does in McKim, Mead & White's Rhode Island State Capitol.

According to the precepts of the École, going back to Vitruvius and following the manifest example of Richardson, McKim, Mead & White believed the architect should always provide the best design, built in the best possible way. As Peabody said of McKim, he brought his clients to build better than they knew or dreamed—the plan often provided for accommodations the client had never thought to specify, the workmen and their crafts-manship were of the highest caliber, and the materials the most durable suited to their task. Both McKim and White took pains in selecting materials or rejecting them when minute imperfections came to light. Alexander Cochrane complained to McKim about the appear-ance of the brick proposed for his townhouse on Commonwealth Avenue, to which McKim replied that "Danvers brick always looks disappointing in the yard. We use it purposely because of its irregular shape and color. Built into the wall it is most satisfactory." It was always kept in mind that in time materials soften and mellow in color, but on occasion McKim wanted a stone that would come from the quarry with a weathered appearance, or as O. W. Norcross put it, would "look old when it is new."[62] White allowed for this effect of time as well. Edward Simmons once pointed out to White that the colors of the brick and terra cotta of Madison Square Garden did not go well together. "Stanny told me not to be silly, but to wait until they were twenty years old. Remembering it the other day, I looked, and behold! the tonality and color in the Madison Square building had come together like smoothing velvet."[63]

The firm and their clients were highly conscious of building for posterity. Samuel Clemens knew this too when he wrote J. P. Morgan in 1909 saying he was pleased that one of his manuscripts had been added to the "august company" of Morgan's collections; he was comforted to know that in that treasury some things would "remain indestructible in a perishable world."[64] What building in this way exemplified was a fundamental belief in the persistence of human institutions, in the continuity of human values across generations. It was also a covenant with the future. McKim, Mead & White never recognized "minimum standards" construction, even when there was every probability that what they were build-ing would shortly be replaced by something larger. Only once did McKim intentionally build a temporary structure—the President's office attached to the White House—hoping in this way to require better construction at a later time. McKim and his partners knew only too well that, once defined, minimum standards soon become the *only* standards.[65]

The reticence of McKim, Mead & White to seize upon the skyscraper as *the* building of the future was part of the indictment against them during the mid-twentieth century. They viewed skyscrapers in much the same way Henry James did on his return to the United States in 1904. The very essence of skyscrapers, it seemed to James, was impermanence: "they never speak to you, in the manner of the builded majesties of the world as we have heretofore known such . . . with the authority of things of permanence or even of things of long duration. One story is good only until another is told, and skyscrapers are the last word of economic ingenuity only until another word be written."[66] Although White may have felt some ambivalence about ever-larger skyscrapers, his Grand Central Terminal project showed his interest in the problem. McKim, however, made clear his dislike as the towers grew taller, packed onto the narrow tip of Manhattan, where they utterly destroyed the scale of the street. Architecture to McKim depended on an explicit scale relationship between the human being and his environment, and the new generation of skyscrapers prevented this. Sullivan's office blocks, it must be remembered, were only thirteen stories tall, hardly more than the firm's Sherry Building, but Ernest Flagg's soaring Singer Tower of forty-seven stories, 1906–08, was of an entirely different order.

How was it that McKim and his colleagues should have wished so to preserve and enhance the street, given the long-standing antiurban bias in American culture?[67] Had not McKim's father habitually avoided the city, settling the family first in suburban Germantown and then in even more idyllic Llewellyn Park? Why, too, did Burnham come to care so passionately about the future of Chicago when he lived on a wooded estate in suburban Evanston? Perhaps both came to respect Renaissance architecture and the clarity of its civic spaces; perhaps, too, there was no escaping the conclusion that laissez-faire uninvolvement in urban development could not continue in the face of ever-increasing urban densities. So both came to view the city's form as paramount, to which any single public or commercial enterprise was to be subordinate. Nevertheless, as they maintained this Olympian view, they kept a close focus on architecture at the scale of the individual, for a building was more than a functional shell. Architecture was for them an environmental art, the creation and manipulation of forms and spaces which shape experience and amidst which people play out their lives, and which at every moment affect human activity physically, psychologically, and emotionally.

If the classical academic Beaux-Arts architecture of McKim, Mead & White does embody positive qualities, how is it that such architecture fell into such profound disrepute? It was the result of a change in the connotation of *function* as applied to architecture during the nineteenth and twentieth centuries, particularly the mechanistic sense "Functionalism" acquired and which then formed the basis of the Modern Movement in Europe during the 1920s. Utility, as defined by the Greeks, simply meant that an object was fitted to its purpose, an idea modified during the Industrial Revolution when it was proposed that just as a machine can be designed to perform one operation supremely well, so too a building should perform its purpose well. This notion of mechanistic utility, pursued by Jeremy Bentham, was enlarged upon by John Stuart Mill in "Utilitarianism" (1863). When, later in the nineteenth century, influenced by the positivism of Auguste Comte, theorists explored what an architecture of empirical realism or utility might be, the logical properties seemed to be simplicity, scientific objectivity, and structural expression. Since Western thought had traditionally insisted on "either–or" dualities (rather than "both–and" as in Eastern views of the world), this meant *ipso facto* that an architecture of complexity, intuitive or formal abstractions, and symbolic expression was illogical and nonutilitarian. It was yet another instance in which syllogistic premises led to a nonsensical conclusion, but the conclusion was nonetheless seductively appealing. Since a functional use could be formulated and quantified, it meant the new architecture would have a purity and machinelike simplicity (often laboriously achieved by hand labor). As Adolf Loos declared, this freedom from ornament was a sign of spiritual strength.

The flaw in this system was in the too-narrow definition of function, for in addition to the quantifiable uses and activities in and around a building, there is its meaning, the image it projects and through which its use is enhanced. Image or cultural association was rejected by the modernist theorists; it was possible, they proclaimed, to free architecture of such outworn tags and devise a new idiom expressive only of utility, but in meaning nothing would it not mean something? As Hannah Arendt proposed in a rather different context, "utility established as meaning generates meaninglessness."[68]

Function in Beaux-Arts design was viewed differently, for it meant not only mechanical utility but also provision of the appropriate character in purely symbolic terms, and, most especially, provision for movement by means of suitably scaled and visually apprehensible spaces where human interaction might occur. The Beaux-Arts formalists recognized, however, that such interactions can never be fully predicted and therefore quantified; as Louis Kahn admitted, "you have no idea about one individual meeting another individual."[69] So Kahn, originally trained in the Beaux-Arts system, came to celebrate human activity in his mature work rather than merely to accommodate utilitarian function.

To analyze academic or Beaux-Arts architecture, it is necessary, as Hitchcock realized, to take into account the fundamental differences in the meaning of *function* as it was understood in the nineteenth century and as it came to be understood in the twentieth. Function for McKim, Mead & White involved aspects of Ruskin's Lamps of Life and Truth, expression of human activity and building materials, but it also included the principles of design taught by the École, later described by Julien Guadet, fidelity to the *character* (not necessarily the *letter*) of the building program, response to vagaries of site and local climate, clear organization, apparent visual strength, and beauty achieved by an optimum of utility and variety.

For McKim, Mead & White, character meant not only properly disposing masses and spaces, creating moods of gravity or gaiety, but also achieving the proper image through historical allusion, using architectural symbols as "crystalized experience." Thus the Rhode Island State Capitol, built in sparkling white marble atop Smith's Hill, is presented as a variation of the national Capitol, but, instead of an assemblage of parts of various vintage, here is a whole of carefully balanced components. It is an image in stone of ideal government, balanced in judgment and untainted; it is certainly not the physical representation of how state governments in this nation actually function, then or now, but it presents a challenge of what government might be. Consider, too, the Low Library at Columbia University, centralized in plan and set on the highest point, its dome and limestone structure strongly contrasting with the surrounding brick buildings. Upon entering the campus one is instinctively drawn toward that commanding element, even without knowing its precise function. Outgrown by the library collections, this "central feature," as McKim called it, has been converted into the administrative center of the university and its symbolic focus thus reinforced. In contrast, when one enters Mies van der Rohe's Illinois Institute of Technology campus there is such a democratic plenitude of directions to take, so many paths to elect, one does not know where to go. Even less does the I.I.T. chapel say anything about its purpose, for the unembellished brick cube could just as easily be a boiler house or handball court.

For a score of years after World War Two the architecture of symbolism and allusion such as that of McKim, Mead & White was torn down as quickly as possible, but when Pennsylvania Station came down, perceptions began to change. One role such buildings were now seen to fulfill was that of ameliorating the diminishing sense of historical continuity in the urban fabric; their presence was soon viewed as vitally necessary. Not only do nineteenth-century monuments reveal an alternative and nonthreatening mode of perception, the mixture they provide of elements from the past and present is what makes the city vital and real. "This multiplicity of experiences, intricately and subconsciously overlaid," claims Theo Crosby, "is the very stuff of cities."[70] Mirrored in serried glass curtain walls, Beaux-Arts classicism reminds us of the continuum of urban life. When Lewis Mumford began calling for a new monumental spirit in the architecture to rise from the ashes of the Second World War, he asked for buildings which celebrated their uses and situations—not merely accommodated but *celebrated*.[71] The new architecture was not just to be something or do something, it was to say something; it was not simply to facilitate use but also to disclose human intentions. The mechanical, the unvarying, was not architecture. "If we want architecture," he proposed, "we must ask for a margin of freedom, a margin above the necessary, the calculable, the economic." Through its expressiveness and the symbolic employment of all the devices available to the architect—mass, volume, color, texture, light, painting, sculpture, and water—the new monumental architecture would declare its place or function to be special, meriting the willing expenditure of the necessary resources. The monument, well conceived and lovingly realized—such as the Boston Public Library for Copley Square—makes its place even more special. These had always been the values given physical expression in the work of McKim, Mead & White. For them, to build was to raise structures of permanent value, such as Mumford wrote should gladden the eye and sustain the spirit. Their credo came from Ruskin: "let it be such work as our descendants will thank us for, and let us think, as we lay stone on stone, that a time will come . . . when men will say as they look upon the labor and wrought substance of them, 'See, this our fathers did for us.' "[72] Such an architecture embodies tradition as a bond of affectionate tolerance, maintaining, as Vincent Scully observed, a continuing dialogue between generations, which creates an environment developing across time. Such architecture requires commitment; it requires the covenant with the future described by Mumford; it requires what McKim, Mead, and White learned early—to build the home of man not with our surplus but with our essence.

Appendix

"An Architect's Service and Remuneration"

Because written statements by either McKim, Mead, or White are so few, this document found in the McKim, Mead & White Archive acquires special importance.[1] Although not signed, it is accompanied by letters to McKim that appear to fix its authorship and date. This is a version of a statement drafted at the annual meeting of the American Institute of Architects in 1903, in response to difficulties numerous architects were experiencing in dealing with governmental bodies as the City Beautiful movement began to result in building commissions. Often architects were being prevented from exercising construction supervision and were denied fees based on the final phase of their work. One letter, from Robert S. Peabody to McKim, June 5, 1903, criticizes McKim for not insisting on the standard 5 percent commission for undisclosed work (perhaps for McKim, Mead & White's War College, Washington, D.C.).[2] However, with Peabody's letter is also a response from George B. Post, to whom Peabody had sent a copy of his letter, which supports McKim's position. Later in the year the draft statement was slightly modified by Frank Miles Day of Philadelphia.[3]

Because of the current issues, the statement is especially concerned with documenting the working relationship of American architects to that of their European counterparts, but of special interest is McKim's assertion that the architect should study the environmental context of a proposed building, giving contextual relationships slight priority over internal functional expression.

The Tarsney Act mentioned here was passed in 1893, largely through the efforts of Daniel H. Burnham and William Rutherford Mead.[4] It provided for, but did not specifically require, the Secretary of the Treasury to procure designs for new Federal buildings by means of open competitions. President Grover Cleveland's Treasury Secre-

tary, John H. Carlisle, declined to do so, and it was not until 1897, under President William McKinley, when Treasury Secretary Lyman J. Gage appointed James Knox Taylor to the position of Federal Supervising Architect, that competitions were organized. Secretary Gage, formerly head of the Chicago businessmen responsible for the World's Columbian Exposition and a good friend of Burnham, was ready to put into practice the lessons of the Fair. Altogether, about thirty-five major Federal buildings or complexes were built through the provisions of the Tarsney Act.

FEW appreciate the time, labor, and skill expended by the architect in the preparation of drawings for a building. There is less appreciation of the fact that to produce artistic and lasting results an architect must have an artistic sense, a broad education, long training, special knowledge in the history of art, and construction, together with business knowledge and executive ability. Without the above qualifications combined in the individual or the firm, the best results in the executed work can never be attained.

It appears that but a very limited number are aware that to attain artistic expression in a building the architect must have full charge from the beginning to the completion of the structure. The life-giving qualities which make a work of art require the solicitous care and guidance of the artist.

Upon receiving a commission or entering a competition, before the drawings are commenced, the architect must study the site and surroundings with reference to its artistic possibilities or expression, and its utilitarian relations to street traffic and existing buildings. He must then investigate and understand the various branches and methods of transacting the business which the building is intended to accommodate. When these questions have been systemized, he is ready to make preliminary drawings. Only the architect is aware of the drawing after drawing, which is made, discarded, and destroyed during this, the most important step in the erection of a building, a step where

1. In "Architects Commission" file, Box M-15, 1968 Coll., MM&W Archive, New-York Historical Society. Reprinted in part in my *America Builds*.
2. R. S. Peabody to McKim, June 5, 1903, loc. cit. For the War College controversy, see ch. 6.
3. F. M. Day to McKim, December 7, 1903, loc. cit.
4. For the Tarsney Act, House Report 1078, 52nd Congress, 1st Session, 1893, see: Charles Moore, *Daniel H. Burnham, Architect, Planner of Cities*, 2 vols., Boston, 1921, 1: 95–109; and Lois A. Craig et al., *The Federal Presence: Architecture, Politics, and Symbols in U.S. Government Building*, Cambridge, Mass., 1978, 202–03 and passim.

the highest skill and the best judgment is required.

Having arrived at a satisfactory solution of the plan, the architect must obtain an artistic expression of the plan in elevation and perspective, an expression that will enhance and dignify the landscape, and be in harmony with the surroundings or the proposed surroundings of the contemplated structure. The solution of this portion of the problem requires the artist. Again, drawing after drawing is made, studied, discarded and destroyed before a solution is reached that is satisfactory to the architect.

The plan and design are evolved during these preliminary stages, the fundamental steps in a building if it is to be a commercial success and a work of art.

The preparation of the scale or working drawings and specifications follow in natural sequence. Foundations, natural and artificial must be investigated, tested, studied, altered and calculated. The various materials must be selected with reference to durability, strength, color, fitness, price, character of the building and the desired expression. Unknown materials and conditions must be tested chemically or physically.

During the progress of this branch of the work innumerable questions of detail are considered and decided. Plans are prepared for drainage, heating, electricity, structural iron, masonry, and carpentry during the preparation of the working drawings. The skill of the economist, constructor, and of the artist is required in adjusting rights of the various claimants to space in the construction. The architect must be vigilantly on guard that no one branch shall monopolize the area which more beneficially belongs to another, that no one or combination of interests shall detrimentally affect the scheme or artistic expression as laid out in the preliminary solution.

In the preparation of the working drawings, the elevations are drawn to a larger scale, artistic details of interior and exterior are more clearly and defi-nitely shown, while all structural features are carefully calculated and their dimensions marked. While the second stage of an architect's service is more mechanical than the preliminary stage, it requires a knowledge of architectural engineering and construction, which includes a knowledge of material, a knowledge of mechanical engineering in heating and electrical or mechanical installation, a knowledge of sanitary engineering in drainage and water supply as well as a knowledge of artistic expression to guide the whole. The architect or his assistants must have this knowledge, even if experts are employed in different branches, otherwise he will soon discover that some one department will monopolize space that will destroy more important features.

The third stage is receiving tenders or bids, and the letting of contracts. Here the business qualifications of the office are called into play. Systematic and methodical business methods of no mean order are required to organize and execute this portion of the work on a monumental building. Contemporaneous with this period of the work and throughout the progress of construction full size detail drawings are being prepared. The drawings require constant attention, both from the structural and the artistic side of the architect. First they must be joined, built, or constructed to stand, to resist weather, decay, water, fire, expansion, contraction, shrinkage, and the various strains of dead and live loads which have all been previously considered in the scale drawings but the ultimate stability of which often depends upon the final details which cannot be shown on small drawings.

A slight deviation in a full size moulding, modillion, pilaster, cornice, or other ornamental feature which an ordinary man would consider an exact interpretation of the scale drawing means the difference between something artistic and beautiful or something crude and ugly.

As soon as the contracts are let the supervision of the work begins.

PART 2ND

The question of supervision is an important one. It appears to be the accepted opinion that when the drawings are prepared, any one familiar or even unfamiliar with construction can erect the building in a satisfactory manner. This might be the fact if the architect and his assistants made drawings so perfect that no alteration would better them, and if it were possible for the superintendent, contractors, and various sub-contractors to carry out the intention of perfect drawings without deviation.

Unfortunately, architects, superintendents, and contractors are no more infallible than other men. According to their ability, they do not produce the best results on the first or second effort. From the inception to the completion of the building, daily arise questions of interpretation, questions of variation, questions for consideration on which depend convenience or inconvenience, economy or wastefulness, refinement or crudity, harmony or discord, a building that will be a work of art or one that will be an aberration.

With an architect of capacity in charge, who has presented a good scheme, and with contractors and other subordinates desirous of producing the best results, no one is as well fitted to weigh and decide such questions as the man who devises the scheme.

It is to be regretted that with the most carefully studied drawings, superintendents do not hesitate to make what they consider slight changes, or changes which they consider an improvement. The contractors have a greater temptation, as they can save money by slight changes in detail, method of construction, substitution of material or device which is (according to statement) as good or better than the one specified. In the opinion of the majority of superintendents, such changes are immaterial; the importance of the idea being unappreciated. All deviations of this character, whether made by a superintendent or contractor, with the best intention, are with few exceptions detrimental to the building.

When the progress of the building reaches the final stage of color and decoration, no one is so well fitted to pass judgment upon what will properly express the architecture of the building as the designer of the scheme. The architect must experiment on the actual work as to what is best, as no man can determine, except on the premises, the effect of shades, shadows, reflections, on tones and tints, or the effect of one color on the other under the varying conditions which exist in every building.

To produce the best results (only the best results should be considered in connection with monumental work) an architect of training and capacity must be in charge from inception to completion.

The selection of an architect: It is considered best for large work to select an architect who has demonstrated his capacity as an executive, constructor, and artist in executed work. Municipal and national governments usually make the selection by some form of competition.

Competitions as conducted in this country have rarely produced the result which they aimed to attain, that is, the best arranged structure for the uses intended and the most artistic building for the site and surroundings. Among the reasons for such failures may be mentioned conditions in the programme such that no one of capacity or dignity will enter the competition. Conditions are imposed which are either unjust and burdensome, the selection of the design not being judged by experts. Under any of the above conditions there is little probability of the best plan or design being selected. Too often intrigue or friendship has entered into awards, and conditions in the competition have been made with this end in view.

To secure satisfactory results an architect should draw up the scheme for competitions and at least three experts should be on the jury.

The American Institute of Architects has adopted an outline for a code of competition as the guide to an architect who may draw up such a scheme.

PART 3RD

Competitions are not a certain means of securing the best building and it is even doubtful if they secure the best design or scheme. Men who have proved themselves capable are usually busy men and cannot afford to spend time and thought on problems where the outcome is so uncertain.

A competition in which the competitors have been selected for their known ability, and paid a small sum to partially cover expenses, is the only certain method of securing competent men.

A brilliant designer does not necessarily insure a good building. In case the designer's capacity as an executive is unknown, provision should be made to associate him with an architect of known ability.

An engineer can not from his education fill such a position on the artistic side of the problem.

To secure the results desired by the client, government, community, or the profession, a scheme for competition should be drawn up by a professional expert. It should be a paid competition, the selection should be by a professional jury, and the successful architect should be awarded the work, at the full commission, with a guarantee that the competitor will have charge of the execution of the work.

The competitions for government work, conducted by the Treasury Department, under the Tarsney Act, have proved very satisfactory. The schemes for the competitions have been drawn up by Mr. J. K. Taylor, Supervising Architect. The competitors are selected, at least half of the selections being made for proved fitness, and half for local or political reasons. The selections have been made by a jury of three or more experts. The decisions of these juries have met the approbation of the profession after the various drawings submitted have been published or exhibited. The successful competitors have in each case been from among the men who were appointed because of proved capacity and never from those who were selected for political reasons.

The programmes being drawn by an architectural expert, they have fulfilled the various conditions necessary to make the preparation of drawings the least burdensome and so as to secure a selection purely upon the merit of the scheme.

One important feature has been unfortunately and unjustly eliminated in these competitions: the payment of each competitor for the actual expense of making sketches.

The work in each case has been awarded to the successful competitor, who has been paid 5 per-cent on the cost of the building for architectural service.

The system adopted by the Treasury Department has been the cause of other government buildings being given out by competition, conducted on similar equitable lines. The Municipal Building of the District of Columbia, in which each competitor was paid $500, the Agricultural Building, the Municipal Hospital for the District of Columbia, the Building for the Insane Asylum, and the group scheme for the War Department at West Point. In the latter competition each competitor was paid $2,000.00 while the average expense or cash outlay of each architect was $3,000.00.

The result of the competition for the Agricultural Department was satisfactory but unfortunately, after the award was made, the Secretary of Agriculture removed the architects and appointed others because of a dispute over the amount of service to be rendered by the architects, the Secretary being determined to limit their service to the preparation of plans, and the architects claiming a contract to have full charge. This decision has been very unfortunate for the community and for the art interest of the country, as only the best results can be obtained by the architect remaining in charge.

In France where the subject of both art and economy have been most thoroughly studied and where they have had the advantage of a long accumulated experience, architects are selected on definite and well considered lines. The government has a technical body of experienced men, in which architects predominate, called a building council to whom all questions relating to government buildings are referred. This council employs the architects who have won the Prix de Rome, after their four years sojourn and study in Rome, in the position of auditors and examining experts. After testing their capacity the government selects from these highly educated and capable artists, as vacancies occur, the architects for municipal, national, and historic buildings. Architects for Gothic work are selected from men who have proved their fitness in ecclesiastical

work. The council may select an architect for special qualifications adapted to the work, or a Secretary of a Department may appoint an architect on the approval of the council, who thus protects himself from outside pressure and political intrigue. Before the work commences the plans must be approved by the council. The council also has charge of selection by competition. The men who have won the Prix de Rome have almost without exception proved successful in the competitions for large government buildings, while the council of architects protects the government interest.

Each Russian ministry has its technical council who are entrusted with questions of building and who must approve all designs. They select for their more ordinary buildings architects who have passed a course of study in a government school of architecture and [who] are known as Court or Palace Architects. The technical committee conducts competitions and selects designs or makes direct selection according to the fitness of the architect for the work to be undertaken.

In England the Office of Works, one of the recognized ministries of the country, is in charge of all government buildings except military barracks, local admiralty buildings, and police stations. The great government buildings in England have been erected by architects who have no connection with the government. The architect for the New Admiralty Buildings was selected by an open competition. The architect for the Queen Victoria Memorial was selected through an invited competition, the Royal Institute of British Architects being asked to nominate the competitors; the New War Offices, by means of known works from a number of architects nominated by the Royal Institute of British Architects.

PART 4TH.

The remuneration of an architect for his services by sufficient sums to reimburse him for the most careful study of the problem, the most explicit and elaborate preparation of drawings, and efficient supervision of the construction, will secure the client or government the best result in the completed building. Anything less should not be considered.

The proper sum for such services can only be ascertained by what experience has proved to be the cost of producing the work by architects in charge of large buildings and who have given the study, prepared the drawings, and conducted business so as to produce good results in completed structures. The expenditure of millions in structures which must permanently beautify or mar the landscape are not proper fields for experimenting with untried methods or inexperienced men.

By an inquiry among the various architects of the country who have been doing such work, I find that the actual office expenses amount from 2 1/2 to 3 per cent on the cost of the building; out of this percentage the architect receives nothing. As 5 per cent is the amount usually paid, the 2 or 2 1/2 per cent which remains, after paying expenses of the office, covers the actual cost of supervision and the remuneration to the architect. If he secures 1 per cent out of this for his service he is fortunate.

The cost of production stated is only for large work; small monumental work costs approximately more.

In this connection, as a proof of what such service costs, and the remuneration usually paid in this country and abroad, the reports of the government officials and statements from foreign countries go to prove that instead of architects receiving less than the usual 5 per cent they should, to properly compensate them, get a greater percentage in most cases.

Taking the [U.S. Federal] Supervising Architect's Office, which in recent years has been conducted in a thoroughly efficient manner, we find that [for] the office expenses in producing drawings and conducting the work, exclusive of the cost of sites and the cost of buildings erected under the Tarsney Act and exclusive of superintendence . . . , the average has been, for the past three years, 6 3/10 per cent for the office work on the amount expended in building, while superintendence during the same period cost 2 4/10 per cent on the amount expended in building, making the total for the preparation of plans and supervision, on an average for the past three years, 8 7/10 per cent on the amount expended by this office, excluding the buildings which have been erected under the Tarsney Act. Captain John E. Sewell, under whose efficient management the Government Printing Office has been built, in his report of November 3, 1903, states the architect's services, draftsmen, and office expenses amounted to $146,198.89, making 6 6/10 per cent on the cost of the work. This is exclusive of cost of experts in heating, ventilation, plumbing, electrical installation, and his own salary. When these items, which would approximate about $20,000.00 during the period of the building covered by the report, [are] added, the expenditures would bring the percentage on the cost of the building up to more than 7 5/10 for drawings and superintendence. The report of the Superintendent of the Capitol for 1902 shows that, his own salary not being included, the reconstruction or fireproofing the central portion of the Capitol cost $153,500.00, and that the pay rolls in the Superintendent's office relating to this branch of the work, together with the fee for [the] consulting engineer, was $25,813.00, or a percentage on the cost of the work more than 16 per cent. The fee of the consulting engineer, $4,760.28, amounts to over 3 per cent on the total cost of the work and 7 7/10 per cent on the cost of structural steel and General Contract as shown in the report of the Superintendent of the Capitol Building and Grounds, June 30, 1902.

In this connection the fees paid by foreign governments to architects for large pieces of construction form a reasonable basis for similar work in the United States at the same rate of compensation. The American architect, with higher salaries paid to draftsmen, higher rents, and no architectural pupils paying for the priviledge of doing work, is receiving smaller remuneration than [his] professional brother across the water.

In England 5 per cent on the cost of the work is paid to the architect, while much of the time and labor is saved to him by the limited sets of drawings

he is expected to furnish and the bills of quantities which are made by the surveyor and for which the owner pays 2 per cent. A clerk of works and an inspector is provided by the owner or government. They are selected by and under the orders of the architect.

In France the same system is in vogue as to payments. The municipality of Paris has recently established a schedule of fees for the payment of architects on municipal work, paying 6 per cent on the first 200,000 and 5 1/2 per cent on the second 200,000 and 5 per cent on the third 200,000 francs, 4 1/2 on the fourth 200,000 and 4 per cent on all additional cost. Thus the fee on the largest building is between 4 and 5 per cent, and the government provides, subject to the order and on the endorsement of the architect, a superintendent and a clerk of works as well as the inspection given by the building council, while his office expenses and draftsmen's wages are from one-third to one-half what is paid by American architects.

In Germany the rates paid by the government on the work when private architects are employed is [in] accordance with the schedule of the Society of Architects and Engineers. These rates vary according to the character of the building and the cost of the structure; simple buildings, like sheds or factories, being done at a less rate than ornate structures. A separate increased rate is charged for decoration in the class under which government buildings are placed. The rate for the most expensive building in their schedule is given at 2,000,000 dollars and the rate for 250,000 dollars worth of decoration and 250,000 dollars worth of furniture makes the rate on the total sum a fraction over 5 per cent. The schedule provides for numerous extra charges for heating, lighting, ventilating, water, sewerage, and electrical arrangements, and salary for building foreman and inspector, traveling expenses, acquisition of building site, [and] per diem to the architect while traveling.

The Russian government pays [paid?] the architect of the building being erected by the Ministry of Marine, at the new port of Liban on the Baltic, 8 per cent on the cost of the building.

In Italy, when an architect or engineer is not working on a salary, he receives a 2 per cent retainer, 4 per cent on the completion of his drawings, and 8 per cent for the total direction of the works.

The Swiss architects and engineers have a very carefully prepared schedule of charges. The buildings are divided into classes; factories, sheds &c, being the first class and for which the smallest percentage is paid. The commission is also graded according to the cost of the structure. In the class to which government buildings belong, 5 per cent on the total cost is the smallest percentage paid for the largest structure, while it runs up to 8 per cent for the small structures of this class. The clerk of works or superintendent is employed or paid by the owner, but he is under the direction of the architect; all travelling expenses and an additional per diem are charged while travelling in addition to the percentage. Some of the special regulations of this schedule are interesting.

By the various schedules it will be seen that the foreign architect protects his interests more carefully than we do usually in this country, against both the government or the owner and the contractor, demanding payment for extra services for many items which an architect does in this country without extra compensation.

In every instance, the answer from foreign countries has been that the architect who designs the building supervises it until completion, although in many countries the government is represented by technical commissions and inspectors, and employs superintendents and clerks of works; they are all, with the exception of the commissions, under the direction of the architect, and the architect is responsible both for design and construction of the building.

After a building of importance is completed, its maintenance, repair, and additions thereto, are not left to the tender mercies of men unfamiliar with design and construction but the architect who designed the building is retained at a small yearly salary to maintain or add to the building until his death when another architect familiar with the structure fills his place. In some countries a technical board of works, on which a majority of the members are architects, has charge of the maintenance of government buildings.

It seems necessary to add that from the foregoing data, the architects in this country do more work for less compensation than do the profession in the other civilized countries of the world.

KEY TO ABBREVIATIONS

AABN	*American Architect and Building News*
AIA	American Institute of Architects
AForum	*Architectural Forum*
ARec	*Architectural Record*
AReview	*Architectural Review* [Boston]
AReview [London]	*Architectural Review* [London]
BPL	Boston Public Library
DAB	*Dictionary of American Biography*
InArch	*Inland Architect*
JAIA	*Journal, American Institute of Architects*
JRIBA	*Journal, Royal Institute of British Architects*
JSAH	*Journal, Society of Architectural Historians*
NCAB	*National Cyclopedia of American Biography*
NYHS	New-York Historical Society
NYSB	*New York Sketch Book of Architecture*
CFM-LC	C. F. McKim Collection, Manuscript Division, Library of Congress
McKim-Maloney Coll., NYPL	C. F. McKim-Margaret Maloney Collection, Manuscript Room, New York Public Library
MCNY	Museum of the City of New York
MM&W Archive, NYHS	McKim, Mead & White Archive, Map and Print Room, New-York Historical Society
CM-LC	Charles Moore Collection, Manuscript Division, Library of Congress
RGW-NYHS	Richard Grant White Collection, Manuscript Collection, New-York Historical Society
RIBA	Royal Institute of British Architects
Scrapbook	Scrapbook, Clippings and Newspaper Notices, 1875–1888, McKim, Mead & White Archive, New-York Historical Society

Notes

PREFACE

1. Charles Herbert Reilly, *McKim, Mead & White*, London, 1924, 7.
2. Much was sent away later, too, as files were cleaned out. In the firm's correspondence, New-York Historical Society, are copies of numerous cover letters accompanying rolls of drawings and specifications being returned to former clients or their children. See, for example, these letters: Burt L. Fenner to Prescott Hall Butler, December 10, 1912, and to Anne W. Cheney, January 8, 1913 (both in Misc. Correspondence File, Box M-3 II, 1968 Collection, MM&W Archive, NYHS); Lawrence Grant White to Benjamin W. Arnold, May 16, 1929, and to Philip L. Godwin, June 10,
1935 (Arnold and Godwin Files, Box M-16, 1968 Collection, MM&W Archive, NYHS).
3. Richardson, who was thoroughly familiar with Viollet-le-Duc, wrote Henry Adams on June 7, 1885, that the French "authority" was "an archaeologist—a theorist—never an architect," and he was pained by "the depths to which you must have fallen in quoting him." See Marc Friedlaender, "Henry Hobson Richardson, Henry Adams, and John Hay," *JSAH* 29 (October 1970), 231.
4. H. Siddons Mowbray, *H. Siddons Mowbray, Mural Painter, 1858–1928*, Stamford, Conn., 1928, 72–73.

PROLOGUE

1. George Santayana, "The Genteel Tradition in American Philosophy," *University of California Chronicle* 13 (October 11, 1911); see also D. L. Wilson, *The Genteel Tradition: Nine Essays by George Santayana*, Cambridge, Mass., 1967, 37–64.
2. Charles N. Glaab and A. Theodore Brown, *A History of Urban America*, New York, 1976, 92–94; Allan Nevins and Milton H. Thomas, eds., *The Diary of George Templeton Strong*, 4 vols., New York, 1952. For the long-standing American bias against the city see Morton and Lucia White, *The Intellectual versus the City from Thomas Jefferson to Frank Lloyd Wright*, Cambridge, Mass., 1962.
3. Edith Wharton, *A Backward Glance*, New York, 1934, 54–55, 2, 6, 44.
4. Carroll L. V. Meeks, "Picturesque Eclecticism," *Art Bulletin* 32 (September 1950), 226–35; "Creative Eclecticism," *JSAH* 11 (December 1953), 15–18; "Wright's Eastern Seaboard Contemporaries: Creative Eclecticism in the United States around 1900," Problems of the 19th and 20th Centuries, *Acts of the Twentieth International Congress of the History of Art*, Princeton, 1963, 64–77. A further refinement of his definition, illustrated by the work of McKim, Mead & White and marking the shift toward greater archaeological accuracy in detail, is proposed in my *Concise History of American Architecture*, New York, 1979, 361–62.
5. Charles B. Hosmer, Jr., *Presence of the Past: A History of the Preservation Movement in the United States before Williamsburg*, New York, 1965, 198–200; William B.
Rhoads, *The Colonial Revival*, 2 vols., New York, 1977, 48–96.
6. O. W. Norcross was the contractor for the bulk of the firm's buildings. See James F. O'Gorman, "O. W. Norcross, Richardson's 'Master Builder': A Preliminary Report," *JSAH* 32 (May 1973), 104–13; O'Gorman, *H. H. Richardson and His Office: Selected Drawings*, Cambridge, Mass., 1974. The only room on the fifth floor of the Mohawk Building, New York, not occupied by McKim, Mead & White, 1891–94, the firm had their offices there, was the branch office of Norcross Brothers manned by a Mr. Reilly, frequently consulted by the partners. The firm also worked with David H. King, Jr.; Michael Reid; Jacob & Young; The Tidewater Construction Company; Charles T. Wills; and George A. Fuller & Company, as noted in the firm's bill books. These notations have been cited in my *Architecture of McKim, Mead & White, 1870–1920: A Building List*, New York, 1978.
7. Howard Mumford Jones, "The Renaissance and American Origins," *Ideas in America*, Cambridge, Mass., 1944; Richard Guy Wilson, *The American Renaissance, 1876–1917*, New York, 1979, 11–25, 39–41.
8. Thomas S. Hines, *Burnham of Chicago, Architect and Planner*, New York, 1974, 268–70.
9. See my catalogue of the firm's work in the *Building List*.
10. William A. Boring to Charles Moore, n.d. (c. 1927), Charles Moore Papers, Manuscript Division, Library of Congress [CM-LC].

11. The six were: Massachusetts Institute of Technology, 1865, first classes 1868; University of Illinois, Urbana, 1867, first classes 1870; Cornell University, 1871; Syracuse University, 1873; University of Pennsylvania, 1874; and Columbia University, 1881. The University of Michigan had a short-lived program, 1876–78, directed by William Le Baron Jenney. See Turpin Bannister, *The Architect at Mid-Century*, New York, 1954, 93–104.

12. C. H. Blackall, in "Architectural Education: Part II, the Office," *AABN* 121 (March 15, 1922), 213–14, singles out McKim, Mead & White as being exemplary for its role in training young architects. See also my "McKim, Mead & White: their Office and Its Influence," *Building List*, xl–xlii.

13. McKim's letter of appointment to head the Columbia atelier, from university president Nicholas Murray Butler, April 18, 1905, in McKim Misc. File, Box M-3, 1968 Coll., MM&W Archive, NYHS. See too the descriptive letter, J. R. Pope to Moore, September 20, 1926, quoted in Charles Moore, *The Life and Times of Charles Follen McKim*, Boston, 1929, 150–51. The atelier system at Columbia is described in Theodor Karl Rohdenburg, *A History of the School of Architecture, Columbia University*, New York, 1954, 20, 96. See too Richard Oliver, ed., *The Making of an Architect, 1881–1981*, New York, 1981, 23–38.

14. S. White to C. T. Barney, September 18, 1901, Architects Education File, Box M-15, 1968 Coll., MM&W Archive, NYHS. See also McKim's replies to Wendell Garrison, March 11, 1893; to Prescott Hall Butler, July 13, 1893; and to Eugene Bigler, December 2, 1895, all in McKim's Letterbooks, Charles Follen McKim Coll., Manuscript Division, Library of Congress [CFM-LC].

15. See Moore, *McKim*, 52–53.

16. See Lucia and Alan Valentine, *The American Academy in Rome, 1894–1969*, Charlottesville, Va., 1973; Moore, *McKim*, 128–81; and C. Grant LaFarge, *The American Academy in Rome*, New York, 1920. Correspondence concerning establishment of the American Academy is found throughout McKim's Letterbooks after 1895, CFM-LC; in the Letterbooks of Daniel Burnham, Burnham Library, Art Institute of Chicago; and in the libraries of the American Academy in Rome and in New York City.

17. Frederick P. Hill., *Charles Follen McKim: The Man*, Francetown, N. H., 1950, 24–25.

18. See Roger Riordan, "The Architectural League of New York," *Century* 25 (March 1883), 698–708; *The Critic* 1 (January 29, 1881), 8; *AABN* 9 (April 16, 1881), 184; "First Annual Exhibition of Architectural Draw-

ings," *The Salmagundi Club and American Black and White Society*, 1886; "Second Annual Exhibition . . . ," *Salmagundi Club* . . . , 1887; The Architectural League, *Proceedings from Organization to January MDCCCLXXXIX*, 1889. An example of a drawing by a member of the League is the townhouse facade done by Cass Gilbert while in the McKim, Mead & White office, *AABN* 9 (April 16, 1881), no. 277.

19. "Prix de Reconnaissance des architectes américaines," *AABN* 22 (September 3, 1887), 113–15, including a list of the various subscribers who had passed through or been influenced by the École.

20. Alfred Hoyt Granger, *Charles Follen McKim: A Study of His Life and Work*, Boston, 1913, 5, 108.

21. Cass Gilbert to McKim, August 4, 1908, CM-LC.

22. *A Monograph of the Work of McKim, Mead & White, 1879–1915*, 4 vols., New York, 1914–20; new edition in one vol., New York, 1973, including my essay, "McKim, Mead & White Reappraised," and notes on the 400 plates. Concerning the publication of the original edition, see the *Monograph*, 1973 ed., 52, and my *Building List*, xl.

23. White did acquiesce to Katherine Mackay's insistence that Harbor Hill, Roslyn, N.Y., 1899–1902, be patterned after François Mansart's Château de Maisons near Paris. See Lawrence Wodehouse, "Stanford White and the Mackays: A Case Study of Architect-Client Relationships," *Winterthur Portfolio* 11 (1976), 213–33. McKim reminded Thomas Kellogg, however, that Richardson had instilled in his students the idea that "your client is going to estimate you at exactly your estimate of yourself"; McKim to Thomas M. Kellogg, August 9, 1893, CFM-LC.

24. Henry H. Statham, *Modern Architecture*, London, 1897, 17.

25. See Vincent Scully, *American Architecture and Urbanism*, New York, 1969, 36–60, and my "McKim, Mead & White Reappraised," *Monograph*, 1973 ed., 40–46.

26. See Reilly's "The Modern Renaissance in American Architecture," *JRIBA* 17 (June 25, 1910), 630–35, and *McKim, Mead & White*, London, 1924. See Le Corbusier's comments in *When the Cathedrals Were White*, New York, 1964, 60 (trans. *Quand les cathédrales étaient blanches*, Paris, 1937).

27. See Glaab and Brown, *Urban America*, 99–119; Blake McKelvey, *The Urbanization of America*, New Brunswick, N.J., 1963; Bureau of the Census, *Historical Statistics of the United States: Colonial Times to 1957*, Washington, D.C., 1957, 14.

28. Thomas Hastings, "The Influence of the École des Beaux-Arts Upon American Architecture," *ARec*, Special Beaux-Arts Number, January, 1901, 89–90.

Chapter 1. F O U N D A T I O N S ,   1 8 4 0 – 1 8 7 0

1. Concerning the Mead family see: "Larkin Goldsmith Mead," *DAB* 12:472–73. Larkin, Sr., was prominent in the Brattleboro community and was one of the founders of the local bank and library. For John Humphrey Noyes see *DAB* 13:585–90; J. H. Noyes, *History of American Socialism*, Philadelphia, 1874; Dolores Hay-

den, *Seven American Utopias: The Architecture of Communitarian Socialism, 1790–1975*, Cambridge, Mass., 1976.

2. See Mildred Howells, ed., *Life in Letters of William Dean Howells*, 2 vols., Garden City, N.Y., 1928, I:11. Howells drew on his years in Italy for articles pub-

lished in 1863 and later his recollection of Larkin's studio provided the basis for the studio described in *Indian Summer*, 1886.

3. "Larkin Goldsmith Mead, [Jr.]," *DAB* 12:472–73; Lorado Taft, *The History of American Sculpture*, rev. ed., New York, 1924, 236–44, 538; Wayne Craven, *Sculpture in America*, New York, 1968, 321–25.

4. William Rutherford Mead, manuscript, "Reminiscences," Box M-3, I, 1968 Coll., MM&W Archive, NYHS, printed in Moore, *McKim*, 40–42. It is significant that Mead saw not the original severely neoclassical building but the reconstructed building with its Renaissance modifications. See Winslow Ames, "The Vermont State House," *JSAH* 23 (December 1964), 193–99; Henry-Russell Hitchcock and William Seale, *Temples of Democracy: The State Capitols of the USA*, New York, 1976, 104–06, 126–30.

5. Mead, "Reminiscences," Moore, *McKim*, 40. George Fletcher Babb (1843–1916) had built three houses in Llewellyn Park, Orange, N.J., before coming into Sturgis's office where he enjoyed a status more like a colleague than an employee. When Sturgis later ceased to practice, Babb moved into the McKim, Mead & White office, leaving shortly afterward to go into partnership with Walter Cook and Willard, though he remained extremely close to White and Joseph Morrill Wells. During the 1880s the two firms worked almost in collaboration, and their work shows marked mutual influence.

6. Peter Bonnett Wight, "Reminiscences of Russell Sturgis," *ARec* 26 (August 1909), 122–31. Emlen T. Trenchard Littell, who had an office at 48 Exchange Place where Richardson first set up practice, specialized in churches and ecclesiastical work; he was not the "engineer" to whom Mead referred.

7. Mead, "Reminiscences," Moore, *McKim*, 42.

8. Mead, "Reminiscences," Moore, *McKim*, 40.

9. McKim's letters, carefully saved, passed to his daughter who presented typescript copies to Charles Moore; these remain with his papers, CM-LC, while the originals were given by Mrs. Margaret McKim Maloney to the New York Public Library, McKim-Maloney Coll., Manuscript Division [NYPL].

10. "James Miller McKim," *DAB* 12:103; Moore, *McKim*, 3–7; Ira V. Brown, "Miller McKim and Pennsylvania Abolitionism," *Pennsylvania History* 30 (January 1963), 55–72. Miller McKim left the ministry because he came to reject the doctrine of the necessity of Christ's death for salvation; his unorthodox views were made public in "A Letter to the Presbytery of Wilmington," printed by Merrihew & Gunn, Philadelphia, 1838. This and other pertinent documents are in the McKim-Maloney Coll., NYPL. See also: pamphlet by J.M. McKim, "The Freed Men of South Carolina," Philadelphia, 1862, 32 pp.; miscellaneous correspondence of J. M. McKim, Houghton Library, Harvard University; Rollo Ogden, ed., *The Life and Letters of Edwin Lawrence Godkin*, 2 vols., New York, 1907; Gustav Pollack, *Fifty Years of American Idealism: The New York Nation, 1865–1915*, Boston, 1915. The only signed article by Miller McKim in the *Nation* is in three parts, March and April, 1870, and concerns "The Vexed Question" of women's suffrage.

11. Miller and Sarah McKim are described in an undated letter fragment, Box 36, McKim-Maloney Coll., NYPL; quoted in Moore, *McKim*, 3–5. Lucy shared in her father's activities, accompanying Miller McKim to the Sea Islands, South Carolina, in 1862 to report on the condition of thousands of slaves suddenly freed. While in the South she collected slave songs, publishing them in *Slave Songs of the United States*, New York, 1867, with William F. Allen and Charles P. Ware, still the best source for this material. Both she and her brother Charles were accomplished musicians. See William Lloyd Garrison's description of a musical evening in the McKim-Garrison home at Llewellyn Park, Walter M. Merrill, ed., *The Letters of William Lloyd Garrison*, Cambridge, Mass., 1979, 5:424.

12. Gordon S. Parker, "The Work of Three Great Architects," *World's Work* 12 (October 1906), 8051–66; see too Moore, *McKim*, 128–81.

13. Benjamin P. Thomas, *Theodore Weld, Crusader for Freedom*, New Brunswick, N.J., 1950, 230; "Theodore Weld," *DAB* 19:625–27. Miller McKim wrote Weld, June 23, 1856, inquiring about school costs, letter, Box 36, McKim-Maloney Coll., NYPL.

14. Jane B. Davies, "Llewellyn Park in West Orange, New Jersey," *Antiques* 108 (January 1975), 142–57; the social climate of "The Park" is discussed by Richard Guy Wilson, "Idealism and the Origin of the First American Suburb: Llewellyn Park, New Jersey," *American Art Journal* 11 (October 1979), 79–90.

15. Sarah McKim to C. F. McKim, June 7, 1866, Box 33, McKim-Maloney Coll., NYPL; quoted in Moore, *McKim*, 15. The Nichols-McKim-Garrison house is illustrated in Davies, "Llewellyn Park," and in Christopher Tunnard, "The Romantic Suburb in America," *Magazine of Art* 40 (May 1947), 184–87. Miller McKim corresponded directly with Haskell, who persuaded him of the advantages of living in the country rather than in Brooklyn; letter, Haskell to J. M. McKim, February 14, 1866, Box 37, McKim-Maloney Coll., NYPL. The McKims moved to Llewellyn Park in May 1866, paying $4,000 for the house and property.

16. C. F. McKim to F. Garrison, c. May, 1866 (?), quoted in Moore, *McKim*, 15–16.

17. J. M. McKim to Wendell P. Garrison, February 9, 1867, CFM-LC. Miller McKim may have been prepared for his son's decision to become an architect through correspondence with his brother, John L. McKim, in September 1866, for, upon asking if Charles might borrow some drafting instruments, he learned that John, Jr., had become an architect and "makes a considerable part of his living at this business"; John L. McKim to J. M. McKim, September 21, 1866, Box 37, McKim-Maloney Coll., NYPL.

18. J. M. McKim to C. F. McKim, March 6, 1867, CFM-LC. This and much more of the preserved correspondence relating to McKim's years at Harvard and the École is quoted in my "Urban Architecture of McKim, Mead & White, 1870–1910," doctoral dissertation, Yale University, 1973.

19. J. M. McKim to H. Villard, June 25, 1867, Box 37, McKim-Maloney Coll., NYPL; quoted in Moore, *McKim*, 21–22.

20. W. H. Furness to J. M. McKim, n.d. (c. spring 1867), Box 37, McKim-Maloney Coll., NYPL; copy in CFM-LC.

21. See David T. Van Zanten, "Jacob Wrey Mould: Echoes of Owen Jones and the High Victorian Styles in New York, 1853–1865," *JSAH* 28 (March 1969), 41–57; Henry-Russell Hitchcock, "Ruskin and American Architecture, or Regeneration Long Delayed," in *Concerning Architecture*, John Summerson, ed., London, 1968, 166–208; "Russell Sturgis," *DAB* 18:181–82; David W. Dickason, *The Daring Young Men: The Story of American Pre-Raphaelites*, Bloomington, Ind., 1953, 71–124; Montgomery Schuyler, "Russell Sturgis," *ARec* 25 (March 1909), 148, 220; M. Schuyler, "Russell Sturgis's Architecture," *ARec* 25 (June 1909), 404–10; Peter B. Wight, "Reminiscences of Russell Sturgis," *ARec* 26 (August 1909), 122–31; and the *Macmillan Encyclopedia of Architects* 4:150.

22. Quoted in Wight, "Reminiscences," 130–31. Later, Sturgis's criticism appeared regularly in *The Nation* and *ARec*, and during 1897–1909 his column, "The Field of Art," appeared in *Scribner's Magazine*. McKim came to hold the same view of the union of the arts, as is evident in a letter to Miss E. G. Hewitt, New York, May 4, 1903, CFM-LC:

> At your request, and in answer to the question as to the propriety of including architecture as an Art, rather than as a scientific course, in the classes of instruction of the Cooper Union, I can only say that, while scientific knowledge and instruction are necessary in the study of architecture, it is essentially an art, as it is the oldest of the Arts. The term "Allied Arts" refers to painting, sculpture and *architecture*. The greatest masterpieces of the painter's art, for instance, are *mural*. Sculpture only reaches its highest expression when associated with *architecture*. The most noble examples of art employ all three. The School of Fine Arts in Paris is an institution founded for the purpose of disseminating the principles of architecture, painting, and sculpture, in the order named. Immediately over the entrance door, the word *"Architecture"* occupies the central position, between "Painting" and "Sculpture," standing for the sister arts.
>
> While mathematics and scientific knowledge are necessary to the practice of architecture, any general course, upon that subject, which did not regard it fundamentally as an Art would be futile.

23. *The Seven Lamps of Architecture*, London, 1849, 191–92. For the profound influence of Ruskin on American architecture see Hitchcock, "Ruskin"; Kristine O. Garrigan, *Ruskin on Architecture: His Thought and Influence*, Madison, Wis., 1973; Roger B. Stein, *John Ruskin and Aesthetic Thought in America, 1840–1900*, Cambridge., Mass., 1967.

24. *Seven Lamps*, 2nd ed., London, 1855, xxvi–xxvii, xxix, 203.

25. *New Path* 1 (September 1864), 56, and (January 1865), 112–13.

26. *The Crown of Olive*, lecture given in 1864, published, London, 1866.

27. Sarah McKim to C. F. McKim, October 4, 1867, CFM-LC. Augustus Saint-Gaudens was also in Paris, in the atelier Jouffroy where he was joined in 1869 by fellow American Olin Warner; McKim did not meet the sculptors until later in New York. For William Robert Ware see *DAB* 19:452–53; Bannister, *Architect at Mid-Century*, 96; and the *Macmillan Encyclopedia of Architects* 4:373–74.

28. Robert S. Peabody, "A Tribute," *Brickbuilder* 19 (February 1910), 55. For Peabody see Wheaton A. Holden, "That Peabody Touch, Peabody and Stearns of Boston," *JSAH* 32 (May 1973), 114–31; and the *Macmillan Encyclopedia of Architects* 3:380–82.

29. William L. B. Jenney studied not at the École des Beaux-Arts but at the École Centrale which emphasized practical arts and industrial design. See Theodore Turak, "The École Centrale and Modern Architecture: the Education of William Le Baron Jenney," *JSAH* 29 (March 1970), 40–47; and the *Macmillan Encyclopedia of Architects* 2:494–96.

30. For the abortive reform see Richard A. Moore, "Academic Design Theory in France after the Reorganization of 1863," *JSAH* 36 (October 1977), 145–74. The essential sources for École training are now: Arthur Drexler, ed., *The Architecture of the École des Beaux-Arts*, New York, 1977, with separate essays noted below; Donald Drew Egbert, *The Beaux-Arts Tradition in French Architecture*, Princeton, 1980; and Robin D. Middleton, ed., *The Beaux-Arts and Nineteenth-Century French Architecture*, Cambridge, Mass., 1982. All of these have extensive notes and bibliographies. For the special impact of the École on American students see: *ARec*, Special Beaux-Arts Number, January 1901; Ernest Flagg, "The École des Beaux-Arts," *ARec* (January through September 1894), essay in three parts; and Joan Draper, "The École des Beaux-Arts and the Architectural Profession in the United States: The Case of John Galen Howard," in Spiro Kostof, ed., *The Architect*, New York, 1977, 209–35. See too: George Chappell, "Paris School Days: How the Student Lives and Works at the École des Beaux-Arts," *ARec* (July 1910 through February 1911), essay in three parts; John Galen Howard, "The Paris Training," *AReview* [Boston] 5 (January 20, 1898), 4–7, and his "The Spirit of Design at the École des Beaux-Arts," *AReview* [Boston] 5 (April 20, 1898), 25–27; and James P. Nofsinger, *The Influence of the École des Beaux-Arts on the Architects of the United States*, Washington, D.C., 1955.

31. Moore, *McKim*, 27.

32. Flagg, "École," *ARec* 3 (April–June 1894), 428.

33. See David T. Van Zanten, "Architectural Composition at the École des Beaux-Arts from Charles Percier to Charles Garnier," in Drexler, ed., *Architecture of the École*, 111–324.

34. Julian Guadet, *Eléments et théorie de l'architecture*, 4 vols., Paris, [c. 1904], 1:134, trans. L. M. Roth and Jean-Francois Blassel. Portions of Guadet's first introductory volume are translated in my *America Builds*, New York, 1983.

35. Walter Cook, "Recent Progress in Architectural Design," *AABN* 71 (January 26, 1901), 27–29.

36. *ARec*, Special Beaux-Arts Number, January 1901, 83.

37. Louis Hautecoeur, *Histoire de l'architecture classique en*

France, Paris, vol. 7, passim; M.-D.-H.-J.-B. d'Espouy, "Honoré Daumet, architect," *L'Architecture* 7 (1912), 17–21; "Les Maîtres de l'architecture française," *La Construction Moderne* 10 (1894–95), 421–24; R. P. Spiers, "The Late Honoré Daumet," *JRIBA* 19 (1911–12), 145–46; Drexler, ed., *The Architecture of the École,* passim.

38. This scrapbook was among various White memorabilia and scrapbooks kept by the White families at Saint James, N.Y.

39. Illustrated in Hautecoeur, *Histoire,* 7:238; *Encyclopédie d'architecture,* 1881, pl. 713.

40. Lassus and Heret are illustrated in Hautecoeur, *Histoire,* 7:61, 223; for Blondel's *portail* see Drexler, ed., *Architecture of the École,* 289.

41. Illustrated in Hautecoeur, *Histoire,* 7:229; *Revue générale d'architecture,* 1868, pl. 32. Néo-grec is used here in the sense given it by most Americans at the time, as discussed by Montgomery Schuyler in "A 'Modern Classic,' " *ARec* 15 (May 1904), 431–44; the more theoretical sense of the term in France is discussed in Neal Levine, "The Romantic Idea of Architectural Legibility: Henri Labrouste and the Néo-grec," Drexler, ed., *Architecture of the École,* 325–46.

42. Peabody, "Tribute," 55.

43. Sarah McKim to C.F. McKim, November 6, 1868, CFM-LC.

44. The originals have been lost, but photographic copies are in the Avery Library, Columbia University; the subjects include a masonry guild hall (?) in Saumur, dated November 1869, and half-timbered houses in Lisieux and Caen, the latter dated August 1869.

45. J. M. McKim to C. F. McKim, January 15, 1869, and February 5, 1869, CFM-LC.

46. J. M. McKim to C. F. McKim, February 7 [1869], CFM-LC. Miller McKim also advised his son to get secondhand copies of Fergusson's *Illustrated Handbook of Architecture,* 2 vols., 1855, and *A History of the Modern Styles,* 1862; whether Charles purchased these is unknown, but his interests were elsewhere as is evident from the news he sent his father that he had begun an English translation of Viollet-le-Duc's *Entretiens,* the first volume of which came out in 1863. He left this unfinished, but an English translation was done by Henry Van Brunt, *Discourses on Architecture,* 2 vols., Boston, 1875, 1881.

47. Lucy McKim Garrison to C. F. McKim, April 3, 1869, CFM-LC.

48. J. M. McKim to C. F. McKim, May 19, 1869, CFM-LC.

49. J. M. McKim to C. F. McKim, August 2, 1869, CFM-LC.

50. J. M. McKim to C. F. McKim, September 21, 1869, CFM-LC.

51. J. M. McKim to C. F. McKim, September 28, 1869, CFM-LC.

52. *NYSB* 1 (January 1874), 2, pl. 2.

53. Mead, "Reminiscences," Moore, *McKim,* 40.

54. Material on Richard Grant White is given in the standard biography of his son, Charles C. Baldwin, *Stanford White,* New York, 1931, 16–30. See also: *DAB* 19:-113–14; Francis P. Church, "Richard Grant White," *Atlantic Monthly* 67 (March 1891), 303–14; *Appleton's Cyclopedia of American Biography* 6:474–75; *National Cyclopedia of American Biography* 1:197; Alden A. Free-

man, "Richard Grant White," *The University Quarterly* [New York University], 4 (May 1881), 87–97; Laura Wood Roper, *FLO, A Biography of Frederick Law Olmsted,* Baltimore, 1973, 109–10.

55. C. Vaux to R. G. White, February 6, 1860, Richard Grant White Collection, Manuscript Division, NYHS [RGW-NYHS]; Baldwin, *White,* 105–07. R. G. White's most specific writing on art included the text of *A Companion to the Bryan Gallery of Christian Art,* New York, 1853, and *A Companion to the Gallery of Paintings of Old Masters . . . ,* New York, 1850. White's large library was broken up in 1870 when a portion was sold at auction (*Catalogue of a Collection of Books . . . forming the Library of Mr. Richard Grant White,* New York, 1870). Altogether 5,500 titles were offered, but some of those which might have had some interest for Stanford were: Archibald Allison, *Essays on the Principles of Taste,* 6th ed.; A. J. Downing's *Cottage Residences* and *The Architecture of Country Houses;* J. Gwilt, *Rudiments of Architecture;* all the major works of James Jackson Jarves; J. Ruskin, *Modern Painters;* C. Vaux, *Villas and Cottages;* Vitruvius, *Ten Books of Architecture* (English trans.); J. J. Winkelmann, *History of Ancient Art* (English trans.). In 1885 after the death of R. G. White a second auction was held to dispose of his paintings, drawings, prints, and musical instruments. R. G. White's most specific writing on architecture concerned Hunt's "Gateways to the Central Park," *Galaxy* 1 (August 1, 1866), 650–56, and editorials against the gates in the *Nation* 3 (September 27, 1866), 255–56. See Baker, *Hunt,* 146–56; Roper, *FLO,* 298; Albert Fein, *Frederick Law Olmsted and the American Environmental Tradition,* New York, 1972, 12–13. Olmsted's grateful appreciation of his friend's defense of the park design is expressed in a letter, July 23 (1866?), RGW-NYHS.

56. Baldwin, *White,* 37.

57. Frederick Law Olmsted to S. White, letter on the occasion of the death of R. G. White, in which Olmsted describes how he first introduced R. G. White to Richardson and arranged for Stanford's apprenticeship, April 9, 1885, Stanford White Collection, Manuscript Division, NYHS; for the full text of the letter see my "Urban Architecture of McKim, Mead & White," 111–12.

58. *NYSB* 1 (December 1874), pl. 45. Vincent Scully discusses the significance of this reproduction in *The Shingle Style,* New Haven, 1955, 26.

59. "Washington's Headquarters, Newburgh, N. Y.," *NYSB* 3 (April 1876), pl. 15; "Cottage at Newport for W. Watts Sherman," *NYSB* 2 (May 1875), pls. 18, 19. For White's work for Richardson see O'Gorman, *Richardson: Drawings,* in which there are a number of cogent attributions, and Hitchcock, *Richardson,* 125–96. At first White had little influence on design; see Theodore E. Stebbins, "Richardson and Trinity Church: The Evolution of a Building," *JSAH* 27 (December 1968), 281–89.

60. Richardson increasingly delegated authority as his worsening Bright's Disease made travel difficult; see O'Gorman, *Richardson: Drawings,* 19–20. A number of White's letters of 1872–78, preserved by the White family, Saint James, N.Y., and printed in part in Baldwin,

White, document his travel for Richardson. For the Blake and Cheney projects see *NYSB* 2 (February 1875), pl. 6, and 3 (September 1876), pl. 35.

61. *AABN* 2 (October 27, 1877), 345, no. 96.

62. Glenn Brown, *1860–1930 Memories,* Washington, D.C., 1931, 28–29; Baldwin, *White,* 47.

63. Augustus Saint-Gaudens, *The Reminiscences of Augustus Saint-Gaudens,* 2 vols., New York, 1913, 1:159–60.

64. Helene Barbara Weinberg, "John La Farge and the Decoration of Trinity Church," *JSAH* 33 (December 1974), 323–53.

65. Hitchcock, *Richardson,* 186; Larry J. Holmolka, "Richardson's North Easton," *AForum* 124 (May 1966), 72–77.

66. *AABN* 3 (May 25, 1878), 183, no. 126.

67. H. H. Richardson to S. White, February 22, 1878, in the collection of the White family, Saint James, N.Y. After White left for Europe, Richardson dissolved the loose partnership with Gambrill and closed his "office" in New York.

68. Baldwin, *White,* 63; Saint-Gaudens, *Reminiscences,* 1:222.

Chapter 2. FLEDGLINGS, 1870–1879

1. MM&W Archive, NYHS.

2. Richard Guy Wilson, "The Early Work of Charles F. McKim: The Country Houses," *Winterthur Portfolio* 14 (Autumn 1979), 243. A perspective of the hall of the John Livermore house, Montclair, N. J., appeared in *NYSB* 1 (July 1874), pl. 27.

3. *Architectural Sketch Book* 1 (January 1874), pl. 26. Sketchy details, perhaps for this interior, are among the early drawings in the MM&W Archive, NYHS. The mounting work caused Charles's mother to write Lucy, March 19, 1872, that "Charlie is . . . on the path of fortune. I have quite lost count of his 'jobs'." (J. M. McKim Papers, Houghton Library, Harvard University, bMS AM 1906, 565).

4. A notice concerning the Child school appeared in the Newport *Journal,* December 2, 1875.

5. Montgomery Schuyler, "Charles Follen McKim," *ARec* 26 (November 1909), 380–82.

6. Editorial statement (McKim?), dated December 23, 1873, *NYSB* 1 (January 1874); reprinted in my *America Builds,* New York, 1983.

7. In 1876 Richardson was still using shingles only for the upper floors of his houses; traditionally William Ralph Emerson's J. C. Morrill house, Mount Desert, Maine, 1879, is credited with being the first completely shingled house, though McKim began to use shingles as a complete envelope in 1876.

8. J. Simpson house, *NYSB* 1 (March 1874), pl. 12.

9. Scully, *Shingle Style,* 16, n. 52.

10. Providence City Hall project, *NYSB* 1 (November 1874), pl. 41.

11. Cayuga Lake Hotel, *NYSB* 2 (April 1875), pl. 16; the original drawing is in the MM&W Archive, NYHS.

12. F. Blake, Jr., house, *NYSB* 2 (July 1875), pls. 25, 26. In the October issue of the *Sketch Book,* pl. 37, McKim published his own drawing of a chimney piece from "an old Newport house."

13. C. G. Francklyn house, *NYSB* 3 (December 1876), pl. 47. Another residence of the same period was McKim's Katherine P. Wormly house, Newport.

14. D. S. Herrick house, *AABN* 2 (June 20, 1877), 206, no. 83. Wilson has suggested that McKim may have drawn the foreground figure, judging from its similarity to those drawn by McKim for the illustrations for W. Nichols, "Misery's Pear Tree," *Scribner's* 16 (June 1878), 270–74. The originals for these illustrations are

in the MM&W Coll., Avery Library, Columbia University.

15. Sarah B. Landau to the author, August 4, 1977. The Elberon Hotel burned, 1914, but the surrounding outbuildings survive with extensive modifications. In 1876 Mead directed the careful dismantling of the Central Presbyterian Church, New York, and its reerection on West 57th Street; see "Correspondence from New York," *AABN* 1 (March 4, 1876), 78.

16. *AABN* 2 (October 27, 1877), 341.

17. Mead, "Reminiscences," Moore, *McKim,* 41. The precise date of formation of the partnership is uncertain, but mid-1877 seems certain. Although Mead indicated 1878, the rendering of the Christ Church Rectory, *AABN* 2 (November 19, 1877), 361, no. 98, drawn sometime earlier, is clearly labeled "McKim, Mead & Bigelow, Architects, 57 Broadway, New York." As of May, 1877, however, Bigelow seems not to have been a partner, judging from the diary comments of client Mrs. Thomas Dunn; see n. 28 below.

For 1877–78, McKim, Mead and Bigelow are listed separately as architects in the New York City directory; for 1879–80, they appear as a firm; and for 1880–81 the designation is McKim, Mead & White. Annie Bigelow was the daughter of Anna Maria Barton and John William Bigelow of New York; he was a highly successful merchant who maintained a summer house, Bayside, in the old section of Newport where McKim was a frequent guest as early as 1872. Here McKim became acquainted with Henry L. Higginson, Henry James, and other prominent Bostonians and New Yorkers who in later years became his clients. His marriage to Annie, then just seventeen, on October 1, 1874, was officiated by the Rev. Octavius Brooks Frothingham, whom McKim had met at Weld's school, and the Rev. William S. Child. On August 18, 1875, a daughter, Margaret, was born. Data on Annie B. Bigelow from material in the McKim-Maloney Coll., Box 36, NYHS, and Maud Howe Elliott, *This Was My Newport,* Cambridge., Mass., 1944, 103.

18. "Note-Book Sketches, by Mr. W. B. Bigelow," *NYSB* 1 (November 1874), pls. 42, 43; other drawings appeared in *NYSB* 3 (October 1876), pls. 39, 40, and 3 (November 1876), pl. 44. They are variously dated April 1873 through September 1874.

19. "Leaves from a Normandy Sketch-Book, by Mr. S. V. Stratton, Architect," *NYSB* 3 (January 1876), pls. 3, 4.

Many of the sketches are dated 1868 when McKim and Stratton were at the École together. See also the drawings by Stratton for a "Country Presbyterian Church," half-timbered, to seat 300, *NYSB* 1 (May 1874), pl. 19. Clearly McKim did what he could to help launch Stratton's career by publishing his work in the *NYSB*. In connection with Stratton, there also appeared a drawing of an "Old Oak Chest in the possession of the Stratton family," *NYSB* 3 (June 1876), pl. 24, signed and dated: "Stanford White meas. & del. May 1876." Stratton was for a very short time a partner in the second firm, for on a letter to C. A. Spofford on company letterhead, April 24, 1882, the partners are listed alphabetically—McKim, Mead, Stratton, White (File 190, Box 35, Henry Villard Papers, Baker Library, Harvard). Other correspondence, 1881–83, in the MM&W Archive, the Cass Gilbert Papers in the Minnesota State Historical Society, and the Henry Villard Papers, Houghton Library, Harvard, is on company letterhead which bears the firm name, address, and the three founders' names, with Stratton's listed below, separated by a line. During the 1880s he rented office space from the firm and appears to have operated as an adjunct partner; see my, *Building List*, xxv–xxvi, nos. 162, 295, 341, 426, 702, 733, and 894.

20. Oakswood, the Samuel Gray Ward house, is illustrated and discussed by Mariana Griswold Van Rensselaer, "Recent Architecture in America: American Country Houses," *Century* 32 (May 1886), 15–16, and (June 1886), 206–208. These two installments, part of a series of nine essays in the *Century* Magazine by Mrs. Van Rensselaer, May 1884 through July 1886, are among three sections reprinted in part in my *America Builds*, New York, 1983.

21. Robert Swain Peabody, "Georgian Homes of New England," *AABN* 2 (October 20, 1877), 338–39. This two-part essay is reprinted in my *America Builds*, New York, 1983. For Peabody's and McKim's contributions to the Colonial Revival see: Scully, *Shingle Style*, ch. 2, and Rhoads, *Colonial Revival*, passim.

22. A photograph of the library interior, Henry A. Page house, Montclair, N. J., appeared in *NYSB* 3 (April 1876), pl. 16.

23. T. Robinson house, fireplace, *NYSB* 2 (October 1875), pl. 37. Scully's suggested date of 1872 (*Shingle Style*, 56n) is corrected by the caption to the plate in *NYSB* which indicates that the work was done in the spring of 1875. See also Antoinette F. Downing and Vincent Scully, *The Architectural Heritage of Newport, Rhode Island, 1640–1915*, rev. ed., New York, 1967, 167, pl. 192. Rhoads, *Colonial Revival*, 54, notes that Clarence Cook, *The House Beautiful*, New York, 1878, praised McKim's retention of authentic eighteenth-century scale.

24. The modifications to the Dennis house were discussed in the Newport *Mercury*, April 29, 1876, 3, and the Newport *Journal*, April 29, 1876, 5; see also Wilson, "Early Work," 250–51.

25. *AABN* 2 (August 18, 1877), 262; William Rotch Ware was the nephew of architect William Robert Ware. No such drawings have come to light, but McKim did commission a portfolio of photographs of selected old Newport houses for the perusal of clients; he later presented them to William Dean Howells who in turn gave them to the Society for the Preservation of New England Antiquities (SPNEA) where they are today. See Walter Knight Sturgis, "Arthur Little and the Colonial Revival," *JSAH* 32 (May 1973), 148. For the formation of the A.I.A. committee, see *AABN* 7 (March 20, 1880), 117; for their report see *AABN* 10 (August 13, 1881), 73, and (August 20, 1881), 83–85.

26. Mead, "Reminiscences," Moore, *McKim*, 41. These drawings have not survived, apparently. The Ben Perley Poor house, Indian Hill Farm, is discussed in Josephine P. Driver, "Ben Perley Poore of Indian Hill," *Essex Institute Historical Collections* (January 1953), 2–12. It may be that sketches of Indian Hill Farm, supplied by McKim, Mead & White to Mrs. Van Rensselaer to illustrate her discussion of the advancing Colonial Revival, *Century* 10 (May 1886), 5, 20, were remnants of that trip in 1877. Also making that trip were R. S. Peabody and Arthur Little; see Holden, "Peabody Touch," 81.

27. "The Lack of an Antiquarian Spirit Among Us," *AABN* 2 (December 29, 1877), 419.

28. *AABN* 2 (July 28, 1877), 241, no. 83. McKim's unidentified preliminary sketch for the Dunn house is in the MM&W Archive, NYHS. The Dunn house design was strongly criticized by Henry Hudson Holly, "The American Style," *AABN* 2 (August 18, 1877), 267, perhaps because of Ipsen's interpretation. See also Ipsen's "Sketches from a Scrap Book," *AABN* 2 (December 22, 1877), no. 104. McKim's design was over budget and the commission was lost to George C. Mason. Although Bigelow traveled to Newport in connection with this, Mrs. Dunn's diary entries for May 1877 suggest he was then an employee rather than a partner (Diary of Mrs. Thomas Dunn, Newport Historical Society). Also Shavian in character was McKim, Mead & Bigelow's Clement W. Williams double house, Germantown, Philadelphia, 1878–79.

29. Elinor Howells to Mead, July 3, 1878, William R. Mead Coll., Amherst College, Amherst, Mass. Redtop, the Howells house, is discussed briefly in Mildred Howells, ed., *Life in Letters of William Dean Howells*, 2 vols., Garden City, N.Y., 1928, 1:244, 270; see also Ginette de B. Merrill, "Redtop and the Belmont Years of W. D. Howells and His Family," *Harvard Library Bulletin* 28 (January 1980), 33–57; and Wilson, "Early Work," 263–64. Howell's letters clearly indicate that McKim, not Mead, was the principal designer.

30. Wilson, "Early Work," 255–57; Scully, *Shingle Style*, 56–58.

31. The incorrect date of 1872–74 in Moore, *McKim*, 38–39, is pushed back even further in Wilson, "Early Work," 240–41. The correct date, 1878–79, is indicated in the detailed journal of the costs of the house kept by Prescott Hall Butler, a lawyer, with entries for purchase of the property, construction materials, and architect's fee (the journal was made available to me by Kyrill Schabert who owned the house). The land was purchased and initial building materials obtained late in 1878; a fee was paid to McKim, Mead & Bigelow in January, 1879. The frontal rendering [35] was painted about 1882–84 by White who purchased the adjoining property after his marriage in 1884. See, too, the book-

case designed by McKim for Butler, *NYSB* 3 (September 1876), pl. 35.

32. Olmsted to H. Y. Attrill, July 8, 1879, in Roper, *FLO*, 372.

33. Christ Church Rectory, *AABN* 2 (November 10, 1877), 361, no. 98. In *AABN* 2 (July 21, 1877), 234, it was noted that D. and L. Jardine, New York, were preparing designs for a frame Queen Anne parsonage for Christ Church, but the November issue carried the masonry design by the firm. The first bill sent to the parish for the rectory was dated November 27, 1878, a year later, and was a retainer only; bills based on construction costs were not sent until March through May, 1879. See, too, Esmond Shaw, "Christ's Church at the Town of Rye, in the County of Westchester and the State of New York: A Historical Review," pamphlet, Rye, [c. 1945].

34. For "Queen Anne" in England see Elizabeth Aslin, *The Aesthetic Movement: Prelude to Art Nouveau,* New York, 1969; Mark Girouard, *Sweetness and Light: The "Queen Anne" Movement, 1860–1900,* Oxford, 1977.

35. A note on the Dickerson house was published, *AABN* 2 (December 8, 1877), 394; Montgomery Schuyler, "Recent Building in New York, III," *AABN* 9 (April 23, 1881), 196, and abridged for *Harper's* 68 (September 1883), 565. Schuyler mentioned the firm's brick William Astor house, New York, 1879–81, which he felt could not be called Queen Anne "in spite of three rows of egg-and-dart moulding" at the top of the rough sandstone base. Interior views of the Dickerson house appeared in D. Appleton, *Artistic Houses,* 2 vols., New York, 1883–84, 1:81–85. Dickerson, a prominent lawyer, was a partner of Charles C. Beaman, another of the firm's clients. Dickerson's house was filled with his own patented designs for heating, ventilating, and lighting equipment. Interiors of the similar Frederick F. Thompson house, New York, 1879–81, were published in *Artistic Houses* 1:47–52; much of this interior finishing was designed by Stanford White after he joined the firm, and Schuyler thought this house better than Dickerson's because of the greater simplicity.

36. Albert Bush-Brown, *Louis Sullivan,* New York, 1960, fig. 8. Among the residents of the Benedict were Albert Pinkham Ryder and Joseph Morrill Wells.

37. The firm's Union League Club entry appeared in *AABN* 5 (June 7, 1877), 180, no. 180; see too *AABN* 6 (August 32, 1879), no. 191, for Bruce Price's entry. For a history of the Union League Club see Reginald Townsend, *Mother of Clubs,* New York, 1936. McKim, Mead & Bigelow were not breaking altogether new ground in turning to Renaissance sources; they had been preceded by George B. Post in his Chickering Hall, Manhattan, 1874–75, the Williamsburg Bank, Brooklyn, 1875, and most especially in the Long Island Historical Society, Brooklyn, 1877–79. See Winston Weisman, "The Commercial Architecture of George B. Post," *JSAH* 31 (October 1972), 176–203; Russell Sturgis, "A Review of the Work of George B. Post," *ARec,* Great American Architects Series, June 1898.

38. Mrs. A. C. Alden house, *AABN* 5 (August 30, 1879), 69, no. 192. About 1882 the house passed to Mrs. Alden's daughter, Mrs. Richard Derby, and her husband, who

for many years were McKim's landlords in New York; see Moore, *McKim,* 47, 166. The house is described in John W. Matheson, *An Historic Sketch of Fort Hill, Lloyd Neck, Long Island,* privately printed, c. 1917; see also M. G. Van Rensselaer, *Century* 10 (July 1886), 432–33.

39. See Bigelow's Methodist Church, Seabright, N.J., *AABN* 26 (November 9, 1889), 218, no. 724. Construction of the Alden house began in July 1879, and by October White had been put in charge of finishing the interiors, judging from notation in the firm's bill books. As the partnership was gradually dissolving during the summer of 1879, Bigelow did several houses on his own, among them the William H. Vanderbilt house, Lowmoor, N.J., published in George W. Sheldon, ed., *Artistic Country Seats,* 2 vols., New York, 1886–87. Sheldon suggests Bigelow alone was responsible for the J. M. Cornell house, Monmouth Beach, N.J., 1879, and this is supported by Bigelow's signature for receipt of payment in the bill books, August 4, 1879.

40. As to the reasons for Annie McKim's suit for divorce, there seems to have been a conspiracy of silence; the decree was noted in the Newport *Mercury,* November 8, 1879, but no information has surfaced in the McKim-Maloney Coll., NYPL. Curiously, no scandal attached to either party. Annie Bigelow McKim later married a prominent Newport Unitarian minister, the Rev. John W. Day (Moore, *McKim,* 43). McKim moved into the inner circles of Beacon Hill society in Boston, precisely that group which, in 1896, forced Ernest Fenollosa's dismissal from the Boston Museum of Fine Arts when he divorced his wife and remarried; see Walter Muir Whitehill, "The Making of an Architectural Masterpiece," *American Art Journal* 2 (Fall 1970), 32.

41. For the European trip see Baldwin, *White,* 63–101. White's letters home are preserved in a scrapbook, with typescript copies, kept by Robert White, Saint James, N. Y., and are quoted nearly in full in Baldwin.

42. D. Maitland Armstrong, *Day Before Yesterday,* New York, 1920, 283. A memento of this jaunt, John Singer Sargent's *Luxembourg Gardens at Twilight,* c. 1878 (oil on canvas, Minneapolis Institute of Arts), is inscribed, "to my friend McKim, John S. Sargent."

43. This and subsequent passages describing the McKim–Saint-Gaudens–White excursion are quoted from White's letters, dated August 20 to September 12, 1878, reprinted in Baldwin, *White,* 76–84.

44. Saint-Gaudens, *Reminiscences,* 1:224–25.

45. The drawings were later arranged and mounted by Lawrence Grant White, filling six large folios, and a selection published by L. G. White, *Sketches and Designs by Stanford White,* New York, 1920. The better finished drawings were later sold, but many sketches are still retained by Robert White, Saint James, N.Y.

46. Two of White's scrapbooks, containing photographs of French and Colonial American architecture, are preserved by the White family, Saint James, N.Y. According to inventories of the firm's library prepared in the 1920s, there were originally exactly 100 of these scrapbooks, containing photographs, sketches, notes, and other material surveying architecture around the world, but with a heavy concentration on antiquity

and the Renaissance. Each of the partners, and Wells also, had personal scrapbooks. Two scrapbooks are at Saint James, and five photographic scrapbooks are in the MM&W Coll., Avery Library, Columbia University; the remainder are now lost.

47. See Jean Schopfer, "Wooden Houses in France during the Middle Ages," *ARec* 9 (April 1900), 333–62, in which the Rouen house is illustrated.

48. Bigelow practiced independently until 1900, when he entered partnership with Frank E. Wallis and Leslie Cotton; his work appeared periodically in *AABN*. See Dennis Steadman Francis, *Architects in Practice, New York City, 1840–1900*, n.p., c. 1980 (for the Committee for the Preservation of Architectural Records). About 1918 Bigelow made the acquaintance of Lewis Mumford, who credits him with much information that appeared in *The Brown Decades*, New York, 1931, rev. ed., 1971, 115.

49. The epigram, quoted in Moore, *McKim*, 46, about White's drawing like "a house afire" may be apocryphal. The dates of White's return from France and the formation of McKim, Mead & White come from let-ters between White and Saint-Gaudens, September 9 and October 17, 1879, Saint-Gaudens Coll., Dartmouth College, Hanover, N.H., published in Homer Saint-Gaudens, "Intimate Letters of Augustus Saint-Gaudens," *ARec* 30 (September 1911), 287, 291. H. Van Buren Magonigle, "A Half Century of Architecture," *Pencil Points* 13 (March 1934), 116, claims that Bigelow left the office June 2, 1879.

50. S. White to his mother, from Boston, n.d., "Sunday, 1873," Stanford White Coll., NYHS. He writes he has been superintending construction of the Springfield courthouse for Richardson; the rainy weather in Boston depressed nearly as much as the Boston City Hall, "the last enough to make a man sad."

51. For a contemporary account of the history of architecture in New York City, see "A Review of Building in New York City," and "A Review of Architecture," in *A History of Real Estate, Building, and Architecture in New York City*, New York, 1898 (new ed., 1967); see also: *Miller's New York As It Is*, New York, 1866; James D. McCabe, Jr., *Lights and Shadows of New York Life*, Philadelphia, 1872.

Chapter 3. A NEW FIRM, 1879–1886

1. L. G. White, *Sketches and Designs*, 15.

2. H. Van Buren Magonigle, "A Half Century in Architecture," *Pencil Points* 13 (March 1934), 116, 226; royal Cortissoz, *The Painter's Craft*, New York, 1930, 429; C. Howard Walker, "The Influence of McKim," *Brickbuilder* 19 (February 1910), 50; letter, William A. Boring to Charles Moore, n.d. but about 1927, CM-LC (quoted in Moore, *McKim*, 57–58). See too, Goldwin Goldsmith, "I remember McKim, Mead & White," *JAIA* 13 (April 1950), 168–72.

3. Granger, *McKim*, 103; Hill, *McKim: the Man*, 16.

4. Henry Bacon, "Charles Follen McKim—A Character Sketch," *Brickbuilder* 19 (February 1910), 38–47.

5. Magonigle, "Half Century," 116.

6. Bacon, "Character Sketch," 39, 44.

7. Royal Cortissoz, "Some Critical Reflections on the Architectural Genius of Charles F. McKim," *Brickbuilder* 19 (February 1910), 23; Granger, *McKim*, 6. This attitude toward materials and workmanship the partners also learned from Richardson. As Olmsted recalled Richardson telling him, "never, never, till the thing is in stone beyond recovery, should the slightest indisposition be indulged to review, reconsider, and revise every particle of [the] work" (quoted in Van Rensselaer, *Richardson*, 1888, 118–19).

8. Bacon, "Character Sketch," 45–47; Granger, *McKim*, 112.

9. Magonigle, "Half Century," 116 (see also ch. 5, n. 142). Paul-Marie Letarouilly, *Edifices de Rome moderne . . .*, text and 3 vols. of plates, Paris, 1843–57; the crisp engraved plates served as models of draftsmanship in the office; Bacon, "Character Sketch," 47. Richardson also acquired a large library used freely by his assistants; see Hitchcock, *Richardson*, 72, 101–02, 139, 182, and O'Gorman, *Richardson: Drawings*, 8–13. The library of McKim, Mead & White has been dispersed, making it difficult to reconstruct its composition during 1890–1910. A few volumes are still retained by the successor firm, Cain, Farrell & Bell, New York, but large portions were removed in 1957–58, when a significant number of volumes were donated to Amherst College; at that time an inventory was prepared and various versions of this exist at Amherst College and in the MM&W Archive, NYHS. Based on these, it is possible to estimate that around 1900 the library numbered 2,500 volumes. Several technical volumes, such as Guadet's *Eléments et théorie de l'architecture*, were given to Ann White Buttrick, Stanford's granddaughter and an architect in her own right, New York City.

10. Hill, *McKim: the Man*, 29.

11. Cortissoz, "Reflections," 33; Moore, *Burnham*, 1:65.

12. Hill, *McKim: the Man*, 23–24.

13. Robert Swain Peabody, "A Tribute," *Brickbuilder* 19 (February 1910), 56.

14. William Dean Howells, *The Rise of Silas Latham*, Boston, 1885, chs. 3, 10, 24.

15. White, *Sketches and Designs*, 40.

16. Cortissoz, *Painter's Craft*, 499.

17. L. G. White, *Sketches and Designs*, 15.

18. See Baldwin, *White*, vii, 1–7, 261–68; Richard Harding Davis, "Stanford White," *Colliers*, August 4, 1906, 17; John Jay Chapman, "McKim, Mead & White," *Vanity Fair* 13 (September 1919), 37, 102, 104.

19. See Bernard S. Perlman, *The Immortal Eight*, New York, 1962, 110–11. There are many letters from Shinn and other artists to White in the Stanford White Collection, Manuscript Division, NYHS.

20. Chapman, "McKim, Mead & White," 102.

21. Edward Simmons, *From Seven to Seventy: Memories of a Painter and a Yankee*, New York, 1922, 238–39. See also F. L. V. Hoppin, "Stanford White as those trained in his office knew him," *Brickbuilder* 15 (De-

cember 1906), 245–46; other articles from this issue dedicated to White's work are cited below.

22. Magonigle, "Half Century," 118, 116–17. A similar description of White's method is found in Egerton Swartwout, "An Architectural Decade," typescript in the office of Cain, Farrell & Bell, New York, which deals with Swartwout's years in the McKim, Mead & White office, 1892–1900.

23. See Phillip Sawyer, "Stanford White . . . ," and Albert Randolph Ross, "Stanford White . . . ," *Brickbuilder* 15 (December 1906), 247, 246. Eero Saarinen worked much the same way, heedless of the hour or energy expended, and this may partly explain why he and his wife, Aline, became so interested in White, beginning a biographical study which remained largely unwritten at the time of Aline Saarinen's early death; the biography has been taken up by Brendan Gill. See Aline Saarinen, "The Splendid World of Stanford White," *Life* 61 (September 16, 1966), 87–108.

24. Magonigle, "Half Century," 116.

25. R. G. White to Alexina White, dated only "July" but about 1880, RGW-NYHS.

26. Ross, "Stanford White," 246.

27. J. Monroe Hewlett, "Stanford White . . . ," *Brickbuilder* 15 (December 1906), 245; Sawyer, "Stanford White," 247; W. A. Boring to C. Moore, in Moore, *McKim*, 57–58.

28. The original agreement, handwritten (by Mead?), on yellow foolscap, is in a scrapbook kept by Laura White, Saint James, and is reproduced in my *McKim, Mead & White . . . Building List*, xiii–xiv.

29. See, for example, *Art Age* 3 (December 1885), 86–87, and 3 (January 1886), 100. The first issue cited contains a note that White alone was the architect of the William Edgar house, Newport, while the second carried White's protest that "no member of our firm is ever individually responsible for any design which goes out from it." Both Granger, *McKim*, 7, and Reilly, *McKim, Mead & White*, 24, stress that it is impossible to speak of a building as being the work of only one of the partners.

30. Phillip Sawyer, *Edward Palmer York*, Stonington, Conn., 1951, 17–27; Magonigle, "A Half Century of Architecture," *Pencil Points* 13 (May 1934), 226; and "Half Century . . . ," *Pencil Points* 13 (March 1934), 116. See also Swartwout, "Architectural Decade," 95.

31. For the Colonial American sources of the Shingle Style see Vincent Scully, *The Shingle Style*, New Haven, 1955. The European connection, noted in my dissertation, is illustrated in Richard W. Longstreth, "Academic Eclecticism in American Architecture," *Winterthur Portfolio* 17 (Spring 1982), 55–82. White's photograph scrapbooks at Saint James and Album XIV, Book of Photographs, Charles F. McKim," MM&W Coll., Avery Library, both contain scores of snapshots of rural French and German buildings covered in slate which has the character of shingle.

32. For the appearance of the casino and country club, beginning with the country club in Brookline, Mass., see: Casper W. Whitney, "Evolution of the Country Club," *Harper's Magazine* 90 (December 1894), 16–33; Robert Dunn, "The Country Club: A National Expression," *Outing* 47 (November 1905), 160–74.

33. For Stewart Hartshorn (1840–1937) see: *NCAB* 28:208 and 36:480; and the New York *Times*, January 13, 1937, 18. For Short Hills see Cora L. Hartshorn, "A Little History of the Short Hills Section of Millburn Township, N. J., developed by Stewart Hartshorn," 1946, reprinted by the Millburn-Short Hills Historical Society, Short Hills, 1979.

34. For the first phase of building in Short Hills see "An American Park," *AABN* 16 (July 12, 1884), 15–16, no. 446. See also Montgomery Schuyler, "Some Suburbs of New York, I: New Jersey," *Lippincott's* 8 (July 1884), 23; and *Sticks, Shingles and Stones: The History and Architecture of Stewart Hartshorn's Ideal Community . . . ,* Short Hills, N. J., 1980.

35. The underscored entries of White's name in the bill books for the Short Hills Music Hall suggest this may have been one of his first responsibilities in the office. The tower and wooden arch may have been suggested by rural French building White had just seen, such as the Château de Plecis Macé near Angers, White's drawing of which was reproduced in L. G. White, *Sketches and Designs*, pls. 1, 13. The Music Hall was published in George W. Sheldon, *Artistic Country Seats: Types of Recent American Villa and Cottage Architecture*, 2 vols., New York, 1886–87 (new ed., New York, 1979), 1:116. This important source was emphasized in Scully's *Shingle Style*; nearly all of the shingled work discussed here is also covered in Scully's seminal study which should be consulted. The auditorium of the Music Hall is shown in Van Rensselaer, "Recent Architecture," *Century* 28 (July 1884), 331–32, with a musical rehearsal in progress.

36. For the Newport Casino see *Artistic Country Seats* 1:67–70; *Monograph* 1:1. The idea for a casino arose as early as 1874, and was noted in the New York *Times*, February 8, 1874, 4, but no steps were taken until Bennett took up the project. Progress in development of the firm's plans is noted in the Newport *Mercury*, August 30, and October 25, 1879; the final approval of plans is noted in the Newport *Mercury*, January 10, 1880. The first entry in the bill books for the casino is February 1, 1880, for a percentage of the construction contract for $64,000. Extant, the building has been modified following a fire in 1953. See William H. Jordy and Christopher P. Monkhouse, *Buildings on Paper: Rhode Island Architectural Drawings, 1825–1940*, Providence, R. I., 1982, 111–12; and also Van Rensselaer, "Recent Architecture," *Century* 28 (May 1884), 327–30.

37. See the Tabard Inn and Stores, Bedford Park, by R. N. Shaw, 1877–80, *Building News* 38 (January 25, 1880), 10; and Andrew Saint, *Richard Norman Shaw*, New Haven, 1976, 208.

38. For the H. Victor Newcomb house see *Artistic Country Seats* 2:95; and Van Rensselaer, "Recent Architecture," *Century* 32 (June 1886), 210–17. The house burned to the foundation line and has been rebuilt as a French château.

39. For the R. Percy Alden house see Van Rensselaer, "Recent Architecture," *Century* 32 (July 1886), 430.

40. See F. L. Olmsted, Jr., and T. Kimball, *Frederick Law Olmsted, Landscape Architect, 1822–1903*, 2 vols., New York, 1922, 1:2. Olmsted had worked with Dr. Agnew on the Sanitary Commission during the Civil War. I

must thank Mrs. Arline Momeyer who occupies the DeForest house and who introduced me to the other residents of the complex.

41. For the Isaac Bell house see: *Artistic Country Seats* 1:23–27; and *Le Moniteur des Architectes* n.s. 11 (1897), pls. 25, 26. For the Goelet house, Southside, see *Artistic Country Seats* 1:7–10; *AABN* 22 (July 2, 1887), 7, no. 601.

42. For the C. McCormick house, Clayton Lodge, see Scully, *Shingle Style*, 136–37; Wayne Andrews, *Battle for Chicago*, New York, 1946, 112–13. The greatly dilapidated house was razed about 1955, but the stables so far have survived.

43. White apparently saw such stucco panels during the sketching trip of 1877; Hitchcock, *Richardson*, 238, notes that samples have been preserved at the Essex Institute, Salem, Mass.; sketches by White showing such decorative work are kept by Robert White at the Davis Gallery, New York.

44. The Osborn house, until recently a yacht club, burned in May 1971. See *Artistic Country Seats* 1:1–5; the *Monograph* 1:12–14; and Van Rensselaer, "Recent Architecture," *Century* 32 (May 1886), 3. Various clippings, including a large article from the *Magazine of Art*, May 1885, are found in the Scrapbook, MM&W Archive, NYHS.

45. For the Narragansett Pier Casino, see *Artistic Country Seats* 1:5–7; the *Monograph* 1:16; "Narragansett and its Casino," *Harper's Weekly* 31 (August 27, 1887), 609, 611; and Jordy and Monkhouse, *Buildings on Paper*, 112–13. Although Scully, *Shingle Style*, 132–34, says that the casino was started in 1881, bill book entries show that travel expenses to the site did not begin until October 1883, and Moore, *McKim*, 319, indicates that plans were accepted September 26, 1883; Eugenia B. Smith, "Rhode Island Architecture of McKim, Mead & White," Master's thesis, University of Wisconsin, 1964, 74, quotes the minutes of the South Kensington town meeting, October 8, 1883, in which permission was granted to build an arch over the coast road. Frederick Law Olmsted was consulted by McKim in landscaping the grounds; see Olmsted and Kimball, *Olmsted*, 1:27. The firm also designed several adjacent cottages for Louis Sherry in 1894, and in 1904–05 added a second casino there for him. All of this is now gone, victim of fire and hurricane, except for the masonry arch over the road and the small masonry lifesaving station about 100 feet south of the arch, built by McKim, Mead & White in 1889.

46. Recounted in Reilly, *McKim, Mead & White*, 20, who says this was told him by an unnamed colleague of McKim's.

47. For the Cook house, see *Artistic Country Seats*, 1:57–60. The partners traveled extensively in the United States, and it was common practice for the partner on the road to visit and inspect whatever buildings might be under construction along his route, whether he was the partner in charge or not. Each of the partners also made annual or semiannual trips to Europe as well. Letters exchanged during these trips appear throughout McKim's letterbooks, LC, and many are published in Moore, *McKim*, passim.

48. See Scully, *Shingle Style*, 134–54; Antoinette Downing and Vincent Scully, *The Architectural Heritage of New-port, Rhode Island, 1640–1915*, 2nd ed., New York, 1967, 162–64; *Artistic Country Seats*, passim.

49. For the Skinner house see Downing and Scully, *Newport*, 166; for the Osborn gate lodge see the *Monograph* 1:13; L. G. White, *Sketches and Designs*, pl. 30; and Van Rensselaer, "Recent Architecture," *Century* 32 (May 1886), 3. For the Cresson house, see *Artistic Country Seats* 2:179; *AABN* 18 (November 21, 1885), 257, no. 517. Of particular interest, too, is the expansive summer house, Rohallion, for Edward Dean Adams, Sea bright, N. J., 1886–88, 1890.

50. William G. Low, a lawyer, was the half-brother of Seth Low, president of Columbia University and later mayor of New York. Despite the great attention recently given to the Low house as a harbinger of modern architecture, the house apparently was never published at the time it was designed and built and was known to only a handful of New York architects who could have seen the drawings, particularly Babb, Cook & Willard (see Scully, *Shingle Style*, 152–53). An undated letter, c. 1886 (CFM-LC), from White to McKim, indicates that the commission was initially White's but was taken over by McKim because of the pressure of office business; the design of the house, now seen as so important, is not attributed to White either by his son in *Sketches and Designs*, nor by Baldwin, nor does it appear in the attribution list prepared by Kendall and approved by Mead in 1920 (see my *McKim, Mead & White . . . Building List*, 3. Fortunately, before the house was wantonly destroyed in the mid-1950s, it was recorded by the Historic American Buildings Survey.

51. For the Davis house, clippings from the Brooklyn *Advance*, March 1885, 308–309, and the New York *World*, April 26, 1885, are preserved in the Scrapbook, MM&W Archive, NYHS. For the Metcalf house see *Artistic Country Seats* 2:95; and the *Buffalo Real Estate & Builders Monthly* for January 1886, 3. Unfortunately, because of greatly deteriorated structural condition, the Metcalf house was demolished, but not before it was completely recorded and the principal ground-floor interiors had been salvaged for the Metropolitan Museum of Art, New York, for eventual incorporation in the American Wing.

52. There are no entries in the firm's bill books for the Wolfe house. McKim lost the commission to Peabody & Stearns whose design was published in *ARec* 1 (October–December 1891), 195. A drawing for McKim's project survives in the MM&W Archive, NYHS, and bears a faint inscription from McKim to Henry Bacon; it is illustrated in Bacon, "Character Sketch," 47.

53. For the Choate house see *Artistic Country Seats* 2:-153–54; *AABN* 24 (December 29, 1888), 300, no. 679. The Scrapbook, MM&W Archive, NYHS, contains various clippings from the Berkshire *Courier* for June 3, 10, and 17, 1885, and October 27, 1886. The notice in the New York *Tribune*, October 17, 1886, in the Scrapbook, is reprinted in Baldwin, *White*, 177. F. L. Olmsted was consulted for landscaping the grounds.

54. Schuyler, "Recent Building in New York," 466; *AABN* 9 (April 23, 1881), 196.

55. Schuyler, "Recent Building in New York," 466.

Schuyler's negative assessment was the inverse of that of Russell Sturgis, who thought the facade original and "a relief"; see his "McKim, Mead & White," *ARec* Great American Architects Series, May 1895, 61–62. See *Building* 5 (October 9, 1886), 175; interiors of the Barney house were discussed in the New York *Sun*, January 14, 1883, 2, and are illustrated in Van Rensselaer, "Recent Architecture," *Century* 31 (March 1886), 681–84. The library of the Barney house is credited to George Fletcher Babb, who was then in the office.

56. The Drayton house is variously attributed to White (New York *Sun*, January 14, 1883, 3; and *Artistic Houses* 2:41) or to McKim (Schuyler, *AABN* [April 23, 1881] 196). See also Sturgis, "McKim, Mead & White," 61; for a number of years Sturgis mistakenly believed the Drayton house to be Richardson's work. The exterior is illustrated and discussed in Van Rensselaer, "Recent Architecture," *Century* 31 (February 1886), 554. For general background on the urban townhouse see Charles Lockwood, *Bricks and Brownstone: The New York Rowhouse*, New York, 1972; Sarah B. Landau, "The Row Houses of New York's West Side," *JSAH* 34 (March 1975), 19–36; Montgomery Schuyler, "The Small City House in New York," *ARec* 19 (February 1906), 83–103.

57. Charles Moore relates that he often accompanied McKim on these twilight walks; Moore, *Burnham* 1:-116.

58. For the Whittier house see Hitchcock, *Richardson*, 218; the *Monograph* 1:13; and *AABN* 14 (November 24, 1883), 246, no. 246. O'Gorman, *Richardson: Drawings*, 76–77, indicates that Richardson received the commission for his half of the complex in February 1881. The interiors of the Whittier house were discussed and illustrated in Van Rensselaer, "Recent Architecture," *Century* 31 (March 1886), 679–80; *Artistic Houses* 1:122–24. The basic history of development of the Back Bay area is Bainbridge Bunting, *Houses of Boston's Back Bay*, Cambridge, Mass., 1967. Besides their own European sketches and snapshots, which they certainly consulted for details, a number of illustrated studies had recently been published: C. Sauvageot, *Palais, châteaux, hôtels, et maisons de la France*, Paris, 1867; Eyrie, *Châteaux historiques de la France*, 2 vols., Paris, 1877–79; and L. Paustre, *La Renaissance en France*, 3 vols., Paris, 1877–85.

59. For the Winans house, now a cluster of doctors' and dentists' offices, see the *Monograph* 1:2; *AABN* 21 (April 30, 1887), 210, no. 592. After 1883, such François Ier allusions were rarely employed by the firm, one exception being the large summer house for Mrs. Mark Hopkins near Great Barrington, Mass., 1885–86; this may have been at the insistence of the client.

60. For the Tiffany house complex see: Charles DeKay, *The Art Work of Louis C. Tiffany*, New York, 1914, 57; the *Monograph* 1:5, 5A; *ARec* 10 (October 1900), 191–202; *AABN* 20 (July 17, 1886), 30, no. 551; *Carpentry and Building* 11 (November 1889), 220. The interiors of the house are discussed and illustrated in: Robert Koch, *Louis C. Tiffany, Rebel in Glass*, 2nd ed., New York, 1966, 63, 95–99; *AABN* 22 (December 10, 1887), 278, no. 624. For the metal frame of the roof see *Carpentry and Building* 7 (August 1885), 152–53. An article from the

New York *World*, March 29, 1884, one of many in the Scrapbook, MM&W Archive, NYHS, is partially quoted in Baldwin, *White*, 122. White's independent work in designing the balcony for the Seventh Regiment Armory for Tiffany and the Associated Artists is noted in Koch, *Tiffany, Rebel*, 14–16, 36–37.

61. Sources once suggested for the Tiffany houses are many: Van Rensselaer, "Recent Architecture," *Century* 31 (January 1886), 556–57, was vague; but the *Sanitary Engineer* 11 (April 9, 1885), 395, proposed the Low Countries; Russell Sturgis, "McKim, Mead & White," 55, said it resembled German townhouses of the sixteenth and seventeenth centuries; Edmund Gosse, *The Critic* 3 (January 24, 1885), 35, said it reminded him of a large Swiss chalet. Much more probable as inspiration is Richard Norman Shaw's Clock House, 8 Chelsea Embankment, London, published in *The Builder* 37 (December 27, 1879), for which see Andrew Saint, *Richard Norman Shaw* (New Haven, 1976), 230–31. Louis C. Tiffany, who apparently had the deciding voice in the design of the house, may have been thinking, too, of H. H. Richardson's Trinity Rectory, Boston, 1879–80. The client of record, Charles L. Tiffany, whom the firm billed, did not move into the lower apartments; they were leased by the Villards upon their return from Germany in 1887.

62. For The Percival, built for O. F. Thompson, see *The Graphic* 15 (January 1883).

63. For the King rowhouse group see Schuyler, "Small City House," 383–85; *Brickbuilder* 7 (March 1898), 65.

64. Arthur D. Gilman, "Architecture in the United States," *North American Review* 58 (1844), 450–53. An early, rather Renaissance house for John Hare Powell, Philadelphia, 1850–51, involved the contributions of several architects including McArthur, Button, and Upjohn; see Charles B. Wood, "The John Hare Powell House," *JSAH* 26 (May 1967), 148–53. This, and the Federal buildings of Ammi B. Young, may have had some impact on McKim; see Lawrence Wodehouse, "Ammi Burnham Young, 1798–1874," *JSAH* 25 (December 1966), 268–80. A striking coincidence to the Villard complex is the well-detailed and novelly arranged Pension Office Building, Washington, D.C., 1882–86, by Montgomery C. Miegs; this, with the Villard group, marks the beginning of the archaeologically correct Renaissance "revival."

65. The German Savings Bank is illustrated in Nathan Singer, *Lost New York*, Boston, 1967, 165. See Post's domed Renaissance submission for the Connecticut State Capitol competition in George L. Hersey, "Replication Replicated," *Perspecta* 9/10 (1965), 223.

66. For biographical information on Villard see *DAB* 19: 273–74; James B. Hedges, *Henry Villard and the Railways of the Northwest*, New Haven, 1930; and Henry Villard, *Memoirs of Henry Villard*, 2 vols., New York, 1902, which concentrates on his journalism and railroad careers. For Thorwood, at Dobbs Ferry, see Van Rensselaer, "Recent Architecture," *Century* 32 (May 1886), 6–7, where two interiors are illustrated. Various photographs and miscellaneous papers relating to Thorwood are in the Oswald Garrison Villard Papers, bMS AM 1323, Box 90, Houghton Library, Harvard University. See also Mosette G. Broderick and Wil-

liam C. Shopsin, *The Villard Houses: Life Story of a Landmark,* New York, 1980.

67. For various accounts of how the Villard houses were designed, see Moore, *McKim,* 47–48; Villard, *Memoirs,* 2:315–21; and Scully, *Shingle Style,* 146–49. The most detailed account is presented in Broderick and Shopsin, *Villard Houses,* which contains quoted material making it clear that Villard personally devised the U-shaped plan of the block with an entrance court at the center. All of Villard's building projects had such plan arrangements, including the stations for Portland and Tacoma, the hotels in Portland and Tacoma (which had H-shaped plans), and even the second hotel in Tacoma, 1891–1906, by Hewitt & Hewitt of Philadelphia (later modified for use as the high school).

68. Biographical information on Wells from: C. Howard Walker, "Joseph Wells, Architect," *ARec* 66 (July 1929), 15–18; Magonigle, "Half Century," 223–24; Royal Cortissoz, *Art and Common Sense,* New York, 1913, 419–20; Cortissoz, *Painter's Craft,* 433; Baldwin, *White,* 230, 357–68; Will H. Low, *A Chronicle of Friendships,* New York, 1908, 275–77; Scully, *Shingle Style,* 147; Joseph M. Wells File, Box M-3, 1968 Coll., MM&W Archive, NYHS (this contains clippings of obituary notices from the New York *Star,* New York *Evening Post,* and the New York *Times,* February 4, 1890); and obituary notice by C. H. W. *AABN* 27 (February 8, 1890), 95. See the drawings for R. M. Hunt's Martin L. Brimmer house, Boston, signed by J. M. Wells, in *AABN* 2 (January 1877), no. 57.

69. William Mitchell Kendall to Royal Cortissoz, June 22, 1928, Wells File, Box M-3, 1968 Coll., MM&W Archive, NYHS, reprinted in Walker, "Wells," 18.

70. Four letters, J. M. Wells to S. White, dated: Paris, August 1, 1880; Paris, October 10, 1880; Florence, January 18, 1881; Florence, January 24, 1881. The originals are preserved in the Stanford White Collection, Manuscript Division, NYHS; they are quoted in part in Baldwin, *White,* 364–67, but the deletions are not indicated, with the result that Wells's use of "Renaissance," meaning French Renaissance (François Ier), is not made clear. The reference to White's higher regard of Italian architecture is deleted from Baldwin's quote. Wells, having written to White that he thought Italian architecture "ill adapted for our domestic country," seems an unlikely candidate to have been given *carte blanche* to redesign the important Villard houses as a palazzo. By 1887, however, Wells's views had changed radically, as indicated by these epigrams from his diary, reprinted in Baldwin, *White,* 361–64:

January 21, 1887: "In architecture, individuality of style is at best a doubtful merit, and in a great majority of cases a positive (if not fatal) defect or weakness."

May 2, 1887: "The classic ideal suggests clearness, simplicity, grandeur, order and philosophical calm—consequently it delights my soul. The medieval ideal suggests superstition, ignorance, vulgarity, restlessness, cruelty and religion—all of which fill my soul with horror and loathing. The Renaissance ideal suggests a fine and cultivated society, with its crowds of gay ladies and gentlemen devoted to the pleasures and elegances of life—which excites my admiration, but

not my sympathies. It is inconceivable to me how any civilized architect can design in the Romanesque or Gothic styles. The absurdity of such a proceeding is immediately evident in painting or sculpture. Why should it not be so in architecture."

71. See Moore, *McKim,* 49, n. 1.

72. Oswald Garrison Villard recalled the drilling in an interview, New York *Sun,* February 25, 1946 (Oswald Garrison Villard Papers, bMS AM 1323, Box 90, Houghton Library, Harvard University). Besides building his own wing of the complex, Villard paid for finishing the court and the decorative iron fence. For the Villard house complex see: the *Monograph* 1:7–11; *Artistic Houses* 2:161–63; Van Rensselaer, "Recent Architecture," *Century* 31 (March 1886), 685; *Building* 2 (December 1883), 38, and 8 (June 1888), 193; *AABN* 22 (December 24, 1887), 302, no. 626. Notices appeared in European journals as well: "A New York Palace," *The Architect* 31 (January 12, 1884), 34; John B. Gass, "Two New York Houses," *Building News* 52 (June 17, 1887), 905–06; "Cheminée hôtel de M. Henry Villard à New York," *Le Moniteur des architectes* n.s. 2 (1888), pl. 19. Concerning the plumbing see George E. Waring, "The Drainage of the Villard House," *AABN* 16 (August 16, 1884), 78, no. 451. There are a number of clippings concerning the Villard group in the Scrapbook, MM&W Archive, NYHS; also in the archive is an album of photographs of the Villard house and interiors taken about 1884–85. For assessments of the Villard house complex see: Scully, *Shingle Style,* 146–47; Hitchcock, *Richardson,* 290–92; H.-R. Hitchcock, "Frank Lloyd Wright and the Academic Tradition of the Early Eighteen-Nineties," *Journal of the Warburg and Courtauld Institutes* 7 (1944), 52–53; Peter C. Neger, "Italian Renaissance Revival Architecture in America: The Villard Houses, 1882–85," *American Art Review* 3 (September–October 1976), 118–28. After serving the Whitelaw Reids, who had purchased the Villard wing and had it enlarged by McKim, Mead & White, the separate units were purchased by the Archdiocese of New York and Random House. When Random House vacated their section in 1967, the future of the complex seemed jeopardized. Critic Ada Louise Huxtable noted that schemes were afoot for "development" of the property, New York *Times* February 14, 1971, Section 2, 25. When developer Harry Helmsley and his architect Emery Roth and Sons proposed demolishing significant sections of the complex to provide for a luxury hotel to be attached to the rear, there went up howls of protest; see the commentary by Ada Louise Huxtable and Robert Goldberger in the New York *Times:* December 9, 1974, 54; January 5, 1975, Section 2, 29; January 26, 1975, Section 2, 30; January 31, 1975, 37; June 6, 1975, 35; June 22, 1975, 31; September 21, 1975, Section 2, 31; June 17, 1976, 37. The grandson and great-grandson of Henry Villard also wrote and testified in behalf of more sympathetic use of the building; see New York *Times,* December 11, 1974, 90; February 10, 1975, 26. Helmsley's Palace Hotel was built, but the entire north and south wings were retained, and Villard's own section was adapted as dining rooms, although the two small center units, once occupied by Artemas Holmes and Edward Dean

Adams, were removed to provide entry into the hotel from Madison Avenue. The stair hall of the E. D. Adams house, however, was removed for the Metropolitan Museum of Art.

73. See Broderick and Shopsin, *Villard Houses*, 86–111.

74. See Letarouilly, *Rome Moderne*, 1:79–90; Hitchcock believes McKim brought a copy of this back with him from France in 1870 (H.-R. Hitchcock, *Rhode Island Architecture*, Providence, R. I., 1939, 59). Other standard references on Italian Renaissance architecture included: A.-H.-V. Grandjean de Montigny, and A.-P. Famin, *Architecture toscane*, Paris, 1815; Percier and Fontaine, *Choix des plus célèbres maisons . . . de Rome*, Paris, 1824; and G. B. Vignola, *Oeuvre complet de . . . Vignola*, Paris, 1812, among others.

75. The Villard interiors are illustrated in Broderick and Shopsin, *Villard Houses*, 62–85, 112–23, using photographs from the album, MM&W Archive, NYHS. Comparison of the relatively restrained Villard interiors with the far more elaborate interiors of the A. T. Stewart house or the W. H. Vanderbilt house is most telling; see *Artistic Houses*, where these and others are illustrated.

76. For the interiors completed by the Whitelaw Reids and for modifications to the house done for them by McKim, Mead & White, see Broderick and Shopsin, *Villard Houses*, 112–23.

77. Information on the various Northern Pacific buildings is drawn from Villard's personal and business correspondence at the Houghton and Baker libraries, Harvard University; the Northern Pacific Railroad Archives, Minnesota Historical Society, Saint Paul; Northern Pacific Railroad papers at the Oregon Historical Society, Portland; and the Washington (State) Historical Society, Tacoma. For the Portland buildings see also Marion D. Ross, "Architecture in Oregon, 1845–1895," *Oregon Historical Quarterly* 57 (March 1956), 61–64. Also useful are: Herbert D. Croly, "Portland, Oregon: the transformation of the city from an architectural and social viewpoint," *ARec* 31 (June 1912), 591–607; Robert C. Sweat, "The Architecture of the Pacific Northwest," *ARec* 26 (September 1909), 166–75; "Notable Examples of Architecture . . . in Portland," *Western Architect* 59 (March 1919), 56–57; M. D. Ross, "125 Years of Building," *JAIA* 49 (June 1968), 120–26; Portland Chapter, AIA, *Guide to Portland Architecture*, Portland, 1968; Thomas Vaughan and George A. McMath, *A Century of Portland Architecture*, Portland, 1967; and Thomas Vaughan and Virginia G. Ferriday, *Space, Style, and Structure*, 2 vols., Portland, 1974, 2:374–75. The Portland station, like the hotel, was to have a rough stone base, with upper walls covered with pebble dash stucco with brick quoins, a treatment White may have had in mind, too, for the Villard house complex; Moore, *McKim*, 48, suggests something to this effect. The Van Brunt & Howe Portland Union Station is illustrated in Vaughan and McMath, *Century of Portland Architecture*, 19–20; it cost $313,500 compared to a projected cost of $1,204,000 for the McKim, Mead & White design. Villard's building enterprises are to be discussed at more length in my "Dreams of Empire: The Architectural Patronage of Henry Villard,"

78. Box 13, Cass Gilbert Papers, Minnesota Historical Society, Saint Paul.

79. Bill books, entry for April 29, 1884, MM&W Archive, NYHS.

80. Henry Villard to W. P. Clough, June 14, 1883, Box 125, Letterbook 51, Henry Villard Papers, Baker Library, Harvard University.

81. See O'Gorman, *Richardson: Drawings*, passim; and Hitchcock, *Richardson*, 177–78, 183.

82. Howard Mumford Jones, "The Renaissance and American Origins," in his *Ideas in America*, Cambridge, Mass., 1944.

83. For the RussWin Hotel see *Building* 8 (April 1888), 137. The use of terra cotta in this and the Phoenix house, 1882, is significant among the early exploitation of this material. Before its prominent employment by George B. Post in a house on 36th Street, New York, in 1877, terra cotta was not considered a fashionable building material in New York. Soon after, Post used terra cotta in his Long Island Historical Society, Brooklyn, 1878, and the Produce Exchange, New York, 1881. As McKim, Mead & White began to use terra cotta, White worked closely with the Perth Amboy Brick Company to create a wider range of base and glaze colors—gray, white, and then buff, with mottled and speckled glazes for both brick and matching terra cotta. This change in color, away from the raw red used by Post, and the later development of true polychromatic glazing, is said to have been due almost solely to the influence of White. See James Taylor, "The History of Terra Cotta in New York City," *ARec* 2 (October–December 1892), 136–48; and also by Taylor, "A Review of Architectural Terra Cotta," in *A History of Real Estate, Building and Architecture in New York City . . .* , New York, 1898, 509–28. See also *Atlantic Terra Cotta* 9 (June 1927), the entire issue devoted to the use of terra cotta by McKim, Mead & White.

84. The Garretts had accumulated significant wealth as heads of the Baltimore and Ohio Railroad. The Robert Garrett house is well preserved by the Engineering Society of Baltimore. See Katherine B. Dehler, "Our Heritage, 11 West Mount Vernon Place," pamphlet published by the Engineering Society of Baltimore, 1969. See also. "The Year's Work in Baltimore," *AABN* 19 (February 6, 1886), 68–69. The easterly half of the present house is an addition by John Russell Pope, 1902.

85. Sullivan and Wright could have been familiar with the Phoenix house through publication in the *Sanitary Engineer* 14 (September 23, 1886), 393, or Russell Sturgis, "The City House, The East and South," *Scribner's* 7 (June 1890), 710. It was later illustrated in Sturgis, "McKim, Mead & White," 62; *Brickbuilder* 5 (January 1896), 16; and *AABN* 87 (February 4, 1905), 40, no. 1519. It is discussed in H.-R. Hitchcock, "Wright and the Academic Tradition," and Vincent Scully, *Frank Lloyd Wright* (New York, 1960), 15, who compare it to the early work of Sullivan.

86. Bill books, entry for September 24, 1884, MM&W Archive, NYHS. For the H. A. C. Taylor house see: *Artistic Country Seats* 2:9–11; the *Monograph* 1:16; and Scully, *Shingle Style*, 149–52. A color "helio-chrome"

view was published in *AABN* 22 (July 23, 1887), 38, no. 604; followed by a view of the entrance gate, *AABN* 40 (April 15, 1893), 46, no. 903. The likely sources of Frank Lloyd Wright's variation on this theme for his classical George Blossom house, Chicago, 1892, are the view in Van Rensselaer, "Recent Architecture," *Century* 32 (June 1886), 427; and *Building* 5 (October 1886), 199. A set of drawings for the Taylor house are among the oldest to survive in the MM&W Archive, NYHS.

87. For the Andrew house and others by the firm in the Back Bay, see Bunting, *Back Bay*. See also: the *Monograph* 1:17; *AABN* 20 (July 3, 1886), 5, no. 549; and my letter to the editor, *JSAH* 32 (December 1973), 348–49.

88. The "survival" of the Georgian idiom in the Back Bay is noted in Douglass Shand Tucci, *Built in Boston: City and Suburb*, Boston, 1978, 145. See also Bunting, *Back Bay*, 322–25.

89. For the Appleton house see *Artistic Country Seats* 1:61–65; and *AABN* 74 (November 16, 1901), 56. no. 1351. Scully, in *Shingle Style*, 145, likened the firm's sensitivity in bending the axis of the house around the tree to Frank Lloyd Wright's response to the landscape.

90. Henry Holt, *Garrulities of an Octogenarian Editor*, Boston, 1923, 110.

91. For the Newburgh YMCA see the *Sanitary Engineer* 16 (July 16, 1887), 179; it is also shown in part in the view of the commercial block by Babb, Cook & Willard, Newburgh, in Van Rensselaer, "Recent Architecture," *Century* 28 (August 1884), 514.

92. Plans and a description of the Algonquin Club appeared in *AABN* 21 (January 15, 1887), 30. no. 577. See also the *Monograph* 1:18.

93. For John F. Goucher see *DAB* 7:442–43. Material on the history of the church from *The Christian Advocate*, New York, November 10, 1887 (Lovely Lane United Methodist Church Archives), and A. A. Cox, "The First Methodist Episcopal Church and Its Associated Buildings, Baltimore, Maryland," *AABN* 36 (June 11, 1892), 166–68. The church appeared in *AABN* 21 (March 26, 1887), 150, no. 587. For a discussion of the church in the context of American Romanesque architecture, see M. Schuyler, "The Romanesque Revival in America," *ARec* 1 (October–December 1891), 151–98. Drawings of the church are in Tube 411, MM&W Archive, NYHS; though none of the general drawings are dated, detail drawings are dated June 1885 through February 1886.

94. For the school see A. H. Knipp and F. P. Thomas, *The History of Goucher College*, Baltimore, 1938. The other buildings by White included the gymnasium (Bennett Hall), 1888–89, and the Latin School, 1892, although he sketched out preliminary designs for a conservatory of music in 1890 and a fine arts building in 1894. See the fragmentary correspondence between White and Goucher in Box M-19, 1968 Coll., MM&W Archive, NYHS. The school buildings are discussed and illustrated with plans in Cox, "Methodist Church," although Goucher Hall, shown there, is now believed to have been designed by Charles L. Carson, c. 1888. I am indebted to David Wright of Baltimore for information regarding this attribution. The Latin School appeared in *InArch* 23 (April 1894).

95. See Margaret French Cresson, *St. Paul's Church, Stock-* *bridge, Massachusetts...*, Stockbridge, Mass., 1951, and also: the *Monograph* 1:14; *AABN* 75 (February 15, 1902), 55, no. 1364; Van Rensselaer, "Recent Architecture," *Century* 29 (January 1885), 333.

96. Why McKim, raised a Quaker and first married by one of the most unorthodox clergymen of the day, Octavius Brooks Frothingham, became an Episcopalian is not recorded. Perhaps, in part, it was a gesture toward Julia Appleton, to whom he was now deeply attached.

97. See J. Elliott Lindsley, *A History of Saint Peter's Church*, Morristown, N.J., 1952, 44–58. In its final form the church is shown in the *Monograph* 1:23; the original shorter scheme is reproduced in Sturgis, "McKim, Mead & White," 105. See also: *AABN* 22 (September 3, 1887), 112, no. 610; and *AABN* 43 (March 17, 1894), 131, no. 951. The stained glass window, designed by Edwin Austin Abbey and constructed by Tiffany and Company, 1890–93, was originally in the chancel but was later moved to the chapel. McKim, Mead & White also designed Saint Peter's Rectory, next door, 1897–99.

The only other church of the period, also Episcopalian, was the shingled summer chapel at Quogue, L. I., N. Y., 1884, designed and constructed in association with Sidney V. Stratton.

98. For a detailed account of La Farge's connection with the Church of the Ascension, see Helene Barbara Weinberg, "La Farge's Eclectic Idealism in Three New York City Churches," *Winterthur Portfolio* 10 (1975), 199–228. The history of the church is given in James W. Kennedy, *The Unknown Worshipper*, New York, 1964, 65–76.

99. The numerous collaborations between Saint-Gaudens, White, and McKim are cited in my McKim, Mead & White *Building List*, passim. J. M. Wells also designed several bases and settings for statuary, including the base for Olin Warner's *William Lloyd Garrison*, 1881–86, on Commonwealth Avenue, Boston, and the Skidmore Fountain, Portland, Oregon, 1886–88, with bronze figures by Olin Warner, and which bears the inscription, "J. M. Wells Architect."

100. For the *Standing Lincoln* see: Tharp, *Saint-Gaudens*, 186–208; Craven, *Sculpture*, 383–404; Saint-Gaudens, *Reminiscences*, 1:350–56, 2:34. The figure and setting were published in *AABN* 39 (March 4, 1893), 143, no. 897.

101. For the Deacon Chapin Monument, *The Puritan*, see: Tharp, *Saint-Gaudens*, 184–86, 209–11; Craven, *Sculpture*, 383–95; Saint-Gaudens, *Reminiscences* 1:353–54, 2:7–14.

102. Saint-Gaudens, *Reminiscences*, 1:353–54.

103. The American Safe Deposit Company building was published in *AABN* 19 (April 24, 1886), 55, no. 527; and Van Rensselaer, "Recent Architecture," *Century* 28 (August 1884), 518–19, 521–22, 527, where it is discussed in connection with other commercial buildings of the period, including the House and School for Industry for Women, 120 W. 16th Street, New York, by Sidney V. Stratton.

104. An undated clipping from the *Record and Guide* (Scrapbook, MM&W Archive, NYHS) describes the Goelet office building as being "very jolly" and an

architectural "entertainment." A view appeared in Sturgis, "McKim, Mead & White," 83. Now destroyed, this small, almost residential building, whose decorative motifs refer to such sources as the Vleeshal, Haarlem, Holland, 1602, was part of a general Dutch Revival in New York during the 1880s and 1890s, comparable to the Flemish allusions in the work of Ernest George and Harold Peto, London, at this time. See also Proctor's Theater, 1888, by H. E. Ficken, in *King's New York* (New York, 1892), 530; the Collegiate Reformed Church, 1891–92, by R. W. Gibson, in *ARec* 1 (July–September 1895), 46; the John Wolfe Building, 1895, by H. J. Hardenbergh, in M. Black, *Old New York*, 35; the Waldorf-Astoria Hotel, 1892–97, also by Hardenbergh, in *ARec* 6 (January–March, 1897), 364–69; and a group of houses on West End Avenue by F. M. Day, in *ARec* 15 (May 1904), 401.

105. The Goelet Building was published in *Building* 8 (May 26, 1888), 169. Between 1920 and 1930 Maynich & Frank added four stories to the building, not replacing the large original cornice, but repeating the features of the building in every other respect. Lewis Mumford, who admired the building, illustrated it in *Brown Decades* (New York, 1931), where he mistakenly attributed it to Joseph Morrill Wells.

106. For Post's Produce Exchange, see my *Concise History*, 162–64; Van Rensselaer, "Recent Architecture," *Century* 28 (August 1884), 523; *AABN* 19 (June 26, 1886) no. 548; and Carl W. Condit, *American Building Art: The Nineteenth Century*, New York, 1960, 44–45, particularly for its structure. See also Winston Weisman, "The Commercial Architecture of George B. Post," *JSAH* 31 (October 1972), 176–203.

107. For Peabody & Stearns see Wheaton Holden, "That Peabody Touch: Peabody and Stearns of Boston, 1870–1917," *JSAH* 32 (May 1973), 114–31. The early New York skyscrapers and commercial blocks are discussed by Sarah B. Landau, "The Tall Office Building Artistically Reconsidered: Arcaded Buildings of the New York School, c. 1870–1890," in H. Searing, ed., *In Search of Modern Architecture: A Tribute to Henry-Russell Hitchcock*, New York, 1982, 136–64. The rounded corner used by McKim, Mead & White and Babb, Cook & Willard was popular in New York from about 1885 through 1915; in its later more classical office and mercantile buildings the firm drew on such models as the Palazzo Almagia' gia Fiano, Rome. For the rounded corner and paneled wall see numerous examples in *King's New York*, Boston, 1892, passim. Gimbel's Store, Philadelphia, 1900, by Francis Kimball, is a direct replication of the Goelet Building, extended horizontally.

108. For Delta Psi, Williams College, see John Addison Porter, "College Fraternities," *Century* 36 (September 1888), 749–60.

109. A brief history in the Jefferson Memorial Library Archives indicates that the ceiling of the reading room was patterned after the twelfth-century library of Merton College, Oxford, and that portions of the screen had been fragments from Morlaix, Brittany, brought back by McKim in 1878. The dedicatory window panel in stained glass and Mexican onyx was executed by D. Maitland Armstrong and Louis C. Tiffany.

110. The interiors of the *Namouna* are illustrated and discussed in S. G. W. Benjamin, "Steam Yachting in America," *Century* 24 (August 1882), 600–607. The firm had already received many other commissions from Bennett, beginning with the Newport Casino, followed by cottages at Newport, alterations to the original New York *Herald* building, alterations to Bennett's own house and interiors for his yacht, the *Polyana*. For White's Pennsylvania railroad car see my *Building List*, 655; no drawings for this have yet come to light, but the project might be compared to the interiors by H. H. Richardson for Boston & Albany cars, illustrated in O'Gorman, *Richardson: Drawings*, 182–83.

111. For the marriages of the partners, see Moore, *McKim*, 49–54, 319–20; and Baldwin, *White*, 158–73.

Chapter 4. RENAISSANCE, 1887–1892

1. Contract values taken from Summary of "Clients Contracts—Cost of Drawings—Commissions," office of Cain, Farrell & Bell, New York; this data was prepared by the office staff of McKim, Mead & White, c. 1920. The precise sum for the total of contracts for the period 1879–1886 cannot be determined but lies somewhere between $4,473,000 and $4,634,415.

2. The Mohawk Building, Fifth Avenue and 21st Street (now destroyed), was a fireproof nine-story block built for wool importers E. H. Van Ingen and Company, completed in May 1892. The arrangement of the firm's office there is shown in E. Everett Waid, "The Business Side of an Architect's Office, The Office of Messrs. McKim, Mead & White," *Brickbuilder* 22 (October 1913), 267–70 (see also my *Building List*, xxviii, xxix). Although the office organization was more systematic after 1894, Mead was quoted by Waid as saying "We never had any system and haven't now." It is true that the office was never as departmentalized as was D. H. Burnham's after 1891; see T. Hines, *Burnham of Chicago*, New York, 1974, 269–72. White's protest, noted earlier, is published in *Art Age* 3 (December 1885), 86–87, and 3 (January 1886), 100. The Kendall attribution list (Attribution file, Box M-16, 1968 Coll., MM&W Archive, NYHS) is the basis of the attributions given in my *Building List*. The checklists for White's assistants, dated December 14, 1892, and May 21–28, 1894, are in Stanford White file I, Box M-3, 1968 Coll., MM&W Archive, NYHS.

3. Melvin Dewey, "The American Library Association," *Library Journal* 1 (1876–77), 247. The history of the Boston Library is best recounted in Walter Muir Whitehill, *Boston Public Library, A Centennial History*, Cambridge, Mass., 1956, ch. 7. See also Douglass S.

Tucci, *Built in Boston, City and Suburb*, Boston, 1978, 132–33. For the filling of the Back Bay see Bainbridge Bunting, *Houses of Boston's Back Bay: An Architectural History, 1840–1917*, Cambridge, Mass., 1967, 1–41, 361–99.

4. Whitehill, *Boston Public Library*, 134. As early as 1881 the Trustees had decided on a scheme using a large reading room with adjacent stack storage of the books rather than a tall court lined with books, the configuration of the Boylston Street building. For a discussion of the four library types then popular—central court or "cathedral," alcoved reading room, departmentalized, and central storage stack—see William H. Jordy, *American Buildings and Their Architects, III: Progressive and Academic Ideals at the Turn of the Twentieth Century*, Garden City, N.Y., 1972, 314–75.

5. See Henry Van Brunt, *Report on the Fitness of the English High School and Latin School Building for the Uses of the Public Library*, Boston, 1882.

6. The competition was discussed in *AABN* 16 (December 20, 1884), 298, where it was called a "discreditable affair," and again in 17 (January 24, 1885), 37; (February 14, 1885), no. 477; and (February 19, 1885), 79, with illustrations of the "winning" entries by Charles B. Atwood, O'Grady & Zerrahn, Clarence S. Luce, and Horace Burr. In *AABN* 17 (April 11, 1885), 169, it was recommended that someone of "greater distinction" than Vinal be appointed library architect. Further commentary appeared in *AABN* 18 (October 3, 1885), 166, and 19 (March 27, 1886), 151, where a design by Van Brunt & Howe is mentioned.

7. Ralph Adams Cram, *My Life in Architecture*, Boston, 1936, 34.

8. In a confidential letter to White, George von Lengerke Meyer writes that the library trustees have been voted full control over the design and that Abbott plans to come to New York to give the commission to the firm, but McKim is to be told nothing of this. Although undated, the letter must have been written c. March 11–17, 1887 (S. White Coll., Manuscript Division, NYHS).

9. The trustees of the Boston Public Library during 1887–95 were: Samuel A. B. Abbott (president of the board, 1888–95), James F. Clarke, William W. Greenough, Henry W. Haynes, Phineas Pierce, Frederick O. Prince, William R. Richards, and William H. Whitmore, who resigned because of strong disagreement with the others as to the increasing cost of the building.

10. Whitehill, *Boston Public Library*, 141–42.

11. *Thirty-seventh Annual Report of the Trustees of the Public Library* [for the year 1888], Boston, 1889, 6. Italics added.

12. Whitehill, *Boston Public Library*, 143.

13. Hitchcock, *Richardson*, 298.

14. Boston *Herald*, April 5, 1888 (Scrapbook Coll., Boston Public Library).

15. Editorial, Boston *Globe*, November 25, 1887 (Scrapbook, MM&W Archive, NYHS).

16. McKim to W. R. Richards, October 11, 1889, Archives of the Trustees, Boston Public Library.

17. Mead to McKim, December 19, 1887, Box 36, McKim-Maloney Coll., NYPL, reprinted in Moore, *McKim*, 65.

18. Reminiscences of William T. Partridge, manuscript dated November 3, 1930, Avery Library, Columbia University. Partridge believed that the similarity to the Bibliothèque Sainte-Geneviève had been unconscious up to this point.

19. Jordy, *American Architects, III*, 333, where he uses the term "thrice-blessed."

20. Crisp line drawings, clearly inspired by the published engravings of P.-M. Letarouilly, of the first and second library designs were bound into the *Thirty-seventh Annual Report of the Trustees of the Boston Public Library* [for the year 1888], Boston, 1889, as a supplement. A selection of these appeared in *AABN* 23 (May 26, 1888, 246, no. 648; and 23 (June 9, 1888), 270. no. 650. Photographs of three plaster model studies are preserved in a scrapbook, Trustees Archives, Boston Public Library. In the Scrapbook, MM&W Archive, NYHS, are excerpts from the Boston *Pilot*, April 21, 1888, Boston *Evening Transcript*, April 21, 1888, Boston *Courier*, April 22, 1888, Boston *Daily Advertiser*, April 23 and 24, 1888, Boston *Post*, April 24 and 25, 1888, and Boston *Herald*, April 25, 1888. The library also attracted attention in European professional journals; see: "The new public library at Boston, U.S.A." *The Art Journal* [London] (April 1893), 126–27; and J. M. Brydon and F. J. Burgoyne, "Public Libraries," *JRIBA* s.3 v.7. (1899), 209–29.

21. Scrapbooks in the Trustees Archives, Boston Public Library, contain newspaper clippings of newspaper comment. The "stately aspect" is called for by C. H. Blackall, quoted in Tucci, *Built in Boston*, 135. Numerous photographs of study models of the cornice raised on scaffolds to the proper height are in the scrapbooks, Trustees Archives, Boston Public Library; one is reproduced in Boston Museum of Fine Arts, *Back Bay Boston: the City as a Work of Art*, Boston, 1969, 60.

22. For the library sculpture groups see: Moore, *McKim*, 70–72; Saint-Gaudens, *Reminiscences* 2:114–23, 304–06; Tharp, *Saint-Gaudens*, 230–31, 366–68. Studies did progress to the point when painted flats were installed to check proportions (see also n. 98); a photograph of this trial is reproduced in Saint-Gaudens, *Reminiscences* 2:304, and other photographs are in CM-LC, and in the photo albums, Avery Library, Columbia University.

23. Whistler did make an oil sketch for *Columbus Discovering America*, now in the Boston Public Library, but he never began work on the mural; for this and the other embellishments see Walter Muir Whitehill, "The Making of an Architectural Masterpiece," *American Art Journal* 2 (Fall 1970), 13–35. For MacMonnies's *Bacchante*, originally intended by McKim for the courtyard fountain, see Walter Muir Whitehill, "The Vicissitudes of Bacchante in Boston," *New England Quarterly* 27 (December 1954), 435–54. French's doors are discussed by Russell Sturgis, *Scribner's* 36 (December 1904), 765–68. For detailed descriptions of all the embellishments to the library see Herbert Small, *A Handbook of the New Public Library in Boston*, Boston, 1895, passim; see also Moore, *McKim*, 69–94.

24. A higher figure of $2,743,284.56 is given in Moore, *McKim*, 66–68, quoted from a letter from McKim to Bernard Green, April 18, 1904, published in *JAIA* 16 (March 1928), 91–93. This figure must represent costs incurred later and on which the architects' fee was not based; it does not appear in the bill books. Whitehill, in "Architectural Masterpiece," says that after Bela Pratt's fee of $30,000 was paid in 1912 the cost of the library stood at $2,558,559. This sixfold increase in the cost of the library, 1881–1912, cannot be attributed to graft, as can the inflated cost of the New York State Capitol (see Hitchcock, *Richardson*, 167–68). The city of Boston kept careful watch over all expenditures. McKim, Mead & White did not realize a profit on the library until the last two payments were made to them in 1895. After all expenses were deducted, the partners netted $22,000. At an interest rate of four percent for the eight years' labor, it averages out to an income of about $2,350 annually, or roughly $785 per partner per year. Clearly this was a labor of love.

25. See George R. Collins, "The Transfer of Thin Masonry Vaulting from Spain to America," *JSAH* 27 (October 1968), 176–201. Trinity Church had been burned out of South Street by the catastrophic Boston fire of 1872, so the memory of disaster by fire and the need for fireproof construction was keen. The Boston Public Library was the largest contract yet given Guastavino, and after this notable success his vaults were widely used by the firm and other architects.

26. Views of the completed library appeared in: *AABN* 48 (April 6, 1895), 3, no. 1006, 48 (May 18, 1895), 70, no. 1012. The entrance lamps appeared in *AABN* 87 (January 21, 1905), no. 1517. See also the *Monograph* 2:100–09. For critical assessments of the library see: *AABN* 48 (April 6, 1895), 3; "The New Library in Boston," *Harper's Weekly* 39 (March 16, 1895), 251; Mariana Griswold Van Rensselaer, "The New Public Library in Boston," *Century* 50 (June 1895), 261. In addition to Herbert Small's *Handbook* (see n. 23), for views and descriptions see: *The Boston Public Library*, photographed by N. W. Elwell, Boston, n.d. but c. 1896; Josiah H. Benton, *The Workings of the Boston Public Library*, Boston, 1909, with drawings by E. C. Peixotto; Horace G. Wadlin, *The Public Library of the City of Boston*, Boston, 1911; *Handbook of the Boston Public Library*, Boston, various eds., 1916–39; Edward W. Hoak and Willis H. Church, *Masterpieces of Architecture in the United States*, Boston, 1930.

27. The strong similarities between the Boston Public Library, the Bibliothèque Sainte-Geneviève, and the Church of San Francesco, Rimini ("Tempio Malatestiano") were discussed by H. Langford Warren, "The Use and Abuse of Precedent," *AReview* 2 (April 3, 1893), 21–25; and Sturgis, "McKim, Mead & White," 82–86. A detailed comparison of these buildings is given in Jordy, *American Architects, III*, 333–44.

28. McKim to White, n.d. but c. December 1887 (Boston Public Library file, Box M-8, 1968 Coll., MM&W Archive, NYHS), indicates that White influenced the decision to return to square-headed windows in the base.

29. Henry James, *The American Scene*, New York, 1907, 241–42.

30. Hill, *McKim: the Man*.

31. Cortissoz, "Critical Reflections," 23–24.

32. For a detailed analysis of the Bibliothèque Sainte-Geneviève, see Neal Levine, "The Romantic Idea of Architectural Legibility: Henri Labrouste and the Néo-grec," in Drexler, ed., *École*, 334–57.

33. For the Sargent mural cycle see Whitehill, "Architectural Masterpiece"; the review by Russell Sturgis, "Boston Public Library," *ARec* 15 (May 1904), 422–30; and Martha Kingsbury, "Sargent's Murals in the Boston Public Library," *Winterthur Portfolio* 11 (1976), 153–72. All of Sargent's studies and sketches for the cycle are now at the library. On the third floor, too, would have been "The Wells Library of Architecture" which McKim proposed to the trustees in a letter of February 27, 1890 (Wells file, Box M-3, 1968 Coll., MM&W Archive, NYHS). This memorial to Joseph Morrill Wells was to have been started with the collection Wells himself had assembled of books, prints, and photographs; the room, it was proposed, would be decorated by Wells's close friends Saint-Gaudens, T. W. Dewing, Sidney V. Stratton, George Maynard, and Francis Lathrop. The proposed memorial was never acted upon.

34. Charles C. Soule to the editor, Boston *Herald*, February 16, 1892. Although there has never been a question as to the central position of the Copley Square library in the city's library system, the reduction in the storage capacity of the stacks and the growth of the collection meant that by the mid-twentieth century the building was no longer large enough; among proposals for expansion see: Boston Public Library, *Building a Great Future upon a Glorious Past*, Boston, 1953; and Milton E. Lord, "Boston Modernizes—Plans for Enlargement," *Library Journal* 78 (December 15, 1953), 1–10. Once the remainder of the block was acquired behind the McKim building, Philip Johnson was engaged to design an addition in 1967 that was constructed 1969–73. In his growing appreciation of the importance of McKim, Mead & White, Johnson retained the general massing of the original, devised a bay system measuring 58 feet square, and clad the exterior with granite from the same quarry used for the original building.

35. For the Adams Memorial see: Ernest Samuels, *Henry Adams, The Middle Years*, Cambridge, Mass., 1958, passim; E. Samuels, *Henry Adams, The Major Phase*, Cambridge, Mass., 1964, 87–90; Saint-Gaudens, *Reminiscences* 1:356–66; Ernst Scheyer, *The Circle of Henry Adams: Art and Artists*, Detroit, 1970, 212–49; Tharp, *Saint-Gaudens*, 219–25, 368–70; Craven, *Sculpture*, 385–87. It was published in *AABN* 59 (February 26, 1898), 72, no. 1157.

36. For Marian Adams's interest in the arts see: Marc Friedlaender, "Henry Hobson Richardson, Henry Adams, and John Hay," *JSAH* 29 (October 1970), 231–46; Samuels, *Middle Years*, 230–39; Ernst Scheyer, "Henry Adams and Henry Hobson Richardson," *JSAH* 12 (March 1953), 7–12. See too the biography, Otto Friedrich, *Clover*, New York, 1979. The heroine in his novel, *Esther* (New York, 1884), Adams based on Marian; the artist, Wharton, "who approached things intuitively rather than intellectually,"

Adams based on La Farge. See *Esther,* 158, 180, 191.

37. John La Farge, *An Artist's Letters from Japan,* New York, 1897, intro., 17, 98, 106–07, 112, 175. The letters were serialized in *Century* during 1890.

38. Samuels, *Middle Years,* 306.

39. Samuels, *Middle Years,* 331–35. A recollection of the first meeting of client and sculptor is given in Scheyer, *Adams,* 222.

40. Saint-Gaudens, *Reminiscences* 1:362.

41. Saint-Gaudens, *Reminiscences* 1:360–61; Samuels, *Major Phase,* 22–23. Drawings for the marble setting, dated June and August 1888, tube 613, MM&W Archive, NYHS.

42. Samuels, *Major Phase,* 22–23.

43. Henry Adams to Charles Francis Adams, August 3, 1891, in Worthington C. Ford, ed., *Letters of Henry Adams (1858–1918)* 2 vols., Boston, 1930, 1:509.

44. Henry Adams, *The Education of Henry Adams,* Boston, 1918, 329. Not all clergy experienced such complete antipathy. D. Maitland Armstrong, in *Day Before Yesterday* (New York, 1920, 315), quotes the Rev. E. Winchester Donald who wrote him: "It haunts one. Out of the human being has gone hope, love, interest, and longing . . . the extinction of all that so much as makes death bearable. . . . She has no secret, that is clear, but the calm inarticulate misery or hopelessness is spread, like a dull sheen, over every feature. And when one has recovered himself, he finds She retains his respect, as certainly the figures, meant to represent hope and faith, do not."

45. Saint-Gaudens, *Reminiscences* 1:362.

46. Saint-Gaudens, *Reminiscences* 1:363–64. The only oblique references to the Adamses are two intertwined wreaths carved on the back of the stele slab.

47. For the Shaw Memorial see: Saint-Gaudens, *Reminiscences* 1:327–28, 332–47, 2:78–96, 120; Tharp, *Saint-Gaudens,* passim; Craven, *Sculpture,* 382–83; and the *Monograph* 2:164–65. More extensive are: Richard Benson and Lincoln Kirstein, *Lay This Laurel: An Album on the Saint-Gaudens Memorial . . . Honoring . . . Robert Gould Shaw,* New York, 1976; and Lois G. Marcus, "The *Shaw Memorial* by Saint-Gaudens," *Winterthur Portfolio* 14 (Spring 1979), 1–23. An early sketch of the Shaw equestrian scheme is reproduced in Tharp, *Saint-Gaudens,* 154; another later study, among Richardson's drawings, is reproduced in O'Gorman, *Richardson: Drawings,* 196–97.

48. McKim to Saint-Gaudens, October 23, 1891, CFM-LC, indicates that the design was finished and drawings ready to go out for estimates.

49. For MacMonnies's *Nathan Hale,* see Craven, *Sculpture,* 422. The bronze figure and marble base were duplicated in Huntington, L. I., N Y., 1894, and New London, Conn., 1935. For other collaborations between White and MacMonnies see my *Building List,* 205. For the Battell Memorial Fountain see L. G. White, *Sketches and Designs,* pl. 46; Saint-Gaudens may have contributed to the relief carvings and bronze sculpture.

50. The final design of 1894 is attributed to Albert Randolph Ross, McKim to Mead, July 6, 1894, CFM-LC, reprinted in Moore, *McKim,* 266–67. An early variant of the monument appeared in *AABN* 30 (December 13,

1890), 169, no. 781, and the finished monument in *AABN* 69 (July 21, 1900), 23, no. 1282. See also: *Monograph* 1:73; Montgomery Schuyler, "The Architecture of West Point," *ARec* 14 (December 1903), 463–92; *ARec* 20 (September 1906), 265–68; *Architects' and Builders' Journal* 48 (August 14, 1918), 74; and *AReview* [London] 38 (December 1915), 106. For background see: Charles W. Larned, *History of the Battle Monument at West Point,* West Point, N. Y., 1898; and Sidney Forman, *West Point,* New York, 1950.

51. For the Washington Arch see Baldwin, *White,* 194–98. The temporary wooden arch is illustrated in *AABN* 23 (May 18, 1889), 238; and M. Black, *Old New York,* New York, 1973, p. 85. White's original design for the marble arch included curved quadrants on each side, marked by freestanding Corinthian columns at the ends, capped by bronze globes and eagles; see drawings in tube 454A, MM&W Archive, NYHS, and photographs of a perspective, MCNY. The permanent marble arch was completed in 1892 at a cost of $128,000, although the sculpture was finished later. See the *Monograph* 1:39–40; *AABN* 65 (September 23, 1899), 103, no. 1239; *Graphic Arts* 7 (November 1914), 210; and *AReview* [London] 38 (December 1915), 110–13. See also: Charles W. Bowen, *The History of the Centennial Celebration of the Inauguration of George Washington,* New York, 1892, designed by White. The spandrel panels were completed by MacMonnies before 1906; the eagle on the keystone was done by Philip Martiny; and the pedestal groups were done by Herman A. McNeil and A. Stirling Calder and finished in 1916 and 1918 respectively; see Adolph Block, "Washington Arch is Among our Forgotten Monuments," *National Sculpture Review* 19 (Spring 1970), 23–26.

52. Manuscript, Washington Arch file, Old Mixed Files 204, 1950 Coll., MM&W Archive, NYHS, printed in Baldwin, *White,* 197–98.

53. John Hamilton to White, September 22, 1888 (Prospect Park file, Box M-7, 1968 Coll., MM&W Archive, NYHS), indicates White had started work on designs. This file also contains copies of contract documents for the Parkside (Willink) and Ocean Avenue entrance, Parkside (Willink) and Coney Island Avenue entrance, Lullwater Bridge, and the Croquet Shelter. Similar Files, Box 176, 1950 Coll., MM&W Archive, NYHS, contain copies of contracts for the Third Street and Coney Island Avenue entrance, and the Vale of Cashmere. The entrances, etc., at Prospect Park are illustrated in: the *Monograph* 1:20–21; *AABN* 65 (September 16, 1899), 95, no. 1238; and *Brickbuilder* 13 (December 1904),

54. Olmsted to William A. Stiles, March 10, 1895, quoted in Roper, *FLO,* 464–65.

55. Other residential work by White during this period included a rustic summer house for the actress Madame Modjeska, and the George Sealy house, Galveston, Texas, 1886–91. The Modjeska cottage, 1888, in Santiago Canyon, twenty-three miles from Santa Ana, California, is discussed and illustrated in Helena Modjeska, *Memories and Impressions of Helena Modjeska,* New York, 1910, 493–94, 540; Marion Moore Coleman, *Fair Rosalind, the American Career of Helena Modjeska,* Cheshire, Conn., 1969, and is illustrated only, in

Sturgis, "McKim, Mead & White," 110. For the Sealy house see E. H. Gustafson, "The Open Gates: The George Sealy House in Galveston," *Antiques* 108 (September 1975), 508–14.

56. For the J. Hampden Robb house, see *AABN* 34 (November 7, 1891), 91, no. 828. When the house was modified for the use of the Advertising Club by McKim, Mead & White in 1924, it was published again: *Architect* 1 (March 1924), pl. 153; *Architecture* 49 (March 1924), pls. 41–43; *Through the Ages* 5 (December 1927), 18–23.

57. Bills for the Patterson house were directed to Elinor Patterson's father, Chicago *Tribune* publisher Joseph Medill. Elinor wrote White, December 30, 1892, that she admired "Mrs. Nicholas Fish's house very much" (Patterson file, Box M-13, 1968 Coll., MM&W Archive, NYHS). For the Robert W. Patterson house see: *InArch* 24 (September 1894); *AABN* 52 (April 4, 1896), 7, no. 1058; and *Prominent Buildings by George A. Fuller*, Chicago, 1893, 97. In 1928 the house was enlarged to the rear by David Adler for the McCormicks; vacant during the mid-1970s, the house was restored externally during 1980–81, and the interiors divided to accommodate a group of luxury condominiums.

→ 58. In 1888 the firm also designed alterations for the Marlborough, another apartment block owned by the New York Life Insurance Company. The Yosemite was published in *AABN* 31 (February 21 and 28), 126, 141, nos. 791, 792.

→ 59. For the Hotel Imperial see *AABN* 30 (October 25, 1890), 57, no. 774; a view of the lobby and staircase appeared in *Architect and Building* 14 (January 3, 1891), 9.

60. The Browne and Meredith apartment block, as well as the earlier Percival, both bachelor apartments, had suites of rooms but lacked kitchens; breakfast was included in the rent and was delivered to the flats. At other times residents dined out. For the Browne and Meredith apartments see *AABN* 43 (March 31, 1894), 155, no. 953. The rise of the apartment block in the city is discussed in D. S. Tucci, *Built in Boston*, 101–30.

61. *The King Model Houses, 138th & 139th Streets, New York City, West Side*, New York, c. 1892, Avery Library, Columbia University. The King Model Houses were admired by Montgomery Schuyler, "The Small City House in New York," *ARec* 8 (April–June 1899), 357–88, especially 378–83. See, too, *Brickbuilder* 2 (October 1893), pls. 73–75, 78–79, for the units designed by Bruce Price. The King Model Houses housed affluent Negroes in the 1920s when this became Black Harlem; see Carl Van Vechten, *Nigger Heaven*, New York, 1926, 77–78; and Jervis Anderson, *This Was Harlem: A Cultural Portrait, 1900–1950*, New York, 1981, 339–41; New York *Times* March 30, 1972, Section L, 39.

62. For the dumbbell tenement and the New Law tenement, see R. W. De Forest and L. Veiller, *The Tenement House Problem*, 2 vols., New York, 1903. To reduce turnover among the residents, and thereby promote stability, King provided liberal sales contracts, excusing thirty percent of the cost of a unit in the event of the death of the purchaser.

63. For the development of the townhouse in New York, see Sarah B. Landau, "The Villard Houses and the New York Row House," in M. G. Broderick and W. C. Shopsin, *The Villard Houses: Life Story of a Landmark*, New York, 1980, 12–19, and her essay, "Row Houses of New York's West Side," *JSAH* 34 (March 1975), 19–36.

64. For the history of the Century Association see Rodman Gilder, ed., *The Century, 1847–1946*, New York, 1947. The division of responsibility is described by Charles Moore, "Charles Follen McKim," *DAB* 12:100; and in a letter to Mead, September 27, n.d. but c. 1889 (Century Club file, Box 37, 1950 Coll., MM&W Archive, NYHS), J. M. Wells discusses his progress with detail development and color selection. For plans and photographs of the Century Club see: the *Monograph* 1:27–29; and *AABN* 36 (May 21, 1892), 123, no. 856; 36 (June 18, 1892), 185, no. 860; 47 (February 23, 1895), 87, no. 1000. It was also discussed in popular journals: "The Century Club," *Century* 41 (March 1891), 673–89; "New Home of the Century Club in New York," *Harper's Weekly* 33 (November 2, 1889), 876. One of the few buildings patterned after the Century Club was the Eureka Club, Rochester, N. Y., by Bolan, Nolan & Stern; see *Brickbuilder* 3 (February 1894), 29, pls. 14–16.

65. *AReview* 1 (September 1892), 78, pl. 63. See, too, J. B. Robinson, "Recent Brickwork in New York," *Brickbuilder* 1 (October 1892), 74, 78–79. It is likely that both White and Wells were familiar with the examples illustrated in color in Ludwig (Lewis) Gruner, *The Terracotta Architecture of North Italy . . .*, London, 1867.

66. An excellent history of the club and its relationship to other clubs in the city is given in Paul Porzelt, *The Metropolitan Club of New York*, New York, 1982. The Metropolitan Club was only one of the many institutions established by disgruntled or blackballed members of the Union Club, which came thereby to be called the "mother of clubs." See, too, the Metropolitan Club files in boxes 79 and 83, 1950 Coll., MM&W Archive, NYHS. Whereas the firm usually did all their own interior work, in this instance, for the ladies' wing, they had the work done by Gilbert Cuel. For plans and photographs see: the *Monograph* 1:57–61; and numerous plates in *AABN* 44 (May 5, 1894), no. 958; 51 (January 11, 1896), no. 1046; 51 (February 8, 1896), no. 1050; 51 (March 7, 1896, no. 1054; 53 (September 6, 1896), no. 1083; and 55 (February 13, 1897), no. 1103.

67. The Johnston Gate was McKim's first work at Harvard, although in 1887 Prof. E. J. Child recommended McKim as architect of Hastings Hall to no avail (see Child to McKim, February 23, 1888, CFM-LC). For the Johnston Gate see: the *Monograph* 1:19–19A; *Boston Record*, November 5, 1889; *Harper's Weekly* 34 (February 22, 1890), 143–45. In the Harvard University Archives is miscellaneous material relating to the gates, including a letter, McKim to Martin Brimmer, April 23, 1889, in which McKim compares the design to the entrance gate of the Château de Dampierre. Other sources noted in Walter D. Swan, "The Harvard Memorial Gates," *AReview* 8 (June 1901), 61–65, pls. 39–44, include the Spanish gates at St. Augustine, and those of St. John's College, Winchester, England, the Banqueting House at Kensington Gardens, and Carshalton and Sherborne Abbeys.

68. Hill, *McKim: the Man,* 34–35.
69. McKim, to Martin Brimmer, March 30, 1889, Harvard University Archives. In a letter to De Wolf Hopper, February 13, 1895 (CFM-LC), McKim describes one inscription on the Johnston Gate

> which had been variously translated, according to the scholarship of the beholder, and perhaps the remark of "Irish John," an aged and time-honored servitor of the college . . . will be longest remembered and regarded by the average Harvard man as the most appropriate that could be suggested. Being discovered by some Freshies, soon after the gate was built, closely scrutinizing the production, they sought to down him in his tracks by a request to decipher what was there—to which he replied: "I dunno, but I guess it means 'To Hell with Yale!!' "

70. D. S. Tucci, *Built in Boston,* 201–205, makes this point.
71. For the Germantown Cricket Club see: the *Monograph* 1:24–26; and *Brickbuilder* 8 (January 1899), 16–17. The outer wings were planned from the start, as an early perspective in an album at the Avery Library indicates. This reveals that the building was originally to be built in rubble fieldstone, in the manner of the Green Tree Tavern, 1748, or Cliveden, the Benjamin Chew house, 1761–67, in Germantown.
72. For Wheatley Hills, see: the *Monograph* 2:147–51; and J. A. Gade, "An Ideal American Country Plan: The Country House of E. D. Morgan," *AReview* 14 (September 1907), 201–03, pls. 51–65. For Beacon Rock, see: the *Monograph* 1:38; and *Country Life* [American ed.] 37 (November 1919), 24–25.
73. See Bunting, *Back Bay,* 326–28.
74. For the Amory-Olney houses see: Bunting, *Back Bay,* 328; the *Monograph* 1:96; *AABN* 43 (February 3, 1894), 59, no. 945; *Brickbuilder* 5 (January 1895), 17, for the Olney portion.
75. To carry out the details of some of the interiors and to supervise overall construction of the Bryan Lathrop house, McKim, Mead & White associated with Chicago architects Holabird & Roche; drawings for the house in the Burnham Library, Art Institute of Chicago, bear the Holabird & Roche nameplate. In 1912 Alfred Hoyt Granger carried out alterations in the house to accommodate the Fortnightly Club; see Historic American Buildings Survey Report ILL-1037, 1964. The Lathrop house was published in *InArch* 24 (October 1894). For Lathrop see Edward F. Dunne, *Illinois, the Heart of the Nation,* Chicago, 1933, 43.
76. Upon completion of the remodeling, the church presented White with an album of photographs of the chancel before and after work; this is now kept by Frederick Lawrence Peter White, Saint James, N. Y., who kindly made it available to me. Letter, Lawrence Grant White to George Conklin, Hanover, N. H., January 15, 1931 (Miscellaneous M-16, 1968 Coll., MM&W Archive, NYHS), indicates that the work was done in the summer of 1889; see also Baldwin, *White,* 234, and John King Lord, *A History of Dartmouth College, 1815–1909,* 2 vols., Concord, N. H., 1913, 2:7–11. The church later burned. Another neo-Colonial building done by the firm two years earlier was the Stockbridge Casino, Stockbridge, Mass., the drawings for which (tube 890, MM&W Archive, NYHS) are dated April and May, 1887. This wooden Georgian hip-roofed structure, containing lounges, game room, and dining facilities, was commissioned by Joseph H. Choate and Prescott Hall Butler, prominent members of the summer community there.
77. For background see Henry-Russell Hitchcock and William Seale, *Temples of Democracy: The State Capitols of the USA,* New York, 1976, 209–26; and William H. Jordy and Christopher P. Monkhouse, *Buildings on Paper: Rhode Island Architectural Drawings, 1825–1945,* Providence, R. I., 1982, 115–17.
78. Public Park Association of Providence, *Rhode Island State House on Smith's Hill* [and] *Grand Boulevard,* Providence, c. 1890, 1, 5 (in Rhode Island State House file, Box M-10, 1968 Coll., MM&W Archive, NYHS).
79. The competition program was published, *AABN* 35 (February 13, 1892), 110, no. 842, with the firm's winning design and other entries. See also *Harper's Weekly* 39 (March 23, 1895), 275; and for the finished building see: the *Monograph* 2:183–90; *American Architect and Contract Reporter* 82 (1903), 1455, pls. 1450–53; *AABN* 81 (July 11, 1903), 15, no. 1437; and 82 (October 10, 1903), 16, no. 1450. The partners had vigorously objected to provisions in the original competition program that stipulated that all drawings were to become the property of the state and not be returned to the architects (Rhode Island State House file, box M-10, 1968 Coll., MM&W Archive, NYHS). For the restoration of the State House see *Interiors* 135 (September 1975), 110–13.
80. McKim to A. S. Jenney, December 17, 1891, and McKim to Prof. Letang, M.I.T., February 29, 1892, CFM-LC. Swartwout, "Architectural Decade," 81, says Henry Bacon was in charge of the drawings and construction supervision.
81. Lyman Farwell, Redlands, California, to Cass Gilbert, November 12, 1894, Cass Gilbert Papers, Minnesota Historical Society, Saint Paul, quoted in part in Hitchcock and Seale, *Temples,* 218. Farwell had been in the McKim, Mead & White office during 1892–93 while the Rhode Island drawings were being restudied.
82. McKim to Mead, August 8, 1901, CFM-LC.
83. Neil B. Thompson, *Minnesota's State Capitol: The Art and Politics of a Public Building,* Saint Paul, 1974, 37–49. The structural scheme devised by Gilbert and the contractor, Butler-Ryan of Saint Paul, was checked and approved by Raphael Guastavino, but the dome was not built by him as suggested by Hitchcock and Seale, *Temples,* 219.
84. Moore, *McKim,* 297, mentioned McKim's work at Montgomery, Alabama; for the other capitols mentioned here see Hitchcock and Seale, *Temples,* passim.
85. William Rotch Ware to McKim, August 26, 1889, MM&W Archive, NYHS. Many of the competition drawings are in the Avery Library, Columbia University, but not the firm's submission. Ware discussed the competition in *AABN* 25 (May 18, 1889), 238, and 25 (June 22, 1889), 196–97; the drawings appeared in *AABN* in various issues from October 1890 through May 1891.
86. Swartwout, "Architectural Decade," 61.

87. Unidentified clipping, Scrapbook, MM&W Archive, NYHS. See too: Charles H. Dorr, "A Study in Church Decoration," *ARec* 33 (March 1913), 187–203; *Art and Progress* 2 (April 1910), 169–74; L. G. White, *Sketches and Designs,* pl. 43. Helene Barbara Weinberg, "The Work of John La Farge in the Church of Saint Paul the Apostle," *American Art Journal* 6 (1974), 18–34, is concerned only with La Farge's contribution.

88. For the sources of the Judson Memorial Church tower see Warren, "Use and Abuse of Precedent," *AReview* 2 (April 3, 1893), 21–25. See also: the *Monograph* 1:55–56; *AABN* 40 (May 15, 1893), 107, no. 907, and 69 (July 14, 1900), 16, no. 1281. The similarity of White's solution to Karl Friedrich Schinkel's Johanneskirche, Zittau, Saxony, appears coincidental, for the firm seems not to have studied the work of this German neoclassicist; see K. F. Schinkel, *Sammlung Architektonischer Entwürfe,* Berlin, 1866, pl. 143.

89. For example, see the cover of *King's Handbook of New York City,* Boston, 1892, which is embossed with views of R. M. Hunt's Tribune Building, the Brooklyn Bridge, and the large night view of the Madison Square Garden Tower. For the history of the Garden, see: Zander Hollander, *Madison Square Garden, A Century of Sport and Spectacle . . . ,* New York, 1973; Andy Logan, "That Was New York: the Palace of Delight," *New Yorker* 41 (February 27, 1965), 41 ff; and Mariana Griswold Van Rensselaer, "The Madison Square Garden," *Century* 25 (March 1894), 732–47.

90. Baldwin, *White,* 199–212. A prospectus of the Madison Square Garden Company, dated May 24, 1887, is among miscellaneous material in the Stanford White Coll., Manuscript Division, NYHS; other founding members included Darius Ogden Mills, Charles Crocker, Charles Lanier, George S. Bowdoin, and Edward Dean Adams. J. P. Morgan owned 3,000 shares, and White had 1,100 shares in his own name and 350 more in the name of McKim, Mead & White.

91. Barnet Phillips, "The Construction of Great Buildings," *Harper's Weekly* 34 (April 12, 1890), 282–83. The arcade enabling legislation (bound with the prospectus) is dated June 9, 1888.

92. For Madison Square Garden see: the *Monograph* 1: 30–37; *Building* 11 (November 16, 1889), 165; *AABN* 34 (December 12, 1891), 170, no. 833; and 37 (July 16, 1892), 43, no. 864; these views were then republished in *AABN* 100 (December 13, 1911) 254, no. 1877, when demolition seemed imminent.

93. Van Rensselaer, "Madison Square Garden," 741. The Garden Theater opened September 27, 1890, with a production of the farcical comedy *Dr. Bill.*

94. A view of the amphitheater interior is reproduced in N. Singer, *Lost New York,* Boston, 1967, 52. The firm's photograph albums, Avery Library, Columbia University, contain numerous views of the Garden. Structural drawings of the amphitheater roof trusses appeared in *Architecture and Building* 12 (April 26, 1890), 199–200, and 12 (May 17, 1890), 234. The iron structure and electrical illumination were described at length in the New York *World,* New York *Herald,* and New York *Times,* October 30, 1887 (clippings in Scrapbook, MM&W Archive, NYHS). The iron and steel work, by Post & McCord, New York, was later analyzed in

"A Thirty-five Years' Test of Materials: A Non-technical Report of an Investigation Conducted upon the Razing of Madison Square Garden," *AABN* 128 (December 20, 1925), 519–42. The building had forced-air heating and cooling, using a system similar to that developed by Dankmar Adler for the Auditorium; see D. Adler, "The Chicago Auditorium," *ARec* 1 (April–June 1892), 415–34; and also *AABN* 26 (November 9, 1889), 223–24, and 26 (December 28, 1889), 299–300.

95. William A. Coffin, "The Tower of the Madison Square Garden," *Harper's Weekly* 35 (October 24, 1891), 819–20. For the framing, see the sources cited in n. 94.

96. The Giralda had just recently been published in *AABN* 18 (December 26, 1885), no. 522. For a comparison to the Garden tower see Warren, "The Use and Abuse of Precedent," *AReview* 2 (April 3, 1893), 21–25; and Sturgis, "McKim, Mead & White," 15, 86, 90–91, where he suggests the high relief terra cotta on the Madison Avenue facade was based on the Hôtel Lavalette on the Quais Célestins, Paris. See also "Campanile, Madison Square Garden, N. Y.," *The Builder* 69 (September 14, 1895), 187.

97. Contrast this with the experiment with full-scale painted flats for the Boston Library terrace groups; see n. 22. The original *Diana,* 18 feet 6 inches tall, a hollow figure of hammered copper sheets, weighed about one ton but was perfectly balanced on one toe so that only about one quarter pound per square foot wind pressure was required to turn her; see *Scientific American* 65 (December 26, 1891), 407; and Coffin, "Tower," 819–20. When the first *Diana* was lifted into place, George Fletcher Babb is reported to have said to White wryly, "Well, you've designed quite a pedestal for Saint-Gaudens, this time" (quoted in Tharp, *Saint-Gaudens,* 257). The first *Diana* was sent to Chicago where she adorned the center dome of the firm's Agriculture Building at the Columbian Exposition. When the buildings were demolished, she is reported to have been purchased by Montgomery Ward but this was not the figure put atop the Montgomery Ward office building by Richard E. Schmidt; the present location is unknown. The second smaller *Diana,* removed in 1925, was put in storage and in 1932 presented to the Philadelphia Museum of Art where she is now prominently displayed. See Tharp, *Saint-Gaudens,* 254–60.

98. The "Tower Studio" is described in some detail in Evelyn Nesbit, *Prodigal Days: The Untold Story,* New York, 1934, 33–35.

99. Clarence Pullen, "Madison Square Garden," *Harper's Weekly* 34 (September 13, 1890), 718; Charles De Kay, "The Madison Square Garden," *Harper's Weekly* 35 (July 18, 1901), 542.

100. Van Rensselaer, "Madison Square Garden," 732, 738, 746–47.

101. *AReview* 1 (May 2, 1892), 42–43, pls. 39–41; Carl W. Condit, *Chicago, 1910–29: Building, Planning, and Urban Technology,* Chicago, 1973, 114–15.

102. There were numerous notices at the time of demolition. See: "Madison Square Garden: An Account of the Passing of One of New York City's Architectural Landmarks," and the accompanying "Thirty-Years' Test . . . ," *AABN* 128 (December 20, 1925), 512–42; *JAIA*

13 (May 1925), 167–70; "For the Preservation of the Beautiful Tower of Madison Square Garden," *Architecture* 50 (October 1924), 340; "The Lesson in the Demolition of Madison Square Garden," *Western Architect* 15 (February 1910), 14; *Pencil Points* 6 (April 1925), 78–79; Harold Sterner, "Madison Square Garden, Old and New," *The Arts* 14 (December 1928), 348–50. When the future of the Garden first seemed in doubt, there appeared "The Passing of Madison Square Garden," *ARec* 30 (December 1911), 513–21.

103. Drawings for the Ramona School, tube 879, MM&W Archive, NYHS; clipping, Horatio O. Ladd, "The Ramona Indian Girls School," *Wide Awake*, n.d., in Clipping Scrapbook, MM&W Archive, NYHS. According to Ralph E. Twitchell, *Old Santa Fe*, Santa Fe, N. M., 1925, 457 n.845, the school was organized in 1885. Richard Longstreth, "Academic Eclecticism in American Architecture," *Winterthur Portfolio* 17 (Spring 1982), 71, discusses this design as the origin of a Southwest regional expression, noting that due to lack of funds it was not built. The local influence of the design is noted in Christopher Wilson, "The Spanish Pueblo Revival Defined, 1904–1921," *New Mexico Studies in the Fine Arts* 7 (1982), 24–29; White's perspective was published and discussed in the Santa Fe *Daily New Mexican*, April 2, 1888, 8.

104. Baldwin, *White*, 154–55. Quoted in Baldwin are White's letters, March and April 1882, from New Mexico to his family in New York. White was scheduled to continue from the Southwest to Oregon, there to join McKim in looking over the Villard building sites.

105. For background see: Louis C. Hatch, *The History of Bowdoin College*, Portland, Maine, 1927; and Montgomery Schuyler, "The Architecture of American Colleges: VII. Brown, Bowdoin, Trinity and Wesleyan," *ARec* 29 (February 1911), 151–56. The building and three murals appeared in *AABN* 70 (November 3, 1900), 39, no. 1297. See also: Richard V. West, *The Walker Art Building Murals*, Brunswick, Maine, 1972; and the *Monograph* 1:45–46. It should be noted that this was only the fourth building specifically designed to house a collegiate art collection, following those for Yale by John Trumbull, 1832; Princeton, 1887; and Stanford, 1891.

106. See Stanley King, *"The Consecrated Eminence": The Story of the Campus and Buildings of Amherst College*, Amherst, Mass., 1951, 107–09.

107. The Whittemore Library was not well published when it was built; it is mentioned in passing by Sturgis, "McKim, Mead & White," 94–95, where he suggests it is derived from Greek work "of Alexandrian times." For the firm's work in Naugatuck see the following chapter and my "Three Industrial Towns by McKim, Mead & White," *JSAH* 38 (December 1979), 331–47.

108. Board of Directors, Chicago Public Library, to MM&W, October 6, 1891, Competitions file, box M-14, 1968 Coll., MM&W Archive, NYHS. Other invited contestants included S. S. Beman, Jenney & Mundie, and Huell & Schmidt of Chicago, and Shepley, Rutan & Coolidge of Boston. McKim, Mead & White are not mentioned in the discussion of the competition in Chicago Public Library, *Twentieth Annual Report of the Board of Directors of the Chicago Public Library*, Chicago, 1892, 9, where other contestants are listed. The winning entry of Shepley, Rutan & Coolidge appeared in *InArch* 19 (March 1892), 24–25, with the text of the competition program. The site of the proposed library included a parcel belonging in perpetuity to the Grand Army of the Republic with covenants that there be a museum on that land. The resulting complexity and the narrow dimensions of the lot may have persuaded the firm not to enter.

109. Mead's responsibility for these two buildings is established in two letters, February 26, 1887 (William R. Mead file, box M-3, 1968 Coll., MM&W Archive, NYHS). Clippings from the Kansas City *Times* and Kansas City *Journal*, both March 10, 1887 (Scrapbook, MM&W Archive, NYHS) indicate that Mead was in the city then, checking the building site. For the New York Life Insurance Company see: James M. Hudnut, *Semi-Centennial History of the New York Life Insurance Company, 1845–1895*, New York, 1895; and Lawrence F. Abbott, *The Story of NYLIC: A History of the New York Life Insurance Company from 1845 to 1929*, New York, 1930. See too Frank Maynard Howe, "The Development of Architecture in Kansas City," *ARec* 15 (February 1904), 134–75. The firm's entry in the competition appeared in *AABN* 21 (April 9, 1887), 176, no. 589, and should be compared to the entry by Babb, Cook & Willard published in *AABN* 22 (November 12, 1887), no. 620. The finished building appeared in *InArch* 14 (December 1889), 86, and 14 (January 1890), 98; and the *Monograph* 1:22. A copy of the competition program is in the New York Life Insurance Company file, box M-8, 1968 Coll., MM&W Archive, NYHS; see also the New York Life Insurance Company file, box 23, 1950 Coll. Although unsuccessful in this competition, Babb, Cook & Willard built office blocks for the New York Life Insurance Company in Minneapolis and Saint Paul, 1888–90; see Montgomery Schuyler, "Glimpses of Western Architecture: Saint Paul and Minneapolis," *Harper's Magazine* 83 (October 1891), 736–55.

110. For the history of the metal frame in New York see the contemporary account, William J. Fryer, "A Review of the Development of Structural Iron," in *A History of Real Estate, Building and Architecture in New York City*, New York, 1898, 455–84. Fryer was a member of the Board of Examiners of the New York Building Department in 1889 when they debated the feasibility of Gilbert's novel metal frame for the Tower Building. See too Winston Weisman, "A New View of Skyscraper History," in Edgar Kaufmann, ed., *The Rise of an American Architecture*, New York, 1970, 115–62. That the firm knew steel framing technology is evident in McKim's response to an inquiry in which he refers to the opinion of Mr. Reilly, the Norcross Brothers New York representative, that there were no problems of destructive expansion or contraction with proper design; McKim expressed his belief that the steel frame is "the strongest, most economical, and least bulky of all forms of construction, as well as the best saver of space" (McKim to a Mr. Meredith, April 21, 1894, CFM-LC).

111. MM&W to the officers of the Home Life Insurance

Company, April 15, 1892, Competitions file, box M-14, 1968 Coll., MM&W Archive, NYHS. When the Brooks brothers of Boston gave Burnham & Root the commission for the Monadnock Building in Chicago in 1884 they specified solid masonry construction, and even in 1892, when they had Holabird & Roche plan an addition to it, Shepard Brooks was still unconvinced as to the long-term structural strength of a steel frame.

112. For the State Street Exchange, see *AABN* 22 (October 22, 1887), 194, no. 617; compare this to Babb, Cook & Willard's design for the Kansas City New York Life Insurance Company building which appeared in *AABN* three weeks later.

113. The Judge Building derived its name from *Judge*, a satirical review, which moved its offices there. The building was published in *Building* 12 (March 1, 1890), 103. Russell Sturgis, "The Warehouse and Factory in Architecture," *ARec* 15 (January and February, 1904), 1–17, 122–33, discusses the Judge Building among others and notes that it was then being topped with added stories.

114. For the Cable Building see: *AABN* 44 (June 16, 1894), 127, no. 964; and *Architecture and Building* 21 (July 7, 1894).

115. For the *Herald* Building see Baldwin, *White*, 218–20, and the *Monograph* 1:62–64A. For a comparison of the *Herald* Building to the Consiglio, Verona, see my "McKim, Mead & White Reappraised," 40–42; Warren, "Use and Abuse of Precedent," *AReview* 2 (February 13, 1893), 11–15; and Sturgis, "McKim, Mead & White," 86, 92–94. For details of the terra cotta see the *Monograph*; *AABN* 46 (December 22, 1894), 131, no. 991; and *Atlantic Terra Cotta* 9 (June 1927), pl. 39. For Bennett's owl fixation, see Richard O'Connor, *The Scandalous Mr. Bennett*, New York, 1962, 221–25.

116. Moore, *Burnham*, 1:67.

117. For varying accounts of the Columbian Exposition see: Moore, *Burnham*, 1:31–68; Thomas S. Hines, *Burnham of Chicago*, New York, 1974, 73–124; David F. Burg, *Chicago's White City of 1893*, Lexington, Ky., 1976; Donald Hoffmann, *The Architecture of John Wellborn Root*, Baltimore, 1973, 220–45; Titus M. Karlowicz, "D. H. Burnham's Role in the Selection of Architects for the World's Columbian Exposition," *JSAH* 29 (October 1970), 247–54; Christopher Tunnard, "A City Called Beautiful," *JSAH* 9 (March–May 1950), 31–35. Of particular importance among unpublished materials is Titus M. Karlowicz, "The Architecture of the World's Columbian Exposition," doctoral dissertation, Northwestern University, 1965.

118. Frederick Law Olmsted, *Report on Choice of Site to Board of Directors, World's Columbian Exposition,* dated August 18, 1890, 1; published in Chicago *Tribune*, August 20, 1890.

119. Karlowicz, "Burnham's Role," 247; Hines, *Burnham*, 80.

120. Resolution printed in *InArch* 16 (January 1891), 93. The tone of the enterprise was echoed, too, by Lyman Gage, head of the Chicago committee, when he addressed the assembled architects at dinner the evening of January 10; he urged self-subordination among the architects in their work, so that "the pride and renown

of each would come out of the success of the work as a whole." Each architect was to view his part not as "a complete thing, but as an element of the general design." Quoted in Daniel H. Burnham, *Final Report of the Director of Works of the World's Columbian Exposition,* Chicago, 1898, 1:7, in Burnham Library, Art Institute of Chicago. Burnham's report does not make it clear who first suggested the classical idiom for the Court of Honor, but its selection seems inevitable in view of the general desire for unity in expression. The fullest account of this stage of deliberations is given in "Lessons of the Chicago World's Fair: An Interview with the Late Daniel H. Burnham," *ARec* 33 (January 1913), 34–44.

121. Louis Sullivan, *The Autobiography of an Idea*, New York, 1924, 320–21.

122. Moore, *Burnham*, 1:47.

123. Moore, *McKim*, 123; Moore, *Burnham*, 1:53–58; and Lucia and Alan Valentine, *The American Academy in Rome, 1894–1969*, Charlottesville, Va., 1973, 1–6.

124. The Agriculture Building was extensively illustrated in *AABN* through the autumn of 1893 and through 1894; other views appeared in *InArch* from April 1891 through August 1893. A recent useful source of visual material is Stanley Appelbaum, *The Chicago World's Fair of 1893: A Photographic Record*, New York, 1980.

125. H. Bacon, "Charles Follen McKim—A Character Sketch," *Brickbuilder* 19 (February 1910), 44. Bacon was the firm's resident superintendent at the fair.

126. *Report of the Board of General Managers of the Exhibit of the State of New York at the World's Columbian Exposition,* Albany, N. Y., 1894, 92, 100. In addition to the Agriculture Building and the New York State Building, the firm designed the ornate Puck Pavilion and the adjacent White Star Steamship Pavilion as well as the display of the American Cotton Oil Company; see my *Building List*, nos. 693, 906; and Appelbaum, *Photographic Record*, 60.

127. Moore, *McKim*, 121, 117.

128. For the New York State Building see: the *Monograph* 1:44; *AABN* in numerous issues February through October 1894; *InArch* 21 (July 1893); and in *Prominent Buildings by George A. Fuller*, Chicago, 1893, 87. Olin Warner carved the portrait busts for the niches in the facade. For a general discussion of the state pavilions see Montgomery Schuyler, "State Buildings at the World's Fair," *ARec* 3 (July–September 1893), 55–71.

129. *Report of the Board . . . State of New York*, 100; the ballroom was illustrated in *AABN* 45 (August 11, 1894), no. 974.

130. Sullivan, *Autobiography*, 325.

131. The exploitation of electricity was one of the attractions of the fair, and the Westinghouse generating equipment, one of the principal exhibits, particularly fascinated Henry Adams. The Columbian Exposition appears to have been the first to be open at night because of its good illumination.

132. See the comments in Hamlin Garland, *Son of the Middle Border*, New York, 1917, 458–61. The wondrous image of the fair was emphasized in the popular press, in such titles as: J. W. Buel, *The Magic City . . . ,* Philadelphia, 1894; or Candace Wheeler, "A Dream City," *Harper's Magazine* 86 (May 1893), 830–46.

133. Montgomery Schuyler, "Last Words About the World's Fair," *ARec* 3 (January–March 1894), 271–301; reprinted in part in my *America Builds,* New York, 1983. Henry Van Brunt's observations on the fair and its effect are collected in W. A. Coles, ed., *Architecture and Society: Selected Essays of Henry Van Brunt,* Cambridge, Mass., 1969. Henry Adams, *The Education of Henry Adams,* Boston, 1918, 343.

134. In his description of his plan for the city of Manila, Burnham wrote: "The delightfulness of a city is an element of first importance to its prosperity . . ."; Moore, *Burnham,* 2:191.

135. For the influence of the Columbian Exposition on the development of American urban planning see: Blake McKelvey, *The Urbanization of America,* New Brunswick, N. J., 1963; John Reps, *The Making of Urban America,* Princeton, 1965; Christopher Tunnard and Henry Hope Reed, *American Skyline,* Boston, 1955; and Mellier G. Scott, *American City Planning since 1890,* Berkeley, 1969. See also Maurice F. Neufeld, "The Contribution of the World's Columbian Exposition of 1893 to the Idea of a Planned Society in the United States," unpublished master's thesis, University of Wisconsin, Madison, 1935. For the fair's influence in Europe see: George R. and Christiane C. Collins, *Camillo Sitte and the Birth of Modern City Planning,* New York, 1965; and Dudley Arnold Lewis, "Evaluations of American Architecture by European Critics, 1875–1900," doctoral dissertation, University of Wisconsin, Madison, 1962. In *Das amerikanische Haus,* Berlin, 1910, F. Rudolph Vogel spoke of the Chicago fair stimulating park and urban planning in Europe; see Leonard K. Eaton, *American Architecture Comes of Age,* Cambridge, Mass., 1972, 105. The laudatory observations of Sir Henry Trueman Wood, a British official at the fair, are quoted in Harvey M. Watts, "The White City," *The T-Square Club Journal of Philadelphia* 19 (May 1931), 24–27; see also the introduction by C. H. Reilly to Patrick Abercrombie, "Town Planning Schemes in America," *Town Planning Review* 1 (1910), 54–65, 137–47.

Chapter 5. ENSEMBLES, 1893–1899

1. For the economics of the period see: Harold Somers, "The Performance of the American Economy, 1866–1918," in Harold F. Williamson, ed., *The Growth of the American Economy,* Englewood Cliffs, N. J., 1951, 646–61. Burnham & Company also survived, but Adler & Sullivan fell victim to the depression.

2. McKim to Mead, July 6, 1894, CFM-LC, printed in Moore, *McKim,* 266–67. McKim to Montgomery B. Pickett, September 28, 1893, CFM-LC (Pickett was then in D. H. Burnham's office, Chicago). McKim wrote a similar negative letter to A. R. Ross, October 24, 1893, CFM-LC. Petition to McKim, Mead & White . . . , MM&W Coll., Avery Library, Columbia University.

3. McKim to Banister F. Fletcher, c/o Barr Ferree, New York, July 12, 1893, CFM-LC. For Fletcher's visit to Chicago to study the Exposition, Mead wrote a letter of introduction to Burnham, May 27, 1893, mounted in D. H. Burnham, *Album of Souvenirs of the World's Columbian Exposition . . . ,* c. 1894, 50, in the Burnham Library, Art Institute of Chicago. Fletcher's observations appeared in the *Report of the Godwin Bursar of 1893* (see the RIBA Library catalogue). See too his "American Architecture through English Spectacles," *Engineering Magazine* 7 (June 1894), 314–21; some of this later appeared in his *History of Architecture for the Student, Craftsman, and Amateur, Being a Comparative View . . . ,* London, 1896, which appeared in later editions as *A History of Architecture on the Comparative Method.*

4. Swartwout, "Architectural Decade," 87.

5. McKim to Thomas M. Kellogg, August 9, 1893, CFM-LC.

6. For the Tarsney Act see: Lois Craig et al., *The Federal Presence: Architecture, Politics, and Symbols in United States Government Building,* Cambridge, Mass., 1978, 149, 202–03; Moore, *Burnham* 1:95–96, 106–109. See also
the firm's correspondence concerning the Ellis Island station, Misc. Competitions file, box M-14, 1968 Coll., MM&W Archive, NYHS.

7. For the Baltimore Courthouse competition, see *InArch* 24 (August 1894).

8. Letter, April 23, 1897, Misc. Competitions file, box M-14, 1968 Coll., MM&W Archive, NYHS. The other signers included: Clinton & Russell; Charles C. Haight; Henry J. Hardenbergh; Edward H. Kendall; James Brown Lord; R. H. Robertson; and Rossiter & Wright.

9. Edward Bok, *The Americanization of Edward Bok,* New York, 1920, 243.

10. For White's frames see Edward Simmons, *From Seven to Seventy,* New York, 1922, 249–50; and the letter of warm thanks "for stopping in the midst of all you have to do to design a frame for our portraits," Anne Cheney to White, May 30, 1889, Cheney file, Box 34, 1950 Coll., MM&W Archive, NYHS. White to Charles C. Beaman, October 20, 1889, Autograph file, Houghton Library, Harvard University. White's most resplendent interiors of the nineties include those of: the Herman Oelrichs house, Rosecliff, Newport, 1897–1902; the William C. Whitney house, New York, 1897–1902; the Henry W. Poore house, New York, 1899–1901; and the Clarence M. Mackay house, Harbor Hill, Roslyn, N. Y., 1899–1902 (the Oelrichs and Mackay houses are discussed below). All of these are illustrated in the *Monograph,* passim. See also: J. Monroe Hewlett, "Stanford White, Decorator," *Good Furniture* 9 (September 1917), 160–79; and Channing Blake, "Stanford White's New York Interiors," *Antiques* 102 (December 1972), 1060–67. For the Poore house see: the *Monograph* 2:155–56; Baldwin, *White,* 270–71; and *ARec* 12 (May 1902), 33–49. The William C. Whitney house was the remodeled Robert L. Stuart house on Fifth Avenue, purchased by Whitney in

1896; the sedate exterior of this conventional brownstone appeared in *InArch* 33 (May 1899), and the interiors were published: *Monograph* 2:144–45; *ARec* 10 (April 1901), 407–16; *House Beautiful* 10 (August 1901), 131–42.

11. Edith Wharton to McKim, n.d. (c. 1897), box 33, McKim-Maloney Coll., NYPL.

12. McKim to Edith Wharton, February 4, 1897, CFM-LC. *The Decoration of Houses*, New York, 1897, was written in collaboration with Ogden Codman, Jr., whom the Whartons engaged to remodel Land's End, in Newport. See E. Wharton, *Backward Glance*, 106–11.

13. White to Shepley, Rutan & Coolidge, January 28, 1895 (Stanford White Letterbook 12, Avery Library, Columbia University), requests elevations of Trinity Church for preparation of Brooks Memorial studies. See also copies of contracts in Phillips Brooks Memorial file, box 467, 1950 Coll., MM&W Archive, NYHS.

14. Elijah R. Kennedy to White, April 23, 1895 (Slocum Memorial file, box M-8, 1968 Coll., MM&W Archive, NYHS), indicates Saint-Gaudens had been offered $35,000 two weeks earlier to do the Slocum Memorial; asks White to exert gentle pressure. In several letters, E. R. Kennedy to White, May through October 1897 (Woodward Monument file, box M-11, 1968 Coll., MM&W Archive, NYHS), Kennedy thanks White for his various studies for placing the Woodward statue in front of the museum "on the Eastern Parkway." McKim's work on the French-Potter *Washington* equestrian detailed in letters, McKim to French, September 11 through October 18, 1899, CFM-LC. Among White's miscellaneous designs of the period were interiors for Royal Phelps Carroll's yacht, *Navahoe*, 1892–93 (see R. P. Carroll yacht file, box M-16, 1968 Coll., MM&W Archive, NYHS), and trophy cups, 1896, for the Goelet Cup Race at Newport (clipping, Stanford White file, box M-3, 1968 Coll., MM&W Archive, NYHS).

15. W. R. Richards to McKim, February 14, 1893 (Copley Plaza file, box M-15, 1968 Coll., MM&W Archive, NYHS), indicates McKim and Ogden Codman, Jr., had already worked out one scheme for the square and that the Boston Society of Architects was going to urge completion. The competition program, dated February 28, is in this file; it was published in *AABN* 39 (March 4, 1893), 129, no. 897. Additional letters in this file and in CFM-LC, dated May through September, concern the firm's second design. Charles A. Cummings to McKim, September 17, 1896 (in the same file, NYHS), specifically blames the depression for lack of work on landscaping. Copley Square eventually was landscaped, 1969, by Sasaki, Dawson & Demay.

16. New York *Times*, January 6, 1898, 5; and February 15, 1898, 3. See also I. N. Phelps Stokes, *The Iconography of Manhattan Island, 1498–1909*, New York, 1909–28, 3:827.

17. For the New York University plan see: Theodore F. Jones, *New York University: 1832–1932*, New York, 1933, 148–91, 423–28; Henry M. MacCracken, *The Up-Town University College: Some Account of the Movement Thus Far*, New York, c. 1892, 1–14; and Henry M. Mac-

Cracken and Ernest G. Sihler, *A History of New York University*, 2 vols., Universities and Their Sons Series, Joshua L. Chamberlain, ed., Boston, 1901; and Baldwin, *White*, 223.

McKim was incidentally involved in the design of the campus of the University of California at Berkeley. Bernard Maybeck wrote McKim asking for advice and comment on the Phoebe A. Hearst campus plan competition program: Maybeck to McKim, August 4, 1897, Misc. Competitions file, box M-14, 1968 Coll., MM&W Archive, NYHS.

18. See *DAB* 11:619–20.

19. MacCracken to White, January 2 and 5, 1892, New York University file, box 129, 1950 Coll., MM&W Archive, NYHS.

20. MacCracken to White, January 22, 1892, loc. cit.

21. Draft of report, White (?) to MacCracken, January 25, 1892, loc. cit.

22. See Jones, *New York University*, 151–55; Jacob Schiff was the chief instigator of the merger proposal.

23. MacCracken to White, December 14, 1893 (New York University file, box 129, 1950 Coll., MM&W Archive, NYHS), says that the estimate of more than $250,000 for removal was far more than several new buildings at $50,000 each.

24. MacCracken to White, December 23, 1893, loc. cit.

25. MacCracken to White, February 28, 1894, loc. cit.

26. MacCracken to White, May 31, 1895, loc. cit.

27. MacCracken to White, June 11, 1895, loc. cit.

28. In Album XII, MM&W Coll., Avery Library, Columbia University, are photographs of the various plan studies. An aerial view, similar to those also in Album XII, was prepared for publication in MacCracken and Sihler, *New York University*, and in *Architects' and Builders' Magazine* 3 (1901), 167.

29. MacCracken to White, April 5, 1897, New York University file, box 246, Old Mixed Files, 1950 Coll., MM&W Archive, NYHS.

30. See the *Monograph* 1:75–77. The New York University buildings are discussed in Montgomery Schuyler, "The Architecture of American Colleges: IV. New York City Colleges," *ARec* 27 (June 1910), 442–69. The Hall of Languages and the Gould Dormitory were published in: *AABN* 73 (September 14, 1901), 87, pl. 1342; *Architecture and Building* 27 (October 9, 1897), *Brickbuilder* 9 (January 1900), pls. 1, 2, and 9 (March 1900), pl. 18. The library was published: *AABN* 73 (September 14, 1901), 87, no. 1342, and (September 28, 1901), 104, no. 1344; *Architecture* 5 (February 15, 1902), 38–43; *Brickbuilder* 10 (July 1901). In 1920–22 the doors of the library were replaced with two bronze valves in memory of the architect, Stanford White. Designed by Lawrence Grant White, the doors were divided into twenty-one panels each, the panels modeled by sculptors who had worked with Stanford: Andrew O'Connor, Philip Martiny, Herbert Adams, and Adolph A. Weinman. The lion's-head door pulls were by Ulysses Ricci, and the inscription in the architrave overhead was by Janet Scudder. Each of the panels, stiles, and rails were cast separately and fastened to a wooden frame. See *American Magazine of Art* 13 (March 1922), 80–81; *American Art News* 17 (March 13, 1920), 1; *Arts and Decoration* 16 (January 1922), 194, 224.

The Cornelius Baker Hall of Philosophy was built on the north flank of the Gould Library, following White's plans, 1912–13. In addition to the buildings mentioned here, the firm also designed the post office for the campus. They did not, however, design the chemistry laboratory perpendicular to the Hall of Languages; that was done in 1894–95 by Arnold Brunner and Thomas Tryon, who closely emulated White's designs and who wrote the firm for material samples (Brunner to White, May 18, 1894, New York University file, box 129, 1950 Coll., MM&W Archive, NYHS).

31. Ramée's own rendered plan for Union College is reproduced in my *Concise History*, 76. This and other Ramée drawings at Union College were not readily available at the close of the century, but many popular versions of a frontal perspective had been circulated during the century, as Paul V. Turner informs me.

32. See Henry M. MacCracken, *The Hall of Fame*, New York, 1901, 1–10; Robert U. Johnson, *Your Hall of Fame*, New York, 1935; Jones, *New York University*, 170, 198–202; and MacCracken and Sihler, *New York University*, 243–46. MacCracken was unduly optimistic as to the northward shift in population, and during the 1960s and 1970s the university focused on its Washington Square campus. The Bronx campus was eventually sold to the Bronx Community College.

33. Journal, "Columbia College: Committee on Site," in Secretary's Office, Columbia University, notes of meetings of May 4 and November 6, 1891. I am thankful to Daniel Gil Feuchtwanger of Columbia University, who brought much of this unpublished and uncataloged material to my attention. The standard description of the campus and its buildings is John W. Robson, *A Guide to Columbia University with Some Account of its History and Traditions*, New York, 1937. See also Moore, *McKim*, 264–72. The best treatment of the evolution of McKim's plan arrangement is Francesco Passanti, "The Design of Columbia in the 1890s, McKim and his Client," *JSAH* 36 (May 1977), 69–84. I am thankful, too, to Francesco Passanti, who provided me with longer versions of his researches prior to publication in *JSAH*.

34. McKim to Olmsted, February 18, 1893, CFM-LC, printed in Moore, *McKim*, 264.

35. Report of the Commission, April 7, 1893, with separate reports by Hunt and Haight; the passages are quoted from a letter by McKim and White accompanying their report, April 10, 1893, Columbiana Collection, Columbia University. The plans by Hunt and Haight are bound in a folder, "Competition Layout Plan for Columbia University on Morningside Site—1893," Avery Library, Columbia University; the plan by McKim, Mead & White has not yet come to light.

36. McKim to Olmsted, February 18, 1893, CFM-LC. Olmsted had designed the landscaping around the national Capitol and the expansive terrace on the west side, 1874–85.

37. McKim to Hunt, September 1893, CFM-LC, printed in part in Moore, *McKim*, 265. The Ware and Olmsted compromise block plan was submitted to the Trustees' Buildings and Grounds Committee, May 26, 1893; the report is in the Columbiana Collection, while the plan itself is in the Avery Library, Columbia University.

38. *Report of the Committee on Buildings and Grounds in Relation to the Development of the New Site*, New York, November 11, 1893, Columbiana Collection. Hill, *McKim: the Man*, 18–19, gives a much different account.

39. John B. Pine, Secretary of the Trustees, to McKim, December 14, 1893; Seth Low to McKim, December 5, 1893; Contract between the Trustees of Columbia College in the City of New York and Messrs. McKim, Mead & White, dated December 28, 1893—all documents in the Columbiana Collection. One important consideration in appointing McKim, Mead & White was the size and stability of their organization and their relative youth in contrast to Hunt and Haight, both of whom were much older and had small offices, clear liabilities in view of the expected protracted period of construction.

40. McKim to Mead, July 6, 1894, CFM-LC, printed in part in Moore, *McKim*, 266–67.

41. McKim credited Kendall and Lord with developing the Low Library scheme in several letters: McKim to Kendall, July 16, 1894, CFM-LC, indicates that Lord had just finished the library drawings during Kendall's illness; McKim to Thomas Nash, July 20, 1895, CFM-LC, credits Kendall with supervising all the Columbia work. Swartwout, "Architectural Decade," 40–44.

42. McKim to White, July 24, 1894, box 10, folder 10, Stanford White Correspondence, Avery Library, Columbia University.

43. Several of McKim's letters in the Columbiana Collection indicate he also was thinking of the Pantheon in Rome as a model; see McKim to Seth Low, December 7, 1894, Office of the Secretary, Columbia University. Passanti noted the connection with Paul Henri Nénot's plan for the new Sorbonne, Paris, published in *AABN* 27 (June 7, 1890), 145, which might be compared to the final Columbia plan in *Harper's Weekly* 38 (November 3, 1894), 1036–42.

44. The Columbia University buildings are extensively illustrated in the *Monograph* 1:47–54, 3:200–203. For Earl Hall see: *AReview* 8 (April 1901), 48, pls. 26–28; *Brickbuilder* 5 (June 1902), The terraces and fountains appeared in *Architecture* 5 (January 15, 1902), pl. 19.

45. Construction of the library was made possible by a large gift from President Low in memory of his father; for the library see the *Monograph* 1:48–54; *Architects' and Builders' Journal* 47 (March 20, 1918). *AABN* ran a number of views of the library during the autumn of 1898. The library was also discussed in English journals: *Building News* 68 (June 14, 1895), 237; and *JRIBA* s.3 v.6 (1899), 209–29. See too Montgomery Schuyler, "The Architecture of American Colleges: IV. New York City Colleges," *ARec* 27 (June 1910), 443–57. It is possible that Seth Low, as patron, had some influence in shifting the design from a rectangular plan to a Greek cross, but his gift was not made until May 6, 1895, four days after Norcross Brothers was awarded the contract for construction. The octagonal reading room has contemporary parallels in Hunt's Administration Building at the Columbian Exposition, and in the reading room of Smithmeyer & Pelz's Library of Congress, Washington, D.C., 1886–97.

46. Hill, *McKim: the Man,* 21–22. See also W. Hallock, "Diffused Illumination," *Progressive Age* 16 (March 1, 1898).

47. Francesco Passanti's research into the construction of the dome indicates that at the base of the brick shell are two steel tension rings; there is also a steel compression ring at the crown, included should it have proved necessary to open the dome for a lantern.

48. McKim to John B. Pine, November 30, 1894, MM&W Archive, NYHS.

49. William H. Goodyear, "Horizontal Curves in Columbia University," *ARec* 9 (July–September 1899), 82–93. Shifting and settling has diminished the effect. The frontispiece to Sturgis's "McKim, Mead & White" shows the Columbia south court with wrought iron gates, about which McKim wrote Henry Villard, September 23, 1895, CFM-LC, suggesting them as a possible gift to Columbia.

50. For the University of Virginia see: Paul B. Barringer, James M. Garnett, and Rosewell Page, *The University of Virginia: Its History, Influence, Equipment and Characteristics,* 2 vols., New York, 1904; Philip A. Bruce, *History of the University of Virginia,* 4 vols., New York, 1921, 4:252–82; William B. O'Neal, *Pictorial History of the University of Virginia,* Charlottesville, Va., 1968. Jefferson's design of the Rotunda itself is detailed in William B. O'Neal, *Jefferson's Buildings at the University of Virginia: The Rotunda,* Charlottesville, Va., 1960; and Joseph L. Vaughan and Omer A. Gianniny, *Thomas Jefferson's Rotunda Restored, 1973–76: A Pictorial Review with Commentary,* Charlottesville, Va., 1981.

51. Faculty Report to the Rector and Visitors, October 31, 1895, University Archives, Alderman Library, University of Virginia. In the closing sections of the report the faculty urged returning to Jeffersonian classicism in an effort to harmonize any new buildings with the original campus. This rather novel idea, for the time, was broached by John Kevan Peebles in "Thomas Jefferson, Architect," *AABN* 47 (January 19, 1895), 29, which advocated a return to classical architecture on the campus. Peebles was a graduate of the university, 1890, and taught there until 1892 when he established an architectural practice in Norfolk. See W. B. Rhoads, *The Colonial Revival,* New York, 1977, 190–91.

52. Copy, John M. Carrère to Charles A. Coolidge, Boston, January 14, 1896, Architects Relations file, box M-15, 1968 Coll., MM&W Archive, NYHS. Carrère, who had been supervising construction of his firm's Jefferson Hotel in Richmond when the Rotunda fire occurred, wrote the university of his firm's interest in serving as architect for the rebuilding; see Carrère to W. C. N. Randolph, Rector, January 20, 1896 in Armistead C. Gordon Papers, Manuscripts Department, Alderman Library, University of Virginia. Mead wrote similarly on behalf of McKim, Mead & White; Mead to Dr. A. H. Buckmaster, November 5, 1895, in Proctors' Records, Box 22, Manuscripts Department, Alderman Library, University of Virginia.

53. Stanford White, for McKim, Mead & White, to W. M. Thornton, faculty president, February 26, 1896, Buildings and Grounds Coll., Manuscripts Department, Alderman Library, University of Virginia. This letter is the subject of careful study in George H. Yetter, "Stanford White at the University of Virginia: Some New Light on an Old Question," *JSAH* 40 (December 1981), 320–25, where the letter is quoted in full. McKim, Mead & White were appointed partly through the efforts of John Kevan Peebles, who made a journey to Charlottesville to speak on their behalf; see William B. O'Neal, *Architectural Drawing in Virginia, 1819–1969,* Charlottesville, Va., 1969, 114.

54. Francis L. Berkeley, Jr., "Mr. Jefferson's Rotunda: Myths and Realities," *University of Virginia Alumni News* 60 (1972), 8.

55. White had written to W. M. Thornton his belief that Jefferson had wanted the larger open space but was forced to subdivide the interior because of circumstances; this idea was repeated in the "Report of the Architects to the Building Committee," *Alumni Bulletin of the University of Virginia* 2 (February 1896), 138–39; and in an article prepared by White, "The Buildings of the University of Virginia," *Corks and Curls* 2 (1898), 127–30, which concludes with a tribute to Jefferson's ability as an architect. The decision to open up the Rotunda was applauded by Montgomery Schuyler, "The Architecture of American Colleges: VIII. The Southern Colleges," *ARec* 30 (July 1911), 78–84. Jefferson's own drawings are reproduced in O'Neal, *Rotunda.* White's rebuilding is illustrated in the *Monograph* 2:110–110A and in Vaughan and Gianniny, *Rotunda Restored,* passim. Strong feelings surfaced in the 1960s for an archaeologically correct restoration of the interiors as they had been built by Jefferson. Plans were prepared, 1966–72, by Louis W. Ballou, and during 1973–76, the McKim, Mead & White interiors were replaced. Considerable controversy was generated by this well-intended work, for to obtain a conjectural Jefferson interior a genuine McKim, Mead & White interior had to be destroyed. For the restoration process, see Vaughan and Gianniny, *Rotunda Restored,* 63–163; and Frederick D. Nichols, "Restoring Jefferson's University," in Charles E. Peterson, ed., *Building Early America,* Philadelphia, 1976, 319–40.

56. For the firm's new buildings see the *Monograph* 2:110–110A; *Brickbuilder* 6 (January 1897), pls. 1–16. White's comment quoted by Edward Simmons, *From Seven to Seventy,* New York, 1922, 241. White's instructions to superintendent Theodore H. Skinner noted in White to Daniel F. Harmon, March 11, 1898, cited in *University of Virginia Board of Visitors Minutes* 7:246, Alderman Library, University of Virginia.

57. For Radcliffe College see David McCord, *An Acre for Education,* rev. ed., Cambridge, Mass., 1958.

58. Data on Sarah, Mrs. Henry Whitman, from a biographical sketch by Ethel M. Desborough, May 28, 1968, Radcliffe Archives, Schlesinger Library, Radcliffe College.

59. McKim to Sarah Whitman, n.d. but c. April, 1897, quoted in Moore, *McKim,* 106–07. It may be significant that McKim's daughter, Margaret, attended Radcliffe for a year and a half before ill health forced her to leave in 1897; see Moore, *McKim,* 166.

60. McKim to Sarah Whitman, April 1, 1897, CFM-LC; and McKim to Sarah Whitman, June 1, 1897,

CFM-LC, printed in part in Moore, *McKim,* 107.

61. For the Radcliffe Gymnasium see: the *Monograph* 2:-122–23; *Brickbuilder* 10 (February 1901), pls. 11, 14.

62. McKim to Edward Hooper, July 8, 1896, CFM-LC, printed in part in Moore, *McKim,* 97–98.

63. See Olmsted and Kimball, *Olmsted,* 1:13, 37. F. L. Olmsted, Jr., discussed the proposed approach in "Harvard and the Charles River," *Harvard Graduates' Magazine* 7 (December 1898), 173–77. The Olmsted approach was illustrated and discussed by Walter Dana Swan, "The Harvard Memorial Gates," *AReview* 8 (June 1901), 61–65; and is reproduced in J. Fabos, G. Milde, and V. M. Weinmayr, *Frederick Law Olmsted, Sr., Founder of Landscape Architecture in America,* Cambridge, Mass., 1968, 85. Planning the Harvard Yard was later entrusted to Burnham and F. L. Olmsted, Jr., in 1905, with no result; see Moore, *Burnham,* 1:246–55.

64. McKim to A. W. Longfellow, n.d., printed in Moore, *McKim,* 99. See also related letters: McKim to Wendell Garrison, July 14, 1896, CFM-LC; and McKim to Martin Brimmer, October 13, 1899, Harvard Archives.

65. McKim to C. E. Norton, n.d., printed in Moore, *McKim,* 100. Norton's proposals are illustrated in the *Harvard Graduates' Magazine* 9 (June–September 1900), 27; and the *Harvard Monthly* supplement for June 1900 (clipping in the Harvard Archives).

66. For the Harvard gates see: the *Monograph* 2:152–54; Montgomery Schuyler, "The Architecture of American Colleges: I. Harvard," *ARec* 26 (October 1909), 243–69; W. D. Swan, "Harvard Gates," *AReview* 8 (June 1901), 61–65, pls. 39–46, 65–70; *Brickbuilder* 10 (September 1901).

67. Henry L. Higginson to McKim, July 18, 1901, Box 36, McKim-Maloney Coll., NYPL.

68. For the history of power at Niagara Falls see Edward Dean Adams, *Niagara Power, History of the Niagara Falls Power Company,* 2 vols., privately printed, 1927. Additional information is given in: *Cassier's Magazine* 8 (July 1895), the entire issue devoted to the power plant at Niagara Falls; Ralph Greenhill and Thomas D. Maloney, *Niagara,* Toronto, 1969; and my "Three Industrial Towns by McKim, Mead & White," *JSAH* 38 (December 1979), 317–47. See too Theodore A. Sande, *Industrial Archaeology, A New Look at the American Heritage,* Brattleboro, Vt., 1976, 54–55.

69. Edward Dean Adams to White, July 14, 1892, Cataract Construction Company file, box M-15, 1968 Coll., MM&W Archive, NYHS.

70. Adams, *Niagara Power,* 2:65–75.

71. The first and second powerhouses were demolished, 1966–67, to make way for the Robert Moses Parkway; the entrance arch of the first powerhouse was saved and reerected on Goat Island. The interiors of the powerhouses were planned by company engineers and incorporated an internal steel frame which carried only the weight of the traveling crane. There was widespread scientific and general interest in the Niagara Falls power plant since it was the first large-scale commercial application of this new technology. *Scientific American* carried a series of articles on the installation during 1892–93, and *Harper's Weekly* also had a number of articles on it from 1891 through 1897.

See too: Mariana Griswold Van Rensselaer, "Niagara," *Century* 36 (June 1899), 184–202; E. A. LeSeur, "Commercial Power Development at Niagara," *Popular Science* 45 (September 1894), 608–30; G. Forbes, "Harnessing Niagara," *Blackwood's Magazine* 158 (September 1895), 430–44.

72. Adams, *Niagara Power* 1:328–29. Echota is discussed in more detail in my "Three Industrial Towns." See too, John Bogart, "The Industrial Village of Echota at Niagara Falls," *Cassier's Magazine* 8 (July 1895), 307–21.

73. Other contemporary housing is discussed in my "Three Industrial Towns," and in my *Concise History* where Oakgrove, Willimantic, Conn., is illustrated, 138–40.

74. White to John A. Chanler, November 5, 1894, Letter-book 12, Stanford White Correspondence, Avery Library, Columbia University.

75. Robert Cheney to White, April 3, 1905, Cheney file, box 594, 1950 Coll., MM&W Archive, NYHS.

76. McKim to H. A. C. Taylor, April 22, 1892, CFM-LC.

77. Similar but somewhat simpler is the firm's William E. D. Stokes (William H. Moore) house, New York, 1898–1900. The Taylor house was published in: the *Monograph* 1:80–82; *AReview* 3 (November 1894), 56, pls. 41–42. See also the H. A. C. Taylor file, box 124, 1950 Coll., MM&W Archive, NYHS. The Florentine model is noted in C. L. V. Meeks, "Wright's Eastern Seaboard Contemporaries: Creative Eclecticism in the United States around 1900," *Acts of the Twentieth International Congress of the History of Art,* 4 vols., Princeton, 1963, 4:64–77. See also my "McKim, Mead & White Reappraised," 43–45.

78. For the Levi P. Morton house see: *Brickbuilder* 11 (January 1902), 2; and *InArch* 33 (May 1899), 28.

79. For the Stuyvesant Fish house see *InArch* 33 (May 1899). For the Philip A. Rollins house see: the *Monograph* 2:162–63; *Architecture* 5 (January 15, 1902), 17; *AABN* 89 (May 12, 1906), 164, no. 1585; and Herbert Croly, "The Renovation of the New York Brownstone District," *ARec* 13 (June 1903), 559.

80. For the adjoining Butler and Guthrie houses see: *AABN* 64 (June 10, 1899), 87, no. 1224; *Brickbuilder* 7 (April 1898), pls. 27–30; *Architecture and Building* 27 (November 27, 1897). For the later conversion of the Butler house for the Women's City Club, see *Architecture* 39 (June 1919), pls. 86–89.

81. The Robert K. Root house appeared in *AABN* 91 (January 12, 1907), 31, no. 1620; and *Brickbuilder* 5 (August 1896), pls. 44–47. The Charles H. Williams house was published in *Brickbuilder* 5 (June 1896), pls. 33–35; and 7 (December, 1898), 266. The George L. Williams house appeared in: *AABN* 91 (February 25, 1907), 88, no. 1626; *Brickbuilder* 6 (October 1897), pls. 81–84, and 9 (April 1900), 88; and *InArch* 34 (August 1899).

82. All the country houses noted here appear in the *Monograph.* For the Vanderbilt house see: Moore, *McKim,* 259, 268–69; *ARec* 10 (October 1900), 188–89; *InArch* 3 (August 1899), 8; *Life* 28 (January 2, 1950), 89–92; and Katherine B. Menz and Donald McTernan, "Decorating for the Frederick Vanderbilts," *19th Century* 3 (1977), 44–50. For the Oelrichs house see: Stuart Bartlett, "Some Newport Villas," *AReview* 15 (March 1908), 41–43, 51–53; *ARec* 17 (January 1905), 50–61; *Brick-*

builder 10 (March 1901). For the E. D. Morgan house see: J. A. Gade, "An Ideal American Country Plan: the Country House of E. D. Morgan," *AReview* 14 (September 1907), 201–03, pls. 51–65. For the Alfred A. Pope house see: *ARec* 20 (August 1906), 122–29; *AReview* 9 (November 1902), 282–83; the reference to Mount Vernon was stipulated by Theodate, Pope's daughter, the actual client, who assisted in preparation of the drawings as is evident in the A. A. Pope files, box 213 Old Mixed Files, 1950 Coll., and in box M-3, II, and M-13, 1968 Coll., MM&W Archive, NYHS. See also Nancy LaRoche, "The Hill-Stead Museum, A Victory for the Muses," *Art News* 74 (December 1975), 70–72. For the James L. Breese house, also inspired by Washington's Mount Vernon, see J. A. Gade "Long Island Country Places," *House and Garden* 3 (March 1903), 117–26. The Breese house also appeared in Barr Ferree, *American Estates and Gardens*, New York, 1904, 173; and John C. Baker, ed., *American Country Homes and their Gardens*, Philadelphia, 1906, 197–203. The Elliott F. Shepard house, Woodlea, Scarborough, N. Y., 1890–05, was published in *ARec* 12 (October 1902), 549–68. The Hamilton McKown Twombly estate, Florham Farms, near Morristown, N. J., 1891–97, was never published.

83. White to Elinor Patterson, January 2, 1901, Album XVIII, MM&W Coll., Avery Library, Columbia University.

84. The extensive grounds of the Mackay estate were laid out by Guy Lowell; the farm and stable buildings were by Warren & Wetmore. For the Mackay house see Lawrence Wodehouse, "Stanford White and the Mackays: A Case Study in Architect-Client Relationships," *Winterthur Portfolio* 11 (1976), 213–33. See also: Herbert Croly, "The Lay-out of a Large Estate, 'Harbor Hill,' the Country Seat of Mr. Clarence H. Mackay, at Roslyn, L. I.," *ARec* 16 (December 1904), 531–55; *ARec* 16 (October 1904), 299–307, 326, 332, 352, 379; and Robert L. Zion, "How our half lives . . . ," *Landscape Architecture* 44 (April 1954), 127–31.

85. For the Nickerson house see: the *Monograph* 1:96–97; Bunting, *Back Bay*, 313; and *AReview* 15 (October 1908), 154, pls. 72–73.

86. For the Page house see: the *Monograph* 1:94–95; *AABN* 75 (March 22, 1902), 95, no. 1369; *ARec* 14 (November 1903), 412, 418, and 30 (October 1911), 438; and *Brickbuilder* 9 (July 1900). Page, well known for his regionalist literature about the South after the Civil War, was instrumental in helping save Mount Vernon; see his *History and Preservation of Mount Vernon*, New York, 1910, for the Mount Vernon Ladies Association. He also was the brother-in-law of Bryan Lathrop, and it was Florence Lathrop who directed Page to the firm; see Thomas Nelson Page file, box M-8, 1968 Coll., MM&W Archive, NYHS. For the Thomas O. Selfridge, Jr., house see: *Brickbuilder* 8 (May 1899), pls. 36–37; *AABN* 90 (September 8, 1906), 80, no. 1602. McKim persuaded the American Institute of Architects to purchase Thornton's Octagon in 1901 for their national headquarters; see Glenn Brown, "Personal Reminiscences of Charles Follen McKim: McKim and the American Institute of Architects," *ARec* 38 (November 1915), 576.

87. The double Taylor houses were published only in the *Monograph* 2:121. For the Goodwin houses see: the *Monograph* 2:120–21; *ARec* 7 (April–June 1898), 462; *Architecture* 5 (January 15, 1902), 5; and *Brickbuilder* 7 (May 1898), pl. 34. Philip L. Goodwin later compiled a history of the houses, *Rooftrees*, 1933, which proved most helpful in the restoration of the duplex; see Ralph L. Walter, "Restoration of Two 19th Century McKim, Mead & White Townhouses," *Technology and Conservation* 6 (Winter 1981), 18–24.

88. H. B. Hollins to Mead, June 2, 1899, H. B. Hollins file, box 251, 1950 Coll., MM&W Archive, NYHS.

89. For Garden City see Vincent E. Seyfried, *The Founding of Garden City, 1869–93*, Uniondale, N. Y., 1969; and M. H. Smith, *History of Garden City*, Manhasset, N. Y., 1963, 50–52, 68–71; Ms. Smith indicates the hotel did much to invigorate the growth of Garden City. Among the heirs to the Stewart estate were Prescott Hall Butler, who led the legal battle, and Stanford's wife, Bessie. White was subsequently named one of the directors of the newly organized Garden City Company.

90. For the first Garden City Hotel see *Brickbuilder* 5 (April 1896), pls. 21–23. For the rebuilt hotel see: the *Monograph* 1:72; *AReview* 19 (April 1913), 142–44; *Architecture* 23 (May 15, 1911), 66. White may have been influenced in his reference by McKim's involvement as a consultant in a restoration of the Independence Hall tower; see McKim's letters to Walter Cope, February 16, 1899, and to Edgar V. Seeler, April 3, 1899, CFM-LC. See also Lee H. Nelson, "Independence Hall: Its Fabric Restored," and Penelope H. Batcheler, "Independence Hall: Its Appearance Restored," in Charles E. Peterson, ed., *Building Early America*, Philadelphia, 1976, 279–97, 298–318; as well as John Maass, "Architecture and Americanism, or Pastiches of Independence Hall," *Historic Preservation* 22 (April–June 1970), 17–25.

91. See Moore, *McKim*, 104–06. The Harvard Union is discussed in letters: McKim to Prof. Warren P. Laird, University of Pennsylvania, September 12, 1899, CFM-LC; and McKim to Charles Eliot, President, Harvard University, November 9, 1899, Harvard Archives. The building was published in: the *Monograph* 2:158–61; *AABN* 76 (April 5, 1902), 6, no. 1371; and *Brickbuilder* 10 (September 1901). For commentary see: Herbert D. Hale, "Recent Buildings at Harvard University," *AReview* 8 (June 1901), 65–70, pls. 45–46; and Schuyler's essay on Harvard, *ARec* 26 (October 1909), 243–69. Higginson's dedicatory address is published in *Addresses by Henry Lee Higginson . . .* , Boston, 1902; see too Bliss Perry, *Life and Letters of Henry Lee Higginson*, Boston, 1921. There were also a series of articles announcing the gift, describing the building, and reporting its opening in the *Harvard Graduates' Magazine* 8 (December 1899), 239–43; 9 (June 1901), 487–91; and 10 (December 1901), 214–33.

92. From *The Letters of George Santayana*, New York, 1955, quoted in D. S. Tucci, *Built in Boston*, Boston, 1978, 202.

93. Lloyd McKim Garrison, "New York's Harvard House," *Harvard Graduates' Magazine* 3 (September 1894), 23–30, printed in part in Moore, *McKim*, 108.

The first phase of the Harvard Club appeared in *AABN* 49 (July 20, 1895), 31, no. 1021. The first addition, 1900–05, was published in: *AABN* 89 (January 6, 1906), 16, no. 1567, 89 (January 13, 1906), 16, no. 1568, and 89 (April 7, 1906), 124, no. 1580; *Architecture* 11 (March 1905), pl. 23; *Brickbuilder* 15 (February 1906), pls. 21–22; and Herbert Croly, "The New Harvard Club House," *ARec* 19 (March 1906), 194–98, 206. The second addition, 1913–16, was published in: *Architecture and Building* 47 (December 1915), 439–42, 455; *Architecture* 32 (November 1915), pls. 132–34; and John T. Boyd, "The Addition to the New York Harvard Club . . . ," *ARec* 38 (December 1915), 615–30. The building, as of 1915, is also reproduced in the *Monograph* 4:340–45.

94. The basic source is James W. Alexander, *A History of the University Club of New York*, New York, 1915, 84–147, condensed in Moore, *McKim*, 255–59.

95. Meeks, "Wright's Contemporaries: Creative Eclecticism" 71 (see n. 77), suggests several Renaissance sources for the University Club. Although the better known Medici and Strozzi palaces are sometimes mentioned as models for the club, it is closer to the Palazzo Spannocchi, Siena, by Giuliano da Maiano, begun 1473, or the Palazzo Bocchi, Bologna, by Vignola, begun 1545, particularly in the use of mezzanine levels. The emphasis on the corner piers seems to derive from Bolognese examples such as the Palazzo Albergati. The heavily banded columns at the entrance may derive from such examples as the Zecca, Venice, by Sansovino, 1537; the courtyard of the Palazzo Pitti, Florence, by Ammanati, 1558–70; the portal of the Palazzo Borghese, Rome, by Longhi, c. 1600; or the entrance to the theater of the Palazzo Barberini, Rome, by Pietro da Cortona, c. 1640.

96. The shields and inscriptions were designed by Daniel Chester French, while the keystones at the windows were designed and cut by Charles Niehaus. Although the club seal over the entrance was designed by Kenyon Cox, it was carved by George Brewster in 1898–1900. The dissension over the shields and inscriptions is described at length by Alexander, *University Club*, 138–47, with photographs of the Palazzo Spada, Rome, used by McKim in his defense.

97. McKim to Lawrence Grant White, Paris, May 18, 1909, Moore CM-LC.

98. The University Club, particularly its interiors, was extensively published; numerous views appeared in *AABN* during the summer and autumn of 1899. See also: the *Monograph* 2:130–40C; *AReview* 6 (December 1899), pls. 79–84, and 7 (May 1900), pls. 27–29; *Brickbuilder* 19 (February 1910), 56–58, pl. 24; *InArch* 47 (July 1906); *Western Architect* 37 (February 1928), 34–35. Egerton Swartwout worked on the drawings for the University Club and in "Architectural Decade," 94–100, gives a good description of how the office handled such a project. The first drawings were made by Weekes and Sawyer. During the last stages of construction, full-scale mock-ups of the cornice were lifted into place atop the walls to study details *in situ*, particularly the lion heads. In the main hall, which Swartwout says was his particular responsibility, the architraves are of white Norwegian marble stained with tobacco juice to obtain a golden color. He also notes that the Connemara quarries in Ireland were exhausted in supplying the material for the columns.

99. The stark white vaults appeared in *AABN* 65 (August 12, 1899), 55, no. 1233.

100. Mowbray's account of the completion of the library murals, reprinted in Moore, *McKim*, 259–63, is adapted from *H. Siddons Mowbray, Mural Painter (1858–1928)*, Herbert F. Sherwood, ed., privately printed, 1928. Mowbray asserts that McKim purposely left the vaults white to generate comment and spur the club into raising funds for the murals. The visit of Prince Henry of Prussia in March 1902 was decisive in persuading the club to have the vaults painted. The furniture especially designed by the firm for the club is discussed in Channing Blake, "Architects as Furniture Designers," *Antiques* 109 (May 1976), 1042–47.

101. For Sherry's see: the *Monograph* 1:98–99; *AABN* 62 (December 24, 1898), 107, no. 1200, 63 (January 7, 1899), 7, no. 1202, and 63 (January 21, 1899), 22, no. 1204; *Architect* 12 (May 1929), 157–71; *AForum* 50 (June 1929), 859–61; *ARec* 7 (April–June 1898), 376; *Architecture and Building* 61 (November 1929), 169, 179–80; *InArch* 33 (June 1899).

102. Had it not been for a hand injury, H. L. Higginson might well have pursued a career in music. His formal academic study consisted of less than a year at Harvard, when failing eyesight caused him to be placed with relatives in Brattleboro, Vermont, there to take Dr. Wesselhöft's water cure. Following this he studied music several years in the United States and Vienna before the injury brought his musical career to an end. He then entered the family banking house of Lee, Higginson & Company, Boston, established by his father and uncle. Successful in this, he gradually acquired considerable means, much of which he immediately dispersed in various philanthropies of which the Boston Symphony was but one. By 1917 he had contributed nearly $1,000,000 to the orchestra and construction of Symphony Hall. His brother, Francis Lee Higginson, also a partner in the business, commissioned the house next to the firm's Whittier house, 1881–83. For H. L. Higginson see *DAB* 9:12, and Bliss Perry, *Life and Letters of Henry Lee Higginson*, Boston, 1921. The Boston Symphony was the third established in the United States, preceded by two in New York. A brief account of the design of Symphony Hall is given in Moore, *McKim*, 101–104, but see, too, M. A. DeWolfe Howe, *The Boston Symphony Orchestra*, Boston, 1914, 3–16, 94–95; and E. Earle Johnson, *Symphony Hall, Boston*, Boston, 1950, 11–19.

103. Higginson to McKim, October 27, 1892, Boston Symphony Hall file, box M-10, 1968 Coll., MM&W Archive, NYHS.

104. Higginson to McKim, November 27, 1892, loc. cit.

105. McKim to Wendall Garrison, November 24, 1893, CFM-LC, notes the plaster model is nearly ready for shipment to Boston. Comments concerning the public reaction to the model, from the Boston *Transcript*, January 15, 1894, are quoted in Moore, *McKim*, 102.

106. Higginson to McKim, October 27, 1898, Boston Symphony Hall file, box M-10, 1968 Coll., MM&W Archive, NYHS.

107. Dedicatory address by Henry Lee Higginson, Octo-

ber 15, 1900, quoted in Moore, *McKim,* 103; see also *Addresses by . . . Higginson,* Boston, 1902.

108. The acoustical analysis of Symphony Hall is discussed in William D. Orcutt, *Wallace Clement Sabine: A Study in Achievement,* Norwood, Mass., 1922, 131–45. Sabine's experiments and his method of analysis are presented in his *Collected Papers on Acoustics,* Cambridge, Mass., 1922. Sabine's reaction to McKim's Greek theater scheme was at first negative, but later, on studying the drawings closely, he changed his mind; his comments are noted in McKim to E. A. Darling, August 12, 1899, CM-LC. McKim's Greek theater design may have had some influence on Burnham's Orchestra Hall, Chicago, 1904–05.

109. Sabine calculated that had the Gewandhaus simply been enlarged seventy percent, with no addition of sound-absorbent materials, the volume would have produced a disastrously long reverberation time of 3.02 seconds.

110. Following the success of the Symphony Hall, Sabine was consulted by the firm on treatment of the walls of the legislative chambers of the Rhode Island State House; see his letters to MM&W, Wallace Sabine file, box M-5, 1968 Coll., MM&W Archive, NYHS. The continuing influence of the Boston Symphony Hall as an acoustical model is demonstrated in the remodeling of Philharmonic Hall/Avery Fisher Hall, New York, 1975–76. To correct serious defects in the original building, acoustical engineer Cyril M. Harris and architects Johnson & Burgee gutted the interior and rebuilt the interior as a rectangular box auditorium with deeply paneled walls and a megaphone-shaped stage, remarkably like Boston Symphony Hall in plan and cross section. See Bruce Bliven, Jr., "Annals of Architecture: A Better Sound," *The New Yorker* 52 (November 8, 1976), 51–54; *Progressive Architecture* 58 (March 1977), 64–69.

111. For Symphony Hall see: the *Monograph* 2:141–43; *AABN* 72 (May 11, 1901), 48, no. 1324; *ARec* 12 (August 1902), 340–41; *AReview* 7 (October 1900), 121, pls. 62–67; *Brickbuilder* 9 (September 1900).

112. Swartwout, "Architectural Decade," 35, says he worked on the project and that the competition drawings were done by Hewlett and Austin Lord; the working drawings were supervised by Sawyer, while Swartwout worked on the details of the central pavilion.

113. For the Brooklyn Museum see: the *Monograph* 1:85–91; *AReview* 6 (December 1899), pl. 78, elevation details initialed by Swartwout; and *Architecture* 18 (July 1908), pls. 54–58. The monumental front staircase was removed in the 1930s.

114. McKim to White, December 27, 1893, CFM-LC. The Reverend Donald, while rector of the Church of the Ascension, New York, had been responsible for the embellishment of the Chancel which White designed. In a letter to Mead, February 14, 1893, MM&W Archive, NYHS, Donald asks if White would be able to undertake completion of the church.

115. For Cullum Hall see: the *Monograph* 2:116–19; *AABN* 69 (July 21, 1900), 23, no. 1282; *AReview* 8 (May 1910), pls. 31–34; *ARec* 14 (December 1903), 462.

116. An undated memorandum from Col. C. W. Larned to MM&W (Cullum Memorial file, box 201, 1950 Coll.,

MM&W Archive, NYHS), lists the other contestants as R. M. Hunt; Babb, Cook & Willard; C. C. Haight; and G. B. Post. McKim to Mead June 6, 1894 (CFM-LC, printed in Moore, *McKim,* 266–67), notes cost trimming. For Cullum's administration at West Point, see: Sidney Forman, *West Point, A History . . . ,* New York, 1950; Edward S. Holden, ed., *The Centennial of the United States Military Academy at West Point, New York, 1802–1902,* 2 vols., Washington, D.C., 1904; Stephen E. Ambrose, *Duty, Honor, Country: A History of West Point,* Baltimore, 1966.

117. Montgomery Schuyler, "A 'Modern Classic,' " *ARec* 15 (May 1904), 431–44, compares Cullum favorably with White's Knickerbocker Trust, New York.

118. Description in Cornell Medical School file, box 219, 1950 Coll., MM&W Archive, NYHS. The building appeared in: the *Monograph* 2:157; *AABN* 72 (June 8, 1901), 80, no. 1328; *Brickbuilder* 9 (October 1900), pls. 76–77. For the connection of the Cornell Medical School with the New York University Medical School and Bellevue Hospital, see Theodore F. Jones, *New York University,* New York, 1933, 172–80; and Morris Bishop, *A History of Cornell,* Ithaca, N. Y., 1962, 317–21.

119. McKim also was consulted on the design of the Harvard football stadium, proposed in 1894 to stand on property given Harvard by H. L. Higginson. The grounds were laid out by F. L. Olmsted, Jr., the concrete structure designed by Professors Ira N. Hollis and J. L. Johnson, and the architectural frame designed by McKim with the assistance of George de Gersdorff. Construction was delayed until 1903, however, and McKim and Burnham meanwhile debated the orientation with Olmsted (see Moore, *Burnham* 1:142). See letters, McKim to Higginson, December 16, 1901, and McKim to Hollis, November 17, 1903, CFM-LC.

120. Higginson to Charles Eliot, July 13, 1899, Harvard Archives. Architectural instruction at Harvard had begun in 1894 in a temporary building on Holmes Field, at some distance from the library and the Fogg Art Museum.

121. McKim to Charles Eliot, October 5, 1899, Harvard Archives.

122. For Robinson Hall see: the *Monograph* 3:204–06; *AABN* 69 (September 22, 1900), 95, no. 1291, and 75 (February 22, 1902) 63, no. 1365; *AReview* 7 (August 1900), pls. 47–50; *Brickbuilder* 10 (September 1901); *InArch* 39–40 (November 1902); and "The University's New Buildings," *Harvard Graduates' Magazine* 9 (September 1900), 23–31, and 10 (December 1901), 252–54.

123. Charles Eliot Norton, *Report of the Board of Overseers,* 1904, quoted in Moore, *McKim,* 111.

124. The work in Naugatuck is treated in more detail in my "Three Industrial Towns," including background material on the town. Basic is Constance McLaughlin Green, *History of Naugatuck, Connecticut,* New Haven, 1948, and the condensation in her *American Cities in the Growth of the Nation,* London, 1957. For John Howard Whittemore see the *National Cyclopedia of American Biography* 15:70.

125. A. C. David, "An Architectural Oasis," *ARec* 19 (February 1906), 135–44.

126. The landscape work is noted in the Whittemore entry in the *Encyclopedia of Connecticut Biography: Representative Citizens* 1:282. Some correspondence and drawings are preserved by the J. H. Whittemore Company, Naugatuck, Conn.

127. For the high school see: the *Monograph* 3:219–21; *ARec* 19 (February 1906), 163–64; *AReview* 12 (April 1905), 117, pls. 21–23.

128. For the Congregational Church see: the *Monograph* 3:220–21; *ARec* 20 (September 1906), 202; and *Brickbuilder* 10 (June 1910), pls. 43–46, which show clearly the riveted steel frame within the steeple. Originally the sanctuary had a smooth segmental barrel vault which caused acoustical problems; the solution, which involved adding deep coffers, is discussed in Wallace C. Sabine, "Architectural Acoustics: Correction of Acoustical Difficulties," *Architectural Quarterly of Harvard University* (March 1912), reprinted in his *Collected Papers on Acoustics*, Cambridge, Mass., 1922, 131–61.

129. This civic consciousness is well illustrated by the treatment of the library and high school. In 1963 the library was enlarged by means of a simple cube at the rear while the original building was cleaned and restored inside and out. In 1961 the high school was gutted by fire, but since the outer bearing walls had suffered no structural damage, the interior was rebuilt using a steel frame, and the exterior was carefully restored. See my "Three Industrial Towns."

130. For the Bowery Savings Bank see: the *Monograph* 1:66–68; *AABN* 74 (October 12, 1901), 16, no. 1346; *AReview* 4 (January 1896), 8, pls. 6–7, and 12 (March 1905), 102.

131. Norval White and Elliot Willensky, *A.I.A. Guide to New York City*, New York, 1967, 39. The bank was restored, 1981–82, by Swanke Hayden Connell Partners, Architects.

132. For Thomas's original New York Life headquarters, see James D. McCabe, Jr., *Lights and Shadows of New York Life*, Philadelphia, 1872, 127; and Winston Weisman, "A New View of Skyscraper History," in Edgar Kaufmann, Jr., ed., *The Rise of an American Architecture*, New York, 1970, 124.

133. New York Life Insurance Company to MM&W, various letters March through May, 1893, NYLIC file, box 23, 1950 Coll., MM&W Archive, NYHS. In renovating the old building, White gutted the interior and inserted a steel frame. Drawings were prepared in 1894; construction commenced in 1896; the new building to the rear was completed in mid-1898; and the renovation of the original building was completed a year later.

134. Interiors only appear in the *Monograph* 1:93, and the Director's Room in *AABN* 79 (January 31, 1903), 39, no. 1414. The Director's Room and the Merchants' Club were decorated by D. Maitland Armstrong; his contribution and Martiny's sculpture are noted in letters in the NYLIC file, boxes 115 and 116, 1950 Coll., MM&W Archive, NYHS. The Director's Room was dismantled and reinstalled in the new headquarters building built on the site of White's Madison Square Garden from designs by Cass Gilbert, 1929.

135. Because of the distance, the firm was associated with architects Donaldson & Meier of Detroit, who supervised construction. See W. Hawkins Ferry, *The Buildings of Detroit*, 1968, 211; and Detroit Savings Bank file, box M-18, 1968 Coll., MM&W Archive, NYHS. The building was published in: the *Monograph* 2:124–26; *AReview* 8 (February 1901), pls. 12–14, and 12 (March 1905), pls. 95–97. Thomas W. Dewing painted the lunette mural, *Detroit Flanked by Commerce and Agriculture*, now relocated in the addition to the rear of the building built in 1914.

136. The firm's description, meant to accompany the drawings, survives as well, Misc. Competitions file, box M-14, 1968 Coll., MM&W Archive, NYHS. For this building a steel frame was proposed. For Bruce Price's winning entry and other skyscrapers of the nineties, see *A History of Real Estate, Building and Architecture in New York City*, New York, 1898, and W. Weisman, "A New View" (see n. 132).

137. McKim to Burnham, March 19, 1897, CFM-LC. The City College competition was won by George B. Post, the Ellis Island competition by Boring & Tilton. Swartwout, "Architectural Decade," 90, says the firm's Ellis Island entry was prepared by White, assisted by Whitney Warren. The firm had at first refused to participate in the City College competition because no professional advisor was engaged by the college; when C. B. J. Snyder was then appointed they accepted the invitation; see MM&W to CCNY, c. July 1897, Misc. Competition file, box M-14, 1968 Coll., MM&W Archive, NYHS. The firm also lost in the competition for a new law building for Yale University, which was given to J. Cleveland Cady; see McKim to R. K. Sheldon, April 19, 1893, CFM-LC. In a letter to Colonel Franklin Bartless, June 1, 1900, CFM-LC, McKim indicates the firm declined to enter the competition for the new Union Club.

138. The twelve finalists for the New York Public Library were: McKim, Mead & White; George B. Post; Cyrus Eidlitz; Carrère & Hastings; Peabody & Stearns; Charles C. Haight; J. H. Freedlander; Haydel & Shepard; Hornbostel, Wood & Palmer; Howard & Cauldwell; W. W. Smith; and Whitney Warren. See Harry Miller Lydenberg, *History of the New York Public Library*, New York, 1923, 442.

139. McKim to Carrère & Hastings, December 9, 1897, CFM-LC.

140. Sturgis, "McKim, Mead & White," 111.

141. For McKim's health see Moore, *McKim*, passim, but especially 148 and 153.

142. Swartwout, "Architectural Decade," 39, points out that McKim often discussed the plates of Letarouilly with him and greatly admired École drawings of the late eighteenth century and nineteenth century: "We had four volumes of Grand Prix of that period . . . and he never tired of looking at them when he saw them on my table. And the wonderful restorations of Despouy [sic] were a standard office bible and he often referred to them." H. D'Espouy edited the restoration drawings made by Prix de Rome pensionnaires and published several collections: *Fragments d'Architecture Antique*, Paris, [1896]; and *Fragments d'Architecture du Moyen Age et de la Renaissance*, 2 vols., Paris, [1897].

Chapter 6. PINNACLE, 1900–1909

1. Contract figures courtesy of Walker O. Cain. Added to the sums already cited, this yields a total, for the period 1879–1910, of approximately $77,800,000–$78,000,000 (figures for the early years are not definite). After 1903 much of the detail development was turned over to the assistants, Kendall (for McKim) and W. S. Richardson (for McKim and White). Mead was assisted by Burt L. Fenner, while Teunis J. Van der Bent was given charge of supervising construction and engineering. Kendall, Richardson, and Fenner were made full partners on January 1, 1906, and Van der Bent was so elevated in 1909.

2. Whitelaw Reid to Mead, January 8, 1908, Whitelaw Reid file, box M-7, 1968 Coll., MM&W Archive, NYHS.

3. Writing to Glenn Brown, October 19, 1901 (CFM-LC), McKim says he has none of the qualities needed in the president of the A.I.A., but he is willing to bow to the wishes of the membership. See also the series by Glenn Brown, "Personal Reminiscences of Charles Follen McKim," *ARec* 38 (November 1915), 575–82; 38 (December 1915), 681–89; 39 (January 1916), 84–88; 39 (February 1916), 178–85. Brown also included this in his *1860–1929: Memories*, Washington, D.C., 1931. For McKim's part in the purchase of the Octagon by the A.I.A., see William B. Hosmer, *The Presence of the Past*, New York, 1965, 200–201; and Glenn Brown, "Dr. William Thornton, Architect," *ARec* 6 (June–September 1896), 50–70.

4. McKim's presidential addresses are printed in *AABN* 78 (December 20, 1902), 91–92, and 82 (October 31, 1903), 35–36; the second is concerned with maintaining professional standards in the face of governmental reluctance to follow accepted plans or pay standard fees. During the 1903 A.I.A. meeting McKim worked with G. B. Post, R. S. Peabody, and Frank Miles Day, drafting a statement of "An Architect's Responsibilities and Remuneration" (see Architect's Commission file, box M-15, 1968 Coll., MM&W Archive, NYHS.) This statement is reprinted in full in the Appendix, and, in part, in my *America Builds*, New York, 1983.

5. See Moore, *McKim*, 128–81, 242–54, and Lucia and Alan Valentine, *The American in Rome, 1894–1969*, Charlottesville, Va., 1973.

6. The award is discussed at length in Moore, *McKim*, 223–41; transcripts of the speeches made by Sir Aston Webb, president of the RIBA, and McKim are printed in *JRIBA* 10 (June 27, 1903), 441–48, and *AABN* 81 (July 18, 1903), 20–22. Other notices appeared in *The Builder* 27 (June 1903) and in the *AIA Quarterly Bulletin* 4 (July 1903), 83–88. McKim's acceptance speech largely repeated what he had said in his A.I.A. presidential address several months previous. In McKim's letterbooks, CFM-LC, are copies of lists of photographs and drawings he supplied to Aston Webb for exhibition in London.

7. McKim's participation in the New York Municipal Art Commission is referred to by Aston Webb in his presentation speech (see previous note). McKim also served as a juror for the competition for the town hall of Irvington, N. Y., as noted in McKim to A. J. Manning, May 24, 1900, CFM-LC. He also organized the annual dinner for the A.I.A., January 11, 1905, arranging for President Roosevelt and other prominent public figures to speak in behalf of the plan of the Senate Park Commission then under attack; these addresses were edited and published by Charles Moore, *The Promise of American Architecture*, Washington, D.C., 1905. The cover design for the dinner program, by McKim, was based on the Cardosso medal of Bramante's Saint Peter's, 1505; see Moore, *McKim*, 254.

8. Mead to Bernard R. Green, September 25, 1905, CFM-LC. Mead enjoyed good health until his death in 1928, aged 82.

9. McKim to Bessie White, March 17, 1905, quoted in Moore, *McKim*, 295–96. The loss was estimated at half a million dollars at the time. See also White's letters to Mead during November 1905, Payne Whitney file, box 508, Old Mixed Files, 1950 Coll., MM&W Archive, NYHS, regarding how items purchased for the Whitney house and destroyed in the fire are to be covered by insurance or by refunds from the monies advanced to the architect.

10. White to Saint-Gaudens, June 23, 1903, Letterbook 29, Stanford White Correspondence, Avery Library, Columbia University. Saint-Gaudens was to cut the intaglio for the embossing.

11. For the Brooks Memorial see: Saint-Gaudens, *Reminiscences* 2:97–98, 313–27; Tharp, *Saint-Gaudens*, 325–398 passim.

12. White to Burnham, April 12, 1904, Letterbook 30, Stanford White Correspondence, Avery Library, Columbia University. Burnham was then beginning work on his Chicago plan, proposing a new lakefront park on made land, in the center of which was to be a museum housing the Marshall Field natural history collection; White wished his design to be related to Burnham's museum project. For the *Seated Lincoln* see: Saint-Gaudens, *Reminiscences* 2:307–11; Tharp, *Saint-Gaudens*, 332 to 397 passim.

13. For the Detroit Memorial Column see: *AABN* 68 (June 16, 1900), 88, no. 1277, with text by White; Anna Mathewson, "The Detroit Bicentennial Memorial," *Century* 60 (September 1900), 706–10; W. Hawkins Ferry, *The Buildings of Detroit*, Detroit, 1968, 219; Aline Saarinen, *The Proud Possessors*, New York, 1958, 126. See also Louis Sullivan's scathing criticism, "A Doric Column," *Kindergarten Chats*, New York, 1947, 58. Belle Isle Park had been landscaped by F. L. Olmsted, 1882–83, although only portions of his plan had been implemented. See Fein, *Olmsted*, Figs. 62 and 63 in comparison to White's scheme. In conjunction with the column, White was also working on a house for Charles Lang Freer, Detroit, which was never carried out; see letters from Freer to White, February through September 1900, Freer file and Detroit Savings Bank file, box M-18, 1968 Coll., MM&W Archive, NYHS. In designing the memorial White donated his time, although he was later awarded an honorarium of $3,750 by the Memorial Association.

The tip of Belle Isle was later embellished, in 1925, with the James Scott fountain by Cass Gilbert.

14. E. R. Kennedy to White, November 18, 1898, Prison Ship Martyrs' file, box M-12, 1968 Coll., MM&W Archive, NYHS. New York *Times* June 18, 1972, 60. The Detroit Memorial and the Prison Ship Martyrs' Memorial provided the model for the Perry Memorial, 1911–15, Put-in-Bay, South Bass Island, Lake Erie, by Joseph H. Freedlander and A. D. Seymour, Jr.; this stands 352 feet high. See Charles E. Frohman, *Put-in-Bay, Its History*, Columbus, Ohio, 1971, 81–107; *Architecture* 25 (March 15, 1912), 38–39; *Through the Ages* 1 (May 1923), 27. In view of these three giant Doric columns, it is not quite so curious why Adolf Loos thought a Doric column skyscraper would be appropriate in the Tribune Tower competition in 1922.

15. White to William E. Dodge, January 21, 1901; CFM-LC.

16. For the Sherman Monument see: Saint-Gaudens, *Reminiscences* 2:77, 123–36, 294–96; Tharp, *Saint-Gaudens*, 320–32; Craven, *Sculpture*, 390–91.

17. John W. Reps, *Monumental Washington*, Princeton, 1967, xiii. See also: Hines, *Burnham of Chicago*, 139–57; Moore, *Burnham*, 1:129–88; Moore, *McKim*, 182–203. For a summary of L'Enfant's plan for Washington see also my *Concise History*, 55–58, 115–16, and 216–18; a selection of L'Enfant's writings on his plan is reproduced in my *America Builds*.

18. For Bingham's proposals see Reps, *Monumental Washington*, 70–82.

19. Reps, *Monumental Washington*, 91; see also 83–93 for the other presentations.

20. Moore, *McKim*, 188. One is reminded, of course, of Burnham's famous aphorism to make no small plans.

21. Scrapbook 8, MM&W Coll., Avery Library, Columbia University, contains photographs of the final drawings and models as well as travel snapshots taken by the commission in Europe, including views of Versailles, Vaux-le-Vicomte, Villa Colonna, Villa d'Este, Villa Pappa Giulia, Villa Madama, Villa Albani, and Villa Lante at Bagnaia; all the major stops of the commission are represented.

22. Moore, *Burnham* 1:167; Moore, *McKim*, 201.

23. McKim's replanning of the Mall drew upon his tree-lined approach to Harvard from the Charles River. The report of the Senate Park Commission is discussed at length in Reps, *Monumental Washington*, 109–38. The official document is *Report of the Senate Committee on the District of Columbia on the Improvement of the Park System in the District of Columbia*, Senate Report No. 166, 57th Congress, 1st Session, Washington, D.C., 1902.

24. When construction of McKim's terraces was proposed, engineers discovered that such extensive disturbance of the grounds around the Washington Monument would threaten its stability; nothing was done. See the suggested landscaping of the grounds around the Monument in the plan of 1964 by Skidmore, Owings & Merrill, in Reps, *Monumental Washington*, 177–91.

25. McKim to Burnham, December 14, 1901 (CFM-LC), thanks Burnham for photographs of the Taj Mahal, whose reflecting pool also served as a reference.

26. L'Enfant to George Washington, September 11, 1789, quoted in Paul Caemmerer, *The Life of Pierre Charles L'Enfant*, Washington, D.C., 1950, 127–29.

27. M. Schuyler, "The Nation's New Capitol," New York *Times*, supplement, January 19, 1902, 4–5, later amplified in his "The Art of City Making," *ARec* 12 (May 1902), 1–26. The warm popular reception of the plan is described in Reps, *Monumental Washington*, 140–43. See Charles Moore, "The Improvement of Washington City," *Century* 63 (February 1902), 621–28, and 63 (March 1902), 747–57; Daniel Burnham, "White City and Capitol City," *Century* 63 (February 1902), 619–20. McKim to Herbert C. Wise, February 21, 1902 (CFM-LC), indicates McKim's great pleasure with the reproduction of the commission's perspectives in *House and Garden* 2 (February 1902), 38–56.

28. Moore, *McKim*, 203.

29. McKim to Moore, March 26, 1902; McKim to the Hon. George Peabody Wetmore, March 29, 1902; and McKim to O. W. Norcross, November 30, 1903, all CFM-LC.

30. For the Lincoln Memorial see: Reps, *Monumental Washington*, 155–59; and Michael Richman, *Daniel Chester French: An American Sculptor*, New York, 1976, 171–86.

31. McKim to Secretary of War Elihu Root, October 10, 1902, CFM-LC (quoted in full in my "Urban Architecture of McKim, Mead & White," 527–28). The proposed granite bridge was to be 1,600 feet long from the Maryland shore to Analostan Island, with fifteen arched spans at 75 feet each, except for a center span of 80 feet (with whatever adjustments were necessary at the ends); each span was to have a rise of 25 feet above mean low tide.

32. McKim to James Knox Taylor, June 13, 1901, CFM-LC.

33. William Howard Taft, "Address in Honor of Mr. Charles Follen McKim," in American Institute of Architects, *Charles Follen McKim Memorial Meeting*, Washington, D.C., 1910, 6.

34. President Roosevelt's address is reprinted in full in Charles Moore, ed., *The Promise of American Architecture*, Washington, D.C., 1905, 13–18.

35. For the Consultative Board and the Commission of Fine Arts, see Moore, *Burnham* 1:228–29, and Reps, *Monumental Washington*, 145–93. For the effect of the Park Commission's plan on the development of Washington see Reps, *Monumental Washington*, 182–93; M. Scott, *American City Planning Since 1890*, Berkeley, Calif., 1969, 47–109; and Charles Moore, "The Transformation of Washington . . . ," *National Geographic Magazine* 43 (June 1923), 569–96.

36. McKim to Moore, January 8, 1903, CFM-LC.

37. McKim to George Dudley Seymour, March 8, 1907; McKim to John F. Weir, Yale University, October 18, 1907, both CFM-LC.

38. For Joseph Pulitzer and his house see: Don Carlos Seitz, *Joseph Pulitzer*, New York, 1924, 13–14, 252–53; and W. A. Swanberg, *Pulitzer*, New York, 1967, 139, 268, 274, 280, 313–14. For background see: George Juergens, *Joseph Pulitzer and the New York World*, Princeton, 1966; and Julian S. Rammelkamp, *Pulitzer's Post Dispatch*, Princeton, 1967.

39. Mead to Pulitzer, November 27, 1900, Joseph Pulitzer file, box M-15, 1968 Coll., MM&W Archive, NYHS. Mead cautions him that the ornament in such a drawing "stands out brutally, where in effect, it is intended to be harmonious and unobtrusive. It is hardly fair for us to be judged by a drawing of this kind."

40. For Longhena see R. Wittkower, *Art and Architecture in Italy, 1600–1750,* 2nd ed., Baltimore, 1965, 191–96. For the Pulitzer house see: the *Monograph* 2:180–82; *ARec* 14 (November 1903), frontispiece; *Architects' and Builders' Magazine* 6 December 1904), 132. For the kitchen see the special issue of *ARec* 16 (October 1904), 384–92.

41. Mead to Pulitzer, October 24, 1900, and White to Pulitzer, February 13, 1902, Joseph Pulitzer file, box M-15, 1968 Coll., MM&W Archive, NYHS.

42. Pulitzer to MM&W, April 16 (1900?), Pulitzer Papers, Columbia University.

43. Mead to Wallace C. Sabine, April 14, 1903, Joseph Pulitzer file, box M-15, 1968 Coll., MM&W Archive, NYHS.

44. Mead to Wallace C. Sabine, November 16, 1903, loc. cit.

45. For the Patterson house see: *AABN* 89 (June 16, 1906), 204, no. 1590; *ARec* 13 (June 1903), 492; *Brickbuilder* 13 (April 1904); and *Prominent Buildings . . . by George Fuller,* New York, 1904, 190. Album XVIII, MM&W Coll., Avery Library, Columbia University, contains correspondence between White and the Pattersons, January 1901, in which Elinor Patterson inquires about the resistance of terra cotta to moisture (see ch. 5, n. 83).

46. For the Payne house see: the *Monograph* 3:289–92; *Architecture* 21 (April 15, 1910), 52–55, pls. 33–37; *New York Architect* 2 (November 1908), 301.

47. A large part of White's time in Europe during 1902–05 was spent in gathering art work and antiques for the Payne Whitney house: see letters and detailed account of all items in the Payne Whitney file, box 502, Old Mixed Files, 1950 Coll., MM&W Archive, NYHS. Letters in the Whitney file, box 508, loc. cit., indicate that Elsie de Wolfe purchased and arranged some of the furnishings.

48. Quoted in Wayne Andrews, *Architecture, Ambition and Americans,* New York, 1964, 196.

49. Helen Payne to White, n.d., Payne Whitney file, box 508, Old Mixed Files, 1950 Coll., MM&W Archive, NYHS.

50. For the Kane house see the *Monograph* 3:285–88. The Kane house inspired the severe William Hayward house, New York, by Guy Lowell; see Walter C. Voss, *Architectural Construction,* New York, 1925, 1: 311–72.

51. For the W. K. Vanderbilt, Jr., house see: the *Monograph* 3:259–60; *AABN* 92 (November 2, 1907), 144, no. 1662; *ARec* 23 (May 1908), 409–12; *Architecture* 15 (June 1907), pl. 60.

52. For the Astor tennis courts at Ferncliffe, see the *Monograph;* 2:113–15; *AABN* 92 (November 9, 1907), 152, no. 1663; *ARec* 18 (July 1905), 20–26; *Country Life* [US] 29 (November 1915), 38–39, and 74 (August 1938), 48–52. See also Virginia Cowles, *The Astors,* New York, 1979.

53. See William D. Orcutt, *Wallace Clement Sabine,* Norwood, Mass., 1933, 233–24, 208–209. As a result of this,

54. Guastavino and Sabine worked to perfect an acoustically porous ceramic tile, patented as "Rumford Tile" in 1914, which absorbed six times more sound than ordinary masonry and about one third that absorbed by felt.

54. For the Coolidge house see: the *Monograph* 3:222–24; *ARec* 20 (September 1906), 232–34; *Brickbuilder* 14 (February 1905). Similar but even more archaeologically correct in its Georgian allusions was the Cass Canfield house, Westbury, N.Y., 1902–03.

55. For the Arnold house see: *AABN* 91 (March 16, 1907), 112, no. 1629; and A. C. David, "A Modern Instance of Colonial Architecture, The House of Mr. B. W. Arnold at Albany, New York," *ARec* 17 (April 1905), 305–17.

56. Clarke's activities as a collector can be inferred from the many published catalogs of his sales in 1891, 1899, 1902, 1910, 1915, 1916, 1917, 1918, 1919, and 1925; see, too, his *Portraits of Early American Artists of the 17th, 18th, and 19th Centuries,* Philadelphia, 1928. Thomas B. Clarke (1848–1930), like White, was an inveterate clubman, and the two often met socially; see Baldwin, *White,* 216, 325.

57. For the Gibson house see: the *Monograph* 2:191–92; *ARec* 15 (February 1904), 172–79; and M. Schuyler, "The New New York House," *ARec* 19 (February 1906), 83–103.

58. H. A. C. Taylor to McKim, January 17, 1906, Misc. MM&W Correspondence file, box M-3, II, 1968 Coll., MM&W Archive, NYHS. McKim to H. A. C. Taylor, January 30, 1906, and McKim to Percy Pyne, February 3, 1906, CFM-LC.

59. For the Pyne house see: the *Monograph* 4:349–51A; and *Architecture* 24 (October 15, 1911), pl. 105. For the later renovation of the house by Walker O. Cain to accommodate the Center for Inter-American Relations, see *Interior Design* 38 (December 1967), 116–21; and *Interiors* 127 (December 1967), 82–93.

60. Roosevelt is quoted in Moore, *McKim,* 205. See also "Roosevelt and the Fine Arts," *AABN* 116 (December 17, 1919), 739–47.

61. McKim to Moore, April 9, 1902, CFM-LC. Accounts of the White House restoration are found in Moore, *McKim,* 204–22; and Charles Moore, ed., . . . *Restoration of the White House,* Senate Document 197, 57th Congress, 2nd Session, Washington, D.C., 1903, which he later adapted for his *Washington, Past and Present,* New York, 1929, 144–56. Portions of this report are quoted in Charles Hurd, *The White House, A Biography,* New York, 1940, 228–44.

62. McKim to Moore, April 17, 1902, CFM-LC.

63. Sundry Civil Act, 1902, quoted in Moore, *McKim,* 213–14.

64. McKim to President Roosevelt, July 11, 1902, CFM-LC.

65. McKim to Thomas Newbold, July 1, 1902, CFM-LC, printed in Moore, *McKim,* 214–15.

66. For descriptions and views of the White House prior to work in 1902, see the *Restoration of the White House* report.

67. See Glenn Brown, "Personal Reminiscences of . . . McKim," *ARec* 39 (February 1916), 84–88. For the renovated White House see: the *Monograph* 2:175–78;

"The Restoration of the White House," *AABN* 79 (February 28, 1903), 67–70; A. Burnley Bibb, "The Restoration of the White House," *House and Garden* 3 (March 1903), 127–39; *InArch* 41 (March 1903). The haste with which McKim had to make his often superficial corrections eventually had its effect. During President Truman's administration, when problems surfaced again, the entire building was gutted, but all fixtures and paneling were carefully removed and stored. Once a steel frame and new utilities had been fitted into the masonry walls, McKim's interiors were rebuilt, with only minor changes in the degree of relief of some of the carved plaster moldings in the ceilings. See Edwin B. Morris, *Report of the Commission on the Executive Mansion*, Washington, D.C., 1952.

68. See Moore, *McKim*, 208, 215, and Charles Moore, "The Restoration of the White House," *Century* 65 (April 1903), 806–31.

69. McKim to Moore, April 17, 1902, CFM-LC.

70. Moore, *McKim*, 206 n. 1. McKim and Burnham understood the realities of Washington well, for the temporary office was reconstructed and enlarged in 1909 and restored after a fire in 1929.

71. McKim to Moore, April 17, 1902, CFM-LC, printed in Moore, *McKim*, 206–07.

72. The office is discussed by McKim in letters to Moore, November and December 1904, CFM-LC. McKim to Senator William Loeb, January 8, 1906, notes that Burt Fenner and Mead had made the office wing their particular responsibility.

73. M. Schuyler, "The New White House," *ARec* 13 (April 1903), 388.

74. For the Brook Club see Thomas B. Clarke, *The Brook . . . its inception, incidents, organization, and progress, 1903–1930*, New York, 1930; and Baldwin, *White*, 228, 289–90, 325. For The Lambs see: the *Monograph* 3: 225–26; *Brickbuilder* 14 (September 1905), pl. 4; *Architecture* 12 (September 1905), pl. 71; and Baldwin, *White*, 228, 290, 324–25. For the Harmonie Club see the *Monograph* 3:228–29; *ARec* 19 (April 1906), 236–43; and *Architecture* 13 (February 1906), pls. 10–14. The Harmonie Club facade's high-waisted design resembles that of the project for a mint for the Duke of Castro by Sangallo the Younger, c. 1530, but it is unlikely that White knew of this (see L. H. Heydenreich and W. Lotz, *Architecture in Italy, 1400 to 1600*, Baltimore, 1974, pl. 202); it is more likely he might have had in mind the Portico dei Branchi, Bologna, by Vignola, c. 1560.

75. A view of the Colony Club appeared in *AABN* 91 (March 9, 1907), 104, no. 1628, with the caption: "We believe this plate will convince our readers that we were fully justified in saying, a while ago, that this building exhibited the 'most immoral piece of brickwork to be found in the city of New York.'" See also: the *Monograph* 3:280–82; *Architecture* 15 (April 1907), pl. 34; *Brickbuilder* 16 (April 1907), pl. 57; *New York Architect* 2 (November 1908), 251, 282–95, 307. For background see: Anne O'Hagan, "Beautiful Club for Women," *Century* 81 (December 1910), 216–24; O. H. Dunbar, "Newest Woman's Club," *Putnam's* 2 (May 1907), 196–206; L. H. French, "New Colony Club," *Harper's Bazaar* 41 (June 1907), 554–59.

76. Alice-Leone Moats, "The Elsie Legend," *Harper's Bazaar* 83 (May 1949), 171. For Elsie de Wolfe's contribution see: Elsie de Wolfe, "Story of the Colony Club," *Delineator* 78 (November 1911), 370–71; Ludwig Bemelmans, *To the One I Love the Best*, New York, 1955, 91; Jane S. Smith and Diana Vreeland, *Elsie de Wolfe: A Life in High Style*, New York, 1982.

77. In addition to White's two churches, McKim was involved in the design of the First Parish (Unitarian) Church of Cambridge, Mass., in the spring of 1900. As there was a strong division in the building committee, both McKim, Mead & White and Cram, Goodhue & Ferguson were asked to submit designs, classical and Gothic. Because the building committee believed the classical proposal was the more costly of the two, they selected Cram's Gothic proposal in May. See various letters: Charles W. Eliot to McKim, April 21, 1900, and McKim to C. W. Eliot 5 and 24 April, 1900, First Parish Church file, box M-3, 1968 Coll., MM&W Archive, NYHS, and Harvard Archives; and McKim to James Barr Ames, May 10, 1900, CFM-LC. Similarly, McKim lost his campaign to have the National Cathedral of Saints Peter and Paul, Mount Saint Albans, Washington, D.C., built in the classical style. He wrote Burnham repeatedly in the summer of 1906 stressing the long association between the Episcopal church and Renaissance classicism, citing the churches of Wren and Colonial churches in America. He also urged a classical design on Bishop Satterlee of Washington, to no avail. The Gothic design by Bodley and Vaughan was selected. See various letters, McKim to Burnham, June 6–22, 1906, CFM-LC, and Moore, *Burnham*, 2:12, 47–68.

78. White's description of Saint-Gilles-du-Gard is reprinted in Baldwin, *White*, 81. For background see E. Clowes Chorley, *The Centennial History of Saint Bartholomew's Church in the City of New York*, New York, 1935, 163–65. For the portals see: the *Monograph* 2: 193–95; *AABN* 87 (January 7, 1905), 8, no. 1515, and 87 (February 11, 1905), 52, no. 1520; *ARec* 13 (June 1903), 508, 511; *House and Garden* 5 (March 1904), 132–38; *AReview* 12 (October 1905), 187–95.

79. The iconographical program is described by Lawrence Grant White in Chorley, *Centennial History*, 164–65; see also Saint Bartholomew's Church, *Architectural and Decorative Features of St. Bartholomew's Church in the City of New York*, New York, 1941. The frieze, almost entirely the work of O'Connor, owes much to the contemporary work of Rodin.

80. M. Schuyler, "Recent Church Building in New York," *ARec* 13 (June 1903), 508–11; Russell Sturgis contrasts the Trinity porch sculpture, totally subordinated to the architecture, to the portals of Saint Bartholomew's, which have their own individual characters; see Sturgis, "A Fine Work of American Architectural Sculpture," *ARec* 15 (April 1904), 293–311; and his "St. Bartholomew's Facade," *International Studio* 38 (July 1909), supp. 19–22, pls. 14–22.

81. See Charles H. Parkhurst, *A Brief History of the Madison Square Garden Presbyterian Church*, New York, 1906. For Parkhurst see *DAB* 14:244–46, and Parkhurst's own writing, especially: *My Forty Years in New York*, New York, 1923, and *Our Fight with Tammany*,

New York, 1895. One of the assistant ministers was Sherrod Soule, who became minister of the Naugatuck Congregational Church shortly before the firm built the new church there. The members of the Madison Square church building committee were: Robert W. De Forest (chairman), Edward C. Bodman, John C. Brown, Arthur C. James, D. William James, John S. Kennedy, William M. Kingsley, Charles H. Parkhurst, Francis L. Slade, William E. Stiger, William C. Sturges, and Louis C. Tiffany. In contrast to the significant cost overruns which were typical in White's houses (notably the Payne Whitney house), in building churches and other buildings with more fixed budgets White was far more careful; building contracts for the Madison Square church totaled $306,022, less than the figure allowed the congregation for their old building and lot.

82. Stanford White, typescript description, Madison Square Presbyterian Church file, box M-20, 1968 Coll., MM&W Archive, NYHS, quoted in full in my "Urban Architecture of McKim, Mead & White," 614–16, and printed in part in Baldwin, *White,* 236. Also in this file are letters dealing with Wallace Sabine's suggested acoustical treatment of the walls.

83. The church was well published; see: the *Monograph* 3:251–57; *AABN* 87 (March 4, 1905), 75, no. 1523, and 90 (July 7, 1906), 8, no. 1593; *ARec* 19 (April 1906), 317, and 21 (February 1907), 156–60; *Architecture* 13 (February 1906), pl. 15; *Brickbuilder* 15 (December 1906), 260, pls. 155–61.

84. The claim appears in *Atlantic Terra Cotta* 9 (June 1927), 2–4, pl. 42. One of the problems which always have affected terra cotta is the unpredictability of color glazing, for minute variations of chemical properties of the clay base or the glaze, the chemical atmosphere of the kiln, and the temperature or duration of the firing produce wide fluctuations in color.

85. Quoted in Baldwin, *White,* 234–35.

86. John Jay Chapman, "McKim, Mead & White," *Vanity Fair* 13 (September 1919), 37, 102, 104, printed in part in Baldwin, *White,* 235. How prophetic was his phrase, "a moon-race of whirl people." Although demolished, the Madison Square church was not lost altogether. Baldwin, *White,* notes two replicas: a church in West Virginia and a synagogue in California replete with the crosses stamped in the bricks! Other derivatives include the Second Church of Christ, Scientist, Los Angeles, California; see *Brickbuilder* 19 (April 1910), pls. 47–50; what is now the Shiloh Baptist Church, Cleveland, Ohio, c. 1925; and the First Christian Church (Disciples of Christ), Eugene, Oregon, 1911, by George W. Kramer of New York. Various portions of the Madison Square church were removed. The main entrance door, with its rich frame, is reported to have been given to the Brooklyn Museum; Weinman's pediment panels are said to have gone to the Metropolitan Museum, New York (neither can now be located). The polished green granite columns, main cornice, and other decorative elements were incorporated by Donn Barber in his Hartford *Times* building, Hartford, Conn., 1919–20.

87. For Trinity Church, Roslyn, see L. Wodehouse, "Stanford White and the Mackays," *Winterthur Portfolio* 11 (1976), 229–33.

88. For background see Reginald C. McCrane, *The University of Cincinnati: A Success Story in Urban Higher Education,* New York, 1963, 175 and passim.

89. Mead to F. L. Olmsted, Jr., August 12, 1903, CFM-LC. For the Amherst plan see Stanley King, "*The Consecrated Eminence*": *The Story of the Campus and Buildings of Amherst College,* Amherst, 1951, 122–25. Norton was also related to McKim through his marriage to McKim's niece.

90. President Seth Low to MM&W, July 17, 1903 (Secretary's Office, Columbia University), requests the firm to design the new South Field. President Seth Low to MM&W, December 8, 1903 (loc. cit.), notes approval of completed plan.

91. There was no effort to push completion of University Hall behind Low Library; eventually the ground floor, the only part constructed, was demolished to make way for a new building in the 1950s. The successor firm continued to design new buildings for Columbia well into the 1920s. Kendall designed the setting for George Gray Barnard's *Pan,* the Clark Memorial, 1907–08, at the northwest corner of the campus. He also completed Kent Hall, 1907–11, although it may have been started by McKim. All the subsequent Columbia buildings were Kendall's: the Philosophy Building, 1910–11; the President's House, 1911–12; the School of Journalism, 1912–13; and Furnald Hall, 1912–14. See Robson, *Guide to Columbia,* passim. For Earl Hall see: the *Monograph* 3:200–02; *AReview* 8 (April 1901), pls. 26–28. For the Avery Library, see: the *Monograph* 4:313–19, 352–53; *AABN* 102 (November 20, 1912), no. 1926; *ARec* 33 (June 1913), 535–49; *JRIBA* 21 (June 13, 1914), 497–512. For Howells & Stokes's Saint Paul's Chapel see: *ARec* 21 (February 1907), 83–95; *AReview* [London] 23 (January and February 1908), 63–73, 108, 112; *Brickbuilder* 15 (December 1906), 261–69. This firm was specifically requested by the donors of the chapel, as President Low informed McKim, September 17, 1903 (Secretary's Office, Columbia University). For an assessment of the development of the campus up to McKim's death see M. Schuyler, "The Architecture of American Colleges: IV. New York City," *ARec* 27 (June 1910), 443–57.

92. For background on the War College see George S. Pappas, *Prudens Futuri: The U. S. Army War College, 1901–1967,* Carlisle Barracks, Pa., 1967, 28. Secretary Root also wrote McKim, April 2, 1902 (CFM-LC), about developing a master plan for the Army base on Governor's Island, New York Harbor, but nothing came of this; some buildings were built on the base by the successor firm in the 1920s.

93. Moore, *McKim,* 201–02.

94. For the War College complex see: the *Monograph* 3: 265–67; and *Brickbuilder* 16 (June 1907), pl. 94.

95. McKim to Capt. John S. Sewell, June 21, 1902, CFM-LC; and numerous letters, Secretary Root and Capt. Sewell to MM&W, May 17–July 9, 1902, Army War College file, box M-11, 1968 Coll., MM&W Archive, NYHS.

96. McKim to Mead, April 2, 1902, CFM-LC. For background on West Point see the sources cited in ch. 5, n. 116. Shortly after the replanning started, M. Schuyler published "The Architecture of West Point," *ARec* 14 (December 1903), 462–92.

97. White to Burnham, November 24, 1902, CM-LC, printed in Moore, *Burnham* 1:190–91.

98. White to Burnham, May 8, 1903, CM-LC, printed in Moore, *Burnham* 1:191–92.

99. It is not clear if the firm actually submitted their large inked drawings; both Moore,, *Burnham* 1:190, and Baldwin, *White*, 322, assert the firm accepted the invitation but did not submit a proposal. The complete set of drawings was photographed, and some of the immense drawings are in the MM&W Archive, NYHS. See also the correspondence and drawings in the West Point files, boxes 544 and 548, Old Mixed Files, 1950 Coll., MM&W Archive, NYHS.

100. Manuscript text (by White?), addressed to Col. Albert L. Mills, dated May 14, 1903, West Point file, box 548, loc. cit.

101. For the Mackay School of Mines and the development of the campus, see Samuel B. Doten, *An Illustrated History of the University of Nevada*, Reno, Nev., 124, 108 ff. Although W. S. Richardson made the initial visit to the campus, prior to designing the School of Mines, its construction was supervised by Bliss & Faville of San Francisco; both Walter D. Bliss and William B. Faville had been office assistants during 1896–97 and thus knew the intricacies of the firm's work well. The Mackay mining school was admired for its technical facilities and functional arrangement by H. O. Hofman, professor of metallurgy at M.I.T., who wrote the firm in August 1912, requesting prints of the floor plans (Mackay Mining Building file, box M-7, 1968 Coll., MM&W Archive, NYHS).

102. Correspondence concerning the development of construction drawings for the Harvard Stadium, Ira N. Hollis to McKim, March 1901–January 1903, Johnston Gate file, box M-17, 1968 Coll., MM&W Archive, NYHS. See too *Harvard Graduates' Magazine* 11 (June 1903), 647–48, 12 (March 1904), 341–48.

103. Brown University to McKim, Mead & White, July 22, 1902, Brown University file, box M-16, 1968 Coll., MM&W Archive, NYHS. McKim to Dr. Charles Hitchcock, July 28, 1902, CFM-LC. For Rockefeller (Faunce) Hall see: *Brickbuilder* 13 (February 1904), pls. 11–12; M. Schuyler, "The Architecture of American Colleges: VII. Brown, Bowdoin, Trinity, and Wesleyan," *ARec* 29 (February 1911), 144–50; and Norman Isham, "The Recent Architectural Development of Brown University," *AReview* 11 (July 1904), 175. The major essay on the firm's work—*ARec* 20 (September 1906), 217—contained a view identified as Rockefeller Hall, Brown University, which was actually the Rockefeller Medical Research Building, New York, by York & Sawyer.

104. See Allan Nevins, *Illinois*, New York, 1917, 167; Leon D. Tilton and Thomas E. O'Donnell, *History of the Growth and Development of the Campus of the University of Illinois*, Urbana, Ill., 1930, 31. Correspondence in University of Illinois file, box 641, Old Mixed Files, 1950 Coll., MM&W Archive, NYHS. For the Women's Building see: the *Monograph* 3:227; and *Brickbuilder* 14 (December 1905), pl. 96. Subsequent additions, c. 1911, closed the area between the wings.

105. McKim to Moses Taylor Pine, Princeton trustee, November 6 and December 3, 1903, and May 24, 1904, CFM-LC. Other correspondence in boxes 632, 642, and 644, Old Mixed Files, 1950 Coll., MM&W Archive, NYHS. For the FitzRandolf gate, see: the *Monograph* 3:283–84; Constance M. Greiff, *Princeton Architecture*, Princeton, 1967; Edwin M. Morris, *The Story of Princeton*, Boston, 1917; and John R. Williams, *The Handbook of Princeton*, New York, 1905. For the Cottage Club, see: the *Monograph* 3:293–93A; and *Brickbuilder* 14 (December 1905), pl. 91. The English source is suggested by W. B. Rhoads, *The Colonial Revival*, New York, 1977, 182.

106. Thomas F. Taylor to MM&W, November 27, 1893, Orange Free Library file, box M-9, 1968 Coll., MM&W Archive, NYHS. For background see Eleanor S. Clark, *The Orange Free Library, A History of the First Seventy-Five Years, 1883–1958*, Orange, N.J., 1958, 16–19. The final design is mentioned in McKim to Wendall Garrison, March 24, 1900, CFM-LC; Brower & Albro, Architects, Orange, N.J., were associated with the firm in supervising construction.

107. For John Pierpont Morgan see: Herbert L. Satterlee, *J. Pierpont Morgan: An Intimate Portrait*, New York, 1940; Frederick L. Allen, *The Great Pierpont Morgan*, New York, 1949; Cass Canfield, *The Incredible Pierpont Morgan*, New York, 1974; Edwin P. Hoyt, Jr., *The House of Morgan*, New York, 1966; Francis H. Taylor, *Pierpont Morgan as Collector and Patron*, New York, 1970.

108. From the will of J. Pierpont Morgan, quoted in Taylor, *Morgan as Collector*, 39.

109. McKim to Whitney Warren, December 27, 1902, CFM-LC. Warren had just completed the New York Yacht Club of which Morgan was commodore. Warren lost this commission because his proposal was floridly ornamented, as was the Yacht Club, whereas Morgan, who was quite austere in his personal taste, wanted something more elegantly simple. Warren's preliminary sketches, from the Cooper-Hewitt Museum Collection, were exhibited at the Morgan Library during the winter of 1981–82, in an exhibition commemorating the seventy-fifth anniversary of the library's opening.

110. McKim to Mead, April 2, 1902, CFM-LC, printed in Moore, *McKim*, 278. In addition, tunnels below the garden were to connect Morgan's house with those of his son and Satterlee and the library. The limestone house for Louisa and Herbert Satterlee, who had been married in November 1900, was a wedding present and was the only nonbrownstone house in the enclave.

111. Harry Siddons Mowbray, *H. Siddons Mowbray, Mural Painter, 1858–1928*, privately printed, 1928, 110.

112. J. P. Morgan to McKim, February 8, 1904, Morgan Library file, box 626, 1950 Coll., MM&W Archive, NYHS. Saint-Gaudens told McKim "not to allow J. P. M. to bully you; I think if you were to sass him back, he would respect you more, I *know* that too; that's been my experience and you will thereby be more able to work in peace." Saint-Gaudens to McKim, August 23, 1905, in Sherman Statue file, box M-8, 1968 Coll., MM&W Archive, NYHS.

113. F. L. Allen, *The Great Pierpont Morgan*, 186, noted that although brownstone was quite good enough for all the Morgan family to live in (except his daughter), when it came to building a house for the books, only marble would do. Concerning the *anathyrosis*, see

Moore, *McKim* 281–82; the episode was apparently related directly to Moore. Moore also relates how McKim was so exhausted during 1905–06 that he asked Morgan if the work might be turned over to White while he took a short rest. McKim was told to get his rest and not worry about the building: "When you go, work on the library will stop until you return. No one else shall touch it"; Moore, *McKim* 282.

114. McKim to Gorham Phillips Stevens, December 14, 1903, CFM-LC, quoted in full in my "Urban Architecture of McKim, Mead & White," 643–44. Credit for the consummate workmanship in construction is due Charles T. Wills, the contractor. Stevens had been an architectural student at M.I.T. and then briefly at the École before entering the office during 1902–03. He then was the first Architecture Fellow of the American School of Classical Studies in Athens, where he began his archaeological work on the Acropolis. In 1905–11 he was again in the office, after which he became Director of the American Academy in Rome, holding that post twenty-one years. See Lucy T. Shoe, "Necrology," *American Journal of Archaeology* 68 (April 1964), 189–90; Charles Picard, *Revue Archeologique* 2 (July 1964), 74–76.

115. McKim to Gorham Phillips Stevens, c. June 1904, CFM-LC.

116. See Wayne Andrews, *Mr. Morgan and His Architect*, New York, 1957; Frederick B. Adams, *An Introduction to the Pierpont Morgan Library*, New York, 1964, 19–23; Canfield, *Incredible Morgan*, passim; detailed description in London *Times*, December 4, 1908, 13, printed in Moore, *McKim*, 279–81 (the correspondent erroneously claims the ceiling in the West Room came from the Aldobrandini Palace, Venice).

117. For the subjects in Mowbray's panels, see W. Andrews, *Morgan and His Architect*, 6–8. The assertion that O'Connor surreptitiously used McKim's likeness for the sphinx is not supported by close examination; see Andrews, *Morgan and His Architect*, 2. McKim to "Bill," August 26, 1904 (CFM-LC), refers to the marbles used in the floor. For color reproductions see *Interior Design* 46 (September 1975), 138–41.

118. Satterlee, *Morgan*, 562. The library served as the setting for an important episode in American economic history. A few days after the panic of October 1907 began, when the federal government was powerless to stop the run on the banks, Morgan gathered in the library all the major financial figures of New York, placing the trust company presidents in the West Room and the bank presidents in the East Room, while he and his secretaries retired to the librarian's office, periodically relaying messages across the hall in search of a solution for halting the panic. Shortly Morgan's guests discovered he had locked the massive bronze doors to keep them from leaving until a settlement had been reached. Eventually, because of a deadlock, Morgan had to force terms upon both sides; he unlocked the doors at 4:45 A.M., Sunday, November 3, 1907. See F. L. Allen, *Great Morgan*, 241–57, and Hoyt, *House of Morgan*, 279–307.

119. The library was widely published; see the description in the London *Times*, December 4, 1908, cited in n. 116. See also: the *Monograph* 3:241–49; *AABN* 89 (February

24, 1906), 76, no. 1574, and 95 (January 6, 1909), 1–2, no. 1724, with commentary by C. H. Reilly; *Architecture* 12 (December 1905), pl. 101; *ARec* 19 (May 1906), 388–93; *AReview* 22 (November 1917), pl. 80–81; *InArch* 47 (July 1906), 6 pls.; *New York Architect* 2 (November 1908), 305. Pursuant to Morgan's wishes the library became a public research collection in 1924, but the increased use necessitated a new wing by Benjamin Wistar Morris; see *New York Architect* 7 (March 1927), 692. In this H. Siddons Mowbray decorated the elevator lobby; see Adams, *Introduction to the Library*, 13. A second addition was made in 1960–62 by Alexander P. Morgan. One of the very few buildings to emulate the Morgan Library was the Memorial Art Gallery, Rochester, N.Y., 1913, by Foster, Gade & Graham.

120. Copy of report, and G. L. Rives to McKim, New York Libraries file, box M-11, 1968 Coll., MM&W Archive, NYHS. See also Harry M. Lydenberg, *History of the New York Public Library*, New York, 1923, 406–12; Theodore W. Koch, *A Book of Carnegie Libraries*, New York, 1917. Eight of the branches are reproduced in the *Monograph* 2:196–99; see also: *AABN* 83 (February 13, 1904), 55, no. 1468, and 87 (April 15, 1905), 123, no. 1529, for the East Broadway, Tompkins Square, 135th Street, and Rivington Street branches. The Rivington Street branch also appeared in *Brickbuilder* 14 (July 1905), and the Saint Gabriel's branch in *Architecture* 17 (April 15, 1908), pl. 32.

121. Russell Sturgis, "The Carnegie Libraries in New York City," *ARec* 17 (March 1905), 237–46. Sturgis wished that industrial metal sash had been used in all the branches.

122. For the early history of Bellevue Hospital see Theodore F. Jones, *New York University*, New York, 1933, 281–304.

123. See John D. Thompson and Grace Goldin, *The Hospital: A Social and Architectural History*, New Haven, 1975, 189; and Robert Bruegmann, "Two American Hospitals in 1876," *JSAH* 35 (December 1976), 280. Dr. Goldwater's views are presented in "Notes on Hospital Planning," *Brickbuilder* 19 (September 1910), 207–10, pls. 115–18. For the impact of technology on hospital design see: Russell Sturgis, "Mount Sinai Hospital," and Josephine Tozier, "An Ideal Hospital," *ARec* 18 (November 1905), 367–83.

124. This version of the plan was published in *House and Garden* 5 (June 1904), 296–99.

125. For Bellevue Hospital see: the *Monograph* 3:274–76; *House and Garden* 5 (June 1904), 296–99; *Pencil Points* 6 (January 1925), 80; and Edward F. Stevens, "Details and Equipment of Hospitals," *AABN* 100 (October 11, 1911), 133–64. For the influence of Bellevue on hospital design see: John A. Hornsby and Richard E. Schmidt, *The Modern Hospital*, Philadelphia, 1914; and Edward F. Stevens, "The American Hospital Development," *ARec* 38 (December 1915), 641–61, and 39 (January 1916), 65–83.

126. For the developmental history of the Metropolitan Museum of Art see: Metropolitan Museum of Art *Bulletin* 24 (Summer 1965), 25–28; Leo Lerman, *The Museum, One Hundred Years and the Metropolitan Museum of Art*, New York, 1969; Calvin Tomkins, *Merchants and Masterpieces*, New York, 1973; August Heckscher,

The Second Century, The Comprehensive Architectural Plan for the Metropolitan Museum of Art, New York, 1971.

127. In McKim to Bernard R. Green, April 18, 1904 (CFM-LC), the museum plan is mentioned for the first time; McKim to Mead, May 11 and 14, 1906, CFM-LC. See also Moore, *McKim,* 324; and Saint-Gaudens to McKim, July 6, 1905, in Sherman Statue file, box M-8, 1968 Coll., MM&W Archive, NYHS.

128. For the museum additions see: the *Monograph* 3:275–77; *ARec* 44 (July 1918), 65–68; *Architects' and Builders' Magazine* 11 (May 1910), 307–14; *Interiors* 104 (June 1945), 67–69, 104.

129. Swartwout, "Architectural Decade," 89–90, notes McKim's failure due to deviation from the program stipulations. For the entries by Cass Gilbert (which won) and Carrère & Hastings see *AReview* 7 (April 1900), pls. 21–26.

130. For the first alteration see *AABN* 21 (April 9, 1887), 175. For background see Merrill Denison, *Canada's First Bank,* 2 vols., New York, 1966–67, 2:20–22, 285–88.

131. For the Bank of Montreal see: the *Monograph* 3:215–216A; *ARec* 20 (September 1906), 203–05, and 25 (January 1909), 11–13; *AReview* 12 (March 1905), 52–53.

132. In the Knickerbocker Trust file, box M-16, 1968 Coll., MM&W Archive, NYHS, are numerous letters, C. T. Barney to White, April and May 1901, requesting that the bearer be allowed to examine the drawings for the trust building. By the time the first bill was sent to Barney and the Knickerbocker Trust for architect's services, it had been decided not to build the uppermost nine floors, although a fee of one percent of their estimated cost was charged. At this point the projected cost of the building was $585,000, but Barney kept trimming the budget; on May 12, 1902, he asked White to lower the cost to $513,000. He also wrote the building was to have "simplicity, dignity, and brightness."

133. White to Baker (?), December 4, 1901, loc. cit. The architect's drawings published in *Architecture* 9 (March 15, 1904), pls. 22–26, show removable panels in the frieze for the insertion of windows later.

134. For the Knickerbocker Trust see: the *Monograph* 3:-208–12; *AReview* 9 (March 1902), 80, pls. 11–12, 9 (November 1902), 282–83, and 12 (March 1905), 82–83. See also J. M. Bowles, "Business Buildings Made Beautiful," *World's Work* 9 (November 1904), 5499–5508.

135. M. Schuyler, "A 'Modern Classic,'" *ARec* 15 (May 1904), 431–44.

136. White's design may have lent strength and credibility to what was a financially weak institution. The Knickerbocker Trust was one of scores established in the period 1898 to 1907 because of a loophole in New York State banking laws that allowed trust companies to operate with much lower reserves than banks. Accordingly, during periods of heavy withdrawals they were liable to collapse. On Monday, October 16, 1907, F. Augustus Heinze, C. T. Barney, and a number of their associates attempted to corner the market in shares of United Copper Company. By Wednesday their attempt had failed, and in trying to buy all offered shares, Heinze's Mercantile Trust's reserves were exhausted, forcing the bank to close. As soon as it became known that Barney was involved, a run began on the Knickerbocker Trust as well, and on Monday, October 23, it too was forced to close. Thus started the panic of October 1907. Under J. P. Morgan's direction, Herbert Satterlee reorganized the bank, replacing Barney as president (shortly afterward Barney took his own life). The Knickerbocker Trust was saved from going into legal receivership and reopened in March 1908, paying six percent on impounded deposits. It is an intriguing historical coincidence that buildings by McKim, Mead & White should have been the scenes where this debacle started and where it was ended (see n. 118).

137. Alfred Bowditch to McKim, February 10, 1904 (New England Trust file, box M-10, 1968 Coll., MM&W Achive, NYHS), appoints his firm architect for the new building. For the New England Trust see the *Monograph* 3:230–31.

138. James O'Gorman points out in *The Architecture of Frank Furness,* Philadelphia, 1973, 66–68, that Furness was specifically excluded from the Girard Bank project. He had already prepared a preliminary design for the bank in 1903–04. What precise role Evans played in developing the design of the bank as built seems to have been minor, for all published references to the building credit the design to McKim and the firm. In his attribution list Kendall also lists W. S. Richardson, who probably handled detail development. Curiously, the firm's bill books contain no bills rendered for services nor any indication of contract figures. O'Gorman sheds little light on this mystery, nor does Evans himself in "Girard Trust Company," *New York Architect* 2 (November 1908), 246–51, 274–79.

139. For the Girard Trust Company see: the *Monograph* 4:329–31; *AABN* 93 (April 22, 1908), 132; *ARec* 25 (January 1909), 73–74; *Architecture* 18 (August 15, 1908), 132, pl. 59.

140. John K. Winkler, *The First Billion: The Stillmans and the National City Bank,* New York, 1934, 112–15, tells of the "auction" of the Merchants' Exchange. For the Merchants' Exchange, before alteration, see *AABN* 65 (July 22, 1899), 31, no. 1230. See also: *ARec* 20 (July 1906), 3, and 24 (December 1908), 441–43; Granger, *McKim,* 45–46. For Stillman, the business successor of Moses Taylor, the firm designed a summer house at Cornwall-on-Hudson, 1882, a city residence in New York, 1900–04, and the country house of his son, James A. Stillman, at Pocantico Hills, New York, 1905, in addition to projects never carried through. Album XIII, MM&W Coll., Avery Library, Columbia University, contains photographs of various early studies for the new bank, including a perspective by Jules Crow, dated 1904, of the final scheme. Moore, *McKim,* 323, indicates that McKim received the commission and began work March 8, 1901.

141. For the National City Bank see: the *Monograph* 3:295–99A; *AABN* 94 (October 21, 1908), 129–31, no. 1713; *ARec* 20 (July 1906), 3, 24 (December 1908), 441–43, and 25 (February 1909), 137–40; *Architecture* 21 (March 1910), pl. 24; *Architecture and Building* 53 (July 1921), 54–55, pls. 100–05, 60 (July 1928), 206–07, pls. 211–12; *New York Architect* 3 (February 1909), 75–77, 128, 135–45, 149, 153–55, and 12 (May 1929), 157–65; *International Studio* 36 (February 1909), supp. 144–45; *Prominent Buildings*

... *by Fuller*, 1910, 6–19. See also the company's booklet, *National City Bank of New York, 1812–1912: A Short Sketch of the Bank with a Description of the Building*, New York, 1914.

142. The Knickerbocker Trust was billed for expenses beginning in October 1906, but Kendall attributes the design to Stanford White. Moore, *McKim*, 343, says White started the design as early as 1904, but both Baldwin and L. G. White give the date as 1906. For the completed building see: the *Monograph* 4:333–35; *AABN* 99 (May 3, 1911), 167, no. 1845; *Architects' and Builders' Magazine* 41 (June 1909), 347–55; *New York Architect* 2 (November 1908), 303; and *Prominent Buildings . . . by Fuller*, 1910, 15. Clearly influenced by the downtown Knickerbocker Trust was Clinton & Russell's East River Savings Bank, New York, 1910.

143. For the American (Havana) Tobacco Company store see: A. C. David, "The Finest Store in the World," *ARec* 17 (January 1905), 42–49; J. M. Bowles, "Business Buildings Made Beautiful," *World's Work* 9 (November 1904), 5499–5508.

144. For background on the Gorham Company, see *National Cyclopedia of American Biography* 23:303. For the Gorham building see: the *Monograph* 3:234–40; *ARec* 22 (July 1907), 8; *Architecture* 10 (July 1904), pls. 56–58, and 12 (August 1905), pl. 52; *InArch* 47 (July 1906); J. S. Holbrook, "The Gorham Building," *New York Architect* 2 (November 1908), 245–46, 249, 253–71, 299.

145. For Charles L. Tiffany and the Tiffany Company see *National Cyclopedia of American Biography* 2:57; and Robert Koch, *Louis C. Tiffany, Rebel in Glass*, 2nd ed., New York, 1966, passim. Although the work produced by Tiffany's (distinct from that of Louis Comfort Tiffany's Tiffany Glass and Decorating Company or Tiffany Studios) was similar to that of the Gorham Company, Tiffany's moved in the direction of fine jewelry and gem stones; Gorham tended toward silver flatware, and one branch of the business did bronze sculpture casting.

146. For the Tiffany building see: the *Monograph* 3:261–64; *AABN* 87 (April 1, 1905), 101, no. 1527; *Architecture* 12 (August 1905), pl. 61; *Architects' and Builders' Magazine* 7 (February 1906), 177–86.

147. Henry James, *The American Scene*, New York, 1907, 179.

148. For the Tiffany stables (garage) see: *Architects' and Builders' Magazine* 7 (February 1906), 186; *Brickbuilder* 15 (February 1906), pl. 23.

149. For the Munsey (*Times*,) building see: *AABN* 89 (May 12, 1906), 164, no. 1585; *Prominent Buildings . . . by Fuller*, 1910, 38.

150. For the Eastman Kodak building see *AABN* 91 (May 4, 1907), 174–75, 187, no. 1636. A few years earlier the firm made additions and alterations to the George Eastman house, Rochester, N.Y.

151. For The Buckingham see: the *Monograph* 3:232; "Two Notable Buildings," *ARec* 19 (February 1906), 163–64; *Brickbuilder* 15 (November 1906), 237. The sgraffito work is illustrated in Maximilian F. Friederang, "An Ancient Art Revived: An Account of Sgraffito," *ARec* 33 (January 1913), 27.

152. White to Nikola Tesla, March 2, 1895, Letterbook 12, Stanford White Correspondence, Avery Library, Columbia University.

153. Nikola Tesla, "The Problem of Increasing Human Energy," *Century* 60 (June 1900), 175–211. The far from scientific account was supplanted by the publication of Tesla's *Colorado Springs Notes, 1899–1900*, Belgrade, Yugoslavia, 1978.

154. Excerpts from Tesla's brochure, "The World System," are reprinted in Arthur J. Berkhard, *Electrical Genius, Nikola Tesla*, New York, 1959, 175–77. The best general account of Tesla and his work is Margaret Cheney, *Tesla: Man Out of Time*, Englewood Cliffs, N.J., 1981.

155. For Wardenclyffe see: Berkhard, *Genius*, 172–79; John J. O'Neill, *Prodigal Genius: The Life of Nikola Tesla*, New York, 1944, passim, but especially 203–17; Leland I. Anderson, "Wardenclyffe—A Forfeited Dream," *Long Island Forum*, August and September 1968, 146–49, 169–72 (I am grateful for the assistance given by Mr. Anderson, the leading technical expert on Tesla's work, particularly at Wardenclyffe). Tesla published some aspects of his work at Wardenclyffe: "Transmission of Electric Energy without Wires," *The Electrical World and Engineer* 43 (March 5, 1904), 429–31, reprinted in *Scientific American*, Supplement, June 4, 1904, 23760–61. See the extensive bibliography by Leland I. Anderson, *Bibliography: Dr. Nikola Tesla (1856–1943)*, 2nd ed., Minneapolis, 1956. White charged Tesla only for draftsmen's time in preparing drawings.

156. In 1943 the U.S. Supreme Court ruled that Tesla was in fact the inventor of the radio, not Marconi. Tesla's many investigations, including his "World System," are still not well understood. His personal papers were seized by the U.S. Government upon his death in 1943, and a large file on his research is still "classified" as top secret, as noted by Cheney, *Tesla*, 309–10. Tesla insisted that the "World System" was practical, "a simple fact of scientific electrical engineering, only expensive—blind, fainthearted, doubting world" (Tesla to J. P. Morgan, July 13, 1913, Library of Congress, quoted in Cheney, *Tesla*, 175).

157. See *Interborough Rapid Transit: The New York Subway, Its Construction and Equipment*, New York, 1904. For their services in contributing to the design, the firm received a flat fee, 1902–03. See also: the *Monograph* 3:207; and *Architecture* 14 (July 1906), pl. 51, where the architect is erroneously identified as Paul C. Hunter.

158. *Interborough Rapid Transit*, 74.

159. For Grand Central Station/Terminal see: Carl W. Condit, *The Port of New York [II] . . . from the Grand Central Electrification to the Present*, Chicago, 1981, 54–100; David Marshall, *Grand Central*, New York, 1946, 22–24, 68, 95; and William D. Middleton, *Grand Central: The World's Greatest Railway Terminal*, San Marino, Calif., 1977. See also: Edward Hungerford, *Men of Iron, The History of the New York Central*, New York, 1938, 121–24, 229–40, 400–409; Alvin F. Harlow, *The Road of the Century*, New York, 1947.

160. For the Pennsylvania Railroad see: George H. Burgess and Miles C. Kennedy, *Centennial History of the Pennsylvania Railroad Company*, Philadelphia, 1949; H. W. Schotter, *The Growth and Development of the Pennsylvania Railroad Company*, Philadelphia, 1927.

161. Lindenthal's bridge was published in M. Schuyler, "Art in Modern Bridges," *Century* 60 (May 1900), 12–25. For Samuel Rea's report see Schotter, *Growth and Development*, 272–73. Alexander J. Cassatt, who earned an advanced degree in civil engineering, was the brother of painter Mary Cassatt. He served the Pennsylvania Railroad for twenty-one years, retiring in 1882. In 1899 he was persuaded to assume the presidency of the company to oversee the difficult job of extending the line into Manhattan. For the Gare d'Orsay see C. L. V. Meeks, *The Railroad Station*, New Haven, 112. For the development of electric traction in the United States see Carl W. Condit, *The Port of New York* [I] . . . *from the Beginning to Pennsylvania Station*, Chicago, 1980, 176–238.

162. Attention here is focused only on the station and its architectural expression, not on the engineering problems of the tunnels or electrification. For the latter see: Michael Bezilla, *Electric Traction on the Pennsylvania Railroad, 1895–1968*, University Park, Pa., 1980; Condit, *Port of New York* [I], 247–58; William Couper, *A History of the Construction Engineering and Equipment of the Pennsylvania Railroad Company's New York Terminal and Approaches*, New York, 1912; James Forgie, "The Construction of the Pennsylvania Railroad Tunnels under the Hudson River at New York," *Engineering News* 56 (December 13, 1906), 603–14, and 57 (February 28, 1907), 223–34.

163. For the limited competition and construction of Grand Central Terminal, see Condit, *Port of New York* [II], 54–100; and Marshall, *Grand Central*, 237–51.

164. Cass Gilbert to William H. Newman, June 11, 1903 (Cass Gilbert Papers, box 12, Division of Archives and Manuscripts, Minnesota Historical Society, Saint Paul), recapitulates their previous conversation.

165. A. J. Cassatt to McKim, April 24, 1902 (Pennsylvania Railroad file, box 981, Old Mixed Files, 1950 Coll., MM&W Archive, NYHS), confirms the verbal commission for the station design; he outlines the firm's specific responsibilities for all work above the level of the waiting room floor. See too the discussion in: Moore, *McKim*, 273–77; Condit, *Port of New York* [I], 259–94.

166. Moore, *McKim*, 274. Newhall, an old friend of McKim's from Germantown, was a purchasing agent for the Pennsylvania Railroad.

167. McKim, himself, never elaborated on the design of Pennsylvania Station, but his intentions were later expressed by his principal assistant in this, William Symmes Richardson: "The Architectural Motif of the Pennsylvania Station," in Couper, *History of the Construction*, 77–78; and also "The Terminal—The Gate of the City," *Scribner's* 52 (October 1912), 401–16, which compares Pennsylvania Station to other major American and European terminals. McKim intended the station, observes Richardson, to give "the appearance of a monumental gateway and entrance to one of the great metropolitan cities of the world."

168. See George Gibbs, "New York Tunnel Extension, Pennsylvania Railroad," *Transactions of the American Society of Civil Engineers* 69 (September–October 1910), 226–383. The track plan and tunneling received special attention in *Scientific American* 85 (December

28, 1901), 426–27, and 90 (January 16, 1904), 42. The volume of excavated material is noted in the booklet published by the contractor for the excavation, foundations, retaining walls, and steel bridging, Westinghouse, Church, Kerr & Company, *The New York Passenger Terminal of the Pennsylvania Railroad*, New York, 1908. Among the paintings see *Excavation—Penn Station* by Ernest Lawson, c. 1910, Minneapolis Institute of Arts. An excellent visual source for the construction of the station is the four-volume set of construction photographs by L. H. Dreyer and others, Avery Library, Columbia University. The first payment to the Norcross Brothers for placement of cut granite was made in April 1905.

169. Richardson's extensive responsibilities are noted in Burt L. Fenner to R. Clipston Sturgis, January 10, 1924, William S. Richardson file, box M-3, I, 1968 Coll., MM&W Archive, NYHS, and in Granger, *McKim*, 82. Van der Bent's contributions to the engineering and building supervision is noted in McKim to Mead, May 14, 1906, CFM-LC.

170. The steel frame of the station was fabricated by the American Bridge Company and erected by George A. Fuller and Company. Construction of the station was reported in detail in *Scientific American* 94 (May 20, 1906), 429; 94 (June 2, 1906), 449, 453–54; and 99 (December 5, 1908), 409–10.

171. Richardson, "The Terminal," 406, presents a table of comparative distances from station entry to train-boarding platform:

1,200 feet	Union station, Washington, D.C. (D. H. Burnham & Co.)
1,100 feet	South Street Station, Boston (Shepley, Rutan & Coolidge)
1,100 feet	Grand Central Terminal, New York (Reed & Stem with Warren & Wetmore)
940 feet	Chicago & North Western, Chicago (Frost & Granger)
480–950 feet	Pennsylvania Station, New York

172. Richardson, "Architectural Motif," 77, indicates that McKim used the Roman bath as a model because it was the largest building type ever designed to accommodate large groups of moving people. He also draws a parallel between the social character of Imperial Rome and the cosmopolitan character of early-twentieth century urban America. See also Moore, *McKim*, 275.

173. Richardson, "Architectural Motif," 78, writes that the travertine was selected because it would take rubbing well, gradually acquiring a deep sheen rather than becoming dirty; furthermore, he says, its pronounced large pattern would give scale to the immense space.

174. For the Baths of Caracalla see: E. Brödner, *Untersuchungen an den Caracallathermen*, Berlin, 1951; and E. Nash, *Pictorial Dictionary of Ancient Rome*, 2nd ed., 2 vols., London, 1968.

175. Richardson, "Architectural Motif," 78. Around the edge of the room were handkerchief vaults of Guastavino tile; see illustrated in *Brickbuilder* 19 (December 1910), 283.

176. Moore, *McKim*, 276–77.

177. Richardson, "Architectural Motif," 78.

178. Schotter, *Growth and Development,* 313. In addition to Pennsylvania Station, the firm designed a delicate umbrella platform cover for the railroad, c. 1905–07.

179. Of all the firm's buildings, Pennsylvania Station was the most extensively published and discussed. A detailed bibliography is given in a special section of the general bibliography, but some of the more important citations are: *AABN* 89 (May 26, 1906), 175–80, no. 1587, 90 (July 14, 1906), 16, no. 1594, 98 (October 5, 1910), 113–18, no. 1815; *ARec* 27 (June 1910), 518–21; *AReview* 13 (May 1906), 77, pls. 24–28; *Architecture* 21 (March 1910), pl. 21, 22 (October 1910), 155, 157, 163–64; *New York Architect* 4 (September 1910), 71–77, 91–115; C. M. Keys, "Cassatt and His Vision," *World's Work* 20 (July 1910), 13187–204.

180. *AReview* [London] 30 (August 1911), 66. Wells Bosworth to MM&W, March 29, 1907, MM&W Archive, NYHS.

181. Richardson, "The Terminal," 410.

182. "Classic Station Modern Improvement," *AForum* 104 (June 1956), 113–15. "Old Setting New Gleam," *AForum* 107 (August 1957), 104–07; Lester C. Tichy's proposal for rebuilding the entire station is also presented in this issue, 108–09.

183. The new ticket counter was "a masterpiece of architectural and visual incongruity," wrote Lewis Mumford, "The Disappearance of Pennsylvania Station," *New Yorker* 34 (June 7, 1958), 106–13, and reprinted in *JAIA* 30 (October 1958), 40–43.

184. *Progressive Architecture* 42 (September 1961), 65, and 43 (September 1962), 63. The "reconstruction" called for a new lower station, with ceilings ranging from nine to twenty feet, inside the old station, with an office slab over the eastern portion and a cylindrical sports arena replacing the glass-vaulted concourse. The new superstructure was designed by Charles Luckman.

185. "Action Group for Better Architecture in New York Proposes a Plan to Save Penn Station," *Progressive Architecture* 44 (January 1963), 48; *AForum* 118 (February 1963), 11; *Progressive Architecture* 45 (November 1964), 49.

186. Lewis Mumford, "Pennsylvania Station: Finis," *Progressive Architecture* 44 (December 1963), 54–55.

187. Some of Ada Louise Huxtable's editorials are reprinted in *Will They Ever Finish Bruckner Boulevard?* New York, 1970. See in particular: "The Impoverished Society," May 5, 1963; "A Vision of Rome Dies," July 14, 1966; and "The Art of Expediency," May 26, 1968.

188. James T. Gardner and Frederick Law Olmsted, *Special Report on the New York State Survey on the Preservation of the Scenery of Niagara Falls,* Albany, N.Y., 1880, 27. See also Olmsted & Kimball, *Olmsted* 1:14–28; and Roper, *FLO,* 378–82, 395–97. For the development of electric power at the falls see the sources cited in ch. 5, n. 68.

189. Quoted in *The Preservation of Niagara Falls,* Final Report of the Special International Niagara Board, Ottawa, Canada, 1930.

190. Quoted from the unpaginated typescript of the report of the Niagara Falls Commission, January 1908, box 559, Old Mixed Files, 1950 Coll., MM&W Archive, NYHS.

191. McKim to Captain Charles W. Kutz, March 5, 1907, CFM-LC. The work of the Niagara Falls Commission is also referred to in various letters: McKim to Olmsted, Jr., Arthur Schoellkopf, and F. D. Millet, February through July, 1907, CFM-LC.

192. *Brickbuilder* 19 (February 1910), 33.

193. Telegrams, White to Burnham, April 25, 1906, copies in CFM-LC.

194. McKim to Mead, May 14 and June 1, 1906, CFM-LC. Charles Moore in *AIA Quarterly Bulletin* 7 (July 1906), 105.

195. The primary sources for the private lives of Evelyn Nesbit and Stanford White are her autobiographical accounts: *The Story of My Life,* London, 1914; and the more detailed *Prodigal Days: the untold story of Evelyn Nesbit,* New York, 1934. In these she draws a sympathetic portrait of White. Harry K. Thaw's *The Traitor,* Philadelphia, 1926, purports to be the "untampered with, unrevised account of the trial and all that led to it." It recounts at length aspects of his life before Evelyn, but it is rambling and in parts unintelligible; the "traitor" of the title is not White but Thaw's first defense counsel who wished to have Harry declared insane immediately, thereby avoiding a sensational trial. A good popular account, rich in social anecdote and background, contemporary with the Baldwin and Moore biographies, is Frederick L. Collins, *Glamorous Sinners,* New York, 1932, in which he ends by citing the headlines which followed Evelyn and Harry during the teens and twenties, marking drug arrests, litigation against Harry for assault on a minor, public brawls, paternity suits, attempts at suicide, and further arrests, closing with this observation: "This is what Evelyn and Harry did with *their* twenty-five years. What would Stanford White have done with his?" A later popular treatment, based closely on the trial transcript, is Charles Samuels, *The Girl in the Red Velvet Swing,* New York, 1953, which led to a Twentieth-Century-Fox film of the same name, 1955, written by Charles Brackett and starring Ray Milland as White, Joan Collins as Evelyn, and Farley Granger as Harry Thaw. The most recent and carefully studied account is Michael M. Mooney, *Evelyn Nesbit and Stanford White: Love and Death in the Gilded Age,* New York, 1976. E. L. Doctorow's celebrated *Ragtime,* New York, 1974, also made into a film, is a highly fictionalized account. A thorough social history, providing excellent background, is Warren Forma, *They Were Ragtime,* New York, 1976. See also "Faces from the Past: Evelyn Nesbit at Thaw Murder Trial," *American Heritage* 20 (June 1969), 64–65.

196. Saint-Gaudens to Alfred Garnier, n.d., quoted in Tharp, *Saint-Gaudens,* 357. As perhaps the most intimate of White's friends, Saint-Gaudens was well aware of Stanford's extramarital liaisons. He himself had a long relationship with his model, Davida Clark, which produced a boy, Louis, whom they called Novy. It was only in 1900, when the boy was eleven, that Mrs. Saint-Gaudens learned of the affair, writing scathingly to her husband, prompting the reply that he had hoped she would follow the example of Mrs. MacMonnies and Mrs. White toward their husbands' failings and remain quietly dignified. "Although my action is a mere peccadillo in comparison to them, it has caused me a misery of mind you do not dream of"

(quoted in Tharp, *Saint-Gaudens,* 318). His autograph letters to Stanford were often graphic; drawn at the bottom of the page in bold calligraphy might be one or a series of erect organs, or comments such as the one on a note of May 5, 1906: "I am glad to know that your Balls are all right. Sometimes mine wabble and sometimes they clink, clink. . . ." (Saint-Gaudens Coll., Dartmouth College Archives). This was largely brave talk by that time, for Saint-Gaudens was dying of abdominal cancer.

197. The letters to McKim are in Box 36, McKim-Maloney Coll., NYPL; his replies (CFM-LC) betray the feeling of gathering darkness and the weight bearing on him. See, for instance, his replies to Dr. Charles Hitchcock and Thomas Newbold, July 7, 1906. The moving portrait of White sketched by Davis, *Collier's* 37 (August 4, 1906), 17, is reported to have caused the removal of Davis's books from a library in New Jersey; noted in A. Logan "Palace of Delight," *New Yorker* 41 (February 27, 1965), 77–78. Davis's eulogy was much appreciated by McKim, as is evident in his reply to Davis, July 11, 1906, CFM-LC. It was also admired by Saint-Gaudens, who wrote a reply to *Collier's,* August 6, 1906, printed in Saint-Gaudens, *Reminiscences* 2:252. Both the Davis article and Saint-Gaudens reply were printed in *AIA Quarterly Bulletin* 7 (July 1906), 100–108, along with testimonial letters by Richard Watson Gilder, Charles Lang Freer, Charles N. ffoulke, Charles Moore, Cass Gilbert, D. H. Burnham, William S. Eames, William A. Boring, and Glenn Brown.

To McKim and Mead fell the task of settling White's incredibly complicated estate. To pay the claims against his estate, White's extensive art collections were auctioned, necessitating a thorough cataloging of the holdings; for the published catalogs, see the special section of the bibliography. The first lot was put on sale April 4–12, 1907, a second lot, on November 25–29. Although the proceeds were ample, they were just sufficient to cover White's debts for the purchase of the art works and entertainment charges for prospective clients. The townhouse on Gramercy Square was sold. Mrs. White then maintained permanent residence at Smithtown-Saint James. For the house at 121 E. 21st Street see L. G. White, *Sketches and Designs,* pls. 47–56, where Box-Hill, Smithtown, is also illustrated. For Box-Hill see also Lionel Moses,

Art World 3 (January 1918), 351–55; Moses had assisted in the remodelings of Box-Hill.

198. Beer's and Adam's remarks quoted in A. Logan, "Palace of Delight," *New Yorker* 41 (February 27, 1965), 78. Two detailed accounts of the trial are: F. A. MacKenzie, ed., *The Trial of Harry Thaw,* Famous Trial Series, London, 1928; and Gerald Langford, *The Murder of Stanford White,* Indianapolis, 1962, both of which include large sections of verbatim quotes from court transcripts. Comparison of these with the same passages "quoted" in Thaw's *The Traitor* reveal how garbled, confused, and biased the latter is. Another moralizing account presenting White as evil incarnate, Evelyn as virtue soiled, and Harry Thaw as the avenging husband is Benjamin H. Atwell, *The Great Harry Thaw Case: or, A Woman's Sacrifice,* Chicago, 1907; in this the court transcript is so bowdlerized as to be misleading.

199. McKim to Saint-Gaudens, December 6, 1897, CFM-LC.

200. McKim to H. A. Bloor, May 28, 1907, CFM-LC. McKim to Aston Webb, June 3, 1907, CFM-LC: The date of this letter suggests McKim was referring to either the Downtown Building for the Knickerbocker Trust or the skyscraper proposed to rise from the Merchants' Exchange. On McKim and skyscrapers see also Moore, *Burnham* 1:200, n.1.

201. Unlike White, McKim apparently had disfavored owning an automobile, for in McKim to Mead, May 14, 1906 (CFM-LC), he writes: "you know my position in regard to automobiling and consistent opposition to the whole subject," but he had relented and rented one: "When you reach home we will have some turns in it, and I think you will find it is good for you." Burnham, like White, was fascinated with automobiles; see Hines, *Burnham,* 238–40.

202. McKim was buried in the family plot in the Rosedale Cemetery, Orange, N.J. McKim had his affairs carefully in order even in death. He left a few personal items and some furniture to friends; all other personal items went to his daughter. The remainder of his estate was liquidated and invested, with the income going to his daughter during her lifetime. Upon her death the invested estate (about $275,000) was divided, a portion going to her heirs, but the bulk (about $250,000) going to the endowment of the American Academy in Rome.

Chapter 7. THE NEXT GENERATION, 1910–1919

1. Misattributions to McKim appear throughout J. Burchard and A. Bush-Brown, *The Architecture of America,* Boston, 1961; see p. 264 where the Municipal Building is said to be his. The firm name was used until 1961 due to the legal instrument which set up the corporation; so long as any partner had known one of the three founders the firm could continue to use the original name. James Kellum Smith, who entered the office in 1924 and was made a partner in 1929, was the last to know Mead. Under L. G. White and Smith, the firm continued in the old style during the middle of the century. White died in 1956 and Smith in 1961,

when the firm McKim, Mead & White came to a legal end. The office was then reorganized as Walker O. Cain Associates and most recently as Cain, Farrell & Bell, in 1979.

2. Although the number of commissions was down, the dollar value went up because of the size of many of the commissions and inflation. For 1910 through 1918 (the last year for which there are summary figures), the total was $55,895,824.

3. For The Architects' Building and Mead and Fenner's role in its construction see *Brickbuilder* 22 (December 1913), 267–70. For Mead's last years see Moore, *McKim,*

326. Mead's letters to the younger partners from Europe are in the Correspondence, MM&W Archive, and the Manuscripts Division, NYHS. The Meads had no children, and he donated large sums to Amherst, which received the bulk of his estate, about $250,000, which supported construction of the Mead Art Building. For Kendall's design of Mead's simple headstone for the Protestant Cemetery, Rome, see Mead tombstone file, box 785, Old Mixed Files, 1950 Coll., MM&W Archive, NYHS; this also contains correspondence concerning Mrs. Mead's interment there in 1936.

4. For Kendall see W. M. Kendall file, box M-3, I, 1968 Coll., MM&W Archive, NYHS. See too: *Bulletin of the Michigan Society of Architects* 15 (October 7, 1941), 3; *Pencil Points* 22 (September 1941), 65; *National Cyclopedia of American Biography*, Current Volume A (1930), 551.

5. For Fenner, see B. L. Fenner file, loc. cit. See too: *AABN* 129 (February 5, 1926), 226; *ARec* (March 1926), 274–75; *JAIA* 14 (March 1926), 129; *DAB* 6:323.

6. For Richardson see W. S. Richardson file, loc. cit., and New York *Times* April 7, 1931, 27.

7. For Van der Bent see T. J. Van der Bent file, loc. cit., and New York *Times* March 27, 1936, 21.

8. For White see the L. G. White file, loc. cit., and *Art News* 55 (October 1956), 58.

9. McKim to L. G. White, April 21 and May 18, 1909, CM-LC, printed in full in Moore, *McKim*, 302–04.

10. McKim to Mead, October 4 and 18, 1907, CFM-LC. McKim repeats his strong opposition to entering the competition to John Russell Pope, October 17, 1907, CFM-LC.

11. Two of Kendall's early sketches for the Municipal Building survive. One, dated March 3, 1908, is in the MM&W Archive, NYHS; the other dated only 1908 and perhaps earlier is in the MM&W Coll., Avery Library, Columbia University.

12. L. G. White to Alfred C. Bossom, London, May 2, 1925, L. G. White file, box M-3, I, 1968 Coll., MM&W Archive, NYHS. White may have meant that the cornice of the base element was at the same height as the main cornice of City Hall. The entries in the competition were published in *AABN* 93 (May 27, 1908), 178, no. 1692. Besides the firm's winning entry are those by Carrère & Hastings, Howells & Stokes, and Clinton & Russell. Other contestants included Trowbridge & Livingston; Helme & Huberty; J. H. Freedlander; Hoppin & Koen; H. Rogers; and Marshall, Heins & Lafarge.

13. For the Municipal Building see: the *Monograph* 4: 320–27; William Walton, "The New Municipal Building," *AABN* 101 (March 20, 1912), 133–40, no. 1891; *Architecture* 17 (May 15, 1908), pls. 39–40, 28 (July 15, 1913), pls. 60–63; *Architects' Journal* 54 (September 12, 1921), 342; *Architecture and Building* 46 (October 1914), 381–96; *Der Städtebau* 11 (December 1914), 143–44, pl. 75; *Graphic* 83 (February 18, 1911), 238.

14. For the Hotel Pennsylvania see: *AABN* 115 (February 26, 1919), 297–306, no. 2253; *AForum* 30 (April 1919), 95–108, pls. 49–58; *AReview* 8 (March 1919), 56–68, pls. 33–39; *Architecture* 39 (April 1919), 91–92, pls. 53–57. The hotel was also published widely in England: "An

American Businessman's Hotel," *Architect* [London] 117 (June 3, 10, 17, 1927), 939–43, 984–86, 1012–18; *Architects' Journal* 49 (April 23, 1919), 250–51; *Architecture and Building* 48 (November 1916), pl. 174, and 51 (March 1919), 18–26; *JRIBA* 36 (November 24, 1928), 158.

15. For 998 Fifth Avenue, see: the *Monograph* 4:346–47; *AABN* 100 (November 29, 1911), 228, no. 1875; *ARec* 33 (January 1913), 69–73; *Architecture* 25 (April 1912), 50, 59 pls. 51–52.

16. These houses appear throughout the fourth volume of the *Monograph*.

17. For the Harvard Club see: the *Monograph* 4:340–45; *ARec* 38 (December 1915), 615–30; *Architecture* 32 (November 1915), pls. 132–34; *Architecture and Building* 47 (December 1915), 439–42, 455. For the Princeton gates see: the *Monograph* 3:283–84; *Architecture* 26 (October 15, 1912), pl. 101. The Columbia University buildings appear in the *Monograph* 3:313–19, 352–53, 376; for the Avery Library see *AABN* 102 (November 20, 1912), no. 1926.

18. For the Andover Free Christian Church, see *AABN* 95 (January 6, 1909), 8, no. 1724. For the First Presbyterian Church, Chattanooga, see: *AABN* 95 (May 19, 1909), 167, no. 1743; *Brickbuilder* 18 (May 1909), pls. 63–65. For construction supervision, the firm was associated with Dearden & Forman, Architects.

19. For the Second National Bank, see: the *Monograph* 4:338–39; *ARec* 25 (January 1909), 44–45; *Architects' and Builders' Magazine* 9 (August 1908), 487–95.

20. For the Waterbury station, see: the *Monograph* 4:311; Samuel O. Dunn, "The Problem of the Modern Terminal," *Scribner's* 52 (October 1912), 416–42.

21. For a more detailed description of the Court of the University and its sculpture, see the *Monograph*, 1973 ed., 72, 4:384–87, as well as the *Official Guide to the Panama-Pacific International Exposition*, San Francisco, 1915.

22. For the New York Post Office, see: the *Monograph* 4:360–64A; *ARec* 33 (March 1913), 187, 222; *Architecture and Building* 45 (March 1913), 155–56; *Architecture* 27 (January 1913), pls. 13–17. A selection of the competition entries appeared in *Architecture* 17 (May 15, 1908), 70–83, pl. 43.

23. Herodotus, *Histories*, 8, 100.

24. See Eileen Michaels, *An Architectural View: 1883–1974; The Minneapolis Society of Fine Arts*, Minneapolis, 1974. The building appeared in: the *Monograph* 4: 369–70; *AABN* 107 (April 21, 1915), 245–48, no. 2052; *AReview* 18 (May 1912), 41–70; *Arts and Progress* 6 (January 1915), 48–50; *Western Architect* 18 (January 1912), 1–11; *Through the Ages* 3 (September 1925), 13–18.

25. For the National McKinley Birthplace Memorial, see: the *Monograph* 4:388–90; *AABN* 107 (February 17, 1915), no. 2043; *Architect* 102 (August 1, 1919), 66; *Architects' and Builders' Journal* [London] 41 (March 24, 1915), 137; *Architects' Journal* 51 (February 18, 1920), 211–13; *AForum* 31 (December 1919), 205–06, pls. 81–84; *AReview* 20 (October 1915), 89, pls. 57–64.

26. For the Racquet and Tennis Club see: the *Monograph* 4:398–99A; *Architecture* 38 (August 1918), pls. 126–34; *Town and Country* 73 (October 10, 1918), 27. Bliss & Faville had already employed a similar blind wall in

their University Club, San Francisco; see *Brickbuilder* 19 (December 1910), pls. 160–61.

27. For the Butler Art Gallery see: the *Monograph* 4:394–94A; *Architecture* 40 (November 1919), 295–96, pls. 163–69; *Country Life* [US] 41 (January 1922), 71–72; *Pencil Points* 6 (July 1925), 73–75. It is possible that Kendall had in mind Cass Gilbert's not far distant Allen Memorial Art Museum, Oberlin College, Oberlin, Ohio, 1915–17.

28. For the Clements Library see W. Hawkins Ferry, *The Buildings of Detroit*, Detroit, 1968, 215. Ferry quotes Kahn as saying that of all his work he wished to be remembered as the architect of this library. Kahn was quite familiar with Vignola's original casino and had photographed it during his European excursions.

29. Lionel Moses, "McKim, Mead & White—A History," *AABN* 121 (May 24, 1922), 413–24.

30. *Vogue la Galère* may be translated variously as "let come what may" or "let's chance it." Figuratively it might be said to mean "against all odds." The founders had first used it in 1879, along with a small image of a sailboat on choppy water, as an identifying mark on their Union League Club competition entry drawings. Professor William Roberts of the French Department, Northwestern University, suggests this may have been inspired by the seal and motto of the city of Paris, *Fluctuat nec Mergitur,* or "tossed but not sunk." It was not until McKim's death that *Vogue la Galère* was revived.

31. The successors published two surveys of their work: *Recent Buildings Designed for Educational Institutions by McKim, Mead & White,* Philadelphia, 1936; and *Recent Work by the Present Partners of McKim, Mead & White,* New York, 1952. See too Teunis J. van der Bent, *The Planning of Apartment Houses, Tenements, and Country Houses,* New York, 1917. A brief list of the major work after Mead's retirement would include: the Eastman School of Music, Rochester, N.Y.; master plan and Olin Library, Wesleyan University, Middletown, Conn.; Harvard Business School; master plan and Ira Allen Chapel, University of Vermont; various new buildings at Columbia University; master plans and numerous buildings for several colleges including Adelphi College in Garden City, the University of Buffalo, George Peabody College for Teachers in Nashville, University of Rochester, University of North Carolina, Trinity College in Hartford, Barnard College, Union College, and Bowdoin College. They also entered numerous competitions including those for the Theodore Roosevelt Memorial, Tennessee Memorial, and the Nebraska State Capitol, all of which were published but were unsuccessful.

EPILOGUE

1. See Henry-Russell Hitchcock, "American Influence Abroad," in E. Kaufmann, ed., *The Rise of an American Architecture,* New York, 1970, 3–48; and Leonard K. Eaton, *American Architecture Comes of Age,* Cambridge, Mass., 1971, 19–31.

2. *The Critic* n.s. 3 (January 24, 1885), 37–38. McKim, of course, was already known to many English architects, having been made an honorary member of the Architectural Association in 1869.

3. Robert Kerr, "The Problem of National American Architecture," *ARec* 3 (October–December 1893), 121–32.

4. James Crowdy to MM&W, July 24, 1892, Misc. MM&W Correspondence file, box M-3, III, 1968 Coll., MM&W Archive, NYHS. This project never materialized.

5. Alexander Koch to MM&W, March 13, 1891, and c. July, 1903, loc. cit. *Academy Architecture and Annual Architectural Review,* published 1889–1931, was edited by Koch, 1895–1919. No material from the firm was actually published in *Academy Architecture.*

6. Richard Harding Davis to White, n.d., Stanford White Coll., Manuscript Division, NYHS. In 1893 A. D. F. Hamlin sent to the firm William Wright of Montreal; Hamlin to MM&W, January 18, 1893, Misc. MM&W Correspondence file, box M-3, II, 1968 Coll., MM&W Archive, NYHS.

7. James F. Muirhead, *America the Land of Contrasts,* London, 1898, 192; this was expanded from the Baedeker guide he wrote in 1892.

8. McKim to Seth Low, April 11, 1899, CFM-LC.

9. McKim to James A. Wright, May 25, 1900, CFM-LC.

10. Cass Gilbert to McKim, August 4, 1908, CFM-LC. The high regard for McKim is evident in the many obituary notices in English journals; see McKim bibliography.

11. Reilly to MM&W, May 25, 1909, and Mead to Reilly, August 25, 1909, Misc. MM&W Correspondence file, box M-3, II, 1968 Coll., MM&W Archive, NYHS. For student work at Liverpool see *JRIBA* 18 (August 28, 1909), 693–94; and *The Architect and Contract Reporter* 82 (October 22, 1909), 257–59. Reilly, an active lecturer and writer, as well as practicing architect, received the Royal Gold Medal in 1942. For Reilly see: *JRIBA* 65 (March 1948), 212–13; *AReview* [London] 103 (April 1948), 180–83; *Architects' Journal* 107 (February 5, 1948), 123–24, and 107 (February 12, 1948), 148.

12. Published *JRIBA* 17 (June 25, 1910), 630–35; see also *AABN* 95 (May 19, 1909), 167.

13. See Eaton, *Comes of Age,* 30–55, for American influence in England. When Reilly retired from the Liverpool School in 1932, a tribute was published: *The Book of the Liverpool School of Architecture,* with a preface by Stanley Ramsey in which he recalled the strong impact of McKim, Mead & White two decades earlier. Their work seemed, he wrote, "to have all the breadth of the French with the refinement of the Italian, and yet somehow was wonderfully Anglo-Saxon."

14. Stanley C. Ramsey, "The Work of McKim, Mead & White," *JRIBA* 25 (December 5, 1917), 25–29.

15. C. H. Reilly, *McKim, Mead & White,* London, 1924. The other volumes in the series dealt with: Inigo Jones (by S. C. Ramsey); Sir John Vanbrugh (C. Barman); Sir William Chambers (A. T. Edwards); Nicholas

Hawksmoor (H. S. Goodhart-Rendel); Fischer von Erlach (H. V. Lanchester); J. F. Bentley (W. W. Scott-Moncrieff), Sir John Soane (H. J. Birnstingl); Jacques Anges Gabriel (H. B. Cox).

16. L. G. White to C. H. Reilly, March 12 and 24, April 6, 1925, L. G. White file, box M-3, I, 1968 Coll., MM&W Archive, NYHS.

17. Reilly refers to Bush House, London, 1925–28, by Hemle & Corbett. The other buildings by American architects in London were D. H. Burnham & Company's Selfridge Department Store (first design), 1906; and Carrère & Hastings's Devonshire House, Piccadilly, 1924–26, in which Reilly was consultant. Although they executed no buildings, McKim, Mead & White were a stronger influence on the English than any other Americans. See Hitchcock, *Architecture*, 3rd ed. 382, 402, 472 n.7, 475 n.11; and T. H. Lyon, "An English Architect's Impressions of New York," *Architecture* 38 (August 1918), 222–25, which focuses on skyscrapers, particularly the firm's Municipal Building.

18. Correspondence with the publisher, the Architectural Book Publishing Company, began in December 1913. Uchida Trading Company (for R. Baba, Osaka, Japan) to MM&W, March 5 and 6, 1923, Monograph file, box M-19, 1968 Coll., MM&W Archive, NYHS. See also MM&W to Wong Chung, August 28, 1914 (Misc. MM&W Correspondence, box M-3, II, 1968 Coll., MM&W Archive, NYHS) in which the firm declines to design a Chinese embassy in an unspecified "foreign capital."

19. Werner Hegemann and Elbert Peets, *The American Vitruvius: An Architect's Handbook of Civic Art*, New York, 1922. See also Jean Schopfer, "American Architecture from a Foreign Point of View," *AReview* 7 (March 1900), 25–30; and observations by Gustav Eberlein quoted in *AABN* 94 (September 2, 1908), 78–79.

20. Werner Hegemann, *Amerikanische Architektur und Stadtbaukunst*, Berlin, 1925; and his "Vergleiche, Fragen und Reisenotizien," *Wasmuth Monatsheft* 9 (1925) 240–52, preceded by an article by Fiske Kimball: "Alte und Neue Baukunst in Amerika: Der Sieg des Jungen Klassizismus Über den Funktionalismus der Neunziger Jahre," 225–39, in which many of the firm's buildings are discussed.

21. Jacques Gréber, *L'Architecture aux Etats-Unis, preuve de la force d'expansion du génie français*, 2 vols., Paris, 1920.

22. Le Corbusier, *Quand les cathédrales étaient blanches*, Paris, 1937 (*When the Cathedrals Were White*, New York, 1964, 60).

23. For the Duquesne Club see: *ARec* 1 (October–December 1891), 138. For the Reid Memorial Library see: *Architecture* 5 (February 15, 1902), 36, and 7 (June 15, 1903), pl. 46. For Pope's Union Station see: *AABN* 116 (July 9, 1919), 31–38, no. 2272. For Rogers's Brooks Art Gallery see: *Through the Ages* 4 (May 1926), 32–35.

24. For the First National Bank of Champaign see: *ARec* 38 (July 1915), 184–85. For the Detroit Trust see Ferry W. Hawkins, *The Buildings of Detroit*, Detroit, 1968, 226. Hawkins also discusses the work of Louis Kamper who had been in the MM&W office before starting his practice in Detroit. For the Bank of California see: *Architecture* 20 (October 15, 1909), pls. 99–100; *ARec* 19

(June 1906), 470–71, and 30 (November 1911), 440, and 31 (January 1912), 12–13. For the U.S. National Bank, Portland, see: *Through the Ages* 6 (May 1928), 4–8; and G. Vaughan and V. G. Ferriday, *Space Style and Structure* 2 vols., Portland, Ore., 1974, 1:332.

25. See A. C. David, "Recent Brickwork in New York," *ARec* 13 (February 1903), 144–56; and Charles Lockwood, *Bricks and Brownstone, the New York Row House*, New York, 1972.

26. See Lee H. Nelson, "White, Furness, McNally and the Capitol National Bank of Salem, Oregon," *JSAH* 19 (May 1960), 57–61. For other misattributions see Brendan Gill, "True White from False," New York *Times Magazine*, October 19, 1975, 14–16, 66.

27. R. Sturgis, "McKim, Mead & White," *ARec*, Great American Architects Series, No. 1, May 1895 (the entire series reissued in book form, New York, 1977). See also Sturgis's candid letters to P. B. Wight, *ARec* 26 (August 1909), 122–31.

28. M. Schuyler, "A 'Modern Classic,'" *ARec* 15 (May 1904), 431–44. See also his satirical pieces: "A Long-Felt Want," *ARec* 7 (September 1897), 118–20; and "Architecture Made Easy," *ARec* 7 (December 1897), 214–18.

29. *The Critic* 49 (August 1906), 104–05.

30. "The Artist in Our World," *The Nation* 83 (July 5, 1906), 5–6, reprinted in *AABN* 90 (July 7, 1906), 6.

31. *AABN* 91 (March 30, 1907), 128. White's Gramercy Square house was in truth a warehouse for the art work continually shipped from Europe. For a more sympathetic view see Channing Blake, "Stanford White's New York Interiors," *Antiques* 102 (December 1972), 1060–67.

32. Thomas E. Tallmadge, *The Story of Architecture in America*, New York, 1927; and his *Architecture in Old Chicago*, Chicago, 1941, 138–39.

33. Fiske Kimball, *American Architecture*, Indianapolis, 1928, 147, 159, 173, and 204.

34. Lewis Mumford, *Sticks and Stones*, New York, 1924, 147.

35. Michael T. Klare, "The Architecture of Imperial America," *Science and Society* 33 (Summer–Fall 1969), 257–84.

36. For example see the remarks by Abram Hewitt at the dedication of the site, printed in *Columbia University, Dedication of the New Site, Morningside Heights*, New York, 1896, 80–84. See also Charles M. Shean, "The Decoration of Public Buildings—A Plea for Americanism in Subject and Ornamental Detail," *Municipal Affairs* 5 (September 1901), 712–17.

37. Hitchcock, *Richardson*, 162, 299.

38. Siegfried Giedion, *Space, Time and Architecture*, Cambridge, Mass., 1941.

39. James Marston Fitch, *American Building: The Forces That Shape It*, Boston, 1947–48, 122–25.

40. John A. Kouwenhoven, *Made in America*, Garden City, N. Y., 1948, 95. Regrettably J. Burchard and A. Bush-Brown, *The Architecture of America*, Boston, 1961, is filled with negative appraisals. See too the derisive comments by Bruno Zevi in Marcus Whiffen, ed., *The History, Theory, and Criticism of Architecture*, Cambridge, Mass., 1965.

41. One of the first expressions of this revision of view was

an address by Siegfried Giedion, "The Need for a New Monumentality," delivered to the RIBA, September 26, 1946. This aroused so much comment that the *Architectural Review* [London] commissioned a series of articles under the rubric "In Search of New Monumentality: A Symposium," to which Gregor Paulson, H.-R. Hitchcock, William Holford, S. Giedion, W. Gropius, Lucio Costa, and Alfred Roth contributed; see *AReview* [London] 104 (September 1948), 117–28. The postscript to this symposium was Lewis Mumford, "Monumentalism, Symbolism and Style," *AReview* [London] 105 (April 1949), 173–80.

42. H.-R. Hitchcock, *Architecture: Nineteenth and Twentieth Centuries*, 1st ed., Baltimore, 1958, 394.

43. Philip Johnson, "Is Sullivan the Father of Functionalism?" *Art News* 55 (December 1956), 44–46, 56–57.

44. James Marston Fitch, *Architecture and the Esthetics of Plenty*, New York, 1961, 20.

45. Wolfgang Pehnt, ed., *Encyclopedia of Modern Architecture*, Munich and New York, 1964, 182–83. See also my extended entries on the firm in: J. M. Richards, ed., *Who's Who in Architecture from 1400 to the Present*, London and New York, 1977, 206–08; and Adolf K. Placzek, ed., *Macmillan Encyclopedia of Architects*, New York, 1983, 3:140–51.

46. Vincent Scully, *American Architecture and Urbanism*, New York, 1969, 135–43.

47. William H. Jordy, *American Buildings and their Architects III: Progressive and Academic Ideals at the Turn of the Twentieth Century*, Garden City, N. Y., 1972, 373–75.

48. Exhibition, "The Architecture of the École des Beaux-Arts," Museum of Modern Art, New York, October 29, 1975, through January 4, 1976. The major publication was Arthur Drexler, ed., *The Architecture of the École des Beaux-Arts*, Cambridge, Mass., 1977. The exhibition elicited much favorable comment. Said Ada Louise Huxtable, "Growing Up in Beaux-Arts World," New York *Times*, November 9, 1975, Sec. 2, 1, 33: "all the milestones of my childhood and adolescence are colored by Beaux-Arts experiences." Most of the commentators asked why such an exhibition had taken so long. See: Stanley Abercrombie, "Beaux-Arts at the Modern," *ArtForum* 14 (February 1976), 52–56; Paul Goldberger, "Beaux-Arts at the Modern," New York *Times*, October 29, 1975, 46; and his "Debate Lingers after Beaux-Arts Show," New York *Times*, January 6, 1976, 38; John Lobell, "Beaux-Arts: A Reconsideration of Meaning in Architecture," *JAIA* 63 (November 1975), 32–37; Franz Schulze, "Architecture of the Beaux-Arts," *Art News* 75 (January 1976), 86–87. See also notices in: *ARec* 158 (October 1975), 37; *Antiques* 108 (November 1975), 834, 854; *Interior Design* 46 (December 1975), 140–41.

49. Jean Paul Carlhian, "Beaux-Arts or 'Bozarts'?" *ARec* 159 (January 1976), 131–34.

50. Ada Louise Huxtable, "The Centenary of a Famous Firm," New York *Times*, December 2, 1979, sec. 2, 31, 37.

51. Baldwin, *White*, 229.

52. As an example of the variety of available materials, consider the catalog published by *Through the Ages*, a trade journal published monthly in Baltimore by mar-

ble producers. From August 1923 through November 1928 there ran an unbroken series by J. J. McClymont surveying available marbles, with an annotated descriptive list of approximately 45 types of marble each month, for a total of more than 2,700 varieties.

53. Archibald Alison, *Essays on the Nature and Principles of Taste*, London, 1790; this volume was in the library of Richard Grant White.

54. Recounted by Frank Lloyd Wright of Shaw in an address of 1918, in Frederick Gutheim, ed., *Frank Lloyd Wright on Architecture*, New York, 1941, 86–87.

55. Hitchcock, *Architecture*, 3rd ed., 227, takes a different position and labels the latter nineteenth-century classicism as an "Academic Reaction." Another label somewhat misleading is "American Renaissance," for although the sculptors, mural painters, and architects worked in collaboration reminiscent of the sixteenth century, this was not the rebirth of a native American tradition but a resurgence of a Western European tradition in the arts.

56. John Ruskin, *The Seven Lamps of Architecture*, London, 1849, ch. 6, sec. 20.

57. Robert Swain Peabody, "Georgian Homes of New England," *AABN* 2 (October 20, 1877), 338–39.

58. M. Schuyler, "Recent Building in New York," *Harper's Magazine* 67 (September 1883), 562. Schuyler was not specific as to what he meant by the "wild work of . . . Fifth Avenue," although he may have had in mind the W. H. Vanderbilt houses, designed by J. B. Snook and C. B. Atwood for the Herter Brothers, which Schuyler thought unworthy of the designation architecture.

59. McKim to H. L. Higginson, April 5, 1894, CM-LC; McKim to G. V. Lengerke Meyer, February 5, 1895, CFM-LC. For the Massachusetts State House see H.-R. Hitchcock and W. Seale, *Temples of Democracy*, New York, 1976, 206–09. According to Baldwin, *White*, 104, during the 1890s White joined in a protest to prevent demolition of the old New York City Hall. During the mid-1880s the firm was approached by Jefferson Levy to make additions to Thomas Jefferson's Monticello, which they refused to do; see Report of Prof. William Thornton to House Committee on Public Buildings and Grounds, "Purchase of Monticello," December 15, 1916, 28, cited in Charles B. Hosmer, *Presence of the Past*, New York, 1965, 159 n. 32.

60. McKim to Dr. Charles Hitchcock, March 30, 1906, CFM-LC. The Alabama State Capitol, built 1846–47 from designs by George Nichols, burned in 1851 and was rebuilt. McKim recommended that wings could be added to the sides, well recessed behind the domed temple front. See Hitchcock and Seale, *Temples*, 226–27.

61. See Kristine O. Garrigan, *Ruskin on Architecture*, Madison, Wis., 1973. The often quoted passage about ornament being the chief part of architecture is from section 59 of the addenda to Lectures One and Two, *Lectures on Architecture and Painting*, London, 1854. The passage concerning structure is from "The Flamboyant Architecture of the Valley of the Somme," lecture, 1869.

62. McKim to Alexander Cochrane, September 16, 1886, Misc. MM&W Correspondence file, box M-3, III, 1968

Coll., MM&W Archive, NYHS. O. W. Norcross to McKim, May 25, 1896, Misc. MM&W Correspondence file, box 231, Old Mixed Files, 1950 Coll., MM&W Archive, NYHS.

63. Edward Simmons, *From Seven to Seventy,* New York, 1922, 243–44.

64. Samuel L. Clemens to J. Pierpont Morgan, September 1909, quoted in Frederick B. Adams, Jr., *An Introduction to the Pierpont Morgan Library,* New York, 1964, 5.

65. On the debilitating effect of minimum standards see Charles W. Moore's comment in John Cook and Heinrich Klotz, *Conversations with Architects,* New York, 1973, 233: "as is usual with the FHA, the minimum equals the maximum."

66. Henry James, *The American Scene,* New York, 1907, 77.

67. The long-standing antipathy is documented in Morton and Lucia White, *The Intellectual Versus the City,* Cambridge, Mass., 1962.

68. Hannah Arendt, *The Human Condition,* Chicago, 1958, 153–54. See also Ada Louise Huxtable, "The Gospel According to Giedion and Gropius Is Under Attack," New York *Times,* June 27, 1976, Sec. 2, 1, 29.

69. Interview with Kahn, Cook and Klotz, *Conversations with Architects,* 186.

70. Theo Crosby, *The Necessary Monument,* Greenwich, Conn., 1970, 63.

71. Mumford, "Monumentalism," 173–80.

72. Ruskin, *Seven Lamps,* ch. 6. sec. 10.

Bibliography

ARCHIVES

New-York Historical Society.
The most important source of information is the McKim, Mead & White Archive deposited in the Map and Print Collection, New-York Historical Society, New York. This consists of various financial records, journals, photographic albums, scrapbooks, over 1000 file boxes of correspondence, and more than 500 tubes of drawings. This mass of material covers the years 1879 through 1948. (See "McKim, Mead & White, Archives," *New-York Historical Society Quarterly* 34 [October 1950], 346; and *New-York Historical Society Annual Report for the Year 1968*, New York, 1969, 21.) The most important items include:

Bill Books, 1878–1947, 17 volumes
Cash Books, 1894–1944, 10 volumes
Contract Books, 1903–1930, 8 volumes
Journals, 1882–1942, 9 volumes
Payments to Engineers, 1917–1931, 1 volume
Scrapbook, Clippings and Newspaper Notices, 1875–1888, 1 volume
Scrapbook, Bank of Montreal, photographs, 1 volume
Scrapbook, E. D. Adams house, Rohallion, photographs, 1 volume
Scrapbook, H. B. Hollins house, photographs, 1 volume
Scrapbook, H. W. Poor house, photographs, 1 volume
Scrapbook, H. Villard house, photographs, 1 volume
Scrapbook, S. White house, photographs, 1 volume
Scrapbook, miscellaneous residences, buildings, photographs, 1 volume
Scrapbook, Senate Park Commission, photographs of models and drawings, 1 volume

Amherst College. Rare Book Room, William R. Mead Collection, consisting of about forty letters. A small portion of the firm's original library was donated to Amherst and is now dispersed in the Amherst College Library.

Art Institute of Chicago. Burnham Architectural Library. Burnham Collection: letterbook containing correspondence regarding the World's Columbian Exposition; microfilmed drawings of the Lathrop and Blair houses; Tallmadge Holograph Collection.

Boston Public Library. Trustees' Records: Trustees' files and records; minutes of Trustees' meetings; Annual Reports.

Columbia University. Avery Architectural Library. McKim, Mead & White Collection.
  Gift of James Kellum Smith and Amherst College, 1963
    Scrapbook 1, Brooklyn Institute (Brooklyn Museum)
    Scrapbook 2, World's Columbian Exposition
    Scrapbook 3, New Municipal Building
    Scrapbook 4, Office work, clippings

Scrapbook 5, Office work, clippings
Scrapbook 6, Photographs of Renderings
Scrapbook 7, Eastman School of Music
Scrapbook 8, Senate Park Commission
Scrapbook 9, William C. Whitney house
Scrapbook 10, World's Columbian Exposition
Scrapbook 11, Arlington Memorial Bridge
Scrapbooks 12–14, Miscellaneous office work, 1927–1934
Gift of Walker O. Cain, 1974
  Album I, Hotel Pennsylvania
  Album II, Pennsylvania Station
  Album III, University Club
  Album IV, The White House
  Album V, University of Virginia, Bank of Montreal, New York Public Library Branches
  Album VI, Bank of Buffalo
  Album VII, Charles T. Barney house
  Album VIII, John Innes Kane house
  Album IX, Payne Whitney house
  Album X, Miscellaneous
  Album XI, Urban Houses
  Albums XII and XIII, Photographs of Renderings
  Album XIV, McKim's European Photographs
  Album XV, Greek Architecture
  Albums XVI and XVII, Italian Gardens
  Album XVIII, Miscellaneous photographs
Gift of Robert White, 1982
  30 letterbooks (29 of letters of Stanford White and 1 of letters of Lawrence Grant White)
  28 file boxes (7,905 letters received by Stanford White)
  826 drawings, mostly projects of Stanford White
Working Drawings for Columbia University Buildings
  560 items in 31 tubes
Miscellaneous: Sketches by McKim; Photographs; Birch Burdette Long renderings of Stanford White's major designs; various drawings

Harvard University. Houghton Library. Correspondence of James Miller McKim, Henry Villard, and between C. F. McKim and Charles Eliot.

Library of Congress. Manuscript Division. Charles F. McKim Collection: 14 file boxes containing diary, original, and typescript copies of correspondence, 1863–1870; McKim's office letterbooks, 1891–1909; Reports of Clerk of the Works, Boston Public Library.

Library of Congress. Manuscript Division. Charles Moore Collection: drafts of *The Life and Times of Charles Follen McKim*, with extracts from bill books and McKim letterbooks; other miscellaneous material.

Library of Congress. Manuscript Division. Frederick Law Olmsted Collection.

Museum of the City of New York. Photographic Archives: major collection of photographs, c. 1,000 negatives, largely post-1892.

Newport Historical Society. Library and Archives: miscellaneous material relating to early work, 1874–1890.

New-York Historical Society. Library; Manuscript Collection. Richard Grant White and Stanford White Collections: varied personal correspondence; S. White's correspondence largely confined to letters to and from artists (S. White correspondence available on microfilm).

New York Public Library. Manuscript Room. Charles F. McKim and Margaret McKim Maloney Collection: c. 150

letters between McKim and his family, 1860–1880; miscellaneous letters relating to office business and personal life. Cain, Farrell & Bell, Architects, New York.

Portions of the original firm library; financial records and personnel records.

White family. St. James, Smithtown, and New York, N.Y.
Laura Chanler White (Mrs. Lawrence Grant White): various memorabilia, personal photographs
Frederick Lawrence Peter White: various renderings and published materials
Robert White: watercolors by Stanford White, scrapbooks of White's letters from Europe, 1878–1879
Ann White Buttrick: published material, scrapbooks, a small portion of the original firm library

THE VISUAL ARTS

Adams, Adeline. *Daniel Chester French, Sculptor*. Boston, 1932.

———. *The Spirit of American Sculpture*. New York, 1929.

Armstrong, David Maitland. *Day Before Yesterday, Reminiscences of a Varied Life*. New York, 1920.

Blashfield, Edwin Howland. *Mural Painting in America*. New York, 1928.

Cortissoz, Royal. *American Artists*. New York, 1923.

———. "An American Sculptor, Frederick MacMonnies." *The Studio* 6 (October 1895), 17–26.

———. *Art and Common Sense*. New York, 1913.

———. *Augustus Saint-Gaudens*. Boston, 1907.

———. *John La Farge, a Memoir and a Study*. Boston, 1911.

———. *The Painter's Craft*. New York, 1930.

Craven, Wayne. *Sculpture in America*. New York, 1968.

Cresson, Margaret French. *Journey into Fame: The Life of Daniel Chester French*. Cambridge, Mass., 1947.

Diamondstein, Barbaralee, ed. *Collaboration: Artists and Architects*. New York, 1981.

Dorr, Charles H. "A Sculptor of Monumental Architecture." *Architectural Record* 33 (June 1913), 518–532.

Dryfhout, John H. *Augustus Saint-Gaudens: The Portrait Reliefs*. Washington, D. C., 1969.

———. *The Work of Augustus Saint-Gaudens*. Hanover, N. H., 1982.

Fairman, Charles. *Art and Artists of the Capitol*. Washington, D. C., 1917.

French, Mary (Mrs. Daniel Chester). *Memories of a Sculptor's Wife*. Boston, 1928.

Koch, Robert. *Louis C. Tiffany, Rebel in Glass*, 2nd ed. New York, 1966.

Low, Will H. *A Chronicle of Friendships*. New York, 1908.

McKean, Hugh F. *The "Lost" Treasures of Louis Comfort Tiffany*. Garden City, N. Y., 1980.

McSpadden, J. Walker. *Famous Sculptors of America*. New York, 1924.

Richman, Michael. *Daniel Chester French: An American Sculptor*. New York and Washington, D. C., 1976.

Robbins, Daniel. "Statues to Sculpture: From the Nineties to the Thirties." Tom Armstrong, ed., *200 Years of American Sculpture*. New York, 1976.

Saarinen, Aline B. *The Proud Possessors: The Lives, Times and Tastes of Some Adventurous American Art Collectors*. New York, 1958.

Saint-Gaudens, Augustus. *The Reminiscences of Augustus Saint-Gaudens*. 2 vols. New York, 1913.

Scheyer, Ernst. *The Circle of Henry Adams: Art and Artists*. Detroit, 1970.

Simmons, Edward. *From Seven to Seventy: Memories of a Painter and a Yankee*. New York, 1922.

Strother, French. "Frederick MacMonnies, Sculptor." *The World's Work* 11 (December 1905), 6965–6981.

Taft, Loredo. *The History of American Sculpture*, rev. ed. New York, 1924.

Tharp, Louise Hall. *Saint-Gaudens and the Gilded Era*. Boston, 1969.

PLANNING AND LANDSCAPE ARCHITECTURE

Baker, John Cordis. *American Country Homes and Their Gardens*. Philadelphia, 1906.

Fabos, Julius G., Gordon T. Milde, and V. Michael Weinmayr. *Frederick Law Olmsted, Sr., Founder of Landscape Architecture in America*. Amherst, Mass., 1968.

Fein, Albert. *Frederick Law Olmsted and the American Environmental Tradition*. New York, 1972.

Ferree, Barr. *American Estates and Gardens*. New York, 1904.

Glaab, Charles N., and A. Theodore Brown. *A History of Urban America*, 2nd ed. New York, 1976.

McKelvey, Blake. *The Urbanization of America: 1860–1915*. New Brunswick, N. J., 1963.

Newton, Norman. *Design on the Land: The Development of Landscape Architecture*. Cambridge, Mass., 1971.

Olmsted, Frederick Law, Jr., and Theodora Kimball. *Frederick Law Olmsted, Landscape Architect, 1822–1903*. 2 vols. New York, 1922.

Reps, John W. *The Making of Urban America*. Princeton, 1965.

————. *Monumental Washington: The Planning and Development of the Capitol Center*. Princeton, 1967.

Roper, Laura Wood. *FLO, A Biography of Frederick Law Olmsted*. Baltimore, 1973.

Tunnard, Christopher. *The City of Man*, rev. ed. New York, 1970.

————. *The Modern American City*. New York, 1968.

Tunnard, Christopher, and Henry Hope Reed. *American Skyline*. Boston, 1955.

White, Morton, and Lucia White. *The Intellectual Versus the City from Thomas Jefferson to Frank Lloyd Wright*. Cambridge, Mass., 1962.

AMERICAN AND EUROPEAN ARCHITECTURE

Andrews, Wayne. *Architecture, Ambition, and Americans: A Social History of American Architecture*. New York, 1964.

————. *Architecture in America: A Photographic History*. New York, 1960.

————. *Architecture in New York: A Photographic History*. New York, 1969.

Artistic Houses. 4 vols. New York, 1883.

Baker, Paul. *Richard Morris Hunt*. Cambridge, Mass., 1980.

Black, Mary. *Old New York in Early Photographs, 1853–1901*. New York, 1973.

Blackshaw, Randall. "The New New York." *Century* Magazine 64 (August 1902), 493–513.

Brooklyn Museum. *The American Renaissance, 1876–1917*. New York, 1979. With essays by Richard Guy Wilson, Dianne H. Pilgrim, and Richard N. Murray.

Bunting, Bainbridge. *Houses of Boston's Back Bay: An Architectural History, 1840–1917*. Cambridge, Mass., 1967.

Burchard, John, and Albert Bush-Brown. *The Architecture of America; A Social and Cultural History*. Boston, 1961.

Bush-Brown, Harold. *Beaux-Arts to Bauhaus and Beyond*. New York, 1976.

Cook, Clarence. "Architecture in America." *North American Review* 135 (September 1882), 243–252.

Cram, Ralph Adams. *My Life in Architecture*. Boston, 1936.

Downing, Antoinette F., and Vincent Scully. *The Architectural Heritage of Newport, Rhode Island*, 2nd ed. New York, 1967.

Drexler, Arthur, ed. *The Architecture of the École des Beaux-Arts*. New York and Cambridge, Mass., 1977.

Eaton, Leonard K. *American Architecture Comes of Age*. Cambridge, Mass., 1972.

Edgell, G. H. *The American Architecture of To-Day*. New York, 1928.

Egbert, Donald Drew. *The Beaux-Arts Tradition in French Architecture Illustrated by the Grand Prix de Rome*. Edited for publication by David Van Zanten. Princeton, 1980.

Hamlin, A.D.F. "The Influence of the École des Beaux-Arts on our Architectural Education." *Architectural Record* 23 (April 1908), 241–247.

————. "Twenty-five Years of American Architecture." *Architectural Record* 40 (July 1916), 1–14.

Hamlin, Talbot. *The American Spirit in Architecture*. New York, 1926.

Hines, Thomas S. *Burnham of Chicago*. New York, 1974.

A History of Real Estate, Building, and Architecture in New York City. New York, 1898.

Hitchcock, Henry-Russell. *Architecture: Nineteenth and Twentieth Centuries*, 3rd ed. Baltimore, 1968. (4th ed., integrated. Baltimore, 1977.)

————. *The Architecture of H. H. Richardson and His Times*. rev. ed. Cambridge, Mass., 1966.

————. "Frank Lloyd Wright and the Academic Tradition of the Early Eighteen-Nineties." *Warburg and Courtauld Institute Journal* 7 (1944), 46–63.

————. "Ruskin and American Architecture, or Regeneration Long Delayed." Sir John Summerson, ed., *Concerning Architecture*. London, 1968.

Hitchcock, Henry-Russell, and William Seale. *Temples of Democracy: The State Capitols of the USA*. New York, 1976.

Holden, Wheaton. " 'That Peabody Touch,' Peabody and Stearns of Boston." *Journal, Society of Architectural Historians* 32 (May 1973), 114–31.

Kaufmann, Edgar, Jr., ed. *The Rise of an American Architecture*. New York, 1970.

Kidney, Walter C. "Another Look at Eclecticism." *Progressive Architecture* 48 (September 1967), 122 ff.

————. *The Architecture of Choice; Eclecticism in America, 180–1930*. New York, 1974.

Kimball, S. Fiske. *American Architecture*. Indianapolis, 1928.

King, Moses, ed. *King's Handbook of New York City*. Boston, 1892.

————. *King's Views of New York, 1896–1915, and Brooklyn, 1905*, new ed. New York, 1974.

Lancaster, Clay. *The Japanese Influence in America*. New York, 1963.

Lewis, Dudley Arnold. "Evaluations of American Architecture by European Critics, 1875–1900." Doctoral dissertation, University of Wisconsin, 1962.

Lockwood, Charles. *Bricks and Brownstone, The New York Rowhouse*. New York, 1972.

Longfellow, W.P.P. "The Course of American Architecture." *New Princeton Review* 3 (March 1887), 200–211.

→ Longstreth, Richard W. "Academic Eclecticism in American Architecture." *Winterthur Portfolio* 17 (Spring 1982), 55–82.

Magonigle, H. Van Buren. "A Half Century of Architecture." *Pencil Points* 14 and 15 (November 1933 through November 1934), a series of seven articles.

Meeks, Carroll L. V. "Creative Eclecticism." *Journal, Society of Architectural Historians* 11 (December 1953), 15–18.

———. "Picturesque Eclecticism." *Art Bulletin* 32 (September 1950), 226–235.

———. *The Railroad Station.* New Haven, 1956.

———. "Wright's Eastern Seaboard Contemporaries: Creative Eclecticism in the United States around 1900." *Problems of the 19th & the 20th Centuries; Studies in Western Art.* Acts of the Twentieth International Congress of the History of Art. 4 vols. Princeton, 1963. 4:64–77.

Moore, Charles. *Daniel H. Burnham, Architect, Planner of Cities.* 2 vols. Boston, 1921.

→ Noffsinger, James P. *The Influence of the École des Beaux-Arts on the Architects of the United States.* Washington, D. C., 1955.

O'Gorman, James F. *The Architecture of Frank Furness.* Philadelphia, 1973.

———. *Henry Hobson Richardson and His Office: Selected Drawings.* Cambridge, Mass., 1974.

———. "O. W. Norcross, Richardson's Master Builder: A Preliminary Report." *Journal, Society of Architectural Historians* 32 (May 1973), 104–113.

→ Platt, Frederick. *America's Gilded Age: Its Architecture and Decoration.* Cranbury, N. J., 1976.

Rhoads, William B. *The Colonial Revival.* New York, 1977.

Roth, Leland M. *America Builds: Source Documents in American Architecture and Planning.* New York, 1983.

———. *A Concise History of American Architecture.* New York, 1979.

Saylor, Henry A. *The A.I.A.'s First Hundred Years.* Washington, D.C., 1957.

Schuyler, Montgomery. *American Architecture and Other Writings.* W. H. Jordy and R. Coe, eds. 2 vols. Cambridge, Mass., 1961.

———. "Schools of Architecture and the Paris School." *Scribner's Magazine* 24 (December 1898), 765–766.

———. "The Work of Charles C. Haight." *Architectural Record,* Great American Architects Series, July 1899.

———. "The Works of Cram, Goodhue and Ferguson: A Record of the Firm's Representative Structures, 1892–1910." *Architectural Record* 29 (January 1911), 1–112.

Scully, Vincent. *American Architecture and Urbanism.* New York, 1969.

———. *The Shingle Style.* New Haven, 1955.

———. *The Shingle Style Today, or the Historian's Revenge.* New York, 1974.

Searing, Helen, ed. *In Search of Modern Architecture: A Tribute to Henry-Russell Hitchcock.* New York and Cambridge, Mass., 1982.

Sheldon, George W., ed. *Artistic Country Seats: Types of Recent American Villa and Cottage Architecture. . . .* 2 vols. New York, 1885–86.

Silver, Nathan. *Lost New York.* Boston, 1967.

Stokes, I. N. Phelps. *The Iconography of Manhattan Island, 1498–1909.* 6 vols. 1909–28.

Sturgis, Russell. "Building of the Modern City House." *Harper's Magazine* 98 (March 1899), 579–594, and (April 1899) 810–822.

———. "A Critique of the Works of Bruce Price." *Architectural Record,* Great American Architects Series, June 1899.

———. "A Critique of the Works of Shepley, Rutan & Coolidge and Peabody & Stearns." *Architectural Record,* Great American Architects Series, June 1896.

———. "Good Things in Modern Architecture." *Architectural Record* 8 (July–September 1898), 92–110. ←

———. "How to Beautify the City." *Scribner's Magazine* 33 (April 1903), 509–512.

———. "Modern Architecture." *North American Review* 112 (January 1871), 160–177, and (April 1871) 370–391.

———. "A Review of the Work of George B. Post." *Architectural Record,* Great American Architects Series, June ← 1898.

———. "Schools of Architecture and the Paris School." *Scribner's Magazine* 24 (December 1898), 767–768.

———. "The Warehouse and Factory in Architecture." ← *Architectural Record* 15 (January 1904), 1–17, and (February 1904) 122–133.

———. "The True Education of an Architect." *Atlantic Monthly* 81 (February 1898), 246–255.

Tallmadge, Thomas E. *The Story of Architecture in America.* New York, 1927.

Tucci, Douglass Shand. *Built in Boston, City and Suburb.* Boston, 1978.

Turak, Theodore. "The École Centrale and Modern Architecture: the Education of William Le Baron Jenney." *Journal, Society of Architectural Historians* 29 (March 1970), 40–47.

Valentine, Lucia and Alan. *The American Academy in Rome, 1894–1969.* Charlottesville, Va., 1973.

Van Brunt, Henry. *Architecture and Society: Selected Essays of Henry Van Brunt.* William Coles, ed. Cambridge, Mass., 1969.

Van Rensselaer, Mariana Griswold. "Recent Architecture in America." *Century* Magazine 28–32 (May 1884–July 1886), a series of nine articles on contemporary American architecture of various types.

Weisman, Winston. "The Commercial Architecture of ← George B. Post." *Journal, Society of Architectural Historians* 31 (October 1972), 176–203.

Wharton, Edith, and Ogden Codman. *The Decoration of Houses.* New York, 1897.

Wight, Peter Bonnett. "Reminiscences of Russell Sturgis." *Architectural Record* 26 (August 1909), 123–131.

→ Wilson, Richard Guy. "American Architecture and the Search for a National Style in the 1870s." *Nineteenth Cen-* *tury* 3 (Autumn 1977), 74–80.

"The Works of Messrs. Carrère & Hastings." *Architectural Record* 27 (January 1910), 1–121, 122–128.

CHARLES FOLLEN McKIM

Honors:

M.A., Harvard, 1890
M.A., Bowdoin, 1894
LL.D., University of Pennsylvania, 1909
Gold Medal, Paris Exposition, 1900
Royal Gold Medal, Royal Institute of British Architects, 1903
Gold Medal, American Institute of Architects, 1909
Fellow, American Institute of Architects, 1877
President, American Institute of Architects, 1902–1903
Academician, American Academy of Arts and Letters
Academician, National Academy of Design
Accadèmia de San Luca, Rome

Obituary Notices:

American Architect and Building News 96 (September 22, 1909), 115.
Quarterly Bulletin, American Institute of Architects 10 (October 1909), 222–224.
Architects' and Builders' Magazine 10 (November 1909), 41–48.
Architectural Record 26 (November 1909), 381–382.
Architectural Review 26 (October 1909), 183–91.
Architecture 20 (December 1909), 189.
Current Literature 47 (November 1909), 522–527.
Harper's Weekly 53 (October 2, 1909), 31.
The Nation 89 (September 23, 1909), 287–288.
New York Architect 3 (September 1909), 113–118.
New York Times, September 15, 1909, 1; September 17, 5; October 2, 2.
Outlook 93 (September 25, 1909), 142–144.
World's Work 19 (November 1909), 12185, 12206–12207.

"The American Institute of Architects Pays Tribute to the Memory of Charles Follen McKim." *American Architect and Building News* 96 (December 29, 1909), 280–281.

"American Memorials in Rome." *American Magazine of Art* 20 (March 1929), 172–173.

Bacon, Henry. "Charles Follen McKim—A Character Sketch." *Brickbuilder* 19 (February 1910), 38–47.

Charles Follen McKim Memorial Meeting, American Institute of Architects, The Corcoran Gallery of Art, Washington, D.C., Dec. 15, 1909. Washington, D.C., 1910.

Cortissoz, Royal. "American Architect." *Scribner's* 47 (January 1910), 125–28.

———. "The Basis of American Taste." *Creative Art* 12 (January 1933), 20–28.

———. "Some Critical Reflections on the Architectural Genius of Charles F. McKim." *Brickbuilder* 19 (February 1910), 23–37.

———. *The Painter's Craft.* New York, 1930, 427–437.

———. "The Secret of the American Academy in Rome." *American Magazine of Art* 13 (November 1922), 459–462.

Exhibition of the Work of Charles Follen McKim, The Art Institute of Chicago, Jan. 18 to Feb. 6, 1910. Chicago, 1910.

Granger, Alfred Hoyt. *Charles Follen McKim; a study of his life and work.* Boston, 1913. Reviews: *Architectural Record* 35 (May 1914), 463–465; *The Dial,* May 1, 1914, 384–385.

"Great Imaginative Interpreter of Renaissance Traditions." *Architectural Record* 35 (May 1914), 463–65.

Hill, Frederick P. *Charles F. McKim: the Man.* Francestown, N.H., 1950.

Memorial Meeting in Honor of the Late Charles Follen McKim held in the New Theater, New York, November 23, 1909. New York, 1909?

Moore, Charles. *The Life and Times of Charles Follen McKim.* Boston, 1929. Reviews: *American Magazine of Art* 21 (March 1930), 178; *Apollo* 12 (July 1930), 60; *International Studio* 95 (April 1930), 70.

Partridge, William T. "Recollections Concerning Charles Follen McKim." Unpublished typescript, Avery Library, Columbia University.

Peabody, Robert S. "A Tribute." *Brickbuilder* 19 (February 1910), 55–56.

"Saint-Gaudens–McKim bronzes given to the New York Public Library." *New York Public Library Bulletin* 43 (September 1939), 643–644.

Schuyler, Montgomery. "Charles Follen McKim." *Architectural Record* 26 (Novrmber 1909), 381–82

Swales, Francis S. "Charles Follen McKim." *Architectural Review* (London) 26 (October 1909), 183–191.

Tallmadge, Thomas E., "Holographs of Famous Architects," *American Architect* 143 (March 1933), 11.

"Tribute of the American Institute of Architects to the memory of Charles F. McKim." *Ohio Architect and Builder* 15 (January 1910).

Walker, C. Howard. "The Influence of McKim." *Brickbuilder* 19 (February 1910), 48–53.

Wilson, Richard Guy. "The Early Work of Charles F. McKim: Country House Commissions." *Winterthur Portfolio* 14 (Autumn 1979), 235–67.

WILLIAM RUTHERFORD MEAD

Honors:

LL.D., Amherst, 1902
M.S., Norwich University, 1909
D.F.A., University of Pennsylvania, 1921
Knight Commander, Order of the Crown of Italy, 1922
President of the New York Chapter, American Institute of Architects, 1907–1908
Gold Medal, American Academy of Arts and Letters, 1913
President, American Academy in Rome, 1909–1928

Obituary Notices:

American Architect and Building News 134 (July 5, 1928), 12.

American Art Journal 25 (1928), 371.
Architectural Forum 49 (July 1928), 37.
Architectural Record 64 (September 1928), 254.
Journal, American Institute of Architects 16 (July 1928), 280.
New York *Herald-Tribune,* June 21, 22, 1928.
New York Times, November 27, 1928, 14; December 5, 1928, 20.
Pencil Points 9 (August 1928), 470, 529.

"As He Is Known, being brief sketches of contemporary members of the architectural profession." *Brickbuilder* 24 (December 1915), 315.

Cabot, M. R. *Annals of Brattleboro, 1681–1895.* Brattleboro, 1922.

Country Life in America 39 (April 1921), 43.

STANFORD WHITE

Honors:

M.A., New York University, 1881

Obituary Notices:

American Architecture and Building News 89 (June 30, 1906), 213; 90 (August 18, 1906), 54.
Quarterly Bulletin, American Institute of Architects 7 (July 1906), 100–108.
Architectural Review 13 (July 1906), 101.
The Critic 49 (August 1906), 105.
The Nation 83 (July 5, 1906), 5–6.
New York Times, June 27, 1906, 2–3; June 28, 1906, 6; June 29, 1906, 2.

Baldwin, Charles C. *Stanford White.* New York, 1931. Reviews: *Architectural Forum* 55 (December 1931), sup. 8.

Davis, Richard Harding. "Stanford White." *Collier's Magazine* 37 (August 4, 1906), 17.

"Exhibition at Davis Gallery." *Art News* 62 (April 1963), 13. (Similar notice in *Art Quarterly* 25 [Winter 1962], 420.)

"Exhibition at Davis Gallery" (second exhibition). *Art News* 64 (April 1965), 56.

"Exhibition at Davis Gallery." *Arts* 39 (May 1965), 71.

Hewlett, J. Monroe. "Stanford White as those trained in his office knew him." *Brickbuilder* 15 (December 1906), 245.

———. "Stanford White, Decorator." *Good Furniture* 9 (September 1917), 160–179. Partially reprinted in *Good Furniture* 11 (October 1918), 198–206.

Langford, Gerald. *The Murder of Stanford White.* Indianapolis, Ind., 1962.

McQuade, Walter. "Stanford White and the Wherewithal," *Architectural Forum* 123 (November 1965), 70.

Memorial Meeting in honor of the late Stanford White held at the Library of New York University for the dedication of the

Stanford White Memorial Doors, December 10, 1921. New York [1921].

Mooney, Michael M. *Evelyn Nesbit and Stanford White: Love and Death in the Gilded Age.* New York, 1976.

Moses, Lionel. "Stanford White house at St. James, L. I." *Art World* 3 (January 1918), 351–55.

Ross, Albert Randolph. "Stanford White as those trained in his office knew him." *Brickbuilder* 15 (December 1906), 246.

Saarinen, Aline B. "The Splendid World of Stanford White." *Life* 61 (September 16, 1966), 87–108.

Saint-Gaudens, Homer. "Intimate Letters of Stanford White, correspondence with his friend & co-worker, Augustus Saint-Gaudens." *Architectural Record* 30 (August 1911), 107–116; (September 1911), 283–298; (October 1911), 399–406.

Sawyer, Philip. "Stanford White as those trained in his office knew him." *Brickbuilder* 15 (December 1906), 247.

Scudder, Janet. *Modeling My Life.* New York, 1925.

"Sentimental approach to antiques: Stanford White Collection." *Arts and Decoration* 41 (May 1934), 58–60.

"Stanford White again; exhibition, Museum of the City of New York." *Architectural Forum* 76 (April 1942), sup. 8.

"Stanford White items are notable feature of March dispersal." *Art News* 32 (March 17, 1934), 14.

Swales, Francis S. "Master Draftsmen, Part I. Stanford White." *Pencil Points* 5 (April 1924), 59–64.

Tallmadge, Thomas E. "Holographs of Famous Architects." *American Architect* 143 (March 1933), 11.

Walker, C. Howard. "Stanford White—His Work." *Brickbuilder* 15 (December 1906), 243–244.

World's Work 9 (November 1904), 5439.

Young, Mahonri Sharp. "Stanford White, the Palace and the Club." *Apollo* 93 (March 1971), 210–215.

McKIM, MEAD & WHITE

*Entries here pertain to interpretive and critical essays or reviews of
groups of the firm's buildings. For publication of specific buildings, see
the citations in footnotes to the text.*

Andrews, Wayne. "McKim, Mead and White: New York's Own Architects." *New-York Historical Society Quarterly* 35 (January 1951), 87–96.

———. "McKim, Mead & White: their mark remains." *New York Times Magazine,* January 7, 1951, 18–21.

Atlantic Terra Cotta 9 (June 1927), entire issue.

Barber, Donn. "The Work of McKim, Mead and White." *Architectural Record* 40 (October 1916), 393–396.

Bowles, J. M. "Business Buildings Made Beautiful." *World's Work* 9 (November 1904), 5499–5508.

Broderick, Mosette G., and William Shopsin. *The Villard Houses: Life Story of a Landmark.* New York, 1980.

Brown, Glenn. "Personal Reminiscences of Charles Follen McKim." *Architectural Record* 38 (November 1915), 575–582, "McKim and the American Institute of Architects"; (December 1915), 681–689, "McKim and the Park Commission"; 39 (January 1916), 84–88, "McKim and the White House"; (February 1916), 178–185, "McKim's Way."

Butler, Alexander R. "McKim's Renaissance: A Study of the American Architectural Profession." Doctoral dissertation, Johns Hopkins University, 1953.

Chapman, John Jay. "McKim, Mead and White." *Vanity Fair* 13 (September 1919), 37, 102, 104.

Cortissoz, Royal. "Architectural Ideas, Old and New." New York *Herald-Tribune,* March 17, 1940.

———. "Ghosts in New York." *Architectural Forum* 53 (July 1930), 87–90.

David, A. C. "An Architectural Oasis." *Architectural Record* 19 (February 1906), 135–144. Essay on the firm's work in Naugatuck, Conn.

Desmond, Henry W., and Herbert Croly. "The Work of Messrs. McKim, Mead & White." *Architectural Record* 20 (September 1906), 153–246. Entire issue; a major study of the firm's work.

Goldsmith, Goldwin. "I remember McKim, Mead and White." *Journal, American Institute of Architects* 13 (April 1950), 168–172.

"Historical Society Exhibits Works." *Architectural Record* 109 (January 1951), 214.

"Hughson Hawley, Scenic Artist and Architectural Painter." *Pencil Points* 9 (December 1928), 761–74.

A Monograph of the Work of McKim, Mead & White, 1879–1915. 400 plates in 4 vols. New York, 1914–1920.

A Monograph of the Work of McKim, Mead & White. Students' Edition. 2 vols. New York, 1925 (new ed., New York, 1981).

Moses, Lionel. "McKim, Mead and White; a History." *American Architect and Building News* 121 (May 24, 1922), 413–424.

Myers, John Walden. "The New York Work of Stanford White." *Museum of the City of New York Bulletin* 5 (March 1942), 46–52.

"One firm and many styles in architecture; exhibition at the New York Historical Society." *Art Digest* 25 (January 15, 1951), 16.

Parker, Gurdon S. "The Work of Three Great Architects." *World's Work* 12 (May–October 1906), 8051–8066.

Ramsey, Stanley C. "The Work of McKim, Mead and White." *Journal, Royal Institute of British Architects* 25 (November 5, 1917), 25–29.

Recent Buildings Designed for Educational Institutions by McKim, Mead & White. Philadelphia, 1936.

Recent Work by the Present Partners of McKim, Mead & White, Architects. New York, 1952.

Reilly, Charles Herbert. *McKim, Mead & White.* London, 1924.

Roth, Leland M. *The Architecture of McKim, Mead & White, 1870–1920: A Building List.* New York, 1978.

Roth, Leland M. "McKim, Mead & White Reappraised." Introductory essay and notes on the plates for *A Monograph of the Work of McKim, Mead & White, 1879–1915.* New ed. New York, 1973.

Roth, Leland M. "Three Industrial Towns by McKim, Mead & White." *Journal, Society of Architectural Historians* 38 (December 1979), 317–347.

Sawyer, Philip. *Edward Palmer York: Personal Reminiscences.* Stonington, Conn., 1951.

Schroeder, Francis de N. "Stanford White and the second blossoming of the Renaissance." *Interiors* 110 (February 1951), 106–109.

Smith, Eugenia B. "Rhode Island Resort Architecture of McKim, Mead & White." Master's thesis, University of Wisconsin, 1964.

Some Recent Buildings Designed by McKim, Mead & White. Privately printed, 1941.

Sturgis, R. Clipston. "Voice from the past." *Journal, American Institute of Architects* 16 (July 1951), 23–28.

Sturgis, Russell. "The Works of McKim, Mead & White." *Architectural Record,* Great American Architects Series, May 1895. A major study of the firm's earlier work.

Swartwout, Egerton. "An Architectural Decade." Unpublished typescript, n.d., c. 1935. Office of Walker O. Cain and Associates, New York.

Valentine, Lucia and Alan. *The American Academy in Rome, 1894–1969.* Charlottesville, Va., 1973.

Van der Bent, Teunis J. *The Planning of Apartment Houses, Tenements, and Country Houses: A Text Book for Students of Architecture.* New York, 1917.

Walker, C. Howard. "Joseph Wells, architect, 1853–1890." *Architectural Record* 66 (July 1929), 14–18.

White, Lawrence Grant. *Sketches and Designs by Stanford White.* New York, 1920.

Wilson, Richard Guy. "Charles F. McKim and the Development of the American Renaissance: A Study in Architecture and Culture." Doctoral dissertation, The University of Michigan, 1972.

Wodehouse, Lawrence. "Stanford White and the Mackays: A Case Study in Architect-Client Relationships." *Winterthur Portfolio* 11 (1976), 229–233.

PENNSYLVANIA RAILROAD NEW YORK TERMINAL STATION, "PENN STATION"

Periodicals:

American Architect and Building News 89 (May 26, 1906), 175, 180, no. 1587; 90 (July 14, 1906), 16, no. 1594; 98 (October 5, 1910), 113–18, no. 1815.

American Society of Civil Engineers, Transactions 69 (October 1910), 226–83.

Architects' and Builders' Journal (London) 42 (October 13, 1915), 164–65.

Architects' and Builders' Magazine 7 (June 1906), 399–408; 11 (July 1910), 379–410.

Architectural Record 27 (June 1910), 518–21.

Architectural Review 13 (May 1906), 77, pls. 24–28.

Architectural Review (London) 30 (August 1911), 65– 88.

Architecture 21 (March 1910), pl. 21; 22 (October 1910), 155, 157, 163–64.

l'Architecture 26 (May 3, 1913), 141–42.

Brickbuilder 19 (February 1910), 63–65.

Builder (London) 101 (August 25, 1911), 219–20; 118 (May 21, 1920), 598, 600–601.

Inland Architect 49 (April 1907).

Monumental News 22 (November 1910).

New York Architect 4 (September 1910), 71–77, 91–115.

Outlook 96 (September 10, 1910), 55.

Pencil Points 7 (October 1926), pl. 34.

Scientific American 85 (December 28, 1901), 426–27; 90 (January 16, 1904), 42; 94 (May 20, 1906), 429, 438–39; 94 (June 2, 1906), 449, 453–54; 99 (December 5, 1908), 409–10; 102 (May 14, 1910), 389, 398–401; 103 (September 10, 1910), 200–201.

Wasmuths Monatshefte 12 (Heft 4, 1928), 164–65.

Baker, Joseph B. "The Mail-Handling System at the Pennsylvania Railroad Station, New York City." *Scientific American* 104 (February 4, 1911), 105, 110–11.

Cochrane, C. C. "The Future Terminal Facilities of New York." *Broadway Magazine* 17 (October 1906), 2–16.

Darvillé, W. "La Nouvelle Gare Centrale de New York." *La Construction Moderne* 25 (November 6, 1909), 67–69.

Keys, C. M. "Cassatt and His Vision." *World's Work* 20 (July 1910), 13187–13204.

Lubchez, B. J. "The Two Great Railway Stations of New York." *Journal, Royal Institute of British Architects* 27 (June 12, 1920), 369–78.

Schuyler, M. "The New Pennsylvania Station in New York." *International Studio* 41 (October 1910), supp. 89–95.

Books:

Condit, Carl W. *The Port of New York [I]: A History of the Rail and Terminal System from the Beginnings to Pennsylvania Station.* Chicago, 1980, 239–311.

Droege, J. A. *Passenger Terminals and Trains.* New York, 1916.

Pennsylvania Railroad Company. *Pennsylvania Station in New York City.* 190(?). (Copy in New York Public Library.)

Prominent Buildings Erected by George A. Fuller. Chicago, 1910.

Westinghouse, Church, Kerr and Company. *The New York Passenger Terminal and Improvements of the Pennsylvania and Long Island Railroads.* New York, 1910.

For other miscellaneous material see the extensive bibliography in the Historic American Buildings Survey No. 7, New York City Architecture, July 1969, 78–84. Structural drawings for the station are preserved in the Engineering Department of Penn Central.

Index

HOTELS 42 [27] Elberon Hotel (Ext)
x 108 Balt. Comp. Cntr.
x 41 (41) Cayuga Lake, NY
216-217 (217) Edn. City
→ 138 (145) Hotel Imperial, NY 1889-91 AABN 30 Oct 25, 1890 for Goelets
→ 339-40 (339) Hotel Pennsyl., NYC 1915-19
138 Park Ave Hot. NYC remod. 1890-91
84 The Percival NYC
92 (93) Hotel Portland, Ore.
94 (95) Russwin, New Brit., Conn.
→ 138 Savoy Plaza NYC HJM Plaza site
223 (224) Sherry's NYC
92 (93) Tacoma
Yosemite Apt. Bldg 1887-90
See AABN 31 (Feb. 21, '28) 126, 141
nos. 791, 792